NING serv

Duchy C

Le

esource is to b
ed below. To

Th

TURF IRRIGATION MANUAL

TURF IRRIGATION MANUAL

The Complete Guide to Turf and Landscape Irrigation Systems

By
Richard B. Choate

H. Gene Johnson
Editor

Rose Torres and Shelley Zander
Graphics Production

Cover Photo
Horticultural Photography
Corvallis, Oregon

A **Weather✳matic** ® *PUBLICATION*

TURF IRRIGATION MANUAL

5th Edition
Copyright 1994
by
Weather-matic Division of
TELSCO INDUSTRIES
All rights reserved

888-4 THE PRO
www.weathermatic.com

Library of Congress Cataloging in Publication Data

Choate, Richard B.
    Turf Irrigation Manual: The complete guide to turf and landscape irrigation systems/
        by Richard B. Choate
    p.   cm.
    Rev. ed. of: Turf Irrigation Manual / by James A. Watkins.
    Includes bibliographical references and index.
    ISBN 0-9635096-0-8
1. Turfgrasses--Irrigation--Handbooks, Manuals, etc. **2.** Lawns--Irrigation--Handbooks, Manuals, etc.
3. Landscape plants--Lawns--Irrigation--Handbooks, Manuals, etc.
4. Sprinkler irrigation---Handbooks, Manuals, etc. I. Watkins, James A., 1915-1988 Turf irrigation manual. II. Title.
SB433.C53 1994
635.9'64287--dc20   93-50092
                                                               CIP

Previous Copyrights
1959, 1965, 1977, 1987

1959 and 1965 editions by M.E. Snoddy (1912-1987) and James A. Watkins (1915-1988),
1977 edition by James A. Watkins (1915-1988).
1987 edition by Richard B. Choate (1932-).

22nd printing
Over 57,000 copies in circulation

Preface

Landscape development provides improved human use of land, aesthetic enjoyment and a positive influence on the environment of the community. Living plants are essential to nature's cycle of oxygen replenishment for our atmosphere. In addition, scientific studies have shown turfgrass and landscaping to be excellent sound insulators, effectively reducing noise levels.

Irrigation is a necessary part of landscape maintenance in most regions of the world. Automatic irrigation systems are very useful in providing and controlling the efficient application of moisture for all types of developed properties.

The Turf Irrigation Manual is designed to serve as a guidebook for engineers, architects, landscape architects, designers and contractors; and as a text for academic students and the interested layperson desiring to obtain proficiency in the field of landscape irrigation. The first edition was published in 1959, followed by expanded editions in 1965, 1977 and 1987. It has become the authoritative text in the field and is currently used by colleges and universities throughout the world. The Turf Irrigation Manual is also a highly recommended study guide for state licensing exams and certification testing by The Irrigation Association.

Education for the required skills of modern system design includes the knowledge necessary for the environmental responsibilities inherent with the use of a natural resource. Local, state and national trade associations are a very important part of the continuing education requirements of an ever-changing industry. The most notable of trade associations is The Irrigation Association, Fairfax, Virginia, USA, an international organization for landscape and agricultural irrigation. In recognition of the increased demand on the world's water supply, we support and recommend the participation of individuals in the efforts of landscape and irrigation associations.

Our purpose in writing this manual is to gather for the benefit of all, the knowledge and techniques accumulated through years of research and field experience, incorporating the most recent changes in technology, methods and the application of landscape irrigation.

Publication of this 5th Edition coincides with Weather-matic's 50th year of providing quality products for the irrigation industry.

We sincerely hope that this work will help to raise the standards of the industry by answering some of the questions of the newcomer and the veteran alike. If this is accomplished, then we will feel that a worthwhile contribution has been made to the field of landscape irrigation.

Acknowledgments

To the many individuals who have provided their knowledge and assistance in the development of this edition, their contribution is acknowledged with sincere thanks. Special thanks is extended to those who aided and guided the development of chapters which, although related to irrigation, are specialized disciplines.

Illustration or mention of specific products in this text is not intended as an endorsement by the author or the publisher, Weather-matic Division of Telsco Industries. Specific product omission is not intentional; other brands may be equally suitable for the applications discussed in this manual. Although the utmost care was used in preparing all tables, formulas, methods, guidelines, etc., the author, editor, and publisher will not be responsible for any errors, omissions, etc., except that items brought to their attention will be corrected in the next printing.

About the Author... Richard B. Choate

Richard B. Choate, Director of Training for Weather-matic's College of Irrigation Knowledge™ , design consultant and co-author of the 1987 edition, has 35 years of professional experience that includes contracting, distribution and manufacturing. He is a licensed irrigator in the State of Texas, an I.A. certified landscape irrigation auditor, associate member of the A.S.I.C. and affiliate member of the A.S.L.A.

He has designed and provided design assistance on landscape irrigation projects throughout the world. The first of his many fully-automatic golf course system designs was installed in 1967. He has developed techniques and formulas that have become the standard for hydraulics calculations. He has participated in over 400 seminars, workshops and training classes with attendees from coast to coast (USA and Canada), Central and South America, Europe, Africa, the Middle East, Australia and Asia.

Richard Choate is a native Texan and U.S. Navy veteran of the Korean War. Richard and his wife, Tress, are the parents of two sons and currently reside in a Dallas suburb.

CONTENTS

PART I IRRIGATION EQUIPMENT AND MATERIALS

1 Irrigation Equipment, 4

SPRAY SPRINKLERS 4, FLOOD HEADS 10, Design Considerations 11, Cost Factors 11, **ROTARY SPRINKLERS 12**, Efficiency 15, Design Considerations 15, Cost Factors 17, **MICRO PRODUCTS 18**, Efficiency 18, Design Considerations 19, **QUICK COUPLER EQUIPMENT 19**, Design Considerations 21, Cost Factors 21, **SYSTEM OPERATION 21**, Automatic Operation 22, Controllers 22, Remote Control Valves 27, Electric Automatic Systems 28, Hydraulic Automatic Systems 30, Remote Sensors 31, **SYSTEM FREEZE PROTECTION 33**, Automatic Drain Valves 33, Manual Drains 34, **ACCESSORIES 35.**

2 Piping, 36

PIPE STANDARDS 36, Piping Terms, General 37, **METAL PIPES 37,** Galvanized Steel Pipe 37, Copper Water Tube 38, **ASBESTOS-CEMENT PIPE 40 ,THERMOPLASTIC PIPE 41,** Physical Characteristics of Plastics 41, Hydrostatic Design Stress 41, Pressure Rating (PR) 41, Material Designations 42, Schedule Wall Thickness Plastic Pipe 42, SDR-PR Plastic Pipe 43, Thermoplastic Pipe Standards 43, Polyethylene (PE) Pipe 44, Poly (Vinyl chloride) (PVC) Pipe 46, Polybutylene (PB) Pipe 47, Non-Potable Water Piping 47, Installation of Thermoplastic Pipe 47.

PART II WATER SUPPLY

3 Hydraulics, 54

NATURE OF WATER 54, PRESSURE 54, Elevation Versus Pressure 55, City Water Supply 55, Local Elevations 56, Determining Elevation 56, Static and Operating Pressure 57, **PIPING SYSTEM DESIGN 59,** Flow 59, Velocity 59, Pressure Loss in Pipes 59, Pressure Losses in Appurtenances 59, Pressure Loss Calculations 60, Pipe Sizing 61, Design Pressure 61, **FLUCTUATIONS IN CITY WATER PRESSURE 64, DETERMINING CAPACITY OF EXISTING PIPING SYSTEMS 65,** Equipment Required 65, Testing Pipe Lines 65, Water Supply Testing -- Basement Meters 67, Water Supply Testing -- Meters Located Outside Of Building 69, General : Testing Existing Piping 69.

4 Water Hammer, 72

VALVE CLOSURE 72, Pipe System Protection 73, Pipe System Design 73, Water Hammer Arresters 76, **UNCONTROLLED FLOW IN EMPTY PIPES 79,** Check Valves 80, Flow Control 80, **AIR ENTRAPMENT 81,** Water Hammer Caused by Air Pockets 81, **REVERSE FLOW 82,** Silent Check Valve 83, Conventional Check Valve Replacement 83.

5 Cross Connection Control, 84

ELEMENTS OF CROSS CONNECTION CONTROL 86, Backflow Due to Back Pressure 86, Backflow Due to Siphonage 86, **BACKFLOW PREVENTION 87,** Vacuum Breakers 88, Atmospheric Vacuum Breakers 88, Pressure-Type Vacuum Breakers 89, Double Check Assembly (DCA) 92, Reduced Pressure Assembly (RP) 94, Air Gap 94, **CROSS CONNECTION CONTROL BY LOCAL PLUMBING CODES 95.**

6 Pumps, 98

Centrifugal Pumps 98, Pump Impeller Lubricating 98, Basic Operation of Centrifugal Pumps 100, **PUMPING TERMS AND DEFINITIONS 100,** Types of Pressure 100, Static Conditions 102, Dynamic Conditions 102, Cavitation 103, Efficiency 103, Net Positive Suction Head 103, **SELECTION OF CENTRIFUGAL PUMPS 104,** Site Conditions 104, Preliminary Selection of Pump 105, **PUMP INSTALLATION 108,** Pump Suction 108, Pump Tappings 110, Pump Mounting 110, Priming 110, **PUMP OPERATION WITH IRRIGATION CONTROLLER 111, HYDRO-PNEUMATIC PRESSURE SYSTEMS 112,** Basic Operation 113, Establishing Air/Water Ratio 114, Maintaining Air/Water Ratio 114, Minimizing Water Hammer 115, Pump System Accessories 115, **VERTICAL TURBINE PUMP SYSTEMS 116, MULTIPLE PUMP SYSTEMS 119,** Manufactured Pumping Stations 121, **WATER STORAGE 124, BOOSTER PUMPS 125.**

7 Source Water And Filtration, 128

FILTRATION 129, Strainers/Filters 130, Automatic Self-Cleaning Strainers 134, Wells 137, Holding Tanks 137, **SEPARATORS 138, IRRIGATION EQUIPMENT SELECTION 139.**

PART III DESIGN

8 Sprinkler Performance and Related Considerations for System Performance, 144

SPRINKLER DISTRIBUTION 144, DISTRIBUTION PATTERNS 145, Diameter of Coverage 146, Wind Effects 147, Pressure Effects 148, Rotational Effects 148, **SYSTEM DISTRIBUTION 148,** Distribution Between Sprinklers 149, Design Spacing 151, **BORDER WATERING 153, PRECIPITATION 154, WIND 156, RELATED CONSIDERATIONS FOR SYSTEM PERFORMANCE 157,** Water Requirement 158, Evapotranspiration 159, Soil-Water-Plant 160, Variations in Planting 161, Method of Irrigation and Zone Separation 163, Water Conservation 163, Conservation by Landscape Design 164, Conservation by Design 164, Conservation by Management 166, Irrigation Audits 166.

9 Plot Plans, 168

MEASURING PROPERTIES 168, Landscape Data Required 169, Drawing Plot Plan 171, **ODD SHAPED PROPERTIES 173,** Triangulation 173, Measuring Odd Shaped Properties 175, Plotting Curves 176, Surveys 176, Professional Surveys 176, Aerial Surveys 176, **ROLLING TERRAIN 176.**

10 Head Layout, 178

INTRODUCTION TO HEAD LAYOUT 178, Head Spacing 179, Triangular Versus Square Spacing 180, Selection of Spacing 180, **BASICS OF SPRAY HEAD LAYOUT 180,** Simple Method To Equal Space 184, Special Layout Methods 185, Spray Beyond Borders 186, Round Corners 186, Curved Borders 187, Parkways and Strips 189, Combined Coverage 191, Lawn and Trees 191, Lawn and Shrubs 192, Planting Beds 192, High Shrubs 193, Flood Watering 194, Planter Boxes 195, Individual Plantings 196, **EXEMPLARY SPRAY SYSTEM HEAD LAYOUT 196,** Spacing Templates 197, Head Labels/Symbols 203.

11 Pipe Sizing and Zoning, 204

Flow Requirement 204, Nozzle Flow Variation 204, Design Flow 204, Zone Flow and Pressure Loss 206, Pipe Fitting Losses 208, Zoning the System 211, Water Supply 211, Zoning the Exemplary System 212, Variations in Precipitation Rate 212, Flow Adjustment 213, Flow Velocity 213, Preliminary Piping 214, Maximum Pressure Requirement 215, Calculating Pressure Losses 217, Final Zones and Piping 219, **LOOPED MAINS 221,** Complex Loops 226, **DESIGN/SYSTEM VARIATIONS 227, COMPUTER-AIDED DESIGN (CAD) 227.**

12 Rotary Systems, 230

DESIGN CRITERIA 230, SITE CONDITIONS 232, DESIGN STANDARDS 232, HEAD LAYOUT 233, Sprinkler Selection 233, Spray Head Layout 238, **DESIGN OF PIPING SYSTEM 241,** Zone Flow and Loss Adjustment 241, Water Supply 243, Zone Flow Versus Piping System Cost 243, **PRELIMINARY PIPING 244,** Pressure Requirement Calculation 246.

13 Micro Irrigation, 252

SPECIAL EQUIPMENT 253, Controllers 253, Electric Zone Valves, 254, Filters 254, Pressure Regulator 255, Tubing/Hose/Pipe 256, Drip Emitters 256, ETO Inches/Day 257, Plant Size 257, Plant Type 258, Irrigation Efficiency 258, Gallons Required Per Day, Per Plant 258, Wetted Pattern (drip emitters) 259, Number of Emitters 259, Unusual Soil Conditions 261, Operation/Programming 261, Micro-Spray Sprinklers 263, Other Types Of Drip Products For Micro-irrigation 269, Low To Medium Flow Products 270.

14 Golf Course Systems, 272

HEAD LAYOUT 272, Greens 273, Tees 276, Approaches and Fairways 277, Effective Coverage 278, Wind Compensation 279, Single-Row Systems 280, Precipitation 281, Two-Row Systems 281, Three-Row Systems 284, Fairway Approaches 286, **ZONING, 288,** Green-Tees 288, Fairways 289, **ALLOWABLE OPERATING TIME 293, EXEMPLARY GOLF COURSE DESIGN 293,** Automatic Control System 295, Development of Operation Program 296, Controllers Required 297, System Piping 302, Swing Joints 303, Main Pipe Sizing 304, Calculations by Computer 309, Design Pressure 310, Pumping System 312, Water Supply 312, Additional Considerations 314, Syringe Watering 315, Supplemental Watering 315, Sprinklers With Check Valves 316, **COMPLETE COVERAGE SYSTEMS 316, SYSTEM CONVERSION 317.**

15 Electrical, 320

VALVE WIRING 320, Type of Wire 320, Wire Sizing With Tables 321, Effect of Water Pressure 322, Electrical Factors 322, Sizing Wire Using Electric Factors 323, Installation 326, **CONTROLLER WIRING 327,** Single Controllers 327, Multiple Controllers 328, **GROUNDING CONTROLLER SYSTEMS 331,** Electrical Leaks 331, Controller Earth Ground 332, **PUMP CIRCUITS 333,** Magnetic Motor Starters 333, **LIGHTNING SUPPRESSION 333.**

APPENDIX OF ENGINEERING AND DESIGN DATA, 336

See separate table of contents for engineering and design data section, 338.

INDEX, 394

Introduction

This manual deals exclusively with the design of permanently installed, automatic in operation, landscape irrigation systems.

Modern landscape irrigation systems cannot be traced to an exact time in history where a particular event or product invention led to the development of the first system. Although certain individuals and companies have been major contributors in the advancement of irrigation products and methods, today's systems have evolved from a century of technology changes in irrigation and all of the other related and necessary products.

Plumbing was the primary skill required for design and installation during the first half of the twentieth century. The majority of these systems consisted of water supply piping to a limited number of outlets for connection of hoses, or in some cases, the piping was located for direct connection of sprinklers, using quick-coupling valves (see Chapter 1). Irrigation was performed by grounds maintenance personnel on large acreage projects, such as estate homes, city parks and golf courses.

In general, manual watering is very inefficient in the application of moisture and labor cost prohibits the use of this method in many parts of the world. Daytime operation will increase the loss of moisture due to evaporation and may not be a practical method in regions where water rationing restrictions do not allow landscape irrigation in the afternoon and evening hours. Daytime watering may also be a problem due to the possible conflict with the required use of land on projects such as athletic fields, office parks, shopping centers and golf courses.

Automatic irrigation systems offer many advantages including a solution for the three basic disadvantages of a manually-operated hose system. However, there are many additional responsibilities inherent with the design of an irrigation system. Although basic plumbing knowledge is still necessary, it is only one of the items on a long list of required skills.

This manual is intended as a book of study and reference on the fundamental requirements of design. Subjects pertaining to the basic elements of engineering a system are covered in Parts I and II. The detailed process of design and explanation of factors for consideration in each phase of system development, are covered in Part III, Design.

The general description of graphics procedures within Part III relates to drafting of design plans on a drawing board. However, designer knowledge, basic consid-erations and stages of development are consistent with the requirements for designing at the property site or using a C.A.D. (Computer Aided Design) system.

Example designs of residential, industrial and golf course systems are provided to cover the practical application of standard irrigation products and related requirements of design. Although each example system is based on design considerations and development that is consistent with the type of property, these systems include basic examples in the use of products that can be applied to any type of property. The word "exemplary" is used throughout the book to indicate "typical example."

The success of landscape irrigation is evidenced by the expanded use of automatic systems for all types of property developments. The increased number of systems, and the related increase in water consumption, has resulted in the expansion of restrictions to control the design, the installation and the use of irrigation systems. A variety of governmental requirements may apply to the designer and/or the system, depending upon the location of the property. Some state laws require irrigation designers and/or installers to be certified by state examination. Water conservation laws in some states place limitations on landscape and irrigation designs. Local government requirements vary from minor to major factors, and compliance may be on a voluntary basis, or may be mandatory.

The basic limitations of irrigation are the result of location and development of the site, and are therefore established before the design of the system. The water supply available at a particular site is the number one factor in controlling the scope of landscape development and the selection of planting material. This includes the combination of quantity, quality, cost and any restrictions that may be applicable to the use of water. Water requirements for irrigation are established by the landscape design, soil conditions and the climate. The amount of moisture necessary for the desired quality of an individual plant does not change with method of irrigation or selection of products.

Local and regional shortages of water cannot be attributed to a decline in the world's water supply. The earth's natural water cycle allows water to be used over and over again, but nature's rate of return in rainfall is not based on man's rate of consumption. Climate conditions that prevail today, around the world, were established many thousands of years ago.

Introduction (cont.)

Water supply problems are inevitable in large populated areas and/or agricultural regions, where water is being pumped from underground aquifers at a rate that is far in excess of recovery. In many cases, the rate of depletion has accelerated due to major shifts of population into semi-arid regions. Man can no longer relocate and develop land as desired without considering the practical limitations of his new environment.

Water conservation in agricultural irrigation is not an option, considering the rate of growth in the world's population and the fact that agriculture has consistently used 75% of the world's consumption. New techniques must be applied for conservation in agriculture and any other use, in regions where the average yearly consumption exceeds the average yearly recovery.

Irrigation in many climate regions is based on the preferable practice of storing water during the rainy season and using it for irrigation during the dry season. Conservation is important, regardless of climate, for a variety of different reasons, including the cost of water. City water rates are based on the combined cost of storage, filtration and distribution. Sewage treatment charges are normally based on water consumption. Comparisons of regional water costs are not necessarily in proportion to the average regional rainfall.

Landscape irrigation systems are judged in many different ways, as the priority in which common standards are applied is not consistent. Performance in maintaining moisture, water conservation and system dependability is often reduced to a lower level of importance by the budget, regional standards and the designer. Designs tend to be based on the established standards of the designer, rather than the variable requirements of different projects. Many property owners and designers will consider that a system is cost-effective if the installation cost is in the desirable range for the property owner. It is easy to assume that high levels of efficiency are obtained when one does not understand the many factors involved in evaluating performance.

System performance, by design, is obtained from a series of related decisions and the importance of each decision is somewhat in proportion to when it occurs in the design process. Basic decisions on the selection and use of irrigation methods, control and products (see Chapter 1), will not only establish levels of irrigation performance and dependability, but will also set up the demand for system development and influence all design decisions that will follow until completion.

Landscape irrigation and water conservation are long-term requirements and the true measure of efficiency is not the theoretical performance of a new system, but the actual performance as measured over time. The difference may be as simple as improper operation, but it is often due to inadequate maintenance, a common problem in landscape irrigation. In most systems, it is necessary to consider the maintenance requirements as a major factor in all design decisions. While it may alter the theory of efficiency in some cases, it is a necessary compromise for long term efficiency.

PART I

Irrigation Equipment and Materials

CHAPTER 1

Irrigation Equipment

Landscape irrigation equipment covers a wide range of products that are designed and manufactured for the special irrigation requirements of turf and other types of ornamental plants.

System design begins with the selection of products for the application of moisture. These components may be for the purpose of providing water to an individual plant or to many different plants. There are many types of products available for different areas of coverage and rates of application. However, almost all of these products are related to one of four broad categories:
(1) Spray
(2) Flood
(3) Rotary
(4) Micro

These four categories are not divisions from a standard system of classification, but they are useful to cover basic differences in irrigation method, products and precipitation rates. Although these are common irrigation terms, they can be confusing to anyone that is not familiar with the implied definition in the use of a single word. As an example, products that spray water are used in three of the four categories. "Micro" refers to components with very low flow rates and includes some spray products.

Complete systems may be developed using only one type of product or with several different types. Variations in precipitation rates must be controlled separately, regardless of method. Product selection for a particular requirement may be based on a variety of different factors, such as: type of planting, size of area, water supply, budget and local governmental requirements. Examples of product application are covered in Part III.

SPRAY SPRINKLERS

This type of product is the most versatile of all methods of applying moisture to turfgrass and almost all varieties of ornamental plants. Spray sprinklers provide efficient coverage for small to large areas and are suitable for use on all types of properties. The majority of all products in the "spray" category will provide precipitation rates from 1 to 2 in/hr, at normal spacings.

Figure 1-1 Spray System Operating

Irrigation Equipment

Although there are no fixed limitations on the size of area to which spray sprinklers may be adapted, there are the practical limitations of cost and maintenance due the quantity of sprinklers that would be required on very large projects.

Spray Head Inoperative   Spray Head During Operation

Figure 1-2 Lawn Spray Head Pop-Up Action

Spray heads discharge a fine, uniform spray that resembles small raindrops. Water droplet size will vary with brand and model, nozzle size and operating pressure at the sprinkler. The majority of this equipment will provide satisfactory performance when operating in the 20 to 30 lb/in^2 head pressure range.

Although performance will vary with different nozzles, these heads develop a certain amount of very fine spray when operating with adequate pressure. Lack of any mist floating within and above the spray indicates low pressure and coverage may be deficient. Conversely, abnormally high pressure will develop an excessive amount of mist that will tend to drift up and/or out of the area of coverage.

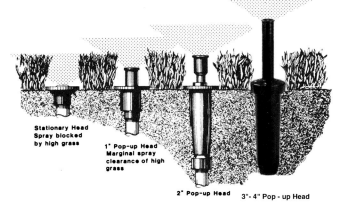

Figure 1-3 Evolution of Pop-Up Heights

Maintaining a range of adequate pressure within the sprinkler piping is not a difficult design problem, except in rare cases. Regardless of the product used to apply moisture, operating pressure that is below or above the desirable range is the direct result of poor system design.

An exemplary layout of a residential spray system is shown in Figure 1-7. It illustrates the wide variety of heads in different capacities, spacings and coverage patterns required to provide complete and uniform watering.

POP-UP HEADS. Spray heads for installation in lawns are pop-up types, often referred to as "lawn heads." These heads are installed flush with the turf. A nozzle pops-up to deliver the spray during operation and recedes within the body when inoperative.

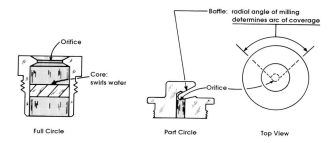

Figure 1-4 Nozzle Construction

Pop-up Heights. Some models of spray heads have a greater pop-up than others. This factor must be considered in relation to spray interference from the grass.

The four sprinklers shown in Figure 1-3 illustrate, from left to right, the progress of sprinkler development for turf. Stationary and one inch pop-up heads are not effective for normal turfgrass applications and are products of the past. Although the pop-up requirement will vary with different types of turfgrass, a two inch pop-up is considered minimum for performance between mowings. Spray heads with 3 to 4 inches of pop-up height are desirable for average turf conditions.

Nozzles. The normal area of coverage for pop-up spray nozzles varies from 12 to 36 feet in diameter, in increments of one or two feet, depending on the nozzle or orifice size. Shorter radii are available in part-circle nozzles. The rate of application is not consistent throughout the diameter of coverage and variations are not consistent for all nozzle series.

Spray nozzles are available in a wide assortment of part-circle patterns from 90° to 270°. Patterns available within this range will vary with brand and nozzle series; increments of coverage may be as low as 15°, or as high as 90°.

Orifices of nozzles are sized to provide a specified radius of coverage and flow at a specified pressure. The specified pressure must be provided by the system designer to obtain proper coverage. If pressure is too low, the spray will not "break-up" into the required fine water droplets necessary to give proper distribution to the entire radius. Also, the specified radius will probably not be attained.

Fixed-orifice nozzles, as shown in Figure 1-4, are available in some brands. This type of nozzle is engineered for a specific performance requirement. Radius, flow rate and arc of coverage are not adjustable. Performance of the system design is maintained by equal performance at the site. Different sizes are selected by the designer for coverage requirements.

Adjustable nozzles feature an adjustment screw for regulating the spray radius. The amount of radius reduction is limited as the flow through the orifice is also reduced. The rate of flow is confined within limits for optimum coverage. Distortion of the spray pattern will occur when the flow is reduced below a certain level.

Figure 1-5 Pop-Up Spray Heads

Spacing. Head spacing requirements vary with the nozzle size, spacing pattern, wind velocity and the distribution profile of the nozzle series. Distance between spray sprinklers will vary from 5 to 24 feet in turf irrigation. Common spacings in open turf areas vary from 12 to 18 feet.

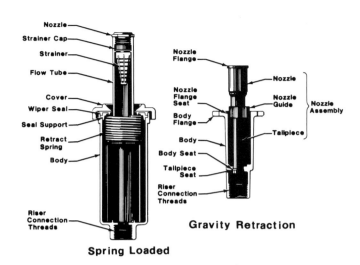

Figure 1-6 Spray Head Construction

Each manufacturer provides nozzle performance tables indicating the diameter of coverage and flow requirements at different operating pressures. Product catalogs are not design manuals and seldom include recommendations on spacings for all types of nozzles. In many cases, spacing information is limited to one or two tables of general recommendations for all types of products. Sprinkler performance is covered in Chapter 8.

Construction. The majority of all pop-up heads available today are of plastic construction and are spring loaded as shown in Figure 1-6. Gravity retraction is the most common method of nozzle retraction for one and two inch pop-up heads of brass construction. The nozzle assembly of gravity retraction heads must contain sufficient weight and clearance within the barrel of the body if it is to recede properly. Spring return of the nozzle offers the advantages of extended pop-up height and a more positive return.

Installation. A lawn head body has a standard pipe thread for connection of the supply piping. A variety of different methods are used for riser piping between the underground lateral and the sprinkler head. Riser assemblies should be flexible to some extent to allow for downward movement without damage to the lateral piping. Flexible plastic nipples or pipe of various lengths are common materials for riser piping. See Figure 1-8. A selection of nipples and elbows provides another common option and allows for movement at each joint. This combination is referred to as a "swing-joint."

Irrigation Equipment

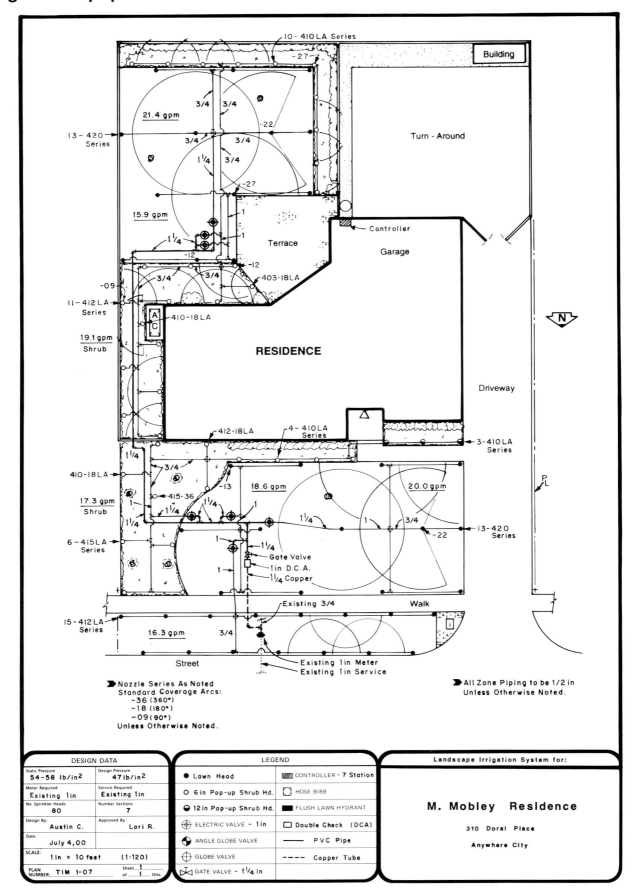

Figure 1-7 Residential Spray System Layout

Standard fittings may be used for swing-joint construction or manufactured products for this purpose are available.

Maintenance. Pop-up spray heads require a minimum amount of maintenance. Dependability of performance is a major advantage with this type of equipment. Operation of each zone for one to two minutes is normally sufficient for visual inspection of sprinkler performance.

It is normally not a problem for spring-loaded heads to be slightly below grade. The wiper-seal prevents soil and other debris from entering the body of the head. See Figure 1-6. Failure of a nozzle to retract is normally the result of an excessive amount of soil being trapped between the wiper-seal and the flow tube. In most cases, this problem is isolated to individual heads where the cover and wiper seal are below grade, or the sprinkler is in a location that is susceptible to the collection of debris on top of the head. Type of soil at the site is also a factor in retraction problems as soil particle size will influence the performance of the wiper seal. Pressure-activated type seals normally provide superior performance.

Extensive turf growth over a long period of time, or the addition of top soil, may require a new nipple length or adjustment of the riser assembly to reposition the head. The sprinkler should be raised only as necessary to compensate for changes in grade. Heads that are set too high will be a hazard and easily damaged from any type of impact or heavy load, including lawn maintenance equipment.

SPECIAL LAWN NOZZLES. A wide selection of spray nozzles with special features is available to the designer. Most of these products are provided as alternatives to the use of standard nozzles and availability will vary with brand and nozzle series. Moisture application rates may or may not be compatible with different brands or nozzle series.

Low Angle Nozzles. The majority of all standard lawn nozzles have a spray trajectory of 30° to 40° above horizontal. However, some nozzle series have a zero degree, flat trajectory, and others have 10° to 15°, low angle trajectory, in part-circle nozzles. In some series, the designer has a choice, with part-circle nozzles available in either a high or low angle of trajectory.

Low angle trajectory reduces the adverse effect of wind drift. This is an important consideration in some areas of coverage, such as part-circle sprinklers along side a walk or street.

Strip Nozzles. Spray nozzles for watering long, narrow strips of turf, or other types of low planting, are available in several different types. Some models must be installed in the center of the strip and others are located along one side of the strip. Width of coverage varies with brand and nozzle series. Spray coverage may not be complete in some models and spacing is an important consideration for the designer.

Pressure Compensating Nozzles. Low operating pressure is one of the most common reasons for poor coverage of spray heads. However, excessive operating pressure will also have a negative effect on cover-

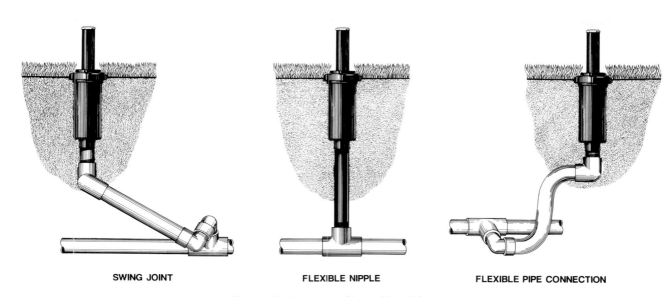

SWING JOINT   FLEXIBLE NIPPLE   FLEXIBLE PIPE CONNECTION

Figure 1-8 Examples of Lawn Head Risers

Irrigation Equipment

age. In most cases, excessive pressure can be controlled at the zone valve and pressure differential between heads can be controlled by pipe sizing; see Chapter 11.

Pressure compensating nozzles, or separate components for use with standard nozzles, are useful if the pressure to the zone is not controlled or zone conditions are unusual. For example, major differences of pressure will occur between heads as the result of extreme differences in elevation between the sprinklers. In most cases, the recommended operating pressure for this type of nozzle is in the 40 to 70 lb/in^2 range and pressure compensation is limited to sprinkler pressures above 30 lb/in^2.

Figure 1-9 Stream Spray System

Figure 1-10 Typical Shrub Spray Heads

Stream Spray Nozzles. This type of nozzle disperses water over the rated coverage area with small streams. Therefore, these nozzles do not provide complete coverage and spacing should be equal to, or less than, the radius of coverage. With such spacing the streams

adequately "crisscross" to provide coverage between the streams. See Figure 1-9.

Most brands and nozzle series are available in full, half and quarter circle patterns only. The very small orifices of stream nozzles require a clean water supply to avoid an abnormal amount of maintenance. These nozzles are often used for ground cover on banks and berms to minimize run-off, as they provide a low rate of application. Precipitation rates are not compatible with other types of spray nozzles.

SHRUB HEADS. Spray heads designed for installation above or below all types of ornamental plants deliver water exactly the same as a lawn head. Shrub heads, as shown in Figure 1-10, are installed on stationary risers. The designer should use caution when specifying this type of head, as pipe risers which extend above grade can be hazardous. Also, some method should be included in the riser piping to allow for movement, such as a flexible nipple or swing-joint. This is important to minimize personal injury and equipment damage. Special consideration should be given to shrub heads that are adjacent to walks, patios, driveways and parking areas.

The visual appearance of a shrub riser is also a factor of consideration, as the property owner may object to the unsightly appearance of a permanent pipe. Risers that are installed adjacent to a building wall or fence are somewhat less obvious, and are normally not as objectionable.

On Fixed Riser   On Retractable Riser

Figure 1-11 Shrub Spray Head

Shrub heads are available in many different combinations of nozzles and connecting bodies. Some are designed specifically for shrub head applications and others use standard lawn nozzles and adapters for connection to riser piping.

Pop-up shrub heads are available as an alternative to a stationary riser. See Figure 1-11. The retractable riser is desirable in many locations to avoid the problems that often exist with stationary pipe risers. They are especially suitable for low ground cover and dwarf planting areas. Several brands have shrub models that will provide either a 6 or 12 inch pop-up height.

FLOOD HEADS

Flood irrigation is a category that covers any type of moisture application that is not limited to coverage over the top of planting. Heads are normally installed on low risers that extend above grade, but at a height that is less than some of the surrounding plant material. This method is often necessary with many varieties of plant material that will grow to a height in excess of 3 feet, at maturity. In some planting beds, it is used to avoid the hazard or appearance of exposed pipe risers. There are also applications where it is not desirable to spray water on the foliage due to the type of planting or the quality of the water.

Complete coverage of the planting bed surface may occur in small areas, but it is seldom attempted in large planting areas, unless the heads are at very close spacings. Spacing for design is often difficult to determine, as requirement will vary with product, soil conditions and quantity, spacing and type of planting. Although it may not be practical to provide separate control for isolated requirements of these products, flood irrigation requires special attention to variations in application rates. Different types of products and spacings are seldom compatible, and separate control valves are recommended. Separate control may also be necessary to allow for major variations of drainage in different beds.

Three common types of products are used for different variations of flood watering. Some of these products have a fixed rate of flow and some have flow rates that vary with operating pressure. However, most of these heads have manual adjustments to regulate the rate of flow. Methods of applying water, in some cases, are the same or similar to methods used in "micro-irrigation", except at higher rates of flow.

BEDSPRAY HEADS. Any type of spray nozzle can be used as a bedspray head, although some nozzles are engineered for this special purpose. Most of the nozzles selected for this application will have a low flow rate and will provide a minimum amount of low-angle spray coverage. Spray nozzles offer the advantage of providing some coverage that is not dependent upon water movement through the soil.

BUBBLER HEADS. Adjustable bubbler heads are very useful to water a very small bed or an individual plant. See Figure 1-12. A pressure compensating bubbler is a good alternative if the actual flow rate requirement is known by the designer. A degree of caution is suggested for any other bubbler head application. Careful consideration of soil conditions is very important when coverage to several plants is totally dependent upon surface flooding. The use of widely-spaced bubblers, for eventual movement of water across the surface, is not an efficient way to water large areas.

JET SPRINKLERS. These heads are known to the trade by such names as "spider", "stream bubbler" and "jet irrigator." They provide directional control of a limited number of jet streams. See Figure 1-12. Each stream will tend to create a small "puddle" of water on the surface of the planting bed unless the stream is dispersed by foliage.

Heads are adjustable and, at low adjustment, the streams reach out only a foot or two, providing a very slow soaking action for close-located shrubs. In the full-open position, radius of coverage will be 3 to 4 feet.

Trickle Bubbler

Umbrella Bubbler

"Jet" Sprinkler

Figure 1-12 Flood Watering Heads

Irrigation Equipment

DESIGN CONSIDERATIONS

Many irrigation systems are designed using spray sprinklers for coverage in all lawn and planting areas. Many others may be complete spray systems, except that some, or all of the planting beds are watered by flood irrigation. In some cases the planting beds are not watered by automatic irrigation.

The majority of spray heads will provide precipitation rates of one to two inches per hour. Actual rate depends on head spacing and flow rate of the sprinklers. Precipitation rates of flood equipment also vary with the quantity and flow of heads and the area of coverage.

Systems are zoned and operated in sections or circuits. Operating zones are developed by considering the basic differences in irrigation requirements and variations in precipitation rates of different equipment. The number of heads per circuit is dependent on the flow requirements of each head and the capacity and pressure of the water supply.

Watering programs for automatic systems are developed to set up a schedule of operation. Programs cover the number of operating cycles per week, the starting time of each cycle and the duration time of each zone. Some zones may be limited to one operating cycle per week and others may operate on multiple cycles per day. Programs for system operation should be changed as necessary to provide irrigation that is in proportion to the demand.

The current trend in automation is to include climate and moisture sensors to minimize the requirement for human monitoring of weather conditions and operating program changes by the user. This trend is likely to continue in the future with new and improved products to measure the irrigation requirement and automatically alter the watering schedule. See Automatic Operation, Remote Sensors.

Watering at night is, for a variety of different reasons, the best time for automatic operation of the system. The percentage of water loss due to evaporation is considerably lower than for daytime operation. Irrigation should be completed as near to dawn as possible for best results. Avoid watering in the late evening hours if possible, as overnight dampness provides ideal condition for growth of moss, fungus, etc. The preferred time for turfgrass irrigation is between 4 and 8 a.m.

The capacity of the water supply must be somewhat in proportion to the size of the property to avoid too many zones and a total watering time beyond reasonable limits.

COST FACTORS

The cost of a spray system, or any other type of system, will vary considerably with such factors as type of equipment, kind of piping, regional labor rates, quality of system design, etc. Due to the many variables, there is no single "rule of thumb" that can be applied to cost estimations. For example, a corner lot will cost more than an inside lot of the same size because a greater number of part-circle sprinklers will be needed for perimeter watering.

Part-circle heads cost approximately the same amount as full-circles, installed. Therefore, a half-circle head will cost twice as much as a full-circle in relation to the amount of area watered. A quarter-circle would cost four times as much, etc.

Ball   **Gear**   **Impact**

Figure 1-13 Typical Rotary Pop -Up Sprinkler Heads

Pipe, fittings and plumbing valves, which serve as a framework for the system, and labor comprise a major portion of the overall cost. Labor is largely a fixed cost (subject only to the economies that may be realized from efficiency and mechanization). The cost of pipe and fittings will naturally change with the grade of materials specified.

These heads are available in both full-circle and part-circle models.

The remaining portion of the cost is made up of irrigation equipment consisting of heads, control valves, automatic controllers and accessories. Trying to seek savings on this equipment can very well lead to false economy when realizing that low cost equipment can be expected to meet minimum standards of performance, at best. Irrigation performance and maintenance are major factors of consideration when selecting products for the development of a system that is environmentally and cost-effective.

ROTARY SPRINKLERS

Rotary sprinklers utilize slow-rotating, high-velocity streams to distribute water over relatively large circular or semi-circular areas. Depending on the model of sprinkler, one to several streams are used to provide coverage.

Diameter of coverage will range from 30 feet to over 200 feet. Rotary sprinklers are suitable for any type of project with large open areas, such as estate homes, parks, schools, athletic fields, public buildings, factories and golf courses.

Rotary sprinklers are used in some cases on smaller properties for economy or due to the flow restrictions of a small water supply. Complete coverage is often difficult to obtain due to trees and other obstructions. Water sprayed on buildings, paved areas and a neigh-

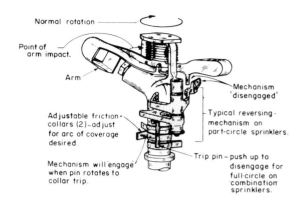

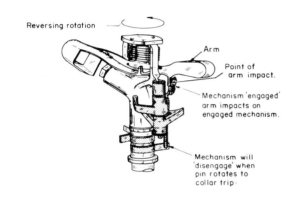

Figure 1-15 Part-Circle Reversing Mechanism

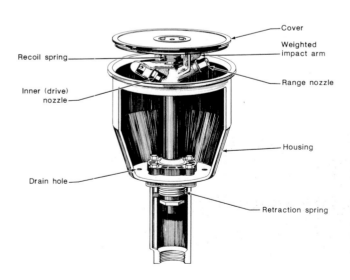

Figure 1-14 Full-Circle, Impact Drive, Rotary Pop-Up Head

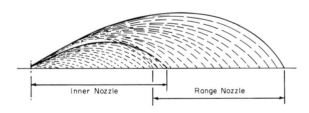

Figure 1-16 Distribution of 2-Nozzle Rotary Sprinklers

bor's property may be objectionable. Low precipitation rates may also be a problem in some climate regions.

Pop-up rotary heads, as shown in Figure 1-13, are used in turfgrass areas. The head is completely concealed in the ground except for the cover plate, which is exposed at ground level. The nozzle portion pops-up for operation and recedes within the sprinkler housing when inoperative.

During operation, water flow through the head will drive any one of several types of mechanisms to rotate the nozzle assembly. Rotary head drives are named to describe the basic component providing the rotational drive force. The three most common types are the "impact" drive, the "gear" drive and the "ball" drive.

IMPACT DRIVE HEADS. The impact drive rotary sprinkler employs a weighted, spring-loaded drive arm to provide the force to rotate the nozzle assembly. The sprinkling stream deflects the arm sideways and the spring pulls the arm back to the nozzle assembly and into the path of the stream. As the drive arm completes each swing cycle it impacts against the nozzle assembly, rotating it slightly. See Figure 1-14. Most models of this type of sprinkler are available in both full-circle and part-circle.

Figure 1-18 Gear Drive Rotary Pop-Up Head

Nozzle	Operating Pressure PSI	Flow GPM	Diameter Coverage (ft.)
E12 x A11 3/16 x 11/64	50 60 70 80 90	12.5 13.8 15.1 16.4 17.8	102 105 107 110 112
E13 x A11 13/64 x 11/64	50 60 70 80 90	15.0 16.4 17.8 19.0 20.2	110 113 117 120 122
*E14 x A11 7/32 x 11/64	50 60 70 80 90	16.2 17.5 18.8 20.1 21.5	114 120 123 126 126
E16 x A11 1/4 x 11/64	50 60 70 80 90	19.0 20.3 21.7 23.0 24.3	116 122 126 129 129

Figure 1-17
Typical Rotary Sprinkler Performance Table

Adjustable Arcs. Part-circles are adjustable for degree of arc to be watered. Adjustment, depending on model, can be from 5 to 355 degrees. Some models have adjustments with detents to retain the arc of coverage selected.

Nozzling. Full-circle, pop-up impact sprinklers generally utilize two opposed nozzles; a "range" nozzle and an "inner" nozzle which make possible larger diameters of coverage. Long streams can't provide "breakup" of the stream into the small water droplets required to give distribution for the entire length. So, the "range" nozzle provides distribution at the outer areas of coverage diameter. And, the "inner" nozzle provides the distribution from the head to where the "range" nozzle begins its distribution.

Part-circle impacts also utilize two nozzles. However, the nozzles both face the same direction.

Only one nozzle is utilized on some smaller impact rotaries (both full-circle and part-circle) where the coverage falls within the range of the "inner" nozzles previously described.

Most brands of impact rotary heads are made in several different physical sizes. The nozzles are changeable, thus allowing each model to accommodate several different orifice sizes. It is important to note that while different size nozzles provide varying coverage diameters, each size also requires different water pressures and flow volumes to operate correctly. There is some overlap in the capabilities of various nozzles. Figure 1-17 is a typical data table. It is included to demonstrate the varying performance of nozzles in impact rotary sprinklers.

To accomplish the distribution pattern with two-nozzle sprinklers, as shown in Figure 1-16, the manufacturer determines the best combination of nozzles. Caution should be used when changing nozzles in the field. Incorrect nozzle combinations will upset the distribution, resulting in areas with deficient coverage. Some nozzles are available with an adjustable "diffuser-pin" to provide a means of improving distribution and coverage. However, improper use of diffuser pins can also have a negative effect on distribution. Two other cautions should be noted: (1) Use nozzle sizes for which water pressure and flow volume can be supplied according to the recommendations of the manufacturer. (2) Design in accordance with manufacturer's recommendation for optimum sprinkler performance.

GEAR DRIVE HEADS. Gear drive rotary heads provide a steady, powerful rotation to the sprinkling streams. Water under pressure enters the base of the head through a stator which converts it into high velocity jets. These jets are then impinged against a turbine-like impeller causing it to spin at high speeds. A gear train, driven by the impeller, reduces the speed and converts the drive into a powerful turning torque. This torque gives the nozzle-assembly the relatively slow rotational speed required for good coverage and precipitation. See Figure 1-18.

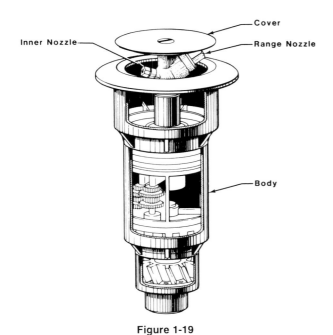

Figure 1-19
Typical Design of Large - Size Gear Drive, Rotary Pop-Up Head

Part-circle models incorporate a reciprocating mechanism that changes the direction of the nozzle flow tube. The arc of coverage is adjustable in most part-circle models. Gear trains are contained in separate housings to protect the gears from debris in the water.

Nozzling. The distribution pattern of gear drive rotary sprinklers is accomplished much the same as it is with the impact drive type. Some models provide a selection of different nozzle sizes with each head. Diameter of coverage and flow volume will vary with nozzle size and

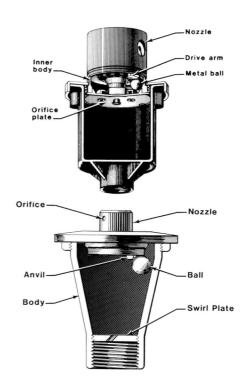

Figure 1-20 Ball Drive, Rotary Pop-Up Heads

pressure at the head. Product performance tables will provide the range of pressure recommended to maintain a good distribution profile within the area of coverage.

Pipe size connection in the base of gear-drive sprinklers varies from 1/2 inch to 1 1/2 inches depending upon the model. Pop-up height, the physical size and the cost of heads will also vary with different models. Figure 1-19 illustrates the typical design configuration of a very large head.

BALL DRIVE ROTARIES. Figure 1-20 illustrates a sprinkler utilizing a spinning metal ball to provide the power to rotate the nozzle. Water under pressure enters the head through a plate with angular openings located in the base of the head. This action causes the water to spin at high circular velocity. This circular flow causes a free metal ball to spin up and around the top inside of the body. As the ball spins, it strikes a projecting drive arm attached to the nozzle. Each impact rotates the nozzle slightly. The impacts occur so rapidly that, in effect, a slow, steady rotation is seemingly accomplished.

Part-circles. Some ball drive sprinklers employ a hood over and around the nozzle to provide part-circle coverage: Figure 1-21. The hood has an opening on one side corresponding to the arc of coverage. During nozzle rotation, the sprinkling streams are "blocked-out" as they enter the closed portion of the hood. The running clearance between the hood and nozzle can cause some degree of puddling near the head.

EFFICIENCY

Sprinkler heads, regardless of type, brand and model are not 100% efficient in providing equal distribution of moisture in every square foot of the coverage area. Performance at the site will vary with model, spacing, pressure and wind condition. Theoretical performance of products, without consideration for wind effect, is not recommended for system design.

Pop-up rotary equipment is the only practical method of providing coverage in very large turfgrass areas. However, there are two potential problems associated with the use of rotary heads. First, there is the obvious problem of obtaining proper coverage should the nozzle assembly fail to rotate. Dependability of rotation is a very important consideration in the selection of products. Visual inspection of sprinkler operation is a necessary requirement of scheduled maintenance. Second, wind will alter the distribution of the long streams. Distortion of coverage will vary with velocity and direction of the wind, and the characteristics of the streams.

Precipitation rates of rotary sprinklers are considerably less than spray heads. Operation time required to apply the same amount of water will average about four times longer. There are advantages and disadvantages of lower precipitation rates. Sprinkler performance is discussed in Chapter 8.

Many different factors will influence the irrigation performance of rotary sprinklers. While most of these are system design considerations, some are based on proper maintenance.

Christiansen, in his bulletin on extensive research of impact rotary sprinkler precipitation (a), reported that these sprinklers are subject to uneven distribution due to variations in speed of rotation. These problems are discussed in Chapter 8, "Sprinkler Operation." Since rotation variation increases with wear, and does not become visible to the eye until the turf shows uneven

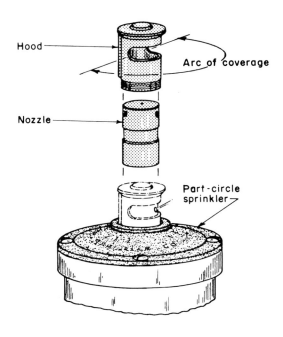

Figure 1-21 Part-Circle Nozzle Hood

distribution, maintenance programs should include a rotation check every year or two.

DESIGN CONSIDERATIONS

Product Selection. Careful selection of model is vital to a good rotary system design. Factors to be considered before selection of rotary heads include: the area to be sprinkled and available water volume and pressure. Chapter 12 covers this consideration in depth. There are rotary heads available for almost every type of situation. For example, rotary heads specifically designed for use in larger plots with small water supply. These heads can be spaced about twice as far apart as spray heads. On the other hand, these rotary heads should never be used in large areas with high pressures.

Conversely, use of large-coverage rotaries in areas that are more suitable for use of the smaller coverage heads, even though the water supply is adequate, will result in a totally undesirable system. With bordered areas, due to overlap required, water waste usually increases as the sprinkler diameter of coverage increases.

Selection of product may include the requirement of certain features which may be standard, optional or not available with some models. The following five features are provided as examples of special requirements:

(1)*Repairable Sprinkler.* Most impact drive heads can be repaired at the site. The majority of gear drive heads available have sealed internal assemblies and the entire drive mechanism must be replaced. Maintenance cost is an important factor for consideration in product selection.

(2) *Rubber Covers.* Rubber covers are recommended for many different types of projects, including schools and athletic fields.

(3) *Non-potable Alert Cover.* "Purple" is the standard color code used to indicate the use of non-potable water in the system. This is a "Do Not Drink" caution.

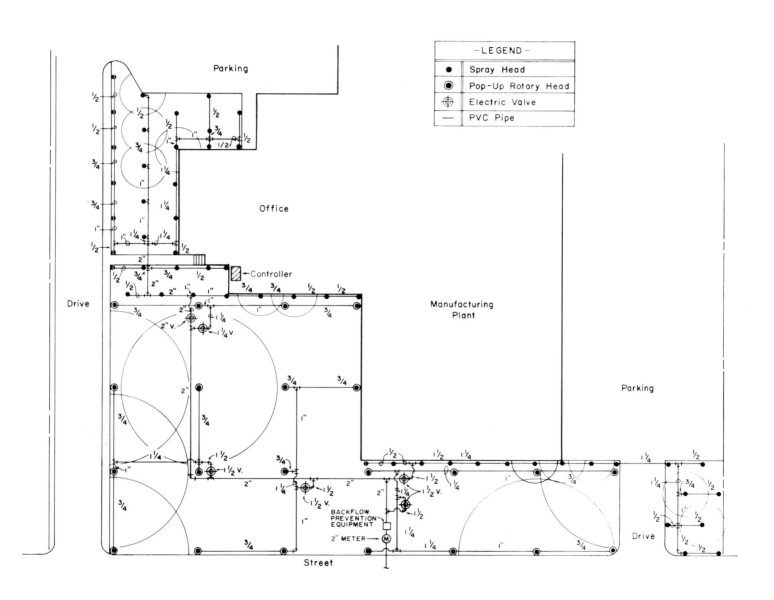

Figure 1-22 Effect of Property Size and Shape on Rotary System Cost

(4) *Check Valve.* An internal check valve (or separate external component) is used to avoid lateral line drainage through the rotary head when not operating. This will eliminate undesirable "puddling" around the head and is useful to control "dryline" shock, as discussed in Chapter 4.

(5) *Valve-in-Head.* A valve within or attached to the head for individual control of large rotary sprinklers. (Valve-under-head option is discussed in Chapter 14).

ZONING. Pop-up rotary systems, like spray systems, are valved and operated in zones, or sections. Again, the number of heads in each zone depends on the volume of water available and the pressure.

Precipitation. The full and part-circle rotary heads of some models are not balanced to provide uniform rates of precipitation. For example, some have the same nozzle orifices for full and fractional circles. Consequently, quarter-circle heads will apply twice as much water as half-circles and four times as much as the full-circles; half-circles will apply twice as much as full-circles. Obviously, each type (full, halves and quarters) must be valved separately from the other types in this case. Otherwise, certain areas will have to be flooded in order to apply enough precipitation elsewhere.

Needless separate valving poses a problem for the designer and adds considerably to the cost of labor and material. Heads that are compatible precipitation-wise may be valved together, making a more compact system at substantial savings.

Because of the character of impact rotary sprinklers, the precipitation rates of full and part-circle models are seldom, if ever, compatible for any given radius of coverage. Therefore, full-circles, part-circles averaging 180°, and those close to 90° should generally be valved separately.

Many models of rotary sprinklers are available with precipitation rates of full and part-circles compatible to the extent that they may be valved together. This is accomplished by selecting nozzles that will provide flow rates in proportion to the area of coverage. While this method is very practical, it will seldom provide exactly the same rate of precipitation, as diameter of coverage will normally change with different nozzle sizes.

Caution. Before valving different types of sprinklers together, consider pressure requirements in addition to precipitation rates. For example: even though two sprinklers have the same precipitation rate, one may require 35 lb/in^2 water pressure at the base of the head while the other requires 60 lb/in^2. Obviously, a piping system cannot be designed to handle this disparity.

Spacings. Coverage ratings are generally given for still air and must be derated to compensate for normal wind conditions in the locale of the system. A standard formula for spacing is not feasible because of the varying stream characteristics of different sprinklers. Manufacturers will normally provide recommendations for different products, spacing patterns and wind conditions. Spacings are discussed in Chapter 8.

SPECIAL CONSIDERATIONS. As previously pointed out, the long streams of rotary sprinklers are affected by wind; even moderate wind. Prevailing winds and site conditions should be carefully considered when designing a rotary system. Care should be exercised that sprinklers are located so that the streams will not blow onto areas where such watering would be objectionable. Water on walks, driveways, and adjacent property is also wasteful.

It should be noted that with rotary systems, there are almost always some relatively confined areas that must be watered with spray sprinklers. The spray sprinklers must be operated independently from the rotary sprinklers because of the large variance in precipitation rates of the two types of sprinklers.

COST FACTORS

The cost of a rotary system will average 50 to 70 percent of the cost of a spray system in the same property. The differential between the two systems tends to diminish with a reduction of area, and increases as the sprinkled area becomes larger. The principal reason for this is that the ratio of part-circle to full-circle heads increases as the property becomes smaller, requiring more perimeter watering.

Unlike spray heads, the unit material cost for part-circle rotary heads is somewhat greater than for full-circles. However, the area of coverage is only one-half as large in the case of half heads and one-fourth as large for quarter heads. Therefore, the cost per square foot of coverage is considerably more than two times greater for half heads and four times for quarter heads. These ratios may vary with model.

The rotary system in Figure 1-22 illustrates the above premise. Because of the shape and size of the property and water supply, a spray system could be installed for very little additional cost.

MICRO PRODUCTS

"Micro" refers to very low flow rates, as compared to standard spray and rotary equipment. Micro products are normally rated in gallons per hour. Micro irrigation covers any method of applying moisture at a very slow rate of application. This includes drip, trickle and spray products. "Low flow" and "low volume" are also common terms used to describe this method of irrigation.

Micro irrigation is normally used, and somewhat limited to, providing water to individual plants or very small areas of coverage. Soil conditions are very important, as the rate of application must be close to the long-term absorption rate of the soil.

Many suggest that low pressure drip systems were first developed in the Middle East in the 1930's. In any event, agricultural irrigation in arid lands is the primary reason for development of low-volume products. Mini-sprays (15 gph) and porous pipe were available for use in landscape irrigation systems before 1960. However, almost all of the drip irrigation products currently used in landscape irrigation are agricultural products. The most common components for the application of moisture above grade are emitters, bubblers and mini/micro-spray nozzles. Subsurface application products have major limitations in permanently installed landscape irrigation systems. Visual inspection of product performance is a necessary requirement for maintenance of any type of micro-irrigation system.

Single   Multiple

Courtesy of Salco

Figure 1-23 Emitters

EMITTERS

There is a wide variety of different emitters available for drip irrigation. Almost all of the emitters used in landscape irrigation are of the pressure-compensating type, and can be used with operating pressures of 10 to 50 lb/in². Single outlet and multiple outlet emitters are available in flow rates of .5, 1.0 and 2.0 gph. Emitters are color-coded for different flow rates. See Figure 1-23. Protective boxes are available for emitters installed below grade.

BUBBLERS

Adjustable and pressure-compensating bubblers are available for low-flow irrigation. Some models provide a "trickle" of water flow down the riser and other models provide a soft, umbrella type of spray coverage. (Jet-Irrigator heads can also be adjusted down for low flow of individual streams). See Figure 1-12. Pressure-compensating bubblers are available in flow rates as low as 15 gph. See Figure 1-24.

MICRO-SPRAY

Small, low-angle trajectory nozzles offer the advantage of dispersing a fine spray of water over a full-circle or part-circle area of coverage. Some models offer a diameter of coverage as small as four feet and a flow rate as low as 5 gph. Micro-spray nozzles are normally installed above grade, using a distribution tube stake. Nozzles with higher flow rates, which may be described as "mini-sprays", are often installed on pop-up spray heads. See Figure 1-25.

Bubbler   **Bubbler Operating**

Figure 1-24 Pressure Compensating Bubbler

EFFICIENCY

Micro-irrigation can be very efficient in maintaining a desired level of soil moisture in the root zone of individual plants and/or trees. It is especially suited for xeriscape projects and regions where water-conservation is a high priority requirement for irrigation. The low oper-

Stake   Pop-Up

Courtesy of Agrifim

Figure 1-25 Micro / Mini-Spray Sprinklers

ating pressure requirement of these products can also be an advantage in some cases.

There are also disadvantages, including a high maintenance requirement of products with very small orifices. System operation must be checked on a frequent basis to allow for inspection of each water outlet. Moisture in the root zone is often very limited, and plant stress can occur in a short period of time. Clogged components should be repaired or replaced as soon as possible.

Pipe, tubing and other equipment exposed on the surface of the planting bed can be unsightly and subject to vandalism, or unintentional damage.

DESIGN CONSIDERATIONS

The systems designer has the responsibility of obtaining some balance between irrigation efficiency and a system that is practical to maintain.

Providing moisture to individual plants at a rate that is somewhat equal to the water use rate of different plants can be difficult, without human monitoring of requirement on a frequent basis.

Planting beds will often have a variety of different types of plants and water requirements are not simply based on the size difference of plant material. Although irrigation design is obviously important in conservation, the basic water requirement is established by the landscape design. Engineering a moisture supply system to conserve water by achieving high levels of efficiency, is limited for very practical reasons.

Higher flow rates have become more common in recent years as a compromise to reduce some of the maintenance problems associated with "drop by drop" irriga-

tion. Low-volume may be more realistic for the average project as compared to flow rates less than 15 gph.

Micro-irrigation circuits are based on the available water supply and zone separation as required for control of application. Piping design to zones is similar to any other method of irrigation. However, special attention is necessary for filtration and pressure control of water supply into the zone piping.

QUICK COUPLER EQUIPMENT

The term "quick coupler" relates to the valve as shown in Figure 1-28. This equipment was very popular for turf irrigation systems during the first half of the twentieth century. These water supply systems were used primarily in golf courses, parks, schools and other large properties. See Figure 1-26. Manual systems of this type are seldom installed today due to the high cost of hand labor and water usage efficiencies.

However, the components of these systems are still used frequently in conjunction with spray or rotary systems. (1) As a temporary means of watering areas in which it is not economical to install a regular system such as areas to be re-developed at a later date, etc. (2) On pressure mains of a system to provide water for a myriad of uses other than normal sprinkling. For instance, deep-watering newly-planted trees. Equipment consists of above-ground rotary sprinklers, couplers (or keys), swivel hose connectors and quick coupler valves. See Figure 1-29.

ABOVE-GROUND SPRINKLERS. Most of these sprinklers are of the basic impact type with a swinging drive-arm. In one variation, the drive arm swings vertically instead of horizontally. Principle of operation is as

Figure 1-26 Quick-Coupler Irrigation System

described for impact drive, pop-up rotary sprinklers which are an adaptation of the above- ground sprinkler.

The coverage arcs of the part circles are adjustable and a "combination-type" permits the part-circle model to be changed to a full-circle by moving a pin or lever.

QUICK-COUPLING VALVES. The quick-coupling valve is used to connect the above-ground rotary sprinkler to the water piping. These valves are installed flush with the turf, the same as sprinkler heads. Valves are sized for flow requirements of the sprinkler.

In the normal method of use, water pressure is maintained continuously at the quick-coupling valve. Water pressure and a spring hold the valve closed when not in use.

METHOD OF OPERATION. The above-ground sprinkler is connected to a coupler. The coupler is inserted into the valve and turned, forcing the seat down and open. This allows water to flow through the coupler and sprinkler.

An accessory (the swivel hose ell) can be attached to the coupler for hose connection. A hose is often desirable for special watering chores. This type hose connection is recommended for all systems using a non-potable water supply. Without the coupler, unknowing persons can't use the water for drinking as they could with a standard above-ground hose faucet. Color-coded valve covers are available for non-potable alert.

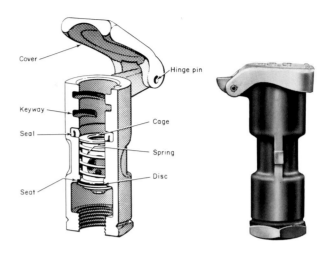

Figure 1-28 Quick-Coupler Valve

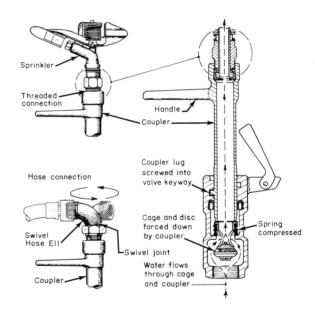

Figure 1-29 Quick-Coupler Valve in Open Position

On smaller, more compact installations, it is customary to design the system so that sprinklers can be attached to successive quick-coupling valves for the sake of convenience. On larger projects, the system is usually planned for connecting sprinklers at alternate valves for each operation; or every third valve, or even alternate rows in some cases. Golf courses using very large sprinklers may be limited to operation of only a few at a time per fairway.

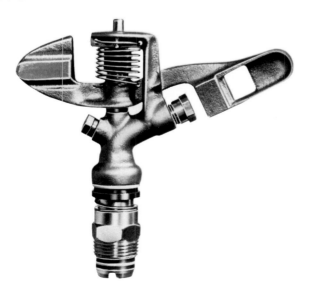

Figure 1-27 Above-Ground Rotary Sprinkler

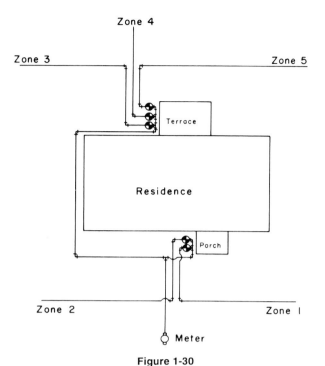

Figure 1-30
System Using Standard Commercial Globe Valves

With operation as outlined in the preceding paragraph, the flow of water is quite well dispersed throughout the system. Spreading out the water load in this manner will permit reduction of pipe sizes, providing initial cost savings without affecting performance. However, some additional cost of moving sprinklers around will be incurred.

DESIGN CONSIDERATIONS

Watering is accomplished by individually plugging the sprinkler-coupler combination into the quick-coupling valve. Sprinklers are left in place until the desired amount of precipitation is attained, then the sprinklers are removed and coupled to another set of valves, usually adjacent to the area just watered. Sprinklers are moved about in this manner until all areas have been watered. Sprinkler rotation is slow enough to enable the operator to plug-in and remove sprinklers without getting wet.

The above-ground sprinklers are available with diameters of coverage similar to those of pop-up rotary sprinklers. In addition, a number of models have a significantly greater range of throw. Spacings must be derated to compensate for wind.

COST FACTORS

Total cost comparison of pop-up rotary vs. quick-coupling systems includes (1) amortization of initial cost, (2) operation labor, (3) maintenance, and (4) water usage. Usage efficiency consistently shows that the automatic pop-up rotary system is actually the least expensive over a period of years.

SYSTEM OPERATION

Control, or operation, of system zone valves may be manual or automatic. Manual control is not recommended and a manual system is seldom cost-effective.

MANUAL CONTROL

Manually controlled sprinkler systems use standard commercial globe valves. Globe valves of either the straight or angle type are acceptable. Angle valves are most commonly used because there is much less pressure loss through this type.

Never use gate valves for zone operating valves. They are not intended for continual use and will soon leak if subjected to such use.

Globe valves with swivel disc holders and soft rubber discs for cold water service should be specified in order to avoid an abnormal amount of maintenance. Brass-to-brass seats inevitably leak under continuous use.

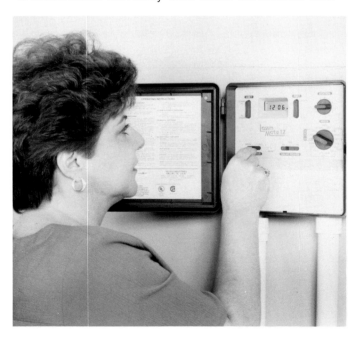

Figure 1-31 Automated Watering

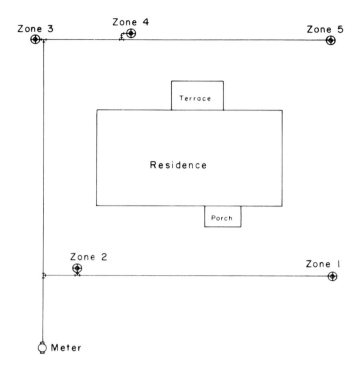

Figure 1-32 System Using Remote Control Valves

Stems should be heavy enough to support key operation without breaking. Stem packing should be generous. Ports through the valves should be full-size to minimize pressure loss.

Manual control valves may be decentralized for economy or manifolded at a central point for control convenience. The latter is more costly, especially on large installations. However, it is accepted practice on residential lawn systems. In any case, manually operated zone control valves should be located so the operator will not get wet, even with wind.

AUTOMATIC OPERATION

Automatic systems have a great advantage over manual control. They offer complete independence from watering chores, release time for leisure, provide continuity of the watering schedule during periods of owner absence, save water and save the cost of labor on larger properties. Automatic systems now comprise a majority of the new installation market. The use of

automatic control to maintain an efficient watering program is a basic requirement for systems where water conservation is desirable or necessary.

Automatic control consists of a conveniently located "controller" which operates "remote control valves." One valve is required for each watering zone.

The remote control valves are dispersed throughout the system, thereby saving considerable quantities of piping. See Figure 1-32. The valves are usually installed at the side entrance to a zone or at the center of a zone, depending on how the main supply pipe is routed. Thus, they are also more efficient and conserve pressure lost in the longer pipe runs of systems with valves manifolded at one or two locations. However, in regions where complete drainage of piping is necessary for freeze protection, control valves may be installed in one location to facilitate "winterizing" of the system.

There are two types of automatic systems: hydraulic and electric. Type refers to the kind of "actuator" employed between the controller and the remote control valves. Almost all modern systems are of the electric type.

CONTROLLERS. Controllers manufactured for the special requirements of landscape and turf irrigation

Figure 1-33 Controller Pedestal

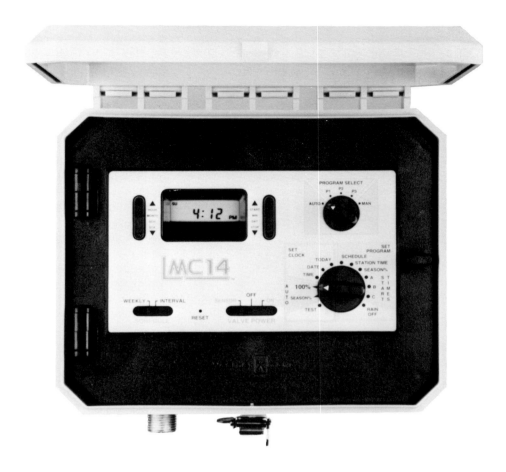

Figure 1-34 Typical Controller Operational Panels

systems vary from electro-mechanical "clock-timers" to complete computer units. Standard units are made to mount on building walls or free standing pedestals. Some models may be mounted either way.

Others are not weatherproof and must be protected. Housings may be plastic or metal. Some are available with industrial-grade plastic or steel enclosures.

Considerations for selection of controller are location, size and type of project, programming features required and cost. Also consider that an automatic system can only be as efficient and dependable as the controller, regardless of the efficiency that may have been engineered into the system for coverage, water requirements, piping and selection of other equipment.

OPERATION. Automatic operation of standard controller:

(1) A clock activates the start of the watering cycle at preset times on preset days.

(2) "Stations" are operated one after the other and in sequence. Operating time of each station is preset. Stations are connected to zone valves with external wiring (tubing for hydraulic control systems).

Standard Features. Most standard controllers will have the following basic features:

(1) A 24 hour clock monitor to set starting time(s) of the watering cycle.

(2) A calendar selector for programming day or days of automatic operation. Number of days on repeating calendar varies with controller model.

(3) Variable station time setting to allow for watering duration of each station independently. Range of setting available will vary with model.

(4) Semi-automatic operation to allow the manual start of the automatic cycle without disturbing the preset starting time.

(5) Manual operation of each station at random or in sequence. Depending upon model, station duration may be at preset time or completely independent of timer setting.

(6) A master switch to omit watering during all scheduled cycles. Use of the master switch should not affect the clock operation or the preset program.

(7) Station omit feature to allow any station or stations to be omitted from the automatic watering cycle.

Optional Features. Some of the more common optional features for standard controllers are listed below (Note: Some brands or models may provide these features as standard).

(1) A master valve circuit to provide for operation of a "master" control valve at the entrance to the entire system. The circuit is activated when any controller station is energized. It can be used to eliminate system flow after a cycle is completed should a zone valve fail to close.

(2) A pump control circuit to energize a pump whenever a station is energized. See Chapter 15, "Electrical."

(3) Multiple programs which allow any pre-selected station(s) to be omitted from the automatic cycle on any day or days of the calendar program. This feature is often used to allow less frequent watering of planting areas. With some controllers, stations to be omitted must be selected at time of installation. Other models provide entirely separate schedules that can be reprogrammed at any time with choice of stations, days, start time and station duration.

(4) Electrical suppression to reduce the effects of lightning and high voltage surges on input line and valve circuits. See Chapter 15, "Electrical."

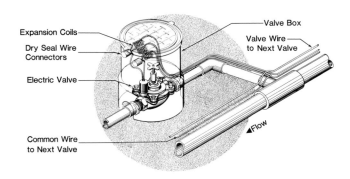

Figure 1-35 Typical Installation of Valve in Valve Box

Hydraulic/Plastic Body

Electric/Plastic Body

Electric/Brass Body

Electric with Pressure Regulation Module

Figure 1-36 Diaphragm Valve Types

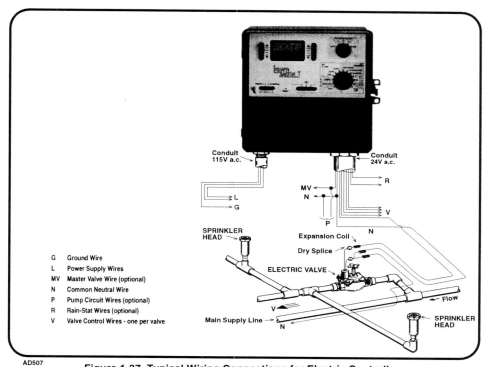

G   Ground Wire
L   Power Supply Wires
MV Master Valve Wire (optional)
N   Common Neutral Wire
P   Pump Circuit Wires (optional)
R   Rain-Stat Wires (optional)
V   Valve Control Wires - one per valve

AD507

Figure 1-37 Typical Wiring Connections for Electric Controllers

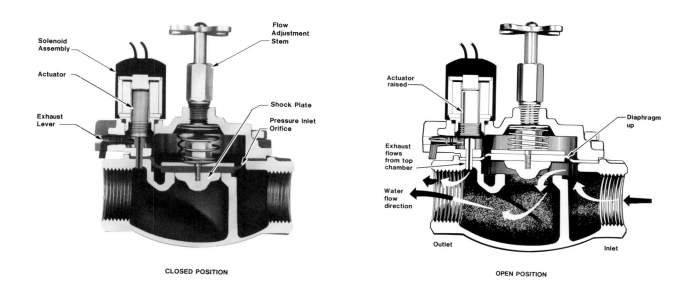

CLOSED POSITION

OPEN POSITION

Figure 1-38 Electric Diaphragm Valve

Irrigation Equipment

Additional Features. Microprocessor based controllers can accommodate many additional features. The ability of a computer to store, retrieve and process data provides a programmable device that is limited only by the zone valves that it controls. Specialized controllers for large or certain types of projects can include video monitors and printers. Sensors can be used to measure soil moisture, temperature, wind, water supply, etc. and alter the scheduled watering program as required.

Multiple Controllers. On larger systems, more than one controller is often used. Some reasons for using multiple controllers are:

(1) Number of zones required exceeds the station capacity of a single controller.

(2) To locate the controller adjacent to that part of the system it controls for visual inspection during manual operation or consideration of valve wiring length.

(3) For convenience of programming when separate watering programs are desired or required for certain areas of the property.

REMOTE CONTROL VALVES. Valves specifically manufactured for automatic irrigation systems are completely buried, therefore less conspicuous. In most cases, valves are enclosed in specially-made boxes with covers installed at grade level. Such installation makes it easier to locate and service the valves when required.

The most important reason for installing remote control valves in burial boxes is to simplify servicing and operation inspection of the system. Most valves have a lever or other device to permit manual opening and closing. This feature eliminates wasted service time for trips back and forth to the controller location.

Material for valve body and cover is, in most cases, either brass (bronze) or plastic. Plastic is, of course, a term that covers a broad range of materials. Other parts may be brass, stainless steel, rubber or plastic. Cost of the more expensive bronze valve is a limiting factor in its application. The majority of control valves used in residential and small commercial systems are of plastic construction. Valve designs, construction and sizes available will vary with brand and model.

Remote control valves are made on the globe valve pattern almost entirely; the straight type being the most prevalent.

Some valves are described as contamination resistant and are recommended for systems using effluent water or what may be described as "dirty" water. This type of valve may also be desirable with some potable water supplies where problems of this type are known to exist. Some models provide added protection from various chemicals by encapsulating the solenoid "actuator" with a protective coating.

Diaphragm-Type Valves. The most commonly used remote control valves for both electric and hydraulic control are the diaphragm type. For the controller to operate these valves, a water pressure differential must be maintained between the top-side and under-side of the diaphragm. For trouble-free operation, a quality diaphragm is required to prevent uncontrolled leakage from one side to the other.

Most diaphragm-type valves have a flow direction based on the globe valve concept, with flow directed "upward" through the valve port. However, some models are designed with a downward flow direction (reverse flow) through the valve port. This concept will minimize stress on the diaphragm since equal pressure is maintained above and below the perimeter of the diaphragm in the closed position. If the diaphragm wall tears, the valve will fail in the closed position. (See Operation - Electric Diaphragm Valves).

There is practically no wear in diaphragm valves. Therefore, parts seldom require renewal. There is no swivel motion on seats to cause leakage as in the case of most types of globe valves. Because of this factor, the seat disc can be molded as a part of the diaphragm to further simplify the valve and reduce the number of parts. See Figure 1-38 and Figure 1-40. In addition, diaphragm valves do not have stem packing, a frequent source of valve leakage.

Flow Adjustment. Most remote control valves include a flow adjustment device. With some valves, this is an optional feature; others provide it standard. This feature is used to reduce flow and pressure to small zones in order to balance them hydraulically with larger zones. Most flow adjustment devices can be used for complete manual shut-off of the valve. See flow adjustment stem, Figure 1-38.

Pressure Regulator. Some models are available with a pressure regulating module to maintain a constant discharge pressure. See Figure 1-36. This feature is useful in systems where the water supply is subject to severe "up and down" pressure fluctuations. In most cases, a single unit can be used at the point of supply and operated by the master valve circuit of the controller.

ELECTRIC AUTOMATIC SYSTEMS. Irrigation systems using electrical circuits between the controller and zone valves are classified as "Electric Automatics."

Wiring. Electrically operated valves manufactured specifically for irrigation systems require less than 30 volts to operate; usually 24 volts. Direct underground burial

of type UF wire (without conduit) is safe with less than 30 volts. However, always check local electric codes before designing systems.

Figure 1-37 illustrates the electric wiring between the controller and electric remote control valves. One control wire is required to each valve from the controller output terminal that controls it. These wires are often referred to as the "station" wires, as they relate to controller stations. However, a variety of different names are used to describe these particular wires. A "common" wire from the controller to all valves is necessary to complete the electrical circuit. Wire sizes depend on the controller model and input voltage, static pressure, length of the wire and the current and voltage requirements of the solenoid.

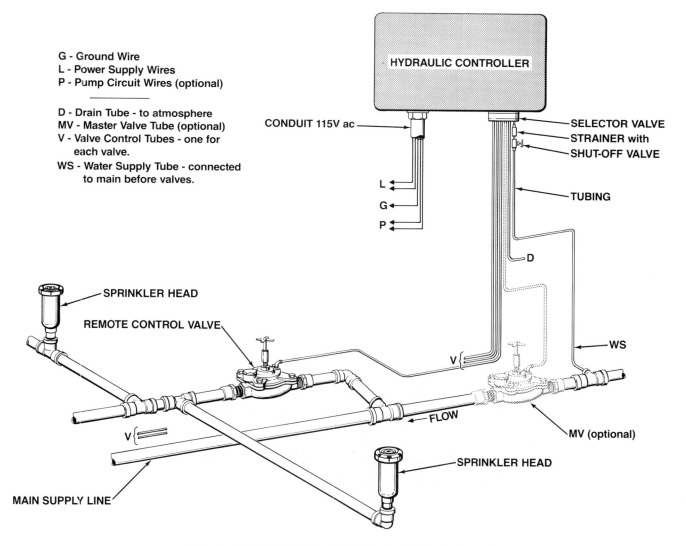

G - Ground Wire
L - Power Supply Wires
P - Pump Circuit Wires (optional)

D - Drain Tube - to atmosphere
MV - Master Valve Tube (optional)
V - Valve Control Tubes - one for
　　each valve.
WS - Water Supply Tube - connected
　　to main before valves.

Figure 1-39 Typical Tubing Installation for Hydraulic Controller

Irrigation Equipment

The electric current "draw" of different brands of valves and the current requirement of different controllers vary. Therefore, wire sizes must be carefully calculated. Most manufacturers furnish tables or other recommendations to simplify controller to valve wire sizing.

Caution should be exercised when "mixing" different brands of controllers and valves. Be sure the controller can supply enough power for the valve and use care in sizing of valve wiring.

Some systems (usually large ones) are designed with one station of the controller operating more than one remote control valve. Before designing such a system, check the capabilities of the equipment that will be specified. Many controllers for electric automatic systems have this capacity, but the number of valves which can be operated varies from model to model. Multiple valves on a single station may require larger wire than for a single valve. And wire sizing is more critical. Again, follow the manufacturer's recommendations.

Operation: Electric Solenoid Diaphragm Valves.
When a valve is not being operated (Figure 1-38, closed position), water under pressure from the sprinkler system "main" pipe line holds the valve closed.

When a controller "station" wired to a valve energizes the solenoid, the magnetic force lifts its actuator off the exhaust port. The pressure of water in the upper (hydraulic) chamber is relieved through the exhaust port which allows the "main" pipe line pressure to force the flexible diaphragm up, opening the valve. (Figure 1-38, open position).

Because a loss of water pressure occurs as water flows through the body of the valve, pressure is greater at the entrance of the inlet port to the upper chamber than at the chamber outlet port. The sizes of the two ports are correlated so water can flow out the exhaust faster than it can enter the upper hydraulic chamber. Therefore, service technicians should be cautioned to never tamper with the port sizing for any reason.

When the controller "station" and solenoid are de-energized, the actuator drops, closing the exhaust port. Pressurized water entering the upper (hydraulic) chamber forces the diaphragm down, closing the valve.

Irrigation water must be clean of debris that could cause the inlet port to be blocked. If this should happen, water could not flow into the upper (hydraulic) chamber and

the valve would remain open. Some valves use an inlet port strainer to keep out larger debris. However, screens can be blocked by build-up of fine debris and require periodic maintenance.

Other valves utilize an inlet port directly through the diaphragm. Large debris that could block the port is normally dislodged as the diaphragm flexes during valve opening and closing. Debris smaller than the inlet port is free to pass through. Since the outlet port is larger than the inlet port, any debris passing through the inlet port will pass through the outlet port.

Normally closed. Electric remote control valves are a "normally-closed" type. The definition means that should the electricity to the valve be interrupted for any reason, such as a power failure, broken wire, etc., the valve will automatically close itself. This feature is of considerable importance.

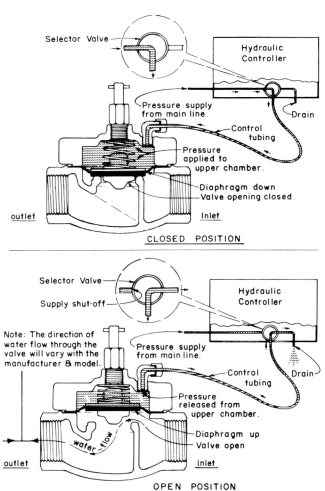

Figure 1-40 Hydraulic Diaphragm Valve Operation

HYDRAULIC AUTOMATIC SYSTEMS. Irrigation systems using water as the "actuator" for remote valves are classified as "hydraulic automatics." Hydraulic controllers apply or release water pressure through "hydraulic tubing" to the hydraulic remote valves. There is more than one method by which the controller operates remote valves. However, since all are quite similar, only the most commonly used method is outlined in detail.

Tubing. Pressurized water is brought into the controller by a tube connected to the "main" pressure pipeline of the irrigation system. This tube must be connected to the "main" in front of all remote valves. Occasionally, an independent water source with pressure as great or greater than that in the system is used.

Water pressure is applied, or released, through tubes connected between the controller and the remote valves. The individual "stations" control this function with a special "selector" valve or with a bank of individual, small, electric solenoid valves commonly referred to as "pilot" valves.

As shown in Figure 1-39, a separate control tube is required for each "station" to operate its valve or valves. Control line, often referred to as "hydraulic" tubing, is usually small plastic tubing . Always check manufacturer's equipment recommendations for size. Also, larger tube may be required when one tube controls more than one valve.

Operation. In the non-operating position, pressurized water from the supply fills the supply tube and valve tubes through the open selector valve or the individual, 3-way solenoid pilot valves. This pressure forces the diaphragm seating disc down and against the body seat, holding the valve closed (Figure 1-40, closed position).

When a controller "station" activates the selector valve, the water supply to the remote valve controlled by that "station" is shut off and pressure in its control tube is relieved through a drain tube (Figure 1-40, open position). Relieving pressure in the control tube also relieves pressure in the upper (hydraulic) chamber of the remote valve. Pressure in the irrigation system main supply pipe forces the diaphragm up, opening the remote valve.

When that "station" is de-activated, the process is reversed and pressure in the control tube forces the

Figure 1-41 Remote Valve Operator Equipment

diaphragm down, closing the valve (Figure 1-40) closed position).

Clean Control Water. The water used to operate remote valves in a hydraulic system must be clean. Most manufacturers specify that a strainer be installed in the supply tube to the controller to avoid clogging of the pilot valve (or valves). Such clogging can prevent the supply of pressurized water to the remote valves, in which case they would not close.

Controller Freeze Protection. Hydraulic controllers must be protected against any freezing if the control tube and/or valves are located in the controller. Also, when the earth freezes to the depth of buried tubing, all tubing must be drained. The small control tubing cannot be drained with the normal methods of draining system piping. The only successful way of removing water from the control tubes is to blow it out with an air compressor.

Normally Open. Unlike electric automatic systems, when the "actuator" source to the hydraulic remote valves-- pressurized water-- is interrupted, the remote valves will open and remain open until pressure is returned. Such failure can be caused by a leak occurring in the control tube, a break in the tube or a clogged or malfunctioning pilot valve.

REMOTE VALVE OPERATOR. A remote valve operator can be very useful on medium and large projects for site testing, maintenance and system operation by grounds maintenance personnel. Handheld transceivers, with a rechargeable battery, communicate by FM transmission to receiver units in the controllers. Equip-

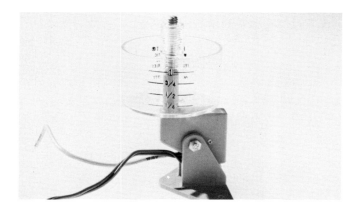

Figure 1-42 Rain Sensor

ment will operate with microprocesser and electro-mechanical controllers. Valves can be operated in sequence, forward or backward. Some models include a syringe feature for "timed" watering of any selected valve station. An example transceiver and receiver unit are shown in Figure 1-41.

FCC License is normally required to transmit in the U.S.A and the use of RVO equipment may not be allowed in some areas of the world. Check regulations and laws that may be applicable for the country in which the project is located.

REMOTE SENSORS

Standard irrigation controllers are "automatic" in that they will start, operate and complete the watering cycles as programmed. Irrigation efficiency can be improved by using additional products to measure the irrigation

Courtesy of Irrometer Co., Inc.
Figure 1-43 Soil Moisture Sensor

Courtesy of Rain Bird
Figure 1-44 Weather Station

requirement, check current climatic conditions and monitor the operation of the system.

A variety of different sensors can be used to override or alter the system operation as programmed. Some of these products are specifically manufactured for use in automatic irrigation systems. However, most of the sensors are standard products of measurement and are available for use in many different types of systems.

Although this equipment can upgrade the level of automation, the designer must consider if it is cost-effective for a particular project. Maintenance requirement and product replacement cost will vary with quality and type of product specified.

Some of the more common types of remote sensor products are listed below:

RAIN SENSOR. Several different types and brands of products are available to collect and measure rainfall. Low-cost units, such as the sensor shown in Figure 1-42, simply prevent valves from operating when a set amount of rainfall has occurred. Rainfall setting to override the controller is usually adjustable. Sensor unit will reset for system operation after excess water evaporates from the cup.

SOIL MOISTURE SENSOR. Various types of measurement devices have been used in automatic irrigation

Courtesy of Glen-Hilton Corp.

Figure 1-45 Low Temperature Sensor

systems since the early 1950's. These include tensiometers which measure soil tension and a variety of different units that measure electrical resistance changes that will occur with different levels of soil moisture. See Figure 1-43.

Although these products are commonly used in agricultural irrigation, they have had limited success in landscape irrigation. Quantity, location and depth of installation in the soil are important considerations. Product cost and maintenance requirements are also important, regardless of type, brand and model.

Products that are suitable for automatic systems must include some type of circuit that is compatible with the remote-sensor circuit of the controller or the electric valve circuit.

LOW TEMPERATURE SENSOR. Use of a low temperature "override" switch is normally limited to climate regions where systems are operated throughout the year and low temperatures during the winter months may be below freezing. This sensor will eliminate any operation that may be scheduled to avoid the hazards of ice development on walks, drives and streets. See Figure 1-45.

FLOW/PRESSURE SENSORS. A flow switch and/or a pressure switch can be especially useful for pump protection. If flow/pressure conditions are not met, pump can be shut down. Pressure sensors can also be used to close control valves should low pressure occur as the result of a major pipe leak. Time delay relays may be necessary in some applications. See Figure 1-46.

CLIMATIC SENSORS. A variety of different instruments to measure temperature, humidity, wind speed and direction, solar radiation and rainfall can be used to assist the user in decisions on water requirement.

Courtesy of Seaflow

Figure 1-46 Flow Sensor

Figure 1-47 Irrigation Management with PC Software

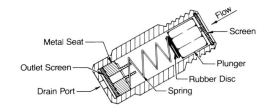

Plunger Style - Open Position

Figure 1-48 Automatic Drain Valve

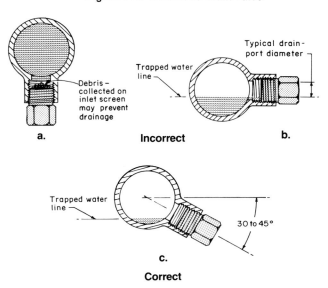

Figure 1-49 Angle of Installation for Automatic Drain

However, use of this data for automatic changes in system operation will require a controller that can collect and process the input data to determine if the operating program should be altered.

Very large projects may include a complete weather station, as shown in Figure 1-44, and a computer system to process the collection of input data.

SYSTEM FREEZE PROTECTION

In many areas irrigation systems must be drained to prevent pipe breakage. In some locales it is only necessary to remove water from certain portions of the piping.

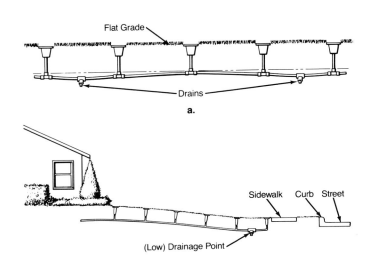

Figure 1-50 Pipe Grading for Drainage

AUTOMATIC DRAIN VALVES

Piping that is not constantly pressurized, i.e., piping on the discharge side of zone control valves or "master" automatic valves, can be drained with automatic drain valves. These valves should never be used to drain pipes under constant pressure during the irrigation season.

A plunger style of drain valve is shown in Figure 1-48 to illustrate the principle of automatic operation. When the control valve is open, lateral line pressure will force the plunger down by offsetting the spring force and the plunger disc will seal off the drain port. When the control valve is closed and operating pressure is removed, the spring will push the plunger up from the seat. Water will flow from the pipe, around the plunger, and out the drain port.

INSTALLATION. For satisfactory operation, proper installation of automatic drain valves is mandatory.

(1) Always install at an angle of 30 to 45 degrees below horizontal.

Theoretically, spring-loaded drains will operate installed in a vertical position as in (a), Figure 1-49. However, any sand, dirt or other grit in the water can be deposited on the inlet screen. Eventual complete clogging of the screen could prevent pipe drainage.

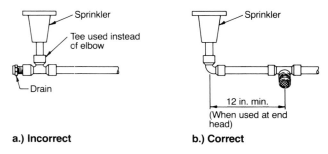

a.) Incorrect　　　**b.) Correct**

Figure 1-51 Automatic Drain Location

Installing the drain horizontally, as in (b), Figure 1-49, will greatly minimize depositing of debris on the inlet screen. However, complete drainage of the pipe does not occur.

The correct installation, illustrated in (c), Figure 1-49, keeps the screen as clean as a horizontal installation, and at the same time, minimizes entrapment of water to an entirely acceptable degree.

(2) Install automatic drains at all low points in the system. On larger flat areas, (a), Figure 1-50, it is necessary to grade the pipe trench in an undulating manner. However, in most residential lots, natural grade changes, (b), Figure 1-50, provide low points for draining with a constant depth trench.

(3) Never install automatic drains at the end of pipe lines. Dirt can easily wash past the tee and into the inlet screen. See Figure 1-51.

(4) Provide sump pits for drainage. A pit like the one shown in Figure 1-52 minimizes the danger of dirty water backing up into and through the drain.

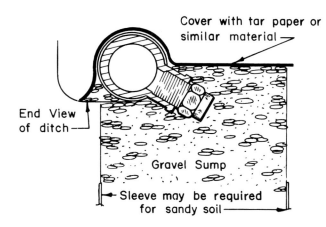

Figure 1-52 Automatic Drain Sump Pit

(5) Automatic drains close with relatively low pressure, usually about 3 lb/in^2. Therefore, do not install automatic drains where water trapped in the piping at elevations above the drain will produce a pressure at, or above, the drain's closing pressure. For example: A drain that closes at 3 lb/in^2 must not have water trapped to an elevation of more than 6 feet above the drain: 6 feet equals 2.6 lb/in^2 (See Hydraulics -- relationship of pressure and elevation).

Caution. In rotary systems, the designer must consider the use of automatic drain valves very carefully. Empty lateral lines are susceptible to problems of dry-line shock, as discussed in Chapter 4.

In many climate regions, water is removed from piping by forcing it out with an air compressor.

MANUAL DRAINS
Small size, manually - operated, valves are often used to drain the constant pressure mains of a system. Occasionally, zone piping is manually drained when long, natural grades will result in relatively large volumes of water.

Manual drains should be installed with a sump pit. Installation should be easily locatable in a manner not detracting from the aesthetics of the lawn area. Figure 1-53 illustrates such an installation.

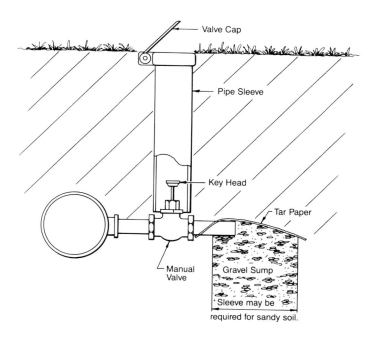

Figure 1-53 Typical Installation of Manual Drain

A sump, as shown in Figure 1-53, may not be sufficient for large irrigation systems using large and/or long pipe lines.

In such cases, an extra large pit must be constructed. Or, preferably, a pipe should extend from the drain valve to a lower point for drainage onto the ground or other suitable area.

Sump pits at drain valves are an important feature to avoid frozen and broken pipe lines.

During periodic thaws in areas where ground freezing occurs, water may enter the piping through heads in low areas. If this should happen when the earth is still frozen at the level of the drain valve, there would be no place for the water to drain without a pit.

Piping does not normally need to be drained in areas where the earth does not freeze. However, in areas where there is occasional above-ground freezing, automatic drains should be installed in zones which consist entirely of shrub sprinklers mounted above-grade on pipe risers. Without a drain, water trapped above ground will freeze, breaking the risers.

ACCESSORIES

Many accessory items are manufactured for landscape irrigation systems, in addition to the products discussed in the chapter. However, almost all of these products are functional items such as filters, pressure gauges, valve caps and boxes, electrical wire connectors and conduit boxes, pump relay kits and a variety of special tools.

BIBLIOGRAPHY

(a) Irrigation by Sprinkling: J.E. Christiansen
Published by:
University of California
Berkeley, California

CHAPTER 2

Piping

The piping network is a major portion of the average landscape irrigation project and a majority of all labor required to construct a system is directly related to water distribution. Selection of piping materials is very important for long-term dependability, as it is the underlying foundation of the irrigation system.

In the early days of irrigation, galvanized steel was used for piping in most systems. Copper tube replaced steel during the 1930's and was the most common material for smaller sizes until the mid-1950's. Thermoplastic pipe became the standard type of pipe by 1960, and is the most common type of material specified in current system designs.

Large size pipe was limited to the use of cast iron until the early 1960's when asbestos-cement pipe became the preferred material for sizes 4 inch and larger. Plastic pipe was not commonly available in large sizes during this time period. Today, plastic pipe is the standard for all types of systems and all sizes of pipe.

This chapter is intended to familiarize the reader with basic information on piping, both old and new. Steel pipe and copper tube are encountered in the supply for almost all systems using city water. Also, some plumbing codes still require partial use of these pipes in irrigation systems.

PIPE STANDARDS

Pipe standards are not consistent throughout the world. Materials, sizes and pressure ratings will vary from one country to the next. This manual is limited to pipe standards and units of measurement, as used in the U.S.A. However, regardless of the country, pipe standards will cover the same essential factors relating to product specifications.

Almost all national piping standards are based on the metric system of measurement, the most notable exception is the United States. Pipe and fittings selected for design should conform to all applicable governmental requirements, including national pipe standards. Irrigation products manufactured in the U.S.A. are normally available with international pipe thread (ISO) as an option.

Pipe standards have been developed for all piping reviewed in this chapter. Standards applicable to the text are indicated by letter symbol and referenced at the end of this chapter. They furnish standard dimensions, pressure ratings and other pertinent data.

The ASTM (American Society of Testing and Materials) Standards for thermoplastic pipe and copper water tube are the most widely recognized and accepted.

AWWA (American Waterworks Association) Standards are generally used for cast iron and asbestos-cement pipe.

Most, if not all, of the above mentioned standards have been accepted by ANSI as American National Standards.

ANSI. The principal function of ANSI (American National Standards Institute, formerly known as American Standards Association) is to act as a clearing house to coordinate the works of standards development in the private sector (which is carried on by nearly 400 different organizations). When a standard not developed by ANSI is approved as an American National Standard, it is assigned an ANSI number. Such standards are then published with both the ANSI standard number and the standard number of the originating organization. The ANSI is also the official representative of the United States in the field of international standards.

Piping

Note: American National Standards numbers may have a prefix of ANSI, ASA, USAA, or USAS, depending upon when the standard was approved.

PIPING TERMS, GENERAL

Common piping terms are listed to avoid any misunderstanding throughout the text of this manual.

PIPING. The word "piping" is a general term used to describe any hollow, cylindrical carrier of liquids. Therefore, the term applies to all materials commonly referred to as pipe and tube.

"Tubing" is a word used to describe many different types of hollow components, but it is not clearly defined in the plumbing trade as a category of classification for piping products. In practice, some will describe tubing as small pipe and/or flexible pipe. However, tubing is not limited to small sizes and may not be flexible.

Copper water tube may be one of the first cases where the word "tube" was used to establish a category of classification for a light-weight standard as compared to the copper pipe standard. Copper tube is a thin wall and seamless type of piping material. Copper pipe is a heavy-weight type of pipe and sizing standards are different than copper tube standards.

Although small sizes of flexible plastic pipe are commonly referred to as tubing, ANSI/ASTM F412-78 defines plastic tubing as plastic pipe in which the outside diameter is essentially the same as the corresponding size of copper tube.

NOMINAL (SIZE). Nominal Size is a term used for the comparative reference of different sizes of pipe and tube rather than actual dimensions. Nominal sizes of piping normally used for water distribution, general plumbing and irrigation systems, are not the actual sizes and are given in inches and fractions of an inch.

OD (OUTSIDE DIAMETER). When the term outside diameter or OD is used, the dimension being referred to is always the actual diameter unless preceded by the phrase "nominal." Piping specifications list actual OD in decimals carried to three places.

WALL (THICKNESS). The actual wall thickness of a pipe and tube is given in decimals carried to three places. Any one nominal size of pipe or tube can be, and usually is, manufactured with more than one wall thickness.

ID (INSIDE DIAMETER). The OD of most pipes is the controlling dimension in order to match with fittings. Wall thickness is important to the strength of the piping. Both the OD and wall thickness specified dimensions are subject to manufacturing tolerance of several thousandths of an inch, plus or minus. If a nominal ID is wanted, twice the specified wall is subtracted from the OD (both dimensions used without tolerances).

Conversely, when the ID is the controlling dimension and the nominal OD is wanted, twice the specified wall is added to the ID; both dimensions again used without tolerances.

IPS (IRON PIPE SIZE). All piping manufactured to the OD of wrought iron pipe is referred to as being iron pipe size, or IPS. IPS pipe can, and is, made of any material; the capability to be threaded is not required for a pipe to be IPS. Wrought iron pipe was the forerunner of piping for general plumbing. Many other piping terms derived from this pipe.

SCHEDULE. A term used to designate a standard series of wall thicknesses for all sizes in which a pipe is made. The term was first used for wrought iron pipe and continued with steel pipe. The most generally used series of wall thicknesses is "schedule 40." Some other schedules are 80, 120, 160. As the schedule number increases, the wall thickness increases.

This term is included as a general term because most kinds of piping are, or have been, made with steel pipe schedule wall thicknesses. Whenever a pipe, made of any material, is designated as "schedule" pipe, the ODs and wall thicknesses are the same as that of steel pipe.

WORKING PRESSURE. The internal water pressure that a pipe can withstand without damage (in a piping system designed according to good engineering practice) is known as working pressure. The working pressure provides a safety factor to allow for reasonable pressure surging due to such conditions as water hammer.

METAL PIPES

GALVANIZED STEEL PIPE

Today, almost all general plumbing piping referred to as "iron pipe" is actually steel pipe. The main reason is that from casual observation it's impossible to differentiate from wrought iron pipe. In addition, when steel supplanted wrought iron pipe, the terms, sizes, etc., were carried over to steel pipe.

Corrosion and chemical deposits accumulate inside steel pipe, reducing the flow capacity. This condition progressively worsens with age, ultimately jeopardizing the operation and coverage of irrigation systems.

Rust and scale flaking may clog water outlets early in the life of steel pipe. This problem becomes progressively worse with the passage of time.

Irrigation system designers need to take these two adverse conditions into consideration when connecting to old, existing steel pipe as a source of water supply. A strainer/filter should be considered at the point of connection.

SIZES [a] [b] The manufacturer of pipe in the nominal sizes of $1/8$ inch to 12 inches inclusive is based on a standardized outside diameter (OD). This OD was originally selected so that pipe with a standard OD and having a wall thickness which was typical of the period would have an inside diameter (ID) approximately equal to the nominal size. Although this relationship no longer exists with current wall thickness standards, these nominal sizes and standard ODs continue in use as "standard."

The manufacturer of pipe in nominal sizes of 14 inch OD and larger, proceeds on the basis of an OD corresponding to the nominal size.[1]

SCHEDULE. [a] [b] "Standard" steel pipe for general plumbing is made with several "schedule" wall thicknesses. Most common is schedule 40.

ELECTROLYSIS. Electrolytic corrosion, caused by stray electrical currents, will affect steel pipe when it is attached directly to piping or appurtenances of dissimilar metals, i.e. galvanized nipple into a brass valve. To avoid this, a dielectric fitting should be used between the two types of metals. A plastic pipe fitting will accomplish the same purpose.

COPPER WATER TUBE

Copper water tube is rarely used in current irrigation systems except at points of connection to water supplies or when used for shrub head risers. In some cases, it is used in locations where pipe will be exposed above grade, or underground in areas where site conditions may result in damage to plastic pipe.

Copper tube is made for many purposes, but only that classified as water tube is of interest here.

SIZES [c] The actual, standard OD of copper water tube is always 0.125 in (1/8 in) larger than its nominal size. Copper water tube is made in three standard wall thickness series. The outside diameters (OD) of each size remain constant regardless of type. As the wall thickness of a given size increases for different types, the inside diameter decreases, reducing the flow capacity.

TYPES [c] Standard series of copper water tube are designated as "types," rather than as "schedules." There are three types: K, L and M. Type K, with the thickest wall, is commonly used for size 2 inch or less water services; i.e., the piping connecting the city water main and outside meters or the curb stop when meters are installed in buildings. Type M, with the thinnest wall section of the three types, is the type generally used in irrigation, when allowed by local code.

All three types are made hard-drawn (rigid) in straight lengths. Type K and L are also available soft-annealed. Up to size 2 inch, soft-annealed tube is available in coils 40 to 100 feet, depending on size. Larger sizes of soft-annealed are available in straight lengths only.

WORKING PRESSURE. The working pressure of copper water tube is sufficient for most, if not all, water pressures encountered in irrigation systems. See tables in Figure 2-1. However, the working pressures of normal soldered fitting joints are well below that of the tube and must be considered, particularly when using sizes over 4 inches. As can be seen in one of the tables, the working pressure of joints can be increased by using "silver solder" rather than regular "soft solder", or by brazing. However, "silver solder" is quite expensive and soldering with it is much slower. These methods should be attempted only by well-qualified personnel because the much higher heat required can easily burn through the tube and/or fitting.

FITTINGS [d] There are several types of fittings available for connecting copper water tubes. Of these, the solder type is used almost entirely for piping systems

(1) Extracted from American National Standard Wrought Steel and Wrought Iron Pipe, ANSI B36.10 -- 1970, with the permission of the publisher, the American Society of Mechanical Engineers, 345 East 47th Street, New York, New York 10017.

Nominal Pipe Size, in	Rated Internal Working Pressures for Tube for Service Temperatures up to 150°F, psi					
	Type M		Type L		Type K	
	Annealed	Hard Drawn	Annealed	Hard Drawn	Annealed	Hard Drawn
1/4	—	—	810	1350	900	1595
3/8	475	840	675	1195	990	1745
1/2	430	760	625	1105	780	1375
5/8	—	—	545	965	640	1135
3/4	350	610	495	875	750	1315
1	295	515	440	770	575	1010
1-1/4	295	515	385	680	465	820
1-1/2	290	510	355	630	435	765
2	300	450	315	555	380	665
2-1/2	235	410	295	520	355	520
3	220	385	275	490	340	605
3-1/2	215	385	270	470	325	570
4	215	380	255	450	315	555
5	205	355	235	410	305	540
6	190	335	215	385	305	540
8	200	350	240	420	325	580
10	205	355	240	425	330	585
12	205	360	225	395	330	585

Alloy Used for Joints	Rated Internal Working Pressures for Copper Tube Joints at Service Temperatures up to 100°F, psi				
	Tube Size K, L, and M (in inches)				
	1/4 to 1 Incl.	1-1/4 to 2 Incl.	2-1/2 to 4 Incl.	5 to 8 Incl.	10 to 12 Incl.
50–50 Tin-Lead Solder	200	175	150	130	100
95–5 Tin-Antimony Solder[1]	500	400	300	270	150
Brazing Alloys (Melting at or above 1000°F)	2	2	2	2	2

[1] Not considered brazing Material.
[2] Rated internal pressure is that of tube being joined.
Reference: Copper Tube Handbook.[d]

Figure 2-1
Working Pressure
Copper Water Tubes and Joints

such as landscape irrigation systems. Check local plumbing codes for solder type recommendations and limitations on use of solder-type connections below grade.

Solder Type Fittings. This type fitting, commonly referred to as a "sweat" fitting, is available in wrought copper or cast bronze.

The socket ends of the fitting are held to a close tolerance to provide a few thousandths of an inch clearance with the outside of the tubing. The areas of the tube and fitting to be soldered must first be cleaned and fluxed. Wire solder flows between the two members by capillary action when the joint is assembled and

heated. Local plumbing code may specify the type of solder that can be used (ratio of tin and lead). Areas to be soldered must be absolutely dry.

Transition fittings, with at least one end threaded IPS, allow connection to other types of piping.

Other Type Fittings. Flared and compression fittings are also available for copper tube. These fittings can easily be taken apart and reassembled. Also, they can be used under wet conditions where soldering is not possible. These fittings are much more expensive.

Flared and compression fittings can be used on annealed tube (c). And, certain types and sizes of compression fittings can be used on types K and L hard drawn tube (c).

INSTALLATION. Certain special precautions are necessary for underground installation of copper tube in particular situations.

Installations Under Paving. Use of annealed tube provides some flexibility for expansion and contraction. Whenever possible, joints under paving should be avoided to eliminate the hazard of leaks. As mentioned previously, coiled tube is available in lengths much greater than straight tube.

If joints under paving cannot be avoided, they should be silver-soldered or brazed, thus making the tensile strength of the joint about equal to that of the tubing itself. Many contractors prefer using "sleeves" when joints cannot be avoided, rather than attempt silver soldering or brazing. Such installations are recommended as excellent practice; not only for copper tube, but all piping.

Installations in Cinders. Any metal pipe laid in cinders is subject to attack by the acid generated when sulfur compounds in cinders combine with water. When installation in such environments cannot be avoided, the tube should be isolated from the cinders with an inert moisture barrier such as a wrapping of insulating tape, a coating of an asphalted paint or with some other approved material [d].

The acids formed by cinders and water erode copper water tube quicker than most other piping.

Installations in Concrete or Mortar. Fittings should never be embedded in, or be in contact with concrete. Elements in concrete and mortar can attack solder.

ELECTROLYSIS. Copper is not affected by electrolysis because it is an excellent electrical conductor. However, when copper is connected to steel or iron, these and other less noble metals should be protected from galvanic and electrolytic corrosion by preventing the creation of a galvanic cell or by blocking the flow of electric currents. Both may be accomplished by using a dielectric coupling or other insulation-type fitting.

CAST IRON PIPE Today, cast iron (CI) is rarely used for any purpose in landscape irrigation systems. However, it was a very common type of pipe for very large systems, before 1960. Internal rust and corrosion are major problems and designers should be very careful if existing cast iron pipe is used as the supply for system additions and/or revisions.

SIZES. [e] Cast iron water pipe is available, standard, in nominal sizes 3 to 60 inches. Certain types are also made 2 and $2\frac{1}{4}$ inches. The OD is the controlling dimension, remaining constant for each nominal size regardless of wall thickness. Standard length is 16 feet.

CLASS. [e] Cast iron pipe is available in Classes 50-350 in increments of 50.

WORKING PRESSURE. [e] The class number of cast iron pipe is also the working pressure which includes a reasonable pressure surging allowance. Also, the laying (depth of installation) conditions for each class determines the recommended maximum pressure that should be applied. The pipe manufacturer should be consulted on the class and wall thickness for each application.

FITTINGS. [e] Cast iron mechanical joint is the most common type pipe and fittings used because it affords the fastest installation, making it the most economical.

INSTALLATION. The technique of installing cast iron pipe is quite critical. Installation should not be attempted without full knowledge. The "Handbook of Cast Iron Pipe" [e] is an excellent source of information.

ASBESTOS-CEMENT PIPE

Asbestos-Cement (A-C) pipe is made of cement, asbestos, and silica. Being non-metallic, it will not con-duct electricity and is free of electrolysis and galvanic action. It combines strength with light weight (as compared to cast iron or steel pipe) and is completely immune to rust and corrosion.

Although A-C pipe is seldom specified for use in modern irrigation systems, many existing systems have A-C pipe in sizes 4 inch, and larger.

SIZES. AWWA standards [f] list A-C pipe in nominal sizes of 4 to 36 inches. Three inch is also commonly made and used. The ID is the controlling dimension and is approximately the same as the nominal size.

CLASS. [f][g] Standard A-C pipe is made in three classes: 100, 150, and 200. Wall thicknesses for each size in a class are designed to provide the specified pressure rating. The external load (backfill and traffic) must also be considered when selecting a class of A-C pipe. [g]

WORKING PRESSURE [f] [g] The class number of A-C pipe is also the rated working pressure.

FITTINGS. A-C pipe is connected with fittings which have a rubber ring placed in a groove near each end. The fitting is forced onto the tapered, machined end of the pipe after coating the rubber ring and surfaces of pipe ends with a lubricant. When assembling fittings onto larger size pipe (8 inch and above), a special "puller" is required. The puller can also be used on smaller sizes.

INSTALLATION. [h] Installation techniques for A-C are critical since the pipe is quite brittle. The pipe must be well supported over its full length. Care must be exercised that soil under, or backfill immediately around and over the pipe, does not contain debris, especially rocks. Such debris can damage the pipe.

Concrete thrust blocks are required at all turns, dead ends, etc., so internal water pressures and/or expansion and contraction cannot force the pipe out of the slip-joints of the fittings (See Chapter 4, Water Hammer).

Because installation techniques are so important for A-C pipe, no attempt is made to detail them. Rather, the user should obtain an installation manual which is available from manufacturers of the pipe. The techniques outlined in the manual should be adhered to strictly, including cautions relating to handling of asbestos material.

THERMOPLASTIC PIPE

Plastic pipe offers many desirable advantages. Without question, it is the thriftiest of all piping materials. Being completely inert, it will not rust or rot. It is also completely immune to electrolysis and all forms of electrolytic corrosion. It is an excellent insulator, not requiring dielectric connectors.

It is lightweight; installation is simple and fast. A mirror-like interior finish yields a greater flow capacity for any given size than other piping material; and this capacity is retained. Life expectancy is considered virtually unlimited.

Several different kinds of plastic materials are used for water piping. There are also different types, grades and size standards for each kind of material. The two most common kinds of thermoplastic materials used for piping in landscape irrigation systems are:
Poly (Vinyl Chloride) -- (PVC) and
Polyethylene -- (PE).

Although flexible PVC pipe is available for some applications, almost all PVC pipe used in irrigation is classed as a rigid pipe. PE is classed as a flexible pipe.

PHYSICAL CHARACTERISTICS OF PLASTICS

CREEP. When pressure of the water being conveyed exceeds the pressure rating of thermoplastic pipe, creep will occur. At the risk of oversimplification, creep may be defined as a "stretching" of the pipe causing a thinning of the pipe walls. Continuous over-pressurizing will cause failure of the pipe sooner or later.

FATIGUE. Plastic piping may also fail when used with water pressures within its pressure rating. Certain conditions (water hammer is the most common) cause a "safe" pressure to momentarily surge several times higher than the pressure rating of the pipe.

Each time the pressure exceeds the rating of the pipe, it will stretch. When the pressure drops below the rating, the pipe walls will only partially return to their previous size. This unrecovered stretch is, of course, creep.

Continually repeated (cyclical) momentary pressure surges cause the pipe to fatigue. Pipe failure due to

fatigue can occur within a few weeks or it may take several years, depending on the frequency and severity of the overload.

It should be noted that an extreme pressure surge can cause pipe rupture immediately.

The piping system will stand the test of time when designed properly, correct plastic pipe is used, and the piping is installed in accordance with recommended procedures.

HYDROSTATIC DESIGN STRESS

"The estimated maximum tensile stress in the wall of the pipe due to internal hydrostatic water pressure that can be applied continuously with a high degree of certainty that failure of the pipe will not occur" is the measure of the strength of plastic pipe and is termed "Hydrostatic Design Stress." The unit of measurement is in pounds per square inch (psi).

Each kind, and type and grade of plastic for pipes is assigned a standard hydrostatic design stress based on test procedures developed by the PPI (Plastic Pipe Institute). (Details can be found in "Standards" for appropriate pipe which are referenced at end of this chapter.)

PRESSURE RATING (PR)

The pressure rating of plastic pipe is defined: "The estimated maximum pressure that water in the pipe can exert continuously with a high degree of certainty that failure of the pipe will not occur."

Pressure ratings of plastic pipe are determined by a formula which considers the hydrostatic design stress of the piping material, size of pipe, and wall thickness.

For PVC pipe:
$$\frac{2S}{P} = \frac{Do}{t} - 1$$
For PE pipe:
$$\frac{2S}{P} = \frac{Di}{t} + 1$$

Where:
S = hydrostatic design stress, psi
P = pressure rating, psi
Do = average outside diameter, inches
Di = average inside diameter, inches
t = minimum wall thickness, inches

Thus, if two pipes had the same diameter and the same wall thickness, but one was made of plastic material with a hydrostatic design stress of 2000 psi and the other 1000 psi, the latter would have a pressure rating of one-half that of the first.

Pressure ratings for plastic pipe are for temperatures at 23° C (73.4F) and must be reduced for higher temperatures.[2] This is rarely of any concern for buried irrigation system piping. The earth covering the piping and normal water temperatures will keep temperatures of the plastic pipe below the rated temperature, or at least close enough to have no practical effect. However, temperature must be considered when selecting piping for above-grade installations.

Pressure ratings are for non-threaded pipe only. Most plastic pipes cannot, or should not, be threaded. When plastic pipe that is suitable for threading is threaded, such threading reduces the pressure rating approximately 50%.

Note: Unlike other kinds of pipes, the pressure rating of plastic pipe is not the safe working pressure that the pipe can be subjected to over the long term. Therefore, the piping system designer must make suitable allowances when selecting plastic pipe. Recommendations are given in Chapter 4: Water Hammer: Pipe System Protection.

MATERIAL DESIGNATIONS (i) (j) (k)
Materials used for the manufacture of thermoplastic pipe are coded by letters representing the kind of material plus four digits. The first two digits identify the type and grade of material; the last two indicate the hydrostatic design stress in units of 100 psi.

Example: PVC1220:
PVC = Poly (Vinyl Chloride)
1 = Type 1
2 = Grade 2
20 = 2000 psi hydrostatic design stress

It should be noted that the first two digits are not indicative of quality. They are assigned in sequence as new compounds are submitted to the PPI for acceptance and classification.

_____

(2) An exception to this temperature rating is CPVC which is produced for hot water piping systems and is not considered in this irrigation manual.

Standard Thermoplastic Pipe Dimension Ratio (SDR) and Water Pressure Ratings (PR) at 23°C (73.4°F) for SDR-PR PE Plastic Pipe

Standard Dimension Ratio	PE PIPE MATERIALS[1]			
	PE 3306[2] PE 3406	PE 2306	PE 2305	PE 1404
	Pressure Rating, psi			
5.3	200	200	160	125
7	160	160	125	100
9	125	125	100	80
11.5	100	100	80	——
15	80	80	——	——
Pressure Rating, psi	Standard Dimension Ratio			
200	5.3	5.3	——	——
160	7	7	5.3	——
125	9	9	7	5.3
100	11.5	11.5	9	7
80	15	15	11.5	9

Standard Thermoplastic Pipe Dimension Ratios (SDR) and Water Pressure Ratings (PR) at 23°C (73.4°F) for nonthreaded PVC Plastic Pipe

Standard Dimension Ratio	Pipe Materials[1]			
	PVC 1120[2] PVC 1220 CPVC 4120	PVC 2116	PVC 2112	PVC 2110
	Pressure Rating, psi			
13.5	315	250	200	160
17	250	200	160	125
21	200	160	125	100
26	160	125	100	80
32.5	125	100	80	63
41	100	80	63	50
64	63	50	NPR[3]	NPR
Pressure Rating, psi	Standard Dimension Ratio			
315	13.5	——	——	——
250	17	13.5	——	——
200	21	17	13.5	——
160	26	21	17	13.5
125	32.5	26	21	17
100	41	32.5	26	21
80	——	41	32.5	26
63	64	——	41	32.5
50	——	64	——	41

(1) These pressure ratings do not apply for threaded pipe.
(2) Material designations.
(3) NPR = not pressure rated.
Note: For available sizes, limitations, and special data see tables 2-3 and 2-4.

Figure 2-2
Standard Thermoplastic Pipe Dimension Ratios and Pressure Ratings

SCHEDULE WALL THICKNESS PLASTIC PIPE
Plastic pipe first used commercially in the U.S.A. was made in IPS sizes with schedule wall thicknesses of steel pipe. It is still available, but its use is limited in irrigation.

The dimensions of wrought iron and steel "schedule" pipe have no relation to the internal pressure the pipe can withstand; however, working pressures exceed, by a considerable amount, the water pressures normally encountered. When plastic pipe is made to these schedule dimensions, pressure ratings, due to its much lesser tensile strength, often are below acceptable limits. In addition, to further complicate piping system design, each size has a different pressure rating. Pressure ratings decrease as pipe size increases. Pressure ratings for schedule 40 PE pipe are listed in Figure 2-3 and for PVC in Figure 2-4.

SDR-PR PLASTIC PIPE

Because of the disparities of pressure ratings for schedule wall plastic pipe, PPI, in cooperation with industry, developed SDR-PR (Standard Dimension Ratio -- Pressure Rated) plastic pipe. The first standards for this pipe were issued in the early 1960's.

Each series of wall thicknesses is based on a "standard dimension ratio" (SDR) which is the ratio of pipe diameter to wall thicknesses. Several SDR values have been separately established for PVC and PE pipe. Tables in Figure 2-2 show the relationship of SDR and pressure rating for the various types and grades of PE and PVC plastic pipe.

Wall thickness required to provide a uniform pressure rating for all nominal sizes for a given pipe material is determined by dividing the SDR value into pipe diameter (OD for PVC and ID for PE). However, if the wall thickness calculated by this formula is less than 0.060 inches, it is arbitrarily increased to 0.060 inches.

The hydrostatic design stress of the material determines the pressure rating as outlined previously. The relationship of SDR, hydrostatic design stress, and pressure ratings is shown in tables accompanying the discussion of PE and PVC pipe later in this chapter.

Today, most plastic pipe used in irrigation systems is the SDR-PR type. The most common exception is due to plumbing code requirements in some regions.

THERMOPLASTIC PIPE STANDARDS
(i) (j) (k)

Comprehensive standards for plastic pipe are extremely important to the user because of the many kinds, types, and grades. Until recently, Product Standards developed by the U.S. National Bureau of Standards (NBS) were commonly used. These standards have now been discontinued in favor of those developed by non-governmental organizations.

Plastic pipe standards developed by ASTM are now generally being used. Slight differences between NBS and ASTM standards are not important to the average user.

Standards include criteria for classifying plastic pipe materials and the pipe itself; a system of nomenclature for each kind of plastic pipe; dimensions, and requirements and methods of tests for materials, workmanship, sustained pressure, burst pressure, methods of marking, etc. Standards for plastic piping systems are also available.

PIPE MARKING. Plastic pipe, according to "standards", must be marked at intervals of not more than 5 feet. This marking is the only way the user can easily identify the type of pipe.

A typical pipe marking for SDR-PR plastic pipe would look like this:

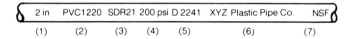

2 in	PVC1220	SDR21	200 psi	D 2241	XYZ Plastic Pipe Co.	NSF
(1)	(2)	(3)	(4)	(5)	(6)	(7)

(1) Nominal pipe size (for example, 2 in).
(2) Type of plastic pipe material in accordance with designation code (for example, PVC1220).
(3) (Paraphrased). Standard thermoplastic pipe dimension ratio in accordance with the designation code. Or, schedule (for example, 40).
(4) (Paraphrased). The pressure rating in pounds per square inch for water at $23°$ C (73.4F) shown as the number followed by psi (for example, 200 psi).
(5) ASTM designation for type of pipe (for example, D 2241 is for PVC SDR-PR plastic pipe).
(6) Manufacturer's name (or trademark).
(7) Seal or mark of the laboratory evaluating the pipe for approval of transport of potable water (example, National Sanitation Foundation [NSF]).

It should be emphasized that all "standards" are voluntary. However, the "standards" are the only convenient method of pipe comparison or determination of suitability for a particular application.

Readers desiring more detailed information on hydrostatic design stress, pressure ratings, standard dimension ratios, etc., should refer to the "standards."

WATER PRESSURE RATINGS[1] at 23°C (73.4°F)[2]

FOR SCHEDULE 40 PE PLASTIC PIPE

Nominal Pipe Size, in	Average Inside Diameter, in	Minimum Wall Thickness, in	Pressure Rating, psi [3]		
			PE 2306[4] PE 3306 PE 3406	PE 2305 [4]	PE 1404 [4]
1/2	0.622	0.109	190	150	120
3/4	0.824	0.113	150	120	100
1	1.049	0.133	140	110	90
1-1/4	1.380	0.140	120	90	70
1-1/2	1.610	0.145	100	80	70
2	2.067	0.154	90	70	60
2-1/2	2.469	0.203	100	80	60
3	3.068	0.216	80	70	50
4	4.026	0.237	70	60	NPR
6	6.065	0.280	60	NPR[5]	NPR

Water Pressure Ratings (PR)[1] at 23°C (73.4°F) [2]

and Standard Dimension Ratios (SDR)

for nonthreaded[3] SDR-PR PE Plastic Pipe

		Pressure Ratings, psi [3]				
PE 2306 [4]		80	100	125	160	200
PE 3306		80	100	125	160	200
PE 3406		80	100	125	160	200
PE 2305		—	80	100	125	160
PE 1404		—	—	80	100	125
Nominal Pipe Size, in	ID in	Minimum Wall Thickness, in				
		SDR 15	SDR 11.5[6]	SDR 9	SDR 7	SDR 5.3
1/2	0.622	0.060	0.060	0.069	0.089	0.117
3/4	0.824	0.060	0.072	0.092	0.118	0.155
1	1.049	0.070	0.091	0.117	0.150	0.198
1-1/4	1.380	0.092	0.120	0.153	0.197	0.260
1-1/2	1.610	0.107	0.140	0.179	0.230	0.304
2	2.067	0.138	0.180	0.230	0.295	0.390
2-1/2	2.469	0.165	0.215	—	—	—
3	3.068	0.205	0.267	—	—	—
4	4.026	0.268	0.350	—	—	—
6	6.065	0.404	0.527	—	—	—

(1). PRESSURE RATINGS ARE THE MAXIMUM THAT SHOULD BE APPLIED. SURGE PRESSURES MUST BE INCLUDED IN THE RATINGS SHOWN.

(2). Pressure Ratings must be reduced for temperatures over 23°C (73.4°).

(3). Pressure Ratings apply only to nonthreaded pipe. The plastic pipe industry does not recommend threading PE plastic pipe.

(4). Code designations.

(5). NPR = not pressure rated.

(6). 2-1/2 to 6 in pipe with a pressure rating of 100 psi is not included.

Figure 2-3 Water Pressure Ratings for PE Pipe

POLYETHYLENE (PE) PIPE

The low strength and high creep of PE pipe results in low pressure rating for polyethylene pipe commonly used in irrigation systems. In most cases, insert type fittings and stainless steel clamps are used for pipe connections.

The flexibility of small size PE pipe makes it a popular choice in regions where pipe pulling machines are used for pipe installation.

Drain valves to prevent freezing of buried pipes are not always successful with flexible pipe, such as PE. In severe climate regions, it is necessary to blow the water out of pipes with a large air compressor.

Polyethylene is a lower strength piping material than Poly (Vinyl Chloride).

MATERIAL. Polyethylene is available in Type I, commercially identified as low density; Type II, medium density; and Types III and IV, high density.

TYPE	GRADE	HYDROSTATIC DESIGN STRESS	CODE
I	4	400psi	PE1404
II	3	500	PE2305
II	3	630	PE2306
III	3	630	PE3306
III	4	630	PE3406

Types I and II are the most flexible and are available in long coils. This feature makes the pipe easier to lay, requiring fewer couplings.

Types III and IV are less flexible and not easily coiled in long lengths. For this reason, larger diameters are furnished in straight lengths.

SIZES. Polyethylene pipe is made in two styles. The one developed first, unlike most other pipes, uses the inside diameter as the controlling dimension. The nominal ID is the same as that of schedule 40 steel pipe throughout the entire range of sizes. As the wall sections become thicker to accommodate higher working pressures, the outside diameter increases. The constant ID for each size permits the use of internal, insert type fittings.

The second style uses a controlled iron pipe size OD for all sizes. The inside diameter varies with the wall thickness.

The two styles are made in both schedule wall and SDR-PR wall pipe.

Schedule Wall PE. Standards have been developed for controlled ID pipe with schedule 40 walls only. For controlled OD pipe, standards include both schedule 40

Piping

Water Pressure Ratings (PR)[1] at 23°C (73.4°F)[2]
and Standard Dimension Ratios (SDR)
for Nonthreaded[3] PVC Plastic Pipe

	Pressure Ratings, psi[3]						
PVC 1120[4]	63	100	125	160	200	250	315
PVC 1220	63	100	125	160	200	250	315
PVC 2116	50	80	100	125	160	200	250
PVC 2112	NPR[5]	63	80	100	125	160	200
PVC 2110	NPR	50	63	80	100	125	160
Nominal Pipe Size, in	OD in	Minimum Wall Thickness, in					
		SDR 64	SDR 41	SDR32.5	SDR 26	SDR 21	SDR 17	SDR13.5
1/8	0.405	(6)	(7)	(8)	—	—	—	0.060
1/4	0.540	—	—	—	—	—	—	0.060
3/8	0.675	—	—	—	—	—	—	0.060
1/2	0.840	—	—	—	—	—	—	0.062
3/4	1.050	—	—	—	—	0.060	0.062	0.078
1	1.315	—	—	—	0.060	0.063	0.077	0.097
1-1/4	1.660	—	—	—	0.064	0.079	0.098	0.123
1-1/2	1.900	—	—	—	0.073	0.090	0.112	0.141
2	2.375	—	—	—	0.091	0.113	0.140	0.176
2-1/2	2.875	—	—	—	0.110	0.137	0.169	0.213
3	3.500	—	—	0.108	0.135	0.167	0.206	0.259
3-1/2	4.000	—	0.098	0.123	0.154	0.190	0.235	0.296
4	4.500	—	0.110	0.138	0.173	0.214	0.265	0.333
5	5.563	—	0.136	0.171	0.214	0.265	0.327	0.412
6	6.625	0.104	0.162	0.204	0.255	0.316	0.390	0.491
8	8.625	0.135	0.210	0.265	0.332	0.410	0.508	—
10	10.750	0.168	0.262	0.331	0.413	0.511	0.632	—
12	12.750	0.199	0.311	0.392	0.490	0.606	0.750	—

Water Pressure Ratings[1] at 23°C (73.4°F)[2]
For Schedule 40 PVC Plastic Pipe

Nominal Pipe Size, in	Outside Diameter, in	Minimum Wall Thickness, in	Pressure Rating, psi[3]			
			PVC1120[4] PVC1220 CPVC4120	PVC 2116	PVC 2110	PVC 2112
1/8	0.405	0.068	810	650	400	500
1/4	0.540	0.088	780	620	390	490
3/8	0.675	0.091	620	500	310	390
1/2	0.840	0.109	600	480	300	370
3/4	1.050	0.113	480	390	240	300
1	1.315	0.133	450	360	220	280
1-1/4	1.660	0.140	370	290	180	230
1-1/2	1.900	0.145	330	260	170	210
2	2.375	0.154	280	220	140	170
2-1/2	2.875	0.203	300	240	150	190
3	3.500	0.216	260	210	130	160
3-1/2	4.000	0.226	240	190	120	150
4	4.500	0.237	220	180	110	140
5	5.563	0.258	190	160	100	120
6	6.625	0.280	180	140	90	110
8	8.625	0.322	160	120	80	100
10	10.750	0.365	140	110	70	90
12	12.750	0.406	130	110	70	80

(1) WATER PRESSURE RATINGS ARE THE MAXIMUM THAT SHOULD BE APPLIED. SURGE PRESSURES MUST BE INCLUDED IN THE RATINGS SHOWN. (See Chapter 4, Water Hammer.)
(2) Pressure Ratings must be reduced for temperatures over 23° C (73.4° F).
(3) These pressure ratings do not apply for threaded pipe. (Most of the plastic industry does not recommend threading PVC pipe with walls less than Schedule 80.)
(4) Code designations.
(5) NPR = not pressure rated.

(6) Available only in nominal pipe size diameters 6 to 12 in.
(7) Available only in nominal pipe size diameters 3-1/2 to 12 in.
(8) Available only in nominal pipe size diameters 3 to 12 in.
SPECIAL NOTES:
(a) SDR 26,21,17 not listed or available because 0.060 in wall thickness is the least permitted.
(b) SDR 32.5,26,21,13.5 normally only SDR-PR PVC plastic pipe used in sprinkler systems.
(c) Nominal pipe size diameters 3-1/2 and 5 in not normally used in sprinkler systems and usually not available from extruders.

Figure 2-4 Water Pressure Ratings for PVC Pipe

and 80. These pipes are rarely used in irrigation systems. Therefore, they are not included in further discussion of PE pipe, except that Figure 2-3 shows sizes in which controlled ID, schedule 40 is made along with the pressure ratings of each for comparison with SDR-PR pipe.

SDR-PR PE Pipe [i] Polyethylene pipe normally used in irrigation systems is SDR-PR, controlled ID. It should be noted, however, that because of the low strength of PE, the higher strength PVC pipe is often used for constant pressure, main line piping to the zone operating valves. Figure 2-3 also shows the relationship of standard dimension ratios (SDR), pressure ratings (PR) and wall thicknesses of PE SDR-PR (controlled ID) pipe.

High Density. In some countries, high density-controlled OD, PE pipe is used for main line pressure piping. Wall thickness varies with different pressure ratings. Pipe is connected by thermo-fusion (butt-welded). Although this type of pipe is available in the U.S.A., it is rarely used for irrigation piping except for areas subject to soil instability.

FITTINGS. Polyethylene pipe cannot be fitted by the solvent-cement process because no solvent has been developed thus far that will penetrate the material.

Molded plastic, cast brass and forged steel insert, clamp type fittings in all types are available for the pipe. These fittings have barbed male ends to resist pullout from pressure when the clamps are secured. The male ends are inserted into the pipe and fastened in place with external clamps. Clamps and bolts should be stainless steel to prevent rusting.

Several kinds of compression fittings are also available along with saddles which are clamped onto the pipe with bolts. These fittings are most commonly used for teeing pipe risers to water outlets. This procedure eliminates the necessity of cutting the pipe at each water outlet location. The fitting is attached to the pipe and a special, heated iron is inserted through the tee branch opening to burn a hole through the pipe.

POLY (VINYL CHLORIDE) (PVC) PIPE

Poly (Vinyl Chloride) pipe is the most common type of pipe used in landscape irrigation systems, primarily because of its higher strength and resistance to a greater variety of chemicals. It also has the longest record of successful usage, dating back to 1940.

When a plasticizer is added during the material compounding operation, finished products are flexible. However, most pipe is made from unplasticized compounds and is semi-rigid. Although classed as "rigid" for practical purposes, the pipe can be "bowed" to some extent when installing.

PVC pipe is used for laterals and pressure mains in all types of systems. Pipe sizes ½ inch through 12 inch are commonly available in pressure ratings suitable for normal irrigation requirements.

MATERIAL (j) (k) PVC pipe is made from four material types. PVC pipe for irrigation systems is usually made with Type I, Grade 2 material. It is one of the three compounds with the highest hydrostatic design stress. Type I, Grade 1, has a greater resistance to chemicals (which doesn't concern piping carrying water). Type IV, Grade 1, commonly called CPVC, was developed to carry hot water at temperatures too high for regular PVC water pipe.

TYPE	GRADE	HYDROSTATIC DESIGN STRESS	CODE
I	1	2000 psi	1120
I	2	2000	1220
II	1	1600	2116
II	1	1200	2112
II	1	1000	2110
IV	1	2000	4120

SIZES. PVC pipe is made in iron pipe size OD which remains constant for each size regardless of varying

wall thicknesses. The ID decreases as the wall becomes thicker to accommodate higher working pressures. PVC pipe is furnished in straight lengths only; 20 ft is most common.

Schedule Wall PVC.(j) There are standards for schedule 40, 80, and 120 PVC pipe. Schedule PVC pipe is seldom specified for irrigation systems because of its varying pressure ratings for each size. An examination of Figure 2-4 shows that the strongest PVC material, schedule 40, has greater pressure ratings than SDR-PR type in sizes 1½ inch and smaller. Larger sizes have lesser pressure ratings. Some designers specify schedule 40 in the smaller sizes because of its greater strength and SDR-PR in the larger sizes. The fallacy of this reasoning should be readily apparent; the additional cost for the schedule 40 is wasteful because a piping system, in its entirety, is no stronger than the weakest pipe. In some cases, local plumbing code will require schedule 40 for mainline piping.

SDR-PR PVC Pipe (k) Usually, when PVC is used for irrigation system piping, SDR-PR pipe is preferred because of the uniform pressure ratings for all pipe sizes. Figure 2-4 also shows the relationship of standard dimension ratios, pressure ratings, and wall thickness of PVC SDR-PR pipe.

FITTINGS (i) PVC fittings are of the socket type and are solvent-cemented to the pipe. Since they are attached to the outside of the pipe, PVC fittings affect carrying capacity much less than PE fittings which are inserted.

In larger sizes, fittings are also made in the "slip-on" gasket type similar to those used with A-C pipe. A rubber ring, seated in a groove in the fitting, seals the joint when the fitting is forced onto the PVC pipe. Such fittings are available made of plastic, fiber glass, cast iron and coated steel.

PVC pipe is also available with a "bell" formed on one end of the length which, with a rubber sealing ring similar to the fittings mentioned above, acts as a coupling.

Pipe installed with gasket-type fittings will require concrete thrust blocks at all turns, dead ends, etc. Pipe installation manuals cover the recommended locations and size requirements of thrust blocks (See Chapter 4, Water Hammer).

The majority of all PVC fittings used in irrigation systems are classified as schedule 40 [l]. These fittings are not rated for working pressure. Experience suggests that schedule 40 pipe ratings should be reduced for schedule 40 fittings. Some suggest a 50 percent reduction is realistic, especially for larger sizes. Expanded use of epoxy-coated steel and ductile iron fittings for large size PVC pipe is due to product failure of standard plastic fittings.

However, there are also many reports of product failure with epoxy-coated steel fittings. Chipping and cracking of the epoxy coating will result in rusting and fitting "blow-outs." Systems designers should be very careful when specifying main line pressure fittings for any large project, such as a golf course irrigation system. See Pipe System Protection, Chapter 4.

POLYBUTYLENE (PB) PIPE

Polybutylene pipe is rarely used for landscape irrigation piping in the U.S.A. However, PB pipe may be encountered in building service and supply lines. It is also used in some countries for irrigation. A variety of different types of fittings are used with PB pipe, including flare, insert and socket fusion.

ASTM [m][n][o] pipe specifications are available for SDR-PR, controlled ID and OD, and copper tube size, controlled OD.

NON-POTABLE WATER PIPING

Many landscape irrigation systems use a non-potable water supply. System designers should include adequate warnings as necessary to alert any person on-site, that the water is non-potable (not suitable for drinking).

Purple is the standard color of identification for products used with non-potable water. Irrigation products such as sprinkler heads and control valves are available with purple-colored components. See Chapter 1, Irrigation Equipment. A variety of different guidelines are used to identify non-potable water pipe. These include the use of purple colored pipe, identification tape marked with caution statements and purple colored polyethylene wrap. Systems designers should always verify that warnings are in compliance with any regulatory standards that may by applicable to a particular project.

INSTALLATION OF THERMOPLASTIC PIPE

HANDLING. Caution should be exercised in handling, loading, unloading and storing pipe and fittings. Any portion of the pipe that has been dented, grooved, or damaged in any way, should be cut out of the section and discarded.

STORAGE. Plastic pipe and fittings should be stored in a way that prevents damage by crushing or piercing. It should be under cover and not in direct sunlight. Care should be taken to protect the pipe from excessive heat or harmful chemicals. Cleaning solutions, detergents, solvents, etc., should be used with caution around the material.

TRENCHING. Trench bottom should be continuous, relatively smooth and free of rocks and rubbish. Where ledge rock, hardpan or rocky soil is encountered, it is advisable to pad the trench bottom with sand or compacted, fine grain soils. Rocks under plastic pipe can cut or otherwise damage the pipe in a manner that will cause pipe failure. Wedging or blocking of pipe should not be permitted.

TRENCH BACKFILL. Sand or fine grain soils should be used for cover to a sufficient depth to prevent damage to the pipe from rocks or other debris in backfill during the compacting operation.

PIPE PULLING. Pulling of pipe through the ground with a special machine is another method of installation which is being used with varying degrees of success in certain areas. This method is rarely successful in obviously dense soils such as clay or gumbo, particularly when damp.

Pipe pulling through rocky ground may result in abrading and grooving the pipe to the extent that it is weakened. PVC, like most other thermoplastics, is extremely "notch" sensitive. If pulling causes excessive grooving, the pipe is likely to rupture at pressures substantially under its rating. In addition, pulling methods prohibit grading of the pipe for drainage, and removal of water to avoid freezing must be done by forced air using an air compressor.

EXPANSION AND CONTRACTION. Plastic pipe is subject to considerable expansion and contraction with temperature changes. To provide for this, pipe with solvent-weld joints should be "snaked" from side-to-side in the trench. Also, backfilling should be done in

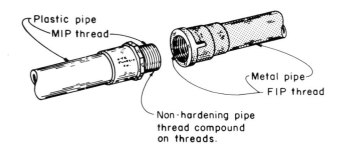

Figure 2-5 Plastic to Metal Thread Connection

the cool part of the day, especially in hot climates. If this is not possible, water flooding of trenches to cool the pipe is necessary before and during backfilling.

THREADED CONNECTIONS. Connections to piping of a type different from that being used for the irrigation system are always required. Such connections are generally by use of adapters which are threaded on one end.

A plastic adapter with external pipe threads should be used when possible, screwing it into metal internal pipe threads. If male metal threads are screwed into female plastic threads, chances are great that the plastic fitting will split as a result of the internal stressing.

Plastic valves with female pipe thread connection require special care by the installer. Male thread adapters and female threads in the valve body will have some variations due to design and normal manufacturing tolerances.

A thread compound such as teflon paste or tape should be used on all threaded connections. Thread lubricant must be suitable for use with the plastic materials of the threaded adapter and the valve body. Using the wrong thread compound and applying an excessive amount of compound are two of the most common problems associated with threaded connections of plastic valves.

Connections must be tight enough to avoid leaks but additional pressure (wrench torque), beyond that necessary for contact of "tapered" threads, may result in a cracked valve body.

PVC PIPE AND FITTING ASSEMBLY. Solvent-cement joining of PVC pipe provides joints which are as strong or stronger than the pipe itself. Skill in making

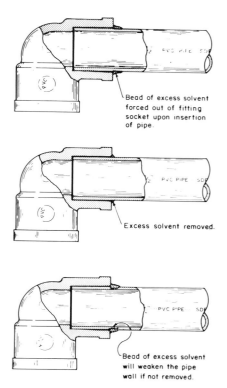

Figure 2-6 PVC Solvent-Cement Joint

these joints can easily and quickly be acquired by following established procedures.

This method consists of coating the outside of the pipe and the inside of the fitting with solvent which quickly (in a matter of seconds) dissolves the two surfaces. When the pipe is inserted into the socket, the dissolved surfaces blend. Upon evaporation of the thinning component of the solvent, the two surfaces become as one.

PVC Solvent (p) Different types of solvents and primers are available for a variety of installation requirements. Air temperature at the site is a factor in selection of the solvent and the procedure required for proper assembly.

Although many installers refer to PVC cement as "glue", it is a welding-solvent and manufacturer's recommendations should be followed, including "cure-time" necessary for maximum strength of the joint. Installers are also advised to read the warning labels on the solvent and primer containers. These products are extremely flammable and exposure to vapor or contact with skin can be very harmful.

Piping

Systems designers and installers should be aware that air quality regulatory agencies in some states measure the emission levels of volatile organic compounds (VOCs) from PVC solvents. The use of pipe solvents in some regions may be regulated by a local or state agency.

Fitting Assembly Guidelines [q] No attempt is made here to detail procedures, rather, the installer is advised to follow the recommendations of the solvent manufacturer. The only exception is to cover a problem due to excess solvent at the joint. Although this is normally covered in assembly instructions, it is often omitted by inexperienced installers.

When the pipe is inserted into the fitting socket after preparation, excess solvent will be forced out and a "bead" will form at the outside juncture of the pipe and fitting. This "bead" must be wiped off immediately. Otherwise, evaporation occurs on the surface and a "skin" forms preventing further evaporation of the solvent. When this happens, the solvent will continue to "eat" into the pipe and the pipe will be weakened at this point, often substantially. See Figure 2-6. If the proper procedure for solvent coating of the two components is not strictly adhered to, this same condition can occur at the inside juncture of the pipe and fitting where it can't be wiped off.

BIBLIOGRAPHY

a. ANSI B36.10: Wrought Steel and Wrought Iron Pipe (published by: The American Society of Mechanical Engineers).

b. ASTM A53 (ANSI B125.1): Standard Specification for Welded and Seamless Steel Pipe.

c. ASTM B88 (ANSI H23.1): Standard Specification for Seamless Cooper Water Tube

d. Copper Tube Handbook (published by: Copper Development Association, Inc.).

e. Handbook of Cast Iron (published by: Cast Iron Pipe Research Association).

f. AWWA C400: AWWA Standard for Asbestos-Cement Pressure Pipe for Water and Other Liquids.

g. AWWA H2: Standard Practice for the Selection of Asbestos-Cement Water Pipe.

h. AWWA C603: AWWA Standard for Installation of Asbestos-Cement Water Pipe.

i. ASTM D2239 (ANSI B72.1): Standard Specification for Polyethylene (PE) Plastic Pipe (SDR-PR).

j. ASTM D1785 (ANSI B72.7): Standard Specification for Poly (Vinyl Chloride) (PVC) Plastic Pipe, Schedules 40, 80, and 120.

k. ASTM D2241 (ANSI B72.2): Standard Specification or Poly (Vinyl Chloride) (PVC) Plastic Pipe (SDR-PR).

l. ASTM D2466: Standard Specification for Poly (Vinyl Chloride) (PVC) Plastic Pipe Fittings, Schedule 40.

m. ASTM D2662: Standard Specification for Polybutylene (PB) Plastic Pipe (SDR-PR) (Re: Controlled ID). ASTM D2666: Standard Specification for Polybutylene (PB) Plastic Tubing (Re: Copper tube OD).

o. ASTM D3000: Standard Specification for Polybutylene (PB) Plastic Pipe (SDR-PR) (Re: Controlled OD).

p. ASTM D2564 (ANSI B72.16): Standard Specification for Solvent Cements for Poly (Vinyl Chloride) (PVC) Plastic Pipe and Fittings.

q. ASTM D2855 (ANSI K65.55): Standard Recommended Practice for Making Solvent-Cemented Joints with Poly (Vinyl Chloride) (PVC) Pipe and Fittings.

ANSI: Attention Sales Department
American National Standards Institute
1430 Broadway
New York, New York 10018

ASTM: American Society for Testing and Materials
1916 Race Street
Philadelphia, PA 19103

ASME: American Society of Mechanical Engineers
United Engineering Center
345 East 47th St.
New York, New York 10017

PPI: Plastics Pipe Institute
250 Park Avenue
New York, New York 10017

PART II

Water Supply

CHAPTER 3

Hydraulics

Hydraulics is a branch of science that relates to a liquid in motion. Landscape irrigation and hydraulics are, therefore, inseparable subjects for the system designer. It is not practical to design an irrigation system without a working knowledge of the basic principles of hydraulics.

Application of hydraulic principles will enable the system designer to select the irrigation products and develop the water delivery system with assurance that the installed system will perform efficiently on the available water supply: volume and pressure.

The following explanation of hydraulics has been simplified so that the behavior of water, both at rest and in motion, can be more easily understood. Technicalities and perplexing theories not related to irrigation system design have been omitted to avoid confusion.

NATURE OF WATER

Water will compress to such a limited degree that for all practical purposes, it is not compressible. Therefore, it must be pressurized for normal domestic and commercial usage. This is accomplished by mechanical force, as in the case of a pump, or by utilizing the weight of water itself.

In the U.S.A, weight of water used in the hydraulics of water systems such as landscape irrigation systems is based on a temperature of 60° F. In the metric system, its weight at 15°C is used.

Volume	Weight (Mass)	
1 cubic foot (ft^3)	62.37	lb
1 cubic inch (in^3)	0.0361	lb
1 U.S. gallon (gal)	8.34	lb
1 cubic meter (m^3)	999.1	kg
1 cubic centimeter (cm^3)	0.001	kg
(1 cubic foot = 7.4805 gallons)		

PRESSURE

Pressure in the U.S.A. is measured in *pounds per square inch* (lb/in^2) and/or *feet of head* (ft H_2O). In the metric system, it is measured in *kilograms per square centimeter* (kg/cm^2) and/or *meters of head* (m H_2O). [A kg/cm^2 is commonly referred to as an (technical) atmosphere(at)]. However, the most common unit of pressure measurement used in the metric system for irrigation is the "bar", which is equal to kg/cm^2 x .98.

POUNDS PER SQUARE INCH -- FEET OF HEAD

As illustrated in Figure 3-1, a column of water 1 foot high with an area of 1 square inch will weigh 0.433 lbs (0.0361 x 12). Therefore, this hypothetical column of water will exert a pressure of 0.433 lb/in^2 at its base due to its weight.

If the 1 foot column of water had an area of 2 square inches, its weight would be 0.866 pounds (2 x 0.433). If the area of the 1 foot column were ½ square inch, its weight would be 0.217 lbs (0.433 ÷ 2). However, in either case, the force or pressure exerted at the base of the columns would still be 0.433 lb/in^2. Therefore, regardless of area, pressure is expressed in pounds per square inch (lb/in^2) and *pressure gauges are calibrated to measure per square inch.*

All liquid pressures can be thought of as being caused by a column of liquid which, due to its weight, will create a pressure equivalent to the weight in pounds per square inch. Such a column of liquid, either real or imaginary, is called the "pressure head."

In common practice, when the word *head* is used to express pressure, the unit of pressure will be the height

Hydraulics

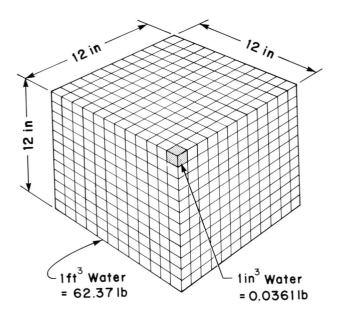

1 ft³ Water = 62.37 lb

1 in³ Water = 0.0361 lb

Figure 3-1 Weight (Mass) of Water

of a column of liquid stated in *feet*. When the word *pressure* is used, the pressure is expressed in *pounds per square inch* (lb/in^2).

PRESSURE EQUIVALENTS. The following equivalents will be used frequently:

1 foot head = 0.433 lb/in^2
1 lb/in^2 = 2.31 feet of head

Metric: 1 meter head = 0.1 kg/cm^2 = .098 bar
1 kg/cm^2 = 10.0 meters of head = .98 bar

Water pressure can be converted to *head* by multiplying lb/in^2 x 2.31. *Head of water* can be converted to pressure by multiplying head x 0.433. For example:

50 lb/in^2 x 2.31 = 115.5 ft H_2O(head)
115.5 ft H_2O(head) x 0.433 = 50 lb/in^2

ELEVATION VS PRESSURE

Every type of water outlet used in landscape irrigation requires a minimum pressure at its base in order to force water through the component and provide flow and/or coverage as specified. It is the responsibility of the designer to provide the required pressure. Examples of pressure calculations included in this chapter are limited to sprinkler systems operated with a city water supply. However, basic considerations included in the examples are typical of calculations required for any type of irrigation system. Additional hydraulics information for systems with private water supplies is presented in Chapter 6, Pumps.

Varying ground elevations cause the pressure in city water distribution systems to differ from one location to another, sometimes considerably. Pressure may even vary substantially from block-to-block. The designer must be aware of and give adequate design consideration to these variances.

CITY WATER SUPPLY. The initial pressure for city water distribution systems is supplied by pumps at the filtration plant. Water is pumped directly through mains to consumers, with any excess going into strategically located, elevated storage tanks, commonly referred to as water towers. When the pumps shut off, pressure is continued by the weight of the water in the towers and their connecting stand pipe.

Assume that a city water distribution system incorporates the elevated water storage tower depicted in Figure 3-2.

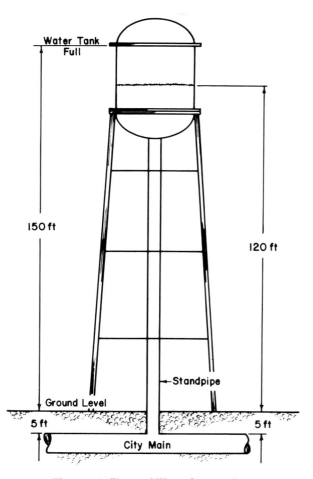

Figure 3-2 Elevated Water Storage Tower

When consumers are not using all water capable of being pumped from the filtration plant, the excess capacity will rise in the tower. Pressure regulatory devices in the distribution system control the height water will rise. Assume that in the example maximum pressure at ground level under the tower is controlled at a maximum of 65 lb/in^2. Then, when ground level pressure reaches 65 lb/in^2, pumps will shut off. The water level in the tower will have raised to 150 feet: 65 x 2.31 = 150. With the distribution pumps shut off, the weight of the water in the tower now provides the 65 lb/in^2 pressure in the city mains: 150 x 0.433 = 65.

In the illustration the pressure in the city main would be 67.1 lb/in^2: water level above city main = 155 ft x .433 = 67.1 lb/in^2. As water is used, the water level in the tower is lowered. When the level falls to 120 ft above ground, the pumps will be automatically turned on again, because the pressure regulatory device is set for a minimum of 52 lb/in^2 at ground level: 120 x .433 = 52 lb/in^2. Pressure in the city main will be 54.1 lb/ in^2.

Figure 3-3 illustrates how varying elevations within the area supplied by the water tower affect pressure.

In this example, the pumps have shut off and pressure is supplied to the main entirely by the weight of the water in the tower. Since the water level elevation is 150 ft above ground level, the pressure at ground level is 65 lb/in^2. No water is moving in the mains.

Therefore, the following conditions will exist:
1. Pressure at hydrant #2 is 65 lb/in^2 because its elevation is the same as ground level at the tower.
2. Hydrant #1 is 30 feet lower in elevation, so the pressure is 78 lb/in^2: 150 + 30 ft = 180 ft x .433 = .78 lb/in^2.
3. Hydrant #3 is 30 feet higher than ground level at the tower. Therefore, the pressure at that point is 52 lb/in^2: 150 ft – 30ft = 120 ft x .433 = 52 lb/in^2.

Special note: If the pressure at ground level under the tower should vary, the pressure at all other points will vary by the same amount; i.e., *available pressure has no effect on gain or loss of pressure due to elevation.*

LOCAL ELEVATIONS: Figure 3-4 illustrates pressure variance on two across-the-street properties connected to a main at the same point. This variance is due to difference in elevation of the two properties. Location of the water tower affects only the static main pressure.

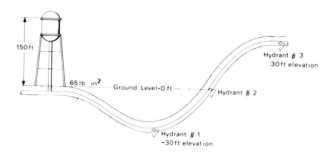

Figure 3-3 Pressure Difference Due to Elevation

With no water moving in the pipes and a pressure of 50 lb/in^2 in the main, the pressure at the lower hydrant will be 56 lb/in^2.

50 lb/in^2 + (14 x .433 = 6) = 56 lb/in^2.

The higher hydrant will have a pressure of only 41 lb/in^2.

50 lb/in^2 – (21 x .433 = 9) = 41 lb/in^2.

If a pressure gauge is connected to each hydrant, it will register the exact pressure at that location including the loss or gain of pressure due to elevation.

Piping designs for the two properties will be different due to a 15 lb/in^2 difference in pressure available for hydraulic design. The following factors must be considered:

A. Upper property:
  1. System must be designed based on pressure at top of grade.
  2. That portion of the system installed on the sloping grade will regain pressure as the piping runs downhill.
  3. If the property continues upgrade behind the house, additional pressure will be lost due to elevation change.
B. Lower property:
  1. Although pressure is gained as piping goes downhill to the hydrant, all of the gain will be lost as system piping goes back uphill to the level of the city water main.

DETERMINING ELEVATION. The preceding example of "Local Elevation" effects was based on the assumption of a definite pressure in the city water main. In actual practice, the main pressure cannot be known at the time pressure is gauged on the property hydrant. Therefore, elevation must be determined before designing an irrigation system.

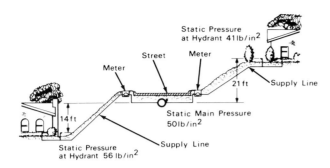

Figure 3-4 Site Pressure Difference Due to Elevation

Topographic Plans. Architecturally designed homes and other buildings will often have a property survey plan showing elevation changes. This is called a "Topographic Plan." Figure 3-5 depicts an exemplary drawing of the results of a topographic survey.

When such a plan is available, it can be used for predetermining pressure changes due to elevation.

Grading plans for new developments may indicate existing and proposed elevations. An inspection of the site will be necessary if topographic plans are not available and the information cannot be obtained from other sources. In many cases, minor changes in elevation can be estimated when a vertical measurement is not practical.

STATIC AND OPERATING PRESSURE

Static pressure (or *static head*) is the pressure when water is motionless. In a closed, level piping system, static pressure is the same at every point. If the system is closed, but not level, *static pressure* will vary at different points only by the amount of pressure equivalent to the difference of elevation.

Operating pressure, also referred to as "working pressure", is the pressure existing at any point in the piping when the irrigation system is operating.

Operating pressure is always less than *static pressure* because the flow of water through a pipe always results in a loss of pressure due to resistance. Figure 3-6 illustrates the difference between *static* and *operating pressure*.

In the upper portion of the illustration, pressure gauges are attached to each of three hose hydrants which are all at the same elevation -- 7 feet above the city water main. Since the water in all pipe from the city main is

motionless, the gauges will all read the same static pressure. Static pressure is the same as the pressure in the main less loss caused by difference of elevation: 47 lb/in^2.

$$50 \text{ lb/in}^2 - (7 \text{ ft} \times .433 = 3) = 47 \text{ lb/in}^2.$$

In the lower portion of Figure 3-6, pressure gauge C has been removed from the last hydrant and water is being allowed to flow out the hydrant. Assume gauge A now reads 42 lb/in^2, which is operating pressure because water is flowing through the pipe to which the hydrant riser is attached.

The difference in static pressure and operating pressure indicated by gauge A of 5 lb/in^2 (47– 42 = 5) is the loss of pressure in the piping from the city main to point 1 caused by the rate of flow from the last hydrant.

Pressure loss equals static pressure minus operating pressure.

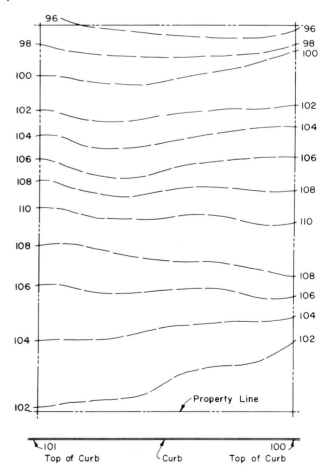

**Figure 3-5 Exemplary Topographic Plan
(Figures Indicate Difference of Elevation in Feet)**

Further assume, with the same rate of flow from the last hydrant, that gauge B reads 39 lb/in^2 operating pressure. Then it is known that the pressure loss in the pipe from point 1 to point 2 is 3 lb/in^2: 42 lb/in^2 (operating pressure at gauge A) minus 39 lb/in^2 (operating pressure at gauge B) equals 3 lb/in^2 loss with that flow.

And, it is known that the total pressure loss from the city main to point 2 is 8 lb/in^2 with that flow: 5 + 3 = 8.

It should be emphasized that the exemplary pressure losses are only for that one particular flow. Any other flows will cause different losses.

The actual pressures in the supply pipe at points 1 and 2, directly under the hydrants, will be more than the gauge reading by an amount equivalent to the height of the gauges above the pipe. However, because the pipe is level, pressure differences will be the same.

Although water in a city main is seldom at rest, its pressure is usually referred to as the *static pressure*. It is the pressure available at the site without flow into the system.

City main pressures are working pressures in a true sense. And, regardless of what terminology is used, the important thing is that *main pressures are subject to considerable fluctuation* which should never be underestimated. The pressure will fluctuate according to the demand, which will vary with month, day of week and time of day.

In addition to variable pressures attributable to the city water plant and elevations, the rise and fall of pressure in the distribution system is caused by the friction of water in the mains. As the flow of water increases, so does the friction and the resulting loss of pressure. Therefore, when the water demand is highest, the pressure will be at its lowest.

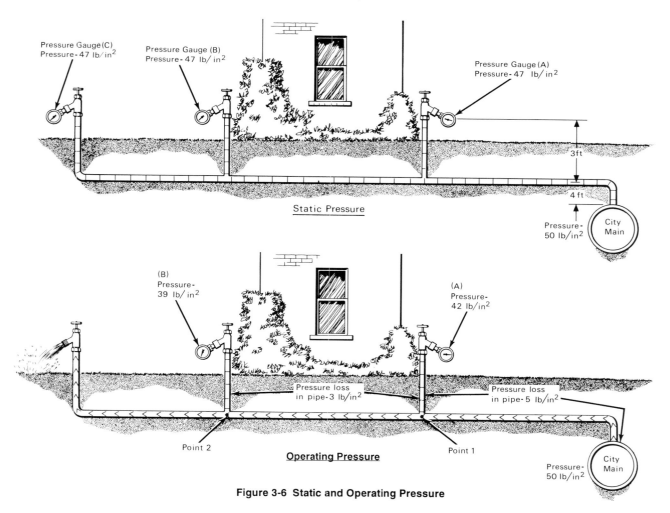

Figure 3-6 Static and Operating Pressure

Hydraulics

These losses are called "frictional loss", "loss of pressure due to friction", "pressure drop", or simply "pressure loss." These are interchangeable terms commonly used to describe energy loss as the result of resistance to water flow in pipes.

In the previous discussion of city water distribution systems regarding pressure and elevation, Figure 3-3, the pressures were true static pressures because it was stated that "no water was moving." With water flowing in the city main, pressures would be reduced at all hydrant locations due to pressure loss in pipe.

PIPING SYSTEM DESIGN

In the previous examples of pressure loss in piping, the pipe was existing and operating pressure could be determined by gauging pressure at various flows. However, in the design of irrigation systems only the static, or available pressure, is known. Therefore, the designer must size all piping and appurtenances in the pipe so that operating pressure (static pressure minus pressure loss) is at least equal to the minimum requirement of specified irrigation products.

FLOW

The volume of flow in irrigation system piping is measured in *gallons per minute* (gpm) and gallons per hour (gph) in the U.S.A. GPM is the standard, except for micro-irrigation systems which use GPH. In the metric system, irrigation rate of flow is measured in cubic meters per hour (m^3/h). However, liters per second or liters per minute are used in some cases.

VELOCITY

The velocity (speed) of flow is measured in linear *feet per second*(ft/s). The flow velocity in pipes, particularly plastic, must be controlled to avoid damage to the pipes.

Velocity is in direct proportion to the volume of flow. For example: If the volume of flow is doubled in the same pipe, the velocity is also doubled.

Flow velocity in pipes varies to the square of pipe diameter. For example: If the pipe diameter is halved, the velocity of the same flow is increased four times.

Note: Velocity flow tables are included with pressure loss charts in the Engineering and Design Data section.

Also, Table 16 provides multiplying factors to determine velocity in most common pipes and tubes.

PRESSURE LOSS IN PIPES

Flow in pipe is always accompanied by a loss of pressure due to the frictional resistance of a liquid to flow. Resistance varies with different liquids and at different temperatures. Hydraulic calculations for irrigation systems are limited to water and normally based on a constant for temperature.

The amount of pressure loss in piping due to friction relates primarily to four conditions:
1. Velocity of flow
2. Diameter of pipe
3. Length of pipe
4. Roughness of pipe (internal surface)

The loss of pressure is completely independent of the amount of pressure forcing water through piping.
The loss of pressure in a pipe due to friction is both progressive and accumulative. That is, as the flow of water progresses through a pipe, the pressure gradually decreases by an amount required to overcome friction. This condition is illustrated in Figure 3-7. If open risers were erected along a pipe in which water is flowing, the water would stand at a lower elevation in each riser successively, indicating the progressive decrease in pressure.

A pressure of 40 lb/in^2 is assumed to exist at the first riser which will cause water to rise 92.4 ft (40 x 2.31). The loss of pressure in the 100 feet of pipe between risers, in this example, is 1 lb/in^2. Consequently, 39 lb/in^2 will exist at the second riser, causing water to rise 90.1 ft (39 x 2.31) and so on.

PRESSURE LOSSES IN APPURTENANCES

Appurtenances in piping systems also cause pressure loss. To simplify calculations, an *equivalent length* of pipe is used to determine losses in standard plumbing valves and pipe fittings. An equivalent length is a length of pipe which has the same pressure loss as the appurtenance.

Pressure losses in specialty-type appurtenances such as water meters, irrigation remote control valves, strainers, etc., cannot be determined by "equivalent lengths." These loss tables or graphs must be obtained from the manufacturer.

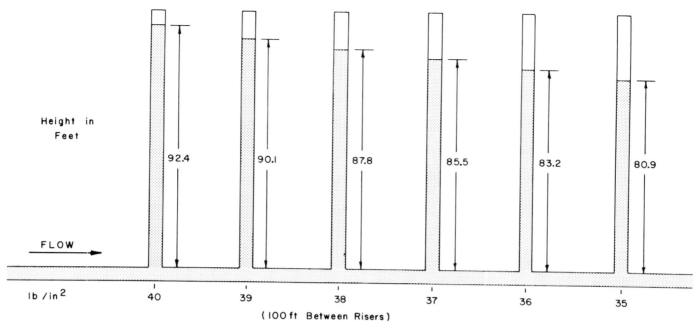

Height in
Feet

FLOW →

lb /in²

| 40 | 39 | 38 | 37 | 36 | 35 |

(100 ft Between Risers)

Flow in horizontal supply pipe causes a pressure loss of 1 lb/in² per 100 linear feet.

Figure 3-7 Pressure Loss Between Risers

PRESSURE LOSS CALCULATIONS

Pressure losses are easily calculated with tables for different kinds of pipe listed in the Engineering and Design Data section of this manual. The results are quite accurate for predetermining pipe and appurtenance sizes to provide sufficient operating pressure at sprinklers or other type of products.

Multiplying factors, Table 3 in Appendix, have been used for pressure loss calculations in this chapter. Standard pressure loss tables, as mentioned above, may be used in lieu of Table 3.

Pressure losses caused by piping appurtenances are also easily calculated with the tables furnished.

Before proceeding to the discussion on pressure loss calculations, the reader is urged to study the pipe pressure loss tables and their explanations, along with companion tables used in conjunction with calculating pressure losses. These tables, in the Engineering and Design Data section, are:

1. Tables 3 to 14 -- pipe pressure losses.
2. Table 16 -- flow velocity multiplying factors.
3. Tables 17, 18 and 19 -- pressure losses for appurtenances.

Formula (and example calculation) used with multiplying factors is provided with Table 3.

The following explanation is provided for Tables 4 to 14 (optional method):

1. Referring to the pressure loss table for 200 psi PR SDR 21 PVC pipe, it will be noted that pressure losses are shown for rates of flow in pipe sizes ½ in to 12 in inclusive. (Tables for other kinds of pipe are basically similar.)

2. The pressure losses listed are for 100 linear feet of pipe. To obtain the loss in longer or shorter lengths, multiply these values by the length of pipe expressed as a decimal equivalent of 100. Thus, 150 feet would be expressed as 1.50, 69 feet as 0.69, 9 feet as 0.09, and so on.

Example: The loss for 24 gpm flowing through 1 in SDR 21 PVC pipe is 7.13 lb/in². The loss in various lengths is calculated as follows:

150 ft (7.13 X 1.5) = 10.7 lb/in² loss
69 ft (7.13 X 0.69) = 4.9 lb/in² loss
 9 ft (7.13 X 0.09) = 0.6 lb/in² loss

The outlet pressure in a level run of pipe is equal to the inlet pressure minus the pressure loss. If the pipe runs uphill, there will be an additional loss of pressure due to elevation, and the outlet pressure will be reduced still further. On the other hand, if the pipe runs downhill, there will be a gain of pressure which will increase the outlet pressure.

Hydraulics

Summarizing: *the outlet pressure of a length of pipe is equal to the inlet pressure minus the frictional loss and plus or minus the gain or loss of pressure due to elevation difference.*

PIPE SIZING

Figure 3-8 illustrates a simple piping system connected to a city water main and supplying three outlets. Each outlet will flow 4.2 gpm at a required minimum pressure of 20 lb/in^2 at its base (In this example, flow is controlled to 4.2 gpm maximum). Piping and appurtenances must be sized so that the total of pressure losses and minimum pressure required at the last outlet (C) does not exceed the minimum available city main pressure.

Note: *If the most distant outlet in terms of pipe length has sufficient pressure, pressure at intermediate outlets will always be sufficient with proper pipe sizing (assuming all outlets are at the same elevation).*

In this example, pipe is sized so that flow velocities in system pipe do not exceed 5 ft/s. Flow velocities for water service pipe and system piping are discussed in Chapter 4.

MEASURING PIPE LENGTHS. Although pipe lengths are given for the example, in practice the designer must measure lengths on the plan. A separate measurement must be made for each length when:

1. Flow changes
2. Pipe size changes
3. Kind of pipe changes

Each separate pipe length with the same rate of flow and pipe size/type is often referred to as a "pipe section."

The length of appurtenances must be shown larger than scale size on plans in order for their symbols to be recognized. Therefore, when measuring pipe lengths on plans, use distance from center-to-center of appurtenances. All measurements which are not exact feet should be rounded to the next larger full foot; i.e., a measurement of 9.3 ft is rounded to 10 ft.

Special Considerations. In the exemplary problem, notice that the 3/4 in type K water service line between the main and meter is 10 ft long on the plan view. However, water mains are almost always several feet deep as shown in the elevation view. The length of pipe for the vertical rise must be included in the total length of water service. Therefore, the total length of type K is 14 ft. Also, the pressure losses through fittings and valves are calculated in equivalent lengths of pipe; these equivalent lengths must be added to the service pipe length.

In addition, allow for pressure losses in appurtenances on each length of pipe beyond the meter.

In the illustration, all piping and appurtenances to outlet "A" are supplying all three outlets so the flow is 12.6 gpm: 4.2 gpm x 3 = 12.6 gpm. Flow through pipe section 7 is 8.4 gpm. And, the flow through pipe section 8 is only 4.2 gpm since it supplies only the one outlet.

DESIGN PRESSURE. Pressure loss calculations shown in Figure 3-9 are made using Tables 17, 18, and 19 for standard appurtenances. Pressure loss shown for the 1 in double-check valve (item 4) was obtained from a manufacturer's table (not provided). Backflow prevention equipment is discussed in Chapter 5, Cross-Connection Control. Pipe pressure loss calculations were made using Table 3 to avoid interpolation of data as provided in standard pipe pressure loss tables.

Note: In actual practice, a variety of different methods can be used to calculate or estimate the loss of individual items, as shown in Figure 3-9. For example, an allowance is sometimes used to cover the combined loss of all pipe fittings. Pressure loss estimates which are based on a "rule of thumb" should be used with caution, as each piping system is different and standard allowances may or may not be realistic.

Pressure losses shown in Figure 3-9 are rounded off in each case to .01 lb/in^2. Many designers round off calculated values to .1 lb/in^2. Actual difference that may occur with different methods is normally unimportant (loss per 100 ft shown for reference).

Item 1. The equivalent lengths for the appurtenances in the type K water service were taken from Table 18. Since the multiplying factor is 1.0 for type K, the "Base Footage Equivalents" were used directly. The "footage equivalents" for the cocks and elbow added to the length of the tube totaled 30.4 feet and was rounded up to 31 feet.

Note: The flow of 12.6 could be rounded off to 13.0 gpm. Rounding off of flows may also be necessary for the 8.4 and 4.2 gpm calculations to avoid interpolation of data when using the standard pipe pressure loss tables.

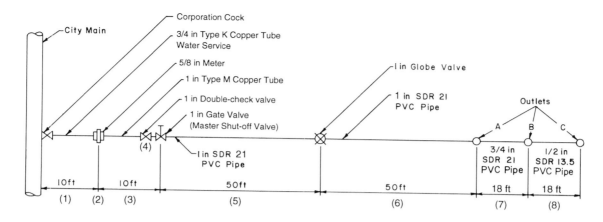

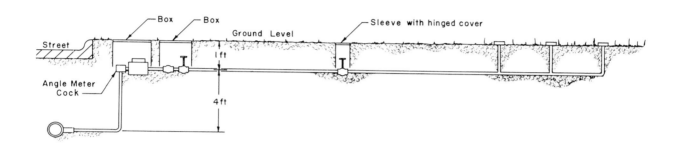

Figure 3-8 Simple Piping System

Pressure loss in item 1, using 13.0 gpm and Table 10, would be: 24.49 x .31 = 7.59 lb/in².

Item 2. Pressure Loss Table 19, Disc Type Water Meters, provides actual losses in lb/in² rather than an equivalent length of piping. Loss of 5.86 was determined by interpolation.

(Note: Most ⅝ in water meters are ⅝ x ¾ and have ¾ in pipe threads.)

Item 3. Some plumbing codes do not allow plastic pipe between the meter and the Master Shut-off Valve for the system. Therefore, in the example, Type M copper tube was used in this location.

In addition to the gate valve, a 1 in by ¾ in bushing is included to connect the tube to the water meter. Losses in individual fittings are considered minor losses. However, the total of all fitting losses can be very important. Many designers develop a "short list" table for equivalent length values. A customized table for normal size, type of pipe and fitting requirements will simplify the

calculations. Loss in pipe couplings is normally not calculated.

Equivalent lengths for the reducing bushing and gate valve were taken from Table 18. Base footage equivalents were calculated using the 1.33 multiplier for type M copper.

Pressure loss per 100 feet of 4.255 was calculated using the formula shown in Table 3. Loss in item 3: 4.255 x .14 = .5957 = .60

Item 4. As previously mentioned, pressure loss for the 1 in double check assembly was obtained from a manufacturer's table (not provided). Backflow prevention equipment and installation must conform to the local plumbing code requirements. Connection fittings are omitted, as pressure loss of this equipment includes normal entrance and exit losses. (This is also true for the majority of valves used in irrigation systems.)

Item 5. Pipe sections (items 5 and 6) of 1 in PVC pipe would normally be combined together. Sections are

Hydraulics

listed separately in Figure 3-9 for explanation only. The first section (item 5) of 1 in pipe is the pressure main to the zone operating valve. In some cases, this would be a different type and/or size of pipe, as compared to item 6. Table 17 was used for the globe valve equivalent length. Straight globe valve length of 29.7 x 1.92 for 1 SDR 21 (multiplier) = 57.0. Pressure loss using Table 3 calculation: 2.162 x 1.07 = 2.31 lb/in^2.

Note: Electric valves are almost always used for zone control valves and a manufacturer's table would be required to determine the pressure loss. A manually operated globe valve was used in this piping example to illustrate the use of Table 17.

Item 6. A reducing tee is required for the pipe size change at outlet "A." Footage equivalent using Table 17: 1.8 for 1 in (run of straight tee) plus 1.5 for a 1 in by $\frac{3}{4}$ in bushing = 3.3 x 1.92 (multiplier for 1 in SDR 21) = 6.4 feet (6.34). Pressure loss using Table 3 calculation: 2.162 x .57 = 1.23 lb/in^2.

Note: Standard reducing tees do not require the use of a bushing. However, "straight" tees with a bushing are commonly used when a size reduction is required. Some designers suggest that the loss in a reducing tee is no greater than the loss in a straight tee, if the flow velocity is approximately the same for both sizes. This theory is discussed in the explanation section of the appendix.

Item 7. A reducing tee is required for the pipe size change at outlet "B." Footage equivalent using Table 17: 1.4 for $\frac{3}{4}$ in (run of straight tee) plus 1.6 for a $\frac{3}{4}$ in by $\frac{1}{2}$ in bushing = 3.0 x 1.84 for $\frac{3}{4}$ in SDR 21 (multiplier) = 5.5 feet. Pressure loss using Table 3 calculation: 3.455 x .24 = .83 lb/in^2.

Item 8. Although SDR 21 PVC pipe is used in this example system, PVC pipe in size $\frac{1}{2}$ in is only available in PR SDR 13.5, 315 psi pressure rating. A 90° elbow is required for the riser at outlet "C." Equivalent length was taken from Table 17: 1.6 for $\frac{1}{2}$ in 90° elbow x 1.96 for SDR 13.5 = 3.136 = 3.2 feet. Pressure loss using Table 3 calculation: 3.534 x .22 = .78 lb/in^2.

Item 9. A $\frac{1}{2}$ in schedule 80 PVC nipple is used to develop a loss allowance for the riser nipple to outlet "C". Many different types of risers are used in landscape irrigation systems. Flexible nipples, tubing and swing-joint assemblies are examples of risers commonly used for sprinkler heads. Pressure loss allowance was

Item No.	Size in	Item	Equivalent Length ft.	Flow gpm	Loss per 100 ft. lb/in^2	Total Length ft.	Unit Loss lb/in^2
1	$\frac{3}{4}$	Water Service					
		Type K Copper Tube	14.0				
		Corporation Cock	6.4				
		Wrought 90° elbow	1.3				
		Angle Meter Cock	8.7	12.6	23.117	31	7.17
2	$\frac{5}{8}$	Water Meter		12.6			5.86
3	1	Type M Copper Tube	10.0				
		Reducing Bushing	2.7				
		Gate Valve	1.2	12.6	4.255	14	.60
4	1	Double Check Valve Assembly		12.6			4.00
5	1	SDR 21 (200 psi PR) PVC pipe	50.0				
		Globe Valve (straight)	57.0	12.6	2.162	107	2.31
6	1	SDR 21 (200 psi PR) PVC pipe	50.0				
		Reducing Tee	6.4	12.6	2.162	57	1.23
7	$\frac{3}{4}$	SDR 21 (200 psi PR) PVC pipe	18.0				
		Reducing Tee	5.5	8.4	3.455	24	0.83
8	$\frac{1}{2}$	SDR 13.5 (315 psi PR) PVC pipe	18.0				
		90° Elbow	3.2	4.2	3.534	22	.78
9	$\frac{1}{2}$	$\frac{1}{2}$ Sch. 80 PVC Nipple (riser)	.5	4.2	13.803	1	.14
					Total pressure Loss		22.92
				Add minimum required pressure at Outlet			20.00
				(DESIGN PRESSURE) Total pressure required			42.92

Figure 3-9
Pressure Loss Calculations for
Piping System in Example 3-8

developed using Table 3: 13.803 x .01 (1 foot) = .14 lb/in^2.

Adding the pressure loss caused by the 9 items of 22.92 lb/in^2 plus the minimum pressure required at the base of the outlets, 20 lb/in^2, makes the total required operating pressure 42.92 lb/in^2. Therefore, a minimum pressure of 42.92 lb/in^2, or more, must be available at all times in the city water main for the outlets to operate properly.

The total minimum pressure required is called the DE-SIGN PRESSURE because that is the pressure with which the system is designed to operate.

ADJUSTING DESIGN PRESSURE. If the calculated design pressure is too high for the available pressure, it will be necessary to reduce the pressure losses by increasing some of the component sizes. Quantity of outlets operating at one time may need to be changed to reduce the flow requirement, if component size changes are not realistic.

In some cases, it may be necessary to consider a larger water meter and service pipe if the number of operating zones required for the complete system is not realistic. Check availability, cost and restrictions that may be applicable before designing to a larger water supply.

Conversely, if the available pressure is considerably greater than the design pressure, some of the component sizes may be reduced in size. Caution: Check increased velocity of smaller sizes, in addition to increased pressure loss. Velocity is discussed in Chapter 4, Water Hammer.

At this point, it is emphasized that the design pressure must never exceed the *lowest available pressure* the water source will provide. Remember that city water system pressures vary at different times of the day and night depending on demand. Peak demands also vary with the season. Also, in piping system design, it is not necessary that all of the available pressure be used; i.e., design pressure can and should be less. However, excessive operating pressure must be reduced by including pressure control products in the piping system as necessary.

FLUCTUATIONS IN CITY WATER PRESSURE

There are many factors that affect pressure in municipal water systems. The designer should have knowledge of these in order to avoid some of the pitfalls that often lead to over-estimating the present and probable future available pressures.

The pressure in a municipal water system will vary due to some or all of these causes:
1. Distance from pumping station to water tower and from water tower to neighborhood in question.
2. Elevation between pump station and water tower and from water tower to neighborhood in question.
3. Size of water mains and whether looped, gridded, or dead-ended.
4. Water demand.

The size of water mains, whether looped or gridded, and water demand are probably the greatest contributing factors to pressure fluctuation. If the mains are relatively small and are single-trunked, a sudden heavy demand will cause a severe drop in pressure. On the other hand, if the mains are of ample size and are gridded with other mains, pressure will probably remain fairly constant despite abnormal loads.

Ordinarily, a city water distribution system will consist of several pump stations and booster stations. The distribution mains will be of the grid-type with water flowing to any one point from several directions. Water towers are dispersed at strategic points and these fill up when the demand is low, then act as an additional supply during periods of excessive demands.

When water mains in the area of concern are less than 6 in, extreme caution should be used when estimating available water pressure. The water pressure in mains of these smaller sizes will drop drastically during periods of heavy demand.

The designer must also make proper allowance for a possible drop in static pressure at some future time, otherwise the irrigation system may be deprived of the pressure required to make it perform satisfactorily. This is a problem often overlooked, especially in the case of expanding communities where static pressures have been known to deteriorate from year to year as mains are extended to accommodate new homes and commercial needs. It is advisable to keep informed on such probabilities by making periodic inquiry at the city water works engineering department.

Static pressure is easily obtained by gauging the pressure on a hydrant at the job site. However, the pressure reading may be inadvertently taken at a time when pressure is highest. Ordinarily, pressures can be expected to vary considerably during any 24 hour period and week-to-week depending on the season.

Lowest pressures usually occur during the hottest summer months when demands are heaviest, and usually during the evening just before sundown when most people without an irrigation system do their watering.

If the designer is not thoroughly familiar with the pressure characteristics in each section of the city, it is best to consult the water department's engineer rather than rely on job site pressure readings.

For existing areas of a city, the water department will usually make periodic recordings of pressure variations. From these checks, they can provide accurate information as to highest pressure, average pressure and lowest summer pressure. Only the low summer pressure should be considered for irrigation system design. Incidentally, these check pressures are taken from fire hydrants, so no consideration need be given

Hydraulics

to the depth of the main below street grade as far as pressure is concerned.

When new areas are developed, the water distribution system is generally designed to provide a minimum pressure after building is completed. This means the immediate static pressure may be considerably higher than the contemplated low. The water department engineers can normally furnish the future low for irrigation system design.

DETERMINING CAPACITY OF EXISTING PIPING SYSTEMS

Existing piping often can or must be utilized as the source and/or as part of a new irrigation system. It is practically impossible to calculate the theoretical pressure loss because the size(s) are not always known and the actual condition of the pipe cannot be determined. Older pipes are often of a type that may be badly choked with rust or deposits.

In addition, it is not uncommon for existing piping systems to have other severe restrictions that impede flow and are not detectable. Included are such restrictions as: malfunctioning water meters, corporation cocks only partially open, faulty taps to the city main, an excessive number of pipe fittings, and kinks in piping made during installation.

Before planning to use an existing piping system, its capacity should be tested on the site; i.e., a flow-pressure test to determine pressure loss in the components. Figures 3-10, 3-11 and 3-12 diagram the basic types of existing piping systems that are encountered. Interpretation of test results differs.

EQUIPMENT REQUIRED
The only equipment required to make a capacity test is one or two accurate water pressure gauges (depending on type of system) and some type of device to measure the rate of flow in gallons per minute. Low-cost flow measurement products are not always reliable and equipment should be checked for accuracy.

Small supply systems can be tested with a plastic container and a stopwatch. Containers should be small enough to locate under water outlets and yet, adequate in size to allow for an accurate measurement. Capacity of container must be marked at one, two, etc. gallon levels.

TESTING PIPE LINES
The following method is for testing capacity of pipe lines incorporating only standard plumbing valves and fittings whose pressure loss can be related to *equivalent lengths* of pipe. Method of test for piping systems including water meters is outlined later. Any strainers in the piping system must be thoroughly cleaned before the test.

In order to obtain a reliable pressure loss test, accuracy must be maintained through the entire test.

Figure 3-10 illustrates the method of test for pressure losses in an existing hydrant system. While it depicts a pump drawing water from a lake, the same test is applicable when the source of supply is city water, either with or without a booster pump, *providing only piping downstream from the meter and pumps is tested.*

METHOD OF TEST. The pressure loss test of the piping in Figure 3-10 would be made as per the succeeding outline. It is imperative that the entire test be made with a *single source operating pressure.* Therefore, to be safe, two gauges should be used, with one person monitoring the source pressure and another conducting the test.

Step 1. Determine static pressure:
Attach a pressure gauge to hydrant "A." Open hydrant and record source static pressure. Leave this gauge on hydrant, displaying pressure during entire test.

Step 2. Container and stopwatch method used to illustrate procedures required. Determine flow rate through pipes 1-2-3:
   A. Open hydrant "E" fully and leave running full force during entire test for pressure losses in this portion of the piping.
   B. Using a stopwatch quickly place the container under hydrant "E" and accurately determine time to fill to a marked level. In this example, assume time to fill to the 3 gallon level is 12 seconds.

Flow rate would be 15 gpm (60 ÷ 12 x 3 = 15).

Step 3. Determine source operating pressure:
   A. With hydrant "E" still flowing full force, obtain and record working pressure at hydrant "A." This pressure is known as source operating pressure.
   B. Caution: If source operating pressure fluctuates at any time during steps 3 and 4, stop tests until pressure stabilizes.

Step 4. Determine *operating pressures* in piping being tested:
 A. With hydrant "E" still flowing full force, obtain and record operating pressures at hydrants B, C, and D.
 B. Caution: These operating pressures must be recorded with the same source operating pressure.

Test Results. The operating pressure difference between each two adjacent hydrants is the pressure loss in the piping connecting the two hydrants.

Example:
 (1) Assume operating pressures in lb/in^2 recorded on the hydrants were as follows:
  A = 62.0
  B = 60.0
  C = 54.0
  D = 47.0
 (2) Then pressure losses in the various pipe sections *with a flow of 15 gpm* would be:
  1. A — B = 2 lb/in^2 (62 – 60 = 2)
  2. B — C = 6 lb/in^2 (60 – 54 = 6)
  3. C — D = 7 lb/in^2 (54 – 47 = 7)

It should be noted that these tests provide the actual pressure loss for a determined flow regardless of the size, roughness, or any adverse condition of the pipe.

For example, there could be two or more sizes of pipe between any two adjacent hydrants. In this case, the pressure difference between the two points represents the accumulative loss for the various sizes, and is the actual loss between the two points. With this information, the pressure loss can be determined for any desired flow in the piping.

A test for pressure loss through piping "A" to "F" would be conducted in the same manner as the test just illustrated. However, the flow rate test would be made at hydrant "G" with hydrant "E" shut off. With a different flow than from hydrant "E", *source operating pressure* would be different. Pressure loss in pipe section A - B would also be different.

These tests do not include the sections of pipe supplying the hydrants which are flowing water. These pipes can be included in the tests, but some difficulty is encountered.

Do not attempt to test these pipes by using a hydrant "wye" with the gauge on one side and water flowing out the other. With such a set-up, the pressure loss in the riser pipe to the hydrant and in the hydrant itself will also be included in the operating pressure reading. And, in all probability, these losses will be greater than the loss in pipe section.

INTERPRETING TEST RESULTS. The following formula can be used to estimate losses in piping for other flows. A calculator with the key y^x (Function: y to the x power) is required.

Formula:
$$\left(\frac{Q_2}{Q_1}\right)^{1.85} \times PL_1 = PL_2$$

where:
Q_1 = test flow
Q_2 = desired flow
PL_1 = test pressure loss
PL_2 = pressure loss at desired flow

Example: Assume that a new pipe connection will be made in pipe section 3 (adjacent to existing tee for hydrant "D") and a flow of 20 gpm is desired at this location. For this example, it is assumed that the pump station can provide 20 gpm at the same discharge pressure.

 Q_1 = 15, Q_2 = 20, PL_1 = 15 (combined loss of pipes 1,2,3)

 $$PL_2 = \left(\frac{20}{15}\right)^{1.85} \times 15 = 25.5$$

Pressure loss in Pipes 1, 2, and 3 equals 25.5 lb/in^2 at a flow rate of 20 gpm.

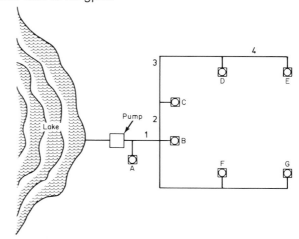

Figure 3-10 Testing Pressure Losses in Hydrant Piping

Hydraulics

WATER SUPPLY TESTING -- BASEMENT METERS

The method for testing the capacity of an existing water supply including a meter and service line is basically the same as the previous test of the hydrant lines. Interpretation of the results is somewhat different.

Figure 3-11 illustrates the capacity test when the meter is located in the basement. Equipment required is the same as for the test of the hydrant system - an accurate pressure gauge and pail or other container of known volume.

METHOD OF TEST. Although the same information is obtained -- pressure loss in piping system components -- the procedure of testing a water service with meter varies considerably from the test of the hydrant line piping.

Step 1. Determine static pressure.
A. Check all valves both inside and out to make certain that they are fully open. A special key for the curb stop is available at wholesale plumbing supply outlets.
B. Request residents not to use water during test. Any water flowing, other than that of the test, will invalidate the test results.
C. Attach pressure gauge to hydrant "A" and record static pressure. Leave hydrant open so gauge will continue to display pressure during entire test.

Step 2. Determine flow rate.
A. Open hydrant "B" fully.
B. Quickly place container under hydrant and accurately determine length of time to fill to a marked level. This information is converted to flow rate as previously explained.

Step 3. Determine operating pressure.
A. With hydrant "B" still fully open and flowing, record residual pressure at hydrant "A." This will be the operating pressure for the flow determined at hydrant "B."
B. Slowly close hydrant "B" and check static pressure now indicated on gauge. If this static pressure deviates from that obtained in Step 1, pressure in the city water main has fluctuated during the test and test is invalid. Repeat entire test to obtain a valid result. The safest procedure to guard against pressure fluctuations during pressure loss test is for a second person to observe the pressure gauge. If operating pressure deviates, stop the test. Repeat test after operating pressure stabilizes.

Test Results. The difference between *static pressure* obtained in Step 1 and *operating pressure* obtained in Step 3 is the pressure loss in the piping from city main to the tee at point "C" for the flow obtained in Step 2. The loss determined includes the resistance through the meter, fittings, valves, bends and any other resistances or restrictions in the piping.

INTERPRETING TEST RESULTS. Interpreting test results for pressure losses in piping systems incorporating a water meter is more complex and requires some compromise. This is because changing flows through meters and pipes *do not* follow the same progression.

The pressure loss in piping incorporating only standard plumbing valves and fittings increases approximately 3.6 times when the flow is doubled through the same piping.

The pressure loss in meters increases about 4.2 times maximum when the flow is doubled through the same meter, depending on meter size and flows involved.

To compromise the preceding differences for flows *greater* than the result of the test of piping including a meter, the theorem -- *to double the flow, increases the pressure loss approximately 4 times* -- is used.

The following formula provides an easy method of estimating pressure loss for flows greater than test flow:

$$\left(\frac{Q_2}{Q_1}\right)^2 \times PL_1 = PL_2$$

Where: Q_1 = test flow
Q_2 = desired flow
PL_1 = test pressure loss
PL_2 = pressure loss at desired flow (approx.)

Example: Assume that in the flow-pressure test the static pressure was 65 lb/in^2 and the operating pressure was 59 lb/in^2. And, assume that the container filled to the two gallon mark in 15 seconds. The test indicated a flow of 8 gpm (60 ÷ 15 x 2 = 8) with a pressure loss of 6 lb/in^2.

For a flow of 15 gpm, the pressure loss to point "C" is determined by the above formula:
Q_1 = 8 gpm, Q_2 = 15, PL_1 = 6

$$PL_2 = \left(\frac{15}{8}\right)^2 \times PL_1 = 21.1$$

Pressure loss to point "C" is approximately 21 lb/in^2 at a flow rate of 15 gpm.

For very short water services the interpolation determined by the theorem formula will be close to actual. As the ratio of pipe length to meter increases, the calculated pressure loss will be increasingly more than actual. But, since the error is on the "high" side, the calculated loss can be used with safety.

The theorem used to interpolate pressure loss for flows *greater than* test results *cannot* be used to interpolate for flows *less than* test results.

When the flow in piping incorporating only standard plumbing valves and fittings is halved, the pressure loss is approximately 28% of the original flow. However, the theorem calculates a pressure loss of only 25% of the

original when the flow is halved. Since the pressure loss of the piping portion of water services contributes the largest portion of the total pressure loss, the above formula will *underestimate* the pressure loss when used for flows smaller than the test flow.

Therefore, the formula used in the previous test (pump system, Figure 3-10) is a safe method for estimating pressure loss when the desired flow is "less" than that measured by test.

Example: Assume a flow of 5 gpm is required at point "C", Figure 3-11.
$$Q_1 = 8, \ Q_2 = 5, \ PL_1 = 6$$

$$PL_2 = \left(\frac{5}{8}\right)^{1.85} \times 6 = 2.5$$

Pressure loss to point "C" is approximately 2.5 lb/in^2 at a flow rate of 5 gpm.

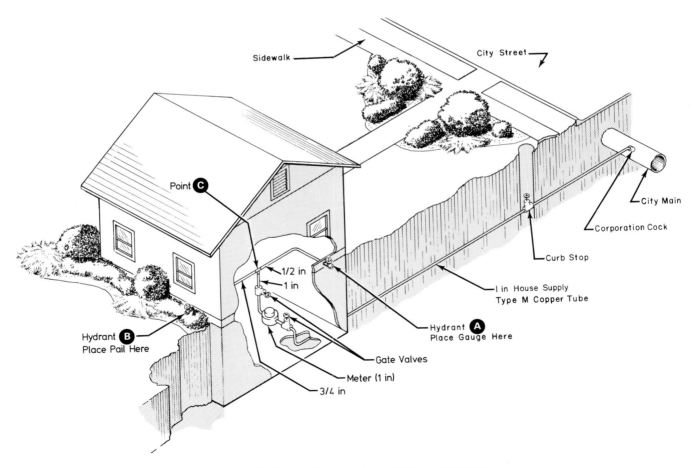

Figure 3-11 Testing Water Supply: Meter in Basement

Hydraulics

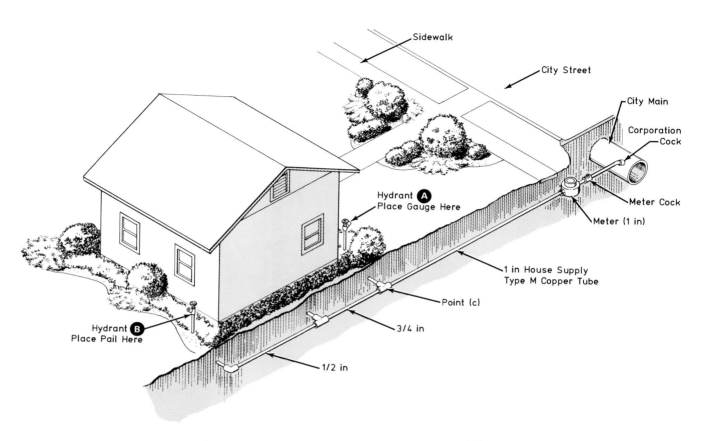

Figure 3-12 Testing Water Supply: Meter Outside Building

WATER SUPPLY TESTING -- METERS LOCATED OUTSIDE OF BUILDING

Figure 3-12 illustrates the capacity test when the water meter is located outside of the building. The test procedure is exactly the same as outlined for the meter supply located in the basement.

The test result will provide the pressure loss to point "C", the tee at base of hydrant riser. Interpolation of the test result is also the same, assuming the connection for the irrigation system is made just prior to point "C"; i.e., on the street side of hydrant connection.

However, when irrigation systems are designed with the supply from an outside meter, common practice is to make the connection at the meter. This permits more of the piping to be increased in size to reduce pressure losses. In this case, the theoretical pressure loss of the pipe between the meter and the front hydrant, "A", is deducted from the loss determined in the test.

To determine the deduction, measure the length of the pipe from the meter to the hydrant. Also, determine the kind and type of pipe (it can be seen in the meter box).

If the pipe type cannot be determined, use the pressure loss table for the type with least loss.

An accurate pressure loss from the main through the meter can be obtained but the method is seldom practical. Before planning the irrigation system, a hydrant would need to be installed adjacent to the meter in the pipe leading to hydrant "A." The pressure loss test is then conducted using the new hydrant in place of hydrant "A."

GENERAL: TESTING EXISTING PIPING

Examples of testing are useful to understand the basic principles of reasoning that must be applied to a flow test. However, individuals who perform actual tests must be able to adapt to the variable conditions of different piping systems and apply the logic as necessary. There are many factors that can influence the accuracy of a particular flow-pressure test. These include the use of proper equipment and procedures, and interpretation of the test results.

WATER PRESSURE GAUGES. Gauges should be tested frequently at all pressures in the range of the gauges. Many suppliers maintain testing facilities and will recalibrate repairable gauges for accuracy.

More accurate pressure readings are obtained when the maximum capacity of the gauge exceeds static pressure by the least amount. Lower capacities provide greater increments of pressure for easier reading. Example: Do not use a 500 lb/in^2 gauge on a 50 lb/in^2 test for accuracy. Gauges are delicate instruments requiring normal care. Do not over-stress by using a 50 lb/in^2 gauge on 60 lb/in^2 and so on. Gauges must also be protected from freezing.

FLOW TEST VOLUME. Accuracy is extremely important when determining flow rate in the pressure loss tests. Conducting the tests with maximum obtainable flow provides best accuracy. However, flowing water at maximum rate into the measuring container often causes so much turbulence that it is impossible to determine exactly when the water reaches the known volume level. Turbulence can be controlled by flowing the water from the hydrant with a hose emitting flow at the bottom of the container.

SUPPLEMENTARY FLOW TESTS. For more accuracy, many designers prefer to make two or three pressure loss tests, each with a different flow. After the initial test is made with the hydrant fully open, a second test is made with the hydrant about ⅔ open. Flow and pressure loss will be less than that of the initial test. The third test is made with the hydrant about ⅓ open.

The three tests are then averaged for final interpretation. Note: The flows of the second and third test can be any amount as long as they are different from each other and the flow of the initial test.

FAULTY METERS. A test indicating an excessive pressure loss as compared to the average results of other tests with the same size piping and meter may indicate a malfunctioning meter. Before using the results of this test, ask the water department to test or replace the meter (generally there is no charge). Then retest the water supply.

UNDER-SIZE METERS. In some cases, existing water supplies will have a meter smaller than the supply pipe from the city water main. Most water departments will install a larger meter, up to the size of the supply pipe. However, flow is primarily limited by the supply piping, so consider the advantage of a larger meter carefully before recommending a change in meter size.

CONNECTION TO BASEMENT METERS. As with all types of existing water supplies, it is best to connect the

irrigation system pressure main as close to the meter as possible. This is especially true when the riser pipe from the meter is smaller than the supply pipe to the meter. Also, the irrigation system is generally designed with the piping from the meter one size larger than the supply to the meter in order to reduce pressure losses.

CHAPTER 4

Water Hammer

Pressure surge occurs when the flow of water in a pipe is abruptly changed or stopped. Therefore, it is a common occurrence in the normal operation of an irrigation system. Water hammer is a standard plumbing term used to describe the surge of pressure in all types of piping systems. In practice, the term is normally only used to describe severe cases where the shock of pressure surging results in noise and/or product failure.

Noise is often a problem when a building water supply is also used for the irrigation system. Pressure surging within the common supply piping may cause pounding, vibration and movement of plumbing components in the building. The absence of noise does not indicate that water hammer is non-existent in a water distribution system.

Forces tremendous enough to rupture piping, weaken or damage connections, damage valves, and damage other equipment can be generated at the point of flow stoppage. (Note: When the word stoppage is used in this text, it means both total stoppage and partial stoppage -- reduction of flow.)

When water hammer occurs, a high intensity pressure wave travels back through the piping system until it reaches a "point of relief." The shock wave then surges back and forth between the "point of relief" and the "point of stoppage" until the extra energy is dissipated. This violent action accounts for the piping noise and vibration.

(*Point of relief* is a larger mass of water in the system. With irrigation systems supplied by city water this may be the city water main. Point of relief can also be a pressure-storage tank of the type used with hydro-pneumatic pumping systems, if of sufficient size).

There are four causes of water hammer which may be encountered in irrigation systems.
1. Valve closure
2. Uncontrolled flow velocity in empty pipes
3. Trapped air in long runs of pipe
4. Reverse flow when pumps stop

The first two causes may be encountered in any type system. The third cause generally occurs only in long runs of pipe such as systems for irrigating golf courses. The last cause is of concern with private pump supplies only.

VALVE CLOSURE

The most commonly known cause of shock is the quick closing of valves. In irrigation systems these can include remote control valves, both electric and hydraulic actuated; pressure relief valves, etc. Even the fast closing of hand-operated globe, gate and quick-coupling valves will cause some degree of water hammer, See Figure 4-1.

Shock intensity is measured by the flow pressure existing before flow stoppage occurs plus pressure rise caused by valve closure.

The degree of shock intensity depends primarily on:
1. Length of pipe (from point of relief to point of flow stoppage)
2. Elasticity of pipe
3. Pipe size
4. Flow velocity
5. Speed of valve closure, *especially during the last 25% of valve closure*
6. Change of flow velocity due to valve closure

Water Hammer

The shock wave created by a quick closing valve will travel back and forth in the piping until the extra energy is dissipated. Graphic illustrations are shown in Figure 4-2. In this illustration, notice that the shock wave alternately expands and contracts the piping during its occurrence. This is the destructive force which may cause damage to the piping and appurtenances.

PIPE SYSTEM PROTECTION

Piping systems must be protected from excessive water hammer to prevent damage. Although not normally encountered, theoretically pressure can surge to 50-60 times velocity due to quick valve closure. It is estimated that pressure surging in the average irrigation system does not approach such intensity. However, it is known that many systems do develop surging of a magnitude that will cause pipe failure.

Complex formulas for determining pressure surging are generally not considered suitable for irrigation system design. Necessary data of sufficient accuracy usually cannot be determined, especially as relates to the most important factor -- the last 25% of valve closure time. Nomographs are also available for estimating surge pressure. When complete valve data is not available, control valves should be considered in the "quick closure" category.

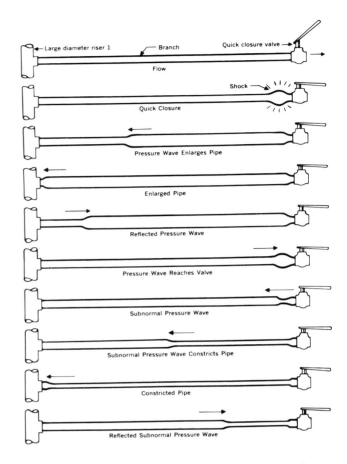

Figure 4-2 Exaggerated Graphic Illustrations of a Shock Wave [1] **(Degree Depends on Elasticity of Pipe Material)**

1. Do not exceed recommended flow velocities.
2. Use valves which are designed with devices to minimize pressure surging when closing.
3. Do not undersize valves.

Plastic Pipe Systems. Methods of plastic pipe system design have evolved over the years to protect against damaging pressure surging from valve closure. This, of course, applies to the piping between the prime source and the section operating valves, referred to as the *pressure main*.

Design recommendations for use of plastic pipe can be divided into two broad categories. The first category covers methods where a wide variety of technical detail is considered for the requirements of an individual project. The second category includes what may be described as "rule of thumb" methods for use with average conditions.

The first category of recommendations is seldom used in irrigation design, except for large or unusual projects.

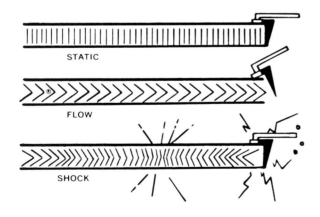

Figure 4-1 Shock Caused by Quick Valve Closure [1]

PIPE SYSTEM DESIGN. Proper design of the pipe system is the best method of controlling water hammer to avoid damage to piping.

---

(1) Reproduced with special permission from Plumbing and Drainage Institute Standard PDI-WH201. [a]

Data and procedures required for methods in this category are not discussed in this manual. Published pipe manuals for piping design and construction are normally available from pipe manufacturers.

There are two basic factors that must be considered with any method in category two:
1. Pressure rating of pipe
2. Maximum flow velocity

Although each factor may be considered separately, pipe protection is limited to the combination of variables as selected by the designer in each case.

Pressure ratings of pipe and maximum flow velocity used for design may vary for several different reasons, including one or more of the following examples:
1. Range of static or operating pressure available
2. Piping material and pressure ratings available
3. Designer experience
4. Local plumbing code requirements
5. Regional practice
6. Water temperature
7. Cost comparison

Pipe failure will seldom occur as the result of static pressure alone. Pressure rating of pipe must include some allowance for surge pressure which will be in addition to the normal operating pressure. Although the combined pressure will only exist for a short span of time, the pipe must be able to withstand the combined total of operating pressure and surge pressure, plus safety factor.

As previously mentioned, flow velocity is one of the prime causes of pressure surging. This is especially important in the selection of pipe as surge pressure levels are directly related to velocity levels (an increase in flow velocity will result in an increase of surge pressure).

Maximum flow velocity used in irrigation mains is normally in the 5 to 7 ft/s (feet per second) range. However, 7 ft/s is normally only used on smaller residential and commercial projects. The most common recommendation is to use a maximum velocity of 5 ft/s for all types of projects.

Although 5 ft/s velocity is considered safe for pipe protection, it does not eliminate the possibility of noise due to water hammer. Building plumbing, as illustrated in Figure 4-4, may be a problem to some degree,

regardless of flow velocity in the system. Conditions shown in this illustration are explained later.

Most of the methods used to determine the pipe pressure rating requirement will include the maximum flow velocity as an important part of the recommendation. In most cases, the only basic difference in general use methods is the static pressure "multiplier." Example: Static pressure (80 lb/in^2) times the multiplier (2.0) equals the minimum pipe pressure rating (160).

Safety factors included for pipe protection will vary with the individual designer and the operating conditions of a particular project. However, a static pressure multiplier of 1.5 should be considered a minimum for an irrigation system with a maximum flow velocity of 5 ft/s. Although this recommendation includes an allowance for surge pressure, the designer must understand that it is based on a minimum amount of surge. Flow velocities of less than 5 ft/s are desirable.

In the U.S.A., SDR-21 (200 psi) PVC pipe is the most common type of pipe for the "average" system. This is due to availability, pressure rating and strength requirements for buried piping. Considering that normal city water pressure is in the 50 to 75 lb/in^2 range, static pressure multipliers would range from 2.7 to 4. In general, system operating pressure (static plus surge pressure) should not exceed 150% of the PVC pipe pressure rating. Thermoplastic pipe standards are discussed in Chapter 2.

The use of additional safety factors is not limited to projects where the most common type of pipe used will automatically provide some degree of added protection. Special attention is recommended for systems with pumps, long mainlines and/or large pipe sizes. Additional safety factors should also be considered in selection of piping materials for systems where extreme cyclic surge conditions may develop. For example, systems with multiple flow outlets operating at the same time can develop high pressure surges within the piping network as controllers cycle through various flow combinations.

Systems with automatic controllers that offer totally independent programming of individual stations will also require special attention if used to control multiple valves operating at the same time. Different combinations of zones operating at one time, as selected by the user, could result in a wide variation of flow velocities within the piping system. Flow limitations may need to

Water Hammer

be established for the user, in at least some portion of the mainline piping system.

Thrust Blocks. Large sizes of PVC pipe are normally connected with a slip-fit type of fitting that includes a rubber sealing ring. This method of connection is also common for asbestos-cement pipe. Earth and thrust blocks are required to hold joints in place. Water flowing in a pipe will exert a thrust force when required to change direction. Blocks are necessary at points where pipe changes direction, at reducers, at valves and at the ends of lines.

Thrust blocks are constructed by pouring concrete between the fitting and the undisturbed bearing wall of the trench, as illustrated in Figure 4-3. The size required depends on the fitting, thrust developed and type of soil. The location of the block is important, and anchorage is often necessary. Pipe installation manuals are available from pipe manufacturers that include guidelines on sizing and construction of thrust blocks.

The piping system is only as strong as the weakest component. With PVC systems (especially those with large pipe sizes), PVC fittings are often the weakest points. Schedule 40 fittings, as discussed in Chapter 2, are the most common type. These fittings are not pressure rated. If pressure rated fittings are not available, the designer should consider the use of alternative materials, such as epoxy-coated steel or ductile iron fittings for larger sizes.

Although steel is much stronger than PVC, there are many reports of product failures with epoxy-coated fittings. Chipping and cracking of the epoxy-coating will result in rusting of the steel fitting. Reports of "blow-outs", within two to five years after installation, suggest that designers must also be very careful when specifying epoxy-coated steel fittings.

Other Types of Pipe. In general, metal pipes can withstand higher surges. However, water hammer can damage other components of the system including plastic pipe if connected to the system. It is advisable to maintain flow velocities consistent with those outlined for plastic pipe. Systems with asbestos-cement pipe are normally limited to a maximum of 5 ft/s.

City Water Supply Piping. Maximum velocity used in service lines tends to increase as the size decreases. This change in design practice is primarily due to the

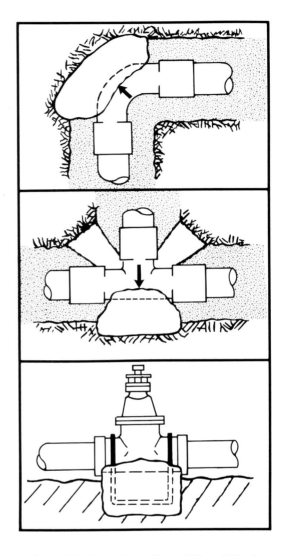

Figure 4-3 Typical Locations of Thrust Blocks

limit that is placed on flow when the recommended maximum velocity is applied to the smaller supply lines.

A greater flow allowance will reduce the quantity of zones required, but it will increase the risk of equipment damage and water hammer noise in the building. Unfortunately, the degree of surge, noise and other problems that may occur are somewhat unpredictable. Small supply lines create a situation involving a choice between two unsatisfactory alternatives.

There is a wide variation in the velocity limit used by different designers for small meter service and building supply lines. The limit may be based on experience or the lack of experience. Some will use 7 ft/s and others 9 ft/s. Most will vary the maximum flow used on different designs with consideration for the other variable factors that influence shock intensity. For economy, some will also use velocities as high as 10 ft/s in small service lines that are short in length. This is not to suggest that these velocities can be used with satisfactory results in every case, as the degree of hazard increases with higher flows. Fewer zones can be more costly if problems develop as the result of higher flows.

Recommended maximum velocities covered in plastic pipe systems are based upon a degree of success under conditions generally encountered in landscape irrigation. There is no guarantee that piping problems will not develop in some of the systems that are designed at or below these maximums. Velocity limits and other safety factors are the responsibility of the designer.

WATER HAMMER ARRESTERS

Use of arresters in lieu of proper pipe system design to control damaging water hammer is not recommended. For systems of any size, their cost is not justified.

However, *engineered water hammer arresters* are often the only answer for water hammer problems that will occasionally occur, regardless of design practice.

Figure 4-4 illustrates an actual system where water hammer noise was a problem even though flow velocities in the plastic pipe were below 5 ft/s and the valves had surge control devices. The design is typical of systems using small existing water supplies. Due to economics, high flow velocities were used in the metal water supply piping. When the zone valve for the largest zone (15 gpm) closed, a water hammer noise problem was created inside the building. In the case of the actual system illustrated in Figure 4-4, a relatively inexpensive, engineered water hammer arrester, PDI (Plumb-

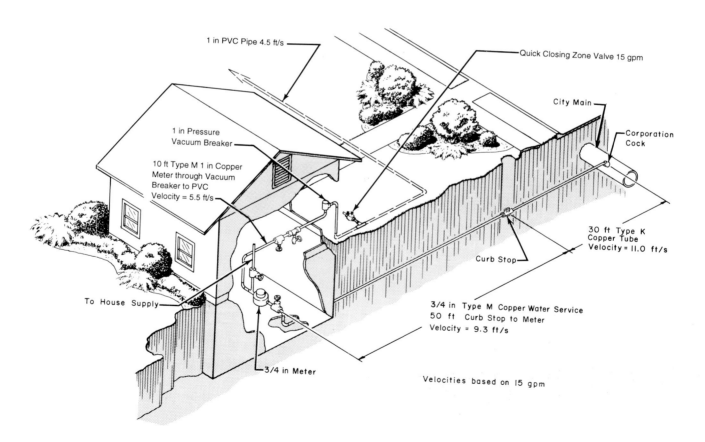

Figure 4-4 Typical System Supplied by Existing Water Service

Water Hammer

ing and Drainage Institute) certified, reduced water hammer noise to an acceptable level. Sizing and installation was made as outlined in the following text.

OPERATION OF WATER HAMMER ARRESTERS.

A water hammer arrester must be placed on the supply side of the valve causing the hammer and as close to the valve as possible. The simplest form of arrester is a vertical, capped pipe. It is sized, diameter and length, so that air is trapped when the piping system is filled with water. If the air chamber has a sufficient volume of air, the shock pressure created by the valve closure will be absorbed by compressing the air. However, such an arrester has a limited life. The air in it is rapidly absorbed by the water until it no longer performs satisfactorily.

Engineered water hammer arresters have a diaphragm to separate the air chamber from water. The model shown in Figure 4-5, and used in the example system illustrated previously, has a molded polypropylene liner below the diaphragm to protect the steel water chamber from rusting. This arrester is pre-pressurized by the manufacturer. An air valve is provided so that air pressure can be changed to provide the most effective pressure for the condition it is to control.

Note: The following text for sizing of the arrester for the example system is included for reference and to illustrate:
1. That arresters must be properly sized to effectively control water hammer.
2. The amount of data and calculations necessary for sizing.
3. And, to emphasize the importance of velocity in piping design. In this case, and many other similar projects, "an ounce of prevention is worth a pound of cure." Using a minimum number of zone valves is not always cost-effective. Although the noise problem from loose pipes in the building was not predictable, the degree of probability was increased by designing the system for maximum economy.

SIZING WATER HAMMER ARRESTERS. To reduce
water hammer to an acceptable level, the arrester must be capable of sufficiently absorbing the Kinetic Energy (KE) which exists in a column of water moving through a pipe.

The formula for determining kinetic energy is:
$$KE = 0.01553WLV^2$$

Courtesy of Amtrol, Inc.

Figure 4-5 Engineered Water Hammer Arrester Absorbing Shock

Where:
KE = Kinetic energy in foot-pounds (ft-lb)
W = Weight of water per foot of pipe length
L = Length of pipe, ft
V = Velocity ft/s

Using the above formula, the kinetic energy in the piping of Figure 4-4 from the city main to the zone valve was determined with the following data based on the characteristics of the zone with the largest flow requirements:

	[1] Weight H_2O lb/ft (W)	[2] Velocity at 15 gpm ft/s (V)	[3] Length Pipe ft (L)
¾ in Type K:	0.189	11.04	30
¾ in Type M:	0.224	9.32	50
1 in Type M:	0.379	5.51	10

(Note: 1 ft of PVC omitted)

[1] From Weights of Water in Pipes, Table 32.
[2] Velocity calculated with multiplying factors of Table 16.
[3] Length of pipe from Figure 4-4.

THEREFORE:

	W	V2	L	Kinetic Energy ft-lb
3/4 in Type K:	0.01553 x	0.189 x	11.04^2 x 30	=10.73
3/4 in Type M:	0.01533 x	0.224 x	9.32^2 x 50	=15.11
1 in Type M:	0.01553 x	0.379 x	5.51^2 x 10	= 1.79

Total Kinetic Energy developed = 27.63 ft-lb

The kinetic energy developed by the flow of water in pipes of the largest zone determines the arrester size, or capacity, in cubic feet for the entire system.

The engineering division of the water department of the city where the example system is located provided necessary pressure information:

1. In the neighborhood where the system is located *high static* pressure during periods of low water usage is 80 lb/in^2.
2. Low summer pressure drops to about 65 lb/in^2.

Based on this information, the system was designed to operate on a pressure of 60 lb/in^2 to allow for possible future pressure reduction.

The required air volume of water hammer arresters to contain the kinetic energy developed in a piping system is determined on the basis of *flow pressure at the valve* and the *maximum shock pressure to be allowed.*

Maximum shock pressure equals flow pressure plus pressure rise caused by valve closure. PDI recommends a maximum shock pressure of 150 lb/in^2 in any piping system.

Flow pressure at the valve must be the maximum that could occur. In the example, maximum possible flow pressure was determined to be 50 lb/in^2:

80 lb/in^2 (high static pressure)
-30 lb/in^2 (pressure loss to valve*)
50 lb/in^2 = maximum flow pressure at valve

*Pressure loss to valve from city water main was extracted from pressure loss calculations for the system piping design.

Based on PDI recommendation of 150 lb/in^2 maximum shock pressure, the pressure rise would be 100 lb/in^2. Volume required is determined by the following formula and the table of "Pressure Factors."

(Kinetic energy, ft-lb) $\dfrac{KE}{PF}$ = equivalent cubic feet air volume required
(Pressure factor)

The equivalent air volume required for the example system was determined to be 0.0090 ft^3.

$$\frac{27.63 ft\text{-}lb}{3048(PF)} = 0.0091\,ft^3$$

Note: "Pressure factor" was determined in the following manner: (See Pressure Factors Table)
1. Enter table on "150" line of left-hand column.
2. Find pressure factor under 50 lb/in^2 heading.

Pressure factor in example above: 3048.

Max. Shock Press. lb/in^2	Line Pressure lb/in^2 - Water Flowing									
	20	30	40	50	60	70	80	90	100	110
50	796	391	105							
60	1156	720	346	92						
70	1509	1074	654	310	81					
80	1851	1434	996	598	280	73				
90	2178	1790	1352	925	550	256	66			
100	2489	2137	1712	1273	862	508	235	61		
110	2785	2474	2069	1630	1199	805	472	218	56	
120	3068	2800	2420	1990	1550	1131	755	441	202	52
130	3337	3113	2763	2348	1909	1475	1069	711	413	189
140	3593	3414	3097	2701	2268	1828	1404	1013	671	389
150	3838	3705	3422	3048	2627	2187	1751	1338	962	635
160	4072	3984	3736	3388	2982	2547	2106	1678	1277	915
170	4297	4253	4041	3720	3331	2905	2465	2028	1609	1221
180	4512	4513	4337	4044	3675	3261	2825	2384	1953	1545
190	4719	4763	4623	4359	4012	3613	3184	2743	2305	1882
200	4917	5004	4901	4666	4342	3959	3540	3103	2662	2229

Courtesy of Amtrol, Inc.

Pressure Factors For Arresters
Factors = Kinetic Energy Held in One Cubic Foot Volume

To allow for variables impossible to calculate, a water hammer arrester with a volume at least 10% greater than the calculated requirement is recommended.

Summary. Although PDI standards recommend controlling shock pressure to a maximum of 150 lb/in^2, this is often too high for irrigation systems. The example, which is an actual installation, had excessive water hammer noise due to loose pipes in the building walls. Tests indicated that 150 lb/in^2 shock pressure would still cause pipes to rattle.

Therefore, a brand of water hammer arrester was selected which, in the smallest size, PDI size A, had an oversize volume of 0.092 ft^3 for safety.

The kinetic energy that can be handled with a given volume can be easily determined:
Volume, ft^3 x pressure factor = kinetic energy, ft-lb

Water Hammer

For the example system and this size arrester:
0.092 ft^3 x 3048 = 280.42 ft-lb.

Since the capacity in ft-lbs substantially exceeded the kinetic energy developed by the system (27.63 ft-lb), noise caused by water hammer was virtually eliminated.

To analyze the results of the arrester installation another way, assume that ideal conditions were wanted: maximum shock pressure not to exceed high static pressure of 80 lb/in^2. Then:

$$\frac{\text{(Kinetic energy, ft-lb)}}{\text{(Pressure factor)}} \quad \frac{27.63}{598} = 0.046 \text{ ft}^3 \text{ (air volume required)}$$

Note that the volume of the arrester used with the example system is almost twice that required for the result wanted.

Since arresters must be installed close to the offending valve, an arrester is required at each valve causing water hammer. When zone valves are scattered, special installation techniques are required.

The only way to avoid having to stand arresters in the lawn area is to install each unit in a box below ground level. This requires laying the main deeper to provide sufficient depth for the arrester. Also, the material from which the arrester is made must be of a type for installation in such an environment. Furthermore, the required additional length of piping to the remotely located arrester will increase kinetic energy which must be absorbed, possibly affecting arrester size.

Installation. As stated previously, in order for an arrester to effectively control water hammer, it must be installed on the supply side of, and adjacent to, the offending valve; preferably within six inches.

Most arresters must be installed upright to provide maximum effectiveness. The arrester should be pre-pressurized equal to the flow pressure for which the unit was selected.

UNCONTROLLED FLOW IN EMPTY PIPES

Flow through the mainline piping is controlled by the total discharge of all water outlets operating at one time. Flow in the supply piping to an individual zone valve, and the resultant velocity, is controlled by the total flow of all outlets supplied by the valve. Each water outlet orifice will only provide a given rate of discharge at a given pressure.

However, when a valve opens to admit water into an empty mainline or lateral pipe, the flow is uncontrolled and will reach velocities far in excess of that for which the system was designed. This uncontrolled velocity can cause damage when filling mainlines or when the zone valve is opened. Longer lines develop a greater shock than shorter lines.

Mainline velocity should not exceed 2 ft/s (preferable 1 ft/s) during initial filling of empty lines. Velocity can be controlled by opening the system shut-off valve slightly to maintain a slow flow until all pipes are filled.

Uncontrolled flow into zone piping is often referred to as "dry-line" shock. It can be a continuing problem with lateral piping if lines are drained each time the zone valve is closed.

Air will escape into the atmosphere at a much faster rate than water. Water will flow through the piping at an accelerated rate, as compressed air will provide a minimum amount of back-pressure when allowed to escape through the orifices of the water outlets. When water reaches the outlets, the velocity is suddenly reduced and a surge is developed in the zone piping. A series of pressure surges will often occur as water replaces air in different parts of the zone piping. Equipment damage can occur before the surge is relieved through the water outlets.

Zone piping will be emptied of water after each operation under two conditions:
(1) When zone piping is installed with automatic drains to prevent freezing.
(2) When at least one water outlet is lower than the rest of the system. The low outlet will drain the piping. CAUTION: This can happen even when the property is comparatively level. A difference in grade of only a few inches may be sufficient to partially drain the piping.

Normally, the zone piping of spray systems, and smaller rotary systems, isn't damaged by the water hammer produced by uncontrolled flow in empty pipes if sized for the same velocities as the pressure main piping.

However, systems with large flows and/or long runs of zone piping may require special equipment in addition to control of normal operating velocities. Two methods are used for the protection of zone piping.

CHECK VALVES
The most common method used to prevent drainage of sprinkler piping is a check valve. Many models of spray and rotary sprinklers are available with an optional check valve. Some models include a check valve as a standard feature (See Figure 4-6). A separate, spring-loaded, in-line check valve is used in some cases. Separate equipment should be selected carefully, as some models have a very high pressure loss.

Check valves are also useful to eliminate undesirable "puddling" around heads at low points and to conserve water.

FLOW CONTROL
Flow control devices, similar to the type used for controlling flow in individual sprinklers, can be used to control flow in empty zone piping. (See Figure 4-7).
1. Install a *flow control* adjacent to and on the discharge side of the remote control valve. Size to permit a flow of approximately 10% more than design flow.
2. Size piping for a flow of not more than 5 ft/s velocity. (An even lower velocity is preferable.)
3. Zones should be designed so that all heads on a single remote control valve are at approximately the same level. Otherwise, a significant difference in elevation will cause additional pressure differentials at the heads.

Using *flow controls* as outlined above provides these results:
1. Flow in empty zone piping *cannot* exceed the rated flow capacity of the flow control regardless of the water supply to the remote control valve. Thus, the flow velocity in the empty pipes will be

Figure 4-6 Rotary with Built-in Check Valve

approximately the same as when the sprinklers in the zone are operating.
2. Because the entire zone flow is controlled, the flow discharge of the sprinklers and the resultant precipitation will be approximately as designed.

Flow controls have a relatively high initial pressure loss. Before designing a system using flow controls, obtain loss data from the manufacturer whose product will be used. Systems must be designed so that available pressure will be enough to offset loss through the controls.

Note: In some climate regions, air compressors are used to winterize the system when piping is installed above the frost line. Surge pressure problems, similar to those previously discussed, can occur when com-

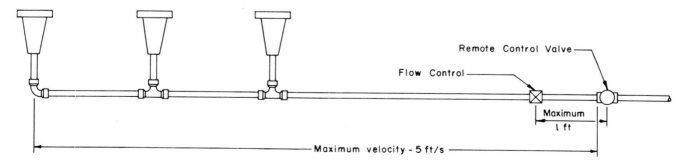

Figure 4-7 Installation of Flow Control to Protect Zone Piping *and* Control Flow Through Heads

Water Hammer

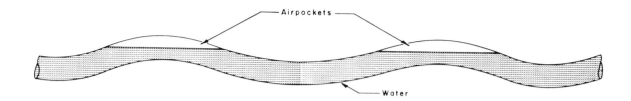

Figure 4-8 Air Pockets in Undulating Pipe Line

pressed air is used to "blow-out" the piping system. Established procedures for the removal of water using this method should be followed carefully.

PUMPS

Irrigation systems with private pumps are most susceptible to water hammer damage when filling empty pipe lines. Because of an inherent characteristic, centrifugal pumps always attempt to deliver water at their rated pressure. When filling an empty pipe, the pump cannot reach its pressure rating and will therefore deliver more water than rated for at extremely high velocities.

Therefore, when the discharge pipe line is empty, pump start should not be attempted until the master shut-off valve on the discharge side of the pump is closed.

After the pump has been primed and is pumping against pressure, use the following procedure:
1. Open valve slightly, just enough to allow a slow flow. Flow velocity should not exceed 2 ft/s (preferable 1 ft/s).
2. Wait until pipes have filled (listen for sound of flow through the valve to stop).
3. Open valve fully only after pipe line has filled.

AIR ENTRAPMENT

Another possible source of water hammer is air pockets in the high points of undulating pipe lines.

These air pockets often develop when the pipe is initially filled, particularly in long lines.

Even if no air is present initially, air may separate from the water over a period of time, causing air pockets to develop. Air separating from water will also cause existing air pockets to increase in size.

Air pockets act as a restriction and cause additional pressure loss just as if a smaller pipe existed. The pressure loss increases as the size of the air pocket increases. Such a condition can cause inadequate system coverage.

WATER HAMMER CAUSED BY AIR POCKETS

If air pockets are exhausted by opening a large valve quickly, water hammer can occur. As previously discussed, water cannot escape at a velocity comparable to the air escaping through the valve. The water flow will essentially come to a sudden stop after filling the area of the former air pocket and pressure surges develop.

Plugged tapping
for optional
test cock

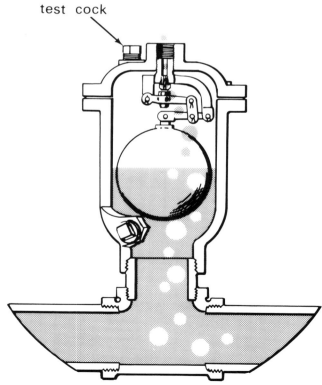

Courtesy of Valve & Primer Corp.

Figure 4-9 Cut-A-Way View of Typical Air Vent Valve

Courtesy of Mueller Steam Specialty

Figure 4-10 Compact Wafer Style Silent Check Valve

AUTOMATIC AIR VENT VALVES. Air pockets in pipe lines can be eliminated with installation of automatic vents at high points of the line. Valves should be installed in a box with removable cover.

Automatic air relief (release) valves with small air outlet orifices are available from several different manufacturers. Location, size and type of air relief valves are important considerations for successful removal of air in the piping system.

In addition, automatic venting precludes any possibility of air pockets causing restrictions that increase pressure loss in the pipe line.

REVERSE FLOW

When a pump shuts down while water is flowing in the discharge pipe line, the water column in the pipe will continue its forward movement until stopped by gravity. If the pipe runs uphill, gravity will then cause the water

column to reverse its direction of flow until stopped by the pump check valve. The weight of the water column impact from reverse flow is another cause of water hammer.

Contrary to popular concept, a small degree of uphill incline and low pressure loss in a pipe line will cause more water hammer from reverse flow than will a pipe line with a steeper uphill incline and higher pressure loss. The reason is that the water column will travel farther after the pump shuts down before gravity can stop the flow. In addition, lower friction losses allow the water column to flow faster in reverse.

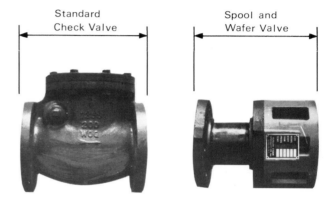

Standard Check Valve   Spool and Wafer Valve

Courtesy of Mueller Steam Specialty

Figure 4-12 Conventional Check Valve and Wafer Type Silent Check Valve with Filler of Same Length

The common swing check valve is designed to be closed by reversal of flow. Water hammer occurs when the column of water, already flowing in reverse, is abruptly stopped by the valve.

SILENT CHECK VALVES

Use of a *silent check valve*, instead of a conventional check valve, will virtually eliminate water hammer from flow reversal. A *silent check valve* opens at a forward flow pressure of about $1/4$ to $1/2$ lb/in^2. Therefore, when a pump is shut down, a silent check valve will completely close while the forward flow still has a pressure of approximately $1/2$ lb/in^2 on the discharge side of the valve. Since a *silent check valve* closes at the same time the forward flow stops, the water column is trapped and *cannot* flow in reverse. Without reverse flow, water hammer cannot occur.

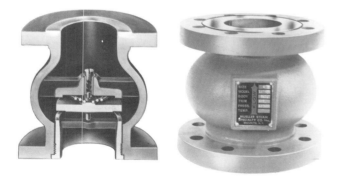

Courtesy of Mueller Steam Specialty

Figure 4-11 Globe Style Silent Check Valve

Water Hammer

Silent check valves normally cause a greater pressure loss than conventional swing check valves. However, the additional loss is relatively minor and will not cause a problem in irrigation system design.

Most *silent check valves* are available in a compact "wafer" style to conserve space and in a globe style.

CONVENTIONAL CHECK VALVE REPLACEMENT

At least one manufacturer can furnish "filler" or "spool pieces" to adapt their wafer type silent check valve as a replacement for any conventional swing check valve.

BIBLIOGRAPHY

(a) Standard PDI-WH201, Water Hammer Arresters: Plumbing and Drainage Institute
5342 Boulevard Place
Indianapolis, Indiana 46208.

(b) USA Standard A112.26.1, Water Hammer Arresters, published by: The American Society of Mechanical Engineers
United Engineering Center
345 East 47th St.
New York, New York 10017

Cla-Val Co.
Newport Beach, California 92663

The Dole Valve Company
Plumbing and Heating Division
6201 Oakton St.
Morton Grove, Illinois 60053

Griswold Controls
2803 Barranca Rd.
Irvine, California 92714

Hayes Manufacturing Company
Erie, Pennsylvania 16512

AUTOMATIC AIR VENTS:

Valve and Primer Corporation
1420 South Wright
Roselle, Illinois 60172

SILENT CHECK VALVES:

Mueller Steam Specialty
29 Meserole Avenue
Brooklyn, New York 11222

Valve and Primer Corporation
1420 South Wright
Roselle, Illinois 60172

PARTIAL LIST OF SPECIAL EQUIPMENT SOURCES

"DIATROL" WATER HAMMER ARRESTERS:

Amtrol,Inc.
1400 Division Road
West Warwick, Rhode Island 02893

FLOW CONTROLS:

Clack Corporation
Duraform Lane
Windsor, Wisconsin 53598

CHAPTER 5

Cross Connection Control

Irrigation systems supplied by domestic or private potable water systems are considered to be a potential pollution hazard to the water supply. These systems must include protection to prevent possible backflow of irrigation water into the potable water supply.

In the U.S.A., federal law requires water suppliers to protect potable water from pollution or contamination by *cross connections*. Although similar methods and products are used for the protection of water throughout the U.S.A., there are variations in requirements for landscape irrigation systems due to differences in local codes or state laws.

The water supplier, plumbing authority and the health department develop the standards for a cross connection control program. Standards, as established for different conditions, include consideration for the degree of hazard (low or high).

Local plumbing code will normally require a permit for connection of a system to a potable water supply and an inspection of the backflow prevention assembly when the irrigation system is installed. In many cases, local authority will also require an inspection at specified intervals to ensure that the assembly is operating properly.

Note: In many rural areas, specific requirements for landscape irrigation systems may not be covered in local plumbing codes and/or enforcement may be limited. However, limitation in local authority does not alter the basic requirement for protection of the potable water supply.

This text is limited to the basics of cross connection control as normally required in landscape irrigation systems. It is not intended as a text that will provide all of the knowledge necessary for the broad range of requirements for backflow prevention. Example installations are provided for reference only. Method, products and installation used for a particular project must be in compliance with the requirements of local authority.

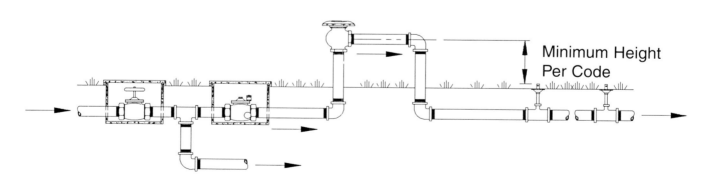

Minimum Height Per Code

Figure 5-1 Vacuum Breaker must be Installed Above Grade and Water Outlets *Courtesy of Febco*

Cross Connection Control

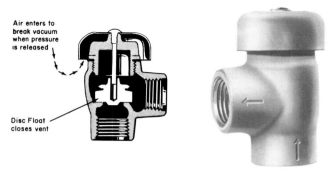

Air enters to break vacuum when pressure is released

Disc Float closes vent

Courtesy of Watts

Figure 5-2 Atmospheric Vacuum Breaker

The following definitions are provided to cover terms as used in this text:

Backflow: The undesirable reversal of water flow or mixtures of water and undesirable substances from any source (such as irrigation water) into the distribution pipes of the potable water system. Water flow, in the opposite direction of what is considered "normal", may occur as the result of back-pressure or back-siphonage.

Back-pressure: Any condition that could create pressure in the user (irrigation) system greater than in the

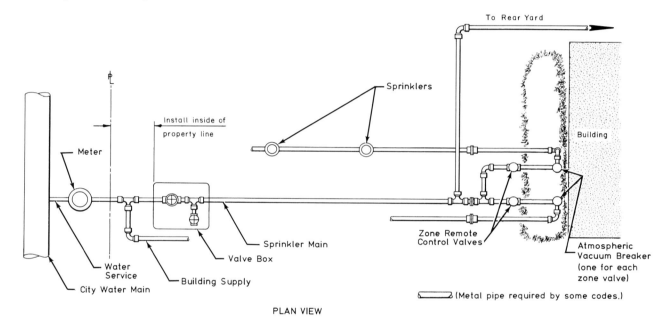

PLAN VIEW

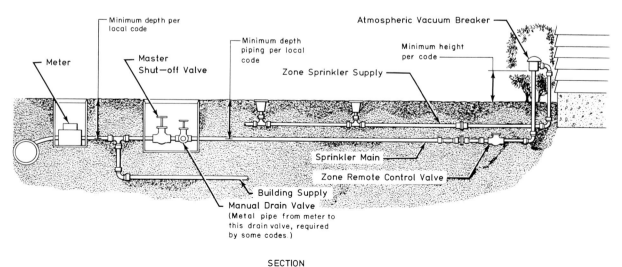

SECTION

Figure 5-3 Typical Installation of Atmospheric Vacuum Breakers with System Using Remote Control Valves

Figure 5-4 Pressure-Type Vacuum Breaker

potable water supply system. Pressure caused by gravity due to elevation difference is one common cause. Pumps can be another cause.

Back-siphonage: Any condition that could create a negative or reduced pressure in the potable supply piping allowing backflow of undesirable substances into the potable water supply.

Continuous Pressure: Pressure that is maintained continuously in a piping system for the immediate delivery of water on demand. In practice, this includes all pipe and related components that are under continuous pressure for a specified period of time (example: 12 hours).

Cross Connection: Any point on a water system where a polluting substance may come in contact with potable water. The permanent or temporary connection of an irrigation system to a potable water supply is an example of a cross connection.

Non-toxic Cross Connection: A cross connection where a polluting substance may come in contact with potable water esthetically affecting the taste, odor or appearance of the water, but non-hazardous to health.

Toxic Cross Connection: A cross connection where a polluting substance may come in contact with potable

water creating a health hazard, causing sickness and death.

Potable Water: Water that is safe for drinking, personal or culinary use.

Within the context of this chapter, water is considered potable in the following two sources.

1. *Distribution systems* supplying water for potable use. Water is considered potable in all piping, including the consumer's piping, until reaching any type fixture, device, or construction from which the potable water is discharged.
2. *Private Wells.* Wells must be protected from backflow of non-potable water regardless of whether the well has been approved as a potable source.

ELEMENTS OF CROSS CONNECTION CONTROL

BACKFLOW DUE TO BACK PRESSURE
Pumping hazards are a potential cause of backflow when there is a cross connection between a potable water system and a non-potable water system supplied by a pump. Such a condition exists when an irrigation system has a dual water source: (1) domestic potable water and (2) an auxiliary or alternate source pumped from a well, pond, lake, river, etc. If the pressure in a domestic water supply should drop below the pressure of the pumped auxiliary supply, the auxiliary supply water would be pumped into the domestic water system.

Note: Health authorities consider a well water supply a cross connection when connected to any system supplied by a city water source, even though the well water has been approved as potable.

BACKFLOW DUE TO SIPHONAGE
Back-siphonage from a consumer's water service can occur when a negative pressure develops in the city water main. Negative or sub-atmospheric pressures in a city distribution system can be caused by main breaks, planned or emergency shutdowns, fire demands, etc. Conversely, if pressure is maintained at the water service connection, back-siphonage *will not* affect the community water supply.

AWWA (American Water Works Association) states: *"With city distribution systems in hilly terrain, high water*

Cross Connection Control

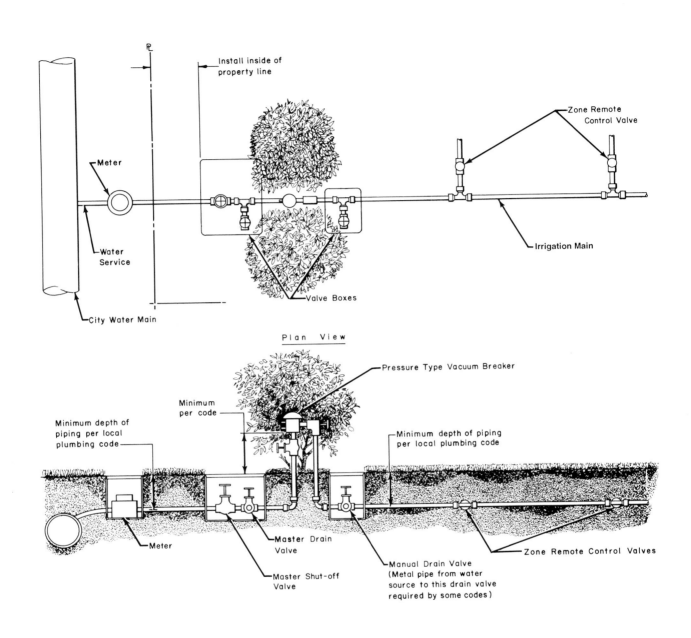

Figure 5-5 Typical Installation of Pressure-type Vacuum Breaker

consumption or main breaks may result in negative pressures developing at high points."

The following text covers various devices, methods and piping arrangements. This section includes general information only and may not conform to the actual requirements of any particular plumbing code.

BACKFLOW PREVENTION

Five different types of backflow preventers and/or methods are commonly used in landscape irrigation systems:

1. Atmospheric Vacuum Breaker
2. Pressure Vacuum Breaker
3. Double Check Assembly (D.C.A.)
4. Reduced Pressure Assembly (R.P.)
5. Air Gap

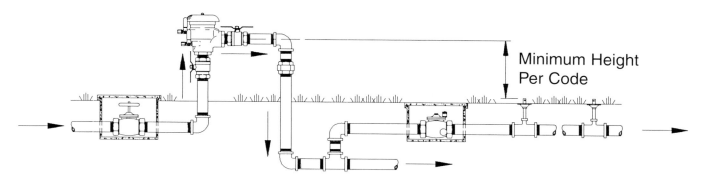

Courtesy of Febco

Figure 5-6 Pressure Vacuum Breaker must be Installed Above Grade and Water Outlets

Each type of device has a specific application and entails different methods of installation. However, there is a considerable lack of uniformity in plumbing codes for landscape irrigation systems. Some local codes will only allow the use of one method and others will allow the use of two or more, depending on the application.

VACUUM BREAKERS

Vacuum breakers are used to prevent back-siphonage only; back pressure against vacuum breakers is prohibited. To avoid back pressure created by gravity due to elevation differences, vacuum breakers must be installed higher than the water outlets. See Figure 5-1.

Plumbing codes will normally specify the minimum dimension allowed for installation. (Example: 12 inches minimum above grade and 6 inches minimum above the highest water outlet).

ATMOSPHERIC VACUUM BREAKERS. (Sometimes referred to as siphon breakers). Continuous pressure on the supply side of this type vacuum breaker is prohibited. Therefore, a separate atmospheric vacuum

breaker must be installed on the discharge side of *each* zone control valve and *before* any water outlets.

When the inlet piping to the atmospheric vacuum breaker is pressurized, the disc float (or poppet) is forced up to seal the air vent for normal operation. Should a back-siphonage condition develop, the disc float will drop and allow air to enter the assembly. The disc float also shields the water inlet to prevent any foreign materials from entering the inlet piping.

Installation. Figure 5-3 illustrates good practice in the installation of atmospheric vacuum breakers. For aesthetic purposes, the vacuum breakers are hidden with shrubbery. The remote control valves are installed in the lawn. Therefore, in the event of service requirements, digging in the planting bed will not be necessary.

Freeze Protection. In areas subject to freezing temperatures, vacuum breakers and the vertical pipes to and from the breaker must be drained to prevent damage. This includes areas where freezing temperatures

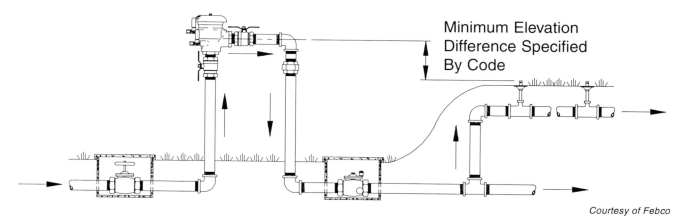

Courtesy of Febco

Figure 5-7 Typical Installation of Pressure Vacuum Breaker with Minor Elevation Differences at the Site

Cross Connection Control

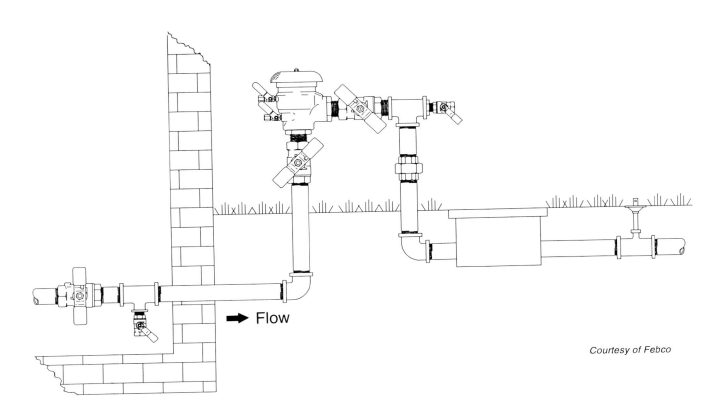

Figure 5-8 Typical Installation of Pressure Vacuum Breaker with Water Supply in the Basement

Courtesy of Febco

do not last long enough to freeze the ground but long enough to freeze pipes and fixtures above ground.

Some plumbing codes will require a drain valve to be installed in the irrigation main, as shown in Figure 5-3. However, there are also codes in some regions that do not allow drain valves at certain locations. Although the installer is responsible for the installation, the designer should be familiar with all piping details as may be required by the local authority.

In regions where systems are operated during the winter months, drainage will be a continuing problem if occasional low temperatures will freeze any piping exposed above grade. Use of automatic drains in this application is not always completely successful, and may not be allowed in some parts of the piping.

Special Conditions. Use of manual operating valves instead of remote control valves does not change the method of installation. In this case, the operating valves are installed in a location where the operator will not be wet by the system, usually next to a porch. The vacuum breakers are installed in the same relative position as shown for the remote control valves.

Pressure loss in a pipe-line size atmospheric vacuum breaker may be a problem on occasion. If so, use a breaker larger than line-size. Or, use line-size breakers manifolded. See "Pressure-type Vacuum Breakers -- Manifolding Vacuum Breakers."

PRESSURE-TYPE VACUUM BREAKERS. With irrigation systems installed in large areas where "hiding" a number of atmospheric vacuum breakers is not economically feasible, a single, pressure-type vacuum breaker can be used. With this vacuum breaker, the irrigation main can remain pressurized at all times; i.e., supply water pressure may exist at all times on both the inlet and outlet sides of a pressure-type vacuum breaker. However, back-pressure is prohibited. In this context, back-pressure means any pressure against the outlet side of the vacuum breaker exceeding the supply pressure against the inlet side regardless of the source of such pressure: elevation differences or pump.

Pressure vacuum breaker assemblies, as shown in Figure 5-4, include shut off valves on the inlet and discharge side of the vacuum breaker and small test cocks. Valves and test cocks are primarily for field testing. The vacuum breaker consists of a spring-loaded check valve and an inlet port that opens should

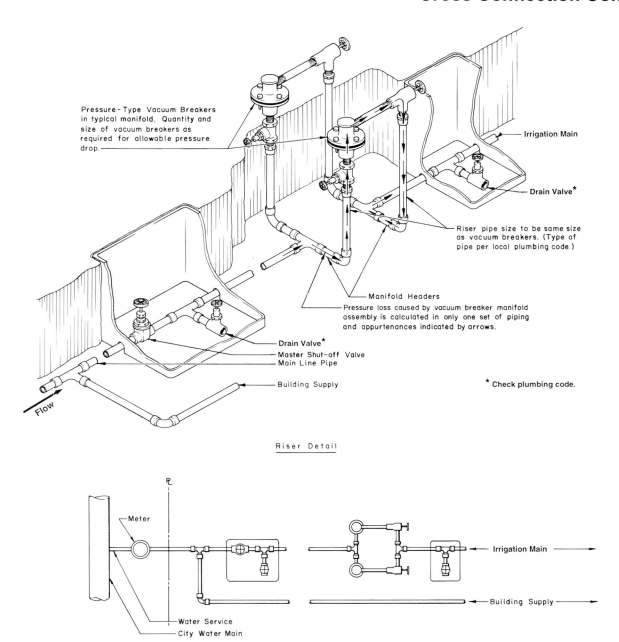

Pressure-Type Vacuum Breakers in typical manifold. Quantity and size of vacuum breakers as required for allowable pressure drop.

Irrigation Main

Drain Valve*

Riser pipe size to be same size as vacuum breakers. (Type of pipe per local plumbing code.)

Manifold Headers

Pressure loss caused by vacuum breaker manifold assembly is calculated in only one set of piping and appurtenances indicated by arrows.

Drain Valve*
Master Shut-off Valve
Main Line Pipe

Building Supply

Flow

* Check plumbing code.

Riser Detail

Meter

Irrigation Main

Building Supply

Water Service
City Water Main

Plan View

Figure 5-9 Manifolding Vacuum Breakers

a back-siphonage condition occur in the potable supply piping.

Figure 5-5 illustrates a typical installation of an irrigation system in a large property using a pressure vacuum breaker for backflow protection.

Since pressure-type vacuum breakers must be installed above the highest water outlet in the system

(See Figure 5-6), the designer should select a suitable location with consideration for the following items:

1. Elevation requirement
2. Personal injury hazard
3. Assembly damage due to maintenance equipment, vandalism, etc.
4. Visual appearance of assembly

Cross Connection Control

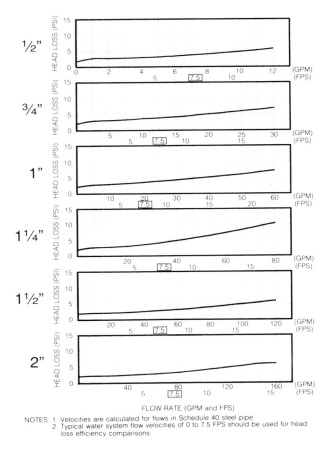

NOTES: 1. Velocities are calculated for flows in Schedule 40 steel pipe.
2. Typical water system flow velocities of 0 to 7.5 FPS should be used for head loss efficiency comparisons

Courtesy of Febco

Figure 5-10 Flow Loss Graph Example for Pressure-Type Vacuum Breakers

Terrain Considerations. Minor elevation differences that may exist at the site can be covered by extending pipe risers above grade as necessary for the plumbing code requirement (See Figure 5-7).

Locating the pressure vacuum breaker near the water source may not be realistic if property is graded upward several feet from the point of connection to the water supply. This type of condition may result in an unrealistic height for the riser piping to the vacuum breaker. Although additional pipe will be required, it is often necessary to route the system main to a higher elevation for the vacuum breaker installation and then back to the zone locations.

In some cases, it may be desirable to use an individual atmospheric vacuum breaker at each zone valve, or some other type of backflow preventer, if allowed by local code. Unusual site conditions may require the system designer to obtain assistance from a product supplier or manufacturer's representative to determine the best solution for backflow prevention. However, regardless of recommendations, the method selected must be approved for the application by the local plumbing authority.

When the water meter is in the basement of a building, the installation of a vacuum breaker is basically the same as shown in Figure 5-6. The only difference is that the supply pipe for the irrigation system comes from the basement, as shown in Figure 5-8. The irrigation main and zone control valves are located as required.

Freeze Protection. Pressure-type vacuum breakers and the vertical pipes to and from breakers must be protected from freezing. With normal installation as shown in Figure 5-5, draining is accomplished by opening specially installed drain valves on each side of the vacuum breaker, after closing the master shut off valve. Test cocks on the vacuum breaker may need to be opened to admit air into the assembly. However, as

Courtesy of Febco

Figure 5-11 Typical Double Check Assembly

previously discussed, some plumbing codes have specific requirements on the location of drain valves.

Manifolding Vacuum Breakers. The pressure loss through some types of pressure vacuum breakers can be substantial. To reduce the loss, vacuum breakers are often sized larger than the irrigation main pipe size. Pressure vacuum breakers are normally only available in sizes ½ through 2 inch. A manifold of two or more vacuum breakers can be used when requirement exceeds that of a single 2 inch breaker.

Figure 5-9 illustrates the method of manifolding vacuum breakers. All other installation details are the same as for a single vacuum breaker.

All vacuum breakers in a manifold should be the same size. To determine the total pressure loss caused by the manifolded vacuum breakers:

1. Divide the total required flow by the number of vacuum breakers in the manifold.
2. Use the flow through each vacuum breaker determined in (1) to determine the pressure loss through a single vacuum breaker.
3. The pressure loss through a single vacuum breaker represents *the total pressure loss through all vacuum breakers in the manifold.*

Example: Assume a required flow of 90 gpm. Using the graph in Figure 5-10, the pressure loss through a 2 inch pressure vacuum breaker is approximately 4 lb/in². Also, the flow rate exceeds the industry standard for 2 inch (normal maximum velocity is based on 7.5 ft/s in schedule 40 steel pipe). *Note:* In practice, use only the loss data provided by the manufacturer of the device which will be used.

1. With two 2 inch breakers, the flow through each will be 45 gpm.

2. Again, referring to Figure 5-10, the pressure loss through one breaker with a 45 gpm flow is approximately 2.5 lb/in².
3. Therefore, since the loss through a single vacuum breaker represents the total pressure loss in all the breakers in the manifold, the pressure loss caused by the breaker is 2.5 lb/in².
4. For the total loss through the manifold, add pressure loss in one breaker and one set of laterals, risers and fittings. See Figure 5-9.

Special Conditions. The use of pressure-type vacuum breakers in relatively small properties can sometimes be advantageous. A situation could be one in which, because of limited water supply, an abnormal number of water zones are required.

In such a case, the total cost of the lower-priced atmospheric vacuum breakers could exceed the cost of a single pressure-type vacuum breaker. Also, "hiding" atmospheric vacuum breakers in planting areas and centralizing instead of "scattering" control valves would increase installation costs substantially.

DOUBLE CHECK ASSEMBLY (D.C.A.)

The double check valve assembly is a good example of the variation encountered in local plumbing codes for backflow prevention in a landscape irrigation system. Some codes allow the use of a D.C.A. and many do not.

Compared to vacuum breakers, a D.C.A. offers advantages and disadvantages depending on site conditions.

Advantages:

1. Supply pressure and back-pressure can exist continuously. Terrain need not be considered.
2. The pressure main and zone control valves can be located in the most economical way.
3. Can be installed below grade level in a valve box "when allowed by local code." *Note:* Manufactur-

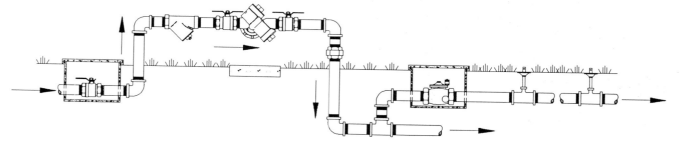

Courtesy of Febco

Figure 5-12 Typical Installation of Double Check Above Ground

ers recommend that the D.C.A. be installed above grade and enclosed in a protective enclosure.

Disadvantages:
1. Unsightly appearance of assembly or enclosure when installed above grade as recommended by the manufacturer or as may be required by local plumbing code.
2. Complete installation can be costly when only a few zones are required for the irrigation system.

A double check assembly consists of two spring loaded check valves, shut off valves on the inlet and discharge side of the check valves and small test cocks. Check valves allow water to flow in one direction only. Double

check assemblies are not approved for backflow prevention of any toxic substance (liquid, solid or gas). D.C.A.s are available from several different manufacturers in sizes ¾ through 2 inch. Some models are available in sizes 2-½ inch and larger.

Figure 5-12 illustrates a D.C.A. installed above grade as recommended by the manufacturer. A 12 inch minimum clearance is recommended under the assembly. Larger size assemblies should include support blocks. Most manufacturers recommend the use of a protective enclosure (not shown in Figure 5-12). Double check valve assemblies must be protected from freezing.

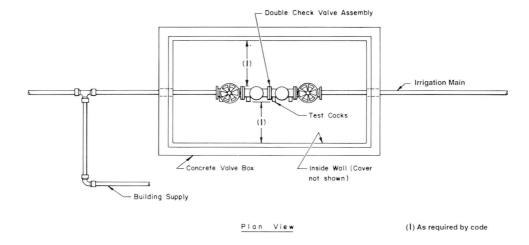

Plan View   (I) As required by code

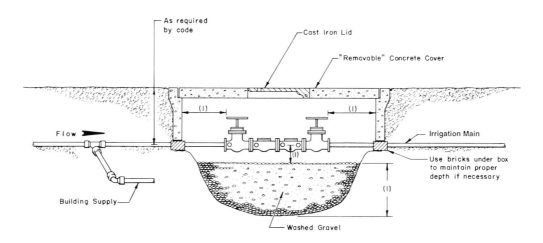

Figure 5-13 Typical Installation of Double Check Assembly Below Grade

In some climate regions of the U.S.A., local codes may allow the D.C.A. to be installed below grade, as shown in Figure 5-13. This method is used to protect the D.C.A. when occasional low temperatures during the winter months will freeze piping exposed above grade. In many areas, irrigation systems are used throughout the year and piping is not drained, except for unusually low temperatures.

Local plumbing codes that allow the double check assembly to be installed below grade will normally include detailed requirements for the installation. In almost all cases, the use of D.C.A. valves for system shut off is not allowed, and a separate valve is required. Location and use of drain valves will vary with different codes.

Multiple double check assemblies are occasionally installed in a manifold when allowed by local code. Installation is similar to the manifold requirements of vacuum breakers, as shown in Figure 5-9.

REDUCED PRESSURE ASSEMBLY (RP).

Some local plumbing codes require the use of a reduced pressure assembly for all landscape irrigation systems that are connected to a potable water supply. Many others require a RP device for certain applications.

The reduced pressure assembly can be used with continuous pressure and back-pressure. It is the only type of mechanical device that is generally accepted for hazardous backflow conditions. The reduced pressure assembly has three disadvantages:
1. Cost
2. Must be installed above grade
3. High pressure loss

A reduced pressure backflow prevention assembly consists of two spring-loaded check valves, a hydraulically dependent differential relief valve, shut off valves on the inlet and discharge side of the assembly and small test cocks.

Under certain conditions, the relief valve will open and discharge to maintain the required pressure differential. A drain must be provided for valve discharge if installed inside a building. A protective enclosure is recommended for outside installation. Assembly must be protected from freezing.

Courtesy of Febco

Figure 5-14 Typcial Reduced Pressure Assembly

RP assemblies are available from several different manufacturers in sizes ¾ through 2 inch. Some brands also have models in sizes 2½ inch and larger.

AIR GAP

The air gap method of physical separation is occasionally used when a potable water supply is used as an alternate source of supply for a system that also uses a non-potable water supply. See Figure 5-15.

This method is also used when the flow rate of an existing potable water supply is not adequate for a direct supply to the irrigation system. Water is stored in a holding tank until an adequate supply is available for system operation. The pump must provide the pressure as necessary for proper operation. The irrigation cycle is limited by the volume of water available in the tank. Equipment and piping required is similar to that shown in Figure 5-15 (without the non-potable supply). In many countries, this is the only method allowed for irrigation systems.

Installation details are very important for a supply system of this type, as protection of the water supply is not based on the use of a manufactured product. Check local authority for approval and installation specifications. A water level control and tank refill system (not

Cross Connection Control

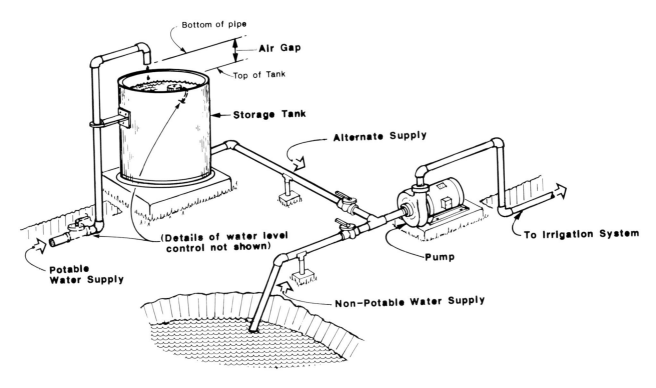

Figure 5-15 Air Gap to Protect Potable Water Supply

shown in illustration) must be included for automatic operation.

CROSS CONNECTION CONTROL BY LOCAL PLUMBING CODES

Protection of a potable water supply is not based on the opinions of the systems designer, general recommendations, etc., but as required by the specifications of the local plumbing authority.

In most cases, plumbing codes will have specific requirements for landscape irrigation systems that are connected to a potable water supply. Requirements may include a plumbing permit, type of device used for backflow prevention, use of approved products, type of pipe, installation details, inspection and testing at specified intervals.

Although local authority may be limited in requirement and/or enforcement, there are very few locations in the world that do not have some type of governmental regulation for the protection of potable water.

Special Conditions. Standard backflow prevention requirements of local codes are based on a "normal" degree of hazard. Use of fertilizer injectors or any other similar type of equipment will create additional hazard. Always check with the local plumbing authority regard-

ing requirements for this type of equipment before designing a new system, or adding to an existing system.

Testing Procedures. As previously discussed, some city ordinances require backflow prevention equipment for landscape irrigation systems to be tested periodically. Shut off valves and test cocks on pressure vacuum breakers, double check and reduced pressure assemblies are provided for testing. Special field test equipment is required and approved procedures must be followed for proper testing. Individuals who perform the test must be trained and approved by the local authority.

ADDITIONAL INFORMATION

Because of the importance of this subject, additional study on backflow prevention is recommended for systems designers and installers. Protection of potable water supplies is one of the primary reasons that some states require irrigators to be licensed. In most cases, the applicant must prove that he or she is competent and qualified by passing a uniform examination. Some tests will include an entire section of questions on cross connection control.

The Irrigation Association (a), an international organization for landscape and agricultural irrigation, offers a certified irrigation specialist program for designers, contractors and irrigation managers. One of the requirements for certification is the successful completion of a written examination. Certified individuals must also follow a code of ethics which includes protection and conservation of water supplies. The Irrigation Association (IA) is an excellent source of information on current trends and industry recommendations for backflow prevention.

Product features, specifications and applicable approval listings for backflow prevention devices are provided in manufacturer's catalogs. Product catalogs may also include additional information on typical applications and installations. It is important for the systems designer to maintain a file on current products, including pressure loss tables.

BIBLIOGRAPHY

(a) The Irrigation Association
  8260 Willow Oaks Corporate Dr., Ste. 120
  Fairfax, VA 22031

Foundation for Cross-Connection Control and Hydraulic Research
University of Southern California
KAP-200 University Park MC-2531
Los Angeles, CA 90089-2531

Partial List of Special Equipment Sources

Febco, a division of CMB Industries
P.O. Box 8070
Fresno, CA 93747

Conbraco
P.O. Box 247
Matthews, NC 28106

Watts Regulator Company
815 Chestnut St.
North Andover, MA 01845

CHAPTER 6

Pumps

A pump system is often required as the water supply for landscape irrigation systems. This chapter is included to acquaint designers with pump technology in a very limited and general way.

Systems designers should understand basic pump operation and variable factors of pumping water before designing an irrigation system for a particular flow and pressure requirement. Final pump selection should always be made by a qualified pump engineer. However, proper selection of the pump can be determined only if the irrigation systems designer provides complete and accurate information relating to pump performance requirement and site conditions.

Considerations during pumping system design include head (pressure), capacity (flow), piping, economics, and pump control requirements.

The important concept of design economics, which begins during pumping system planning and continues throughout its useful life, is too often neglected. For example, careful examination of pressure requirements and pump location can affect long-term energy savings with little increase in initial cost.

CENTRIFUGAL PUMPS
Pumps used for landscape irrigation systems are referred to by several names. However, all are *centrifugal pumps.* Figure 6-1 illustrates several of the more common types used in irrigation.

CLOSED-COUPLED VOLUTE. Figure 6-1a illustrates a typical *close-coupled volute type centrifugal pump.* Its distinctive feature is that the pump is mounted directly on a special motor frame. This allows the pump impeller to be mounted directly to the motor shaft, thus eliminating need for shaft alignment.

VOLUTE WITH FLEXIBLE COUPLING. With this type, Figure 6-1b, a volute centrifugal pump with its own impeller shaft is mounted on one end of a frame and the electric drive motor on the other end. To facilitate alignment, a flexible coupling is used to connect the two shafts.

HORIZONTAL SPLIT CASE. Figure 6-1c shows a *horizontal split-case centrifugal pump* with double suction (water inlet). Although available in smaller capacities this type pump is commonly used for flow requirements exceeding 700 gpm.

VERTICAL TURBINE. The *vertical turbine* pump, Figure 6-1d, is often preferred for pumping systems on large projects. The drive motor is installed above ground with a long drive shaft that operates a pump located below water source level. With the pump actually located in the water supply, many problems of supply to the pump are eliminated. Vertical turbine pumps are discussed in more detail later.

PUMP IMPELLER LUBRICATING
Some centrifugal pumps use a "stuffing box" with packing to control leakage between the pump housing and impeller shaft; see Figure 6-2a. Water in the pump is used as a lubricant for the shaft. Therefore, a slight amount of water must leak out between the shaft and packing during operation.

Compression of the packing around the shaft is adjustable to control leakage. *Never compress packing to eliminate drippage completely; otherwise, damage to the packing and shaft will occur.*

Pumps

a. Close-Coupled Volute

b. Volute with Flexible Coupling

c. Horizontal Split-Case

d. Vertical Turbine

Figure 6-1 Some Types of Centrifugal Pumps

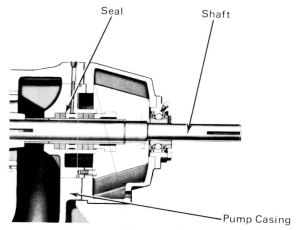

a. Packing Seal

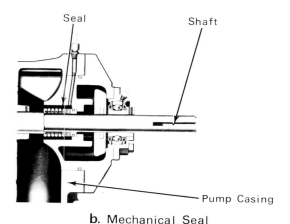

b. Mechanical Seal

Figure 6-2 Pump Shaft Seals

A bronze sleeve is most commonly used to protect the drive shaft in the packing area. When water source contains sand or other abrasives, hardened sleeves are recommended.

"Packless" pumps use *mechanical seals* (Figure 6-2b) to eliminate drippage.

In most cases, this is the preferred type of seal since maintenance of the seal is not necessary.

BASIC OPERATION OF CENTRIFUGAL PUMPS

The operating principle of all types of centrifugal pumps is basically the same. For illustrative purposes, the operation of the most common -- the *volute type* -- is described.

Rotation of an impeller inside a housing causes circular motion of the contained water. The rotating water is

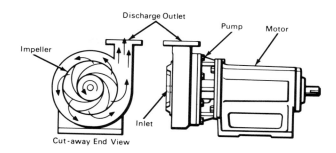

Figure 6-3 Flow of Water in Centrifugal Pump

forced through the discharge outlet of the housing by centrifugal force generated by centrifugal velocity. See Figure 6-3. As the water exits from the pump, its velocity is converted to pressure.

PERFORMANCE. Centrifugal pumps are ideally suited for the water supply of irrigation systems. By controlling flow requirements -- reducing or increasing the number of flow outlets in a zone -- pressure developed by a pump can be controlled. The graph in Figure 6-4 illustrates the varying performance of one pump model.

Note that with discharge flow controlled at 60 gpm, pump discharge pressure will be 206 ft head (89.2 lb/in^2). At 120 gpm discharge, pressure will be 190 ft head (82.3 lb/in^2), etc. If a valve on the discharge side of the pump is completely closed, stopping all flow, pressure will rise to 209 ft head (90.5 lb/in^2). Pressure produced with flow completely stopped is known as the *shut-off head.* This head is important to the operation of "hydro-pneumatic" pumping systems reviewed later in this chapter.

PUMPING TERMS AND DEFINITIONS

Exact pumping terms should be used to avoid misunderstandings. To avoid confusion, only terms normally used in conjunction with landscape irrigation systems are included. Definitions have also been worded to apply directly, but are still technically correct for this purpose.

TYPES OF PRESSURE

Pressure in *feet of head* (height of a column of water) is generally used in pumping rather than lb/in^2. See Chapter 3, "Hydraulics", for relation of these pressure measurements.

Among other pressure terms used in pumping are: *absolute* and *gauge* pressure. The term *vacuum* is also

Pumps

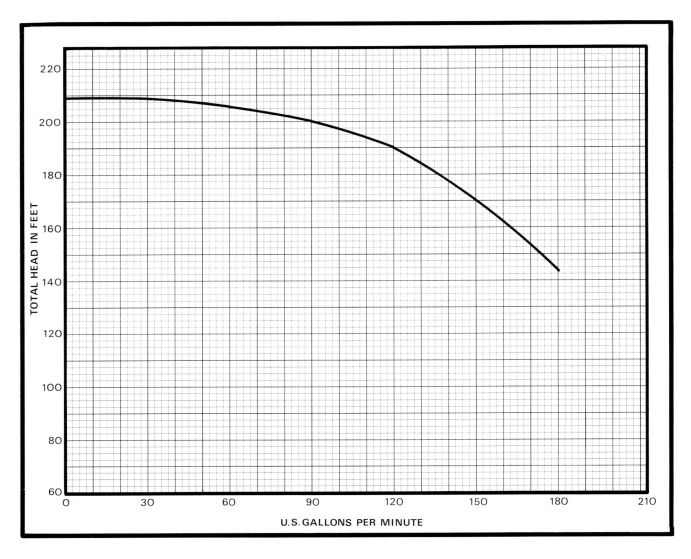

Figure 6-4 Varying Performance of a Pump Model

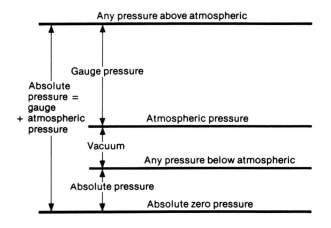

Figure 6-5 Relation of Pressure Terms Used in Pumping

used, but it is not a pressure term in the same sense as the others. Figure 6-5 illustrates the derivation of these terms.

ATMOSPHERIC PRESSURE. The weight (mass) of atmosphere above the earth's surface is termed *atmospheric pressure.* It varies with altitude above sea level and climatic conditions. For irrigation pumping calculations, *standard atmospheric pressure* at project site elevation is used. Climatic conditions are ignored because the effect overall is inconsequential. Figure 6-7 lists standard absolute pressures for various altitudes in commonly used units of measurement.

ABSOLUTE PRESSURE. Total pressure above absolute zero is termed *absolute pressure.*

lb/in^2	ft hd	kg/cm^2	m hd
0.5	1.2	0.03	0.3

Figure 6-6 Vapor Pressure of Water at Normal Temperatures Used in Irrigation Systems

Pressure gauges measure only pressure above atmospheric pressure. For example, assume the pressure in a tire is gauged at 30 lb/in^2. Then, absolute pressure would be 30 lb/in^2 plus the atmospheric pressure at a certain elevation. If the pressure were being gauged at sea level under standard climatic conditions, absolute pressure in the tire would be 44.7 lb/in^2: 30 + 14.7 = 44.7 lb/in^2; 14.7 lb/in^2 being standard atmospheric pressure at sea level (see tables, Figure 6-7).

Whenever confusion could exist as to whether a pressure is gauge or absolute, it should be identified. For example:

gauge pressure = lb/in^2 gauge (psig*)
absolute pressure = lb/in^2 abs. (psia*)
* These symbols are obsolete, but are still commonly used in the U.S.A.

VACUUM. The amount pressure is reduced below atmospheric is termed a *vacuum.*

STATIC CONDITIONS

Pumping terms and definitions prefaced by the word *static* relate to conditions when pump is not operating.

STATIC SUCTION LIFT. When a pump is above the water supply level, the vertical distance in feet (or meters) from the pump centerline to the supply level is termed the *static suction lift* (see Figure 6-8). Pump engineers commonly recommend that static suction lift should not exceed 15 ft for installations up to 5000 ft above sea level. Then, lift is reduced 1 ft for each 1000 ft of additional elevation.

It is not uncommon for other installation factors to limit static suction lift to less than the above distances.

STATIC SUCTION HEAD. A static suction head exists when the pump is below the water supply level. It is the vertical distance in feet (or meters) between the pump centerline and the water supply level.

DYNAMIC CONDITIONS

Conditions that exist or develop when water is flowing in a pumping system are prefaced by the word *dynamic* in this text. The trend today is to omit this word in defining conditions of an operating pumping system.

Altitude Below or Above Sea Level ft	Standard Barometric Pressure in Hg	Atmospheric Pressure		Altitude Below or Above Sea Level m	Standard Barometric Pressure mm Hg	Atmospheric Pressure	
		lb/in^2	Head H$_2$O @ 60°F ft			kg/cm^2	Head H$_2$O @ 15°C m
− 1000	31.02	15.2	35.2	− 300	787.4	1.07	10.71
− 500	30.47	15.0	34.5	− 150	773.6	1.05	10.53
0	29.92	14.7	33.9	0	760.0	1.03	10.34
+ 500	29.38	14.4	33.3	+ 150	746.6	1.01	10.16
1000	28.86	14.2	32.7	300	733.4	0.997	9.98
1500	28.33	13.9	32.1	450	720.3	0.979	9.80
2000	27.82	13.7	31.5	600	707.5	0.962	9.63
2500	27.32	13.4	31.0	750	694.8	0.945	9.45
3000	26.82	13.2	30.4	900	682.3	0.928	9.28
3500	26.33	12.9	29.8	1050	670.0	0.911	9.12
4000	25.84	12.7	29.3	1200	657.9	0.894	8.95
4500	25.37	12.5	28.8	1350	646.0	0.878	8.79
5000	24.90	12.2	28.2	1500	634.2	0.862	8.63
5500	24.43	12.0	27.7	1650	622.6	0.846	8.47
6000	23.98	11.8	27.2	1800	611.2	0.831	8.32
6500	23.53	11.6	26.7	1950	600.0	0.816	8.16
7000	23.09	11.3	26.2	2100	588.9	0.801	8.01
7500	22.65	11.1	25.7	2250	578.0	0.786	7.86

Figure 6-7 Atmospheric Pressures at Various Altitudes

Pumps

However, since the word *dynamic* helps express the idea of motion, it is believed that its use will eliminate confusion to the reader and make the text more understandable.

VAPOR PRESSURE. At temperatures above their freezing point, liquids exert a pressure due to formation of vapor at their free surface. This is called *vapor pressure.* As temperature increases, vapor pressure increases.

Vapor pressure will stop liquid flow into the pump if the pressure in the suction pipe drops below vapor pressure.

Vapor pressure of water at normal temperatures used in landscape irrigation systems is listed in Figure 6-6.

SUCTION FRICTION HEAD. Pressure loss in the pipe and appurtenances to the suction entrance of the pump must be considered in the design of the pumping system. Entrance and exit losses and losses due to sudden enlargement or reduction of pipe size are also included in suction friction head.

When water enters from a free or submerged source of supply, or discharges into a similar area, there is a loss of pressure. Entrance loss occurs at the pipe inlet. Exit loss occurs at the pipe outlet. A similar pressure loss occurs at any sudden pipe size enlargement or reduction.

DYNAMIC SUCTION LIFT. The sum of *static suction lift* and *suction friction head* is numerically the *dynamic suction lift.* Suction friction head must include pressure losses in all pipe and fittings in the suction line plus entrance loss, if any, and losses due to sudden enlargements or reductions in the piping.

DYNAMIC SUCTION HEAD. Numerically, *dynamic suction head* is the *static suction head* minus the *suction friction head* plus any pressure in the suction line.

DYNAMIC DISCHARGE HEAD. When used as the source of water supply for irrigation systems, *dynamic discharge head* is the sum total of (1) discharge velocity head, (2) pressure at the highest outlet above the pump in an operating zone, (3) elevation of that outlet above the pump, and (4) all pressure losses in piping and appurtenances from the pump discharge to that outlet computed in *feet of head.*

DYNAMIC TOTAL HEAD. Adding *dynamic suction lift* and *dynamic discharge head* provides *dynamic total head.* Capacity of pumps is rated by their flow and dynamic total head.

CAVITATION

Excessive suction lift or insufficient pressure at the entrance to the pump often causes *cavitation.* When the entrance pressure is reduced below vapor pressure, vapor pockets form bubbles on the impeller vanes nearest the pump inlet. These bubbles move from the low pressure area at the inlet to the high pressure area near the tip of each vane where they collapse. The bubbles break quickly, causing water to hit the vanes with considerable force, resulting in an identifiable noise.

Vibration and excessive noise are usually evidence of severe cavitation. In this event, the force of the water is often sufficient to gouge small pieces out of the impeller, thus pitting it. Mild cavitation may cause only a small reduction in pump efficiency and moderate wear of pump parts. Any cavitation should be avoided.

EFFICIENCY

The efficiency of any pump is the ratio of work expended to work accomplished. For example: If flow and pressure produced are equal to 2½ hp of work and the pump is driven by a motor requiring 5 hp work input, then pump efficiency is 50%; 2.5 divided by 5 = 0.50.

Pump efficiency changes with varying flow and pressure requirements. One of the services expected from the pump engineer is the selection of the most efficient pump for a given project. Conversely, the designer must zone the irrigation system within limits that will allow use of the most efficient pump.

NET POSITIVE SUCTION HEAD

As water is forced out of a centrifugal pump, water is forced into the pump through its inlet by some type of pressure. *Entrance pressure is critical* because water must be forced into the pump as fast as water is discharged through the outlet. This force or pressure is termed *net positive suction head (npsh).*

REQUIRED NPSH. The amount of pressure necessary for pump operation is termed *required npsh* which varies from one make of pump to another, between different models of one manufacturer, and with the capacity and speed of any given pump.

AVAILABLE NPSH. Pressure from any source existing at the suction inlet of a pump is termed *available npsh;* it must always be equal to, or more than, the required npsh of the pump being used.

Incorrect determination of npsh results in more pump troubles than any other single cause according to pump engineers. Insufficient npsh can reduce pump capacity, leading to cavitation damage. It can also cause priming problems.

Water Supply Below Pump. If a water column flowing into and out of a centrifugal pump becomes separated in the pump (and no air is in the pump), a perfect vacuum of absolute "zero" pressure would exist in the separation. Therefore, pumps installed above a water source level, exposed to atmosphere, can use the atmospheric pressure to force water into the suction inlet and provide the required npsh.

Atmospheric pressure *decreases* as elevation above sea level *increases;* this reduction must be considered when pumping systems are designed. Atmospheric pressures at various altitudes are listed in Figure 6-7.

Use of atmospheric pressure to furnish suction requirements is explained later.

Water Supply Above Pump. When a water supply exposed to the atmosphere is above the pump centerline, available npsh is the sum of atmospheric pressure *plus* the static suction head, *minus* friction head loss in the suction piping and vapor pressure.

SELECTION OF CENTRIFUGAL PUMPS

The landscape irrigation designer must furnish complete, accurate information regarding site conditions and requirements for a pumping system.

SITE CONDITIONS
Generally, information needed for the pump installation is obtained at time data for developing a plot plan is acquired.

PUMP LOCATION. Many factors must be considered when determining a location for the pumping system.

Often the level of the water supply is not constant. The highest and lowest levels must be known. The pump must be installed above the high level to avoid the risk

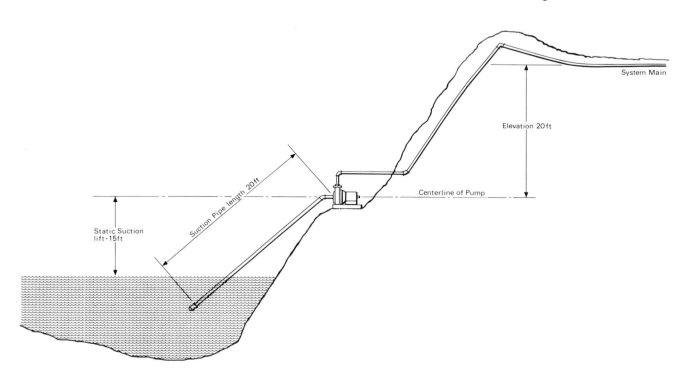

Figure 6-8 Example: Pump Installation Conditions

Pumps

of flooding. At the same time, the pump cannot be placed any higher above low level than the maximum limitation on its static lift.

In addition, care should be exercised to require the shortest suction pipe possible, thereby minimizing pressure loss.

ELECTRIC POWER. Compare long-term cost of using the existing power supply versus the initial and long term cost of providing a new electric service.

In general, 110-120V, single phase, electric power results in the highest motor and power costs. The cost of motor and power with 220-240V, single phase electricity is considerably less.

Three phase electric service should be strongly considered for requirements of 10 hp and above.

Usually a qualified electrician is required to properly analyze existing electrical service (wiring from power company lines to proposed pump site) and determine the cost and availability of required changes in electrical service.

PRELIMINARY SELECTION OF PUMP

The first consultation with a pump engineer should occur before the irrigation system design proceeds too far. But, only after preliminary design data has been developed.

In the theoretical example outlined below, the irrigation systems designer has analyzed a property and prepared the head layout on a plot plan; see Chapter 10. The system has been tentatively zoned; see Chapter 11, zoning the system. Maximum flow and pressure requirement zones have been determined and tentatively piped and sized. Minimum pressure requirement at the source was determined by adding the calculated pressure loss of the zone with the greatest loss, to the operating pressure requirement of the heads (elevation loss is not included).

Pipe added for elevation changes, Figure 6-8, must be included in pressure loss calculations. Since the length of the pipe is more than the vertical rise above the pump, the length should be determined when the plot plan is prepared; see Chapter 9, Plot Plans: Rolling Terrains. The vertical elevation must be taken into account when pump size is selected.

In the first consultation with the pump engineer, the designer furnished the data listed below. Based on this data, the pump engineer will determine if a suitable pump can be furnished. The engineer might also recommend changes which could result in a more efficient pumping system. For example, changing zone sizes a little, with less flow and pressure required, could reduce initial cost and long term power costs considerably.

DATA FURNISHED PUMP ENGINEER. Flow and pressure requirements are usually increased 10% or more to provide a safety factor for future possible reduction of pump capacity from wear or other causes.

1. Design flow requirement; see Chapter 11. Example flow requirement is 90.9 gpm. Therefore, with 10% added, required pump discharge will be 100.0 gpm. Be sure to advise the pump engineer so he/she won't add a second safety factor.
2. Calculated design pressure requirement is 40 lb/in^2. Adding 10% makes required pressure 44 lb/in^2, or 102 ft head.
3. Water must be pumped uphill. It is 20 ft from the centerline to the elevation of the highest sprinkler head.
4. The conditions of desired pump installation are shown in Figure 6-8.
   a. Pump to be located 15 ft above lowest possible water supply level.
   b. 20 ft of suction pipe is required to place end below lowest water level and above lake bed; see Pump Installation, this chapter. A 2 inch suction pipe and foot valve are preferred. Pressure losses in the suction pipe and appurtenances should be calculated by the designer and furnished to the pump engineer for checking.

PUMP ENGINEER'S CALCULATIONS. With the information furnished, the pump engineer will first calculate the npsh (net positive suction head) available to determine if a suitable pump can be fitted to the desired conditions. Figure 6-12 diagrams the calculations made to determine available npsh at pump.

Elevation. The lake is slightly less than 1000 ft above sea level. Therefore, atmospheric pressure at 1000 ft elevation is used to offset Dynamic Suction Lift and other suction requirements. At that elevation, atmospheric pressure is equivalent to 32.7 ft H_2O head, Figure 6-7. Subtracting all suction pressure reductions from atmospheric pressure provides head available for npsh to the pump.

Vapor Pressure. Atmospheric pressure is reduced 1.2 ft by vapor pressure of water at temperatures normally encountered for irrigation system supply; see Figure 6-6.

Suction Friction Head. The irrigation system designer furnished the following computation of friction head in the pump suction line, Figure 6-9.

Flow l00 gpm:

2 in 200 lb/in² PVC suction pipe:	20	ft
2 in x 1½ in reducing coupling:	5	ft
2,2 in 90° elbows:	14	ft
TOTAL EQUIVALENT SUCTION PIPE:	39	ft

Loss per 100 ft.: 5.40 lb/in² (Table 5):
5.40 lb/in² x .39 = 2.11 lb/in² x 2.31 =   4.9 ft hd loss
2 in foot valve (Figure 6-11):   2.2 ft hd loss
TOTAL SUCTION FRICTION HEAD   7.1 ft

Figure 6-9 Designer's Calculations of Suction Friction Head

Foot valves are required on the end of centrifugal pump suction pipes when pump is installed above water supply level. These valves close by weight of water when pump operation is stopped. This keeps the column of water in the suction pipe and pump from flowing back into the water supply. If any part of this water is lost, the pump loses its prime and it will not pump water the next time operation is started. There are two basic types of foot valves as shown in Figure 6-10.

The Poppet type foot valve causes the most pressure loss. Since pressure in the suction pipe is normally critical, the hinged type is the most commonly used. Water quality and dependability are also important considerations.

Figure 6-11 provides pressure loss through Hinged Disc foot valves. Loss is given in ft of head for water at 60 F. Losses are accurate enough for average water temperatures. Pressure losses for Poppet valves vary by product and should be obtained from the manufacturer.

Foot valves do not open fully until flow exceeds certain minimums. Hinged foot valves should be sized so that flows cause a pressure loss of not less than 1 ft head. Lesser flows cause greater losses of undeterminable amounts because the disc will not have fully opened. If necessary to obtain flows greater than lower limit of table, use foot valve smaller than line size.

In the example, Figure 6-9, loss caused by the 2 in foot valve was estimated by interpolation (between 97 and 120 gpm).

Available NPSH. The pump engineer's calculations, Figure 6-12, illustrate that the conditions prescribed provide a head pressure of 9.4 ft to satisfy the net positive suction head requirements.

PUMP PERFORMANCE. A pump is selected which has a performance rating suitable for the project with a required npsh less than the available npsh calculated.

Pump Rating. The minimum capacity, or rating, required for the pump is then determined. Rating is the amount of work the pump can do in terms of "lifting" and "pushing" water. The rating for a pump to be used in the example is determined as follows.

1. Flow discharge: irrigation system design requirement 90.9 gpm + 10% safety factor equals 100 gpm.

2. Pressure:

Irrigation system design pressure	101.7	ft
40.0 lb/in² + 10% = 44.0 lb/in² x 2.31:	20.0	ft
Elevation, pump to highest outlet	121.7	ft
DYNAMIC DISCHARGE HEAD REQ'D:		

Suction requirement:			
Friction Head:	7.1		
Static Suction Lift:	15.0 ft		
DYNAMIC SUCTION LIFT:		22.1	ft
VAPOR PRESSURE:		1.2	ft
DYNAMIC TOTAL HEAD REQUIRED:		145.0	ft

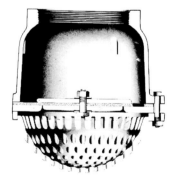 

Foot Valve With Strainer; Hinged Type   Foot Valve With Strainer; Poppet Type

Figure 6-10 Two Types of Foot Valves

PUMPS

DO NOT USE STANDARD FOOT VALVES WITH LESS THAN 1 FOOT H₂O HEAD LOSS

Head loss ft H₂O	Nominal Pipe Sizes: Inches									Head loss ft H₂O
	1½	2	2½	3	4	6	8	10	12	
	Flow:gpm									
1	39	66	96	152	268	632	1122	1805	2603	1
2	57	97	140	221	390	919	1632	2625	3786	2
3	71	120	175	275	486	1145	2032	3269	4713	3
4	83	141	204	322	568	1337	2374	3819	5507	4
5	94	159	230	363	641	1509	2678	4308	6213	5
6	104	175	254	401	707	1665	2956	4755	6836	6
7	113	190	276	435	769	1810	3212	5168	7452	7
8	121	205	297	468	826	1945	3453	5555	8010	8
9	129	218	317	499	880	2073	3680	5920	8636	9
10	137	231	335	528	932	2195	3896	6267	9037	10

Figure 6-11 Pressure Losses: Foot Valves with Hinged Disc

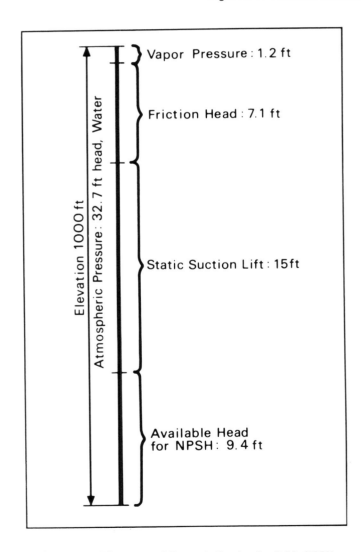

Figure 6-12 Diagrammed Computation for Available NPSH

Therefore, a pump for this project would be selected with a rating (rounded-off) of 100 gpm @ 150 feet of head.

Pump Performance Curves. A pump is selected by comparing requirements against the performance of several pump models as shown in graph, Figure 6-13.

1. Using pump rating required, enter graph from bottom at 100 gpm and from left side at 150 ft hd. Lines drawn from these two reference points would intersect at the point where an asterisk has been placed.
2. Pump with impeller providing the performance requirements is tentatively selected. In this case, an impeller diameter of 6 ⅜ in is used. (Proportional interpolation is made on curve in increments of ⅛ in.).
3. Reading down from performance point to required npsh curve, it is seen that available npsh, 9.4 ft hd, is safely more than required: approximately 6 ft hd (See vertical scale on right).
4. The dashed lines from upper left to lower right specify the horsepower of the motor required for the various model pumps graphed. Since the pump requirements fall between 5 and 7 ½ hp, a 7 ½ hp motor will be required.
5. The lines curving from top center to the upper right indicate pump efficiency. In this case, efficiency exceeds 65%.

FINAL SELECTION OF PUMP. After the entire irrigation system has been designed (flow and design pressure for all zones determined), the designer should consult with the pump engineer if there are any changes in requirement, or to review and confirm the original pump selection.

Pump performance should be checked for normal variations of flow and/or pressure requirement that occur with different zones. Final selection of a pump must be based on the range of requirement of all zones in the irrigation system.

PUMP INSTALLATION

Careful selection of the best pump for a particular project can be defeated if proper installation methods are not followed.

PUMP SUCTION

Installation of the suction pipe for a pump that must *lift* water is the most critical part of a pumping system.

Installation must be such that *complete* removal of air from the suction pipe and the pump can be accomplished. Also, leakage of air into the suction must be prevented. Otherwise, it is possible that the pump could not be primed or prime may be lost.

SUCTION PIPE JOINTS. All joints of the suction pipe must be *absolutely air-tight.* Joints that are only watertight can leak air into the pipe.

Normally, the pump inlet will be smaller than the suction pipe, requiring a reducing coupling. The reducer should be placed as close to the pump as possible to minimize pressure loss. Always use an eccentric coupling as shown in Figure 6-14a.

A standard reducing coupling will allow an air pocket as shown in Figure 6-14b.

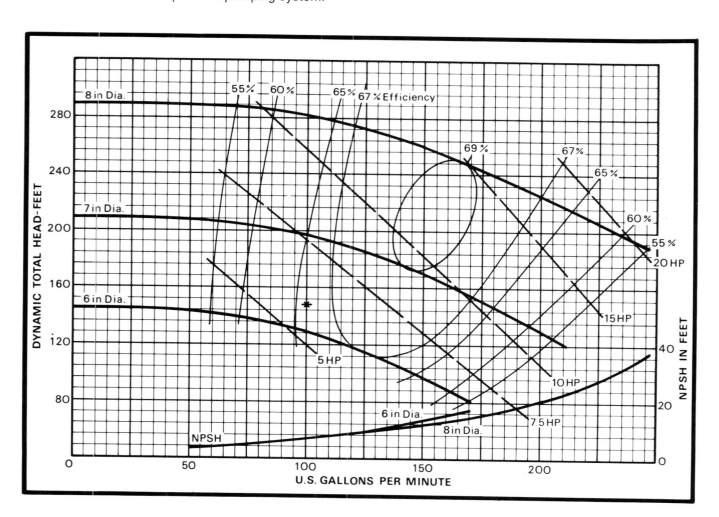

Figure 6-13 Typical Pump Performance Curves

Pumps

SUCTION PIPE GRADE. Suction pipes must be installed with a straight, unbroken incline to the pump as shown in Figure 6-15a. Figure 6-15b shows a suction pipe with a sag. Note that air is trapped in a pocket. Entrapped air eventually works its way into the pump and either causes a loss of prime or a reduction of output.

End-suction centrifugal pumps are normally installed with the inlet facing the water supply (Figure 6-8). However, the angle of suction pipe incline grade often does not coincide with the angle of standard fittings. In this event, a *swing joint* consisting of two elbows can be "rolled" to provide any angle of incline.

Installing the pump parallel to the water supply eliminates the double-ell swing-joint. As can be seen in Figure 6-18, only one elbow is required to obtain any angle of suction pipe incline.

Swivel assemblies are particularly desirable where suction pipe incline angle may require changing frequently;

angle can change without affecting seal of joint if suitable for operating under vacuum.

SUCTION INTAKE. The suction intake (foot valve) must not be located too near the surface or bottom of the water source. Turbulence created by water being drawn into the supply pipe will cause air or debris floating on the surface, or mud and silt from the bottom, to be sucked into the pump.

There are many ways to protect the intake. Consult with the pump engineer for the best method to suit specific conditions. Figure 6-16 illustrates one solution for placement of foot valve near the bottom of a shallow body of water.

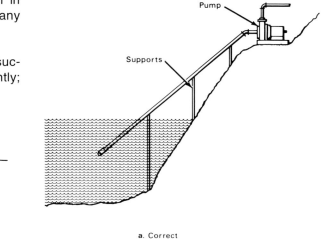

a. Correct

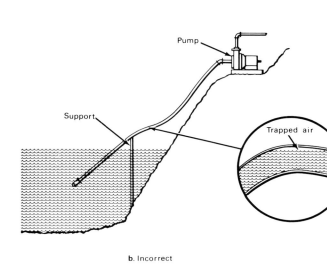

b. Incorrect

Figure 6-15 Grading Pump Suction Pipe

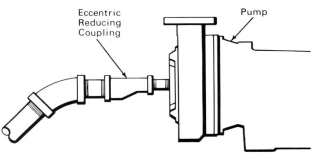

a. Correct

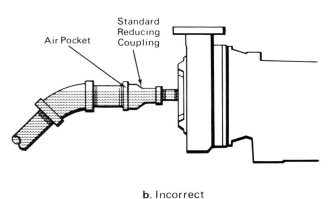

b. Incorrect

Figure 6-14 Reducing Coupling Connection at Pump

The example illustrates a round concrete septic tank with one end closed. If the tank is a minimum of 2 or 3 feet high, intake turbulence cannot stir up the bottom of the water source. A frame (made of angle iron or similar material) is covered on the top and sides by hardware cloth with openings of about 1/4 inch. Since debris is more apt to be drawn and collect against the top, the vertical portion of the screen should be high enough to accommodate several times the total flow requirement.

Centrifugal pumps can handle any debris that might pass through the 1/4 inch openings of the hardware cloth. Finer debris, sand, etc. should be strained from the water supply to the irrigation system by a strainer installed on the discharge side of the pump. See Chapter 7, Clean Water: Strainers.

Fine screening of the suction intake should be avoided. A fine screen tends to clog more quickly, causing abnormal pressure loss and pumping failure. Figure 6-17 illustrates an alternate method of protecting the suction intake using special products manufactured for this purpose.

SUCTION TESTING. As previously emphasized, the greatest number of pump operation failures are due to improper suction conditions. Therefore, whenever a pump does not perform properly, including discharge flow and pressure, suction conditions should be checked first.

The suction test consists of gauging the amount of vacuum existing at the entrance to the pump when it is pumping at maximum flow requirement; amount of vacuum can be used by a pump engineer to determine available npsh.

A plugged tee installed in the suction pipe as close to the entrance of the pump as possible will provide a means of gauging suction vacuum. The side outlet of the tee must be parallel to the earth so the gauge reading will be at the centerline of the pump. Reduce the side outlet to 1/4 in internal pipe thread for acceptance of standard gauge connections. See Figure 6-18.

Never use a valve on the suction test tee. Although the packing of a valve may provide a water-tight joint, it probably would leak air into the suction causing pump failure.

SUCTION AND DISCHARGE UNIONS. Unions, either screwed, ground-joint or flanged type, should always be

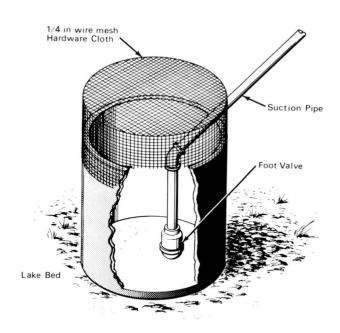

1/4 in wire mesh Hardware Cloth

Suction Pipe

Foot Valve

Lake Bed

Figure 6-16 Protection of Suction Intake

installed in the suction and discharge pipes to facilitate maintenance and servicing. See Figure 6-18.

PUMP TAPPINGS

A pump with plugged tappings at intervals of 90° on the circumference of the pump housing should always be used. See Figure 6-18. These plugged openings are used for draining the pump and venting air when necessary. Pump tappings are optional and must be specified when placing an order for a pump.

PUMP MOUNTING

Pumps should always be mounted on a sturdy base, preferably concrete. Rubber pads between the base and mountings of pump are usually recommended to absorb vibration during operation.

PRIMING

When installed above water supply level, centrifugal pumps must be *primed* before start of initial operation. *Priming* a pump consists of introducing water into the pumping system above the pump itself until water has *completely* replaced air in the pump and its suction piping.

Pumps

Air in a centrifugal pump can cause serious problems.

1. Pump will lose its prime and, if pump continues to run, serious damage will occur, or
2. Pump will discharge water, but pressure and flow may not be adequate.

Starting a pump, after priming, without first closing the discharge valve can create two serious conditions if the irrigation main is empty. Both conditions result from uncontrolled flow. See Chapter 4, Water Hammer: Uncontrolled Flow in Empty Pipes.

1. When pipes fill, damaging water hammer can occur.
2. Pump delivers flow of water exceeding design; dynamic suction head will increase reducing npsh below requirement and pump will lose its prime.

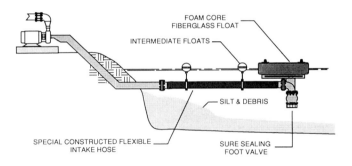

Courtesy of Greenscape Pump
Figure 6-17 Suction Intake with Float

AUTOMATIC AIR VENTS. Installation of a small automatic air vent in the top of a pump will pay for itself many times over as an aid to removal of air from the pump and suction. It removes air during the initial priming and any entrained air which may escape from the column of water under suction. Note: The vent usually cannot remove air when the pump is operating. Automatic air vents are the same as those used to remove "entrapped air" in irrigation system mains reviewed in Chapter 4, Water Hammer.

AUTOMATIC PRIMING. Priming can be accomplished automatically by several means. One method uses a vacuum pump to remove air from the pump. Self-priming pumps are also available, but they are more costly and less efficient.

PUMP OPERATION WITH IRRIGATION CONTROLLER

Pump operation can be controlled with most automatic irrigation controllers. Generally, the controller does not operate the pump directly. Most, if not all controllers, operate a relay which switches power on and off to a motor starter.

Irrigation controllers with a pump circuit energize an internal or external relay at the same time any station on the controller is energized. In automatic sequential operation, this provides continuous pump operation from time first station is energized until controller sequence is ended. Care should be exercised that controller does not "dwell" on an unused station (set all unused stations to 0 timing). Some controllers, with automatic back-up timing on each station, are available with a pump protection circuit to override the back-up program time on unused stations. A pressure relief valve can also be used to prevent a no-flow condition. In any case, the pump should not operate without being able to discharge water.

With this type pump control, used principally with smaller installations, water in the irrigation system is relied on to maintain pump prime. This requires special installation methods resulting in some disadvantages.

The irrigation main must run uphill so that gravity can cause water to back flow into the pump to maintain prime.

A check valve should be used in the discharge pipe to prevent potential damage of the pump caused by flow reversal when a pump operation stops (see Chapter 4, Water Hammer: Reverse Flow). Therefore, a bypass pipe around the check valve is required. A small diameter -- $1/4$ or $3/8$ in -- will provide sufficient backflow to replace loss of water in the pump chamber due to leakage around the impeller shaft. A pipe of sufficient size to replace water lost due to the foot valve not closing cannot be used. A larger bypass would recirculate enough water through the pump to affect its efficiency and capacity.

The amount of water available to maintain prime is limited to the volume of water flowing back from the system. Pump must be operated often enough to keep piping system from draining completely.

In addition to the standard type of pump circuit, a variety of special features relating to pump systems are available with some models of irrigation controllers (See Chapter 1, Remote Sensors).

HYDRO-PNEUMATIC PRESSURE SYSTEMS

Automatic control of pump operation with a *Hydro-Pneumatic Pressure System* eliminates disadvantages of control with the irrigation controller. This system consists of a suitable pump, a suitable size pressure tank and necessary control devices. Pressure controls pump operation.

The following information is provided to cover the basic operation and requirements of a hydro-pneumatic pumping station. Pre-engineered and pre-assembled water supply systems may be similar in operation or there may be major differences, depending on brand and model. "Manufactured Pumping Stations" are discussed later in this chapter.

Figure 6-19 diagrams a basic Hydro-Pneumatic Pressure System for smaller irrigation systems. Actual details may vary depending on requirements and recommendations of the pump engineer. Pump control is entirely independent from the irrigation system except for pressure required.

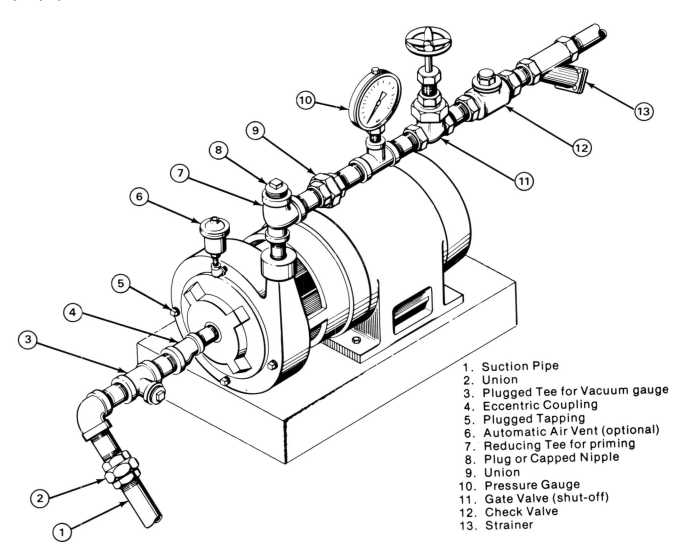

1. Suction Pipe
2. Union
3. Plugged Tee for Vacuum gauge
4. Eccentric Coupling
5. Plugged Tapping
6. Automatic Air Vent (optional)
7. Reducing Tee for priming
8. Plug or Capped Nipple
9. Union
10. Pressure Gauge
11. Gate Valve (shut-off)
12. Check Valve
13. Strainer

Figure 6-18 Typical Pumping System

Pumps

Hydro-Pneumatic Pressure Systems have several advantages because the main is pressurized at all times.

1. Water is available for other uses such as supplemental watering of newly planted trees with hoses, etc.
2. Water hammer does not develop due to uncontrolled flow in empty main.
3. Provisions can be made for bypass of water from pump to eliminate loss of prime.

In addition, a properly sized pressure tank will dampen water hammer developed by closing zone valves.

BASIC OPERATION

The pressure tank is filled with about $\frac{1}{2}$ to $\frac{2}{3}$ water and $\frac{1}{3}$ to $\frac{1}{2}$ compressed air for irrigation systems (water to air ratio may be different on "Manufactured Pumping Stations"). The pressure switch is set for high and low pressures required.

Assume that the air in the tank has been pressurized to the high limit of the pressure switch and the pump is not operating. When a zone valve opens (or any flow demand is made), the pressure of the tank will force water out to supply the demand. As water leaves the tank, the air expands and pressure reduces. When pressure

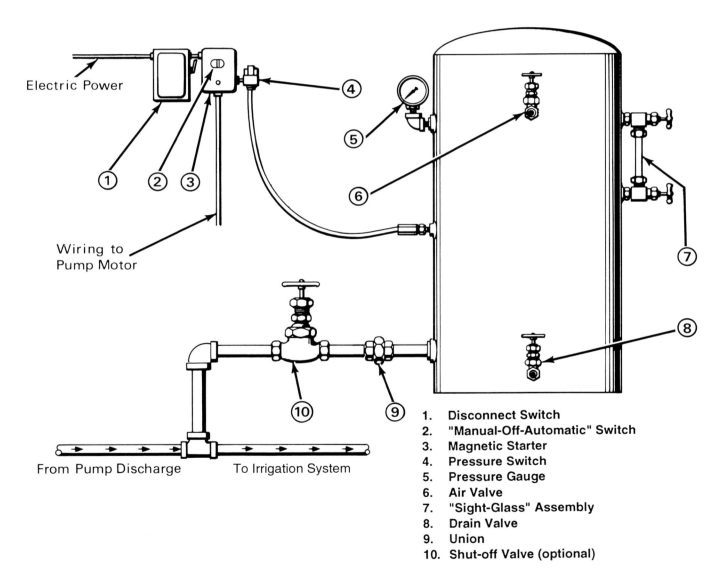

Electric Power

Wiring to Pump Motor

From Pump Discharge   To Irrigation System

1. Disconnect Switch
2. "Manual-Off-Automatic" Switch
3. Magnetic Starter
4. Pressure Switch
5. Pressure Gauge
6. Air Valve
7. "Sight-Glass" Assembly
8. Drain Valve
9. Union
10. Shut-off Valve (optional)

Figure 6-19 Basic Hydro-Pneumatic Pressure System

drops to the low limit of the pressure switch, the pump is started.

The pump will continue to operate as long as pressure is not developed equal to the high limit setting on the pressure switch.

When flow demand is low enough that the pump can develop pressure equal to the high limit setting of the pressure switch, the pump operation will be stopped. If a zone is operating at this time, pressure will immediately drop to the low limit and the pump will be restarted. An irrigation system designed so that pressure remains between the high and low limits, provides the best operating condition.

PRESSURE SWITCH. The high limit pressure setting (pump off) of the pressure switch must not exceed the "shut-off" head of the pump (maximum pressure the pump can develop). For safety, after allowing for accuracy tolerance of the switch, the setting should be at least 3 or 4 lb/in^2 less.

Best low limit setting is the required pump discharge pressure for operation of the zone with highest pressure requirements. However, low limit setting must be somewhat lower than the high limit to minimize the number of times the pump will cut "on" and "off."

As an example, refer to pump selection for the pumping system previously analyzed, Figure 6-8. Minimum Dynamic Discharge Head required was 121.7 ft hd (52.7 lb/in^2). Shut-off head of the pump was 168 ft (72.7 lb/in^2), Figure 6-13 performance curve.

Pressure switch setting would be as follows:
High Limit:
72.7 lb/in^2 2% mfg. tolerance (1.5) 2 lb/in^2 (safety) = 69.2 lb/in^2; setting rounded to 69.0 lb/in^2.

Minimum Low Limit:
52.7 lb/in^2 + 2% mfg. tolerance (1.1) = 53.8
setting rounded to 54.0 lb/in^2.
Caution: Check for proper installation after putting system into operation. Slight adjustments may be necessary due to manufacturing tolerances of switch accuracy.

PRESSURE TANK. Several considerations affect pressure tank selection.

Size. Many formulas exist for sizing tanks for Hydro-Pneumatic Pressure Systems. However, some of these consider the amount of water that may be used without causing pump to be started and may not be applicable to the operation of irrigation systems.

The only function of the tank, as shown in Figure 6-19, is to monitor pressure and operate the pump as needed. Disappointing results accompany under-sized tanks. Recommended size in gallons is at least ten times the maximum flow per minute. For example: When maximum flow requirement is 100 gpm, tank size should be not less than 1000 gallons.

Type. For smaller sizes, vertical tanks are used as shown in Figure 6-19. Vertical or horizontal tanks are used in larger sizes (Figure 6-23).

Tappings. Standard tanks are available with pipe thread outlets for mounting the various accessories required. Outlets are usually oversized; reducing bushings are used where required. Unused outlets are plugged. When outlets are not properly sized or not suitably located, tanks with specified outlets are available.

AIR VALVE. In order to maintain proper water level, air will periodically need to be added to, or released from the pressure tank. The air valve, which is used for this purpose, must be a type specifically made for air control. A standard valve will leak air, causing problems and additional maintenance.

ESTABLISHING AIR/WATER RATIO
The ratio of air and water in the pressure tank is vital to proper operation of a Hydro-Pneumatic Pressure System. As stated previously, the ratio for operation of an irrigation system is about 1/3 to 1/2 air by volume. This ratio must be established at the time the system is first put into operation and maintained at all times.

A "sight glass" (Figure 6-19) should always be installed on the tank so the water level can be monitored. Height of water required for the ratio wanted can be determined from Table 27 for vertical round tanks and from Table 28 for horizontal round tanks.

MAINTAINING AIR/WATER RATIO
Low water level in the pressure tank will delay the pump from establishing its normal operating pressure. High water level may result in cycling the pump "on" and "off" too frequently. Normally, water levels will rise due to air leaks in the tank or absorption of air by the water.

Pumps

Water level should be monitored and proper level re-established as frequently as required. With lower pressures, water can be drained to correct level. With higher pressures, not only must water be drained, but air must be pressurized with an air compressor.

"WATER-LOGGED" PRESSURE TANKS. The condition commonly referred to as a *water-logged tank* exists when air volume is too small. When this condition exists, the pump will cycle "on" and "off" with little, or no hesitation between cycles. Continuous cycling can result in damage to the pump.

SPECIAL TANKS. Tanks are available which reduce or eliminate air charging.

Floating Wafer Type Tanks. Vertically installed pressure tanks are available with "floating wafers." The wafer rides on the surface of the water reducing the air and water contact area as shown in Figure 6-20. It is pressurized at time of installation. Since the wafer doesn't completely separate the water from the air, periodic recharging is still necessary.

Diaphragm Type Tanks. Figure 6-21 shows a pressure tank with a flexible diaphragm which isolates water from the air. The tank is pre-charged with air by the manufacturer to a specified pump start pressure. An air charging valve allows the installer to change air pressure if necessary. No other tank connections are provided.

The pressure switch is connected to the system water piping. Ratio of air and water is not controllable. Ratio is self-establishing depending on system pressure.

Bag Type Tank. All details of bag type tanks, Figure 6-22, are the same as those for the diaphragm type listed above except that a bag is used in place of a diaphragm.

MINIMIZING WATER HAMMER

Air storage in the pressure tank can help to reduce water hammer in the irrigation system by absorbing some of the energy that may develop. To provide this added advantage, the tank must be of ample size and the pipe to the tank the same size as the irrigation main. Or, in the case of very large irrigation mains, a size as recommended by the pump engineer.

PUMP SYSTEM ACCESSORIES

Many other items are available for Hydro-Pneumatic Pressure Systems, but they are rarely used on smaller projects because of cost. However, long-term service costs may exceed initial cost for some accessories. For example, automatic maintenance of air pressure in tanks would eliminate many periodic service costs. In such cases, the added investment may be justified when all operating costs are fully analyzed.

AUTOMATIC AIR/WATER LEVEL CONTROL. The "Nu-matic Water Control" functions as a compressor for supplying air into a pressure tank. By means of a float and special valves, it utilizes the tank pressure for manipulating air into the tank while at the same time establishing and maintaining the desired high water level. No other power is required.

This unit (7) is installed on the end of horizontal tanks (see Figure 6-23) and on the side of vertical tanks. It operates only when a change of water level or air volume is required. Pressure rating is 125 lb/in^2 maximum.

The Nu-matic has only two minor disadvantages which are far outweighed by its advantages. The unit is slow in establishing the desired water level when the pumping system is first put into operation. Additionally, the waste water from the control must be drained by gravity

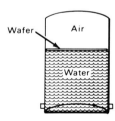

Figure 6-20 Floating Wafer Type Tank

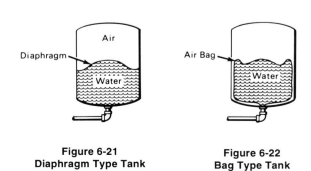

Figure 6-21	Figure 6-22
Diaphragm Type Tank	Bag Type Tank

and may be objectionable unless a method of disposal is provided.

PRESSURE RELIEF VALVES. Pressure surging (water hammer) can be dampened with a pressure relief valve. The valve must be of a type that is fast opening and slow closing. If the valve does not open fast enough, maximum pressure surging can still develop momentarily. A valve that closes too rapidly can, itself, develop water hammer.

A pressure relief valve(s) (17) is installed on the downstream side of the pump and as close to the check valve (15) as possible (Figure 6-23). Provision must be made for disposal of water discharge that occurs when valve relieves pressure. Usually the water is returned to the source.

The combined use of a pressure relief valve, ample size pressure tank, and a silent check valve can virtually eliminate pressure surging. When irrigation system mains are long, such as on a golf course, secondary relief valves are recommended at points most distant from the pump(s).

Note: In most cases, "Manufactured Pumping Stations" are used for large projects, such as a golf course irrigation system. Although a pressure relief valve is available as an optional item with these systems, an automatic pump control valve is the primary method of controlling the discharge pressure. These systems are discussed later in this chapter.

NPSH MONITORING. Reduction of npsh below that required, can cause damage to an unattended pump. Reduction of npsh below design can result from several conditions.
1. Suction intake clogged by debris.
2. Debris does not allow foot valve to open fully.
3. Break in irrigation system piping. Note: Centrifugal pumps will always try to deliver flow at pressure for which it is rated. If a pipe on the discharge breaks sufficiently so that the pump cannot reach its rated pressure because of too much flow, the electric motor will overload and could burn out.

Pressure control switches are available to monitor npsh and shut down pump if necessary. These control switches are installed in the suction adjacent to the pump. If npsh drops below switch setting, this control can be wired to accomplish either of the following:

1. Stop pump operation and turn on a red signal lamp.
2. By wiring a time delay into the circuit, further control can be obtained. If such a malfunction occurred, the signal lamp is first turned on. Then, if the malfunction does not correct itself within the length of time delay, the pump is stopped. Signal lamp remains lit.

Caution: When this method of npsh monitoring is used with multiple pump installations, a control switch is required in all suction pipes. And, the controls must be wired so that all pumps are stopped even though npsh is insufficient for only one pump. Continued operation of only one of the pumps can result in the same condition that a broken pipe causes.

VERTICAL TURBINE PUMP SYSTEMS

For larger landscape irrigation systems, where the additional cost can be justified, Vertical Turbine Pumps often provide a preferred pumping system. See Figure 6-1d. The advantages of a vertical turbine pump include the following.
1. No suction lift.
2. Suction pipe not required.
3. Foot valve not required.
4. No priming required, consequently pump cannot lose prime.
5. In the average capacity range required for landscape irrigation systems, these pumps are commonly more efficient than pumps used when water must be lifted from the supply source (see examples earlier in this chapter).

Actually, the vertical turbine pump itself is not as costly as pumps which must lift water when the elimination of a suction pipe, foot valve, priming, etc., are considered. The requirement for a pump pit and the water supply to it are the features which add cost. Conversely, it is not unusual for site and water supply conditions to make the pit requirement the least costly of the two types of pumping systems. In addition, the initial cost of the pit will often be more than offset by the reduction of other costs long-term.

MULTI-STAGE
For most flows and pressure requirements of vertical turbine pumps, multi-stages are used. Each stage, which can be thought of as an individual pump, utilizes an inherent characteristic of centrifugal pumps.

Pumps

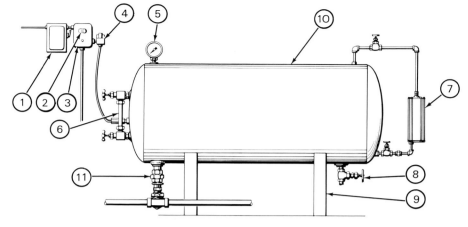

Side View

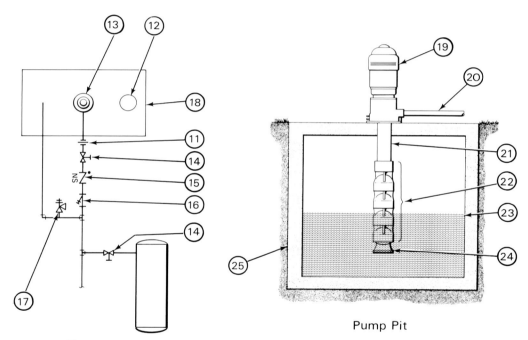

Top View

Pump Pit

1. Disconnect Switch
2. "Manual-Off-Automatic" Switch 15.
3. Magnetic Starter
4. Pressure Switch
5. Pressure Gauge
6. "Sight Glass"
7. Nu-Matic Water Level Control (optional)
8. Drain Valve
9. Tank Saddles
10. Pressure Tank
11. Union
12. Manhole
13. Vertical Turbine Pump

14. Shut-off Valve
    Silent check Valve
16. Strainer
17. Pressure Relief Valve
18. Concrete Pit
19. Motor
20. To Irrigation System
21. Column Pipe
22. Multi-stage Pump
23. Minimum water level
    at least 2 ft. above pump entrance
24. Bell-mouth inlet
25. Water supply inlet: see Figure 6-26
    6-27

Figure 6-23 Composite Vertical Turbine Pump Installation

As explained previously, pumps are rated by the amount of work the pump can do in terms of "lifting" and "pushing" water. Thus, if the total dynamic suction lift required of a pump is reduced, the difference is added to the amount of "pushing" developed in the form of pressure.

This characteristic can be carried further. When water under pressure is forced into the inlet of a pump, the pressure of the incoming water is added to the discharge pressure of the pump. The preceding characteristic is utilized by all multi-stage pumps.

As an example, a pump is required that will provide a flow of 300 gpm at a dynamic discharge head of not less than 120 lb/in^2 (277.2 ft hd). A vertical turbine will be installed with a column pipe approximately 10 ft long. The column pipe is the pipe through which water is pumped from the top pump stage to discharge into the irrigation system main. Elevation of water supply is 1000 ft above sea level.

Note: Length of column pipe is cut to fit sump pit.

The pump engineer selected the pump with performance curve ② in Figure 6-24. This curve furnishes the best characteristics at a flow of 300 gpm, as follows:

Head (pressure) produced per stage: 71.0 ft
Npsh required: 16.0 ft
Horsepower required per stage: 6.8
Efficiency: 79%

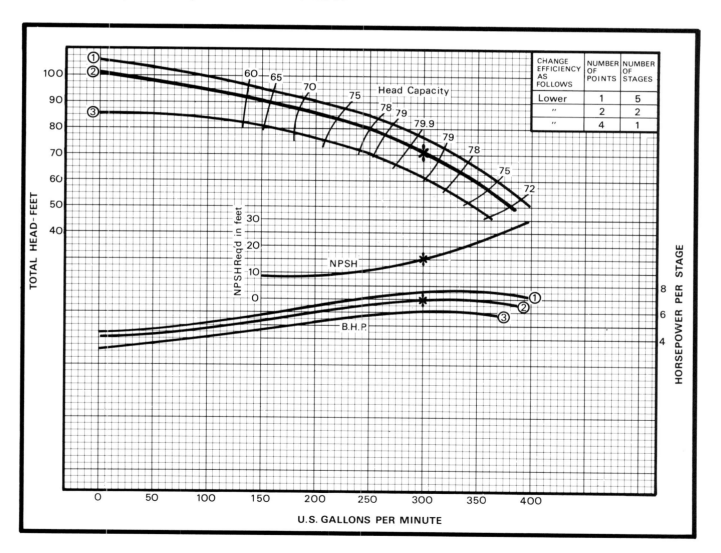

Figure 6-24 Performance Curves of One Model Vertical Turbine Pump

Pumps

ATMOSPHERIC PRESSURE: abs   32.7 ft hd
   Less vapor pressure   -   1.2
   Plus submergence: +   3.0
   NPSH of 16.0 ft satisfied by: abs   34.0 ft hd

    1st stage   gauge + 71.0 ft hd
    2nd stage   + 71.0 ft hd
    3rd stage   + 71.0 ft hd
    4th stage   + 71.0 ft hd

Dynamic Discharge Head (123.0 lb/in^2)   gauge   284.0 ft hd
less loss in pump column,
@ 6.4 ft hd/100 ft x .10:   -   0.7 ft*
Net Dynamic Discharge Head (122.7 lb/in^2) gauge 283.3 ft hd**

* Loss in column is insignificant and is normally ignored
  except for greater lengths that have a pronounced effect on
  pressure loss.

**Subject to adjustment for efficiency.

**Figure 6-25 Determination of Dynamic Discharge Head
for Multi-stage Pump**

Pressure that will be provided to the irrigation system is determined as shown in Figure 6-25.

Note: Npsh needs to be satisfied by atmospheric pressure and submergence only once for multi-stage vertical turbine pumps. Any unused atmospheric pressure is not added to dynamic total head when pump entrance is flooded.

Efficiency: Figure 6-24 also indicates reduction of pump efficiency from 79% to 78% with four stages. This affects Dynamic Total Head of pump or horsepower of motor required. The adjustment for reduction of efficiency was made as follows:

Total specified hp (6.8 hp per stage -- 4 stages)   27.2
Plus efficiency loss factor, approximately 1%   + 0.3
HORSEPOWER REQUIRED*   27.5
Or:
Dynamic Discharge Head   122.7 lb/in^2
Less efficiency loss factor, approximately 1%   - 1.2
Adjusted Dynamic Discharge Head   121.5 lb/in^2
Less loss in pump column   - 0.7
NET DISCHARGE HEAD*   (279.0 ft) 120.8 lb/in^2

* This data should be developed only by pump engineer for pump model being
  considered.

PUMP INLET

A bell-mouth entrance of a vertical turbine virtually eliminates entrance loss. This type pump is also available with a basket strainer below the entrance. However, strainers on the pump inlet may clog, at least partially, causing pressure problems.

INSTALLATION

Vertical turbine pumps require special installation techniques; particularly as concerns water supply to the pump.

PUMP PIT. The pump engineer should specify size and configuration of pump pit which varies with amount of water to be pumped and method of supply. Interior pit configuration must provide protection against excessive turbulence as water enters the pit.

WATER SOURCE. Figures 6-26 and 6-27 diagram two common methods of providing water to the pump pit.

Pipe Supply. Figure 6-26 illustrates an intake pipe from the lowest point in a pond to the pump pit. Pipe must be sized so that pressure loss for maximum required flow is non-existent for all practical purposes. The only pressure which can "push" the water is the head caused by height of water over the inlet, which is usually only a few feet.

Bottom of reservoir should be graded to reduce length of pipe as much as possible. With existing reservoirs, it is often advantageous to regrade for this purpose.

Inlet to pipe supply should be screened to eliminate large debris from entering intake. Screening can be similar to that illustrated for a basic pumping system in Figure 6-16. At least one manufacturer offers an alternative method for large projects to keep the end of the intake away from silt and debris at the bottom of the reservoir. A flexible hose is connected to the intake pipe from the pump pit. An intake screen is connected to the end of the reinforced hose and maintained at the desired location (off the bottom of the reservoir) with a float on the surface. Hose connection and float are similar to the intake shown in Figure 6-17.

DIRECT SUPPLY. Figure 6-27 illustrates a direct supply from the reservoir to the pump pit. This method provides the best supply. Removable screens should be installed at the entrance to the pit.

MULTIPLE PUMP SYSTEMS

Very large irrigation systems, requiring a substantial water supply, are usually supplied by multiple pump systems. These systems can incorporate centrifugal pumps with individual suction pipes or vertical turbine pumps using a single pit. Discharge pipes from the

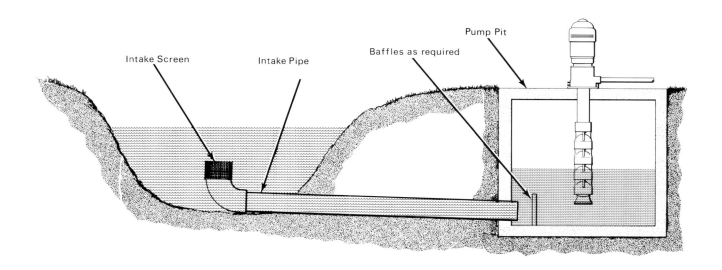

Figure 6-26 Pipe Supply to Vertical Turbine Pump Pit

pumps usually connect to a single irrigation system main.

A hydro-pneumatic system with a single pressure tank is most often used for control. Basics of multiple pump systems are the same as for single pump systems which have been reviewed in this chapter. Special aspects required are outlined below.

PUMP SIZING

A multiple pump system consists of one or more main pumps and a jockey pump. A typical system for an 18-hole golf course consists of two main pumps and a jockey pump. Larger systems may incorporate three or more main pumps and a jockey pump.

In a three pump system, each of the main pumps is usually sized to provide approximately one-half the maximum flow requirement for any irrigation system operation. As flow requirements change, the various pumps are automatically started or stopped by pressure switches maintaining pressure as programmed.

Multiple pump systems also provide back-up capability. If one of the main pumps fails, irrigation can still be continued for the most critical planting areas. For example, a golf course could continue watering greens while a malfunctioning pump is out of service.

The jockey pump serves several purposes.
1. Maintains pressure in the irrigation main at all times to prevent water hammer that occurs when water is pumped into empty lines.
2. Provides small flows without starting the main pumps, such as for deep-watering trees or newly-planted shrubbery with hoses.
3. Allows for special supplementary watering of selected zones without main pumps operating.
4. When flow requirement is more than can be supplied by one main pump, and not enough to require full capacity of both main pumps, one main pump and the jockey pump can often supply the requirement.

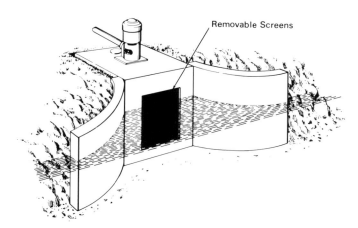

Figure 6-27 Direct Supply to Pump Pit

Pumps

CONTROL OF MULTIPLE PUMPS

Special controlling of multiple pump systems is required. When the irrigation system is turned on, water flows from the pressure tank; pressure reduces, and the pressure switch signals the pump controller to start pumps. A typical sequence of control follows:

1. Jockey pump starts.
2. If pressure cannot be maintained, main pump 1 starts and jockey pump is turned off.
3. If pressure still cannot be maintained, jockey pump is restarted.
4. If pressure still cannot be maintained, main pump 2 is started, operating in parallel with main pump 1 and jockey pump is stopped.
5. When flow requirements reduce, less pump capacity is required and the preceding sequence is reversed.

A pump controller which alternates sequence of main pump start is extremely desirable. Alternate starts balance wear of the pumps.

Switches are available which can be wired to provide the operation outlined above or any variation. Time delays should be wired into the circuits to allow pressure to stabilize before another pump is started or stopped. Pre-wired package pump controllers are available in cabinets for most desired pump sequences (Figure 6-28).

MANUFACTURED PUMPING STATIONS

Pre-engineered and pre-assembled water supply systems are available from several different manufacturers. These pump stations offer many design and installation advantages for large size irrigation systems.

Figure 6-28 Hydro-Pneumatic System with Multiple Pumps

Figure 6-29 Installed Pre-assembled Pump Station

Different models are available to cover typical requirements from a few hundred gpm to several thousand gpm.

Figure 6-29 illustrates a pre-assembled pump station installed over a vertical turbine pump-pit. In the pumping station shown, the water is pumped through the tank. Pumps discharge into the hydro-pneumatic surge-control tank and the tank discharges into an automatic control valve. Air in the tank is provided by the turbine pumps. This type of system must be properly designed to allow the air to separate and rise from the flow before entering the irrigation main. Excessive air in the tank is removed by an air release valve.

VARIABLE FREQUENCY DRIVE (VFD). Development of solid-state pump control technology has provided a new type of pumping station that does not require a hydro-pneumatic tank and a pressure regulating valve.

Pressure in the discharge pipe is maintained by using an electronic control system to vary the speed of the pump (pressure output of a centrifugal type pump is related to the impeller diameter and speed of rotation). In most cases, only one pump of a multiple pump station is controlled by variable frequency drive. Additional pumps operate at a fixed speed.

Motor speed of the VFD pump is changed by varying the frequency of alternating current (A/C). An electronic pressure sensor (transducer) is connected to the computer controller. The controller determines the speed requirement and regulates the pump motor speed through a frequency inverter.

Additional cost and concerns about service are disadvantages associated with VFD pump stations. However, VFD pump control systems are more efficient than conventional control systems, and cost difference may be recovered within a few years due to power savings.

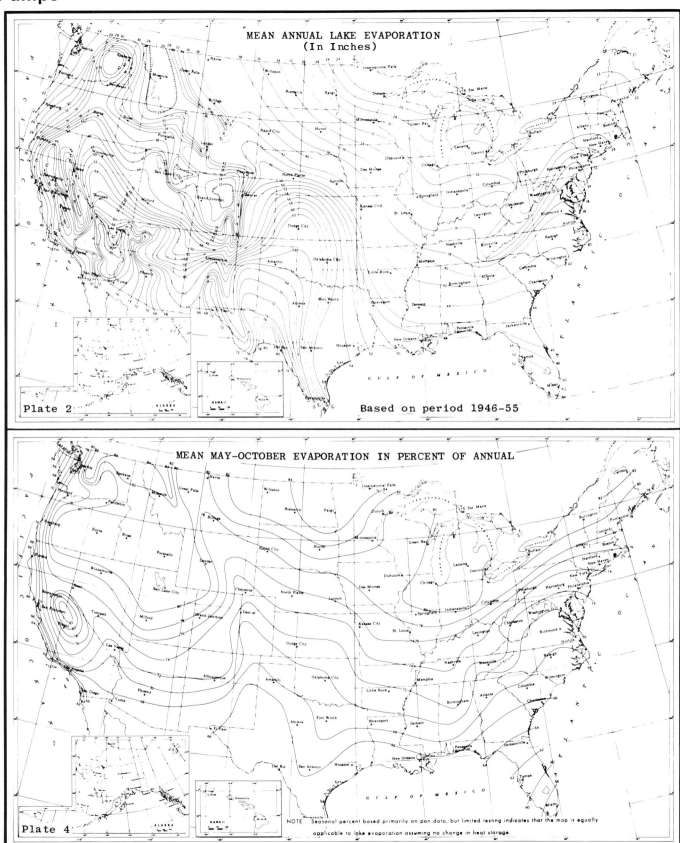

Figure 6-30 Mean Lake Evaporation
(From: Weather Bureau Technical Paper No. 37, prepared by Hydrologic Services Division, Office of Hydrology)

WATER STORAGE

Reservoirs must be of sufficient volume to supply the maximum requirements. Irrigation systems cannot be designed to adequately irrigate with a water supply less than that required.

When natural water reservoirs (lakes, ponds, rivers, etc.) are not available, construction of a reservoir should include considerations for conservation of impounded water.

Ecologists recommend reservoirs with large surface areas so that withdrawing water does not lower the level enough to expose the banks to any extent. However, this approach requires storage of greater amounts of water because water loss due to evaporation is directly proportional to the surface area.

WATER EVAPORATION

Evaporation[b][c] is the natural process of changing water into vapor. The rate of evaporation depends on the temperature of the water, the temperature of the air that is in contact with the water, the amount of water vapor already in the air and velocity of the wind. Dry air has a greater capacity for absorbing moisture. Hence, evaporation increases as humidity decreases. Wind increases evaporation from water surfaces by replacing moist air with dried air moving in from a distance. Evaporation also increases as temperature increases.

Figure 6-30 shows average evaporation in the United States. While this information serves as an alert to the consequences of evaporation, more detailed local data should be obtained. For example, the map indicates an average of 45 inches evaporation at Amarillo, Texas. Thus, an average of 7.5 inches per month is indicated. However, more detailed local data showed losses varied in the five month period of May to September from over 7 inches in September to a maximum of over 11 inches in July.

Local data is usually available from one of the state universities. This data, applied to a reservoir at Amarillo, for example, indicates that the average loss by evaporation during the month of July per acre of water surface is 298,696 gal or 9,635 gal per day. Thus, if water surface is halved and depth of water doubled, water storage capacity remains the same but loss by evaporation is reduced by 50 percent.

a.

b.

c.

Courtesy Staff Industries, Inc.

Figure 6-31 Lining Beds of Reservoirs with Plastic Film

Pumps

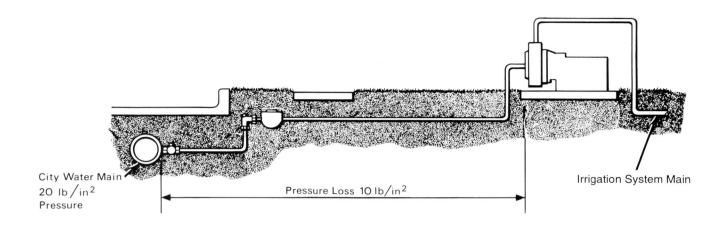

City Water Main
20 lb/in^2
Pressure

Pressure Loss 10 lb/in^2

Irrigation System Main

Figure 6-32 Booster Pump Installation

WATER LOSS BY SEEPAGE

Loss of water from reservoirs by seepage into the earth can be considerable. This is particularly true of man-made lakes. Loss by seepage will, of course, vary with type of soil; loss is greater in sandy soils than in clay-type soils.

Seepage can be virtually eliminated by lining the reservoir with plastic film. This technique is now well established. Figure 6-31 illustrates lining of lakes with vinyl film; note that pictures are not of the same project.

BOOSTER PUMPS

Booster pumps are used when the existing pressure in a water supply is insufficient to offset all losses in the system piping and provide adequate pressure at the irrigation outlets. These pumps are ordinary centrifugal pumps. The function of booster pumps, as the name implies, is to boost an existing pressure to a higher pressure with a given flow.

Booster pumps utilize the inherent characteristic of centrifugal pumps described when multi-stage pumps were discussed earlier in this chapter.

SIZING BOOSTER PUMPS

Figure 6-32 diagrams a simple booster pump installation. Pressure in city water main is 20 lb/in^2 and pressure loss from city main with a flow of 50 gpm is 10 lb/in^2, leaving 10 lb/in^2 pressure at the pump. Irrigation system requirements are 50 gpm at 40 lb/in^2 from the pump.

Pump is sized to provide a 10% safety factor for both flow and pressure.

Final pump requirements are then 55 gpm at a pressure of:

System pressure requirement	44.0 lb/in^2 (40 + 10% = 44)
Less residual city pressure	10.0
Pump Requirement	34.0 lb/in^2

Note: In the case of booster pumps the inlet is under positive pressure. Therefore, npsh is generally not a factor but must be considered by the pump engineer.

Caution: Many potable water distribution systems (city or otherwise) do not permit direct connected booster pumps. Always check with the authorities beforehand.

SPECIAL APPLICATIONS

Booster pumps can provide the solution to unusual pressure design problems. This can best be illustrated by a composite example. Assume that two holes of a golf course are at a considerably higher elevation than the balance of the course. And, to provide enough pressure to offset this extra elevation, abnormally high pressures would be required in the piping of the sprinkler system for the other sixteen holes.

In this case, basic design pressure requirements would ignore the two holes at the higher elevation. A single pipe would branch from the sprinkler main to supply the system for the two holes. A booster pump would then be installed in the branch main to provide additional pressure. A flow switch would also be installed in the branch main to control pump operation.

Whenever any zone control valves are opened at the higher elevation, the resulting flow would cause the flow switch to start the pump. When flow ceases, the booster pump is stopped.

Flow switches can also be used to operate booster pumps that are connected to domestic water supplies.

CONCLUSION

Pumps with weather-proof electric motors are available at relatively small additional cost. These pumps allow installation without protection from rain.

Pumps without weather-proof motors must be installed in a pump-house or other building for protection. Smaller, volute-type centrifugal pumps are often installed with a removable sheet metal housing placed over the pump. Housing must be well louvered to provide adequate ventilation for the motor.

BIBLIOGRAPHY

(a) Hydraulic Institute Standards
Hydraulic Institute
122 East 42nd Street
New York, NY 10017

(b)"Evaporation from Pans and Lakes"
Research Paper No. 38
by Hydrologic Services Division,
U.S. Weather Bureau, 1955

(c)"Water Evaporation Studies in Texas"
Bulletin 787 by Texas Agricultural Station
Texas Agricultural Extension Service
in cooperation with the Texas
Board of Water Engineers and the
U.S. Department of Agriculture

PARTIAL LIST OF SPECIAL EQUIPMENT SOURCES

ACCESSORY CONTROL SWITCHES

The Mercoid Corporation
4201 Belmont Avenue
Chicago, IL 60641

Seaflow Inc.
P.O. Box 1589
Kent, WA 98035

AUTOMATIC AIR VENTS

Valve and Primer Corporation (APCO)
1420 South Wright
Roselle, IL 60172

Armstrong Machine Works
Three Rivers, MI 49093

AUTOMATIC WATER LEVEL CONTROLS FOR PNEUMATIC TANKS

Nu-Matic Company
P.O. Box 1325
Newport Beach, CA

PLASTIC FILM RESERVOIR LINING

Staff Industries, Inc.
78 Dryden Rd.
Upper Montclair, New Jersey 07043

MANUFACTURED PUMPING STATIONS

Flowtronex PSI
10717 Harry Hines
Dallas, TX 75220

Carroll Childers Co.
P.O. Box 12951
Houston, TX 77017

PRESSURE REDUCING AND PRESSURE RELIEF VALVES

Cla-Val Co.
P.O. Box 1325
Newport Beach, CA 92663

PRE-WIRED PACKAGE PUMPING CONTROLLERS

Well-Guard
Square D Company

Pumps

1601 Mercer Rd.
Lexington, KY 40405

Frank W. Murphy Manufacturer
P.O. Box 470248
Tulsa, Oklahoma 74147

SUCTION PIPING/FLOATS/SCREENS

Greenscape Pump Services
556 Coppell Road
Coppell, TX 75019

CHAPTER 7

Source Water And Filtration

The source water for a landscape irrigation system can be from a potable or non-potable water supply, or a combination of both. The need for water conservation in many regions of the world has resulted in a rapid increase in the use of recycled water for irrigation. Regardless of the water source, the systems designer must consider the limitations and general requirements associated with the use of a water supply.

Quantity, quality and cost of available water, and applicable governmental regulations must be determined before an irrigation system can be designed for any property. Any one of these variable factors can prevent, alter or limit to some degree, the development of an irrigation system.

Total volume of water required during a given time period (day, week, etc.) is normally only considered when estimating the cost of water or water storage requirements, or for water conservation considerations (as desired or required by law). System development and operation is always limited by the maximum flow rate (combination of volume and time) available for a particular project.

Maximum flow rate may be due to:
1. Standard design practice limitations -- new or existing supplies.
2. Limitations of existing supplies as discussed in Chapter 3, Determining Capacity of Existing Pipe Systems.
3. Actual limitations or cost considerations of a new water supply.
4. Limitations of flow (or volume) as established by governmental regulations -- new or existing supplies.

Water quality is an important consideration for all water supplies, including potable water supplies. A water suitability analysis may indicate that the supply is not suitable for landscape irrigation, or that the water should only be used to irrigate certain types of tolerant plants.

Some city water supplies in the U.S.A. have a total salt content that is fairly substantial. When this water is used for landscape irrigation, systems must be designed to avoid water application to the foliage of broad leaf plant material. Soil amendments may also be necessary with some types of soil. In most cases, excess amounts of water will be required to minimize the tendency of soluble salts to accumulate in the root zone.

Water quality must be associated with the intended use of the water. However, in landscape irrigation, the suitability of the water for planting material is not the only concern for the systems designer. In some cases, an unpleasant odor or staining of building walls, fences and paved areas can be a problem due to minerals in solution.

In all cases, adequate protection and warnings should be included when a non-potable water supply is used for the irrigation system. This includes the use of products with color-coded components for non-potable alert.

Recycled Water. The use of recycled water is an accepted principle of water conservation. In semi-arid or arid regions of the world, it is necessary or at least desirable to use a limited supply of water for more than one purpose. However, in most climate regions, the use of recycled water as a source of supply for a landscape irrigation system is limited for practical reasons.

Source Water and Filtration

Figure 7-1 Sprinkler System Operating at a Sewage Treatment Plant

The intelligent use of water must include the best methods available from modern technology, but application of methods must also include consideration for limitations that may exist at the site or as may be established by the property owner, or governmental authority. Examples of common limitations and considerations for landscape irrigation systems are provided below:

1. Requirement of a waste collection, treatment (if necessary), storage and pumping system at the site.
2. Make-up water or separate systems, as may be required if recycled supply is not adequate for maximum irrigation water requirement.
3. Irrigation limitations due to water quality and/or soil conditions.
4. Waste water systems will impose additional cost and liability.
5. Systems must conform to all local, state and federal laws relating to the use of recycled water. Although necessary for health and protection of the environment, laws may not allow the use of recycled water in some cases, or requirements may make the use of recycled water impractical for a particular project.

Gray Water. In some regions, the use of gray water is allowed for landscape irrigation, but only when guidelines for safety are followed by the systems designer and the property owner.

Gray water is the "untreated" waste water from various acceptable household sources such as showers, bath tubs, bathroom sinks, and the washing machine.

These water sources, if properly used, can be recycled for some landscape irrigation requirements.

The building plumbing system must provide collection and separation of usable gray water from unacceptable waste water. Untreated waste water from toilets, dishwashers, garbage disposals, kitchen sinks and utility sinks is unacceptable for irrigation.

For safety, gray water is normally only released underground. Using gray water does carry the potential risk of transmission of disease-causing organisms. Fruits and vegetables which come in direct contact with gray water should not be eaten.

Landscape irrigators should not design, install, alter or service any type of system that uses recycled water (treated or untreated) unless the design, installation and use of the water is specifically allowed by local and state laws, and approved by public health departments.

Treated Waste Water. Irrigation can be part of a waste water reclamation project for private or public land when adequate quantities of water will be available at or near the site. Source water is treated so that water does not create problems for wildlife, fish and other aspects of the environment. Sewage effluent which has been subjected to secondary treatment and chlorination is generally considered as the minimum acceptable effluent for landscape irrigation.

In most cases, an attractive landscape is a secondary benefit, as the primary purpose of the irrigation system is to disperse water over the land for additional water treatment that occurs when water percolates down through soil. Large projects of this type, including the irrigation system design, are controlled by engineering firms that specialize in waste water engineering and management. All water reclamation projects, large and small, must conform to all applicable codes and environmental laws relating to the use of water.

FILTRATION

The designer must consider many different categories of protection when designing an irrigation system, including the protection of individual components in the system. Foreign matter in the water supply is one of the primary causes of irrigation equipment malfunction. In many cases, filtration of the source water is necessary to prevent the damaging effects of dissolved and

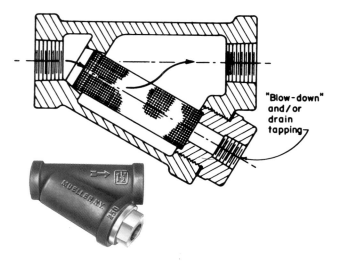

Typical Screwed "Y" Type Strainer

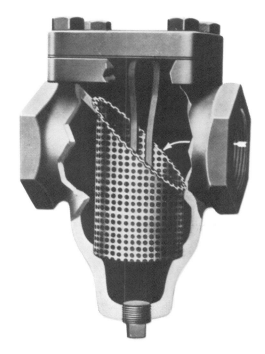

Typical "Basket" Type Strainer

Courtesy Muessco

Figure 7-2 Types of Strainers

suspended solids which can clog water outlets, damage components or cause failure of moving parts.

Foreign matter enters an irrigation system during installation or service, or from a "dirty" water supply. Un-wanted foreign particles that enter the piping system during installation or service should be removed by proper flushing of the piping system. Note: Follow procedures of flushing lines as recommended for different types of equipment. Example: Piping of rotary systems should be flushed before heads are connected to pipe risers.

Source water that contains suspended particles will be a constant problem for an irrigation system unless contaminants are removed from the water supply. Common sources of contamination include:

Potable city water supplies.
1. Flaking of rust particles from inside cast iron and steel pipe.
2. Sand particles. A common problem when source of city supply is ground water.

Raw water supplies.
1. Sand pumped from wells or any other water source.
2. Leaves, sticks, weeds, peat moss, algae, etc. pumped from pond, lake and river sources.

Sandy water causes a multitude of problems. The more troublesome are fouled orifices, eroded orifices, sticking sprinklers, sticking valves, frozen bearings, and accelerated wear.

Installation and service-introduced contaminants can only be eliminated by good workmanship. Source water contaminants must be removed by filtration.

STRAINERS/FILTERS
A strainer is a simple protective device to remove unwanted particles from a fluid. A filter may be similar or more complex, and may include different types of filter media. In general, a filter is considered to be a more precise type of device to remove particles above a critical size. These definitions are not adequate to distinguish the difference between the limited types of strainers and filters discussed in this chapter. Many irrigators use a simple rule, if the screening device is "fine" to remove very small particles, it is a filter and if the screen is "coarse", it is a strainer. However, for practical purposes, strainers and filters are used as interchangeable terms in this text to describe the same type of general filtration products.

Source Water and Filtration

Courtesy of Argricultural Products Inc.

Figure 7-3 Typical Wye Filter for Individual Operating Zones

Screen openings are usually specified by "mesh" or "micrometre" (m)(1) size. See Engineering Data Table No. 29 for relationship of these terms and the relationship to inches.

Many brands and models of strainers are not available with fine mesh sizes as required for some types of irrigation systems, or as necessary for the filter definition using the above general rule. Strainer mesh sizes "in stock" at supply stores may or may not provide adequate protection for some water supplies and some types of irrigation equipment.

A strainer should always be used with any raw water supply. Additional fine mesh filters may also be required for the system or individual zone requirements. Micro-irrigation zones should always have a filter, regardless of the type of water supply. A fine mesh "wye" filter for individual zones is shown in Figure 7-3. Filtration requirements of micro-irrigation systems are discussed in Chapter 13.

Pump intake pipes must also include a strainer. However, these are required to keep large size debris out of the pump station and are not sized for irrigation water quality requirements. See Chapter 6, Suction Intake.

PRODUCT SELECTION. Products discussed in this chapter are primarily used for system protection by removing suspended solids. This equipment will not remove contaminants in solution. Additional methods of filtration may be necessary with some water supplies and/or types of irrigation equipment.

---

(1) The "Micrometre" was formally known as the "Micron." This latter term is still in common use.

The ultimate selection of a product should be made only after considering its capability to screen out the expected particulates, the loss of pressure it will cause and the amount of maintenance it will require. Although product cost must be considered, low cost products will not result in savings if the product does not provide the necessary filtration to minimize problems in the irrigation system.

Pressure losses through strainers and filters vary:
1. With flow rate.
2. With mesh size. Pressure loss increases as the mesh size decreases.
3. With the ratio of the screen area to its pipe area; the larger the ratio, the less pressure loss. Generally, a "basket" type unit will have a larger ratio than a "wye" type.
4. With the amount of strainer clogging.
5. With make and model of strainer product.

Pressure loss tables furnished by manufacturers are generally for clean strainers and standard screen mesh. For finer mesh screens, request the manufacturer provide multiplying factors to use with the standard pressure loss data. Rate of pressure loss increases due to clogging is generally available too, and should be considered when designing a system. Do not use data of one manufacturer for another manufacturer's product.

Note: As strainers increase in size, their cost is usually disproportional to smaller sizes. Quite often, manifolding two smaller strainers will be less expensive than a single large strainer, without any greater total pressure loss.

INSTALLATION. Equipment must be installed so that the screen element is readily accessible and removable for periodic cleaning. "Basket" strainers are usually easiest to clean because the screen-basket is designed for removal from the top.

The "Y" or "wye" type strainer screen is removed from the bottom; consequently, the strainer must be installed in a way to allow for removing the screen. This type of strainer requires the removal of a full sized plug first. A large wrench is required in most cases.

The recommended method of installing both types of strainers is "above-ground" as diagrammed in Figure 7-4. Screen removal is much simpler with this method. Above-ground installation also permits certain other

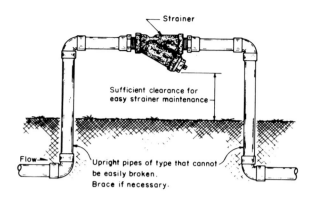

Figure 7-4 Recommended Strainer Installation

refinements which simplify maintenance. These will be discussed later.

Note: Installation recommendations are somewhat different for filters in micro-irrigation systems, see Chapter 13.

CLEANING. The frequency of cleaning must be timed to coincide with the rapidity of clogging, at least. It should be noted that there is no "average" cleaning frequency; requirements vary with the kind and amount of contaminants in a given volume of water.

Screens cannot be cleaned too often. Some types of contaminants become more difficult to remove the longer they are left on the screen. The ideal method would be to clean the screens after every watering cycle.

The cleaning schedule, if not properly programmed, can cause as many other problems as the strainer eliminates. Since the build-up of contaminants on the screen is gradual, the increase of pressure loss through the strainer is also gradual and progressive. This is hazardous, because at a certain point the pressure loss will still allow the system to operate even though coverage may be inadequate. The operator may not realize this condition has developed until visible planting material damage has already occurred.

The installation of two pressure gauges, one on either side of the strainer, is well worth the cost; see Figure 7-5. They enable the operator to monitor the gauges and clean the strainer when the pressure differential reaches a predetermined limit. Since the designer must allow for pressure loss of a partially clogged strainer, the allowable pressure differential is known.

IMPORTANT! Use gauges marked with the smallest increments possible.

Cleaning strainers on a frequency schedule, or even on a pressure differential basis, has a serious drawback since there are times when the water supply will be "dirtier" than usual, and a regular cleaning program cannot take this into account. Some examples are:

1. Heavy rains cause supply sources such as ponds, lakes and streams to become unusually turbid.
2. During drought periods, the water level in wells may drop causing an increase in the amount of sand pumped with the water.
3. Work on city water mains will dislodge rust, scale, etc. from the inside of the pipe which can be carried into the irrigation system.

Cleaning by "Blow-down." Cleaning can be greatly simplified by using a strainer designed for "blow-down." This is a method of washing contaminants off the screen and out of the strainer through a "dump" valve. A "basket" type strainer is easiest to install for this type operation. However, they are usually not readily available and may be quite expensive as compared to "Y" strainers.

Strainer cleaning by "blow-down" should never be attempted with a strainer not specifically designed for this purpose.

IMPORTANT! Successful washing of debris from the screen by "blow-down" depends to a large extent on the velocity of the water washing across the screen. Therefore, blow-down should never be initiated when the

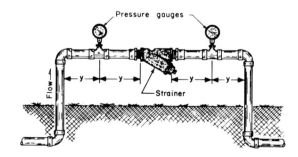

"Y" equals not less than 6 times pipe diameter.

Figure 7-5 Pressure Gauges Installed with Strainer

Source Water and Filtration

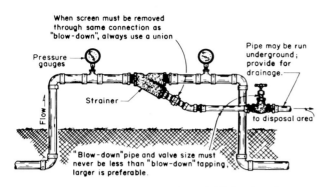

Figure 7-6 Typical Installation of "Y" Strainer for "Blow-down" Cleaning

system is operating. The entire water flow should be directed across the screen.

Although smaller screen area will affect pressure loss and frequency of cleaning, oversize units may be a problem due to low "flush" velocity. With manual or automatic flush filter systems, consideration must be given to the flow velocity that is necessary to flush contaminants from the screen.

Automatic Strainer Blow-down. With automated irrigation systems, strainers can be flushed automatically, if designed for blow-down. An electric operating valve is installed in the blow-down line. The valve is then wired to the first unused station of the irrigation controller. Thus, at the end of every watering cycle, the valve is automatically opened and the screen is flushed for a pre-set length of time.

When extremely dirty water is encountered, wiring the blow-down valve to a station midway through the watering cycle will provide more frequent cleaning and consequently less build-up of pressure loss through the strainer.

The length of strainer wash-time is determined by how quickly the screen is cleaned. In order to determine controller station time setting, gauges should be installed with the strainer to judge the time and pressure differential relationship.

Maintenance. When relying on blow-down cleaning, preventive maintenance is essential. The screening element should be removed and inspected periodically. At the first sign of deterioration, or damage, replace the screen. Monthly inspection would not be too often.

ALGAE AND PEAT MOSS. In most cases, algae and peat moss cannot be successfully removed from strainer screens by blow-down. Blades of grass may also be a problem. An analysis of algae, peat moss and straining is contained in the "CONCLUSION" of "STRAINERS" segment of this chapter.

MESH SIZE CONSIDERATIONS. Screen mesh size should be carefully considered with regard to the needs of irrigation equipment being used in the system. Obviously, all particles that are equal to or larger than the smallest outlet orifice must be removed from the water supply. In practice, all particles larger than a percentage (example: 20%) of the smallest orifice size should be removed by filtration.

In many cases, automatic control valves (including contamination resistant type) and/or sprinklers (especially rotary type) may require a smaller mesh size than the smallest outlet orifice.

The following example information on comparisons is provided to illustrate practical considerations that may be necessary when selecting the mesh size for a particular project:

1. A 60 mesh (250 m, 0.0098 in) strainer for a hypothetical system will eliminate an estimated 50% of maintenance problems caused by dirty water.
2. A 120 mesh (125 m, 0.0049 in) strainer will eliminate an estimated 90%.
3. A 325 mesh (45 m, 0.0017 in) strainer will eliminate an estimated 99%.

Assuming the exact mesh size requirement (or recommendation) is not known for products in the example system above, the 120 mesh strainer may be the most practical choice. This is based on the limited information of rough percentage estimates for only three different mesh sizes.

The 325 mesh size may not be worth the extra costs involved, both direct and indirect. Indirect costs include higher pressure losses and more rapid clogging which affect system cost and strainer maintenance cost. In addition, the added protection may not be required in this example.

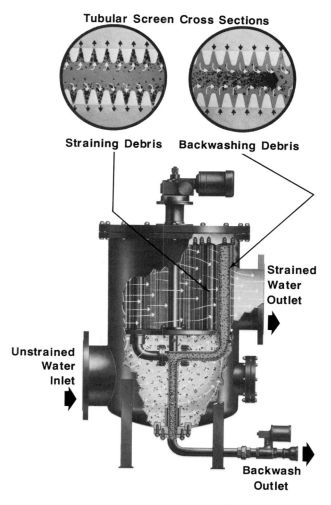

Tubular Screen Cross Sections

Straining Debris | **Backwashing Debris**

Strained Water Outlet

Unstrained Water Inlet

Backwash Outlet

Courtesy of R.P. Adams

Figure 7-7 Adams "Poro-Edge" Automatic Self-Cleaning Strainer

ormal mesh size for micro-irrigation systems is in the 100 to 200 mesh range. Some products will require 200 plus mesh size.

Information on filter requirements should be obtained from the manufacturer or product distributor of the irrigation equipment being used. In most cases, manufacturer's recommendation for micro-irrigation products will be included in the product catalog.

AUTOMATIC SELF-CLEANING STRAINERS

Automatic self-cleaning strainers are units which go through a complete cleaning cycle, using some of the fluid flowing through the strainer to flush out the col-

lected debris, with little or no attention by maintenance personnel.

Automatic strainers are recommended for large irrigation systems using contaminated water supplies operating for long periods of time unattended.

ADVANTAGES. Automatic strainers are normally more expensive than the manually cleaned units but the extra cost can usually be justified for one or more of the following reasons:

1. The frequency of cleaning of a manual unit and the cost of labor for doing this may often offset the extra cost of the automatic strainer.
2. If there is any danger the strainer or the equipment it is protecting may be damaged because the strainer is not cleaned when required.
3. Manual cleaning cannot be properly scheduled because clogging of the strainer is unpredictable due to a variable loading rate.
4. Insufficient available personnel to perform the manual cleaning.
5. The cost of cleaning irrigation equipment and flushing the piping of a large sprinkler system with a "dirty" water supply and improper straining can approach, or exceed, the cost of an automatic strainer during just one irrigation season.

TYPES OF AUTOMATIC SELF-CLEANING STRAINERS. Figures 7-7 and 7-8 are examples of some basic types of automatic self-cleaning strainers.

Figure 7-7. Raw water enters into this unit from the bottom flowing into tubular strainer screens mounted in a circle in the upper housing. The water is strained as it flows through the trapezoidal wire tubes on the way to the outlet of the unit.

Each tube is cleaned -- one at a time -- in consecutive order as a backwash arm rotates over the ends of the tubes. As the backwash arm passes over each tube, entry of raw water is closed at the bottom. Strained water then flows in reverse through the screen to wash it. Since the reverse flow is to atmosphere, full water pressure is utilized for washing.

Straining down to 125 microns (approximately 0.005 in) is available. However, the manufacturer recommends screen apertures not less than 0.010 in for types of water pumped to irrigation systems since particles re-

Source Water and Filtration

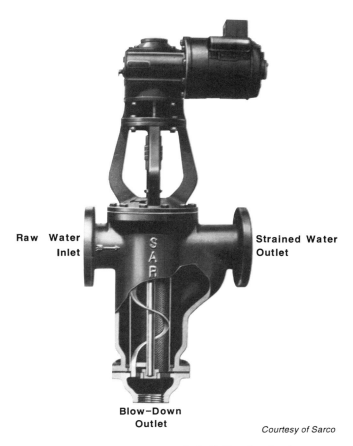

Raw Water Inlet

Strained Water Outlet

Blow-Down Outlet

Courtesy of Sarco

Figure 7-8 Sarco Automatic Self-Cleaning Strainer

tained in this type screen provide a smaller straining effect.

Initial pressure loss through the unit can be less than 2 lb/in^2. The unit can be programmed so that an additional 2 lb/in^2 pressure loss due to screen clogging will activate a back washing cycle.

Figure 7-8. The strainer shown in this illustration depends primarily on a scraper to clean the screen. Raw water flows into the strainer element from the top, then through the element to the outlet connection. The spiral blade, driven by an electric motor, scrapes the inside of the screen. Debris collects in the sump at the bottom which requires periodic flushing. Nylon or wire brush type rotors are available.

Continuous scraper rotation during irrigation system operation provides the best results. This can be accomplished several ways:

1. Irrigation system controller(s) energize the motor drive whenever a zone is being operated.
2. A "flow switch" installed in the discharge will activate the motor whenever flow occurs.
3. With pump systems, the scraper motor can be wired to operate whenever the pump operates.

Periodic, automatic blow-down will also help to clean the screen. Automatic control equipment for blow-down is not available as an integral part of this unit. However, such controls are easily obtained. See also "Types of Control" for Automatic Self-Cleaning Strainers.

Screens are available for straining down to 100 m (approximately 0.004 in).

Pressure loss with a clean screen is determined by sizing of strainer unit.

This "scraper" strainer is also available in a manual model in sizes 3/4 in through 10 in illustrated in Figure 7-8.

TYPES OF CONTROL. There are many types of automatic controls for strainers; among these are:

1. Pressure differential switches which sense the pressure drop through the strainer and initiate a cleaning cycle at a preset pressure differential.
2. Timer which initiates cleaning cycle of strainer at preset intervals or times.
3. Pushbutton start for which an operator pushes a button to initiate a cleaning cycle.
4. Differential pressure switch alarms which signal the operator that the strainer needs cleaning.
5. Any combination of the above controls.

GENERAL: AUTOMATIC SELF-CLEANING STRAINERS. Several factors must be considered when designing irrigation systems incorporating automatic self-cleaning strainers:

1. Automatic backwash or blow-down uses a considerable amount of water. Therefore, if these cycles are controlled by pressure differential, water supply must be sized to provide sufficient flow for system operation plus the flow required for cleaning. Otherwise, the irrigation system would not have enough pressure to operate satisfactorily during the cleaning cycle.

A.

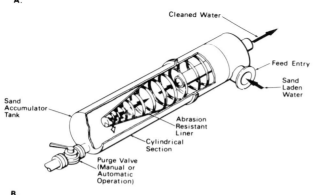

Cleaned Water

Feed Entry

Sand Laden Water

Sand Accumulator Tank

Abrasion Resistant Liner

Cylindrical Section

Purge Valve (Manual or Automatic Operation)

B.

Courtesy of Krebs Engineers

Figure 7-9 Krebs Engineers Desander, Model KCSS

The cleaning cycle of each of the two backwash type strainers reviewed requires 2 to 3 minutes, average. Thus, if the cleaning cycle occurs during the operation of a zone with short duration time, the zone would not be sufficiently watered.

2. System should be designed to maintain possible water hammer below the level that could result in damage to the strainer.

3. Excessive clogging can occur in strainers due to malfunction or due to type of contaminant. This is particularly true of material that tends to entwine in the screens, resisting removal by backwash or blow-down. Such materials include algae, peat moss, weeds, etc.

Excessive clogging can cause pressure loss through the strainer, reducing system pressure enough to cause deficient operation. In addition, if the strainer cannot clean itself sufficiently to reduce the loss to below that programmed into a pressure differential automatic control, the unit will continue to operate a cleaning cycle until the water supply is discontinued. Therefore, a safety device to signal when such a condition exists is recommended.

Relatively inexpensive auxiliary controls are available for situations such as the above which will provide any or all of the following or similar functions:

    a. Turn on a signal lamp if pressure loss exceeds allowable amount programmed into the pressure differential control for a predetermined length of time.

    b. Turn on a signal lamp and shut-off pump(s) supplying the system if excessive loss continues for a predetermined length of time, or exceeds pressure loss by a selected amount.

    c. Some strainer manufacturers can provide these, and other, additional controls as a part of the overall package. If not, such controls are easily obtained.

Automatic self-cleaning strainers should not be considered as "off-the-shelf" merchandise. When requesting a quotation, furnish the manufacturer with all criteria. Information required includes range of flows, pressure loss allowable, type and size of particles to be strained from the water, etc. To their credit, many manufacturers will not quote without full product application information.

CONCLUSION: STRAINERS/FILTERS

Certain general information regarding use of strainers with irrigation systems follows.

PUMP SUCTION. Use of standard type strainers in pump suction piping is not recommended because this portion of the pumping plant is most critical; see Chapter 6, Pumps: Suction. The main reason is the limited amount of pressure that can be lost in the suction piping.

Do not rely entirely on a strainer to remove debris from water pumped from ponds, lakes, rivers, etc.

Even though a filter will be used in the supply to the irrigation system, always provide a screen at the suction intake to remove larger debris; see Chapter 6, Pumps: Suction Intake.

Source Water and Filtration

"STRINGY" MATERIAL. Materials of a "stringy" nature sometimes entwine into the screen elements, making them difficult or impossible to remove by backwash or blow-down. At the same time, this type material can cause problems with operation of irrigation equipment if allowed to enter the system. Screens must be removed from the strainer body and hand-cleaned, often frequently, in addition to other methods of cleaning.

Peat Moss. The "stringy" nature of peat moss varies in degree. Normally, most of it can be brushed from screens after drying.

Algae.[b] Only algae is more difficult than peat moss to remove from strainer screens. Unless the water source has been treated, algae is alive and it will, therefore, "grow" into the screen making it virtually impossible to remove by normal methods.

About the only successful method of removing live algae from strainer screens is to remove the element and soak it in a weak solution of acid. Consult with the manufacturer as to strength and kind of acid that can be used with the unit. When such procedure is necessary, spare screens should be stocked for continued use of the strainer while a screen is being cleaned.

Growth of algae can be prevented (or at least retarded) by application of copper sulfate to the water source. Caution: Do not apply or recommend the use of any type of chemical, regardless of the amount, to the water supply unless the chemical and measured amount (dosage) is approved for the particular application by the manufacturer and allowed by governmental regulations. Generally, dead algae can be removed from strainer screens by normal methods.

Note: Algae can also be controlled in a lake or pond by using aeration to add oxygen.

WELLS

As previously stated, water quality is an important consideration for all water supplies. In some cases, water from an aquifer will require treatment or may not be suitable for irrigation.

Wells are often used as the only source of water. They are sometimes used as a supplemental supply when the prime source is a small lake or pond. In either case, it is best to pump well water into the lake or a holding tank. Separate pumps are then used to operate the sprinkler system. This method provides better control of the water supply to the system and may be as economical as pumping directly from the well to the system.

Water from wells is normally clean except that considerable sand is often pumped. Removal of sand from the water at the well-head by pumping into a holding tank reduces or eliminates straining when the water is pumped into the irrigation system. The tank should be covered to prevent other debris from falling into it.

Pressure loss through strainers installed at the well-head when pumping into a holding tank is not as critical as when the strainer is installed in the irrigation main. This is because discharge pressure of the well pump is immaterial when discharging into a lake, holding tank, etc., provided flow is sufficient.

HOLDING TANKS

Reservoirs used to store water pumped from another source until pumped into a system are called by many names. For simplicity, this manual uses the term "Holding Tanks." These tanks are used with "dirty" water supplies to reduce demand on strainers installed in the main piping to irrigation systems. The irrigation system pumps draw water from the holding tank rather than directly from the water source.

Another use of holding tanks is when pumping from an extremely "dirty" water source where debris can obstruct the suction pipe of the pump(s). In these cases, a special pump is used to pump from the water source into the holding tank from which other pumps draw water for the irrigation system.

The pump used to supply the holding tank is commonly called a "contractor's pump." It is a diaphragm pump which handles large volumes of water at very low head, can pass relatively large debris, and does not require "priming."

When a holding tank is used for receiving very dirty water, the tank is divided by several removable screens of varying sized mesh. Water pumped into the tank flows through these screens to the suction of the irrigation system pump(s). The water flows through the largest mesh first with each subsequent screen having a smaller mesh. A typical set of screens is $3/8$, $1/4$, $1/5$ and $1/16$ in mesh.

Screens in the holding tank should be cleaned at a frequency determined by observation.

For a water supply like that being discussed, complete straining in the tank is not normally attempted. Further straining is completed by a strainer on the discharge side of the main pump.

Holding tanks vary in size according to the pumping capacity. A rule-of-thumb is to size the tank to hold at least 10 times the maximum flow requirement for the system. For example, if maximum flow requirement is 500 gal/min then tank volume would be at least 5000 gal: 500 x 10 = 5000.

Supply to the holding tank must be controlled to match rate of withdrawal. When the water source is a lake, pond, or such, the controlling can be simplified by utilizing an overflow pipe from the tank back to the source.

SEPARATORS

Separators, often called "Desanders" or "Sand Separators", are used primarily for the removal of sand from water. These units will also remove scale and many other materials with a specific gravity greater than water. Figure 7-9a shows a large volume unit being used to remove sand in water from a well.

Although configurations vary from one brand to another, Figure 7-9b illustrates the principle by which desanders remove particles. There are no moving parts. Inlet design produces a spiral flow of the entering water. As the water spirals through the unit, high centrifugal forces push the sand toward the cylinder wall. Sand particles then progress in a spiral path to an integral accumulator chamber. The manufacturer of the illustrated unit claims high collection efficiency and that, even at low pressure drops, separation of 95% of sand coarser than 200 mesh (74 m, 0.003 in) is common.

The solids collected in the accumulator must be purged periodically, either manually or automatically. A simple, efficient automatic purge can be provided by the irrigation controller. With this method, an electric valve is opened about one minute at the end of each irrigation cycle.

Since the desanding process depends on the centrifugal velocity of water, flow velocity through the unit should be maintained within specified limits for the brand desander used. The manufacturer of the unit illustrated recommends velocities which create a pressure loss through the unit of 5 to 12 lb/in^2, which is more or less typical of such units. Various size models provide for a wide range of flows.

Flows not within recommended limits of each size unit, particularly lower flows, will not provide the sand removal normally desired.

Specific flows must be considered when using desanders in irrigation systems. For example: Assume that a 9-hole golf course system is designed for flows of 400 to 500 gal/min in normal operation. Further assume that only one green is watered at a particular time (as often happens) and that the water flow is only 100 gpm. In this case, removal of sand would be deficient and could contaminate the irrigation equipment for that green. Special methods of desander installation can overcome the problem.

The manufacturer of the illustrated desander recommends two methods of maintaining ideal flow velocities in units:

1. Use a multiple number of desanders so that minimum flow is handled at an adequate pressure drop; i.e., as the flow rate goes up or down, units are cut in and out of service as required to maintain an acceptable pressure drop across each desander. The on-off cycle is controlled by pressure transducers and automatic switches and valves. As an example, two units of the make illustrated would accommodate flow ranges from 110 to 600 gal/min. Or, only 3 units are required for flow ranges from 110 to 1300 gal/min.

2. The second method is to provide a constant flow through the desander at all times. To accomplish this, a bypass is connected at the discharge of the desander and piped to the pump suction. A flow control valve regulates the amount of water returned to the suction in order to maintain proper flow through the desander.

The manufacturer has given special permission to reproduce Figure 7-10 illustrating a method developed to provide a constant flow through a desander with differential pressure control.

Source Water and Filtration

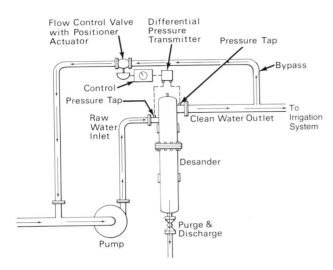

Figure 7-10 Flow Control with Differential Pressure Control

The required velocities of sand-laden water through desanders can result in considerable abrasion on the inside surfaces. Therefore, desanders with abrasion-resistant liners or made with abrasion-resistant metal are considered desirable.

IRRIGATION EQUIPMENT SELECTION

Quality of the available water supply is often a factor to consider in the selection of irrigation equipment. Selecting a particular type, brand, or model of water application equipment will not eliminate the requirement of proper filtration. However, some types of products are less susceptible to problems that are often associated with water quality.

It may also be advisable to use remote control valves that are listed as contamination resistant. This type of valve is normally recommended for systems using recycled water or "dirty" water as described in this chapter.

Note: There is not an industry standard of established design parameters for valves designated as, "contamination resistant." Valve performance to resist corrosion of materials and blockage of ports by contaminants will vary by design and water quality. For example, some models do not include adequate protection of materials that are susceptible to corrosion. Accelerated deterioration may occur when components are exposed to water that contains substantial quantities of common corrosive elements.

BIBLIOGRAPHY

(a) "Guide for the Selection, Installation and Maintenance of Pipe Line Strainers" prepared by the Pipe Line Strainer, Separator and Filter Section, Fluid Controls Institute, Inc.

(b) "Algae in Water Supplies," Public Health Service Publication No. 657

A PARTIAL LIST OF STRAINER/FILTER MANUFACTURERS

REGULAR TYPE

Muessco Strainers
Mueller Steam Specialty Co.
72 Jericho Turnpike
Mineola, NY 11501

Armstrong Machine Works
Three Rivers, MI 49093

AUTOMATIC SELF-CLEANING STRAINERS

R. P. Adams Company, Inc.
225 East Park Drive
Buffalo, NY 14240
Sarco Company, Inc.
1951 26th Street
Allentown, PA 18105

Lakos-Plum Creek
1365 North Clovis Ave.
Fresno, CA 93727

Perfection Sprinkler Co.
2077 S. State St.
Ann Arbor, MI 48106

CONTROL SWITCHES

The Mercoid Corporation
4201 Belmont Avenue
Chicago, IL 60641

SEPARATORS

Krebs Engineers
1205 Chrysler Drive
Menlo Park, CA 94025

SUCTION PIPING/FLOATS/SCREENS
PUMP SYSTEMS

Greenscape Pump Services
556 Coppell Road
Coppell, TX 75019

PART III

Design

CHAPTER 8

Sprinkler Performance and Related Considerations for System Performance

Distribution of water to each area of coverage should be as uniform in application as possible. Assuming moisture requirement is equal per square foot, as in the case of turfgrass, then uniform application of moisture is desirable to maintain consistent turf quality and efficient use of water. Uniformity of water application is one of the important factors used to measure irrigation efficiency. Efficiency is a measure of equipment performance and management at the site. Although variable site conditions will alter performance of sprinklers during operation, distribution uniformity is, in large part, established during system design.

Regardless of type, brand and model of product, and other factors of influence, distribution of moisture is never completely equal in each square foot of the coverage area.

Distribution uniformity of a sprinkler zone is dependent on the coverage and precipitation characteristics of individual sprinklers which vary with:

1. The geometric distribution profile (cross section of precipitation pattern) of individual nozzles as in Figure 8-3.
2. Wind which distorts precipitation and coverage patterns.
3. Spacing patterns and distance between sprinklers.
4. Operating pressure at sprinkler.

And, additionally, in the case of rotary type sprinklers:

5. Speed of rotation.
6. Uniformity of rotation (including inconsistent or lack of rotation due to product failure).

SPRINKLER DISTRIBUTION

Although some sprinklers and nozzles will perform better than others, all products have limitations that preclude the equal distribution of moisture in all areas of the wetted pattern.

There are inherent limitations of ejecting water from a small orifice into the atmosphere to provide coverage over a large surface area. For example: a $\frac{1}{8}$ inch diameter orifice, half-circle spray nozzle, with a 12 foot (144 in) radius of coverage. Water is dispersed from an

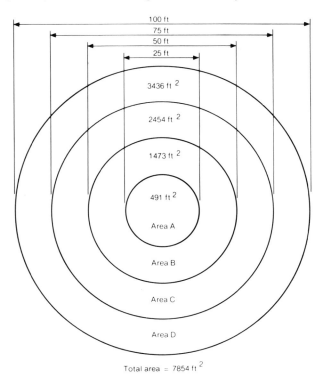

Figure 8-1 Comparison of Circle Areas

orifice area of .012 in^2 onto a coverage area of 32,572 in^2, an area that is 2.7 million times larger than the orifice.

Although the nozzle flow of a rotary sprinkler is not sprayed over the entire area at one time, the diameter and total area of coverage is normally much greater.

Figure 8-1 illustrates the square footage difference of 4 areas within a 100 ft diameter circle. The total area of the 100 ft diameter circle is 7,854 ft^2. Area A, closest to the center, represents only about 6% of the total area. Each succeeding increase of diameter by the same amount increases the area by ever-increasing amounts. Area B represents approximately 19% of the total; Area C, 31%; and Area D, 44%.

Assume that the stream being discharged from a rotary sprinkler spreads the *same amount* of water over its entire length. When the stream rotates it will distribute an ever-decreasing amount of water from the sprinkler to the extremity of its throw as the circumferential area increases. The resulting cross-sectional distribution profile will therefore be a *triangle* as illustrated in Figure 8-2a.

Conversely, assume that the stream being discharged spreads an ever-increasing amount of water over its entire length in proportion to the ever-increasing area it must cover. When the stream rotates, it will distribute an equal amount of water from the sprinkler to the extremity of its throw over the entire area. The resulting cross-sectional distribution profile will therefore be a rectangle as illustrated in Figure 8-2b.

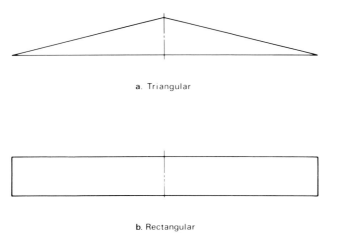

a. Triangular

b. Rectangular

Figure 8-2 Triangular and Rectangular Distribution Profiles

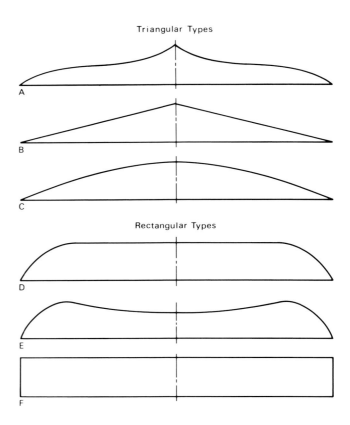

Figure 8-3 Theoretical Distribution Profiles [a]

DISTRIBUTION PATTERNS

Figure 8-3 illustrates several basic profiles representing various geometric shapes of distribution. Complete profiles would include a horizontal scale along the bottom base line to indicate distance from the sprinkler (vertical center line) and a vertical scale to indicate the depth of water.

Profiles A through E in Figure 8-3, are examples of theoretical shapes to illustrate typical and possible variations and limitations of sprinklers to provide an even distribution of moisture in all areas of coverage, as illustrated by Profile F. Many additional shapes would be necessary to illustrate common variations that occur with different sprinkler nozzles.

A rotary sprinkler, when rotated at a uniform speed in perfectly still air, will theoretically deliver a distribution pattern symmetrical about the center. However, this is of limited importance to the system designer, as wind effect at the site is not equally proportional in all directions from the sprinkler.

Water dispersed from a spray sprinkler is not equally distributed in all directions from the nozzle. For example, the amount of water applied at four feet from the nozzle in one direction, will not be exactly equal to the amount applied at four feet from the nozzle in a different direction. Depending on the individual nozzle type and series, arc of coverage, operating pressure, etc., the amount of precipitation difference applied to different sectors of the coverage area, may be small or large, or a combination of both. Sector variations in distribution of spray sprinklers are determined by test, using catch pans on grid pattern in all areas of coverage.

Therefore, a single, cross-sectional distribution profile is normally not realistic for a spray sprinkler, unless the profile is used for practical purposes to illustrate the "average" depth of precipitation applied in all sectors, from the sprinkler to the outer limits of coverage.

Although distribution profiles (developed from test under controlled conditions) are useful to estimate or compare sprinkler performance, there are major limitations in using a single sprinkler profile to extrapolate performance with different:

1. Operating conditions that may occur at the site, including wind conditions.
2. Arc of coverage (adjustable or fixed).
3. Radius adjustments that may be required at the site with adjustable nozzles. This includes adjustment by stream diffusion and flow reduction.

Different types of distribution profiles, including the examples shown in Figure 8-3, will have an effect on the uniformity of distribution to a greater or lesser extent. This is true with the performance of an individual sprinkler or when installed at spacings to allow for partial or complete overlap of sprinkler coverage.

Sprinklers can be more, or less efficient than other methods of applying moisture when common factors of consideration are used to rate irrigation efficiency. However, sprinkler irrigation is generally considered to be the most "cost-effective" method of irrigation for turfgrass, or other types of closely-spaced ground covers. This includes consideration of long-term cost (including maintenance cost) and dependability.

DIAMETER OF COVERAGE. Radius or diameter of coverage as listed in sprinkler manufacturer's performance tables may or may not be based on an industry standard of measurement. ASAE (American Society of

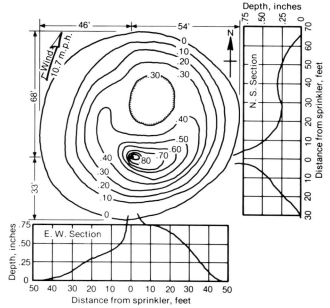

Figure 8-4 Distribution Pattern Distorted by 10.7 mi/h Wind [a]

Agricultural Engineers) Standard S398.1 for testing and performance reporting [b], is considered to be the standard for landscape irrigation.

Tests are performed with controlled conditions and without wind effect. Radius is the measured distance from the sprinkler to the most distant point at which .01 in/hr (.3 mm/hr) precipitation occurs within the area of coverage.

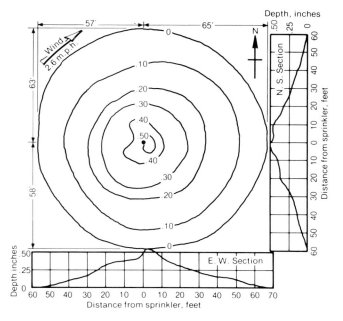

Figure 8-5 Distribution Pattern Distorted by 2.6 mi/h Wind [a]

Sprinkler Performance

WIND EFFECTS. The factor which affects the distribution pattern of a sprinkler, and which can't be controlled by system design or sprinkler manufacture, is wind. Variable wind conditions (velocity, direction and uniformity of both) will alter the distribution profile to some degree, each time the sprinkler is operated. With all other factors remaining constant, distribution uniformity of a sprinkler can range from very good to poor when operated at different times and with different wind conditions.

Figures 8-4 and 8-5 illustrate some actual test results of rotary sprinklers operated in wind[a]. In still air the sprinklers have a slightly modified version of Profile C, Figure 8-3.

Figure 8-4 shows the distorted pattern of a sprinkler operating in a 10.7 mi/h wind. The effects, easily discernible, are several:

1. The radius of coverage is shortened on the windward side of the sprinkler. And, the wind into which the stream is discharged also blows the droplets back toward the sprinkler increasing precipitation above normal close to the sprinkler.
2. On the leeward side, the stream is carried by the wind, increasing area of coverage which, in turn, decreases precipitation under the stream. In addition, note that some of the water discharged windward is also blown back past the sprinkler and deposited on the leeward side close to the sprinkler.
3. It is also readily apparent that as the sprinkler rotates and is discharging at right angles to the wind, the stream is shortened.

When winds have a velocity of less than 3.0 mi/h, a condition of *dead calm* is considered to exist. Figure 8-5 shows the distribution pattern of a sprinkler operating in a dead calm of 2.6 mi/h. Notice that the distribution pattern is affected in a similar way to higher winds, except to a lesser extent. *Therefore, since sprinkler systems almost always operate in winds above the dead calm category, spacing of sprinklers during design must consider this factor.*

A single precipitation test will provide a limited amount of information relating to distribution. For example, assume that an installed rotary sprinkler is operated twice a week. And, Figure 8-4 indicates the distribution that occurs on the first day of operation and Figure 8-5

indicates the distribution on the second day. Total moisture depth applied will be the sum total of both applications and not two times the amounts shown on either one of the test profiles.

Droplet Size. Wind distortion of distribution depends on size of water drops as well as wind velocity. The trajectory of large drops is less affected by wind than small drops. However, wind effect is only one of several factors of consideration relating to droplet size.

Different size droplets are essential to disperse water into all areas of coverage. Large size drops tend to fall in the outer areas of the wetted area and smaller drops, commonly referred to as "fall-out", tend to fall in areas nearer to the sprinkler.

In planting bed areas, the impact of large drops on the soil surface can breakdown particles into smaller sizes. Air and moisture movement into the soil are directly affected by surface sealing. Velocity and energy expended upon impact increases with an increase in size of droplets.

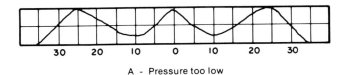

A - Pressure too low

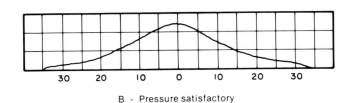

B - Pressure satisfactory

C - Pressure too high

Figure 8-6 Effect of Different Pressures on Distribution Profile (d)

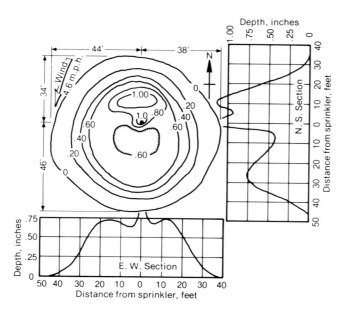

Figure 8-7 Effect on Distribution Due to High Speed Rotation[a]

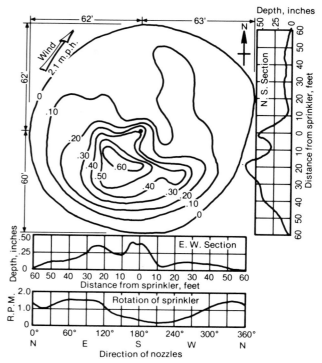

Figure 8-8 Effect on Distribution: Erratic Rotation of Sprinkler with Dual Nozzles Pointing Same Direction[a]

Small drops (mist in some cases) are generally preferred for improved coverage and protection of ornamental plant foliage.

The actual wind effect on different drop sizes cannot be determined unless tests are made under controlled conditions, drop size measurements are accurately determined and all factors relating to wind distortion are considered.

The drop size measuring process used by CIT (Center for Irrigation Technology) includes a flat beam of laser light, directed by mirrors to a horizontal array of photosensitive diodes. As each drop passes through a screening area, it crosses the beam, casting a shadow sensed by the diodes. The number of diodes in shadow determines the width of the drop[c]. The interested reader is referred to Solomon, et. al (1991) for a more complete discussion of the measurement process.

PRESSURE EFFECTS. Pressure, higher or lower than that recommended for a sprinkler or individual nozzle, affects distribution. Figure 8-6 illustrates the possible effects on a rotary sprinkler with different operating pressures.

Note the reduction of area covered when pressure is too high. This same effect will also occur when pressure is reduced too much. Also note the drastic change in the precipitation profile when pressure is too low. Similar effects occur with spray sprinklers.

ROTATIONAL EFFECTS. Abnormal rotation of sprinklers will also distort the distribution pattern.

High Speed Rotation. Figure 8-7 illustrates how a sprinkler rotating at a speed faster than recommended affects a basically triangular distribution pattern. The area covered is reduced and a corresponding increase in rate of application occurs.

Erratic Rotation. Figure 8-8 illustrates the effect on distribution when a sprinkler does not rotate at a constant speed. The effect was produced with a sprinkler using two nozzles pointing in the same direction (graph indicates measured RPM during rotation). A similar effect would occur with a single nozzle sprinkler.

SYSTEM DISTRIBUTION

System coverage is normally accomplished by blending the distribution of two or more adjacent sprinklers together to obtain a relatively uniform distribution of moisture. System design spacings to obtain overlap of coverage may be based on an analysis of sprinkler distribution profiles, manufacturer's recommendation, experience, general (rule-of-thumb) formulas, cost considerations, water conservation, or a compromise between some or all factors. Although complete uniformity

Sprinkler Performance

in the system is unattainable, distribution can be improved by careful selection of the sprinkler and the related spacing used for design.

Wind distortion of individual sprinklers, as previously discussed, will have a significant effect on the uniformity of a sprinkler system. Although wind effect is not in direct proportion to wind velocity, sprinkler spacings are commonly derated in proportion to the wind velocity.

DISTRIBUTION BETWEEN SPRINKLERS. Distribution profiles, without wind distortion, are often used to analyze the combined coverage of sprinklers at different spacings and with different spacing patterns. Uniformity of water application will change as distance between sprinklers is changed and spacing pattern is changed, with or without wind effect.

Figure 8-9 illustrates the theoretical distribution of four sprinklers on a square spacing pattern. Spacing distance is equal to radius of coverage (50% of diameter). Values shown in Figure 8-9b indicate the depth of water (in/hr) at 221 example locations within the area of coverage. Distribution was determined by a computer after input of performance data from the sprinkler distribution profile (not shown). Profile was developed from a sprinkler test under controlled conditions and without wind effect.

Although a computer is very useful for this type of output, including graphic displays, uniformity coefficients, etc., it is important for the designer to consider the limitations and practical use of the information provided. All output information is limited by the quality of input data and the level of knowledge included in the computer software.

Depth of moisture, as indicated in Figure 8-9b, is the total amount applied at each location by all sprinklers. The variable amount applied by each sprinkler depends on the sprinkler distribution profile at that particular location. Figures 8-10 and 8-11 illustrate overlap points of consideration for triangular and square spacing patterns.

1. Point of beginning of overlap, O, on a straight line between adjacent heads, A-B.
2. Midway point, M, between three adjacent heads with equilateral triangular spacing and between four adjacent heads with square spacing.
3. Point of beginning of overlap, 00 and 000, between each head and midpoint, M.

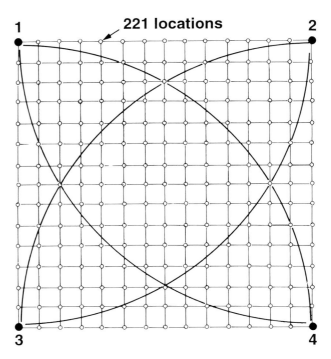

A. Sprinkler Layout and Distribution Grid

```
 1.                                                    2.
(X) .23 .21 .27 .30 .30 .28 .33 .28 .30 .30 .27 .21 .23 (X)
.23 .25 .23 .30 .33 .36 .33 .32 .33 .36 .33 .30 .23 .25 .23
.21 .23 .27 .30 .34 .35 .39 .41 .39 .35 .34 .30 .27 .23 .21
.27 .30 .30 .31 .33 .33 .40 .39 .40 .33 .33 .31 .30 .30 .27
.30 .33 .34 .33 .33 .36 .32 .32 .32 .36 .33 .33 .34 .33 .30
.30 .36 .35 .33 .36 .31 .27 .24 .27 .31 .36 .33 .35 .36 .30
.28 .33 .39 .40 .32 .27 .23 .21 .23 .27 .32 .40 .39 .33 .28
.33 .32 .41 .39 .32 .24 .21 .21 .21 .24 .32 .39 .41 .32 .33
.28 .33 .39 .40 .32 .27 .23 .21 .23 .27 .32 .40 .39 .33 .28
.30 .36 .35 .33 .36 .31 .27 .24 .27 .31 .36 .33 .35 .36 .30
.30 .33 .34 .33 .33 .36 .32 .32 .32 .36 .33 .33 .34 .33 .30
.27 .30 .30 .31 .33 .33 .40 .39 .40 .33 .33 .31 .30 .30 .27
.21 .23 .27 .30 .34 .35 .39 .41 .39 .35 .34 .30 .27 .23 .21
.23 .25 .23 .30 .33 .36 .33 .32 .33 .36 .33 .30 .23 .25 .23
(X) .23 .21 .27 .30 .30 .28 .33 .28 .30 .30 .27 .21 .23 (X)
 3.                                                    4.
```

B. Computer Print-out of Distribution - in/hr

Figure 8-9 Example of Theoretical Distribution: Four Sprinklers on Square Spacing

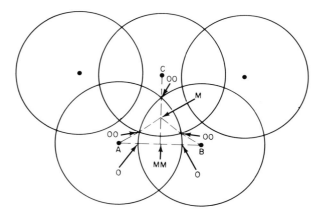

**Figure 8-10 Points of Consideration:
Equilateral Triangular Spacing**

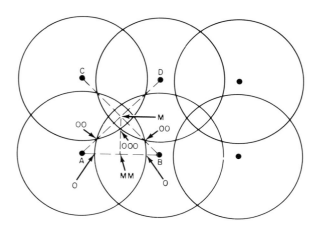

Figure 8-11 Points of Consideration: Square Spacing

No single ratio of head spacing to diameter of coverage is suitable for all sprinklers. The determining factor is the characteristics of streams from rotary sprinklers and characteristics of spray from spray heads.

The hypothetical sprinkler distribution profile shown in Figure 8-12 is used to demonstrate combined coverage between sprinklers. Detail 2 illustrates single and combined coverage along the A-B line as shown in Figures 8-10 and 8-11. Sprinkler spacing is 60% of the coverage diameter. Uniformity is considerably better than that shown in Detail 3 when spacing is reduced to 50% of coverage diameter. Distribution profiles along the A-M and MM-M lines could also be developed for comparison.

Note: Figure 8-12 is not an example to suggest that performance will improve with extended design spac-

ings, it is used only as a comparison of an individual sprinkler at different spacings, and with controlled operating conditions.

Combined distribution along the A-B line in Figure 8-13 is based on the hypothetical sprinkler profile shown in Detail 1. Radius of coverage shown is the most distant point at which .01 in/hr (.3mm/hr) precipitation occurs within the area of coverage.

Detail 2 illustrates the combined distribution when sprinklers are spaced at 50% of diameter. Head to head coverage is commonly used as a rule-of-thumb spacing to provide additional coverage in the area adjacent to the sprinkler (also commonly used for wind deration). Coverage at sprinklers A and B is basically limited to that provided by the individual sprinklers, as minimum additional precipitation (overlap point O) is provided by adjacent sprinklers due to the limited amount of droplets required to produce .01 in/hr (.3 mm/hr).

Detail 3, Figure 8-13, illustrates an example of spacing reduction (40% of diameter) that would be necessary to increase coverage at sprinklers. Distribution uniformity also changes along the A-B line when spacing is reduced.

SUMMARY. The preceding discourse on sprinkler performance illustrates the dilemma of sprinkler manufacturers and systems designers. Many variable factors directly influence the performance of sprinklers that must spray moisture into the atmosphere and cover relatively large areas. Sprinkler design and system design must also contend with a variety of different standards that may be used to judge if a system is cost-effective.

Application uniformity can also be measured in different ways, including Christiansen's (CU) formula[a]. Methods of rating uniformity vary primarily in the manner in which deviations from the mean are considered in the rating system. Some consider all types of deviations (over, under, etc.) as equal and influence on uniformity is considered only in proportion to the amount of deviation. Others have established different penalties for certain types of deviations. For example, Distribution Uniformity (DU) emphasizes the importance of the low application amounts collected.

$$DU = 100 \ (LQ/AD)$$

Sprinkler Performance

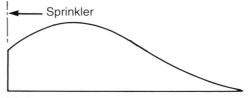

(1) Sprinkler Distribution Profile

(1) Sprinkler Distribution Profile

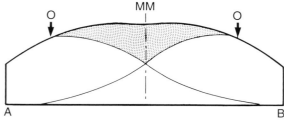

(2) Distribution A to B-Spacing at 60% of Diameter

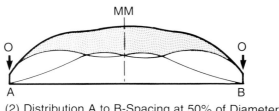

(2) Distribution A to B-Spacing at 50% of Diameter

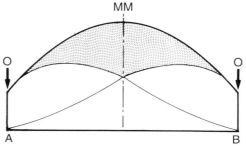

(3) Distribution A to B-Spacing at 50% of Diameter

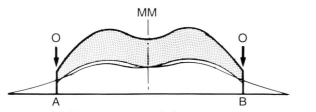

(3) Distribution A to B-Spacing at 40% of Diameter

Figure 8-12 Distribution A to B
Hypothetical Sprinkler

Where LQ is the average of the lowest ¼ of all catch can amounts collected and AD is the average depth of all catch can amounts.

DESIGN SPACING. The effects of wind on sprinkler distribution cannot be altered except by providing control of when the system is operated. However, distribution with wind effect can be improved by sprinkler spacing. Figure 8-14 shows a theoretical composite of typical wind effect on coverage and compensating spacing. Note that, with reduced spacing, adequate coverage overlap is obtained regardless of wind direction.

Parts A and B of Figure 8-14 show the effect of wind perpendicular to rows of heads. Spacing (% of diameter) is shown for reference only and is not necessarily the recommended spacing of a particular distribution profile. A-1, A-2 and A-3 illustrate theoretical coverage with wind at 5, 10, and 15 mi/h respectively. Note the

Figure 8-13 Distribution A to B
Coverage at Sprinkler

increase in deficient coverage at the midpoint between each three heads as wind velocity increases and spacing remains constant.

Parts B-1 to B-3 demonstrate how improved midpoint coverage is obtained by reduced spacing at the same wind velocities as indicated in A-1 to A-3. Spacing is decreased as wind velocity increases.

Parts C and D of Figure 8-14 illustrate that the effect on coverage with wind blowing parallel to the rows of heads is quite similar to the effect when wind is perpendicular to the rows.

Square spacing of a particular sprinkler is almost always less than that used for triangular spacing. However, similar results are obtained when spacing is decreased as wind velocity increases.

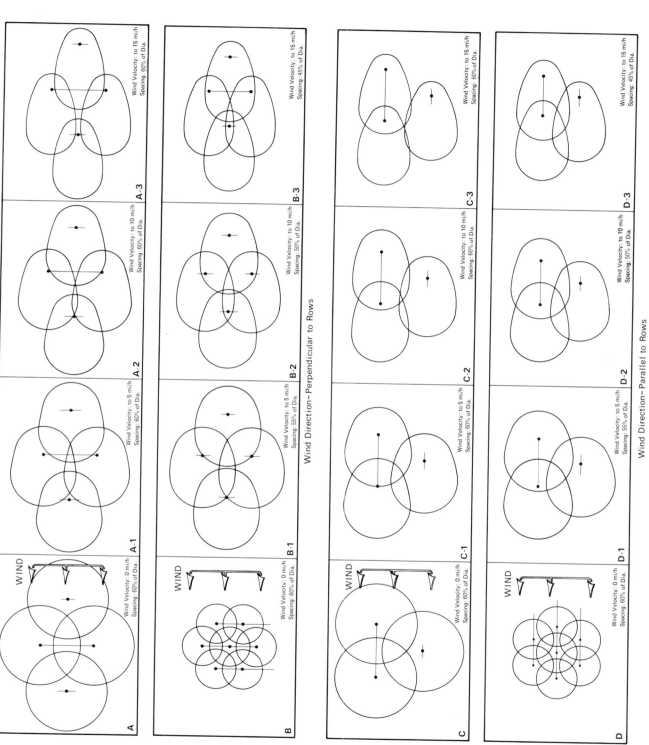

Figure 8-14 Theoretical Wind Effect to Rotary Sprinklers: Triangular Spacing

Sprinkler Performance

The "egg-shaped" wetted patterns shown in Figure 8-14 are typical for the wind velocities indicated. Actual distortion of a rotary sprinkler will also depend on the individual sprinkler (angle of trajectory, droplet size, etc.). For example, a small, low-volume stream of water may produce a good distribution profile when tested under controlled conditions, but the performance may be totally destroyed when operated with normal wind conditions.

Reduced spacing is a necessary compromise to ensure coverage with variable wind conditions. Uniformity of water application will vary to some degree, each and every time the system is operated.

While uniformity in water application (at wind speeds of less than 5 mph) is important, it is only one factor of consideration for the designer. Methods commonly used to measure efficiency in application can be misleading if limited to theoretical coverage, or the results of a single test. Three additional factors should be considered for sprinkler performance in landscape irrigation systems:

1. *Wind Effect.* A significant change in uniformity will occur if the average wind speed during normal system operation is considerably greater than the wind speed during a sprinkler test. Performance of a single sprinkler at 2.6 mi/h and 10.7 mi/h can be compared in Figures 8-4 and 8-5.
2. *Dependability.* Regardless of other considerations included for design, and on-site adjustments to the operating program, uniformity is limited to the performance of sprinklers during the time period between scheduled maintenance. This is an important factor, considering maintenance on the average system is less than adequate. For example, uniformity of a rotary sprinkler is possible only if it is rotating, and streams are spraying in the right direction.
3. *Overthrow.* Water on walks, driveways, streets, etc. is not only the result of "run-off" from planting areas. In many cases, it is the result of coverage onto the areas by the sprinkler layout.

BORDER WATERING

Special design considerations are required for watering at borders of sprinkled areas. There are two basic kinds of borders, each requiring different handling:

1. *Unprotected borders.* With this type border, full-circle sprinklers water to and beyond the edge of the area. No attempt is made to minimize sprinkling out-of-bounds. An example would be sprinkling fairways of a golf course. Normally, full-circle sprinklers run the length of the fairway. The sprinklers are placed close enough to the edge to sufficiently water the fairway width without regard to overthrow into the rough.

2. *Protected borders.* A protected border is any area that requires sprinkling to be confined within bounds. For example, boundary lines bordered by streets, public sidewalks, other properties, etc.

UNPROTECTED BORDERS. When full-circle pattern sprinklers are used to provide coverage, the distribution of a single sprinkler must be considered in order to locate the sprinklers for adequate coverage up to an unprotected border. Figure 8-15 illustrates the need for this consideration.

In this illustration, the circumferences are for the manufacturer's rated maximum diameter of coverage. Water distribution ends completely, for all practical purposes, at the circumference. A line drawn through the intersections of coverage arcs (E), (G), etc., is called the Mean Coverage (MC) of the head layout pattern; it is measured from the row line of heads.

Sufficient precipitation in relation to the average within the system will not be provided along the line of mean coverage. In still air, the amount of application will depend on the sprinkler profile and the spacing between the sprinklers. If radius is measured by the manufacturer at the most distant point at which .01 in/hr (.3 mm/hr) precipitation occurs, then the combined application at points E and G would be .02 in/hr.

In order to sufficiently water an unprotected border, a row of full-circle sprinklers must be located so that the mean coverage occurs some distance outside of the area border for which irrigation is being designed. This distance will vary with different precipitation profiles.

Calculating Mean Coverage. The mean coverage of sprinklers for any diameter of distribution in still air can easily be determined with Table 30 (Table 31 for metric dimensions with sprinkler coverage specified in feet).

Example: Assume sprinkler coverage diameter is 100 ft. and spacing is 60% of diameter. Table 30 shows that

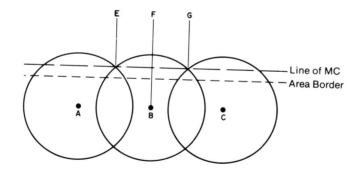

Figure 8-15 Mean Coverage

MC (mean coverage) with 60% of coverage diameter is determined by multiplying diameter with the factor .40. Therefore, MC in this example is 40 ft: 100 x .40 = 40 ft.

Summary. In actual practice, watering to the edge of unprotected areas usually will not be the same as the theoretical coverage just discussed. The actual location of points E and G in Figure 8-15 will depend on wind effect. Mean coverage will also vary depending on whether the stream is discharged against or with the wind.

PROTECTED BORDERS. Sprinklers with part-circle arcs of coverage should be used along borders requiring protection from overthrow outside of the area. With wind blowing from the sprinkled area toward the border, the fact must be accepted that wind will blow the water across the border as illustrated in Figure 8-16a. Conversely, wind blowing into the area may reduce coverage along the border as illustrated in Figure 8-16b.

In some cases, spray nozzles are available with arcs of coverage that are slightly less or slightly greater than 180° to offset the effects of wind. However, the nozzles are useful only if the wind direction and velocity are somewhat constant during the irrigation season. See Figure 8-17. With wind, the edges of the coverage arc will theoretically be "pushed" back to provide 180° of coverage.

Most part-circle rotary sprinklers have adjustable arcs of coverage and degree of arc can be set after installation. In some cases, the use of part-circle rotary sprinklers along protected borders in not recommended. The long streams and the height the streams reach at the peak of their trajectory subject them to abnormal deflection even in light winds.

Sprinklers along walks, driveways and streets are good examples of the difference between performance on the "drawing board" and actual performance at the site. Although system cost is a necessary consideration, the systems designer must also consider the waste and liability of water on paved areas; property owner dissatisfaction and, in some cases, local ordinances that do not allow sprinkler over-spray into the street. While the designer cannot control the wind, he/she can be expected to consider effects of average wind conditions.

PRECIPITATION
The precipitation rate (PR) of individual sprinkler operating zones is an important factor for design and system operation. Precipitation rate describes the length of time required to deposit a given depth of water on an area. PR is normally measured in inches per hour (in/hr) or millimeter per hour (mm/hr).

Example: A sprinkler operating zone that has a precipitation rate of 1 in/hr (25.4 mm/hr) will apply .25 inches (6.4 mm) of moisture in 15 minutes of operation.

The precipitation rate can be estimated by considering volume/time and size of area. Average PR can also be determined by a "catch can" test after the system is installed.

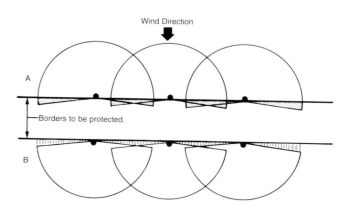

Figure 8-16 Wind Distortion - Part Circle Sprinklers on Protected Borders

FULL-CIRCLE SPRINKLERS. The following formulas provide average precipitation for a system of full-circle sprinklers. The calculation relates to the shaded area as shown in Figure 8-18. The constant 96.25 (96.3) is used to establish inches per square foot per hour.

Sprinkler Performance

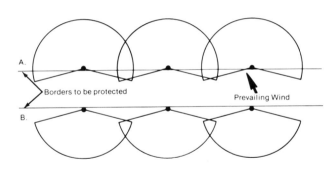

Figure 8-17 Sprinklers Along Borders to be Protected (Arcs of Coverage Shown with No Wind)

$$\frac{gpm\ (one\ head)\ x\ 96.25}{head\ spacing\ on\ row,\ ft\ x\ row\ spacing,\ ft} = {}^{in}\!/_h\ precipitation$$

or:

$$\frac{m^3h\ (one\ head)\ x\ 1000}{head\ spacing\ on\ row,\ m\ x\ spacing,\ m} = {}^{mm}\!/_h\ precipitation$$

or:

$$\frac{{}^l/_{min}\ (one\ head)\ x\ 60}{head\ spacing\ on\ row,\ m\ x\ row\ spacing,\ m} = {}^{mm}\!/_h\ precipitation$$

Example: Determine the average precipitation rate of a full-circle rotary sprinkler zone. Flow per sprinkler is 6.0 gpm; sprinklers are on a 42 ft triangular spacing; row spacing equals 36.4 ft. Note: Row spacing equals .866 (constant) x spacing between heads for equilateral triangle spacing.

$$PR = \frac{6.0\ x\ 96.25}{42\ x\ 36.4} = \frac{577.5}{1528.8} = .38\ {}^{in}\!/_{hr}$$

The general-use formula is somewhat confusing for the above triangular spacing calculation. However, a different formula that relates directly to the total flow into the triangle and the actual area of the triangle will provide the same answer. Actual total flow in the triangle is equal to one half of one sprinkler (⅙ of each sprinkler flow x 3 heads). Area of the triangle equals head spacing^2 x .433.

$$PR = \frac{3.0\ x\ 96.25}{42^2\ x\ .433} = \frac{288.75}{763.81} = .38\ {}^{in}\!/_{hr}$$

PART CIRCLE SPRINKLERS. For precipitation purposes, part-circle sprinklers are often compared to the PR of full-circle sprinklers and categorized as compatible or non-compatible. Compatible sprinklers are sometimes described as "matched precipitation" sprinklers.

Compatible part-circle sprinklers are those which have a radius of coverage that is approximately equal to the

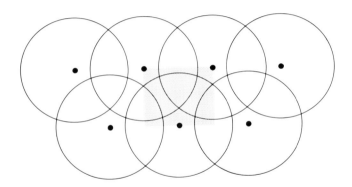

Figure 8-18 Area of "Average Precipitation"

full-circle radius and a flow rate that is in proportion (or within reasonable limits) to the arc or coverage. For example, a 3.0 gpm half-circle and a 1.5 gpm quarter-circle sprinkler would be considered compatible to a 6.0 gpm full-circle sprinkler. Precipitation rates would be equal to the full-circle, and full, half and quarter-circle heads could be combined together for coverage and connected to the same zone valve. Comparison of radius and flow is a practical method to determine if precipitation is compatible within reasonable limits.

Distribution uniformity of the system must be judged with consideration of practical limitations, including cost and the fact that there will be some variations in the distribution profile of the full, half and quarter-circle sprinklers.

Non-compatible sprinklers have a precipitation rate that is not compatible with the full-circle (or some other arc of coverage) and should not be connected to the same control valve. Different types with significant variations in PR should be controlled with separate zone valves.

The general-use formula for PR is based on the flow rate of a full-circle sprinkler. The systems designer must consider the difference if the formula is used for a separate zone of part-circle sprinklers. The formula can be altered as necessary to adjust for a different proportion of the sprinkler flow in the same area of coverage. For example, if the same formula is used for two rows of half-circle sprinklers, the calculated value can be doubled to allow for the fact that the proportion of a half-circle flow in the area is twice that of a full-circle flow.

PR formulas can be developed as desired to cover variations in flow, area and spacing pattern. The following examples relate to two rows of half circle sprinklers:

1. Triangular Spacing/Half-Circles:

$$PR = \frac{gpm\ (one\ head)\ x\ 96.25}{head\ spacing,\ ft^2\ x\ .433} = \frac{in}{hr}$$

Note: gpm based on $\frac{1}{3}$ of each sprinkler flow - 3 heads total.

2. Square Spacing/Half-Circles:

$$PR = \frac{gpm\ (two\ heads)\ x\ 96.25}{head\ spacing,\ ft^2} = \frac{in}{hr}$$

Note: gpm of two heads based on $\frac{1}{2}$ of each sprinkler flow - 4 heads total.

WIND

A basic understanding of the characteristics of wind will help the designer plan for required compensation in sprinkler system design. Extreme differences in wind condition exist depending on location, season and time of day or night.

The United States National Weather Service publishes condensed weather information compiled from more than 300 reporting stations. These reports include information on temperatures, precipitation, humidity and wind.

> 1. An annual summary of Comparative Local Climatological Data is generally available from any weather station. Data is listed by month with yearly averages. Although data is for a particular year, monthly average wind information will vary only slightly from year to year.
> 2. Weather data is also available monthly by subscription.

In addition, records of hourly observations may be examined at the station.

The systems designer should obtain information on wind conditions at the site or as close to the site as possible. Figure 8-19 lists wind information for selected cities. An examination of the data provides the following examples of diverse wind conditions:

> 1. Winds in San Francisco average about 40% greater velocity than in Los Angeles. And, they are more northerly. However, during the mid-summer months, velocity is 75% greater.

> 2. Average wind velocity in Columbia and Greenville, South Carolina is almost exactly the same. However, in Greenville (only about 100 miles further inland) average wind direction is the exact opposite.
> 3. Richmond, Virginia (about 75 miles inland) has wind velocity about 25% less than Norfolk, located on the coast.
> 4. Average winds in most cities listed in Figure 8-19 are relatively constant year-round. However, in five cities, the average falls in the category of low velocity winds, 4-8 mi/h. Four fall in the category of medium winds, 8-11 mi/h; and three fall in the category of high winds.

Certain general characteristics of different kinds of wind provide some guidance in designing sprinkler systems.

> 1. Low velocity winds can affect sprinkler systems as much or more than winds in the medium category because they are usually the most constant in velocity and direction. For example, along some stretches of the west coast, constant, low velocity, westerly winds cause the branches of trees to grow in a pronounced easterly direction.
> 2. Medium velocity winds usually vary in direction and velocity, almost constantly. This tends to offset somewhat the effect of wind on sprinkler coverage.

An examination of the *hourly* wind observation records for July, 1971, at many weather stations revealed additional variances. Some are listed below.
> 1. Charleston, South Carolina:
> Day average, 8 am - 7 pm: 9.4 mi/h.
> Night average, 8 pm - 7 am: 5.4 mi/h.
> Small difference within each time period.
> 2. Los Angeles, California:
> Day average, 8 am - 7 pm: 10.4 mi/h.
> Night average, 8 pm - 7 am: 5.9 mi/h.
> Small difference within each time period.
> 3. Dallas, Texas:
> Day average, 8 am - 7 pm: 10.1 mi/h.
> Night average, 8 pm - 7 am: 9.5 mi/h.
> Wind velocity after midnight decidedly less than before midnight.
> 4. Amarillo, Texas:
> Day average, 8 am - 7 pm: 13.5 mi/h.
> Night average, 8 pm - 7 am: 12.2 mi/h.
> Small difference within each time period.

Sprinkler Performance

City	State	Annual Dir. Vel.	Jan. Dir. Vel.	Feb. Dir. Vel.	Mar. Dir. Vel.	Apr. Dir. Vel.	May Dir. Vel.	Jun. Dir. Vel.	Jul. Dir. Vel.	Aug. Dir. Vel.	Sept. Dir. Vel.	Oct. Dir. Vel.	Nov. Dir. Vel.	Dec. Dir. Vel.
Los Angeles	CA	W 7.4	W 6.7	W 7.3	W 7.9	WSW 8.4	WSW 8.2	WSW 7.8	WSW 7.5	WSW 7.5	WSW 7.1	W 6.7	W 6.6	W 6.8
San Francisco	CA	WNW 10.5	WNW 7.1	WNW 8.5	WNW 10.3	WNW 12.1	W 13.2	W 14.0	NW 13.7	NW 12.9	NW 11.1	WNW 9.3	WNW 7.1	WNW 6.8
Boston	MA	SW 13.0	NW 14.6	WNW 14.5	NW 14.5	WNW 13.7	SW 12.7	SW 11.8	SW 11.3	SW 11.3	SW 11.5	SW 12.3	SW 13.2	WNW 14.1
Detroit	MI	SW 10.0	WSW 11.2	WSW 11.3	WSW 11.2	WSW 11.2	WSW 10.1	SW 8.7	SW 8.4	SW 8.2	SW 8.6	WSW 9.2	SW 10.7	SW 10.8
St. Louis	MO	S 9.5	NW 10.2	NW 10.7	WNW 11.7	WNW 11.3	S 9.5	S 8.5	S 7.6	S 7.4	S 8.0	S 8.6	S 9.9	WNW 10.2
Columbia	SC	SW 7.0	SW 7.1	SW 7.7	SW 8.4	SW 8.5	SW 7.1	SW 6.8	SW 6.7	SW 6.1	NE 6.2	NE 6.2	SW 6.5	WSW 6.7
Greenville	SC	NE 7.1	NE 7.4	NE 8.3	SW 8.2	SW 8.4	NE 7.3	NE 6.5	WSW 6.3	SE 6.0	NE 6.2	NE 6.9	SW 6.9	NE 7.3
Amarillo	TX	SW 13.7	SW 13.2	SW 14.3	SW 15.5	SW 15.4	S 14.8	S 14.4	S 12.4	S 11.8	S 13.1	SW 13.0	SW 13.2	SW 13.0
Dallas	TX	S 10.9	S 10.5	S 11.3	S 12.8	S 13.1	S 12.1	SSE 12.0	S 10.1	SSE 9.6	SE 9.4	SSE 9.4	S 10.2	SSE 10.4
Houston	TX	SSE 7.2	WNW 7.9	SSE 8.9	SSE 8.9	SSE 8.9	SSE 8.1	SSE 6.6	S 6.1	SSE 4.6	SSE 6.6	ESE 5.7	SSE 6.9	SSE 7.4
Norfolk	VA	SW 10.5	SW 11.7	NNE 12.0	SW 12.4	SW 11.8	SW 10.2	SW 9.4	SW 8.1	SW 8.7	NE 9.6	NE 10.4	SW 10.7	SW 11.0
Richmond	VA	S 7.6	S 8.1	NNE 8.6	W 9.0	S 8.9	SSW 7.9	S 7.3	SSW 6.8	S 6.5	S 6.7	NNE 7.0	S 7.5	SW 7.5

Source: National Weather Service Local Climatology Data, Annual Summary, 1971

Figure 8-19 Average Winds: Selected Cities

Special Note. The relationship of wind at different times of each 24 hour period will hold true, in general, in other months too, year after year. However, the relationship must be considered as secondary to the average of each month.

For example: Referring to Figure 8-19, it will be seen that although the time relationships of wind velocity in Amarillo are shown for July, most of the months during which sprinkling is required have greater average wind velocities.

In summary, before designing a sprinkler system, all information regarding wind should be considered. In addition, obtain recommendations from the manufacturer of the equipment that will be used. And, especially consider experience that has been garnered in each locale, including the experience of others.

RELATED CONSIDERATIONS FOR SYSTEM PERFORMANCE

Irrigation Performance is not limited to the uniform distribution of water. While equal application is important, the water requirement of different areas may not be equal. Sprinkler coverage zones need to be established for control of operation.

Frequency of application and the length of zone watering time can be changed within certain limitations. Method and rate of application, zone control and uniformity of precipitation are fixed in place by design.

Total length of watering time available per day may also be restricted. This is particularly true where systems cannot interfere with daytime use of the property; for instance, golf courses, office buildings and parks.

In most cases, it is desirable to complete the watering cycle around sunrise to avoid problems, such as mildew and fungi, that can occur if water remains on the planting for an extended period of time. There may also be less wind velocity and/or maximum city water pressure during the early morning hours. However, systems should not be designed based on these advantages alone. Remember that all systems must be operated during the day at times. For example, watering-in of fertilizers, germinating newly seeded lawns, testing and inspecting system, etc.

A watering program is one of the first steps necessary in irrigation design to avoid a possible conflict between the volume of water required and the time available to operate the system. The water supply (volume and pressure), the piping system and the control system must be adequate for the maximum irrigation requirement per day or per week.

The demands of the watering program will establish the basic criteria for many of the design decisions that will follow, including the precipitation rate of the sprinklers and/or other types of moisture application products. Volume required is a major factor in the necessary compromise between the application rate that may be desired and the actual rate required to provide volume in a limited period of time.

The required program of operation will also affect the total number of zone valves allowed or the number of valves that must be operated at the same time. The controller must include the programming features to control the operation of individual zone valves as necessary per day or per week.

Depending on the type of project and the experience of the systems designer, the watering program may be a rough concept of the required operation, or a detailed program of days, cycle start times and zone duration timing. In any case, the system should be designed with the capacity and control to provide the potential water requirement within the time period available for operation.

A detailed irrigation schedule should be developed for the initial programming of the controller. The preliminary schedule is based on an estimate of requirements at the time the system is installed. Some adjustments may be necessary for the unique requirements of the site and the system. Future programming adjustments may be based on a visual inspection of the site, changes in weather conditions or the recommendations of an irrigation auditor. Automatic changes or interruption of the watering schedule will depend on the type and features of the controller, and related sensors that may or may not be included with the system.

This text is limited to the basics of engineering a sprinkler system (the practical application and necessary delivery system for landscape irrigation). It is not intended as a text that will provide all of the knowledge necessary for the many phases of system design. Of the subjects beyond the scope of this text, none will provide more useful information that relates to landscape irrigation than agronomy and the science of ornamental horticulture. There is a wide variety of literature available that will provide the desired ratio of theory and practical application. This includes trade magazines, which offer many articles relating to horticulture and the practice of grounds maintenance.

Although often attempted, it is not realistic to undertake the design of a system without some degree of knowledge of agronomy. An individual plant can be watered incorrectly with a bucket, garden hose or an irrigation system. Economy-priced systems, in many cases, provide automation with minimum improvement. Often, these economy systems are merely "the permanent installation of incorrect watering."

The designer should have at least a basic understanding of the soil-water-plant relationship. A limited explanation is provided to illustrate the relationship and combined effect on irrigation requirement. The old rule of watering hose sprinklers until one inch of water is collected in an open container is somewhat less than adequate information for an irrigation designer.

WATER REQUIREMENT. Plants require soil, water and air to survive. Daily loss of water from the soil must at some point be replaced by rainfall or irrigation. The purpose of an irrigation system is to provide moisture to the plants and not simply to wet the surface of the land. The designer should, therefore, consider the movement of water from the surface to the root system.

Downward movement from the surface and storage of moisture in the soil will vary with the underground environment. Water loss also occurs at a variable rate and, therefore, there is not a standard schedule of replacement that is correct for all irrigation systems.

There are many factors that can influence the water requirement of a particular project. Turf specialists, for example, indicate that water consumption of turfgrass can be altered by cultural practice. There are some variations in cultural practice that are common for different types of projects, such as residential, parks, athletic fields, and golf courses. Cutting height, mowing frequency, application of fertilizer and irrigation frequency are examples of cultural practice variations for turfgrass.

Grounds maintenance managers are often required to maintain a turf color, texture and general appearance that is based on the judgment of others. They are seldom allowed the opportunity to develop and maintain a turf where considerations are based entirely on the most efficient use of water and maintenance.

Water consumption is equal to the total amount of water required for plant growth plus the amount lost. This total will vary, but it can be as high as .5 inches per day for

Sprinkler Performance

turfgrass in arid regions of the United States. Average monthly rainfall can be deducted from monthly losses to estimate the average irrigation requirement. However, average rainfall should be adjusted to obtain a realistic value, as natural rainfall is not 100% effective. Many systems designers reduce the average rainfall amount by ⅓ (.67 multiplier) to roughly estimate effective rainfall.

EVAPOTRANSPIRATION. Transpiration and evaporation are the two principal ways in which water in the soil is depleted. Transpiration is the process by which plants consume water. Evaporation is the direct loss of water from the soil surface. See figure 8-20. Water loss can also occur with runoff and percolation below the level of root absorption.

Evapotranspiration rate is often used to indicate the total loss due to evaporation and transpiration. Evapotranspiration is sometimes referred to as "consumptive use." Factors affecting evapotranspiration are plant species and related variables, cultural practice, water quality and the environment, above and below ground. Principal climatic factors are temperature, solar radiation, humidity and wind velocity. Evapotranspiration rates available for a regional area are, in most cases, based on a formula using the average of long term weather data. While this does not include all of the variables, it is a practical solution for design and is considered to be reliable for estimating water requirements.

Many different formulas (and modified formulas) have been developed for use in agriculture. Estimating methods may be based primarily on temperature or radiation or humidity, or a combination of factors. Evapotranspiration (ET) estimates will vary depending on the formula, input data and type of crop. Several of these formulas have been used to estimate water-use in landscape planting.

ET rates, commonly used in landscape irrigation, include general-use tables with monthly rates for a city, region or type of climate. Listed rates for a regional area are based on average weather conditions using historical data. While useful to estimate water loss, rates do not indicate the actual loss for a given day, week or month in the future. Actual weather conditions are rarely equal to the average of variations that have occurred in the past.

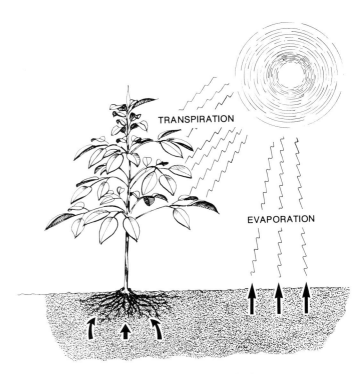

Figure 8-20 Evapotranspiration

In most cases, ET rates in standard tables indicate the consumptive use of a high water requirement plant under well-watered conditions. Listed values must be adjusted to estimate the rate for a particular type of plant.

Reference Evapotranspiration (ETo) rates are used in most applications in landscape irrigation. A plant factor (crop coefficient) is used as a multiplier to adjust the ETo for a particular plant species.

Note: ETo adjustment for type of crop is discussed later in this chapter; see Variations in Planting.

In some climate regions of the U.S.A., ET rates that are based on actual weather conditions, are provided to the general public on a regular basis (newspaper, radio, computer modem service, etc.) to promote water conservation in landscape irrigation. In some cases, the watering schedule of individual systems can be automatically adjusted. Adjustments to the watering program can be made using a communication link to the controller from an outside source. Adjustments may also be the result of information developed at the site, if the system is equipped with a computer that can calculate ET data using input from a weather-station located at the site.

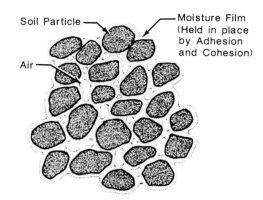

SOIL−WATER−AIR

Thin Film of Moisture−
High Tension

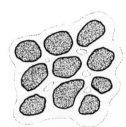

Thick Film of Moisture−
Low Tension

Figure 8-21 Water Storage in Soil

SOIL-WATER-PLANT. Plants are subject to stress whenever a negative water balance occurs as the result of transpiration exceeding root absorption. Soil tension increases as moisture is depleted and the energy required by the plant to remove water from the soil particles increases. Plant color and other general changes in appearance are visible evidence of stress. Plants cannot extract moisture at a certain level of soil tension and will wilt and die.

Water holding capacity and infiltration rates vary with soil type. Particle size of soil varies with classification. Spaces between soil particles are called pores. Pores provide the space for the necessary supply of water and air to the roots. See Figure 8-21. Compaction of soil particles will reduce pore size and therefore will change the water capacity and infiltration rate of the soil.

Excessive amounts of water can also create problems as most commonly used plants cannot survive for an extended period of time with excessive wetness in the soil. Water fills the pores and eliminates the necessary supply of oxygen to the roots, a common problem in areas with poor surface drainage.

Frequency of irrigation and station timing are primarily determined by sprinkler performance, type of planting, cultural practice, soil conditions and the evapotranspiration rate. Water conservation, due to rationing or cost of water, could alter the entire watering schedule. Slopes, drainage problems and light intensity are examples of additional factors that may influence the schedule for individual areas of coverage.

Standard recommendations, such as: "water only when there are visible signs of stress and apply adequate water at a single setting to develop a deep root zone", are logical methods to produce a more drought tolerant turf. Frequent irrigation will maintain moisture only in the first few inches of soil and produce a shallow-rooted grass. However, these type of recommendations do not necessarily provide the turf appearance required in many lawn areas.

Application rates of sprinklers are often recommended to be equal to, or less than, the infiltration rate of the soil. This type of general recommendation is realistic in theory, but is seldom practical and may also be misleading if common "rule-of-thumb" infiltration rates are used for comparison without consideration of time. Infiltration rates are important for proper scheduling.

Most spray sprinklers that cover relatively large areas have a precipitation rate in the 1 to 2 in/hr range when used at normal spacings. Although this is a high rate of application, it is a necessary compromise to develop an acceptable diameter of coverage with an acceptable distribution profile. In general, low-volume sprinklers have major limitations when used to cover large areas.

The infiltration rate of soil is much higher at the beginning of irrigation than it is 20 minutes later, as illustrated in Figure 8-22. Operating time per cycle decreases as the sprinkler precipitation rate increases. Spray sprinkler operation is based on the fact that a relatively high rate of application is possible when elapsed time is measured in minutes.

Repeat cycles (two or more) on the same day are often necessary to reduce surface run-off. A second watering after all zones have watered on the first cycle will allow time for some level of absorption. Repeat cycles are often required on sloping terrain. The greater the slope, the more acute the run-off problem.

Soil infiltration rates vary with different types of soil. Ground cover and soil modification will increase the rate

Sprinkler Performance

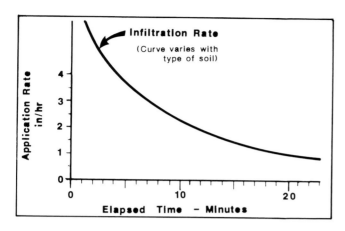

Figure 8-22 Typical Comparison Curve - Soil Infiltration Rate/Time

of a given soil type. While there are many soil types, the infiltration rate will consistently decrease from coursesand (high) down to clay (low). However, of equal importance is the fact that the water-holding capacity of the soil types is in the reverse order of high and low. Therefore, soil type will also influence the frequency of irrigation cycles.

Regardless of soil type, the amount of water applied at the surface must be sufficient to produce a moisture supply in excess of field capacity (amount retained in the soil against the pull of gravity). Light applications of water may not be adequate to move water down into the root zone. It is also important to consider that the majority of evaporation occurs in the first two inches of soil.

Regional standards of efficiency for the average system tend to rise and fall in proportion to irrigation requirement. A similar comparison can be made with regional requirements for air-conditioning systems. While factors that influence efficiency are somewhat constant, demand by regions is not equal and minimum standards for design are not equal.

Irrigation efficiency is a general-use term that is applied in a qualitative manner. It is a measure of how much of the irrigation water applied is beneficially used by the planting. Efficiency is the ratio of water used by the planting to the total quantity of water applied, the efficiency being expressed as a percentage. Although it can be estimated by formula, actual efficiency would be difficult to measure, as there are many variable factors in the soil-water-plant relationship.

There are inherent losses with any method of irrigation and a calculated efficiency of 80% would indicate a very good system. An efficiency of 100% cannot be obtained as this would require an irrigation system to provide moisture without losses, including runoff and percolation below the root zone.

Efficiency of a landscape irrigation system must be based on the total amount of water used for irrigation. It is not limited to the theoretical rates of application and losses in the planting area, but must also include consideration for water applied on walks, drives or any other area that does not require coverage. Also, if efficiency is measured by a limited comparison of water applied to water used by the plant, then under-watering could be very efficient.

Regions where irrigation is necessary for plant survival may have poor soil conditions, poor water quality, harsh climate and a limited water supply...conditions that are not conducive to irrigation efficiency. In this environment, the requirement for efficient use of water increases as the need for water conservation increases. However, efficiency may be limited by an irrigation schedule (frequency and duration) that is necessary for plant survival.

VARIATIONS IN PLANTING. Landscape irrigation would be considerably less complicated if planting was limited to turfgrass only. However, many different varieties of planting are used in landscape design to provide variations in size, shape, texture and color. Plants may be located in planters or beds of various sizes and shapes. Some may be exposed to full sun and others in partial or complete shade.

All plants have a different set of growing conditions that they prefer. A common factor for most types used in exterior landscapes is the ability of the plant to thrive in the local climate. There are ten hardiness zones on the North American continent with different average minimum temperatures. Hardiness of a particular plant in a particular region is not simply limited to the lowest winter temperature, but to a number of factors, including the local climate throughout the year and local soil conditions.

Foundation planting around buildings is often limited to types that are very hardy when minimum grounds maintenance is desired. Some types can exist under extreme environmental conditions above and below ground. However, landscape designs are not always limited to plants with such a degree of hardiness. Selection will often include plant material that requires a special set of growing conditions for quality desired, or even survival.

In some climatic regions, the list of available native or hardy plants is very limited and the landscape may include many exotic plants. The region may also have a very limited amount of rainfall and irrigation performance will be a major factor in maintaining the landscape quality.

All plants require water but not the same amount. Most plants can adapt to soil moisture levels within the normal range. Few can survive extended periods of time in dry or water-logged soil. Some plants are more sensitive to variations and prefer a constant, even amount of moisture. The limited range of soil moisture preferred will vary from dry to moist conditions, depending on the type of plant. While good soil drainage is generally considered to be desirable, it will be an essential requirement with some plant varieties.

Unlike agricultural crops, the water requirements of ornamental plants are not well known. Although research has increased significantly in recent years, much of the current data relating to the water requirements of turfgrasses and other ornamental plants is based on very limited information.

There are also practical limitations in irrigation design when a wide variety of different plant material with different water requirements is used on a project, or mixed together in a planting bed.

Trees are an example of plant variations that often exist in mixed planting. Trees are common for turf and planting bed areas. Watering programs are normally based on the requirements of shallow-rooted plants.

Additional water will be required for newly planted trees and separate irrigation is sometimes provided. The addition of hose outlets to the piping system is a common alternative. Hose watering may also be necessary for mature trees.

In some regions of the U.S.A., plant lists are available with general water requirements of different plant species. Lists may also include information to cover plant size variations. Some plant lists provide daily and yearly requirements with amounts listed in gallons or cubic feet.

As previously discussed, ETo rates are base values and must be adjusted for the type of crop (plant). Plant factors (crop coefficients) should be obtained from agriculture extension services or other reliable sources in the region where the irrigation project is located. Tables which provide "rule of thumb" plant factors should be avoided when possible. Plant factors are used as multipliers to adjust the ETo rate for the requirement of the particular type of plant. For example, a plant factor of .80 indicates that the ET rate for the plant type is 80% of the ETo rate.

System design is normally based on the average irrigation requirement for the "worst-case" month. Since future requirement will be above the historical average, in some cases, an additional allowance should be added to irrigation requirement, when practical. In most regions of the U.S.A., July is the month of greatest requirement.

$$\text{Irrigation Water Requirement} = \frac{(ET_O \times K_c) - ER}{IE}$$

where: ET_O = Reference ET for month (historical data)
  K_c = Plant-Type Coefficient for month.
  ER = Effective Rainfall (67% of monthly average)
  IE = Irrigation Efficiency

Requirement Plant coefficient values will vary with different types of plants and month of the year. Turfgrass will vary by species and water demand (kc) will be higher in the spring and lower during the winter. Plant factors available for different types of ornamental plants are very limited. In many cases, different varieties are limited to one of three plant factors for broad categories of water use (low, average or high).

Actual irrigation efficiency will depend on many variable factors. Many designers use 70% (.70) as a practical goal for sprinkler system design and to estimate the irrigation requirement.

Plant identification through recognition is a basic requirement for most irrigation designers. While there is a minimum level of knowledge necessary to identify plants and determine water requirements, there is no limit on the extent of knowledge that can be of assistance. There are many reference books available that can provide photographic assistance, habit of growth and special water considerations. Landscape texts are also helpful to determine the scientific or common name of a particular plant.

Sprinkler Performance

METHOD OF IRRIGATION AND ZONE SEPARATION. Sprinklers are the most common method of applying water in landscape irrigation. While the amount of water required by an individual plant is not changed by the method used to apply moisture, site conditions, plant selection and plant location may require other methods of watering. Examples are:

1. Plant size and location obstructs the spray coverage.
2. Planting bed is too small for normal spray coverage.
3. Plant type is susceptible to problems from water spray on the leaves.
4. Water quality is poor and should not be sprayed on plants.
5. Individual plants at scattered locations.

Bubblers, stream or mist heads with very small areas of coverage are available as an alternative to standard spray and rotary sprinklers (see Chapter 1, Flood Heads). Micro-irrigation systems, as discussed in Chapter 13, also provide alternate methods of applying moisture to individual plants when very low rates of application are desirable. Variations in planting and common methods of watering with sprinkler systems are also discussed in Chapter 10.

There are many factors that can influence the area of coverage that will be controlled by a single valve. These include basic considerations, such as: method of watering, application rate variations, logical areas of division and water supply or pressure limitations. Basic factors of this type are explained in Chapters 11 and 12.

Separate zone control should also be considered for areas with major variations in site conditions and/or plant water requirements. Separate coverage and valve control are recommended for lawn and shrub beds. In addition to the normal differences in water requirement there is the basic difference of root zone depth between turf and shrubs. It is also necessary in many climates to water grass several times a week to maintain the desired quality during the months of consistent high temperatures.

Soil, sun/shade and slope are common site variations in lawn and planting areas that should be considered for possible separation of control. In some cases, control separation is provided for planting beds on each side of a building.

There are practical limits of control for any system. There is always a degree of compromise between the level of moisture an individual plant may prefer and the average that is practical due to cost considerations.

Recommended design practice is often established with emphasis on one of the following factors.

- Cost of installation
- Equipment performance
- Regional standards
- Water conservation
- Experience
- Theory

Irrigation design should be a blend of these factors in some proportion that is consistent with the parameters of the individual project and any applicable laws.
A minimum level of performance is often used for residential systems where the owner's desire is limited to minimum improvement over "sprinklers at the end of a garden hose."

Client dissatisfaction may occur when the level of performance desired is not obtained due to the limitations of the designer. Problems will often occur when the priority placed on landscape quality by the owner is considerably above that of the designer.

The designer should allow the owner, owner's representative and landscape designer the opportunity to become involved in development of design criteria.

WATER CONSERVATION. There are many regional areas and individual projects that will require a design with special emphasis on water conservation. Restrictions on the use of water in landscape irrigation are common in many regions of the United States. This will often include the use of private water supplies in addition to public water systems. Conservation laws, in some cases, apply to the landscape and the irrigation system design. There may also be specific requirements relating to schedules, maintenance and water audits.

Water rationing may occasionally be required in all public water supplies due to lack of normal rainfall or other reasons. However, conservation may be necessary on a long-term basis in certain areas. This is common in locations where underground supplies are used and/or the annual rainfall is very limited.

While some climatic regions have always had a limited supply of water, many areas which had adequate supplies in the past are now confronted with supply problems. This is often due to the depletion of an underground aquifer or rapid growth of population as the result of relocation. In some cases, there is adequate annual rainfall but development of reservoirs, filtration and delivery systems occur at a slower rate than population growth. It is not uncommon for rationing to occur in the summer months as the result of high consumption demands exceeding the capacity of the water mains to deliver water.

An aquifer is an underground zone or layer of gravel, sand, etc. and water. Water will seep down to this level and remain in place due to a watertight layer of rock below the aquifer. If water is removed at a rate that exceeds replacement, the water table or supply is reduced. Water moves very slowly underground and rainfall may take months or years to replenish the aquifer. Many cities and industries obtain their water from wells drilled down into an aquifer. In some cases, a supply that may have taken many centuries to develop is being depleted in a short period of time.

Note: The use of recycled water is discussed in Chapter 7.

Regardless of the reason for water conservation, it will influence the irrigation design and system operation. Normally this will be in proportion to the need for conservation. There are two separate categories for factors that can influence the design:

    1. Those that may be desired and...
    2. Those that may be required.

Many systems are designed to meet the minimum requirements of local restrictions without regard for improvements in system performance. Although this practice may seem necessary for cost considerations, it is not the best long-term solution for the owner, the water supply, the designer or the irrigation industry. Curtailment of lawn watering is one of the first methods used by cities to reduce consumption when rationing is required. This is very effective, especially in regions where a high percentage of normal consumption is used for landscape irrigation. While improved performance will not eliminate the need for restrictions, over-all improvement of design standards will assist in solving the problem and not be part of the problem, as is the case in many regional areas.

Local regulations may limit the water meter and service pipe size or establish a watering schedule. The schedule may restrict watering to certain days of the week or a particular frequency and may also set limitations on the time of day. Water rates may be set at high levels to promote conservation. An even higher rate may be used during the summer months or a surcharge may be added to normal rates above a certain level of consumption.

Independent water supply systems that are privately owned may also be regulated. Use of water from wells may be controlled by setting a limit on the flow rate allowed. There may be minimum distance requirements between wells and in some cases, new wells are not allowed. A nearby lake may have what seems like an abundance of water, but installation of pumps for private use may be prohibited.

CONSERVATION BY LANDSCAPE DESIGN. The first criteria affecting water conservation on a property is the selection of turfgrass and landscape plant materials to be utilized. A concept of landscape design which is growing in popularity is called "xeriscaping." Xeriscaping involves emphasis on landscape design featuring native plant materials and/or other concepts which will require less supplemental watering while providing an aesthetic setting.

Obviously, the irrigation designer may not be involved in the landscape design process. In fact, the irrigation designer's role is often limited to providing the most efficient design for watering landscape requirements which have already been specified. A discussion of sprinkler system design elements which can affect water conservation is covered in the following section.

CONSERVATION BY DESIGN. In regions where water supplies are limited and water costs are high no single individual will be more concerned about conservation than the owner. However, the owner(s) cannot make a decision on the level of performance desired unless they understand that major variations can occur with different designs. Without this knowledge, they will consider that the most economical system is also the most cost-effective. Cost is not limited to the initial cost of installation and effect is not limited to a standard set of equal benefits.

Figure 8-23 illustrates two problems that often exist in systems where design considerations were based primarily on the cost of installation without regard for the cost of operation. While this approach to design may be considered necessary in some cases, it is not realistic in regions where water conservation is required.

The "Sprinkler in Each Corner" layout, sometimes referred to as the "Four-Poster", is illustrated in Fig. 8-23a and is a good example of poor performance by design. Coverage across walks and drives or over-spray onto buildings, adjacent properties, parking areas and streets are obviously not recommended as methods that will conserve water.

In most cases, there will be adequate concern for loss of water due to wind, without intentionally watering the walk as indicated by the small rotary sprinkler layout in Fig. 8-23a. Ten percent of the water applied to this area or 125 gallons per week (1 inch per week) would be sprayed on the walk. This is based on the assumption that water would be applied equally to the 40 x 50 ft. area. However it will not, and this is the second problem that is often associated with this type of design. Sprinklers are in logical locations and coverage seems adequate, but spacings exceed the maximum distance recommended for the sprinkler. Lack of uniform coverage is considered by many to be the greatest cause of water waste.

Figures 8-23b and 8-23c demonstrate additional waste by design, over-spray beyond the area of planting and onto adjacent paving. Designs for water conservation require careful consideration for each area of coverage and the quick placement of a sprinkler symbol in each small area of the plan is not sufficient.

Sprinkler systems on public property are always subject to criticism by local taxpayers. Common complaints refer to "the system that was operating during the day or at the same time that a rainstorm was in progress."

There are many special problems that exist with irrigation systems on public land and caution is advised in design and equipment selection. Unfortunately, some are designed with the same layout methods and equipment that are used for residential properties. Systems that should be designed with more than average consideration for long-term cost and performance are, in many cases, developed with less than average consideration. This is often due to the fact that an adequate budget was not included and the system is the last item on the design list.

Figure 8-24 illustrates another example of waste and poor performance, but it is also based on an actual design that was used for medium strips of a two mile long, major thoroughfare. After operation, the street is partially covered with water from run-off due to over-spray and slopes. Coverage is less than adequate as the result of spacing, trees and street light standards. Operating time has been extended in an attempt to provide water to areas that are not covered.

Problems of operation are further complicated by product specifications that dropped to a lower standard in favor of low bid. This is unfortunately a common occurrence in public and commercial projects. Low price tends to promote the mythology that all sprinklers with the same diameter of coverage are equal and all valves of a given size are equal, etc. In this example, equipment used has been somewhat less than dependable and valves have often stayed open longer than expected. (Usually during the morning rush hour when system deficiencies are most apparent to the public!)

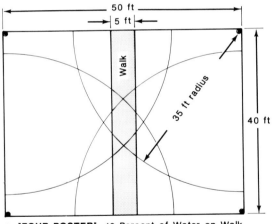

a. "FOUR POSTER" 10 Percent of Water on Walk
125 Gallons Per Week

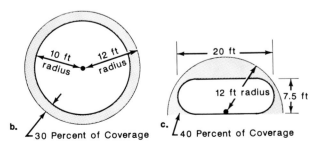

b. 30 Percent of Coverage **c.** 40 Percent of Coverage

Figure 8-23 Poor Performance by Design

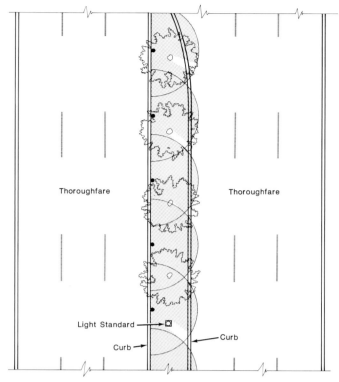

Thoroughfare

Thoroughfare

Light Standard

Curb

Curb

Figure 8-24 Inefficient Median Strip Design

This system is located in the Southwestern region of the United States, in a city that must advise its citizens each summer that they must conserve water or rationing will be necessary. While this example may seem extreme, it does demonstrate that water conservation must be by design. The designer must make an effort to improve efficiency and reduce waste. This is not necessary simply to satisfy the owner but to conserve water. The level of water conservation in landscape irrigation that can be obtained for any region will be limited to the benefits produced on individual systems. This includes residential, commercial and public properties.

CONSERVATION BY MANAGEMENT. The design, installation and maintenance of a permanently-installed system are very important, but irrigation efficiency is not permanently established at a given level by the performance of the water delivery system.

While water distribution and the rate of application provided by the system are somewhat constant, the amount of irrigation water required is not consistent throughout the irrigation season. Irrigation efficiency is therefore related to irrigation management. Changes in the watering schedule should be consistent with changes in the water requirement.

The average system design and operation during the irrigation season would be different if the average property owner understood how irrigation efficiency is measured. In many residential and commercial systems the watering schedule is seldom changed and management is often limited to changes in the position of the controller power-output switch.

Water conservation by landscape and system design is based on considerations during the design phase. Water conservation by management of the system operation is based on considerations over the life span of the irrigation system.

IRRIGATION AUDITS. Improvement in irrigation efficiency at a very large site is especially important due to the size and total water requirements of the turfgrass area.

Management of automatic operation requires a watering schedule that is based on the actual performance of the system, site conditions and different amounts of water that are necessary throughout the irrigation season.

Development of a watering schedule with emphasis on conservation may require the services of a Landscape Irrigation Auditor to evaluate the system performance, determine irrigation requirement and provide a monthly schedule for each controller.

The benefit for site managers is a month-by-month schedule to maintain turf appearance with efficient use of water. In most cases, improved management of controller operating programs will also result in monthly and/or yearly savings in water use and cost.

A watering schedule that is developed from a site audit will include the frequency of operation (days per week), cycles required per day and duration timing for each controller station.

The base schedule will be calculated using historical weather data (ETo) for the local area. The site manager can modify the schedule for more or less watering based on the actual weather conditions. Current ETo rates are available to the general public in some climate regions. Sources for this information would include university extension agents and state Department of Water Resources. Weather-stations and computer systems are used in some cases to collect and process the data at the site.

Sprinkler Performance

Courtesy of The Irrigation Association

Figure 8-25 "Catch-can" Test in Progress

A complete irrigation audit is not a simple task and includes a considerable amount of field work to obtain the necessary site data. This includes "catch can" testing to determine the actual distribution uniformity and precipitation rate of the system.

The cost of a landscape irrigation audit for a particular site will depend on several factors including the size of the irrigated area. In most cases, an audit is cost-effective for very large properties due to the potential savings in water cost.

For additional information on irrigation audits, auditor training programs and certification, the interested reader is referred to:

The Irrigation Association
8260 Willow Oaks Corporate Drive, Ste. 120
Fairfax, VA 22031

SUMMARY. Sprinkler performance will vary with product, and product performance will vary with system design. Design will vary with product, landscape, climate, site conditions and budget.

Irrigation systems are judged in many different ways, including the most economical way to scatter water across the land. However, the essential worth consists of performance in the control of soil moisture. Levels of performance are directly related to the levels of design compromise.

The designer should have some understanding of the basis on which industry techniques are recommended. Suggested methods of irrigation must be adapted to the conditions of the individual project. In many cases, it is necessary to deviate from accepted practice and, therefore, knowledge required for design is a blend of theory and practical application.

BIBLIOGRAPHY

(a) Irrigation by Sprinkling: J. E. Christiansen published by University of California, College of Agriculture.

(b) ASAE (American Society of Agricultural Engineers) 2950 Niles Rd. St. Joseph, MI 49085-9695

(c) Kenneth H. Solomon, David F. Zoldoske and Joe C. Oliphant. Drop Size Measurement and Sprinkler Performance Evaluation. Proceedings, IA 1991, San Antonio, Texas. CIT California State University, Fresno, California 93740-0018.

(d) Soil Conservation Service National Engineering Handbook, Section 15, Irrigation.

CHAPTER 9

Plot Plans

The first phase of an irrigation design is the preparation of a plot plan of the property. This phase is very important and should be done accurately to avoid errors in the design and cost estimate. Considerable time can be saved if a professional survey can be obtained from the owner.

An architect's plot plan, mortgage survey or landscape plan will be helpful in preparing the irrigation system plot plan. However, the major dimensions on any of these drawings should always be checked on the job site. The house or other buildings may not be located on the lot according to the plan, or the length and width of the lot may not be correct. It is not uncommon when construction is started that buildings, walks, driveways, etc., may be shifted relative to the location shown on the architect's original plot plan.

In many cases, minor differences that may exist between the plot plan and the site can be resolved by on-site adjustments before installation. However, a re-design may be necessary in some cases, including the use of different equipment and/or additional equipment. An error of one foot may be very important at one location (or in one direction) and of minor importance at another location (or in a different direction). Obstructions (trees, poles, etc.) that are shown in the wrong location, or not shown on the plan, can create as many problems as errors relating to the size of the area.

MEASURING PROPERTIES

Plans are usually not available for existing residential properties. In addition, they are often not available for commercial and institutional sites. Therefore, the designer must measure these properties in order to draw a plot plan for the irrigation system.

When measuring, first make a freehand sketch of the property as shown in Figure 9-3. Show all buildings, walks, driveways, flower and shrub beds and any other permanent objects. All of these have some effect on the design of the irrigation system which is discussed in the design chapters.

Measure the house or main building first. Then use the main building as the base for measuring the location of all other objects including the boundary lines. It is generally assumed that measuring the landscape area is the primary concern. Actually, the opposite is true. If everything but the planting area is measured accurately, the final drawing will show the correct size and relative location of all planting areas.

The *imaginary extension of building walls* from an accurately measured main building will solve most measurement problems of reasonably sized properties with the use of only a tape measure. The logic of this method will be understood if you imagine that the property is a huge drawing board, and a "T" square and triangle are being used to mark off parallel lines and intersecting lines at 90°. This is the way the plot plan is drawn from the measurements of the sketch.

Often, lots are not perfectly rectangular even though the property lines and streets may seem parallel to the house on all sides. Therefore, it is safer to assume that a property is not rectangular. Two *widely separated* measurements taken from four sides of the building, as shown in Figure 9-1, will establish the property lines, street(s), and building in true relationship when transferred to scale on the final drawing.

The dimension lines in Figure 9-1 are all imaginary extensions of the building lines. These lines can be established quite accurately by sighting of the building walls from the furthermost point. For example: the 38.7 ft and 42.8 ft measurements were measured from a point on the curb *after* sighting the building wall.

Although the property in Figure 9-1 was thought to be perfectly rectangular, the measurements show that the west lot line and the street are not parallel to the building. Also, comparison with the measurements of the other two lot lines shows that the property is not a true rectangle.

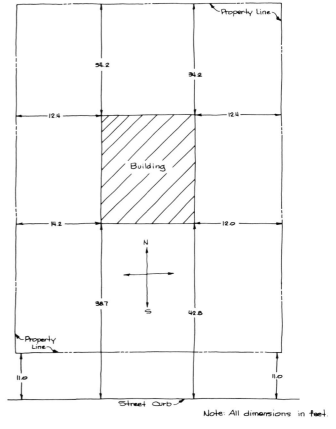

Figure 9-1 Imaginary Extension of Building Lines

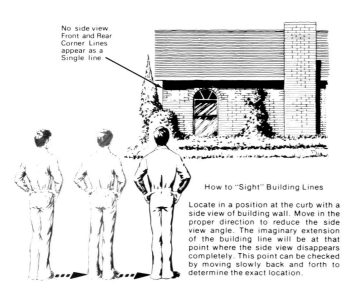

No side view. Front and Rear Corner Lines appear as a Single line.

How to "Sight" Building Lines

Locate in a position at the curb with a side view of building wall. Move in the proper direction to reduce the side view angle. The imaginary extension of the building line will be at that point where the side view disappears completely. This point can be checked by moving slowly back and forth to determine the exact location.

Conversely, a property could be an exact rectangle with the building not placed parallel to the lot lines. Using the "imaginary extension of building lines" method of measuring will also indicate such a condition.

MEASURING HINTS. Two simple hints will help to avoid errors in measuring.
1. Since most plot plans are drawn to an engineering scale (1 in = 10 ft, etc.), measure with a tape that has feet divided in 10 increments rather than inches.
2. When measuring, particularly around a building, measure from left to right. This way the figures on the tape will be right side up instead of upside down as is the case when measuring the opposite way.

LANDSCAPING DATA REQUIRED

Note on the sketch all types of plantings. Indicate shrubs, planting beds, trees, retaining walls, abrupt grade changes, sunlight exposure variations, soil types, etc. As discussed in Chapter 8, plant identification through recognition is a basic requirement for individuals who visit a site with existing plant material. It is necessary to identify plants for zone separation requirements and in many cases, to estimate the size and height of the plant at maturity.

A variety of different graphic symbols are used to show the various kinds of plants and trees on sketches, irrigation designs and landscape plans. In most cases, the drawing scale and the necessary piping detail of the irrigation design will limit the use of common landscape symbols as shown in Figure 9-2. The circled figures in Figure 9-2 illustrate a common method used to indicate the existing heights of planting material on the survey sketch.

Size and height of planting are important for a sprinkler system due to the height limitations of spraying water over the top and the possible obstruction of foliage to spray coverage in other areas. Additional planting bed detail may be required for flood irrigation or micro-irrigation, due to the importance of spacing and individual plant locations.

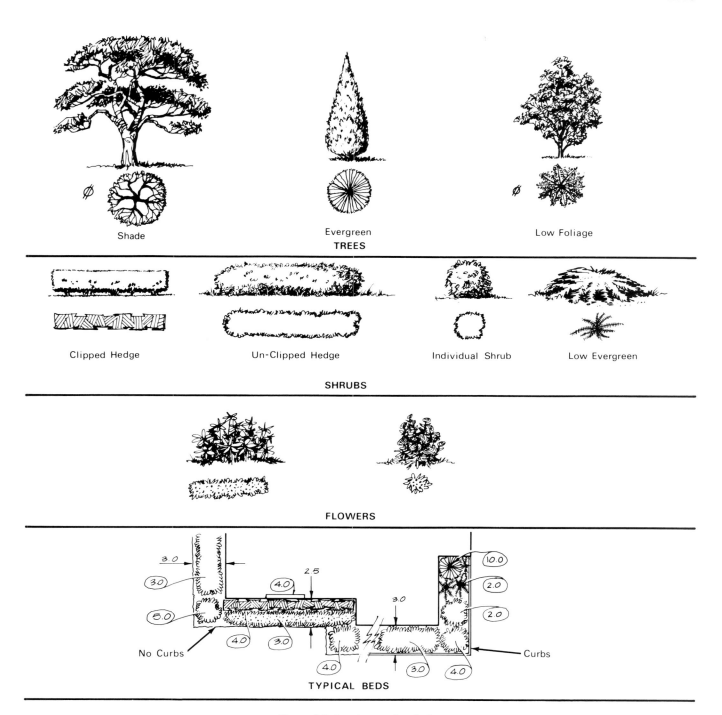

Figure 9-2 Landscape Symbols

Trees obstruct coverage of all types of sprinklers. Those with low hanging branches like willows and magnolias cause the most obstruction. The location of the trunk and the hanging branches should both be correctly noted on the sketch.

Even tall, small-trunked trees affect sprinkler coverage. The lower branches may interfere with the streams of long-range rotary sprinklers. The trunks of trees over 2

inch caliber block the coverage of spray heads. It should be noted that trees with small trunks, at time of system design, will soon grow to a size that will affect sprinkler coverage. So, all trees of any size or shape should be plotted on the sketch.

OTHER REQUIRED DATA
In addition to landscaping details, other types of required information can be obtained from a site visit.

Plot Plans

Information necessary for design considerations will depend on the type of irrigation products (sprinklers, flood, micro, etc.) used in the system. The following items are provided as examples:

1. Location of city water main in relation to the property. (If not readily apparent, this information can be obtained from the engineering division of the water department.)
2. Location and size of existing water meter and service (piping from city water main to an outside meter; or curb stop in cases where meter is located in building). Also, when meter is in building, determine size and type of piping from curb stop to meter.
3. Static water pressure measured with pressure gauge attached to a hydrant with no water flowing. (Note: This pressure reading is for reference only. The system must be designed to the lowest pressure that will exist in the area at time of highest water usage.)
4. If existing water supply will be used, a flow-pressure loss test may be necessary.
5. Elevation differences (plus or minus) on the property.
6. Soil type and general conditions. Will rock or shale be encountered during installation?
7. Suitable location for automatic controller and availability of a non-switched electrical circuit.
8. If a pump will be used, obtain information on electric service, site conditions for pump location, etc. (See Chapter 6, Pumps).

Four additional examples for sprinkler designs:

9. Window locations. Windows are shown on the sketch only if low enough and so located that preventing their being sprayed might be a design consideration. Or, if the bottom of a window is close to the height of shrubbery in front. In this case, the information is necessary so that shrub heads will not inadvertently be placed so that the head and its riser pipe can be seen through the window.
10. Adjoining neighbors, walks, patios, etc., requiring protection from sprinkler sprays.
11. Is there a street curb to set half-circle heads against, or is it a suburban area where the lawn grows to a non-curbed street? Without curbs, a row of full-circle sprays are set back from the street with the spray throwing to the street edge. This is necessary because heads located next to a non-curbed street will be constantly damaged by vehicles running off the edge.
12. Approximate compass direction, so allowance can be made for prevailing wind.

Figure 9-3 is a measured freehand sketch for which a spray system is designed in Chapters 10 and 11.

The freehand sketch need not be, and rarely is, drawn to scale. This is because only the measured dimensions are used in drawing the plot plan to scale. All objects, and dimensions locating them, should also be shown on the sketch because all this information will be required in making the plot plan and designing the system.

DRAWING PLOT PLAN

Although training and experience will be very useful, a limited amount of drafting skill and equipment is necessary to draw a plot plan and design an irrigation system. Individuals who have never used the basic tools of drafting may find it somewhat difficult the first time. However, as with any new endeavor, performance will improve very quickly with each new drawing.

Design drawings for normal engineering reproduction (blue-line prints) require the use of drafting vellum or a suitable plastic material. The plot plan can be drawn using pencil (.5mm mechanical or lead holders). Many professional designers use ink pens for improved contrast and appearance of the blue-line prints. Irrigation designs developed on computers with CAD (Computer Aided Design) software also produce ink drawings from the plotter (printer).

Regardless of the drafting methods, dimensions are used to develop a plan of the property at a very small scale, and with all areas and details in correct proportion. The scale selected for the drawing is based on a compromise between the requirement to show the necessary detail and the overall size of the plan. The standard (U.S.A.) engineering scale of 1 in = 10 ft (1:120 ratio) and the standard (metric) scale of 1:100 are often used for smaller size properties. With consideration for the drawing sheet size, the drawing ratio will increase as the property size increases. Scales of 1 in = 20 ft (1:240), 1 in = 30 ft (1:360), etc. are used as required to maintain a practical drawing size.

Since the plan is drawn to scale, dimensions are normally not provided on irrigation design drawings. The system design is therefore limited by the accuracy of

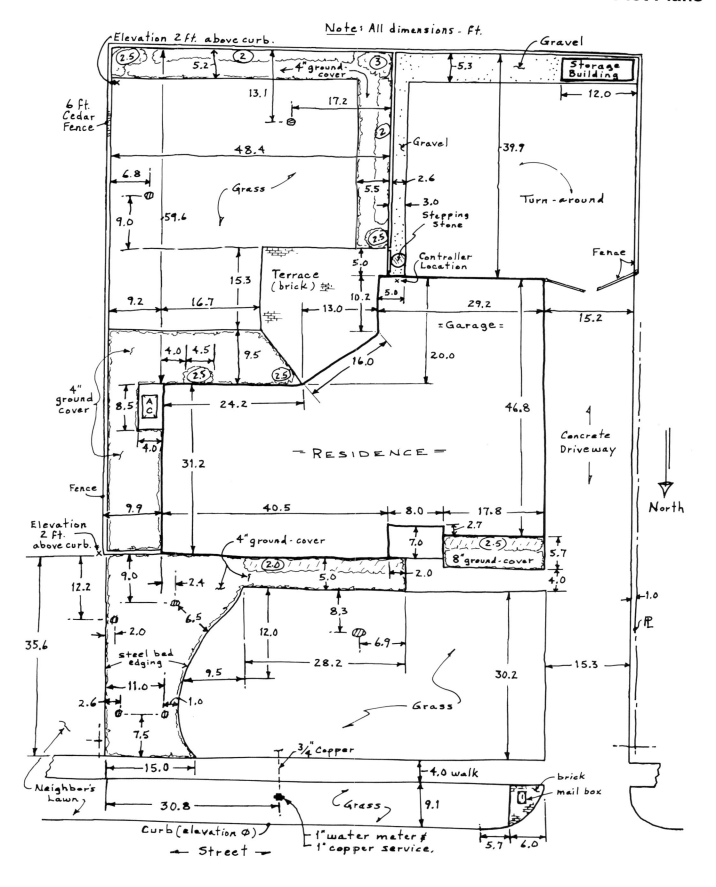

Figure 9-3 Freehand Sketch - Exemplary Rectangular Property

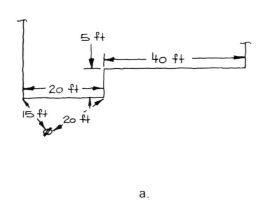

a.

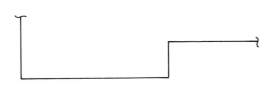

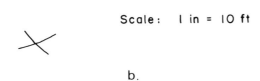

Scale: 1 in = 10 ft

b.

Figure 9-4 Location of a Tree by Triangulation

the plot plan. The listed scale of the drawing is also used to lay-out the location of components at the site for installation. Note: Dimensions as necessary to locate mains, valves, etc. are added after installation for "as-built" drawings.

ODD SHAPED PROPERTIES

Non-rectangular lots can also be successfully measured with a tape measure. The imaginary extension of the building is the basis. In addition, *triangulation* is generally required.

TRIANGULATION

With this supplementary measuring method, two measurements to a given point from a known length of a line will accurately locate the point.

Example 1. A tree was measured from two ends of a building wall to the center of a tree, Figure 9-4a. The 20

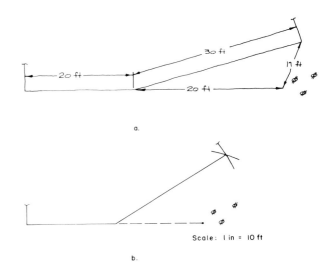

a.

Scale: 1 in = 10 ft

b.

Figure 9-5 Developing Angles

ft building wall is the "known length of line." To locate the tree on a plot plan, Figure 9-4b, the building was first drawn to scale. Then a compass was used to lightly draw arcs; a 20 ft radius from the right end of the 20 ft building wall and a 15 ft radius from the left end. The intersection of the two arcs locates the tree exactly as it is on the property.

Example 2. Figure 9-5 illustrates a building with walls at an angle other than 90°. The building cannot be drawn on the plot plan without knowing the angle. In lieu of determining the angle, measurements were made which, when used on the plot plan, establish the proper angle between the two walls.

In a freehand sketch, Figure 9-5a, the 20 ft building wall was imaginarily extended 20 ft and from this point a measurement was taken to the end of the 30 ft wall. When establishing angles by this method, the preferred procedure is to extend the wall about the same distance as the length of the angling wall; in this example, 30 ft. However, the wall could be imaginarily extended only 20 ft because the grove of trees would have prevented a straight measurement to the corner of the 30 ft long wall.

When drawing the scaled plot plan, Figure 9-5b, the 20 ft long wall was drawn first, with the building line extended 20 ft. A 30 ft radius arc was struck from the right end of the wall. Then a 17 ft radius arc was struck from the end of the imaginary extension of the building line. The intersection of the two arcs locates the end of the 30 ft wall with the proper angle between the two walls.

Application of the two previous examples of triangulation, and various versions, will solve most problems of

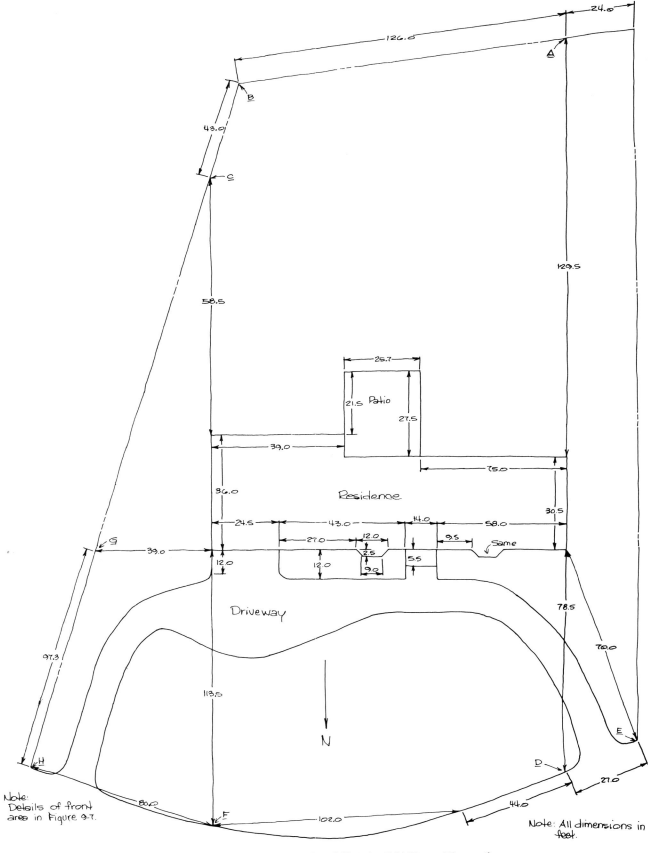

Figure 9-6 Dimensioned Freehand Sketch - Odd Shaped Properties

MEASURING ODD SHAPED PROPERTIES

The imaginary extension of building walls was used as the basis for measuring the odd shaped property in Figure 9-6. The west wall was extended to provide points for both the front (D), and rear (A), boundary lines. Imaginary extension of the east wall provided boundary line points (C) and (F).

The second point required to establish the rear property line was developed by triangulation. First, the east building wall line was extended 58.5 ft south to the east property line (C). Then a measurement was taken from this point to the southeast corner of the property.

On the scaled plot plan, a 126.0 ft radius arc was struck from point (A). A second arc with a radius of 43.0 ft was struck from point (C). The intersection of these two arcs located the southeast corner, (B), of the property. Extending a line through points (B) and (A), 24.0 ft west of (A) located the southwest corner.

A 27.0 ft radius arc from the end of the 78.5 ft imaginary extension north of the west building wall, (D), was drawn. Then a 70.0 ft arc from the northwest corner of the building was drawn. The intersection of these two arcs located the northwest corner, (E), of the property. A line drawn through points (E) and (D) and extended eastward from point (D) 44.0 ft then depicted the westerly, straight portion of the front boundary.

Although not readily apparent, the northeast corner of the property was also located by triangulation. The east building line was extended 113.5 ft, (F), to the front boundary line. The front building wall was extended to the east property line 39.0 ft, (G). Then a 97.3 ft radius arc struck from the developed point (G) and an 80 ft arc from point (F) located the northeast corner of the property, (H), at the intersection of the two arcs.

Note: Exactly locating points on a property line will probably be impossible unless there is a fence or other means to identify the line. But, that is the advantage of triangulation; it doesn't matter if the point is not on the property. As long as the dimension is on a true extension of the building line, (as the dimensions 58.5 ft and 39.0 ft), the results will be the same. However, never

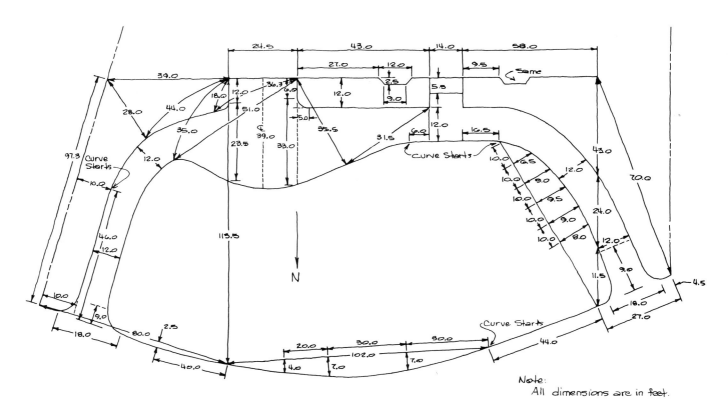

Figure 9-7 Freehand Sketch - Curve Detail

use these indefinite points to lay out property lines. When the plot plan was made for the property sketched in Figure 9-6, the points representing the two east corners of the property, (B) and (H), were connected to establish the east property line in true relationship to the building.

Whenever possible, obtain a property survey plat of any property that is similar in shape to that shown in Figure 9-6. The actual location or number of property line points may be different than "assumptions" made at the site.

PLOTTING CURVES
Curves are easily plotted with a tape measure, too, as illustrated in Figure 9-7 showing the details of the driveway and street in the front half of Figure 9-6. A careful study of the sketch will show that a strategic number of points on the curves were located by either an extension of building lines or triangulation.

Where more details are needed to plot curves, another simple method requiring only two tape measures is used. This method is illustrated by the measurements taken for the curve in the street of Figure 9-7. From the point indicated by the notation "curve starts", a tape measure was stretched "straight" to the point established when the east building line was extended 113.5 ft. Then, at intervals indicated by the dimensions, measurements were taken at right angles from the tape to the street. The same method was used to plot the curvature of the west portion of the driveway.

When drawing the plot plan, points are located by the measurements. Then a smooth, unbroken line is drawn through the points with a French Curve or an adjustable curve template.

SURVEYS
Most residential and institutional properties can be measured with a tape by the methods already discussed. However, in some instances property corner stakes cannot be found, especially on new properties. A plot of all properties is registered in the city or county records building.

This official survey drawing, which can be examined, provides the length of all property lines and the angles at which they intersect. With this data, property lines can be established from only two property corner stakes.

PROFESSIONAL SURVEYS. Larger and more complicated properties may be beyond the scope of the methods of measuring previously outlined. In this event, the services of a registered surveyor should be used if the owner cannot furnish a copy of the survey.

The fee for a professional survey is usually not exorbitant, if only the property lines, buildings, walks, drives, etc., are requested. With such a survey, all other details lacking can easily be added by the designer. Requesting such details from the surveyor would increase the cost of the survey considerably.

AERIAL SURVEYS. Extremely large and irregular properties like golf courses are best surveyed by means of an aerial photograph. When contracting for this type survey, advise the scale of photograph desired. Usually, the scale for the plot plan of an 18-hole golf course is 1 in = 100 ft and a 9-hole course, 1 in = 50 ft. The photographs should be checked for accuracy and distortion.

An aerial survey is usually quite accurate in the center. The accuracy deteriorates towards the sides and ends, and especially at the corners of the photograph. To verify accuracy, two points on each side of the photograph, two on the ends, and two near the center should be tape measured on the site. A comparison of the actual measurements against the scaled distances between the same points on the photograph will determine accuracy. Any discrepancies should be allowed for in the system design and estimate.

Aerial photographs are easily traced to make a plot plan of the property. Angular shots have a tendency to cast shadows which blur some areas, especially the outlines of trees and buildings. Fairways, tees and greens offer sharp outlines against the rough if shot just after mowing.

ROLLING TERRAIN

Professional surveys, aerial surveys and topography surveys, (such as Figure 3-5 in Hydraulics Chapter), show proper dimensions on a level plane. However, piping lengths and spacing of irrigation outlets follow the ground surface even though it may be of an undulating nature.

Figure 9-8a shows an elevation view of a theoretical rolling property. The length of the property according to a professional survey, a topography survey, and in

Plot Plans

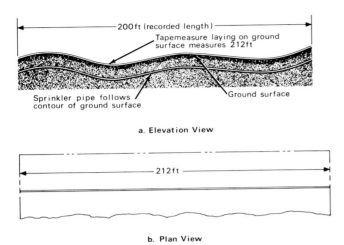

a. Elevation View

b. Plan View

Figure 9-8 Diagram of Rolling Property

property records, (such as deeds, etc.), is recorded as 200 feet. This dimension was measured on a level plane as shown.

To compensate for the additional 12 ft length of property, the plot plan is drawn using 212 ft for the length as if the ground surface were on a level plane, Figure 9-8b. With this method, pipe lengths and head spacings will be correctly depicted. Otherwise, the system design and estimated cost would be incorrect.

When verifying aerial surveys, as discussed above, compensation for rolling ground surface should also be determined. With professional surveys and plat records, properties, if of a rolling nature, should also be measured to provide compensation. When the designer measures the property to develop a plot plan, measurements should be made as illustrated in Figure 9-8a to provide proper compensation.

CHAPTER 10

Head Layout

INTRODUCTION TO HEAD LAYOUT

The second phase in preparation of a system design is the "head layout", a term used to describe the detailed process of locating the necessary quantity of sprinklers in each area of desired coverage. This includes specifying the required performance of each head as to diameter of coverage and degree of arc. Manufacturers product numbers are often used to simplify the specification.

Basic areas of coverage and the uniformity of water distribution are determined by the sprinkler layout. It is necessary that the designer understand the limitations of an individual sprinkler and the requirement of coverage overlap from adjacent sprinklers. This subject is explained in Chapter 8.

There are many factors that can influence system performance, but none are more directly related than head layout. Layout can be as simple as locating large coverage sprinklers in each corner of a landscaped area, or it can be extensive, with consideration for the requirements of individual plants. Layout recommendations can vary from the most economical to the most efficient. Cost of installation and efficiency of performance will normally rise and fall together.

An irrigation design is developed in phases with a continuous and connected series of decisions. This is necessary for a system that will be formed by a group of interacting and interdependent items. Each phase should be developed to a level that is consistent with the overall performance desired.

The extent of system development required and, therefore, cost, are directly related to the sprinkler layout. However, regardless of any improvements that may follow in other phases, system performance will always be limited by the level of efficiency provided in the application of water.

Head layout is often the most difficult part of design. While there are many standard methods of layout, there is not a standard that is correct for each situation in different designs. There are basic considerations of coverage for various sizes and shapes, in addition to water requirement, site and planting variations, as discussed in Chapter 8.

System cost and water supply limitations are factors that always result in a degree of design compromise. The size of an existing water meter or pump and the related supply piping can be a very limiting factor in the system. The cost of a new, larger size should be determined if the existing supply is not adequate when compared to the area of coverage. Flow capacity and pressure of the supply will influence the selection and quantity of sprinklers and, therefore, the entire system. The effect of flow capacity on operating zones is discussed in Chapter 11.

There are obvious restrictions in the amount of coverage when the supply is limited in quantity. Rate of recovery must be considered when a well or pond is used for the water supply.

All of the normal layout considerations to avoid waste are elevated to a higher level of importance when water conservation is more than an occasional requirement. Examples of items requiring special consideration are:

1. Selection of sprinklers. Also valves and controllers.
2. Uniformity of sprinkler distribution.

Head Layout

3. Spray beyond borders of coverage requirement.
4. Surface runoff.
5. Separate layouts for areas with water requirement variations.
6. Variations in sprinkler operating pressure. Discussed in Chapter 11.

Although methods of layout and related examples provided in this chapter are limited to spray heads, many of the considerations discussed will also apply to rotary sprinkler layout. Basic considerations of a rotary sprinkler layout are discussed in Chapter 12, Rotary Systems.

Separation of sprinkler coverage and zone control for lawn and shrubs is always desirable, as discussed in "Related Considerations," Chapter 8. Additional separation of planting areas is also recommended when there are significant differences in water requirement, including frequency of irrigation cycles.

However, in most cases, some degree of compromise is necessary for practical reasons or cost considerations. The level of compromise required will depend on the individual project, including the influence of regional design standards for landscape irrigation. Regional design standards are based primarily on the minimum requirements of the regional climate. Although recommended design methods for improved irrigation performance are somewhat constant, the performance of individual systems will vary for many reasons, including the regional variation of basic need for irrigation and efficiency. Irrigation in one climate region may be a desirable option to improve plant quality for a short period of time, and in another region, irrigation may be necessary for plant survival over an extended period of time.

HEAD SPACING

Sprinkler heads are rated by the manufacturer for area of coverage, flow and operating pressure requirements. Head spacing and performance for a given diameter of coverage will vary from one model to another. Coverage diameters, as listed in manufacturer's catalogs are commonly used on irrigation designs to visualize the area of coverage. However, circles drawn on a plan can also be very misleading if the designer does not understand the limitations of distribution, as discussed in Chapter 8.

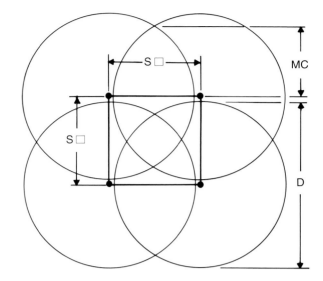

Square Spacing

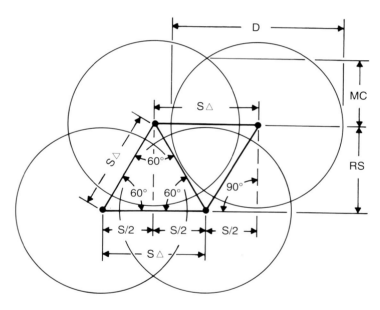

Equilateral Triangular Spacing

S□	=	Square Spacing of heads
S△	=	Equilateral triangular spacing of heads
S/2	=	Equilateral triangular 1/2 spacing of heads
RS	=	Spacing between rows of heads
D	=	Diameter of coverage
MC	=	Mean Coverage

Figure 10-1 Triangular vs. Square Spacing

The designer should establish the maximum spacing that will be used on the design for each nozzle size available in the nozzle series selected. The spacing should be based on the overlap requirements of the nozzle series and with consideration for average wind conditions at the site.

The inexperienced designer does not have the advantage of a standard spacing formula with an established set of variable factors. Although a formula could be developed, it would be of very limited value due to the lack of knowledge that would be necessary to predict the infinitely variable effects of wind on sprinkler performance.

Most spacing recommendations for a particular nozzle series are based on years of experience, and are intended as a practical compromise for the permanent installation of sprinklers that must operate with wind conditions that will change to some degree, each time the system is operated.

TRIANGULAR VS. SQUARE SPACING. In square spacing, shown in Figure 10-1, heads are located at each of the four corners formed by a square. And, in triangular spacing, heads fall at each of three points formed by an equilateral triangle in which the included angles are 60°.

SELECTION OF SPACING. Spray head spacing can vary from a few feet to over 20 feet for landscape areas that can vary in size from a small planter box to relatively large areas of turf or other types of ground cover. The spacing (or spacings) used for head layout in an individual area will be controlled primarily by:

1. The size and shape of the landscape area.
2. The size, type and spacing of planting material and obstructions to spray coverage, if applicable.
3. The influence of budget on product selection and design criteria.
4. The designer's knowledge and experience relating to distribution and spacing requirements of the sprinkler model and nozzle series selected, and spray head spacing, in general.
5. Site conditions, such as, the capacity of the water supply, pressure available for design and average wind velocity.

Spray head layout can be comparatively easy for areas where a somewhat constant spacing is possible. The layout process will become increasingly more difficult as the need for different spacings increases due to size and shape variations within the area.

Triangular spacing is generally preferred over square spacing due to the improved distribution characteristics of triangular spacing. Also, heads on triangular spacing can be spaced further apart as compared to square spacing. Reduced spacing for a square pattern is necessary to provide sufficient water at the center of the square where the four circles of coverage must overlap.

The only basic disadvantage of triangular spacing is the over-spray that will occur beyond borders which are perpendicular to the rows of sprinklers. This can be a problem (unless corrected) on rows where a head is located one-half space from the border. See rows (f) and (h), Figure 10-2.

Even though triangular spacing is preferred, the pattern is not always practical for the many different sizes and shapes that a systems designer will encounter in landscape irrigation design. The use of triangular, square and single-row, or a combination of spacing patterns on a particular project is often necessary for practical reasons.

Triangular spacing is used for the layout examples provided in this chapter. A square spacing layout is similar and somewhat less complicated.

BASICS OF SPRAY HEAD LAYOUT

NOTE: To facilitate the explanation of the design of spray systems, "Exemplary Performance Data: Spray Nozzles," Figure 11-3, is used for the majority of examples discussed in Chapters 10 and 11.

The performance of this nozzle series is fixed (non-adjustable). Nozzles are available in seven different sizes and up to eleven different areas of coverage.

Although nozzle sizes, spacings and arcs of coverage available will vary with brand and model, basic methods of layout are the same for most types of standard spray heads.

Very few areas will be of an exact size to accommodate a true equilateral triangular (all sides of a triangle of equal length) sprinkler pattern. However, a good layout can be obtained, in most cases, by compressing an

Head Layout

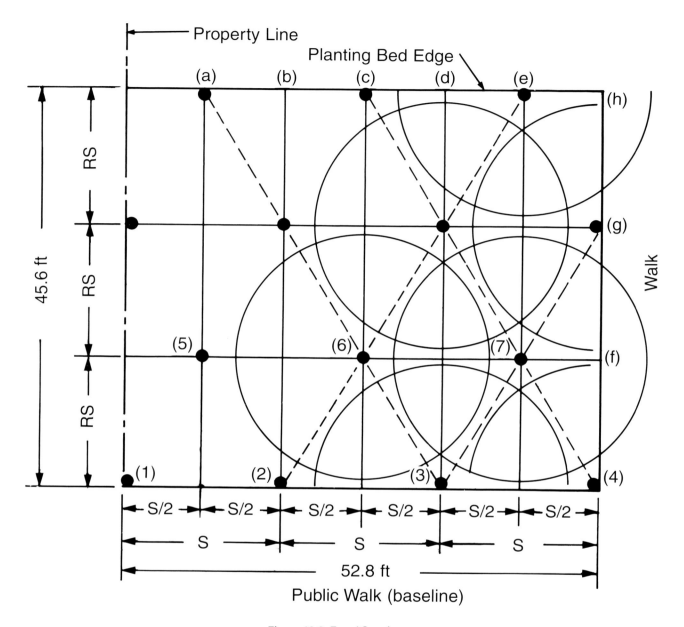

Figure 10-2 Equal Spacing

equilateral triangular pattern from one or both directions.

Triangular sprinkler head patterns cannot be accurately developed by drawing triangles on the plot plan. Instead, a rectangular grid is drawn; heads placed at the intersection of the lines forming the grid produce an "equal spaced" triangular pattern.

This pattern can easily be plotted with the following rule:
1. Use the same spacing for all heads on all rows of heads.
2. Use the same spacing between all rows of heads.

Figure 10-2 depicts an area which is not of an exact size for a true equilateral triangular sprinkler pattern. Therefore, the layout was adjusted to provide an "equal spaced" pattern.

In layout of an area that is suitable for equal spacing, the first step is to compare the available spacings (maximum for design) of the nozzle series selected to the size of the area.

In open areas, such as the area shown in Figure 10-2, larger spacing nozzles are normally considered first to reduce the total number of heads required for the area.

However, nozzle sizes used for layout in open areas are not limited to a selection based on the number of heads alone. Performance, flow and pressure requirements must also be considered for a cost effective sprinkler spacing.

For example, in the nozzle series shown in Figure 11-3, the 412, 415, 418 and 420 series are commonly used for layout in areas where multiple rows of sprinklers will be required. The 424 series is seldom used for large, open areas due to the flow requirements of this series. In most cases, and with most water supplies, the 420 series is a more practical choice. However, the "practical choice" can change with different projects and with an area size that is not suitable for normal spacings.

The 420 nozzle series is used for the triangular spacing layout shown in Figure 10-2. Radius of coverage is 14 ft at 25 psi operating pressure; see note (2), Figure 11-3. Maximum design spacing is based on a common method of deration for this nozzle series; see note (1), Figure 11-3. Row spacing is calculated using the spacing multiplier of .866 (constant for equilateral triangle):

Design Spacing = 18 ft (20 ft. maximum x .90 = 18 ft)

Row Spacing = 15.6 ft (18 ft. spacing x .866 = 15.59 ft)

There are many possible considerations that may be necessary for the head layout of a particular area. However, to simplify the explanations of the layout used in Figure 10-2, the primary consideration for the layout is the requirement of part-circle sprinklers along the public walk.

The part-circle requirement can be accomplished in two different ways using a triangular pattern. A row of part-circle heads along the walk is the most obvious way and is considered to be the first choice for this example layout. This simple decision will also establish the required direction of the sprinkler rows as being parallel to the public walk. Row direction is optional with a triangular pattern and, in this example, rows could be considered in the opposite direction, if necessary. Alternate layout methods for consideration are discussed later in this chapter.

The following explanation is provided to illustrate the head spacing to area size comparison.

1. Head spacing for the row along the public walk is compared to the 52.8 ft dimension. Three spaces

(4 heads) at design spacing of 18 ft for the 420 series nozzles equals 54 ft. This indicated that this nozzle series is suitable when used at a slightly reduced spacing (52.8 /3 = 17.6).

2. Row spacing is compared to the 45.6 ft dimension from the public walk to the planting bed. Three row spaces (4 rows) at 15.6 ft equals 46.8 ft. This confirms that 420 series nozzles are suitable for the area since 45.6 ft is less than the 46.8 ft (maximum distance allowed for four rows). Row spacing will be compressed to 15.2 ft (45.6 ft /3 = 15.2 ft).

Alternate spacings (different nozzles) would be considered if the 420 series was not suitable for the area. Since the size of the area is rarely equal to the exact dimensions required in both directions, compressed spacing is a common requirement. Within practical limits, reduced spacing is not undesirable.

After the head spacing is determined for an area, the "equal spacing grid pattern" is developed for a triangular spacing layout.

1. Half-Space Lines. Equally spaced lines are drawn perpendicular to the public walk. The public walk is used as the "base line" for the grid layout. In this example, lines (a), (b), (c), (d), and (e) are drawn from the base line to the planting bed. Half-space distance, S /2 = 17.6 /2 = 8.8 ft, or 52.8 /6 (spaces) = 8.8 ft.

2. Row Lines. Lines (f) and (g) are drawn parallel to the "base line." Lines are equally spaced between the public walk (base line) and the planting bed. Lines extend from the property line to the walk on the opposite side of the area. Row space distance, RS = 45.6 /3 (spaces) = 15.2 ft.

After the equal spacing grid pattern is completed, sprinkler heads are located at the intersection of grid lines. Although the complete grid is necessary, approximately half of the intersection points will not be used to locate heads on triangular spacing.

Note: The grid is used only for the head layout phase of design. This should be considered if the grid is developed on a plan that will be used for the final design drawing.

Head Layout

1. Locating heads on one row at a time is advisable for a triangular spacing pattern. For example, heads (1), (2), (3) and (4) are located on the row along the public walk before any heads are located on row (f). Heads (1) and (4) will require 90° arc of coverage nozzles and heads (2) and (3) will require 180° arc of coverage nozzles.

2. Next, heads are located on row (f). Since a triangular spacing pattern is being developed, heads (5), (6) and (7) are located at the intersection of the half-space lines (a), (c) and (e). Full-circle nozzles are required for row (f).

3. Heads on row (g) are located at the intersection of row (g) and the same half-space lines used for heads (1) through (4). Two half-circle and two full-circle coverage nozzles are required for row (g).

4. Heads on row (h) are located at the intersection of the planting bed and the same half-space lines used for row (f). Half-circle nozzles are required for row (h).

Circles are added to illustrate the diameter of coverage without wind distortion. In some cases, the final drawing can be misleading if circles are omitted. For example, the "over-spray" of sprinkler (7) onto the adjacent walk may not be apparent without a circle. However, in most cases, it is not necessary to show circles of coverage for all heads. There are also practical limits on the amount of detail that can be shown clearly on a small scale drawing.

When heads are equal spaced, the result is a symmetrical pattern. In the example layout, all heads are in a straight line along the rows, on the full spacing lines, and on the half spacing lines. Dashed lines have been drawn to illustrate that the heads are also on straight diagonal lines forming a series of like triangles.

Symmetrical layout patterns help to accomplish the aims of a good layout:

1. The most uniform distribution possible.
2. A plan that has a "professional appearance."
3. An installed system that will reflect a "professional appearance" in operation.

Alternate Layout. Primary requirements must be considered before selecting the pattern of heads for a

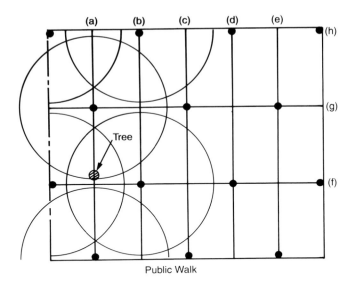

Figure 10-3 Equal Spacing Alternate Layout with Same Grid Pattern

layout. In the example, Figure 10-2, the primary requirement for the system was the use of part-circle heads along the public walk. And, the spacing pattern was developed with consideration for the requirement.

In many cases, the layout selected for an area may also be based on additional considerations. For example, assume that a tree was located near sprinkler (5) in Figure 10-2. The location of a tree (or any other type of obstruction to spray coverage) can be a problem depending on the head layout selected.

Figure 10-3 shows the property of Figure 10-2 with the same grid pattern. However, due to the addition of the tree, the head layout has been shifted one-half space. All heads are in a different location as compared to Figure 10-2. A grid pattern for triangular spacing provides at least two possible layouts. In this example, the alternate layout, shown in Figure 10-3, is an improvement due to the location of the tree. The same arc of coverage nozzles are required, but at different head locations.

EQUAL SPACING: HALF-SPACE PATTERNS. Figure 10-4 illustrates another advantage of triangular spacing layout. The 30.6 ft dimension is less than the maximum allowed for two row spaces of an 18 ft spacing head (18 x .866 = 15.6 x 2 = 31.2). Three rows of heads can be used with a row spacing of 15.3 ft.

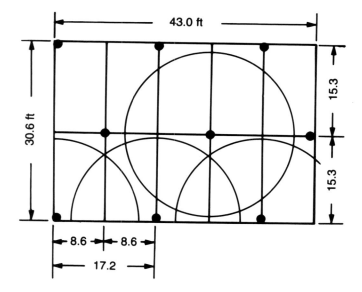

Figure 10-4 Equal Spacing: Half-Space Pattern

However, the width of the area is 43.0 ft, and this dimension is not suitable for multiples of 18 ft spacing (2 x 18 = 36 ft and 3 x 18 = 54 ft). In this case, the 43 ft dimension is suitable if half-spaces are considered rather than full-spaces (43.0 /5 half-spaces = 8.6). Head spacing on each row is 17.2 ft (2 x 8.6). Half space patterns are not available with square spacing.

Note: As previously mentioned, 18 ft triangular spacing heads are used for example only. Any triangular (or square) head spacing that may be used will be suitable in some cases, and not suitable in others.

SIMPLE METHOD TO EQUAL SPACE

More often than not, the dimensions of an area preclude determining equal spacing easily. For example, in Figure 10-5, 6 half-spaces are required for an area that is 51.8 ft wide. It would be difficult to measure 6 equal spaces on the plan at 8.63 ft each (51.8 /6 = 8.63). However, using a scale and the "Rule of Proportion" will simplify equal spacing of grid lines on the drawing.

When developing a layout, it is advantageous to work from two "base lines", each as long as possible and forming a 90° "base corner." The primary "base line" should be the line controlling the pattern. In Figure 10-5, this is the public sidewalk. When one line is considerably longer than the other, the longest line is usually selected as primary.

In the example, there are two lines at 90° to the public sidewalk; the driveway was arbitrarily chosen as the second "base line."

To equally divide a distance, select a length on the scale that is longer than the distance and which is exactly divisible by the number of divisions required.

Figure 10-5 is drawn to a scale of 1 in = 10 ft. Therefore, 6 inches represents 60 feet on the drawing. 60 ft is more than the width of the area to be layed out and is divisible by six.

The 51.8 ft width is divided into 6 equal spaces as follows:

1. Place the scale on the drawing in a diagonal position so that "0" is on the "base corner" and 6 inches (representing 60 feet) is on the line of the walk as shown.

2. Mark the plan at each inch (representing 10 feet).

3. Remove the scale and draw lines perpendicular to the primary "base line" through the one-inch marks previously placed on the drawing.

A "T-square and triangle" (or alternate equipment) will be necessary to draw the lines perpendicular to the primary base line and parallel to the secondary base line.

Row lines can be equally spaced using the same method; except different dimensions are used, and in the example, the measurement would be between the base corner and the building.

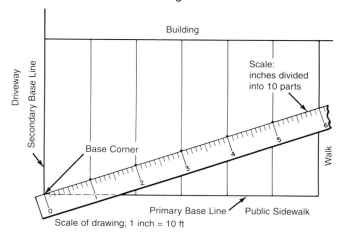

Figure 10-5 Equal Spacing by Proportion

Head Layout

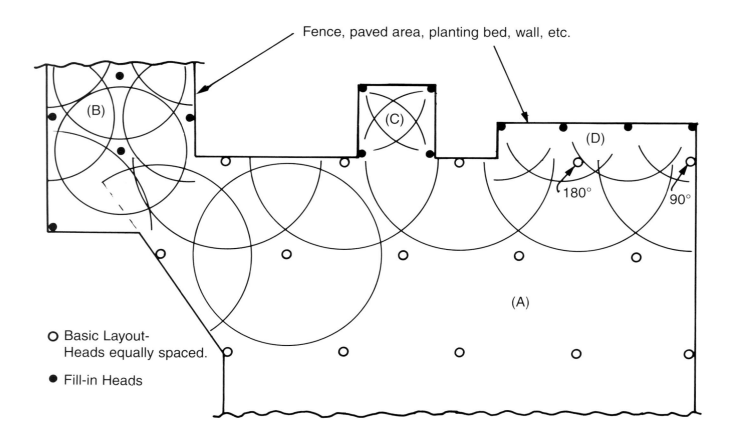

Fence, paved area, planting bed, wall, etc.

(B)

(C)

(D)

180°

90°

(A)

○ Basic Layout-
Heads equally spaced.

● Fill-in Heads

Figure 10-6 Example of Fill-in Head Requirements

Note: It is not mandatory that the preceding method of equal spacing be made from a "base corner." However, use of the corner is the handiest method. There will be plans on which a "base corner" cannot be used. In such cases, all that is necessary is that the length selected (60 ft in the example) be placed diagonally on the plan so that the two extremities fall on two parallel lines.

Half-space grid patterns can be developed just as easily with the "Rule of Proportion." Only the accumulated total of half-spaces is used to determine the length to be compressed in the area width, or length.

SPECIAL LAYOUT METHODS
The previously reviewed methods of layout can be used in the major areas of almost all properties for which sprinkler systems are designed. However, almost all layouts will have areas requiring special layout methods. The following examples provide methods for some types of areas that will be encountered.

Note: Although the special layout examples provided are limited in number, the examples are infinite in scope if applied to similar areas. Similar areas may not be readily apparent, but a little study will clarify the logic of the preceding statement.

FILL-IN HEADS. Although equal spaced layout patterns are usually designed for the major portion of areas to be sprinkled, there are almost always some areas where the sprinkler pattern cannot be maintained. In these cases, the system is designed with fill-in heads.

Fill-in heads may be defined as heads not located on the basic symmetrical pattern and/or which may not have the same coverage as the sprinklers in the pattern.

Figure 10-6 illustrates three common conditions where fill-in heads are required due to an irregular border. Adjacent areas are not identified and the border lines shown could represent a fence, wall, planting bed or any type of paved surface.

In the example, the head layout for area (A) was developed first. Heads are equally spaced at 16 ft using the 418 nozzle series. Areas (B), (C) and (D) required a special layout for the requirements of each area.

1. Area (B) is an extension of the main area, but at a reduced width. The head layout and nozzle series used in this area are based on the width and shape of the area, and the necessary blending of coverage with area (A). Although the spacing is not equal in the transition zone between areas (A) and (B), overlap is fairly consistent between the heads.

2. Area (C) is a small square-shaped area and is provided only as an example of many possible sizes and shapes that will require a totally independent layout.

3. The four fill-in heads in area (D) are required to cover the strip between the boundary line and the row of part-circle sprinklers in area (A). Spacing and nozzle size required will depend on the width and length of area (D). The two sprinklers (90° and 180°) in area (A) are located on one of the "base lines" used for the layout in this area.

Since fill-in heads are normally connected to the same operating zone as heads used in the basic layout, the performance of all nozzles should be compatible. In most cases, it will be necessary to consider compatible performance within practical limits.

In Figure 10-6, matched precipitation nozzles are used in all areas. However, there will be some variations in performance, due to nozzles (flow ratio is not exact for each size and arc), different spacing patterns, and different amounts of overlap. For example, triangular spacing is used in areas (A) and (B), square spacing is used in area (C), and single-row coverage is provided in area (D).

SPRAY BEYOND BORDERS. The overthrow of water beyond borders is a common problem with any type of spacing pattern and is always a factor of consideration with a triangular spacing layout. Wind distortion of spray is discussed in Chapter 8, "Protected Borders."

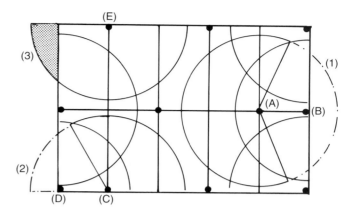

Figure 10-7 Back-up Heads

While overthrow beyond the planting areas is not desirable, it is normally a problem that varies by degree. For example, water sprayed onto a neighbor's lawn is seldom equal to the potential problem created when water is sprayed onto a neighbor's driveway. Water dispersed onto many types of adjacent areas is objectionable for many reasons, including the loss of water.

Figure 10-7 illustrates an equal-spaced, triangular layout with spray coverage beyond the borders. Dash line (1) indicates the overthrow of head (A) into the adjacent area, if the sprinkler was equipped with a full-circle nozzle. The overthrow can be eliminated by the addition of the "back-up" head (B). In this case, head (A) is equipped with a 225° arc of coverage nozzle and head (B) has a half-circle (180°) nozzle. The added sprinkler is a practical and low cost solution if, for example, the adjacent area is a walk, drive, street, etc.

Dash line (2) illustrates the coverage onto the adjacent area, if head (C) is equipped with a half-circle nozzle. An alternate layout is shown with the addition of back-up head (D). Head (C) is shown with a 120° arc of coverage nozzle and head (D) has a quarter-circle (90°) nozzle.

Shaded area (3) is shown to emphasize the amount of coverage beyond the border with a half-circle nozzle. The systems designer should examine each location where overthrow will occur and decide if an alternate layout is required.

ROUND CORNERS. Providing coverage at round corners always includes some overthrow beyond the border. Head layout options are limited and the layout selected for a particular location will depend on the

Head Layout

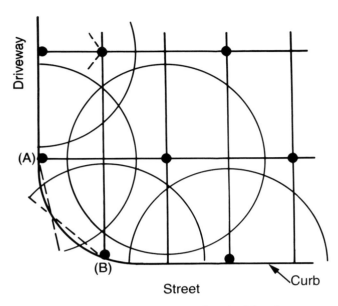

Figure 10-8 Round Corners - Standard Spacing

spacing pattern, nozzle selection available, the characteristics of the curve and any special considerations.

Figure 10-8 illustrates an equal-spacing layout. The rounded-corner is typical of an entrance to a driveway. Head (A) is located at the intersection of the row line and the driveway, and head (B) is located at the intersection of the half-space line and the curb line. In this example, head (A) is shown with a 165° part-circle nozzle and head (B) has a 135° part-circle nozzle. These nozzles are approximately correct for the curve and are used to reduce the amount of overthrow that would occur with half-circle nozzles.

Note: Figure 10-8 is an example only. There are many possible variations of rounded-corners, including those encountered at the entrance to a driveway.

Figure 10-9 illustrates the same driveway entrance as shown in Figure 10-8. In this example, the head layout is shifted one-half space on the same grid pattern. Head (B) is a "back-up" for head (A), which has a 225° part-circle nozzle to avoid the overthrow of a full- circle nozzle. Head (B) is shown with the coverage of a 165° part-circle nozzle. Fill-in head (C) is also equipped with a 165° part-circle nozzle and is used to maintain overlap with adjacent heads (substitute for a quarter-circle head in the corner).

Although any sprinkler that is located along a driveway or street is subject to damage, head (C) is at a location where damage is a common problem. The following

options are provided for head (C) to illustrate the degree of compromise that may be necessary for a practical solution:

1. Provide additional clearance between the head and curb by moving the head in, and away from the paving edge. Coverage along the curve will be reduced by a comparable amount.

2. Relocate the head by moving it several feet into the planting area, and with the spray directed in the opposite direction. The amount of overthrow onto the paved entrance will depend on the location of the head and the radius of coverage.

3. Omit head (C) and related coverage.

4. Use a completely different layout for the area.

CURVED BORDERS. Curved border lines are common for walks, driveways and planting beds. Border lines may curve inside or outside, or both. The degree of difficulty in providing coverage along a curved line depends on the characteristics of the curve and the amount of overthrow allowed. Since the shape of the curve will rarely conform to the location of heads on a standard spacing pattern, fill-in heads are required for locations with reduced spacing, and, when back-up heads are necessary to avoid excessive overthrow beyond the border.

Figure 10-10 illustrates a curved border along one side of an area with a triangular spacing layout. Head (A) is the only head along the curved line that is located at the

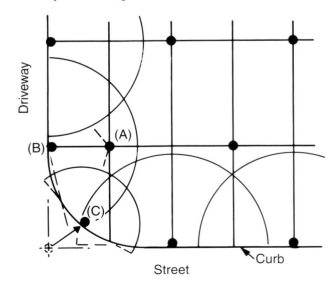

Figure 10-9 Round Corners - With Back-up and Fill-in Heads

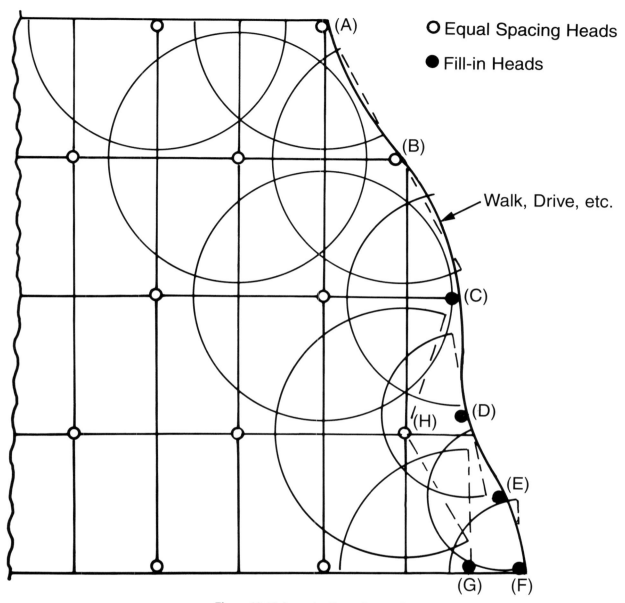

O Equal Spacing Heads

● Fill-in Heads

Walk, Drive, etc.

Figure 10-10 Irregular Curve Across Rows

intersection of a row line and a half-space line. Head (B) is a standard size, half-circle nozzle and is shown as an equal-spacing head since it is only slightly off pattern.

Head (C) is shown with a smaller size nozzle and 165° arc of coverage. Head (C) is located approximately two feet off the row line to balance the overlap with heads (B) and (D). Heads (D), (E) and (F) are small size, part-circle heads to back-up heads (G) and (H). Head (G) is shown as a fill-in head, as it is not located on the equal spacing pattern.

Single Curves. A layout for an area bounded on one side by a long, inside curve is illustrated in Figure 10-11. The area is symmetrical about the center line. An equal spacing grid is shown in the area north of the center line. In this example, the grid is for an 18 ft triangular spacing layout.

Although not shown, an identical grid pattern was used to locate the equally-spaced heads in the area south of the center line. Head locations (A1), (B1) and (C1) on the grid are related to heads (A2), (B2) and (C2) in the head layout shown for the area south of the centerline.

Head Layout

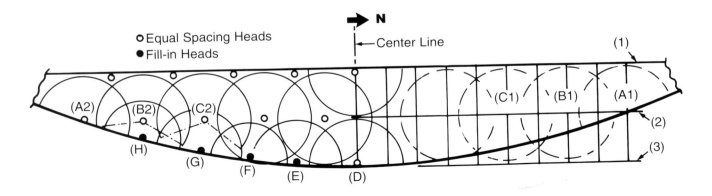

Figure 10-11 Layout for Long Inside Curve

Using location (A1) as a reference, head (A2) is a half-circle sprinkler, located at the intersection of row line (2), the half-space grid line and the curve. Head (B2) is shown with a 225° arc of coverage nozzle to avoid the overthrow of a full-circle nozzle, as shown at location (B1). Head (C2) is shown with a 240° arc of coverage nozzle and relates to location (C1) on the grid. Head (D) is located at the intersection of row (3), the half-space line (centerline) and the curve.

Head (E) was moved into the area from row (3) and is located on the half-space grid line. Heads (F), (G) and (H) are sized and located as necessary to cover the area along the curve from head (E) to (A2). A completed layout for the area would include a duplication of the layout shown for the area north of the centerline.

Figure 10-12 illustrates an alternate head layout for the area shown in Figure 10-11. The only difference is the use of fill-in heads on all rows. Nozzle sizes and spacing are reduced somewhat in proportion to the gradual

reduction of row spacing in the area where three rows of sprinklers are required. The application of this method will range from necessary to not suitable, depending on the size and shape of the area. In this example, two additional heads are required, as compared to the layout shown in Figure 10-11.

PARKWAYS AND STRIPS. Parkways (planting strips between public sidewalks and street curbs) and similar types of narrow strips are very common on residential and commercial projects. The type of equipment and the head layout used for a particular location will depend on the width and length of the strip, and the type of planting in the area.

"Strip nozzles" are used in most cases for very narrow turfgrass areas in the 2 to 5 ft width range. These nozzles discharge a narrow, wedge-shaped spray. Coverage distance (radius) is adjustable within certain limits. The most common complaint for this type of nozzle (and other types of rectangular pattern nozzles) is the lack of uniform coverage. Head-to-head spacing is a typical requirement for these nozzles. Wind distortion is also a common problem and low-angle trajectory nozzles are preferred in most cases.

Strip nozzle performance is listed in product catalogs by width and length of coverage. The majority of strip nozzles available are designed for installation in the center of the strip. A side strip version is available for installation along one side of the strip.

Most strip nozzles are available in a "center strip" and "end strip" pattern. The center-strip pattern nozzle provides two directly opposed streams of spray. The end-

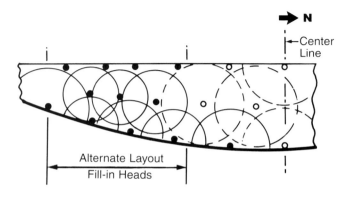

Figure 10-12 Alternate Layout for Long Inside Curve

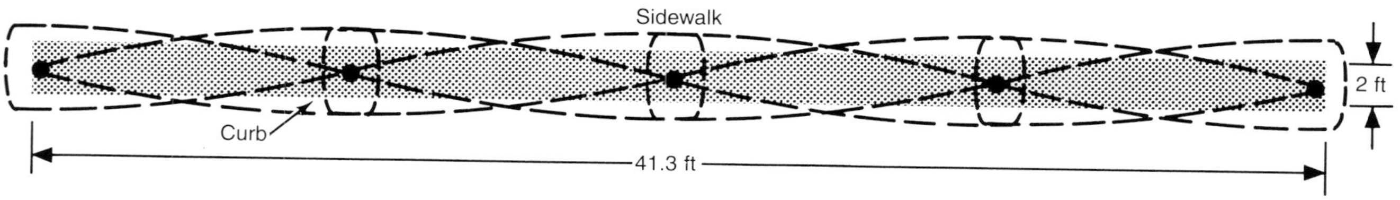

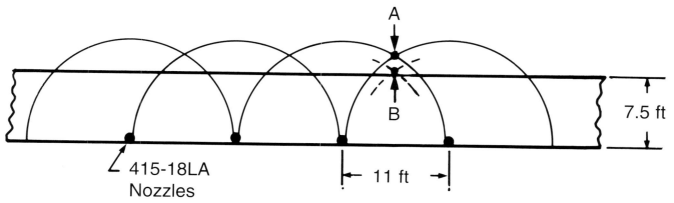

Figure 10-13 Strip Head Layout in Narrow Parkway

strip pattern nozzle has a single stream for use at each end of the strip.

Figure 10-13 illustrates a typical layout using strip heads in a narrow parkway. Three center-strip and two end-strip nozzles are equally spaced along the center-line of the 2 ft wide parkway.

One or two rows of part-circle spray heads are commonly used for strips that are too wide for strip heads. Figure 10-14 illustrates a single row of sprinklers along one side of a 7.5 ft wide strip. Although this is a practical solution to provide coverage in some cases, the obvious disadvantage is the necessary overthrow beyond the border on one side or the other. If, for example, the strip in Figure 10-14 was a parkway, overthrow would be sprayed onto a walk or street. While neither choice is desirable, water into the street is normally the least desirable of the two options, and in some cases, it is not allowed by a local ordinance.

Note: In a limited number of cities, local ordinance will not allow the installation of any pipe or irrigation equipment within the street "right-of-way", including the parkway.

The amount of overthrow that is necessary for single row coverage depends on the degree of compromise allowed in coverage (distribution uniformity) along the border, and therefore, it depends on the characteristics of the sprinkler distribution profile.

In Figure 10-14, sprinklers are equally spaced at 11 ft along one side of the strip. Low-angle nozzles are used to reduce the effects of wind. Referring to the example spray performance table, Figure 11-3, the 415LA performance is derated according to note (4).

In this example, radius and "effective radius" (ER) are derated by 10% to allow for reduced coverage when the nozzle is used on a typical turfgrass pop-up head. The listed radius of 12 ft (at 25 psi) is reduced to 11 ft (10.8 ft) and the listed ER of 10 ft is reduced to 9 ft.

Since the radius of this nozzle series is based on the A.S.A.E. Standard, as discussed in Chapter 8 (see table note 2), the amount of water applied at point A is .02 in/hr. This is the total amount applied at this point from two adjacent sprinklers (.01 in/hr each), and without any allowance for wind distortion.

Point B represents the intersection of ER arcs at the border line. Referring to note (3) of the example spray performance table, .5 in/hr will be applied at this point (2 nozzles at .25 in/hr each). While this amount will be less than that applied in some areas, it can be considered as a practical deviation from the average, considering the limitations of single row coverage.

Figure 10-15 illustrates an alternate head layout for the strip shown in Figure 10-14. Radius of coverage is 7 ft for the 410-18LA nozzles (listed radius of 8 ft, less 10% for LA). Although the triangular spacing layout shown

Figure 10-14 Strip with Single Row of Part-Circle Heads

Head Layout

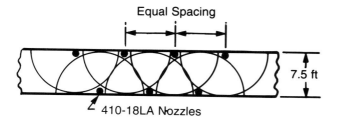

Figure 10-15 Alternate layout for 7.5 ft Strip

in Figure 10-15 is preferred, the improvement is achieved by added cost, as additional heads are required for the two row layout. However, the system designer (and property owner) should also consider that the long-term cost will be less with improved performance.

Wide Parkways and Strips. Many strips will require two rows (or more) of sprinklers due to the width of the strip.

The triangular spacing required for a two-row layout can be determined by multiplying the width of the strip by the constant 1.16. The width is equal to row spacing for a two-row layout.

Figure 10-16 illustrates a two-row triangular spacing layout on a curved strip. The row spacing (RS) or width of the strip is 13.8 ft. Triangular spacing required is 16.0 ft (13.8 x 1.16 = 16.0). However, since the strip is on a curve, spacing will not be equal in all directions.

Heads are located along the curb first, as this is the greatest distance for spacing on a row. Head spacing of 16 ft is measured on a straight line between head locations. Actual spacing may be less than 16 ft due to

equal spacing requirements between the ends of the strip.

Reduced spacing is necessary for sprinklers along the inside curve, Row 2. Heads are equally spaced between the head locations established on Row 1, as indicated by the dash lines. In many cases, this method is limited to two or three rows since the spacing on each successive row will decrease.

COMBINED COVERAGE

In addition to turfgrass, many other types of ground cover, shrubs and trees are commonly used in landscape designs. Different varieties of planting material will have different water requirements, and separate coverage and zone control should be provided when there are significant differences in requirement. Variation in landscape planting is discussed in Chapters 8 and 13.

However, there are practical limitations in providing separate coverage and control when many different types of plants are mixed together in one area.

LAWN AND TREES. In most cases, separate or additional watering is not provided for trees at scattered locations within an area of turfgrass. Turf sprinkler systems are designed and operated on a watering schedule for the requirements of the turfgrass, and will not provide sufficient water for most types of trees.

Property owners of new systems should be advised of the need for supplementary watering. Established trees should be watered with a slow-flowing hose periodically during long drought periods. Newly planted trees should receive a frequent soaking of the roots by rainfall or hose watering.

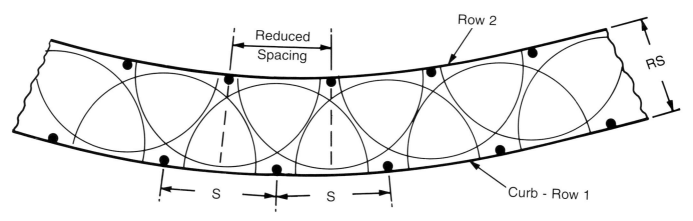

Figure 10-16 Two Row Layout on Curved Strip

Often lawns under trees are of very poor quality. This may be due to the turf species. Some types will survive in shaded locations and others will not. A degree of quality change is common for areas with a major reduction of light intensity. While water loss is reduced in shaded areas, the soil must provide moisture for turf and trees.

Therefore, sprinkler coverage under trees is very important. The designer should provide complete coverage by adding fill-in heads as required. However, in large areas where trees are very dense, it may not be practical to provide complete coverage.

The system in Figure 10-17 shows excellent coverage of a wooded area. Such areas should be separately zoned so that longer or shorter watering periods can be scheduled to meet specific conditions.

Note: In some climate regions, it may be necessary to provide separate watering for all trees.

LAWN AND SHRUBS. Separate watering should be provided for lawn and shrub areas. This general rule for improved efficiency is recommended for all landscape irrigation systems, where applicable. This is considered to be a minimum recommendation, as water requirements are not the same for all types of plants that may be described as "shrub."

However, complete separation of lawn and shrubs may not be practical due to the mixture in the landscape design. Plant selection and arrangement in landscape designs are seldom conducive to irrigation efficiency. There are exceptions, including a landscape design that is based on the principles of "Xeriscaping." See Water Conservation, Chapter 8.

The climate, type of plants, budget, water supply and other factors will influence the design standards for a particular project. In some climate regions, an irrigation system is a desirable option to improve the quality of planting material, but is not necessary for the survival of hardy plants. Adequate rainfall may be available throughout the year, except for a 2 or 3 month period of time, when supplemental water is necessary and a sprinkler system is a convenient alternative to a garden hose.

Although recommended methods for irrigation improvement are somewhat consistent, minimum design standards and water conservation considerations are not

Figure 10-17 Spray System in Wooded Area

consistent for all climate regions. In some regions of the world, sprinkler systems are designed primarily for the turfgrass areas. These systems are used to improve the appearance of turf in selected areas. Some will include coverage for planting beds and some do not. Shrub coverage may be separate or combined with the lawn, as illustrated in Figure 10-18. Combined coverage is not a realistic option for systems in semi-arid or arid regions. In any case, it is a design compromise that will require careful attention by the systems designer, as there are practical limitations, regardless of the climate.

PLANTING BEDS
Coverage of most planting beds can be accomplished with layout methods that are similar to those used for the lawn. Shrub nozzles mounted on permanent risers or pop-up shrub heads are used to spray over the planting. This method is commonly used for ground cover or small, closely-spaced plants of any type. There are three design considerations that require special

attention when sprinklers must operate at a higher elevation to obtain coverage over planting:

1. Coverage deficiency may occur in the area adjacent to the riser. This will vary with the nozzle performance and height of the riser. Low-angle nozzles are normally preferred for part-circle sprinklers to reduce the effect of wind drift.

2. Permanent risers can be hazardous. The designer should carefully consider the risk of each sprinkler head, in addition to coverage. Pop-up shrub heads may be necessary in certain locations and all permanent risers should be installed with flexible connections. Appearance is also a factor if risers are not concealed within the planting.

3. Type of planting. The ultimate height and size of individual plants at maturity should be determined.

Control of spray coverage will diminish as the nozzle is extended to higher levels on a shrub riser to spray over planting. Three feet is often considered to be the maximum height of planting that can be watered with this method.

HIGH SHRUBS. Plants that are over three feet in height will require a different method of providing coverage. In many cases, when complete coverage of the bed is necessary due to ground cover or other types of low plants, coverage can be provided by using a row of heads which spray under and/or into the larger plants. Figure 10-19 illustrates two common conditions where low-angle nozzles on risers (or pop-up shrub heads) are located along one side of the bed. Nozzle size and spacing requirements will vary with the width of the bed, plant spacing and clearance available for spray coverage.

The head layout shown in Figure 10-19a provides relatively broad coverage from each nozzle. This method is commonly used to reduce the total number of heads and maintenance requirements of other methods, even though coverage is combined for different types of plants.

Two rows of sprinklers will normally be necessary if the larger plants are located in the center of the planting bed with low plants located on each side of the bed.

The many variations of planting material that may be located in a single planting bed by a landscape designer (amateur or professional), or additional variations that may occur in the future, create a dilemma for the irrigation designer. In many cases, it is not practical to

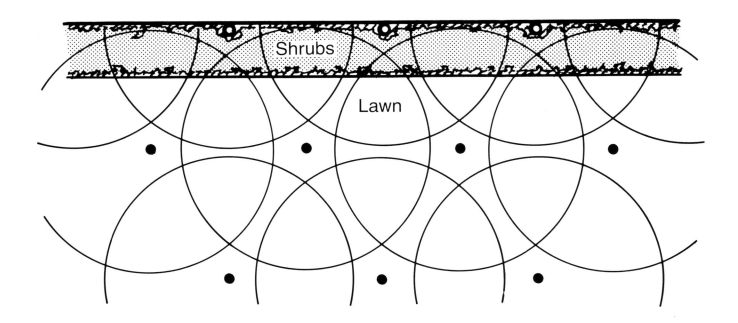

Figure 10-18 Combined Coverage - Lawn and Shrub

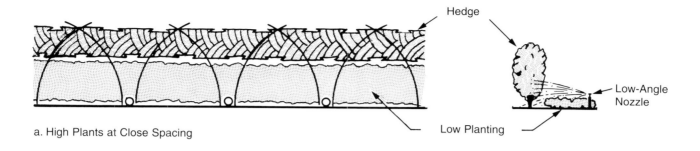

a. High Plants at Close Spacing

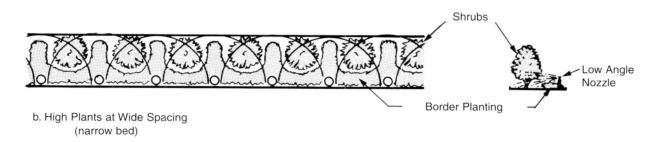

b. High Plants at Wide Spacing
(narrow bed)

Figure 10-19 Spray Coverage into Larger Shrubs

separate coverage when several different types of plants are entwined together, regardless of the method used for irrigation.

FLOOD WATERING. A variety of different products can be used to flood water planting beds. Diameter of coverage applied above the surface will vary from an inch (flow down a pipe riser) to several feet, depending on the type of product. The majority of products used for flood watering applications are commonly described as bubbler heads or spray heads.

Although the word "bubbler" is used to describe the flow from some products, the term is also used in the trade to describe heads with similar methods of ejecting water at specific locations. For example, some bubblers provide a small, umbrella-shaped spray around the riser and others provide streams of water that create small puddles of water at several locations. Stream bubblers are also known to the trade by such names as "spider" and "jet" irrigators.

Almost any type of low-angle or flat trajectory spray nozzle can be used for flood watering applications. However, in most cases, shrub nozzles that are designed for special treatment in planting beds are used at relatively close spacings. Nozzles are installed on low permanent risers (or pop-up heads) to spray under the planting.

Spacing of heads (spray or bubbler) will vary with product performance, type and spacing of plants, and soil conditions. Spray nozzles offer the advantage of providing improved coverage on the surface. However, coverage is often limited to a very small area due to the obstruction of foliage.

Coverage of an individual bubbler is as limited as the open-end flow of a garden hose. The important difference is that the hose can be moved if the location is not suitable to flood water the bed. The wetted pattern on the surface and below the surface from an individual bubbler is very limited, and considerable differences will occur with different types of soil. This is an important consideration for planting beds which may have soil conditions that are completely different than other areas at the site.

Areas with different types of equipment should always be zoned separately. This recommendation normally includes the separation of stream bubblers from other types of bubblers. The flow rate of individual bubblers is adjustable, except for the pressure-compensating type.

Note: There is a degree of deception that will often occur with close spacings on small scaled drawings. Quantity of heads required may appear somewhat ridiculous for the size of the planting area. In these cases a larger scale drawing may be helpful.

Water Quality. Water is the most versatile solvent of all known liquids. Common water supplies are a solution of many substances. Water quality should be associated with the intended use. Therefore, the designer is concerned with irrigation quality and the influence it may have on methods of irrigation. Quality varies from place to place and with the season of the year.

Quality of water for irrigation should be determined if unknown. In some cases, water analysis will indicate that irrigation systems should be designed to avoid water application to the foliage of broadleaf plant material. Continued application of spray may result in salt accumulation and leaf burn. In some regions this quality condition exists with potable water supplies provided by the city. Methods of flood watering may be necessary for planting beds. Excess amounts of water may also be required for leaching of the soil. Source water is discussed in Chapter 7.

Special Plantings. Some types of plants should not be watered by spraying over and/or onto the foliage. Roses are an example of plants in this category. Methods of irrigation should be used to flood irrigate the bed or to water individual plants. Micro-irrigation may also be considered as an option. See Chapter 13.

While flood irrigation is often preferred in planting beds, the designer must also consider the cost of such methods. Even distribution of water is seldom obtained without very close head spacings.

Figure 10-20 illustrates a method of watering a bed by flooding. Small diameter of coverage, flat trajectory shrub heads were used. Full circle heads are located with consideration for plant spacing. Two small ½-circle shrub heads were included in the layout.

With close-spaced planting and the heads installed about an inch or two above grade, the sprays are directed against the main stems of the plants under the foliage. The throttle valve was included to control pressure and thus, performance. Sprinklers in this example are non-adjustable.

Flooding of the bed can be controlled by the throttle valve and station timing of the zone. A properly sized pressure reducing valve may be an alternative solution.

Fig. 10-20 is typical of head spacings required for flood watering with small spray or stream heads. Careful examination of the layout will illustrate some of the problems common to this method. Some plants are watered by a single head and others by two heads. The center row could be eliminated and all plants would receive some water, but very little coverage and flooding would not occur in the center of the bed.

PLANTER BOXES. Many different types, sizes and shapes of planters are encountered in landscape irrigation design. Separate zone control is desirable and often necessary due to planter construction and/or the type of equipment used for irrigation.

Figures 10-21a and 10-21b illustrate the typical construction of a planter box at a building. Weep holes are located through the planter wall to provide drainage. Drainage may range from good to bad depending on the soil, and the design of the planter. Natural rainfall into planter boxes is often restricted or eliminated by roof overhangs.

Figure 10-21 also illustrates one method of watering a narrow planter box using low-flow spray nozzles at spacings in the range of 2 to 3 feet. This method is preferred in some cases when complete coverage is difficult to obtain with bubblers or other equipment, due to drainage. A throttle valve (globe, ball, etc.) is necessary to control the performance (pressure and flow) even when very small (orifice size) nozzles are used in a narrow bed.

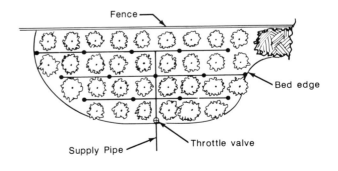

Figure 10-20 Spray/Flood Watering

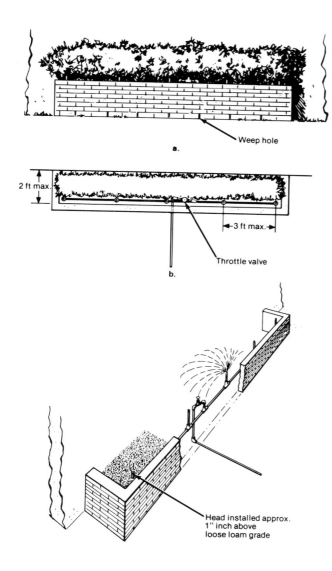

a.

Weep hole

2 ft max.

3 ft max.

Throttle valve

b.

Head installed approx.
1" inch above
loose loam grade

Figure 10-21 Watering Planter Boxes

INDIVIDUAL PLANTINGS. In some cases, it is necessary to water individual plants due to the isolated location of a single plant or when plants are widely-spaced along a row, and it is not desirable to water between the plants. Covering a large area just to water sparsely located plants would be wasteful.

Individual plants can be watered with a small coverage spray head or some type of bubbler head. Micro-irrigation equipment should also be considered if there is a sufficient quantity of plants. Micro-irrigation is a common method of providing coverage to individual shrubs when the landscape design is suitable for this type of irrigation system. See Micro-Irrigation, Chapter 13.

SUMMARY. There is no single method, product or design recommendation that is correct for all of the many possible variations that may be encountered in landscape irrigation. Common factors that can influence the head layout of a single planting bed or all planting areas at the site are:

1. Size, type and quantity of plants.
2. Climate (average rainfall and irrigation requirement).
3. Quality, quantity and cost of the available water supply.
4. Local and state laws.
5. System cost and maintenance cost.

In addition, there may be other factors that will only affect the system design of a particular project or designs in a regional area. For example, building foundation damage is a special problem in some regions due to very unusual soil conditions. In some cases, irrigation systems should not be installed adjacent to buildings due to the expansion characteristics of the soil.

However, there are also regions where a certain range of soil moisture should be maintained along the foundation during dry periods to avoid the sudden expansion of soil due to a short period of heavy rain. Although the systems designer cannot be responsible for any existing problems with building foundations, it is important for the designer to understand the possible effect of a soil moisture supply system in areas adjacent to any type of structure.

EXEMPLARY SPRAY SYSTEM HEAD LAYOUT

The plot plan drawn to scale from the property sketch with dimensions, Figure 9-3, is used to demonstrate the exemplary spray system head layout on the following pages.

It is important to explain that this plan is used primarily to illustrate common pattern adjustments and spacings that are necessary due to size and shape variations. Although separate layouts are used in the lawn and shrub areas, separate coverage is not provided for ground cover and the small size shrubs shown in several locations.

The finalized layout, shown in Figure 10-24, illustrates the degree of coverage that can be obtained with spray sprinklers. Careful examination will also provide visual evidence of the design compromise included in this residential system. For example, the head layout includes some overthrow onto paved areas, fences and adjacent property.

Although a certain level of design compromise was intentionally included in the exemplary head layout, the advantages and disadvantages of any layout must be compared to the design criteria, as established for the individual project. In this example, there are several different ways in which the system could be designed and be more or less effective. The finalized layout is not intended as a design that illustrates the best possible option in each area of coverage.

SPACING TEMPLATES

A spacing template is used as a visual aid to assist in the selection of a head layout for some areas of the design. Transparent templates made from tracing paper or plastic sheets provide an easy way for the designer to see and analyze different layout patterns without actually drawing the spacing pattern on the original drawing. Templates of commonly used design spacings must be accurate and at the proper scale for the plot plan. Triangular spacing grid lines should be included on the template. Circles indicating the diameter of coverage are not necessary but are often helpful to visualize coverage. Symbols (dots) to indicate the head locations, or circles of coverage (or both) are necessary to use the templates.

The transparent template is placed over each area of the plot plan separately because each area must be analyzed separately. Normally, each area will require a completely different layout. For illustration, two small size templates are shown over the two major lawn areas in Figure 10-22. Rows of sprinklers run in opposite directions in the two examples.

Templates can be shifted along a row one half-space, and then turned 90° and shifted again to analyze the options and select the most suitable pattern. In the areas shown, there are at least four possible layouts that can be considered with the template.

In many cases, some of the possible patterns can be considered as unsuitable at first glance. This may be due to the fact that one or more of the heads are in locations that are obviously not acceptable, or the spacing pattern is simply not compatible for the size and shape of the area.

Selection of the best layout is not always apparent as the spacing grid will seldom conform exactly to the size of the area in both directions. In some cases, two different patterns may require similar adjustments, including the possible requirement of fill-in heads. Although the template is used to consider the options, the final layout will normally be a modified version of the spacing pattern on the template. Therefore, the designer must visualize the modified version when analyzing the possible use of each option available.

TRIAL LAYOUT PATTERNS. In Figure 10-22, 18 ft spacing templates are laid over the front and rear turf areas of the property.

Rear Area. The grid is postioned with a row of sprinklers along the east fence line and with a half-space line along the edge of the planting bed at the north end of the turf area. The four rows shown would need to be compressed within the turf area since the row on the west side is located several feet into the planting bed.

In the other directions, the half-space line at the south end of the area is only slightly into the planting bed. The major problem with this pattern is in the area around the terrace. Many changes would be necessary to avoid excessive amounts of overthrow onto the terrace. Shifting of the template one half-space to the north (or south) does not improve the layout possibilities around the terrace and one head would be very close to a tree.

Front Area. The grid is positioned with a row of heads along the public walk and with a half-space line along the driveway. The distance between the public walk and entrance walk (and planting bed line) is only slightly less than the three row requirement on the 18 ft spacing template. The only disadvantage to the head layout is the amount of overthrow onto the driveway and the planting bed at the opposite end of the turf area. In this case, the two patterns available with the template rotated 90° are not suitable for the distance between the walks and the amount of over-spray onto the public walk.

Note: If none of the available 18 ft spacing patterns are suitable for the area, a different spacing template may provide an improvement in options available for selection.

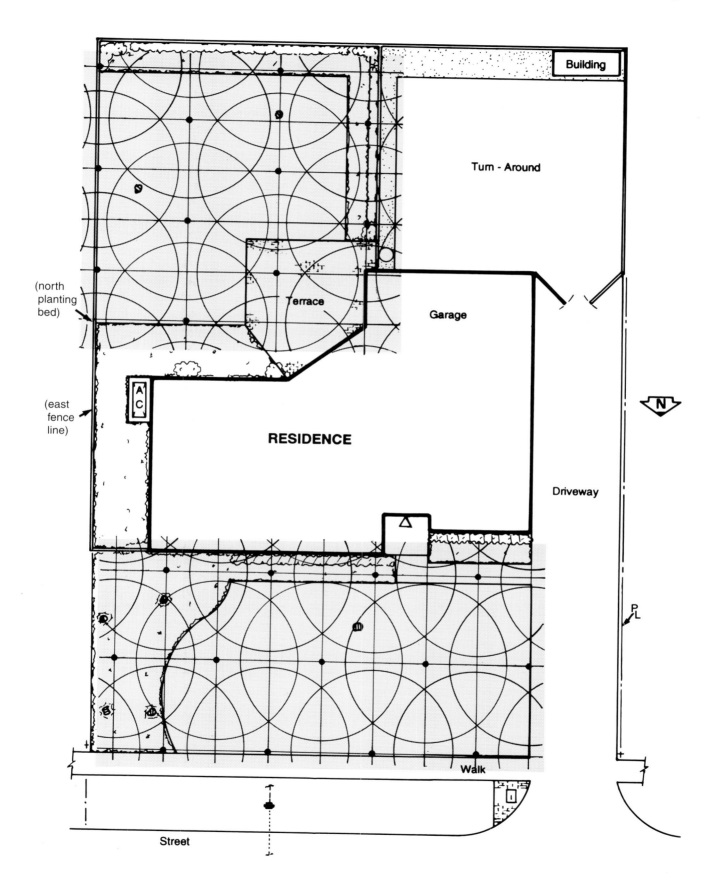

Figure 10-22 Templates on Plot Plan

Head Layout

ALTERNATE LAYOUT PATTERNS. Figure 10-23 illustrates an alternate layout pattern for the front and rear turf areas.

Rear Area. The template has been rotated 90° from the pattern shown in Figure 10-22. The grid is positioned with a row of heads along the edge of the planting bed at the north end of the turf area and with a half-space line along the east fence line. The four rows shown will need to be compressed since the row on the south end of the area is located approximately in the center of the planting bed. In the other direction, half-spaces will also need to be compressed since the half-space line on the west side of the area is located within the planting bed.

The pattern shown in Figure 10-23 is considered to be an improvement, as compared to the pattern shown in Figure 10-22, due to the improved possibilities of head layout around the terrace.

Front Area. The template in Figure 10-23 is located in the same position as shown in Figure 10-22, except the template has been shifted one half-space to the west (or east). The only improvement in the pattern shown in Figure 10-23 is the head layout possibilities available to reduce the amount of overthrow beyond the borders at each end of the turf area.

ADJUSTING LAYOUTS. The layout patterns shown in Figure 10-23 are used for the final layout. Front and rear patterns are modified and fill-in heads are added as necessary. The finalized layout in Figure 10-24 illustrates the adjustments that were made to the standard 18 ft spacing pattern.

Rear Area. The pattern was compressed in both directions. Equal spacing of rows and half-spaces was accomplished by using the "Rule of Proportion" as previously explained.

Note: The grid lines on the template can be used in place of a normal scale. Row spacing can be equally spaced using a half-space line as a scale. Half-spaces can be equally spaced using a row line.

The following nozzles are required for the area:

Quantity	Nozzle No.	Arc of Coverage
2	420-36	360°
4	420-18	180°
4	420-09	90°
1	420-12	120°
1	420-22	225°
1	420-27	270°

Heads (A) and (B) were added as back-up heads to avoid overthrow onto the planting bed and terrace. Head (C) is equipped with a full-circle nozzle and head (D) is equipped with a half-circle nozzle. Both of these heads will spray onto the fence along the east side of the area. Although this amount of overthrow is considered to be a practical compromise for this particular system, it may not be acceptable for some projects. Two additional back-up heads would be necessary to eliminate the overthrow.

Front Area. The only pattern adjustment necessary for the front area was a minor reduction in row spacing.

The following nozzles are required for the head layout as shown in Figure 10-24:

Quantity	Nozzle No.	Arc of Coverage
2	420-36	360°
7	420-18	180°
2	420-09	90°
1	420-13	135°
1	420-22	225°

Head (E) was moved off-pattern and equipped with a 135° arc of coverage nozzle. Head (F) was added as a back-up head to avoid the overthrow of a full-circle onto the driveway. Although head (G) will provide some overthrow onto the planting bed, a back-up was not added.

PARKWAY HEAD LAYOUT

Two rows of part-circle heads are shown in the finalized layout for the 9.1 ft wide strip between the curb and the public walk. Low-angle nozzles are specified for this turf area to reduce the amount of spray drift onto the adjacent walk and street. Diameter of coverage and spacing are reduced to allow for the use of low-angle nozzles. See Figure 11-3, Exemplary Performance Data, Note 4.

Head (H) will overthrow onto the brick surface near the driveway and head (I) will overthrow onto the neighbor's lawn. With consideration for the practical limitations of

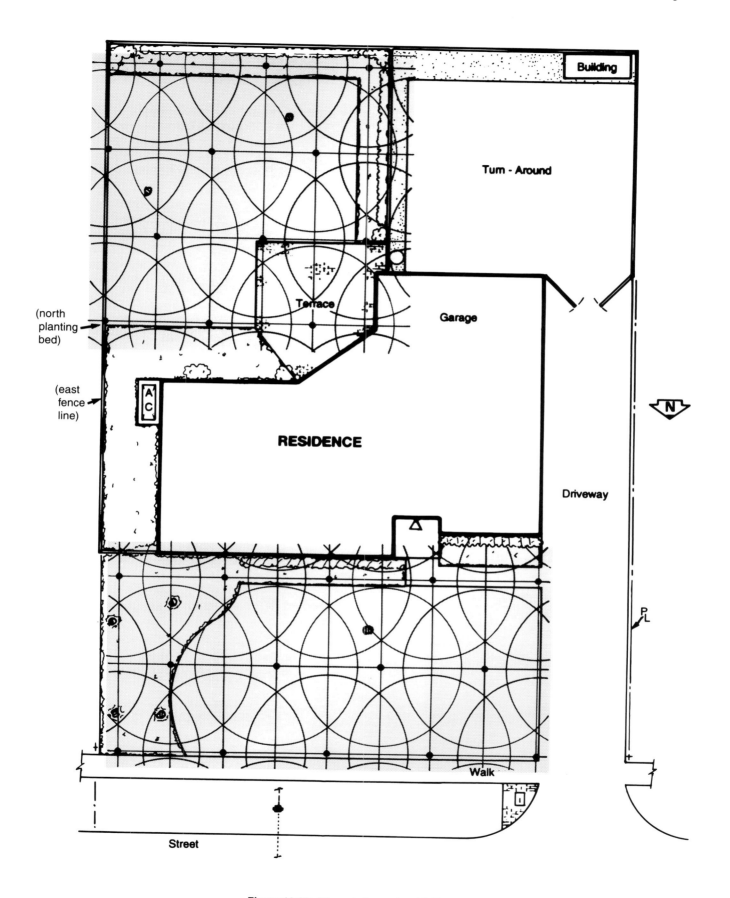

Figure 10-23 Alternate Layouts with Templates

Head Layout

this project, back-up heads were not added, due to the total number of heads required for this 70 ft long strip.

PLANTING BEDS

As previously stated, separate coverage and zone control is not provided for the ground cover and the small size shrubs that are located within the same planting beds. In this example, water requirements of planting material are considered compatible to the extent that combined coverage is a practical compromise. This includes consideration for the added system cost and maintenance requirements of additional equipment, as compared to the degree of improvement in irrigation efficiency.

Note: Systems designers should not assume that combined coverage is a practical solution for all types of plants that may exist at a particular site. See "Variations in Planting", Chapter 8.

PLANTING BED NO. 1. As shown in Figure 10-24, ten pop-up shrub heads are equally spaced along the front edge of planting bed number 1. Heads will require the following part-circle nozzles:

Quantity	Nozzle No.	Arc of Coverage
8	410-18LA	180°
1	410-09LA	90°
1	410-27LA	270°

The low-angle nozzles and the row of small shrubs along the back side will minimize the amount of spray onto the fence.

PLANTING BED NO. 2. The triangular spacing layout in planting bed number 2 is somewhat consistent considering the shape of the bed which extends around the corner of the building. Nozzles required for the two row layout are as follows:

Quantity	Nozzle No.	Arc of Coverage
7	412-18LA	180°
3	412-09LA	90°
1	412-12LA	120°
1	410-18LA	180°
1	403-18LA	180°

The primary consideration in the layout of this bed was to protect the building and terrace as much as possible. The 403-18LA nozzle is used as a small coverage fill-in head in the area near the less than 90° corner of the bed. The 410-18LA nozzle is also used as a fill-in head between the air-conditioner unit and the fence.

Alternative. Stationary shrub heads, mounted on pipe risers, could be considered as an alternative to pop-up heads in several locations. However, the appearance and possible hazard of a permanent pipe riser must be considered for this type of shrub head.

PLANTING BED NO. 3. The head layout for this planting bed was developed by the "trial and error" method due to the size, shape and number of trees in this area. Heads are spaced on a combination of square and triangular patterns. Although adequate overlap between heads is important, it is seldom equal, since nozzles are sized and located where necessary for coverage.

Nozzles required for the nine heads in this large, ground cover bed are as follows:

Quantity	Nozzle No.	Arc of Coverage
1	415-36	360°
4	415-18LA	180°
2	415-09LA	90°
1	412-18LA	180°
1	410-18LA	180°

The 415-36 full-circle head is necessary for the width of the bed in this area and to provide coverage between the trees. Although the amount of water applied will be minimum due to the low precipitation rate at the outer perimeter of coverage, overthrow will occur onto the lawn and neighbor's lawn.

PLANTING BEDS NO. 4. Four part-circle sprinklers are equally spaced along the front edge of planting bed (4a) on the east side of the building entrance and three heads are equally spaced in bed (4b) on the west side. Nozzles required for the two beds are as follows:

Quantity	Nozzle No.	Arc of Coverage
4	410-18LA	180°
3	410-09LA	90°

12-inch pop-up shrub heads are specified for the three heads on the west side due to the height of the ground cover in this bed. Low-angle (or flat trajectory) nozzles are recommended for the combined coverage in these beds to avoid an excessive amount of spray onto the building wall. Although a minimum amount of the wall is exposed (between plants) due to the close-spac-

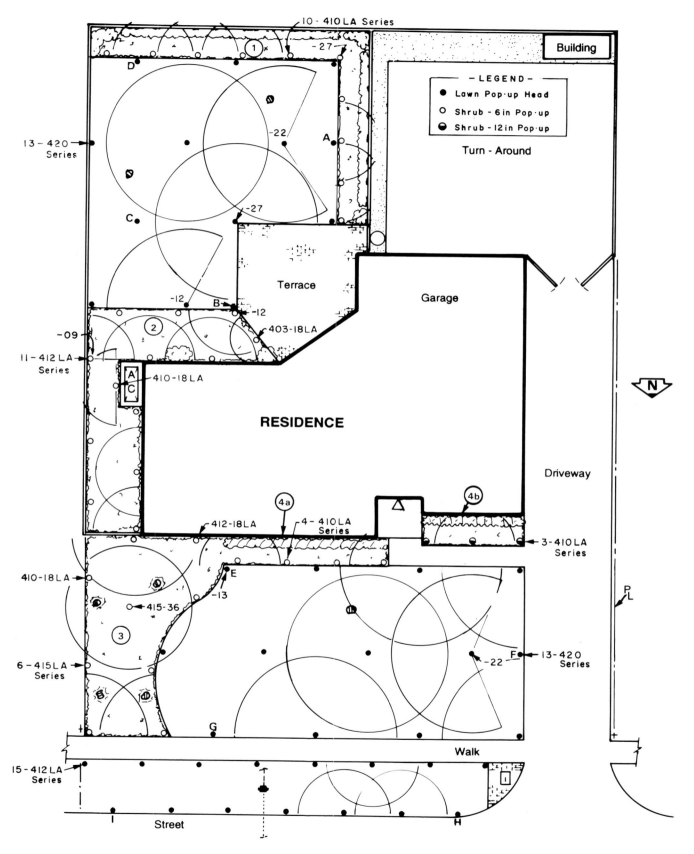

Figure 10-24 Finalized Layout

ing of the foundation planting, water sprayed over the top of the low shrubs could be a problem on the wall and any windows that may be located along the wall.

HEAD LABELS/SYMBOLS

Nozzle and type of sprinkler should be indicated on the plan. This information will be needed: (1) to determine flow requirements when sizing the pipe system; (2) to prepare a bill of material required; (3) for installation; and for future reference and service.

There are many methods for indicating the type of head and nozzle required. One procedure uses different symbols for each type of nozzle used in the design. See Table 2, Appendix, for examples. This method may not be practical for very small scale drawings with many different types of nozzles. In any case, a legend is required to identify each symbol used on the plan.

The method of identification used in the exemplary layout utilized the manufacturer's numbering code for each type of nozzle. The quantity and nozzle size (series) is noted for each area. This method is based on the assumption that anyone can easily determine which heads will require a full, half or quarter-circle nozzle by the location of the head. Any other arc of coverage required is noted by the manufacturer's code for the arc. Fill-in nozzles are identified by the nozzle number. The type of head required at each location is identified in the legend (an additional symbol would be necessary for locations on the plan where a stationary shrub head is required if this optional method is used for shrub heads in some locations).

SUMMARY

There are necessary limitations that must be placed on the amount of material provided in each chapter of this book. Selection of the exemplary spray system was based on this limitation.

The final head layout and related design decisions included for this residential system are typical for any type of landscape irrigation system using spray sprinklers. The layout does not represent the most economical design that is possible for the property, nor is it intended as a recommendation of the most efficient design possible.

Each property is different in size, shape and landscaping, and each will have a different sprinkler layout and design requirement. However, regardless of design criteria and the size of the project, basic system performance will be established and limited by the head layout provided.

Methods of layout, use of spacing templates and pattern adjustments provided in this chapter are limited to explanation and procedures that are common for design at the drawing board. Computer systems with special operating programs can offer assistance in head layout by providing visual patterns that are similar to those illustrated in Figure 10-22 and 10-23. Design considerations for sprinkler location and coverage remain the same regardless of method used to develop the plan: drawing board and 'T'-square or computer graphics. Computer-aided design is discussed in Chapter 11.

Pipe Sizing and Zoning

The final phase in the preparation of a sprinkler system design is the layout of the piping. Figure 11-1 is used to demonstrate the development of a piping system after the head layout phase is completed.

Fundamentally, pipe system design entails grouping the sprinkler heads (and/or other types of water application products) into operating zones, developing a piping schematic, and sizing all pipe and valves as necessary for proper operation. The entire process can be relatively simple or somewhat difficult, depending on the designer's experience and the requirements of the system.

A basic understanding of system hydraulics is necessary, see Chapter 3.

FLOW REQUIREMENT

Flow requirement is determined as a preliminary step to zoning the system. However, in order to simplify pressure loss calculations, adjustments must first be made to the manufacturer's performance specifications.

NOZZLE FLOW VARIATION. Manufacturers' specifications list the performance of spray nozzles (and other type of nozzles) at one or more operating pressures. The rate of flow at each pressure listing is the nominal flow rate. The actual flow of a given nozzle may be equal to the listed flow or it may be higher, or lower than the listed flows. Flow variations due to manufacturing tolerances will vary with the brand and nozzle series.

Nozzle flow will also vary due to pressure variations at different outlets within the operating zone. Nozzle flow increases as operating pressure increases.

Example: Assume that 20 lb/in^2 operating pressure exists at the most distant outlet in a row of four heads and there is a pressure loss of 1.0 lb/in^2 in each of the three connecting pipes. Pressure at the next to the last head will be 21 lb/in^2 at its base. And, each head progressively nearer the source will have more pressure than the preceding head as illustrated in Figure 11-2.

The approximate effect on the flow rate of the sprinklers in Figure 11-2 is shown below (using a base flow of 4.0 gpm at 20 lb/in^2):

Operating Pressure, lb/in^2	gpm
20	4.0
21	4.1
22	4.2
23	4.3

The total flow of 16.6 gpm for the four heads is approximately 4% higher as compared to the total flow of the same heads at 4.0 gpm each. A similar flow increase will also occur in pressure-compensating devices if the range of pressure within the zone is below the pressure at which the device is effective. Also, an allowance should be considered for common flow variations of pressure-compensating devices when there is a significant difference in the operating pressure within the zone.

DESIGN FLOW. In most cases, the flow rates provided in product catalogs should be adjusted for design purposes. The amount of adjustment required will depend on the type and brand of equipment, and the extent of pressure variations that will exist within an individual zone.

Pipe Sizing and Zoning

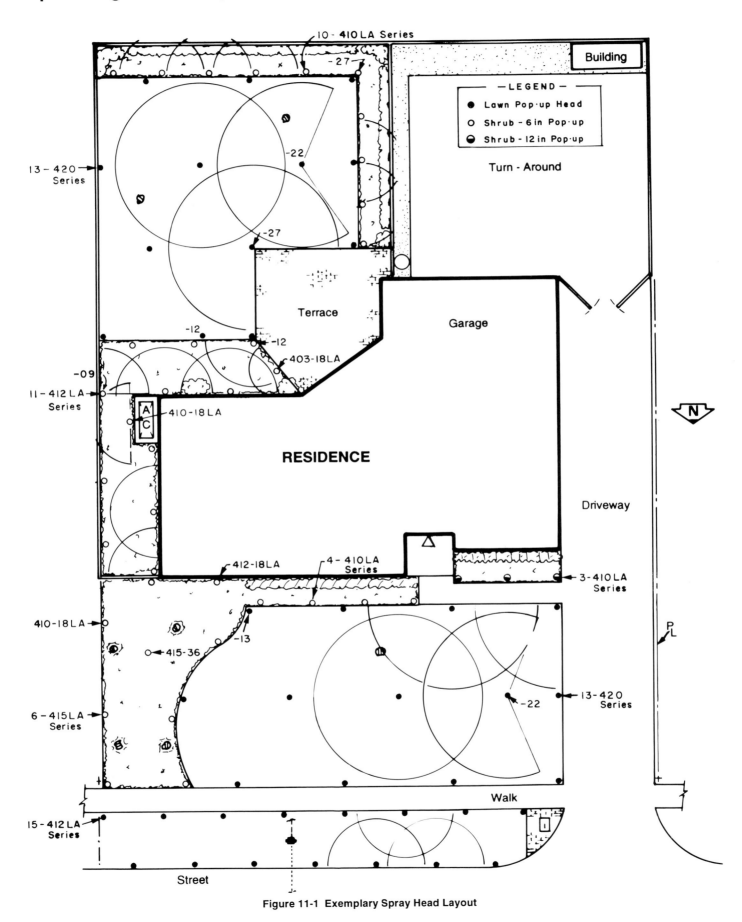

Figure 11-1 Exemplary Spray Head Layout

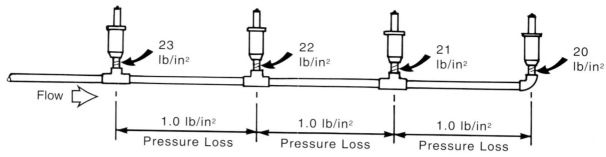

Figure 11-2 Sprinklers Operate at Varying Pressure Due to Losses in Piping

System designers use a variety of different methods to compensate for normal flow variations that result in an increase of flow, and an increase in pressure loss. Many designers use a multiplier to increase the catalog flow by a percentage. Some will use the same multiplier for all projects and others will use a variable factor that relates to the individual zone or system.

The spray performance table shown in Figure 11-3 was used in preparing the head layout for the property in Figure 11-1. This example table is used to determine the catalog flow requirements in this chapter.

ZONE FLOW AND PRESSURE LOSS

The following explanation is provided for the method used in this chapter to adjust the total zone flow (derived from catalog data) and the total zone loss (pipe and fittings) as calculated at catalog flow.

The flow rate increase of a standard nozzle, due to an increase in pressure, will depend on the amount of increase as compared to the base sprinkler pressure. A 1 lb/in^2 increase in pressure will provide a very small increase in the flow of a nozzle operating at 50 lb/in^2, since the increase from 50 to 51 lb/in^2 is a minor change. However, the same 1 lb/in^2 increase in pressure will have a greater effect on the flow increase of a nozzle operating at 5 lb/in^2, since the increase from 5 to 6 lb/in^2 represents a 20% increase in pressure (flow will increase approximately 10%).

Pressure differential between outlets in a zone is due to pressure loss (gain is also possible due to elevation difference) as indicated in Figure 11-2. However, in most cases, the actual operating pressure and flow at each outlet in a zone is difficult to determine since an increase in flow will result in an increase in pressure loss and an increase in pressure loss will reduce the operating pressure. A reduction in operating pressure will reduce the flow and reduce the pressure loss, and "back in the circle", with new variables. The difficulty is due to the fact that pressure, flow and pressure loss are interrelated.

The exact flow and pressure is seldom determined during design. In most cases, it is impossible to determine, since the flow rate of individual outlets can vary up or down at a given operating pressure. This applies to any type of water outlet product used in irrigation.

A table of adjustment factors for zone flow and zone pressure loss is shown in Figure 11-4. These factors are based on the average flow increase of all outlets in a typical zone of sprinkler heads. The multiplying factors are used to adjust the total catalog flow of the individual zones to allow for a normal flow increase.

Multipliers are selected from the table with consideration for the following two factors:

1. Total pressure loss calculated (or estimated) from the zone entrance (ZE) through the piping to the point where the greatest total loss will occur in the zone. Loss is calculated using the nominal (catalog) flow at each outlet.

   NOTE: The zone entrance (ZE) is the first tee (or cross) in the piping on the discharge side of the zone control valve.

2. The catalog listed operating pressure relates to the flow rates used in the zone pressure loss calculations. This pressure is normally considered the minimum sprinkler operating pressure for the zone.

The same multiplier is used to adjust the total zone pressure loss (pipe and fitting loss). This method is used to simplify the flow and pressure loss adjustment and is based on the theory that the zone flow and loss ratio will remain somewhat constant with the increased flow dispersed throughout the zone. The percentage of flow increase at a particular sprinkler within a zone or pressure loss increase in a particular pipe may be more or less than the average flow and pressure loss increase.

Pipe Sizing and Zoning

NOTE: This spray performance table is provided for reference only. Sprinkler heads for use with this nozzle series are available in 2.5, 3.5, 6 and 12 inch pop-up models. A threaded shrub head adapter is also available for stationary risers.

Standard 30° and Low Angle 15° Trajectory/Spacings Triangular/ Matched Precipitation.

Type	Arc	PSI	403 No.	GPM	Radius (2)	ER (3)	410 No.	GPM	Radius (2)	ER (3)	412 No.	GPM	Radius (2)	ER (3)	415 No.	GPM	Radius (2)	ER (3)	418 No.	GPM	Radius (2)	ER (3)	420 No.	GPM	Radius (2)	ER (3)	424 No.	GPM	Radius (2)	ER (3)
					3' to 5' Spacing (Varies with application)				10' Maximum Spacing (1)				12' Maximum Spacing (1)				15' Maximum Spacing (1)				18' Maximum Spacing (1)				20' Maximum Spacing (1)				24' Maximum Spacing (1)	
360°	20		-	-	-	-	-	-	-	-	-36	1.7	9	8	-36	2.4	11	10	-36	3.4	12	11	-36	4.2	13	12	-36	5.9	16	15
	25											1.9	9	8		2.7	12	10		3.8	13	12		4.8	13	13		6.2	17	16
	30											2.1	11	9		3.0	12	11		4.2	13	12		5.3	15	14		7.0	18	16
180°	20		-18LA	.3	5	4	-18LA	.6	8	7	-18/-18LA	1.0	9	8	-18/-18LA	1.4	11	10	-18/-18LA	2.0	12	11	-18/-18LA	2.4	13	12	-18	3.3	16	15
	25			.3	6	5		.7	8	7		1.1	9	8		1.6	12	10		2.3	13	12		2.7	14	13		3.5	17	16
	30			.3	7	5		.7	9	8		1.2	11	9		1.8	12	11		2.5	13	12		2.9	15	14		4.0	18	16
90°	20		-09LA	.3	5	4	-09LA	.3	8	7	-09/-09LA	.5	9	8	-09/-09LA	.7	11	10	-09/-09LA	1.0	12	11	-09/-09LA	1.2	13	12	-09	1.8	16	15
	25			.3	6	5		.4	8	7		.6	9	8		.8	12	10		1.1	13	12		1.4	14	13		1.9	17	16
	30			.3	7	5		.4	9	8		.7	11	9		.9	12	11		1.2	13	12		1.5	15	14		2.1	18	16
105°	20														-10/-10LA	.8	11	10	-10/-10LA	1.1	12	11	-10/-10LA	1.4	13	12				
	25															1.0	12	10		1.3	13	12		1.6	14	13				
	30															1.1	12	11		1.5	13	12		1.8	15	14				
120°	20		-12LA	.3	5	4	-12LA	.4	8	7	-12/-12LA	.7	9	8	-12/-12LA	1.0	11	10	-12/-12LA	1.3	12	11	-12/-12LA	1.6	13	12	-12	2.2	16	15
	25			.3	6	5		.5	8	7		.7	9	8		1.1	12	10		1.4	13	12		1.8	14	13		2.4	17	16
	30			.3	7	5		.6	9	8		.8	11	9		1.2	12	11		1.6	13	12		2.0	15	14		2.7	18	16
135°	20		-13LA	.3	5	4	-13LA	.5	8	7	-13/-13LA	.7	9	8	-13/-13LA	1.1	11	10	-13/-13LA	1.5	12	11	-13/-13LA	1.8	13	12	-13	2.5	16	15
	25			.3	6	5		.6	8	7		.8	9	8		1.2	12	10		1.7	13	12		2.1	14	13		2.9	17	16
	30			.3	7	5		.6	9	8		.9	11	9		1.4	12	11		1.9	13	12		2.3	15	14		3.2	18	16
165°	20														-16LA	1.3	11	10	-16LA	1.8	12	11	-16LA	2.3	13	12				
	25															1.5	12	10		1.9	13	12		2.6	14	13				
	30															1.7	12	11		2.3	13	12		2.9	15	14				
195°	20										-19/-19LA	1.0	9	8	-19/-19LA	1.5	11	10	-19/-19LA	2.2	12	11	-19/-19LA	2.8	13	12	-19	3.9	16	15
	25											1.1	9	8		1.7	12	10		2.5	13	12		3.2	14	13		4.4	17	16
	30											1.3	11	9		1.9	12	11		2.8	13	12		3.5	15	14		4.9	18	16
225°	20		-22LA	.3	5	4	-22LA	.7	8	7	-22/-22LA	1.3	9	8	-22/-22LA	2.0	11	10	-22/-22LA	2.5	12	11	-22/-22LA	3.0	13	12	-22	4.3	16	15
	25			.3	6	5		.9	8	7		1.4	9	8		2.3	12	10		2.9	13	12		3.4	14	13		4.9	17	16
	30			.3	7	5		.9	9	8		1.6	11	9		2.6	12	11		3.2	13	12		3.8	15	14		5.4	18	16
240°	20		-24LA	.3	5	4	-24LA	.8	8	7	-24/-24LA	1.3	9	8	-24/-24LA	2.2	11	10	-24/-24LA	2.7	12	11	-24/-24LA	3.3	13	12	-24	4.6	16	15
	25			.3	6	5		.9	8	7		1.5	9	8		2.4	12	10		3.2	13	12		3.7	14	13		5.2	17	16
	30			.3	7	5		1.0	9	8		1.7	11	9		2.6	12	11		3.5	13	12		4.1	15	14		5.7	18	16
270°	20		-27LA	.3	5	4	-27LA	.9	8	7	-27/-27LA	1.4	9	8	-27/-27LA	2.4	11	10	-27/-27LA	3.1	12	11	-27/-27LA	3.8	13	12	-27	5.2	16	15
	25			.3	6	5		1.0	8	7		1.6	9	8		2.6	12	10		3.5	13	12		4.3	14	13		5.5	17	16
	30			.3	7	5		1.1	9	8		1.8	11	9		2.9	12	11		3.8	13	12		4.7	15	14		6.1	18	16

All full circle and Model 424 part-circle series are available in standard trajectory only.

403 and 410 series are available in low-angle trajectory only.

412 through 420 (part circle) nozzles are available in standard or optional low-angle trajectory.

(1) *Maximum triangular spacing.* Climate, wind and nozzle performance should be considered for design spacing. Example: Many designers derate spacing by using 90% of maximum for average site conditions.

(2) *Listed radius determined by ASAE industry standard measurement .01 in/hr.*

(3) *ER "Effective Radius"* indicates the most distant point at which .25 in/hr precipitation will occur within the area of coverage.

(4) *Low-Angle Nozzles:* Radius and ER are measured with nozzle mounted on a 12" riser. Derate radius (10-15%) if used with pop-ups of 6" or less.

(5) *Precipitation:* 1.2 in/hr for Full Circle/20psi/Maximum Spacing.

Figure 11-3 Exemplary Performance Data: Spray Nozzles

Figure 11-5 illustrates an example zone of spray sprinklers. Zone flow is 24.0 gpm and the total pressure loss is 3.5 lb/in^2 (7 pipe sections at .5 each). Base sprinkler operating pressure is 15 lb/in^2. Flow and pressure loss are adjusted for design using the multiplier of 1.08 from the table provided in Figure 11-4. Flow is adjusted to 26.0 gpm (24 x 1.08 = 25.92) and the zone pressure loss is adjusted to 3.8 lb/in^2 (3.5 x 1.08 = 3.78). The zone has a minimum requirement of 26 gpm at 18.8 lb/in^2 (15.0 head pressure + 3.8 loss) at the zone entrance (ZE) to provide 15 lb/in^2 at the most distant head.

Elevation differences within a zone can also affect the operating pressure and flow rate at one or more sprinklers. For example, increased pressure may be required at some sprinklers to obtain the pressure necessary at higher elevations within the zone.

Any pressure loss due to elevation difference within the zone is included in the zone loss when selecting the multiplier for adjustment. However, the pressure loss due to elevation is not adjusted as it does not relate to the flow rate.

Zone[1] Loss (lb/in²) At Nominal Flow	Multipliers[2] to Adjust the Total Zone Flow (gpm) and Loss (lb/in²)			
	Base Sprinkler Pressure (lb/in²)			
	15	20	25	30
1.0	1.02	1.02	1.01	1.01
1.5	1.03	1.03	1.02	1.02
2.0	1.05	1.03	1.03	1.02
2.5	1.06	1.04	1.03	1.03
3.0	1.07	1.05	1.04	1.03
3.5	1.08	1.06	1.05	1.04
4.0	1.09	1.07	1.05	1.05
5.0	1.11	1.08	1.07	1.06
6.0	1.13	1.10	1.08	1.07
7.0	1.15	1.12	1.09	1.08
8.0		1.13	1.10	1.09
9.0		1.15	1.12	1.10
10.0			1.13	1.11
11.0			1.14	1.12
12.0				1.13
13.0				1.14

(1) Maximum pressure loss from "zone entrance" to any outlet. Total of pipe, fitting and elevation losses within the zone.

(2) Multipliers to adjust the total zone flow (catalog flow at base pressure) and the total zone loss (calculated at catalog flow). Factors are based on the average flow/pressure ratio and "typical" pressure variations that occur within a zone.

(3) No allowance is included for manufacturer's nozzle flow variations.

Figure 11-4 Example of Adjustment Factors for Total Zone Flow and Pressure Loss

Elevation differences that are below the zone entrance (ZE) may also increase the pressure at one or more sprinklers within a zone. In most cases, the designer can analyze the elevation differences (higher, lower or both) and include an adequate adjustment without a detailed examination of the operating pressure and flow rate at each sprinkler in the zone.

PIPE FITTING LOSSES

The pressure loss of fittings within the piping of a spray system will depend on the type of fitting specified, the pipe size, the rate of flow and the quantity of fittings (tees, elbows, bushings, etc.) required for the piping arrangement. Fitting loss, as compared to pipe loss, will

vary over a wide range, including fitting losses that exceed the pipe loss.

Unfortunately, there is a very limited amount of information available to estimate the pressure loss in standard type (pipe O.D.) fittings, and even less information is available for insert-type fittings. Almost all of the tables used for threaded and socket-type (IPS) PVC fittings are based on pressure loss tests of threaded steel fittings. This includes Table 17 in the Appendix.

System designers use different methods to allow for pipe fitting losses in landscape irrigation systems. Some designers will calculate all pipe losses and then add an allowance for all fitting losses, using a percentage of the total pipe loss. This is a very practical method if the allowance is based on a percentage of pipe loss that is realistic for the particular piping arrangement.

It is seldom realistic to use the same percentage allowance for fitting losses in the zone piping and the mainline piping. Normally, a greater number of fittings are required for a given pipe length in the zone, as compared to the mainline. In any case, there is no percentage of pipe loss that is correct for all zones, or a percentage that is correct for all mainlines.

Figure 11-6 illustrates an example table of percentages used to estimate PVC fitting losses within a zone. The average pipe section length in the table relates to head spacing for a straight single-row of sprinklers or the average pipe section length in the run of pipe from the zone entrance (ZE) to the most distant head (or point used for the pipe loss calculation).

Percentage variations listed in Figure 11-6 are based on common variations in the ratio of fittings required for a given length due to spacing between connections. The percentages should be adjusted if the fitting requirement for a particular zone is not "typical" due to the piping arrangement. Also, the ratio of fitting loss, as compared to pipe loss, will vary with the type of fitting and the fitting loss table used by the designer.

It may also be practical for the designer to develop a table of percentages to allow for fitting losses in the piping from the water supply to the zone entrance. However, at least two different percentages would be necessary to cover the average (and less than average) requirement, and the occasional supply piping layout that requires an unusually large quantity of tees and/or elbows.

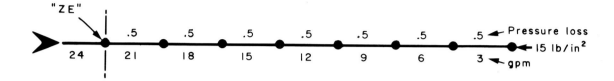

Base Sprinkler Pressure — 15 lb/in²

Flow per Outlet (catalog)— 3 gpm

Total Zone Flow = 24.0 gpm (catalog)

Total Calculated Loss = 3.5 lb/in²

Figure 11-5 Example of Zone Catalog Flow and Calculated Pressure Loss

Some system designers calculate the loss in each fitting by adding the equivalent footage total to the length of each pipe section calculated. Data is obtained from Table 17 in the Appendix, or a similar type of table. This method is also commonly used to allow for fitting losses in the mainline, when a different method is used for zone fitting losses.

A modified version of calculating each fitting loss is also used by many designers to include an allowance that is approximately correct for the piping arrangement of a particular system. This method is used as a compromise to reduce the amount of detail that is often necessary in pressure loss calculations, when each fitting, bushing, etc. is considered separately.

Figure 11-7 illustrates an example of a "short-list" of equivalent lengths that is used with the modified version of calculating each fitting. This example table is used for (socket-type) fitting loss calculations in this chapter. When a very rough fitting allowance is possible, an even simpler table can be developed by reducing the number of variables to one or two per size.

For example, the table below provides a single equivalent length value for one or more sizes and type of fittings. The result is an additional compromise in accuracy to reduce the amount of time required for calculations. However, it offers the advantage of simply counting the elbows and tees (tee with branch flow is

equal to two fittings) and converting the total quantity of fittings to pipe length using a single factor.

PVC Pipe Sizes:	Equivalent SDR21 Pipe	Length (ft) Sch. 40 Pipe
½	3	2
¾	4	2
1	5	3
1¼ - 2	6	5
2½ - 3	9	7

NOTE: Regardless of the method, or methods used to cover fitting losses, the allowance should be adequate to cover piping changes that are often necessary during installation of the system.

PRELIMINARY FLOW REQUIREMENTS. The manufacturer's specified flow is used to determine the preliminary flow requirements of an area or an individual zone, when using the flow adjustment method (Figure 11-4) as previously discussed.

NOTE: Specified (catalog) flow may or may not include an adequate allowance for flow variations due to manufacturing tolerances.

Figure 11-3 shows the Exemplary Performance Data for the sprinklers used in preparing the head layout for the property in Figure 11-1. To simplify determination

Average Pipe Section Length (ft)	Fitting Loss Allowance [1] Percentage of Total Zone Pipe Loss	
	Typical Zone Piping Arrangement	Single-Row Tees Only
5.0	80%	65%
7.5	70%	55%
10.0	60%	45%
12.5	55%	40%
15.0	50%	35%
17.5	45%	30%
20.0	40%	25%

(1) Actual percentage of pipe loss will vary with each zone due to fittings required and pipe sizing. Calculated loss will vary with different fitting loss tables, allowance for bushings, etc

Figure 11-6 Example of Percentages Used to Estimate Zone Fitting Losses - PVC Pipe and Fittings

of zoning, flow requirements are determined (using this table) for logical areas of division and/or areas where separate zoning is required. Areas of division should be as small as possible; small areas can be combined later if zoning consolidation is feasible. Flow requirements of each of the logical areas of division in the example system are shown below (25 lb/in^2 base pressure):

REAR LAWN AREA

Quantity	Nozzle	gpm	Total gpm
2	420-36	4.8	9.6
4	420-18	2.7	10.8
4	420-09	1.4	5.6
1	420-12	1.8	1.8
1	420-22	3.4	3.4
1	420-27	4.3	4.3
		Total Flow	35.5

REAR SHRUB BEDS

1. At rear fence

Quantity	Nozzle	gpm	Total gpm
8	410-18LA	.7	5.6
1	410-09LA	.4	.4
1	410-27LA	1.0	1.0
		Total Flow	7.0

2. Around building

Quantity	Nozzle	gpm	Total gpm
7	412-18LA	1.1	7.7
3	412-09LA	.6	1.8
1	412-12LA	.7	.7
1	410-18LA	.7	.7
1	403-18LA	.3	.3
		Total Flow	11.2

FRONT LAWN AREA

Quantity	Nozzle	gpm	Total gpm
2	420-36	4.8	9.6
7	420-18	2.7	18.9
2	420-09	1.4	2.8
1	420-13	2.1	2.1
1	420-22	3.4	3.4
		Total Flow	36.8

PARKWAY STRIP

Quantity	Nozzle	gpm	Total gpm
13	412-18LA	1.1	14.3
2	412-09LA	.6	1.2
		Total Flow	15.5

FRONT SHRUB BEDS

Quantity	Nozzle	gpm	Total gpm
1	415-36	2.7	2.7
4	415-18LA	1.6	6.4
2	415-09LA	.8	1.6
1	412-18LA	1.1	1.1
5	410-18LA	.7	3.5
3	410-09LA	.4	1.2
		Total Flow	16.5

Pipe Sizing and Zoning

ZONING THE SYSTEM
In order to section the system into operating zones, factors that should be considered are:

1. Water Supply - Capacity, flow velocity, pressure and operating time requirements.
2. Size of mainline and related equipment.
3. Zone separation for system control.

WATER SUPPLY. The capacity of an existing municipal or private water supply is normally the first factor of consideration since zone sizes are limited by the flow rate available. In some cases, an existing water supply may be too small, due to the number of zones that would be necessary and the total period of time that would be required for a complete operating cycle of the system. Water pressure available at different flow rates may also affect the flow rate that is available for zones.

A larger water service and water meter (or pump system) may be required for a practical system. However, it is often necessary to compromise on the size of a new water supply, due to cost and a variety of possible restrictions that may be applicable for a particular project.

Flow velocity in the water service of municipal supplies to a building water meter (or to an irrigation meter) is normally the limiting factor that will establish the maximum flow rate for the system. This limitation is discussed in Chapter 4, "City Water Supply Piping."

The table shown in Figure 11-8 includes the most common sizes of domestic water meters available for smaller projects in the U.S.A. In most cases, the water service pipe is Type-K copper and is the same nominal size as the water meter. However, there are exceptions in the type of pipe, and the size as compared to the meter size. For example, most 5/8 in meters are 5/8 x 3/4 (5/8 in meter with 3/4 in connections) and are used with a 3/4 in service pipe.

The "Maximum Safe Capacity" values in Figure 11-8 relate to the water meter flow and pressure loss. These rates do not relate to the safe flow for irrigation systems. The maximum flow rate through each pipe size for irrigation design will depend on the maximum velocity used by the designer for the service pipe. The flow for Type-K copper at 9 ft/s is listed for comparison. For the reasons discussed in Chapter 4, some designers use 9 ft/s as the maximum velocity for service lines to water meters.

ZONE SIZING-LARGE SUPPLIES. In some cases, an existing water supply can be much larger than necessary for the flow requirements of the irrigation system. This condition is common when the landscaped area is small as compared to the size of the building.

Equivalent Feet - PVC/SDR-21								
Type of Fitting:	**Nominal Pipe Size: inches**							
	1/2	3/4	1	1 1/4	1 1/2	2	2 1/2	3
Elbow -90°[1]	3	4	5	6	6	7	9	10
Elbow -45°[1]	2	2	3	3	3	4	5	5
Tee - Run of -Standard[1]	2	3	4	4	4	5	6	7
-Reducing[2]	-	5	6	6	6	7	9	10
Tee - Branch Flow -Standard[1]	6	8	10	11	12	13	17	20
-Reduced[2]	-	10	12	13	14	16	20	23

Threaded Adapters - Assume loss is included in allowance used for valve or other equipment.
Couplings - No allowance due to minor loss in socket - type couplings.
Cross - Use two tees for loss allowance (tees commonly used for installation).

Notes: (1) Steel pipe equivalents adjusted for PVC/SDR-21 (re: Table 17).
(2) Rough allowances only. Based on approximately the same velocity for entrance and exit flows.

Figure 11-7 Example of "Short-List" for Estimating PVC Fitting Losses

When zone flow is not limited by an undersized water supply, the designer should consider a maximum flow rate for the zones that is cost-effective for the size of the irrigation system. This consideration is necessary since the cost of pipe, fittings, valves and other required equipment will increase significantly with some nominal size increases.

Although the total number of zones required must be realistic, considering the size of the system and the time available for operation per day, large zones in a relatively small system may not be cost-effective.

ZONE SEPARATION FOR CONTROL. Development of individual zones is not limited to separation as required for different rates of application and/or to establish a zone that conforms to the flow limitations of the available water supply. Separation of some areas may also be desirable for improved system performance by providing separate control for areas with different watering schedule requirements. See Chapter 8, "Related Considerations."

ZONING THE EXEMPLARY SYSTEM
The flow requirements of the exemplary system were previously determined using catalog flow at 25 lb/in^2 sprinkler pressure:

Rear Lawn Area	35.5 gpm
Rear Shrub Beds	18.2
Front Lawn Area	36.8
Parkway Strip	15.5
Front Shrub Beds	16.5

These flow rates do not include an allowance for increased flow due to head pressure variation, as previously discussed in this chapter.

VARIATIONS IN PRECIPITATION RATE. Increased flow for pressure loss calculations is not the only consideration for system design, as head pressure variations will also have an effect on the average precipitation rate between sprinklers within a zone. The following comparisons show the effect that variable head pressures have on the rate of precipitation.

Pressure differential between heads	Effect on rate of precipitation
10%	4%
15%	7%
20%	10%
30%	14%
40%	18%

Meter Size	Maximum Safe Capacity		Flow in Type K
	Flow	Pressure Loss	© 9 ft/s
_in_	_gpm_[1]	_lb/in² [1]_	_gpm_[2]
⅝	20	15.0	
¾	30	15.0	12.2
1	50	15.0	21.8
1½	100	20.0	48.3
2	160	20.0	84.6

(1) From Table 19.
(2) From Table 10A.

Figure 11-8 Capacity of Water Meters and Type K Copper Tube Water Services

Since the theoretical effect on the precipitation rate is based on a percentage of the head pressure, the actual amount of the pressure difference will depend on the head pressure. For example, at the typical design pressure of 25 lb/in^2 for spray heads, the actual pressure difference within the zone for 10, 15, and 20% is listed below:

Percentage Increase	Pressure Difference	Precipitation Difference
10%	2.50 lb/in^2	5%
15%	3.75 lb/in^2	7%
20%	5.00 lb/in^2	10%

Pressure differential within each circuit should be limited to a maximum that is consistent with the level of performance desired. However, regardless of the budget available, pressure differential over 20% is normally not recommended. Many designers will attempt to achieve a 10-15% maximum pressure differential. Except for unusual cases, it is not difficult to maintain the pressure difference below 20% when flow velocity is controlled at recommended levels within the zone piping.

Once the differential is established for the circuit, the ratio of the pressure at any sprinkler to the pressure at any other sprinkler will remain constant. Precipitation may increase in the zone with additional pressure, but the precipitation difference between sprinklers will remain at the same ratio.

Although the effect on the precipitation rate can be significant if not controlled, the systems designer should compare the theoretical effect of pressure difference on a standard nozzle to other common flow variations. This procedure will help the designer understand the practical limitations of control. The flow rate of any type of water outlet device can vary up or down from the

Pipe Sizing and Zoning

nominal flow rate. This includes various types of pressure-compensating products (emitters, bubblers, spray heads, etc.) which can have a 10% (plus or minus) variation in the flow rate at normal operating pressures.

FLOW ADJUSTMENT. A maximum of 15% (3.75 lb/in^2) head pressure increase will be used for the zones in the exemplary system. It will be necessary to control the total pressure loss within the zones to a maximum of 3.75 lb/in^2. Pipe for the system will be PVC, SDR-21, and sizes will be as necessary to control the pressure loss in each zone.

The flow requirement for each area is adjusted by using the 1.05 multiplier from the table in Figure 11-4. This is the listed adjustment factor for 25 lb/in^2 base pressure and 4 lb/in^2 zone loss. This adjustment will provide the approximate flow necessary for each area, and can be used to consider the zone requirements for each area. The adjusted flow rates are listed below for each area.

Rear Lawn Area	37.3 gpm
Rear Shrub Beds	19.1
Front Lawn Area	38.6
Parkway Strip	16.3
Front Shrub Beds	17.3

FLOW VELOCITY. The maximum flow velocity for all PVC pipe in the system will be 5 ft/s for the reasons discussed in Chapter 4, "Pipe System Design."

The exemplary system has a 1 in. water meter (located in the parkway strip) and a 1 in., Type-K copper water service from the city water main to the meter. The maximum flow rate allowed for the system is 22 gpm (21.8). This is the listed flow in Table 10a (Appendix) for a 1 in. pipe at 9 ft/s velocity. This velocity was selected as a compromise due to the flow limitations of a small service pipe, as discussed in Chapter 4, "City Water Supply Piping."

Based on the maximum flow rate of 22.0 gpm, seven zones are required for the system. Two zones are required for the rear lawn area (37.3 gpm) and two zones are required for the front lawn area (38.6 gpm). The rear shrub beds, the parkway strip and the front shrub beds require only one zone for each area.

The seven zone requirement is based on the assumption that the available water pressure at 22.0 gpm is adequate for the pressure losses that will occur due to elevation and water flow through all pipe, fittings and valves from the water supply (city main) to all sprinklers, and provide a residual operating pressure of at least 25 lb/in^2 at the inlet to all sprinklers.

CONDITIONS. The design must allow for all conditions that will influence the piping design of the individual system.

Although the existing water supply to any type of building (or plumbing system) is similar in some ways, there are many possible variations including the location, size, capacity and dependability of the water supply. There are also many possible variations in plumbing code requirements for an irrigation system, including the type and location of backflow prevention equipment, as discussed in Chapter 5.

This exemplary system will be designed without an allowance for flow into the residence during system operation. In this case, this was considered to be necessary, due to the small size service pipe and the fact that the system will start operation after midnight and will be completed before sunrise. However, in some cases, the piping design for an irrigation system must allow for other flow requirements in the water supply.

The following listed conditions must be considered for the seven zones in the exemplary system.
1. 6 in. city water main is located in the street and 25 ft. from the water meter.
2. Existing 1 in. water meter and 1 in. Type K copper service.
3. 55 lb/in^2 static water pressure gauged at the site.
4. Pressure range available in the city main per water department records: 54 to 58 lb/in^2.
5. Plumbing code requires a Double-Check Valve assembly for backflow prevention. Equipment can be installed in a valve box below grade. Piping from the point of connection to the equipment must be copper tube.

The systems designer should use caution in selecting a pressure that is safe for system design, unless reliable information is obtained on the normal range of pressure available at the site throughout the year.

Water distribution systems are designed in new neighborhoods to allow for future building construction, extension of mains into even newer areas, and reduction of main capacity due to deterioration from aging. Thus, immediate pressure in a new neighborhood is usually substantially greater than the planned future low pressure. For example: gauged pressure in a new neighborhood when only a few homes have been built may be 85 lb/in^2. After the area has been completely built, gauged pressure may be only 55 lb/in^2. A check with the city engineer would probably have revealed that planned future low pressure would be 50-55 lb/in^2. A sprinkler system for a property in the area should be designed based on the planned minimum future pressure of 50 lb/in^2.

As a general rule, systems should be designed to operate on less pressure than the anticipated low pressure in new neighborhoods and known low pressure in older ones. This protects the system from unanticipated pressure drops.

An allowance for such pressure depreciation is usually graduated in proportion to the low static pressure, anticipated or existing. All other factors being duly considered by the designer, it would be appropriate to consider allowances on the following sliding scale:

When low static pressure is:	Allow:	Design for:
50 lb/in^2	10%	45 lb/in^2
75 lb/in^2	15%	65 lb/in^2
100 lb/in^2	20%	80 lb/in^2
125 lb/in^2	25%	95 lb/in^2

NOTE: The 80 and 95 lb/in^2 design pressures are normally not practical for a spray system design.

A further argument in support of conservatism is the necessity to design systems to function properly on hot days when pressure will be lowest. This is obviously the time when good, dependable, artificial watering is needed most. It could be argued that such a degree of conservatism is not required with automatic systems since sprinkling is normally programmed for early morning hours. However, a marginal design would not allow for "watering-in" of "hot" fertilizers during the day; burned turf areas might occur due to lack of coverage.

The exemplary system will be designed to operate on a minimum pressure of 48 lb/in^2 (or less) in the city water main. This is based on the low of 54 lb/in^2 with a 10% depreciation allowance.

PRELIMINARY PIPING. In most cases, a preliminary piping layout is recommended to allow for possible

changes in the number of zones that may be necessary. For example, 23.0 lb/in^2 is available for the total of all pressure losses in the exemplary system. This is based on the difference between the 48 lb/in^2 available for design in the city main, and the 25 lb/in^2 residual requirement for sprinkler operation. The 23.0 lb/in^2 may, or may not, be adequate for the total of all losses that will occur in a cost-effective piping design for this particular system.

Pipe Layout Guidelines. There are some variations in the piping layout of a system due to the location of the water supply (inside or outside the building), the type and location of the backflow prevention equipment, the desired location of the zone control valves (one location or scattered), the type of pipe, and the type of equipment that will be used to install the piping (trencher or pipe-puller).

In most cases, the routing of the mainline piping will be determined by the location of the zone control valves and any other equipment that will require a water supply. The routing of the mainline will also be influenced by the location of zone piping when a trench will be available for the installation of multiple pipe lines and valve wiring.

The zone piping layout is primarily controlled by the location of the heads in each zone. However, it is necessary to consider the material cost (amount and size of pipe), labor cost, site conditions and pressure variations that will occur within the zone as a result of the piping arrangement. These considerations are interrelated and a compromise is often necessary for practical reasons.

The following guidelines are provided to assist the designer in the development of the piping layout:

1. Although pipe routing is considered diagrammatic, the pipe layout should be as realistic as possible for the design and installation of the system.

2. Zones should be as compact as possible and the zone entrance (ZE) should be located with consideration for the distribution of flow within the zone. The total flow into the ZE should be divided as soon as possible to distribute the flow in different directions.

Pipe Sizing and Zoning

Therefore, the best piping arrangement would be a compact zone with the ZE located in the center of the zone, and the least desirable piping arrangement would be a long, single-row of heads with the ZE located at one end. Although piping arrangement is of minor importance in small zones, the level of importance in flow and pressure loss distribution increases as the size of the zone increases.

3. Pipe should be routed around all obstructions (including trees), but should be routed as directly as practical between all points of connection. Headers within a zone should be located to intersect laterals as near to the center of the laterals as practical to create an approximate balance in flow and pressure between the extreme ends of the lateral.

   NOTE: A "header" is the pipe that supplies the lateral(s) and is perpendicular to the lateral(s) at point of connection; example, (L) in Figure 11-9. A "lateral" is any pipe which connects sprinklers to the "header;" example, (K) in Figure 11-9.

4. All piping should be laid out in a symmetrical fashion with intersecting lines forming a simple grid pattern. Lines are rarely run diagonally because it disrupts the pattern, usually serves no practical purpose, and makes installation more difficult.

5. When a trench is available, parallel pipe lines should be moved together for installation in the same trench, whenever possible. Pipes that are to be installed together are drawn on the plan approximately 1/8 in. apart.

6. Pipes should be located with consideration for the limitations of the equipment that will be used to install the pipe. For example, most trenching and pipe-pulling equipment cannot be used along a fence or building wall.

Maximum Pressure Requirement. The preliminary piping layout should be developed as necessary for the zone (or zones) that will have the greatest pressure requirement. The following four factors should be considered when selecting the zone(s):

1. Head pressure requirement.
2. Total zone flow.
3. Distance from the water supply.
4. Elevation difference from the water supply.

Since the operating pressure requirement is the same for all heads in the exemplary system, and the 2 ft elevation difference is minor, the zone of maximum pressure requirement will be the zone with the largest flow and/or the greatest distance from the water supply.

The rear lawn area is divided into a south and north zone. Zones are separated with two rows each and flow is not equal for the two zones. This flow imbalance will be changed only if necessary.

The front lawn area is divided into an east and west zone. Zones are separated by a north-south line through the center to equally divide the total flow as close as possible.

The flow requirements (catalog flow x 1.05) of the seven zones are:

Rear Lawn - South	21.4 gpm
Rear Lawn - North	15.9
Rear Shrub - Two Beds	19.1
Front Lawn - East	18.6
Front Lawn - West	20.0
Parkway Strip	16.3
Front Shrub - Two Beds	17.3

The rear lawn-south zone has the largest flow requirement and is also the most distant zone from the water supply.

All zones need not be (and seldom are) equal in flow requirements. The flow differences of the seven zones in the exemplary system are typical of the variations that will occur in a landscape irrigation system. These differences are due to lawn and shrub separation, the size of the individual areas, and the logical separation of the lawn areas.

The best hydraulic balance is attained when the zones near the water supply are the largest and progressively become smaller until the most distant zone has the smallest flow requirement. However, this is seldom practical except for very large areas that must be divided into several zones.

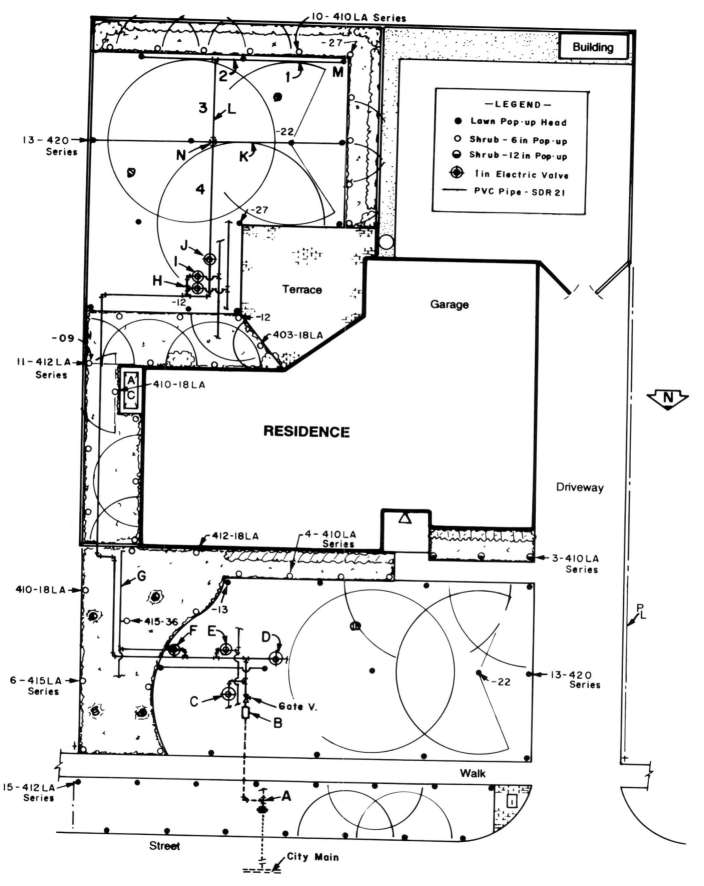

Figure 11-9 Preliminary Piping Layout

Pipe Sizing and Zoning

Figure 11-9 illustrates the preliminary piping required for the exemplary system. Some of the valves and piping shown are not necessary to determine the pressure requirement of the rear lawn-south zone. This detail is included only to explain the logic used to route the mainline through the system.

Since the existing building supply line from the water meter is ¾ in, a new copper line will be required from the meter (A) to the location of the double-check valve assembly (B).

The PVC main is routed from (B) with consideration for the front zone valve requirements and to allow for installation of the mainline in the same trench with zone piping where possible. Zone valve (C) is for the parkway strip, valves (D) and (E) are for the two lawn zones (east and west), and valve (F) is for the front shrub zone.

The main is routed between the small trees in the ground cover bed and parallel to the zone piping (G) that will be required in the area. Zone valve (H) is for the rear lawn area-north zone, and valve (I) is for the rear shrub zone. Zone valve (J) is for the rear lawn-south zone.

Calculating Pressure Losses. A pressure loss calculation is required from the city main through the system and the south zone to head (M). This is the most distant head within the zone from the zone entrance (N). The pressure loss for the zone piping will be calculated using catalog flow. When completed, the total flow and pressure loss from (M) to (N) will be adjusted using the proper adjustment factor from Figure 11-4, plus a safety factor if desired.

The loss in pipe sections (1), (2) and (3) will be calculated to determine the total loss from (M) to (N). The flow in a zone is accumulative. That is, when starting with the most distant head (M) and tracing the natural flow pattern back to the zone entrance (N), the flow will increase with each section and the flow for each section will be equal to the total of all heads served by the pipe section.

Pipe sizes for pipe sections in the zone are based on the flow requirements of each pipe section. Two common methods are used to select the sizes for the zone loss calculation. These preliminary sizes can be changed if necessary, when the total zone loss is known.

Method One. This "rule of thumb" method is useful for the average spray zone requirement. Maximum flow rates are established for each pipe size, using the maximum velocity allowed in the zone piping to determine the maximum flow rate. For example, using Table 5a, Appendix, the maximum flow rate at 5 ft/s is listed below:

Pipe Size	Flow, gpm
½	5.9
¾	10.1
1	16.7
1¼	26.9

Method Two. This method relates to the conditions of an individual zone. However, it does not provide a limit on flow velocity and is seldom useful with a small zone, unless the allowable zone loss is very low. The allowable loss per 100 ft is determined for the zone piping and sizes are selected from a pressure loss table that is based on loss per 100 ft; example, Table 5, Appendix.

The allowable loss for zones in the exemplary system is 3.75 lb/in^2, as previously stated in "Flow Adjustment." The combined length of all pipe sections from the most distant head (M) to the zone entrance (N) is 36 ft [pipe section (1) = 17 ft, (2) = 4 ft and (3) = 15 ft].

The combined length is adjusted to include an allowance for normal fitting losses. The fitting percentage of zone loss in Figure 11-6 can also be used as a "length" percentage. The three pipe sections have an average length of 12 ft (36 /3). The adjusted total length using the fitting percentage of 55% is 56 ft (36 x 1.55).

Pipe Section	Size/Type	Flow gpm	Length, ft Pipe & Fittings	Loss lb/in^2
1	½ in PVC 315	1.4	17 + 3=20	.09
2	½ in PVC 315	4.1	4 + 2=6	.20
3	¾ in PVC 200	6.8	15 + 10=25	.58
	Sprinkler Riser Pipe			0
Pipe and Fitting Loss at Catalog Flow				.87
Zone Elevation (+/-lb/in^2)				0
Adjusted Pipe/Fitting Loss (x 1.05 See Explanation)				.91
Sprinkler Operating Pressure				25.00
Operating Pressure Required at ZE				25.91

**Figure 11-10 Zone Pressure Calculation
Exemplary System - Rear Lawn**

$$\frac{Allowable\ Zone\ Loss}{3.75} \div \frac{Length/100}{.56} = \frac{Allowable\ Loss\ Per\ 100\ ft}{6.7\ ^{lb}/_{in^2}}$$

Using Table 5, Appendix, the flow rate required for each size to develop 3.75 lb/in^2 loss in 56 ft of pipe (and fittings) is approximately:

Pipe Size	Flow, gpm
1/2	6
3/4	12
1	23
1 1/4	43

These flow rates would not be useful in the exemplary system if the flow is to be maintained at 5 ft/s velocity, or less. The flow velocity at these rates would range from 5.1 to 8.0 ft/s. These allowable flow rates are high for each size since 3.75 lb/in^2 is a rather high pressure loss for 56 ft of pipe (and fittings). Although a different set of flow rates can be established using a lower zone loss, the flow rates will seldom relate to the actual flow rates in a limited number of pipe sections.

Pipe sizing methods are limited by the number of standard pipe sizes available. An unrealistic number of sizes would be necessary to provide the "correct" size for each flow rate and pressure loss that may be required in a pipe section.

The pressure calculation for the rear lawn-south zone is shown in Figure 11-10. Flow in each section is based on catalog flow requirements from the table in Figure 11-3. The length for each section is the pipe length plus the fitting equivalent length, using the data provided in Figure 11-7:

    Section (1) - 1/2 in 90° Elbow at head (M)
    Section (2) - 1/2 in Run of Tee (connection at section 1)
    Section (3) - 3/4 in Tee, branch reducing (at Sect. 2).

NOTE: Fittings at the zone entrance (N) will be included with pipe section (4).

Pressure loss for each pipe section was calculated using Table 3 (RC formula). Appendix pressure loss tables can also be used (example, Table 5). The following two items are listed in the calculation for reference only:

1. The sprinkler riser pipe will be a short - 1/2 in nipple, and no allowance is included.

2. Elevation: there is no elevation difference within the zone.

As previously discussed in "Pipe Fitting Losses", the amount of design time required to consider an equivalent footage for each individual fitting, may not be practical (or necessary) for the average zone. For example, the total loss of the three pipe sections is .57 lb/in^2, when calculated using the pipe length only. A 55% fitting allowance from the table in Figure 11-6 (12 ft average length) is .31 lb/in^2 (.57 x .55). The pipe and fitting loss would be .92 lb/in^2 (.57 + .31 x 1.05) as compared to .91 lb/in^2 in Figure 11-10.

NOTE: This fitting loss example is somewhat misleading since a "rough" percentage allowance of this type will rarely provide a loss that is this close to the calculated loss of individual fittings.

The total zone pressure loss of .91 lb/in^2 in Figure 11-10 is the adjusted loss using a multiplier of 1.05 (.87 x 1.05 = .91). This multiplier is used to include a safety factor in the zone pressure loss and the total zone flow. The multiplier in Figure 11-4 for 1.0 lb/in^2 zone loss at 25 lb/in^2 sprinkler pressure is 1.01. The catalog zone flow of 20.4 gpm (6.8 from Figure 11-10 plus 13.6 gpm for 4 additional heads) will be adjusted to 21.4 gpm (20.4 x 1.05).

The maximum zone loss allowance of 3.75 lb/in^2 for the exemplary system was established only to set a limit on the level of compromise between the cost of pipe and fittings, and head pressure differential within the zone.

Although the total zone loss of .91 lb/in^2 is very low, it is not uncommon for a small and compact spray zone. The total loss is low due to the pipe sizes available for the flow rates, and the fact that the combined distance from (M) to (N) is only 36 ft. It would also not be uncommon for the total zone loss in large spray zones to be considerably higher than this example.

Figure 11-11 illustrates the pressure loss calculations required to estimate the total loss from the city main to the zone entrance. Pressure losses for the three pipe sections (Copper and PVC) were calculated using Table 3, Appendix.

Pipe Sizing and Zoning

The loss for the 1 in. water service includes an allowance for a corporation cock at the city main connection, 2-90° wrought elbows, and a straight meter cock at the water meter. Equivalent footage for these items was determined using Table 18, Appendix.

The pressure loss in the water meter of 2.6 lb/in^2 is based on interpolation of the data provided in Table 19, Appendix. The elevation loss of .87 lb/in^2 was included to cover the 2 ft elevation increase from the meter to the building and rear lawn area (2 x .433). In this case, the loss allowance may not be necessary since city water pressure data is normally based on a pressure test at a fire hydrant, which may be two feet above the meter.

The loss in the 1¼ in type L copper from the meter to the D.C.A. includes an allowance for a 1¼ in tee (at the connection to the existing ¾ in building line) and a 90° elbow. Equivalent footage for these wrought-type fittings was determined using Table 18, Appendix, including the use of the 1.08 multiplier for type L copper. However, the minor difference in footage was omitted in the total pipe length.

NOTE: Backflow prevention is discussed in Chapter 5. The type and location of the backflow prevention equipment, and the type of pipe required at the point of connection (P.O.C.) must be in accordance with the requirements of the plumbing code. The requirement for the system is an example only.

The pressure loss in the Double Check Assembly (D.C.A.) was obtained from a product manufacturer's pressure loss table (table is not provided). The flow of 21.4 gpm is the maximum (approximate) flow rate recommended by the manufacturer for the 1 in size unit. The loss allowance should be based on the type of equipment required. Some types of backflow prevention equipment can have a pressure loss as much as 15 lb/in^2.

NOTE: No allowance is included for the minor loss in the 1¼ in gate valve (system cut-off valve) located on the discharge side of the D.C.A.

The 218 feet of PVC main includes the equivalent footage allowance for all fittings from the D.C.A., and the two tees (run of tee, reducing) at the zone entrance. In some cases, different types (or pressure ratings) of pipe are used for the mainline and the zone piping.

The pressure loss in the 1 in electric (zone control) valve was obtained from a product manufacturer's pressure loss table (table is not provided). The valve size selected is based on the pressure loss through the valve and is not necessarily the same size as the pipe. The 1 in valve, in this example, is commonly used with ¾, 1 and 1¼ in pipe. The zone flow rate should be within the flow range recommended for the valve size by the manufacturer.

The 1¼ in pipe size for the type L copper and the PVC main was selected with consideration for the flow velocity and pressure loss. Regardless of the flow requirement and pressure available for an irrigation system, the size selection for the mainline is based on the flow velocity, pressure loss and the cost of materials.

The mainline size can be increased to 1½ in if the combined loss of 4.9 lb/in^2 (.94 + 3.96) is too high. However, the related increase in cost should be compared to the cost increase of other possible size changes that may be used to reduce the loss. These include the D.C.A., the electric valve, or increasing the number of zones to reduce the flow rate.

Although the pressure loss of the miscellaneous items (plumbing valves and fittings) in the mainline piping can be included by using a different type of loss allowance, the combined loss of these items is an important consideration when estimating the pressure loss. While the following percentages only relate to the exemplary system, the percentages illustrate the level of importance of these, and similar items:

Pipe:	Equivalent Footage:	Percent of Pipe	Pipe Length
Type K Copper	14.7	59%	25
Type L Copper	5.4	36%	15
PVC Main	73.0	50%	145

FINAL ZONES AND PIPING

The pressure requirement of 46.8 lb/in^2 in the city main, as shown in Figure 11-11, is slightly below the 48.0 lb/in^2 available for design (54 less 10%). Therefore, no changes are necessary for the seven zone requirement previously established for the system. This decision is based on the fact that the rear lawn-south zone is considered to be the zone of greatest pressure requirement. This zone has the largest flow requirement of the seven zones, and is also the most distant zone from the water supply.

Item:	Length ft	Flow gpm	Velocity ft/s	Loss lb/in^2
1 in type K copper service	25.0			
1 in corporation cock	7.3			
1 in 90° ells-2 at 1.5	3.0			
1 in Straight Meter Cock	4.4			
Water Service=	40.0	21.4	8.8	6.02
1 in Water Meter		21.4		2.60
Elevation (2 ft above curb)				.87
1¼ type L copper to DCA	15.0			
1¼ branch of tee	3.2			
1¼ 90° ell	2.2			
P.O.C. Piping = (20.4)	20.0	21.4	5.5	.94
1 in Double Check Valve		21.4		4.00
1¼ PVC, 200 Main	145.0			
1¼ in branch of tee [1]	11.0			
1¼ in run-of-tee (5)	20.0			
1¼ in r. of t. reducing (2)	12.0			
1¼ 90° ell (5)	30.0			
PVC from DCA to ZE =	218.0	21.4	4.0	3.96
1 in Electric Valve		21.4		2.50
	Total Pressure Loss from City Main to ZE			20.89
	Zone Pressure Requirement (Fig. 11-10)			25.91
	Operating Pressure Required at City Main (at 21.4 gpm)			46.80 lb/in^2

Figure 11-11 Pressure Requirement for Rear Lawn Zone. Exemplary System

The number of calculations required for an irrigation design will depend on the number that is necessary to prove that all zones will have adequate operating pressure. One zone calculation may be sufficient, or it may be necessary to check the pressure requirements of several zones. The amount of "proof" that is necessary, will in large part, depend on the experience of the systems designer.

Since the copper, D.C.A., PVC main and zone valve are adequate in size for the zone of maximum pressure requirement, the same sizes are suitable for the other six zones. The same comparison can be applied to the zone piping. However, the length and flow requirements within the zone will vary with each zone.

In the exemplary system, the total pressure loss in the zone piping can be somewhat greater for the other six zones. This is due to the fact that the other zones will have less loss in the main supply system (less flow and pipe length). However, it is difficult to compare the requirements of different zones without additional calculations or experience, or both.

Figure 11-12 illustrates the zone piping of the rear shrub zone. The two planting areas are combined together and connected to the same zone valve. The zone entrance (A) is approximately in the center of the zone piping. The distance from the ZE (A) to head (B) is 88 ft and 70 ft to head (C).

The total flow for the rear shrub zone is 19.1 gpm (18.2 catalog x 1.05). The pressure calculation for the zone is shown in Figure 11-13. The total pressure loss in pipe sections (1) through (7) is almost equal to the loss in pipe section (8), due to the length of pipe section (8). The adjusted total zone loss is 2.53 lb/in^2, using a multiplier of 1.05. A different multiplier can be used to increase the safety factor, if desired (basic multiplier of 1.03 in Figure 11-4).

Pipe Sizing and Zoning

The operating pressure required at the city main for the shrub zone is 44.93 lb/in². This is approximately 2 lb/in² less than the lawn zone requirement in Figure 11-10, even though the zone loss is almost 2 lb/in² higher. This is due to the reduced pressure loss in the supply system from the city main. The zone piping from the ZE (A) to head (C) will have a slightly less total pressure loss, if the size selection is based on approximately the same loss per foot (or per 100 ft).

NOTE: The pressure requirement at the source is often referred to as the "zone design pressure." The maximum zone pressure requirement in the system is referred to as the "system design pressure."

The zone piping for the other five zones will be sized using the two zone calculations as a reference. The 2.5 lb/in² zone loss in the rear shrub zone will represent the maximum head pressure difference within a zone, and the maximum (theoretical) precipitation difference within a zone will be 4%.

The flow control on each zone valve can be adjusted to control the pressure into each zone as necessary. In some system designs, a master electric valve is used on the mainline, before the first zone valve. This additional valve will offer a degree of safety by providing an automatic cut-off to the main supply piping when the system is not operating. The valve is connected to the master valve circuit of the controller.

An automatic pressure regulating option is available on some electric valve models to maintain a constant discharge pressure. This option is recommended for the master electric valve (or individual zone valves) when there are extreme variations in the city water pressure at the site.

The completed exemplary spray system is shown in Figure 11-14.

SUMMARY

The procedures and considerations discussed for zoning and pipe sizing of the exemplary system are typical for any type of sprinkler system, small or large, residential or commercial properties. Although the number of zones and the zone flow rate may be different with a smaller or larger water supply (or a different system), the same basic steps of design development are necessary.

Flow and pressure calculations for a system that has a meter (or point of connection) inside the building are similar to the examples provided, if the size, type and condition of the existing pipe is known. In some cases, a flow test may be necessary to determine the capacity of an existing supply. See Water Supply Testing, Chapter 3.

Flow and pressure calculations for a system that has a pump on a private water supply (well, lake, etc.), will be based on the pump discharge requirement, as compared to the city water main in the exemplary system. The zone flow rate and pressure available for design will be limited by the performance at the pump discharge, or at some other point of connection. See Chapters 6 and 7 for additional considerations that may be necessary with this type of water supply.

LOOPED MAINS

When feasible, looping an irrigation main has several advantages:
1. Reduced pressure loss with same size piping.
2. Reduced pipe size and cost with same pressure loss.
3. Reduced pipe size and cost and reduced pressure loss.

In a conventional system like Figure 11-15, the main would be branched from A to C and A to E, as shown by the solid lines, in a manner to keep each leg as short as possible. With a looped main, gap C - E is breached by a connecting pipe represented by the broken line. Joining the mains in this manner allows water to supply any outlet from two directions.

Not all properties lend themselves to looped mains. A property must be of a size and shape that two "legs" are required for the main, and the legs must naturally terminate near each other. Exceptionally large properties like parks and golf courses are normally suitable, regardless of shape.

In Figure 11-15, assume that each zone requires 90 gpm and only one zone operates at a time.

EXAMPLE 1: CONVENTIONAL MAIN. Assume a 2½ in 200 psi, SDR 21 PVC main. Pressure loss from A - B - C is computed thus: Flow of 90 gpm produces a loss of 1.74 lb/in² per 100 ft. Then, loss in the 400 ft = 7.0 lb/in². Thus, with a pressure of 40 lb/in² at A, flow pressure at C will be 33 lb/in² (40 − 7 = 33).

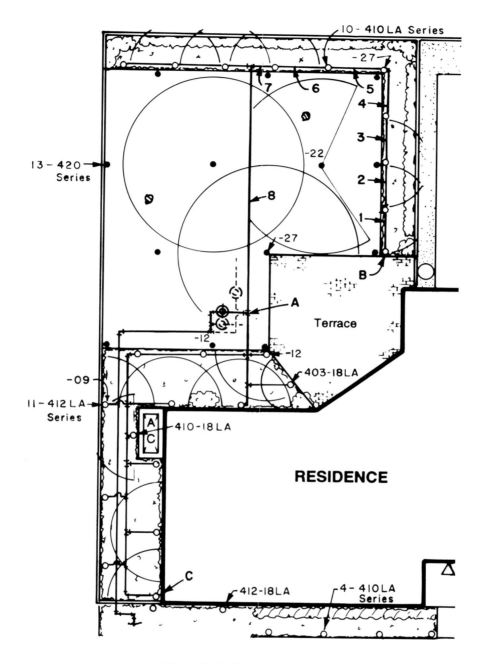

Figure 11-12 Piping for Rear Shrub Zone

EXAMPLE 2: LOOPED MAIN. The operating valve at C is exactly midway in the total length (800 ft) of the looped main. Therefore, one half of the total flow of 90 gpm will flow to the valve through pipe A - B - C, and the other half through pipe A - D - E - C. Pressure in either leg of the main is calculated on the basis: *One half of total flow in one half total length of looped main equals pressure loss in either leg.*

Therefore:

With a flow of 45 gpm (90 ÷ 2 = 45) through 2½ in 200 psi PVC, pressure loss equals .48 lb/in^2 per 100 ft, (Table 3).

Then:

The total pressure loss through each leg (800 ÷ 2 = 400 ft) of the main is 1.92 lb/in^2: .48 x 4 = 1.92; a reduction of 5.1 lb/in^2 if compared to the conventional main of the same size, example 1.

Pipe Sizing and Zoning

Thus:
With a pressure of 40 lb/in^2 at A, flow through each leg of the main will converge at C with a pressure of 38 lb/in^2; instead of 33 lb/in^2 with a conventional main.

EXAMPLE 3: LOOPED MAIN. In many cases, a looped main can be made one size smaller than a conventional main with no more, or possibly less, pressure loss. With the same flow as Example 2 (45 gpm), the loss through 2 in 200 psi PVC pipe is 1.23 lb/in^2 per 100 ft.

Then:
The total pressure loss through each leg of the main (400 ft) is 4.9 lb/in^2: 1.23 x 4.0 = 4.92.

Thus:
With 800 ft of 2 in looped main as compared to 400 ft of 2½ in conventional main, the loss at C is still 2.1 lb/in^2 less.

In addition, the cost of the longer 2 in main and fittings will be substantially less than for the 2½ in conventional main and fittings. The increased cost of labor for installation of the longer main may be insignificant because trenches for circuit piping will normally accommodate the extra length of main.

Caution: The loss calculated for a looped main is for that portion of piping only. Additional losses must be considered for the supply piping (in the example to A), as well as through the zone valves and circuit piping. Often, pipe supplying loop and zone is larger than loop size.

EXAMPLE 4: LOOPED MAIN. The pressure loss in a looped main of smaller systems is generally calculated with one half the flow through one half the total length regardless of valve locations. This loss is then used for all points in the looped main even though losses to other

Pipe Section	Size/Type	Flow gpm	Length, ft Pipe & Fittings	Loss lb/in^2
1	½ in PVC 315	.4	7 + 3=10	.00
2	½ in PVC 315	1.1	7 + 2=9	.03
3	½ in PVC 315	1.8	7 + 2=9	.07
4	½ in PVC 315	2.5	7 + 2=9	.12
5	½ in PVC 315	3.5	8+ 5=13	.33
6	½ in PVC 315	4.2	8+2=10	.35
7	½ in PVC 315	4.9	8+2=6	.28
8	¾ in PVC 200	7.0	40+10=50	1.23
				2.41
	Zone Loss Adjusted (x1.05)			2.53
	Sprinkler Operating Pressure			25.00
	Operating Pressure required at ZE			27.53
1in type K Service		19.1	40*	4.88
1 in Water Meter		19.1		2.00
Elevation (2ft)		19.1		.87
1 ¼ in type L P.O.C.		19.1	20*	.76
1 in D.C.A.		19.1		3.90
1 ¼ in PVC Main		19.1	190*	2.79
1 in Electric Valve		19.1		2.20
	Total pressure Loss from City Main to ZE			17.40
	Zone Design Pressure (required at 19.1 gpm)			lb/in^2 44.93
	*Includes fitting equivalent footage (see Fig. 11-11)			

Figure 11-13 Design Pressure - Rear Shrub Zone

points are less than the calculation for the mid-point of the loop.

With larger systems, it is often advantageous to determine actual loss to a zone supply located other than at the midpoint of the loop. In these cases, the two legs of the loop are different lengths. This causes different flows in the two legs because the pressure loss in the legs must be equal. With different pipe lengths, flow will self-adjust to cause equal losses, because pressure will equalize itself where the legs join.

Assume, in Figure 11-15, that the pressure loss in each leg of the loop from (A) to the zone supply (B) must be determined for the same flow previously used: 90 gpm total.

A simple method of determining the flow can be accomplished with a calculator that is equipped with an exponential function power key (Y^x or X^y) and the following formula:

Loop Formula:

$$F = \frac{TF}{LR^{.5405} + 1}$$

Where:

F = Flow in leg being considered
TF = Total flow from a single outlet
LR = Length ratio

Flow/Short Leg:

$$LR = \frac{Short\ Length}{Long\ Length}$$

Flow/Long Leg:

$$LR = \frac{Long\ Length}{Short\ Length}$$

NOTE: This method is limited to loops with only one zone operating at a time.

Flow and loss in Short Leg: (Figure 11-15)

$$LR = \frac{200}{600} = .3333$$

$$Flow = \frac{90}{.3333^{.5405} + 1} = \frac{90}{1.5522} = 58\ gpm$$

Pressure Loss: 2 in PVC, SDR 21 - 200 ft (A - B)

Loss = 3.95 lb/in² (Table 3)

Flow and loss in Long Leg:

$$LR = \frac{600}{200} = 3$$

$$Flow = \frac{90}{3^{.5405} + 1} = \frac{90}{2.8100} = 32\ gpm$$

Pressure Loss: 2 in PVC, SDR 21 - 600 ft (A-D-E-C-B)
Loss = 3.94 lb/in² (Table 3)

The total pressure loss to the zone supply (B) is 3.95 lb/in². Only one of the above calculations (short or long leg) is necessary to determine the pressure loss to (B).

EXAMPLE 5: LOOPED MAIN WHERE PIPE IS OF DIFFERENT SIZES AND/OR DIFFERENT KINDS. In this type loop, the same basic computations are used as in previous examples. However, pipe sizes and types must be converted to "one size and type" by using length equivalents.

The following formula can be used to determine the conversion multiplier for equivalent length:

Pipe Conversion Formula:

$$CM = \left(\frac{F_2}{F_1}\right)^{1.85}$$

Where:

CM = Conversion Multiplier
F_1 = "F" factor for size and type to be used as the standard - from Table 3.
F_2 = "F" factor for size and type to be converted from Table 3.

In Figure 11-16, the 3 in. PVC in each leg of the loop will be converted to an equivalent length of 4 in. AC pipe.

Leg A:

$$CM = \left(\frac{.0089}{.00508}\right)^{1.85} = 1.75197^{1.85} = 2.822$$

Pipe Sizing and Zoning

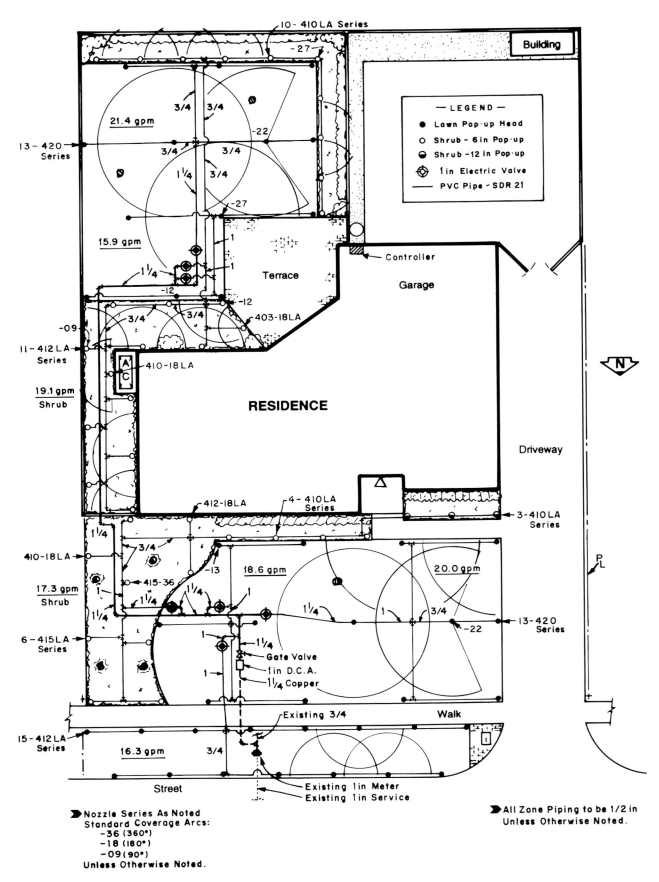

Figure 11-14 Completed Exemplary Spray System

100 ft of 3 in. PVC x 2.822 = 282 ft of 4 in. AC (100 ft of 3 in. PVC, SDR 21 will have a pressure loss equal to 282 ft of 4 in. AC).

Leg A = 300 ft of 4 in. AC + 282 ft equivalent length
       = 582 ft of 4 in. AC

Leg B:

200 ft of 3 in. PVC x 2.822 = 564 ft of 4 in. AC (200 ft of 3 in. PVC, SDR21 will have a pressure loss equal to 564 ft of 4 in. AC).

Leg B = 400 ft of 4 in. AC + 564 ft equivalent
        length = 964 ft of 4 in AC

The pressure loss in the loop from the source to the outlet can be determined using the loop formula:

Flow/Short Leg: (Short = 582 ft Long = 964 ft)

$$LR = \frac{582}{964} = .6037$$

$$Flow = \frac{200}{.6037^{.5405} + 1} = \frac{200}{1.7613} = 113.6 \; gpm$$

Pressure Loss: 4 in. AC - 582 ft
    Loss = 2.10 lb/in^2 (Table 3)
    or, with actual size/type and length:
    4 in. AC - 300 ft = 1.08
    3 in. PVC - 100 ft = 1.02
    Leg A - Loss   = 2.10 lb/in^2

The following pressure loss calculation for Leg B is used to check the above loop loss (leg A) calculation:

Flow in Leg B = 200 – 113.5 (leg A) = 86.40 gpm
4 in. AC - 400 ft   = .87
3 in. PVC - 200 ft   = 1.23
                                 2.10 lb/in^2

The total loop loss is 2.10 lb/in^2 (Figure 11-16).

COMPLEX LOOPS

Some systems will require the operation of more than one zone at the same time, due to the total number of zones required and the limited amount of time available per day for system operation. In these cases, the loop is not complex, but the flow rate and direction, and the pressure loss in various pipe sections is more difficult to analyze.

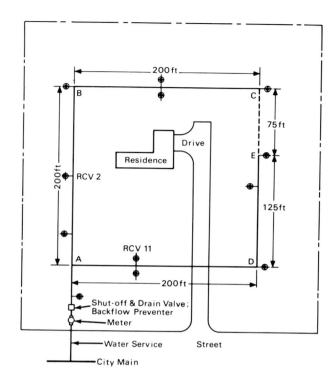

Figure 11-15 Diagram of Looped Main

The designer must assume flow directions and the flow rate in each pipe section. A number of corrections and recalculations may be necessary to establish the flow distribution within the loop and estimate the pressure loss to a particular zone. The flow may not be evenly divided in the supply lines to the zone, but the total pressure loss from the supply will be equal in each supply (leg) to the zone.

In addition, many large systems will have multiple loops (two or more) which are connected together with some portion of the piping in each loop being part of an adjacent loop. Since the pipe sections between the loops are common to two different loops, the flow in the common pipe and each loop will be influenced by the combination.

The water distribution network will become increasingly more difficult to analyze as the number of loops increases, and/or the number of zones operating at the same time increases. See Complex Loop Mains, Chapter 14.

Pipe Sizing and Zoning

DESIGN/SYSTEM VARIATIONS

This chapter is limited to basic considerations and procedures as required for the hydraulic design of landscape irrigation systems. There are always exceptions to any rule, and allowances as suggested are based on common variations of flow and piping arrangements. Additional or different allowances may be necessary for any particular design.

Considerations recommended for hydraulic design, and related allowances included, are provided as a blend of theory and practical application. The extent to which pressure calculations and time are required should be based on the individual design and the designer's ability to evaluate data and compare hydraulic conditions. It is not realistic to develop or recommend a standard procedure that is correct for all designs and all designers.

When pumps are required, it is important to adjust the flow requirements to an even higher level for pump selection. This is also true for pressure requirements, as discussed in Chapter 6.

Irrigation systems are developed by methods of design that range from "Trial and Error" to various levels of engineering. This includes the "Rule of Thumb" method where a standard design concept is adapted, in one form or another, to each property.

COMPUTER-AIDED DESIGN (CAD)

Computers have been used for various phases of plumbing design for many years. Complex piping networks require hydraulic calculations that are tedious and time-consuming. Projects with multiple loops and flow outlets are especially difficult due to the number of iterations that are often necessary. Computers are useful devices to solve difficult and repetitive calculations of this type. They can perform complex calculations, alter data and re-calculate with incredible speed.

The application of computers in irrigation design was limited for many years. This was primarily due to the high cost and limitations of available computer systems. Few designers had access to the computers or the knowledge necessary to operate the systems. Operating programs were limited to hydraulic calculations, as mentioned above.

Technology has developed to the point, that in most design and engineering companies of today, the computer is as common as the drawing board. In many cases, "CAD" (Computer-Aided Design) systems have replaced the "T-Square" and the drawing board. They have not, as yet, replaced the designer or engineer. Use of computers in irrigation design, or any other application, is limited primarily by the operating program (Software); the extent to which it is developed, and the quality of any design decisions included.

Business computer systems that are purchased for the daily requirements of bookkeeping/accounting or word-processing are seldom used for design. Limited time available for use and location of equipment are common problems. Also, programs that are necessary for design assistance may not be available for this equipment.

A computer system that is purchased primarily for design is preferable, but this will require careful consideration to justify the cost. "Brand-name" equipment will, in most cases, provide a more dependable product with added features and improved operation and service assistance. This equipment is recommended when the system will be used for design on a regular basis, and

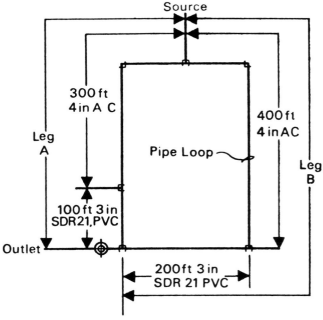

Total loop length: 1000 ft
Total flow: 200 gpm

Figure 11-16 Looped Main with Different Sizes and Kinds of Piping

the cost of such equipment can be considered as cost-effective. A computer is a "tool" and, therefore, the investment should be based on requirement, quality of performance, frequency of use and replacement.

Courtesy of Kaden Landscape

Technology continues to change with improvements in performance and cost of computer systems. While this is desirable, it does introduce a degree of additional concern into the decision making process... concern that next year's model may have added features and at less cost.

"CAD" systems for irrigation design are limited to those units that have the required software. Design programs that operate on brand "X" will not necessarily operate on brand "Y". There is no single deciding factor more important in selection of product, than the software available. Computer-aided design can range from simple calculations to development and print-out of a complete plan. A system that can furnish plans requires several different pieces of equipment (Hardware), in addition to the operating program. These include a digitizer pad and plotter.

The quality of output, regardless of volume, is controlled by the software and the quality of input. Software is developed by programmers who create operating programs from specifications. The fact that designs vary with budgets, climate, water supplies, planting, clients and designers illustrates the difficulty of developing a program that could design the entire system with all of the possible variations included. While computer-aided design is very practical at the present time, irrigation systems that can be completely designed by a computer may be so simple that a computer is not necessary.

Computer-aided design is not limited to complete "CAD" systems. Various levels of design assistance can be provided with any computer system. Output is limited by equipment and the operating program, which is necessary in all cases. Small micro-computers can solve most of the hydraulic problems encountered in landscape irrigation design. This includes pressure loss calculations for operating zones, mains and simple loop mains as discussed in this chapter; also complex loop mains with multiple flow outlets. Data must be collected from a piping schematic for input. Many users of small "personal computers" have developed their own operating programs. There are many advantages in programs that are custom-made for a particular output requirement.

Small computer systems offer a compromise that is often necessary to accomodate budget requirements. Figure 11-17 illustrates a zone pressure calculation produced by a small, inexpensive computer using "custom" software developed by an irrigation systems designer. Most of the necessary design considerations explained in this chapter are included in the software. Basic input data relating to piping requirement was obtained from Figure 11-9. Input is also required to cover flow and pressure loss variations that occur with different irrigation products.

Figure 11-17 is an example only and details of use, input requirements or scope of the decision process in this program are not explained. However, some of the features are listed below to illustrate the level of output quality and to partially explain variations that exist in previous calculations for the rear lawn zone of the exemplary design:

```
                  PROJECT: M.MOBLEY RESIDENCE
                      ZONE: REAR LAWN

                      ** PRESSURE DATA **
        PRESSURE FOR SYSTEM DESIGN  =   48 PSI
        MAXIMUM AVAILABLE PRESSURE  =   58 PSI
        SPRINKLER PRESSURE REQUIRED=    25 PSI

                  ** ZONE PIPING DATA **
                       @ INPUT FLOW
    -->PIPE SECT.NO. 1 <--          -->PIPE SECT.NO. 2 <--
            GPM= 1.4                 GPM ADDED= 2.7    GPM= 4.1
    LENGTH= 17 -- 3 F/U UNITS +      LENGTH= 4 -- 2 F/U UNITS +
    -.0-= 3.1 --TOTAL= 20.1 FT.      -.0-= 2.1 --TOTAL= 6.1 FT.
    PIPE SIZE/TYPE=1/2 IN.315        PIPE SIZE/TYPE=1/2 IN.315
    LOSS= .09 PSI  VEL.= 1.2 FPS     LOSS= .21 PSI  VEL.= 3.5 FPS

    -->  PIPE SECT.NO. 3 <--
    GPM ADDED= 2.7 ---  GPM 6.8
    LENGTH= 15 - 6 F/U UNITS +
    RED.= 9.3 --TOTAL= 24.3 FT.
    PIPE SIZE/TYPE=3/4 IN.200
    LOSS= .57 PSI  VEL.= 3.4 FPS.

                  --> ZONE ENTRANCE <--
                   GPM ADDED= 13.6
              DATA BEFORE ADJUSTMENT:
        ZONE GPM= 20.4  ZONE LOSS= .87 PSI

               ADJUSTED DATA:
        ZONE FLOW FOR DESIGN  = 21 GPM
        PRESS.REQ'D. AT 'ZE'  = 25.9 PSI
        MAX.ZONE PRECIP.DIFF.= 2 %

            ** SYSTEM SUPPLY AND CONNECTION **
                    @ DESIGN FLOW

    SERVICE PIPE:
    PIPE SIZE AND TYPE= 1 IN.-K
    PIPE LENGTH= 25 + 10.7 F/U UNITS= 11.3 FT.= 36.3 TOTAL FT.
    PRESSURE LOSS= 5.03 PSI    -VELOCITY= 8.7 FPS

    1 IN. WATER METER LOSS= 2.6

    CONNECTION PIPE:
    PIPE SIZE AND TYPE= 1-1/4 IN.-L
    PIPE LENGTH= 15 + 3.9 F/U UNITS= 5.3 FT.= 20.3 TOTAL FT.
    PRESSURE LOSS= .87 PSI    -VELOCITY= 5.4 FPS

    1 IN.D.C.A. LOSS= 4
     2  FEET OF ELEVATION= .87 PSI

               * SINGLE MAIN *
    MAIN LINE LENGTH- =  145  FT.
      37 F/U UNITS---- =  69.6 EQUIV.FT.
    TOTAL LENGTH----- =  214.6  FT.
    MAIN SIZE/TYPE--- =  1-1/4 IN.200
    MAIN PRESSURE LOSS=  3.77
    MAIN VELOCITY---- =  3.9 FPS

    1 IN.ZONE VALVE 11000 --LOSS= 2.5
                  --> ZONE REAR LAWN <--
                   DESIGN PRESSURE= 45.54 PSI
                   DESIGN FLOW --  = 21 GPM

        --------REF.DATA AT MAX.STATIC OF 58 PSI----------
            APPROX.SYSTEM FLOW AT 58 PSI= 25 GPM
            APPROX.VELOCITY AT MAX.STATIC :
               SERVICE= 10.4 FPS
               CONNECTION= 6.4 FPS
               SINGLE MAIN= 4.6 FPS
        --------------------------------------------------
                      93- RC/ 1S
```

Figure 11-17 Example Pressure Loss Calculation

- Zone pipe sizes are selected by the program (software) for pipe sections entered (Sections 1-3).

- PVC main line and copper connection pipe sizes were also selected by the program. Loop main option is available.

- Zone flow (all sprinklers at 25 lb/in^2) and pressure loss are adjusted for design by the program.

- Fitting losses determined from input codes.

- Optional building flow allowance available, but not required.

- Approximate flow and velocity at 58 lb/in^2 included for consideration of flow conditions at maximum pressure.

"CAD" systems can provide a plan that is professional in appearance which can be extremely valuable as a sales tool, but irrigation quality is limited to the design considerations included in the software and/or the design knowledge of the user. "Designed by Computer" does not necessarily indicate the design is superior in quality.

BIBLIOGRAPHY

IRRIGATION DESIGN SOFTWARE

Landcadd, Inc.
7519 East Highway 86
Franktown, CO 80116
or
P.O. Box 604
Franktown, CO 80116-9900

Green Thumb Software
73 Manhattan Drive
Suite 100
Boulder, CO 80303

CHAPTER 12

Rotary Systems

The design of a rotary sprinkler system is based on the same design principles used for a spray system. See Chapters 10 and 11. However, there are special considerations that are necessary due to the rotating-stream method of providing coverage. In general, rotary sprinklers are used to provide coverage in large, open areas. The system designed in this chapter was selected to illustrate the typical application of spray and rotary equipment in small and large areas.

Diameters of coverage available with different brands and models will range from 30 feet to over 200 feet. However, the majority of rotary head layouts will require a diameter of coverage in the 50 to 120 ft range.

While there are advantages in providing coverage in relatively large areas with a minimum number of heads, there are three disadvantages that are inherent with the use of rotary sprinklers:

1. Drive Mechanism. Although some types may be more dependable than others, all have moving parts that are subject to malfunction. Some models are repairable and some are not.

2. High Operating Pressure. Most rotary systems are designed at sprinkler operating pressures between 35 and 65 lb/in^2. Some models will operate below 35 lb/in^2 and some large diameter of coverage sprinklers (or nozzles) will require pressures above 65 lb/in^2.

3. Sprinkler Coverage:

   a. Head layout can be somewhat difficult for the average property that includes walks, driveways, streets, buildings, etc., since the amount of possible overthrow beyond borders will in-

crease in proportion to the increase in the diameter of coverage.

   b. At low winds speeds, moisture application by a rotary sprinkler is reasonably consistent in different sectors of the coverage area due to the rotation of the nozzle assembly. However, higher wind speeds will significantly alter the distribution profile and reduce coverage on the windward side while increasing coverage on the leeward side of each sprinkler. See Chapter 8, Figure 8-14.

DESIGN CRITERIA

There are many possible approaches to the design of an irrigation system for properties that are similar to the example shown in Figure 12-1. Each approach will have a different affect on performance, cost, maintenance requirement and owner's satisfaction. A pre-design conference between the owner (or owner's representative) is always recommended. The owner's preconceived opinion of a cost-effective system is subject to change when informed of the possible variations that are available.

Although the actual system cost cannot be determined until the design is completed, the designer must have some guidance for the many design decisions that will be necessary. The following criteria were established for the exemplary system:

1. Gear-drive rotary sprinklers will be used in all areas where practical. However, overthrow beyond the planting areas should be avoided as much as possible.

Rotary Systems

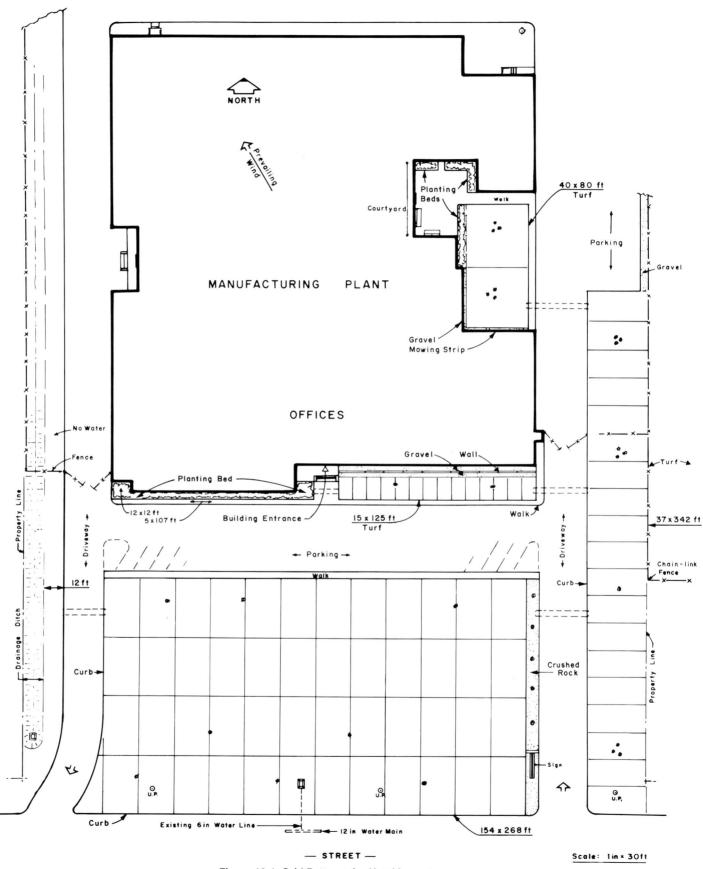

Figure 12-1 Grid Patterns for Head Layout

2. The system will be automatic. A maximum of 8 hours per day, 6 days per week is available for system operation. There are no local watering restrictions. Design for the normal maximum irrigation requirement of 1.25 in/week.

An outside, wall-mount controller will be located on the front wall, at the southeast corner of the building. Owner will furnish a 115V, 60 Hz power supply in the area between the screening wall and the building.

3. A separate irrigation meter will be used for the system since the city water department does not include a sewage charge on irrigation water. A new 2 in water service and meter will be furnished by the owner. Irrigation meter will be located approximately 40 ft West of the sign.

4. No irrigation will be provided between the west property line and the driveway, except for the turfgrass strip on the east side of the drainage ditch. Coverage will be limited to the area along the driveway from the street to the fence line (gate) at the front of the building. No irrigation will be provided for the area on the north side of the building.

5. Five existing 6 in sleeves are available for irrigation pipes and valve wiring. The owner will be responsible for locating the sleeves.

6. Five, 1 in quick-coupling valves will be provided at the following locations for hose connections:

   a. Turf area along west driveway.
   b. Crushed rock area along the east driveway. Note: No additional irrigation equipment will be provided for the trees in this area.
   c. Turf strip along the east property line. One valve for the north end and one for the south area.
   d. Turf area on the east side of the building.

7. All irrigation piping to be PVC, SDR-21, except as may be required at point of connection. Fittings will be PVC, Schedule 40.

SITE CONDITIONS

The following site conditions were also determined for the exemplary system design:

1. City water main is 12 in and is located 10 ft. from the curb.
2. Water pressure gauged at the site: 73 lb/in^2. Water department records indicate a normal pressure range of 70 to 75 lb/in^2. Maintenance department at site suggests 65 lb/in^2 should be safe for system design.
3. Prevailing wind in the area is from the southeast at an average velocity of 8 mi/hr during the irrigation season. Average velocity is 6 mi/hr during the nighttime hours.
4. Local plumbing code requires a vacuum-breaker for an irrigation system. Unit must be installed 12 in above the highest outlet (sprinkler head). Pipe risers for the assembly must be copper tube or steel pipe.
5. Elevation difference from the curb is no more than plus or minus one foot in any area.
6. The plot plan for the site was provided by the owner. The drawing scale is 1 in = 30 ft (1:360).

DESIGN STANDARDS

No special design standards have been developed for the exemplary system design in this chapter. The following standards are similar to those used in Chapters 10 and 11:

1. Lawn and Shrub areas will be watered and zoned separately. Rotary sprinklers will also be zoned separately due to the precipitation rate difference.
2. Sprinkler spacing will be equal to or less than the manufacturer's recommendation.
3. Sprinkler catalog flow will be used for zone loss calculations, but will be adjusted to allow for pressure variations and a degree of safety in the total zone flow.
4. A swing-joint loss allowance will be included for all rotary zone calculations.
5. The PVC main line velocity will be maintained at 5ft/s or less.
6. PVC Zone piping will be maintained at approximately 5 ft/s or less.
7. Service piping velocity will be a maximum of 9 ft/s (preferably less).

8. Reference only. Valve wiring will be Type UF, direct-burial (without conduit), and will be installed in the main line pipe trench. See Chapter 15, Valve Wiring.

HEAD LAYOUT

Regardless of the type of equipment used in irrigation, product performance is based on a given flow and pressure requirement. Since the pressure requirement of rotary heads can be high, as compared to other types of equipment, the selection of heads, nozzles and spacing will require special consideration. The importance of the pressure requirement will increase for a project that has relatively large areas, and is limited by the pressure available from an existing water supply. Booster pumps are often required with rotary systems when the available pressure is below a level that is considered necessary for a particular project.

SPRINKLER SELECTION

The sprinkler performance selected from a product catalog must be based on an operating pressure that is practical, considering the pressure available for design and normal pressure losses that will occur in the piping system. For example, all sprinklers (or nozzles) and spacings that require 50 lb/in^2 or more, cannot be considered for head layout if the available pressure at the source is only 50 lb/in^2. This example is based on the assumption that there will be pressure losses in some type of piping system, and the use of a booster pump will not be considered.

Note: Sprinkler pressure requirement is also very important when a booster pump or a new pump station at a private water source is used for the system. The discharge pressure requirement will directly affect the size, cost and energy requirements of the pump. See Chapter 6, Pumps.

The precipitation rate of sprinklers should also be considered when selecting heads for a particular system design. Low precipitation rates offer some advantages, but there are also disadvantages, including additional station duration time to apply an adequate amount of water. For example, assuming an irrigation requirement of 1.5 in/wk, it would be necessary for a sprinkler with a precipitation rate of .20 in/hr to operate 7.5 hours per week. If the system operated every day and there were 10 rotary zones, the system would operate 10.7 hours per day, or 75 hours per week.

Very low application rates can also be wasteful due to evaporation losses. In at least one case, state law requires the precipitation rate used for sprinklers to be above a given rate (minimum rate varies by climate zones).

The precipitation rates of full and part-circle models should be compatible to the extent that both types can be valved together. If the rates are not compatible, the two types should be valved separately. See Chapter 8, Precipitation.

The sprinkler performance of the gear-drive head selected for the exemplary system design is shown in Figure 12-2. Spray sprinklers and nozzles are the same series used in Chapters 10 and 11. See Figure 11-3 for spray nozzle performance table.

SOUTH AREA BETWEEN DRIVEWAYS. The size of this large area is 154 x 268 ft. The 154 ft dimension is from the street curb on the south side, to the walk along the parking area on the north side. The 268 ft dimension is from the driveway curb on the west side, through the center of the area to the crushed-rock strip on the east side. Several trees and two utility poles (u.p.) are located within this turfgrass area.

Sprinkler rows that are parallel to the street are preferred to allow for a row of part-circles along the curb and along the walk on the north side. The 154 ft dimension can be divided by a number of different row spaces to establish row spacing dimensions for triangular spacing. Row spacings can be converted to head spacings by using the 1.155 (1.16) multiplier. Example:

1. 154 ft /2 spaces = 77 ft R.S. x 1.155 = 88.9 ft spacing
2. 154 ft /3 spaces = 51.3 ft R.S. x 1.155 = 59.3 ft spacing
3. 154 ft /4 spaces = 38.5 ft R.S. x 1.155 = 44.5 ft spacing
4. 154 ft /5 spaces = 30.8 ft R.S. x 1.155 = 35.6 ft spacing

The manufacturer recommends a triangular spacing of approximately 50% of diameter for an 8 mi/h wind velocity (see 10 mi/h listing in Figure 12-2). The sprinkler radius is equal to spacing at 50% of diameter. In the spacing examples above, the approximate sprinkler radius required would be 89, 59, 45 and 36 ft.

The 89 and 59 ft radii (178 and 118 ft diameters) are not available with the gear-drive model that will be used for the exemplary design. Although these radii are available with some rotary head models, the sprinkler pressure requirement would be too high for the pres-

T3-360 (Full Circle)
Maximum Operating Pressure 65 PSI

Nozzle	Operating Pressure PSI	Flow GPM	*Maximum Diameter Coverage (ft.)
4	20 35 50	1.0 1.4 1.8	56 68 76
5	20 35 50	1.2 1.7 2.1	56 68 76
6	20 35 50	1.5 2.2 2.7	56 68 76
7	35 50 65	2.6 3.1 3.6	76 82 88
8	35 50 65	3.6 4.4 5.1	76 84 88
9	35 50 65	4.6 5.7 6.6	80 88 92
10	35 50 65	6.0 7.3 8.6	84 94 102
11	35 50 65	7.0 8.8 10.3	84 94 102
12	35 50 65	10.6 13.0 15.0	84 96 106

* Diameter of coverage shown is for still air with no diffusion. Derate for wind. See formulas to calculate deration and to determine precipitation.

T3-ADJ (Part Circle)
Maximum Operating Pressure 65 PSI

Nozzle	Operating Pressure PSI	Flow GPM	*Maximum Radius Coverage (ft.)
4	20 35 50	1.0 1.4 1.8	28 34 38
5	20 35 50	1.2 1.7 2.1	28 34 38
6	20 35 50	1.5 2.2 2.7	28 34 38
7	35 50 65	2.6 3.1 3.6	38 41 44
8	35 50 65	3.6 4.4 5.1	38 42 44
9	35 50 65	4.6 5.7 6.6	40 44 46
10	35 50 65	6.0 7.3 8.6	42 47 51
11	35 50 65	7.0 8.8 10.3	42 47 51
12	35 50 65	10.6 13.0 15.0	42 48 53

* Radius of coverage shown is for still air with no diffusion. Derate for wind. See formulas to calculate deration and to determine precipitation.

Wind Deration

- Diameters of coverage shown in tables are for still air.

Head Spacing = Diameter of coverage
(selected from Perf. Table)

x Deration factor
(listed below)

- Spacing with wind deration as follows:

Miles/Hour	Multiply Diameter in Table by:	
	△	❏
5	.55	.50
10	.50	.45

Figure 12-2 Exemplary Performance Data: Rotary Sprinklers

Rotary Systems

sure available for this design. Large coverage heads of this type will require 70 lb/in^2 (or more) at the sprinkler.

Sprinkler performance listings in Figure 12-2 are limited to three pressure listings for each nozzle size. However, interpolation can be used to determine performance at pressures between the listings provided. For example, the following data at 40 and 45 lb/in^2 is an estimate of performance for a full-circle head with a number 11 nozzle:

Pressure	GPM	Diameter-ft	Radius-ft
35	7.0	84	42.0
40	7.6	87	43.5
45	8.2	90	45.0
50	8.8	94	47.0

These estimates are in proportion to the difference between 35 and 50 lb/in^2, as provided in the catalog performance table. The estimate of radius at 45 lb/in^2 for the number 11 nozzle is equal (for design purposes) to spacing example (3), with 4 spaces and 5 rows of sprinklers. The 45 lb/in^2 head pressure requirement is realistic since this will provide 20 lb/in^2 for all system pressure losses (65 − 45 = 20 lb/in^2).

Head spacing of 45 ft can be compared to the 268 ft width of the area to determine if the spacing is suitable, and the actual head spacing requirement on the row. Example:

$$268 \div 45 = (5.96) \text{ 6 spacings required.}$$
$$\text{or, } 268 \div 22.5 = (11.9) \text{ 12 half-spacings for grid.}$$
then,
$$268 \div 6 = 44.67 \text{ ft head spacing on row.}$$
$$268 \div 12 = 22.33 \text{ ft half-spacing for grid.}$$

The width and length of this area is suitable for a 45 ft, triangular spacing layout (grid pattern shown in Figure 12-1). However, the actual area sizes (width to length) encountered in rotary head layout will seldom be this close to the dimensions required in both directions.

Spacing templates, as discussed in Chapter 10 for spray heads, can also be used to assist the designer with a rotary head layout. In this example, assuming a selection of 35, 40 and 45 ft transparent templates where available, each spacing could be considered visually by placing the templates over the area. Spacings that are not suitable can be rejected very quickly. The templates can also be useful to select half-spacing, alternate layouts.

Part-Circle Nozzles. Theoretically, matched-precipitation rates would require that part-circle heads provide the same diameter (or radius) of coverage and a flow rate that is in proportion to the arc of coverage, as compared to the full-circle (or some other arc). Example:

(at 45 lb/in^2)	Arc	Gpm	Radius (ft)
Full - 360°		8.20	45
Half - 180°		4.10	45
Quarter - 90°		2.05	45

It would also be necessary to have additional nozzles available that would provide the proper flow rate for part-circle arcs of 120°, 240°, 270° or whatever arc of coverage that may be required.

However, a compromise is necessary in the selection of nozzles that can be considered compatible for design purposes, as the theoretical flow rates are not available (fixed or adjustable) for the same pressure, diameter of coverage and with the same distribution profile.

The head locations on the grid pattern are shown in Figure 12-3. The half-spacing used for head locations was selected as the best choice, considering the tree locations in the area (see alternate layouts in Chapter 10). The completed head layout, including nozzle numbers, is shown in Figure 12-4. The following nozzle numbers were selected from Figure 12-2:

Nozzle Number	Coverage: Arc	% of 360°	GPM	Interpolated for 45 lb/in^2 % of #11	Radius (ft)
5	90°	25%	2.0	24%	37
7	120°	33%	2.9	35%	40
8	180°	50%	4.1	50%	41
9	225°	63%	5.3	65%	43
11	360°	100%	8.2	100%	45

Comparing the arc percentages and the flow percentages, all part-circle nozzles are approximately correct for the number 11 full-circle nozzle. However, all of the part-circle nozzles provide less radius than the full-circle nozzle, and the ratio of water applied to area size will be different.

Note: It is important for the designer to understand the practical limitations of providing coverage and equal distribution. Precipitation applied will not be equal if all nozzles had the same catalog listed radius. Wind effect is not consistent for all types of rotary streams (volume, droplet size, etc.) and in all directions of rotation. The actual amount of water applied per square foot from an individual rotary sprinkler will also vary due to wind distortion. This includes the "break-up" of the stream and the actual area of coverage. See Chapter 8, Sprinkler Performance.

Arc of coverage was changed on 5 heads, and back-up heads (A, B, C, D and E) were added to avoid overthrow beyond the borders. The actual arc of coverage required for part-circles along the walk (Row 5) can be adjusted at the site as necessary for the prevailing wind direction. The radii of sprinklers on Row 4 may require adjustment to reduce the overspray onto the parking area. Reduction of coverage on Row 2 may not be necessary due to the prevailing wind direction.

EAST AREA ALONG PROPERTY LINE. The size of this area is 37 x 342 ft. A chain-link fence is located across the area at 93 ft from the north end. A driveway curb is located along the west side and the property line is on the east side of this turfgrass strip. A few trees and one utility pole (u.p.) are located approximately in the center of the strip at five different locations.

Adjacent Property - East Side. There is an existing (7 ft) chain-link fence on the adjacent property. The north-south fence line is located approximately 1 ft east of the property line. All areas east of the property line are primarily grass and there are no walks, driveways, parking areas or buildings within 20 ft of the property line.

Sprinkler Spacing. Strips can be difficult to lay out with rotary heads when there are borders on each side that require protection from excessive overthrow. A head spacing compromise may be necessary, depending on the width and length of the area and the amount of overthrow that will occur with the required radius of coverage.

Recommended spacing in Figure 12-2 for 10 mi/h (8 mi/h average at site) is 50% of diameter for triangular spacing. Equilateral spacing with a required row spacing of 37 ft would be 42.7 ft. This spacing was determined using the 1.155 row spacing multiplier to obtain spacing (37 x 1.155 = 42.7). The total length of 342 ft is suitable for 8 spaces at 42.75 each (8 x 42.75 = 342). A 42.8 ft radius will be required for a spacing at 50% of diameter. The number 9 nozzle will provide a 42.7 ft radius (interpolated) at 45 lb/in^2. The only problem with the 42.7 ft spacing is the 42.7 ft radius requirement. Coverage (without wind effect) will overthrow 5.7 feet on each side of the strip.

A compromise spacing can be considered as an alternative to the equilateral triangular spacing of 42.7 ft. Spacing to be considered will be based on a 37 ft radius to avoid the overthrow problem. The length of 342 ft is suitable for a compressed spacing of 36 ft on each row (342 ÷ 36 = 9.5 half-spaces). Row spacing is established by the width at 37 ft. This will provide a spacing triangle with 36 ft head spacing on the rows (49% of diameter) and 41 ft head spacing, row to row (55% of diameter). The 41 ft side of the triangle can be determined by plan measurement, or by calculation if desired. The half-spacing grid pattern is shown in Figure 12-1.

The number 6 nozzle will provide a 37 ft radius (interpolated) at 45 lb/in^2. The number 4 nozzle, which can be used for quarter-circle coverage, will also provide a 37 ft radius at 45 lb/in^2. However, due to wind distortion problems of low-volume rotary streams, many designers prefer the use of a larger nozzle size on half-circle coverage heads.

For example, at 45 lb/in^2, the number 8 nozzle at 4.1 gpm will provide a 64% increase in flow as compared to the number 6 nozzle at 2.5 gpm. The 40.6 ft radius of the number 8 nozzle at 45 lb/in^2 can be reduced approximately 3 ft by using the range adjustment provided for the nozzle. The number 5 and number 7 nozzles can be used for 90° and 120° arc of coverage requirements. These are the same nozzle combinations previously selected for the south area, between the driveways.

The nozzle changes for this area are not intended as a general recommendation that higher flow nozzles should always be specified for improved performance. The changes are included only as an example of additional considerations that may be included in the selection of nozzle sizes for a rotary system. Low flow nozzles are often necessary due to the flow restrictions of a small water supply, or when lower precipitation rates are required.

NOTE: The nozzle sizes selected will establish the flow requirements and related pipe sizing for the area. All nozzles listed in Figure 12-2 are provided with the rotary sprinkler model selected for this design. Nozzle sizes can be changed at the site, assuming the piping system is adequate for the flow requirements.

The head locations on the grid pattern are shown in Figure 12-3. Back-up heads have been added at each

Rotary Systems

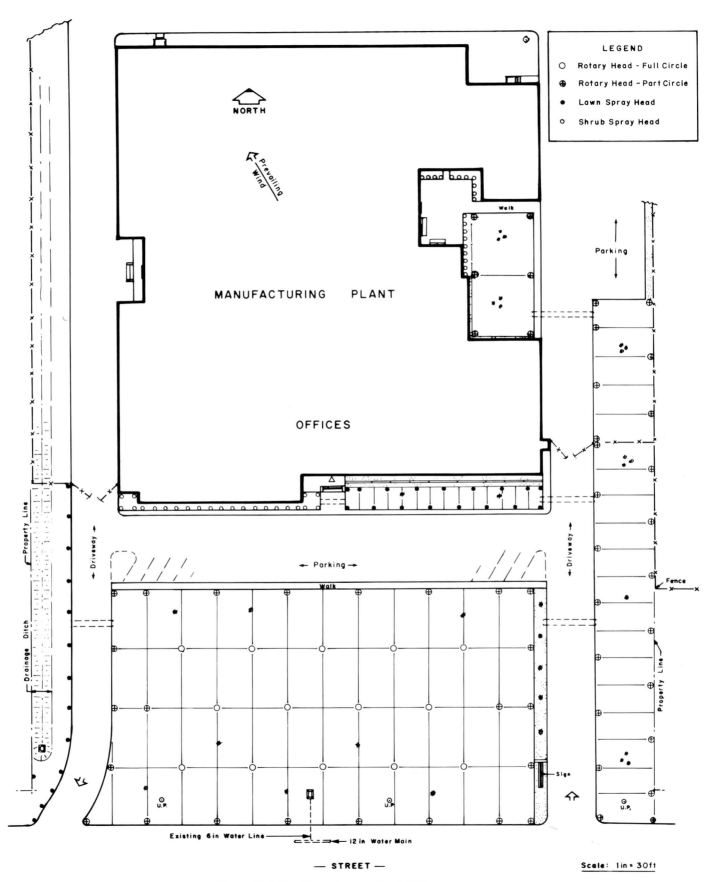

Figure 12-3 Head Locations on the Grid Patterns

end of the strip to avoid overthrow into the street and the parking area. Half-circle heads (F and G) on each side of the fence across the area will spray onto the fence. One, 90° arc of coverage head, is located on each side of the gate post (heads H and I). The completed head layout, including nozzle numbers, is shown in Figure 12-4.

AREA ON EAST SIDE OF BUILDING. The size of this turfgrass area is 40 x 80 ft. A walk is located along the east side and north end of the area. A 2 ft gravel strip separates the turf area from the building wall at the south end. The gravel strip and a planting bed separates the turf area from the building on the west side.

A spray head layout can be used in the area, using the 424 series nozzles as listed in Figure 11-3. Three rows of heads on triangular spacing would be required for the 40 x 80 ft area. Head spacing along each row would be 20 ft with 22.4 ft head spacing, row to row. A total of 16 heads would be required, including two back-up heads to avoid the overthrow of two full-circles. However, the design criteria for this system includes the use of rotary heads, where practical.

Triangular Spacing. The 40 ft width of the area creates a row-spacing problem for a rotary head layout with triangular spacing, when all borders must be protected from overthrow.

A triangular spacing layout would require 3 heads on one side (at 40 ft spacing) and 4 heads on the opposite side, including 2 back-up heads. Head spacing, row to row, would be 44.7 ft due to the 40 ft row spacing. 45 ft (44.7) radius would be required for spacing at 50% of diameter. The number 10 nozzle will provide a 45 ft radius at 45 lb/in^2.

However, the 45 ft radius requirement would result in overthrow beyond the borders in several areas. A 40 ft radius nozzle would be suitable for the 50% of diameter spacing requirement along each row, but head spacing, row to row, would be at 56% of diameter (56% of 80 ft diameter = 44.8 ft). Although maximum head spacing should not exceed the manufacturer's recommendation, this area provides an example where it may be necessary to compromise on spacings, as compared to the diameter of coverage.

Square Spacing. The width and length dimensions of this area meet the exact requirements of a 40 ft square spacing layout. However, recommended spacing in

Figure 12-2 for 10 mi/h is 45% of diameter for square spacing. A 44.5 radius (89 ft diameter) of coverage would be required (89 x .45 = 40 ft spacing). This is not practical for the area since a 4.5 ft overthrow would occur in all directions.

Square spacing will be used for this area and radius of coverage will be limited to 40 ft. A reduction in sprinkler overlap is a practical compromise, as compared to the alternative with a larger nozzle. The number 7 nozzle will provide a 40 ft radius of coverage at 45 lb/in^2, and will be used for the quarter-circle heads. The number 9 nozzle was selected for the half-circle heads to maintain a compatible flow rate with the number 7 nozzle. The number 9 nozzle will require a range adjustment to reduce the 42.7 ft radius available at 45 lb/in^2. Radii of the nozzles were determined by interpolation, using the data provided in Figure 12-2.

The six sprinklers and the simple grid pattern required for this area are shown in Figure 12-3. The completed layout, including nozzle numbers, is shown in Figure 12-4.

SPRAY HEAD LAYOUT
Pop-up spray heads will be required in two turfgrass strips and shrub spray heads will be used in the two planting bed areas.

Spray head layout is discussed in Chapter 10 and a very brief explanation will be provided in this chapter on the nozzle selection and layout of each area.

Exemplary performance data in Figure 11-3 will be used for all lawn and shrub nozzle requirements in this chapter.

TURF STRIP-WEST SIDE. Coverage between the driveway and west property line will be limited to the narrow strip along the driveway, from the street to the fence line at the southwest corner of the building.

There is a gradual slope from the driveway curb down to the edge of the drainage ditch. A single row of heads will be required at the curb line due to the variable conditions along the edge of the ditch. Width of coverage required is approximately 12 ft.

The completed head layout for the area is shown in Figure 12-4. The layout at the south end of the strip was developed by the "trial and error" method due to the size and shape of the area. The width of coverage required

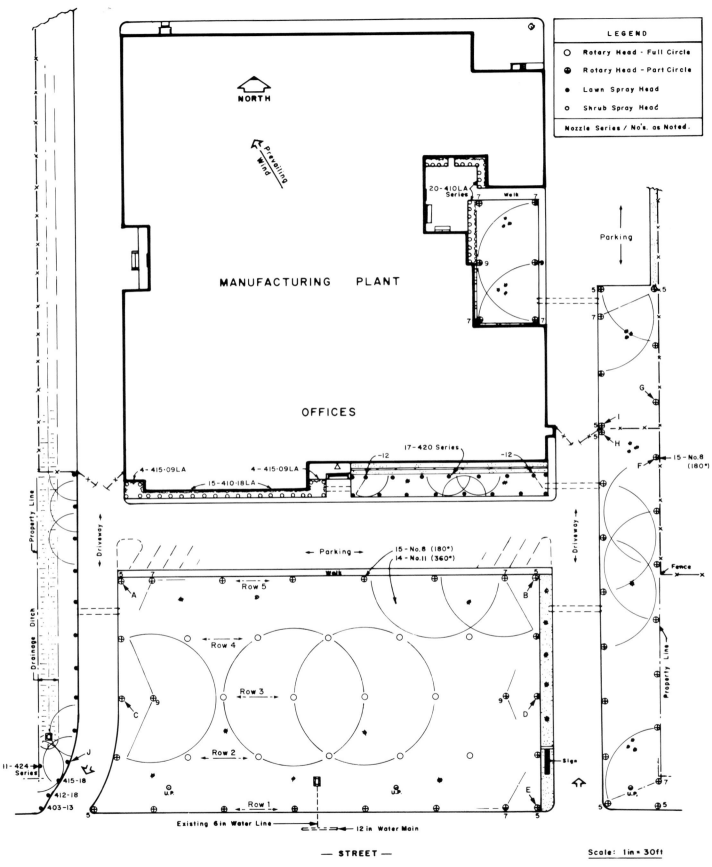

Figure 12-4 Completed Head Layout

Average Pipe Section Length (ft)	Fitting Loss Allowance[1] Percentage of Total Zone Pipe Loss	
	Typical Zone Piping Arrangement	Single-Row Tees Only
25-35	30%	20%
40-50	25%	15%
55-65	20%	10%
70-90	15%	10%

(1) Actual percentage of pipe loss will vary with each zone due to fittings required and pipe sizing. Calculated loss will vary with different fitting loss tables, allowance for bushings, etc.
(2) See Figure 11-6 and explanation, Chapter 11.

Figure 12-5 Example of Percentages Used to Estimate Zone Fitting Losses - PVC Pipe and Fittings

Zone[1] Loss lb/in² at Nominal Flow	Multipliers[2] to adjust the Total Zone Flow (gpm) and Loss (lb/in²)			
	Base Sprinkler Pressure (lb/in²)			
	30-35	40-50	55-65	70-90
1-2	1.02	1.02	1.01	1.01
3-4	1.05	1.03	1.03	1.02
5	1.06	1.04	1.03	1.02
6	1.07	1.05	1.04	1.03
7	1.08	1.06	1.04	1.04
8		1.07	1.05	1.04
9		1.08	1.06	1.04
10			1.06	1.05
12			1.07	10.6
14				1.07
16				1.08

(1) Maximum pressure loss from "zone entrance" to any outlet. Total of pipe, fitting and elevation losses within the zone.
(2) Multipliers to adjust the total zone flow (catalog flow at base pressure) and the total zone loss (calculated at catalog flow). Factors are based on the average flow/pressure ratio and "typical" pressure

Figure 12-6 Example of Adjustment Factors for Total Zone Flow and Pressure Loss

in this area varies from a few feet to over 20 ft, and nozzle sizes selected vary from small to large.

The distance along the curb from head (J) to the fence is 190 ft. The 424 series nozzle will be used at 21.1 ft spacing (190 ft ÷ 9 spaces = 21.1 ft). This nozzle series will provide a 16 ft effective radius at 25 lb/in² (see note 3, Figure 11-3) and will, in theory, intersect with the 16 ft radii of adjacent heads at 12 ft from the curb, when spaced at 21.1 ft.

TURF STRIP AT BUILDING ENTRANCE. The size of this turfgrass area is 15 x 125 ft. A walk is located at each end and along the south side. The area is separated from the building wall on the north side by a gravel strip and screening wall.

The two rows of 420 series, part-circle nozzles used in this area, are shown in Figure 12-3. The 125 ft length is divided into 14 half-spaces of 8.9 ft each (125 ÷ 14 = 8.93 ft). Head spacing along each row will be 17.9 ft. Head spacing, row to row, will be 17.5 ft with the required row spacing of 15 ft. One back-up head is added at each end of the strip to avoid overthrow. The completed layout is shown in Figure 12-4.

SHRUB BED AT BUILDING ENTRANCE. The shape of the shrub bed along the front of the building provides 3 separate areas for head layout. A 12 x 12 ft, square area is located at each end. These two areas have small shrubs (1 to 1.5 ft high) at close-spacing.

A 5 x 107 ft planting strip is located along the building, between the two end-areas. The planting in this bed is limited to two rows of shrubs. One row of 2.5 ft high shrubs is located along the building wall. A second row

of dwarf (1.0 ft high) type shrubs is located between the walk and the row of shrubs along the building.

The head layout for this area is shown in Figure 12-4. Four, 415-09LA nozzles on a square pattern will be used in the planting areas at each end of the bed. A single-row of 410-18LA nozzles will be located along the front side of the 5 ft wide bed. Heads will be located to spray over the dwarf planting and into the larger plants along the building.

SHRUB BEDS - EAST SIDE OF BUILDING. Three separate shrub beds are located in the courtyard area on the east side of the building.

The head layout for these beds is shown in Figure 12-4. These beds have low, ground-cover planting in all areas with several dwarf-size shrubs at scattered locations. A single-row of the 410LA series nozzles will be used for spray coverage in these 5 ft wide beds.

Gate valves will be provided in the supply piping to the two beds on the north side and to the single bed on the south side. These valves will be used to adjust spray

Rotary Systems

performance to a 5 ft radius (approximately). Pressure reduction will also reduce the amount of fine mist that can occur with very small nozzles.

Note: The electric valves for all spray zones will require adjustment at the site to control the zone operating pressure. Gate valves (or some other type of plumbing valve) as mentioned above, are included by some designers to control specific areas, or as a secondary adjustment to allow for "fine-tuning" of the performance in shrub zones.

Depending on site conditions, the designer should also consider the use of electric valves with automatic pressure regulating control, and the use of pop-up shrub heads in some, or all locations. The typical application of this equipment is discussed in Chapter 11.

DESIGN OF PIPING SYSTEM

Design of piping systems for rotary sprinklers follows, in general, the same basic methods discussed in Chapter 11 for spray systems. Although flow rates can be considerably higher with some types of rotary heads, most of the differences between spray and rotary piping design are related to pressure. Examples of design considerations that will require special attention with rotary systems are listed below:

    A. Pressure Requirement. In most cases, the operating pressure requirement at rotary heads is substantially greater than that required for sprays, or any other type or irrigation equipment.

    B. Pressure Loss. The higher operating pressure requirement of rotary heads will influence the allowable pressure loss throughout the piping system.

      1. When a domestic water supply is used for a rotary system, the pressure available may require a lower zone flow rate to reduce the pressure loss in the water service and meter.

      2. Mainline piping, backflow prevention equipment and zone control valves may require larger sizes (at a given flow rate) to reduce the combined pressure loss in these items. Also, main lines are often much longer in a rotary system and pressure loss can increase significantly due to the additional length.

      3. Zone piping loss will also increase due to additional pipe length. Heads are spaced at greater distances and individual pipe sections can be 2, 3 or 4 times longer in length, as compared to spray systems.

Fitting losses, when compared as a percentage of pipe loss, are normally less for rotary systems. The quantity of fittings (tees, elbows, etc.) does not increase with the added distance between heads. Fitting losses are discussed in Chapter 11.

The example fitting loss allowance table in Figure 12-5 provides percentages based on normal rotary head spacings. This table is similar to the table provided in Figure 11-6. Standard fitting loss (equivalent footage) tables are provided in the Appendix section, Tables 17 and 18. The example "short-list" table, Figure 11-7, will be used for pressure loss calculation in this chapter.

ZONE FLOW AND LOSS ADJUSTMENT

Manufacturer's specified flow (or flow interpolated from tables) should be adjusted for design purposes. A pressure loss adjustment is also recommended when the total zone loss is based on calculations using catalog flow requirements. Flow variations due to product and pressure differences between heads are discussed in Chapter 11, ZONE FLOW AND PRESSURE LOSS.

Some systems designers add a standard percentage (5%, 10%, etc.) to all catalog listed flows, regardless of the type of product or pressure variations that may occur within a zone. The adjusted flow is also used to calculate pressure losses within the zone, mainline, supply piping, etc.

The method used in Chapter 11, to adjust the total zone flow and pressure loss, will also be used in this chapter for all rotary and spray zones. A table of adjustment factors for rotary zones is shown in Figure 12-6. This table is similar to the table of adjustment factors provided in Figure 11-4. The multipliers listed in these tables are considered "minimum" to cover common flow variations. These multipliers do not include a safety factor. A slightly higher flow and pressure loss adjustment is recommended.

AREA FLOW REQUIREMENTS. The manufacturer's specified flow (interpolated at 45 lb/in^2) is used to determine the total flow requirements for each area. Spray nozzle flow is based on 25 lb/in^2 (Figure 11-3).

South Area between Driveways

Quantity	Nozzle	gpm	Total gpm
4	5	2.0	8.0
3	7	2.9	8.7
15	8	4.1	61.5
2	9	5.3	10.6
14	11	8.2	114.8
		Total Flow =	203.6

East Area along Property Line

Quantity	Nozzle	gpm	Total gpm
6	5	2.0	12.0
2	7	2.9	5.8
15	8	4.1	61.5
		Total Flow =	79.3

Area on East Side of Building

Quantity	Nozzle	gpm	Total gpm
4	7	2.9	11.6
2	9	5.3	10.6
		Total Flow =	22.2

Turf Strip - West Side

Quantity	Nozzle	gpm	Total gpm
1	403-13LA	.3	.3
1	412-18LA	1.1	1.1
1	415-18LA	1.6	1.6
10	424-18	3.5	35.0
1	424-09	1.9	1.9
		Total Flow =	39.9

Turf Strip at Building Entrance

Quantity	Nozzle	gpm	Total gpm
4	420-09	1.4	5.6
2	420-12	1.8	3.6
11	420-18	2.7	29.7
		Total Flow =	38.9

Shrub Bed at Building Entrance

Quantity	Nozzle	gpm	Total gpm
8	415-09LA	.8	6.4
15	410-18LA	.7	10.5
		Total Flow =	16.9

Shrub Beds - East Side of Building

Quantity	Nozzle	gpm	Total gpm
6	410-09LA	.4	2.4
13	410-18LA	.7	9.1
1	410-27LA	1.0	1.0
		Total Flow =	12.5

The total catalog flow for each area can be adjusted by using a standard percentage of adjustment as previously mentioned, or a multiplier can be selected from Figure 12-6 based on a preliminary allowance for zone pressure loss.

The maximum loss allowed for zone piping is normally based on an amount that is selected to control the head pressure difference and the related effect on precipitation rate, as discussed in Chapter 11, VARIATIONS IN PRECIPITATION RATE.

For example, a maximum of 15% head pressure increase was used for the preliminary flow adjustment for the exemplary system design in Chapter 11. If the same maximum allowance is used for system design in this chapter, the maximum zone loss will be 6.75 lb/in^2 (45 x .15 = 6.75) for rotary zones and 3.75 lb/in^2 (25 x .15 = 3.75) for spray zones.

Referring to Figure 12-6, the flow adjustment multiplier is 1.06 for the rotary zones (45 lb/in^2 base pressure at 7 lb/in^2 zone loss). Referring to Figure 11-4, the flow adjustment multiplier is 1.05 for the spray zones (25 lb/in^2 base pressure at 4 lb/in^2 zone loss). A multiplier of 1.06 will be used to adjust the catalog flow of all zones. The difference between 1.05 and 1.06 is due to the limitations of the tables, since the flow increase will be the same in both cases, with a 15% head pressure increase.

Note: This method of adjustment only provides an allowance for flow increases. The actual increase (and zone flow rate) will depend on the product and the actual pressure available at each head in the zone. Head pressure will vary within the zone due to differences in pipe loss and elevation. The preliminary design flow for each area is listed below:

South Area between Driveways	-	215.8 gpm
East Area along Property Line	-	84.1
Area on East Side of Building	-	23.5
Turf Strip - West Side	-	42.3
Turf Strip at Building Entrance	-	41.2

Rotary Systems

Shrub Bed at Building Entrance   -   17.9
Shrub Beds - East Side of Building -   13.3

WATER SUPPLY. Flow velocity in the water service of municipal supplies is discussed in Chapter 4, City Water Supply Piping. A 2 in type K, copper water service and a 2 in (disc-type) irrigation meter will be available for the system. The city water main is 12 in and is located in the street, 10 ft from the curb.

Although many suggest that flow velocity should not exceed 5 ft/s in all pipes, it is seldom practical for water service piping, size 2 in and smaller. A maximum of 9 ft/s will be considered for the 2 in service pipe in the exemplary design in this chapter. This will establish the maximum flow rate available for individual zones (rotary and spray) at 84.6 gpm, see Table 10a, Appendix.

Flow velocity in the water service is only one factor of consideration to determine a suitable flow rate from the municipal water supply. The distribution system of the municipal supply must have the capacity to provide the flow requirement at the system design pressure, in addition to other normal water supply requirements.

The water pressure available at the site may also influence the selection of a suitable flow rate. Flow reduction is often necessary when the available pressure is below normal and/or when medium to large size rotary heads are used in the system. Regardless of the water volume that may be available in the supply, the system piping design will be limited by the pressure available at the required flow rate.

ZONE FLOW VS PIPING SYSTEM COST. The flow rate selected for design (municipal or private water supply) will directly affect the size of pipe, fittings, valves and related equipment that will be necessary for the piping system. Although the number of zones must be realistic, considering the size of the project and the time available per day for system operation, the systems designer must also consider the related cost of the piping system.

For example, a total of 9 zones would be required for the exemplary design, if the allowable flow rate for the system was based only on the maximum velocity desired in the service pipe (2 in, K: 9 ft/s = 84.6 gpm). The 9 zone requirement is based on one zone each for 6 areas (84.1 gpm maximum) and 3 zones for the South Area between Driveways. A 3 in (minimum) PVC, SDR-

21, main would be required to maintain the flow velocity at 5 ft/s, or less (see Table 5a, Appendix).

However, if one additional zone was used in the South Area between Driveways, and the East Area along the Property Line was divided into 2 zones, the maximum zone flow would be reduced to approximately 54 gpm (215.8 ÷ 4 = 53.95 and 84.1 ÷ 2 = 42.5). Two additional zones would reduce the flow rate requirement by 35%. The mainline (minimum) size for 5 ft/s maximum would be reduced to 2 in.

Note: The actual zone flow required will depend on the nozzle combinations of each zone. The mainline sizes are included for comparison only, as the actual size required will also depend on the allowable pressure loss.

Development of a cost-effective system is not limited to cost considerations. The system cannot be considered effective unless it conforms to the basic criteria established for the system design. The use of 11 zones (or any other number) cannot be considered for the exemplary system unless the precipitation requirement per week (per day, etc.) can be provided within the time available per day for system operation.

Note: The irrigation requirement of 1.25 in/wk is low since the estimated turfgrass requirement has been adjusted to allow for irrigation efficiency. Maximum time available for system operation is 8 hours per day, 6 days per week.

A watering program of system operation should be developed to check the total operating time required for the 11 zones to apply the necessary amount of water per day and per week. Although this preliminary program does not include the necessary details required for an irrigation schedule, it should be realistic and include consideration for irrigation frequency requirements.

Note: Frequency required for water replacement will depend on the water use per day and the water-holding capacity of the soil within the root zone. Water replacement will be required when the available water supply is near the maximum allowable depletion (50% of the total water-holding capacity is often considered the maximum).

Precipitation rates for each area must be calculated by the designer to determine the operating time required for each zone. Precipitation rates and formulas are discussed in Chapter 8, Precipitation. The following rates (theoretical at catalog flow) are used to develop a watering program:

South Area between Driveways:
  44.7 ft spacing (38.5 ft R.S.) = .46 in/hr
East Area along Property Line:
  36.0 ft spacing (37.0 ft R.S.) = .59
Area on East Side of Building:
  40.0 ft square spacing
  (estimate, using two rows w/#9 nozzles) = .64
Turf Strip - West Side:
  21.1 ft single-row spacing
  (estimate for 12 ft width) = 1.33
Turf Strip at Building Entrance:
  17.9 ft spacing (15 ft R.S.) = 1.94
Shrub Bed at Building Entrance:
  7.2 ft single-row spacing
  (estimate for 5 ft width) = 1.87
Shrub Beds - East Side of Building:
  5.0 ft single-row spacing
  (estimate for 5 ft width and nozzle
  flow reduced to approximately .5) = 1.93

The following program of system operation is based on 3 operations per week for all turfgrass areas, and one operation per week for the shrub beds. This program is used only to check the total operating time requirement of the 11 zone system. The actual watering schedule will be determined after the system is installed, including adjustment of moisture requirement for the shrub zones.

South Area between Driveways:
4 zones at 55 minutes each   = 3.67 hours
(3 times a week = 1.27 in/wk)

East Area along Property Line:
2 zones at 42 minutes each   = 1.40
(3 times a week = 1.24 in/wk)

Area on East Side of Building:
1 zone at 39 minutes   = .65
(3 times a week = 1.25 in/wk)

Turf Strip - West Side:
1 zone at 19 minutes   = .32
(3 times a week = 1.26 in/wk)

Turf Strip at Building Entrance:
1 zone at 13 minutes   = .22
(3 times a week = 1.26 in/wk)

Turf Areas --- 6.26 hours

Total cycle time per day (2 days) - - - - - - 6 hrs, 15 mins

Shrub Bed at Building Entrance:
1 zone at 40 minutes   = .67
(1 time per week = 1.25 in/wk)

Shrub Beds - East Side of Building:
1 zone at 39 minutes   = .65
(1 time per week = 1.25 in/wk)

Shrub Areas -- 1.32 hours

Total cycle time per day (1 day) - - - - - - - - 7 hr, 34 min

The 11 zone system can provide the weekly irrigation requirement in 3 days. A maximum of 7.5 hours per day will be required. If desired, the shrub zones can be programmed to operate on a different day, or days, if multiple cycles are required. An additional day of operation for the turf areas would increase the weekly precipitation by 33%.

PRELIMINARY PIPING

In many cases, a preliminary piping layout is recommended to allow for possible changes that may be necessary due to pipe sizing requirements. Sizes required may, or may not, be practical, depending on the amount of pressure available to offset losses. The preliminary piping layout should be developed as necessary for the zone (or zones) that will have the greatest pressure requirement. Preliminary piping and pipe layout guidelines are discussed in Chapter 11, Preliminary Piping.

Head pressure requirement, zone flow, distance from the water supply and elevation difference from the supply are the common factors of consideration to determine the zone (or zones) with the greatest pressure requirement. The 4 spray zones in the exemplary system can be eliminated, since all spray zones have an extra 20 lb/in^2 available for pressure losses. The spray head requirement is only 25 lb/in^2 as compared to the 45 lb/in^2 head pressure requirement of the rotary sprinklers.

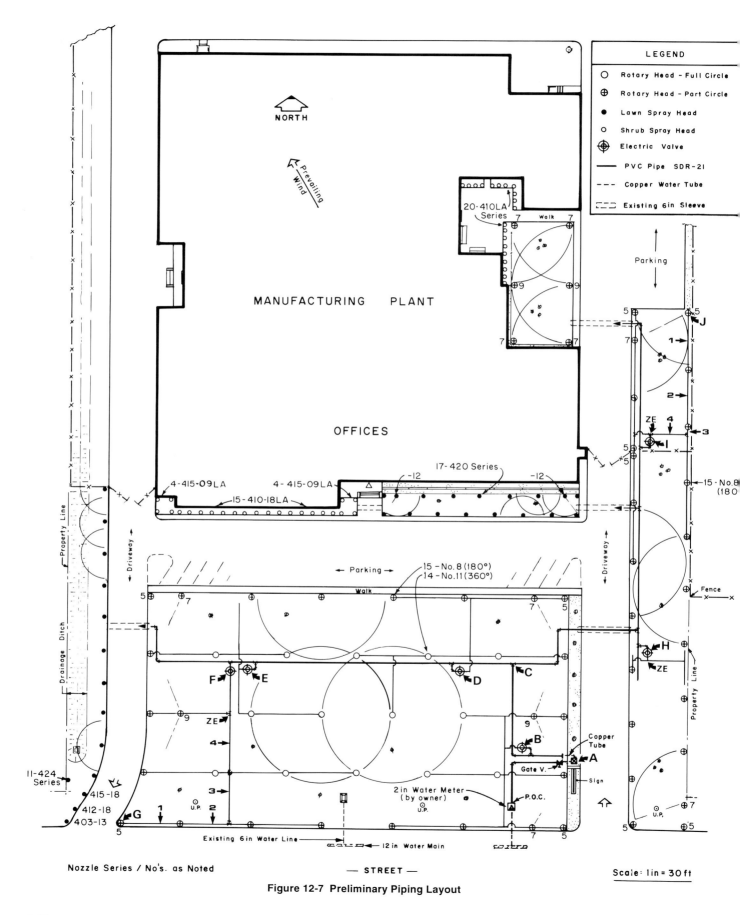

Figure 12-7 Preliminary Piping Layout

The South Area between Driveways was divided into 4 logical areas of division to establish the zones. The combination of heads in each zone and the shape of the logical areas were changed as necessary to divide the total flow of 215.8 gpm into 4 zones with approximately the same flow rate. The 4 zones have a design flow rate that ranges from 53.0 to 55.5 gpm.

The East Area along the Property Line was divided into 2 zones of approximately 42 gpm each. The zone at the north end of the strip has a design flow rate of 41.98 gpm and the zone at the south end has a flow rate of 42.08 gpm (catalog flow x 1.06 = design flow).

Considering the flow requirements and the location of the 7 rotary sprinkler zones, the 55.5 gpm zone in the South Area between Driveways was selected for a pressure requirement calculation. The zone is located in the southwest corner of the area and piping for the zone is shown in figure 12-7, Preliminary Piping Layout.

A limited amount of preliminary piping is necessary to determine the piping requirements to an individual zone. However, the mainline piping layout should be realistic with consideration for the water supply requirements of other zones and/or the supply for the entire system.

The point-of-connection (P.O.C.) for this system is the 2 in water meter (new water service and meter will be installed by the city water department). PVC pipe (SDR 21) is routed from the meter to a suitable location for the vacuum breaker (A), which must be installed above grade (see Chapter 5, Vacuum Breakers). Copper tube will be used from the gate valve (system cut-off) to the pressure-vacuum breaker and to a point below grade, on the discharge side of the assembly. The PVC main is routed from the copper tube to the location of zone valve (B).

The main continues to the tee (C), which is required for routing of the main under the driveway on the east side. The location selected for the mainline from the tee (C) to zone valves (D), (E) and (F) was based on a compromise, considering the location of the existing sleeves and trees in the area, and to allow for installation of the mainline in the same trench with lateral piping in the area.

PRESSURE REQUIREMENT CALCULATION. A calculation is required from the city main through the system to the zone valve (F), and through the zone to head (G). This is the most distant head within the zone from the zone entrance (ZE). Pressure losses for the zone, pipe sections (1) through (4), will be calculated using catalog flow. The total zone flow and pressure loss will be adjusted as required, or desired.

Since the flow is accumulative from head (G) to the zone entrance (ZE), pipe sections are numbered in the order of accumulation to determine the flow rate required in each section. The initial sizes selected for each section will be based on a flow velocity of 5 ft/s or less. A minimum pipe size of ¾ in will be used for the rotary zones.

The pressure requirement calculation for the 56.0 (55.5) gpm zone in the South Area between Driveways, is shown in Figure 12-8. A fitting loss allowance is included for each PVC pipe section, using the "short-list" of equivalent lengths for SDR-21, in Figure 11-7. The following fittings were included for the zone pipe sections:

> Section (1) - ¾ in 90° elbow at head (G).
> Section (2) - ¾ in run of tee (connection to Section 1).
> Section (3) - 1 in branch of tee - reducing (at section 2).
> Section (4) - Two reducing tees are used for connection shown. 2 in run of tee (2 x 1½) and 1½ in run of tee (1½ x 1) to section 3.

The ¾ in swing-joint (riser assembly) allowance is based on the use of 3 - 90° elbows at 4 ft (3 x 2.1 each = 6.3 x Sch. 80 factor of .6 = 3.8, see Table 17, Appendix) and 4 threaded nipples at 1.5 ft (total length). Pressure loss was calculated using maximum rotary flow of 8.2 gpm (5.5 ft of Sch. 80 = .56 lb/in^2).

Pressure loss for all pipe sections was calculated using the "RC" Formula, Table 3, Appendix. Pressure loss tables (loss per 100 ft) can also be used; example, Table 5. Elevation difference within the zone (converted to lb/in^2) is listed for reference only, since there is no elevation difference in this example zone.

The total zone pressure loss of 3.36 lb/in^2 was adjusted to 3.56 lb/in^2, using an adjustment multiplier of 1.06.

Rotary Systems

Pipe Section	Size/Type	Flow gpm	Length, ft Pipe & Fittings	Loss lb/in^2	
1	¾ in, PVC 200	2.0	41+4=45	.11	
2	¾ in, PVC 200	6.1	32+3=35	.67	
3	1 in, PVC 200	14.3	39+12=51	1.39	
4	2 in, PVC 200	43.0	39+13=52	.59	
	¾ in, Sch. 80		Swing-Joint Allowance	.60	
		Pipe and Fitting Loss at Catalog Flow		3.36	
		Zone Elevation (+/-lb/in^2)		0.00	
		Adjusted Pipe and Fitting Loss (x1.06)		3.56	
		Sprinkler Operating Pressure		45.00	
		Operating Pressure Required at ZE			48.56 (lb/in^2)
		Zone Flow: 52.4 x 1.06 = 56.0 (55.54)			

City Main to Zone Entrance:					
Item:	Length ft.	Flow gpm	Velocity ft/s	Loss lb/in^2	
2 in type K copper service	25.0				
2 in corporation cock	9.2				
2 in 90° elbows - 2 @3.5	7.0				
2 in gate valve	1.7				
Water Service = (42.9)	43.0	56.0	5.9	1.42	
2 in Water Meter (disc-type)		56.0		2.30	
Elevation (+/-lb/in^2) Meter to Zone				0.00	
2½ in PVC 200	70.0				
2½ in 90° elbow	9.0				
Meter to P.V.B. =	79.0	56.0	3.4	.57	
2 in type M copper	12.0				
2 in 90°elbows - 3 @ 4	12.0				
2 in gate valve (system cut-off)	1.9				
P.V.B. Piping = (25.9)	26.0	56.0	5.7	.76	
2 in P.V.B. Assembly		56.0		3.00	
2½ in PVC 200 Main	285.0				
2½ in branch of tee	17.0				
2½ in branch-reducing	20.0				
2½ in run of tee (3)	18.0				
2½ in 90° elbow	9.0				
PVC Main to Valve =	349.0	56.0	3.4	2.53	
2 in Electric Valve		56.0		2.70	
2 in PVC to ZE	39.0				
2 in run of tee (at ZE)	5.0				
PVC-Valve to ZE =	44.0	56.0	5.0	.81	
		Total Pressure Loss from City Main to ZE			14.09 (lb/in^2)
		Zone Design Pressure (City Main at 56 gpm)			62.65 (lb/in^2)

Figure 12-8 Pressure Requirement for 56.0 gpm Zone - Exemplary System

Pipe Section	Size/Type	Flow gpm	Length, ft Pipe & Fittings	Loss lb/in²	
1	¾ in, PVC 200	2.0	36+4=40	.10	
2	¾ in, PVC 200	6.1	36+3=39	.75	
3	1 in, PVC 200	10.2	7+6=13	.19	
4	1¼ in, PVC 200	18.4	35+13=48	.66	
	¾ in, Sch 80	Swing-Joint Allowance		.20	
	Pipe and Fitting Lose at Catalog Flow			1.90	
	Zone Elevation (+/-lb/in2)			0.00	
	Adjusted Pipe and Fitting Loss (x1.05)			2.00	
	Sprinkler Operating Pressure			45.00	
	Operating Pressure Required at ZE				47.00(lb/in²)
	Zone Flow: 39.6 x 1.05 = 42.0 (41.58)				

City Main to Zone Entrance:

Item:	Length ft.	Flow gpm	Velocity ft/s	Loss lb/in²	
2 in type K copper service	25.0				
2 in corporation cock	9.2				
2 in 90° elbows - 2@3.5	7.0				
2 in gate valve	1.7				
Water Service = (42.9)	43.0	42.0	4.5	.84	
2 in Water Meter (disc-type)		42.0		1.30	
Elevation (+/-lb/in²) meter to zone				.00	
2½ in PVC 200	70.0				
2½ in 90° elbow	9.0				
Meter to P.V.B. =	79.0	42.0	2.6	.34	
2 in type M copper	12.0				
2 in gate valve (system cut-off)	1.9				
2 in 90°elbows - 3 @ 4	12.0				
P.V.B. Piping = (25.9)	26.0	42.0	4.2	.45	
2 in P.V.B. Assembly		42.0		2.50	
2½ in PVC 200 Main	105.0				
2½ branch-reducing	20.0				
2 ½ in run of tee	6.0				
2½ in 90° elbow	9.0				
PVC Main to tee (c) =	140.0	42.0	2.6	.60	
2 in PVC 200 Main	235.0				
2 in 90° elbow- 3 @7	21.0				
2 in branch -2 @ 13	26.0				
2 in branch - reducing	16.0				
PVC Main to ZE =	298.0	42.0	3.8	3.24	
1½ in Electric Valve		42.0		3.30	
Total Pressure Loss from City Main to ZE					12.57 (lb/in²)
Zone Design Pressure (City Main at 42.0 gpm)					59.57 (lb/in²)

Figure 12-9 Pressure Requirement for 42.0 gpm Zone - Exemplary System

Rotary Systems

The same factor is used to adjust the total zone (catalog) flow. The 1.06 multiplier was selected previously from Figure 12-6 to establish the preliminary flow rates for design. The selection was based on an "allowance" for zone loss. A different multiplier can be used for the adjustment, if required (or desired), after the pressure loss calculations for the zone are completed.

Referring to Figure 12-6, a minimum adjustment of 1.03 is listed for a 3 to 4 lb/in^2 zone loss, at a design head pressure of 45 lb/in^2. However, the 1.06 multiplier (preliminary adjustment factor) was used to adjust the zone loss and flow in the pressure requirement calculations shown in Figure 12-8. The 3% difference will provide a small safety allowance for zone loss and flow, and loss in the system.

Note: As previously discussed in this chapter, some designers use a "standard" allowable zone loss and a related "standard" percentage of adjustment for pressure loss and flow. Regardless of method, some type of adjustment is recommended, since the actual zone flow will rarely be equal to the combined flow of nozzles (any type) at catalog listed flow rates.

The loss for the 2 in water service includes an allowance for a corporation cock at the city main connection, 2 - 90° wrought elbows, and a gate valve at the water meter. Equivalent footage, for these common items in the service pipe, was determined using Table 18, Appendix. The pressure loss in the water meter is based on interpolation of the data provided in Table 19, Appendix.

The pressure loss in the 2 in Pressure Vacuum Breaker (P.V.B.) assembly was obtained from the flow loss graph provided in Figure 5-10. The backflow prevention product and installation, including the above-ground location of the vacuum breaker, must be in accordance with the requirements of the local plumbing code. The pressure loss in the 2 in electric zone control valve was obtained from a manufacturer's pressure loss table (table is not provided). The zone flow rate should be within the flow range recommended for the valve size by the manufacturer.

The 2½ in PVC main from the meter (79 ft) and vacuum breaker (349 ft) was necessary to reduce the loss in the mainline. A 2 in mainline would have approximately 5 lb/in^2 more pressure loss. Velocity would be at the maximum normally recommended.

A minimum of 63.0 (62.65) lb/in^2 is required in the city main at a flow rate of 56.0 gpm. The pressure requirement is often referred to as the "zone design pressure".

The single calculation is adequate for the 4 rotary zones in the South Area between driveways, since the 56.0 gpm zone has the greatest flow requirement and is also the most distant zone from the water supply. This calculation will be used as a guide to determine all pipe sizes required in the 4 zones. All zones will require a 2 in electric control valve.

The other 3 rotary zones are located in the East Area along the Property Line (2 at 42 gpm) and the Area on the East Side of Building (1 at 23.5 gpm). The zone at the north end of the East Area along the Property Line was selected for a pressure requirement calculation. The zone at the south end of the strip has approximately the same flow requirement, but with approximately 100 ft less mainline length. The zone west of the driveway at the north end (in Area on East Side of Building) is small as compared to the other zones. Although this zone is the most distant of the 3 zones from the water supply, the flow requirement is 40% less than the other 2 zones.

The pressure requirement calculation for the 42.0 gpm zone is shown in Figure 12-9. The zone and piping arrangement is shown in the preliminary piping layout, Figure 12-7. The zone calculation includes the 4 pipe sections (1 through 4) from the most distant head (J) to the ZE, at zone valve (I). The calculated zone loss of 1.90 lb/in^2 was adjusted to 2.0 lb/in^2 using an adjustment factor of 1.05. The zone catalog flow of 39.6 gpm was adjusted to 42.0 gpm.

Note: The adjustment factor of 1.05 is based on the minimum multiplier of 1.02 from Figure 12-6 (1 to 2 lb/in^2 zone loss), plus an additional 3% to maintain a consistent safety factor. The preliminary flow adjustment factor was 1.06. This zone calculation provides an example of the minor difference that will occur in adjustment, with a minor difference in zone pressure loss. In most cases, the same adjustment factor will be used for all zones, unless there is a significant difference in the zone loss. The use of a consistent multiplier for all zones is a practical method of adjustment, considering the fact that the multiplier is only an "allowance" for flow increase, and is not necessarily correct for a particular zone.

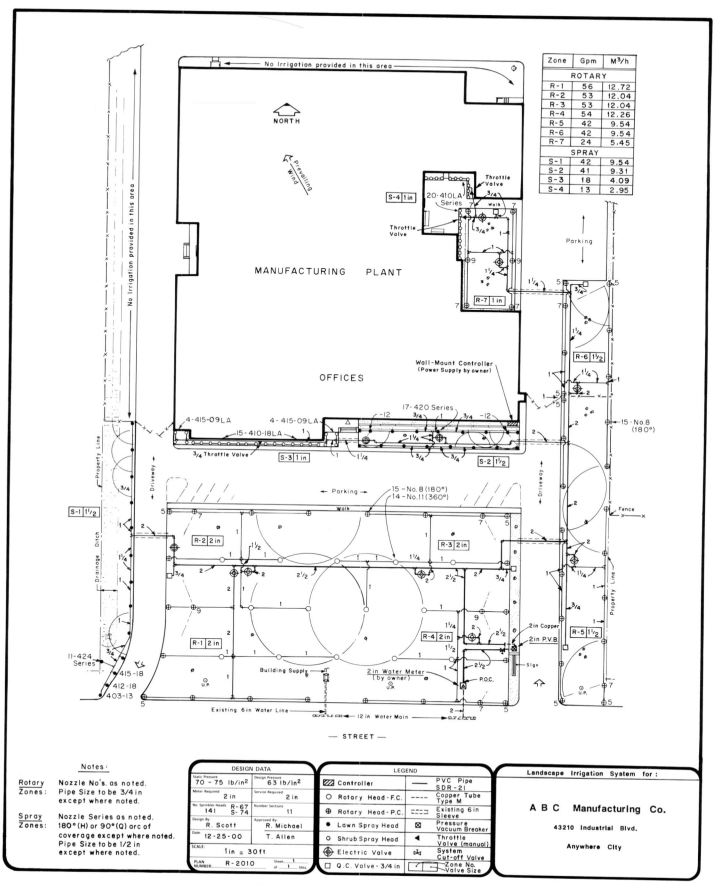

Figure 12-10 Finalized Exemplary System

Zone	Gpm	M³/h
ROTARY		
R-1	56	12.72
R-2	53	12.04
R-3	53	12.04
R-4	54	12.26
R-5	42	9.54
R-6	42	9.54
R-7	24	5.45
SPRAY		
S-1	42	9.54
S-2	41	9.31
S-3	18	4.09
S-4	13	2.95

Notes:

Rotary Zones: Nozzle No's. as noted. Pipe Size to be 3/4 in except where noted.

Spray Zones: Nozzle Series as noted. 180°(H) or 90°(Q) arc of coverage except where noted. Pipe Size to be 1/2 in except where noted.

DESIGN DATA

Static Pressure 70 – 75 lb/in²	Design Pressure 63 lb/in²
Meter Required 2 in	Service Required 2 in
No. Sprinkler Heads R-67 141 S-74	Number Sections 11
Design By R. Scott	Approved By R. Michael
Date 12-25-00	T. Allen
SCALE: 1 in = 30 ft	
PLAN NUMBER: R-2010	Sheet 1 of 1 Shts.

LEGEND

▨ Controller	— PVC Pipe SDR-21
○ Rotary Head - F.C.	---- Copper Tube Type M
⊕ Rotary Head - P.C.	☰☰☰ Existing 6 in Sleeve
● Lawn Spray Head	⊠ Pressure Vacuum Breaker
○ Shrub Spray Head	◀ Throttle Valve (manual)
⊕ Electric Valve	⋈ System Cut-off Valve
▢ Q.C. Valve - 3/4 in	Zone No. Valve Size

Landscape Irrigation System for:

A B C   Manufacturing   Co.

43210 Industrial Blvd.

Anywhere City

The swing-joint allowance in Figure 12-9 is based on the maximum head flow in the zone of 4.1 gpm. A 2 in PVC main is used from the $2\frac{1}{2}$ in main at tee (C) to the 42.0 gpm zone. The zone valve (I) size is $1\frac{1}{2}$ in, with a pressure loss of 3.30 (manufacturer's pressure loss table is not provided). The zone design pressure is 60.0 (59.57) lb/in^2.

Fitting Losses. An equivalent footage allowance was included for all zone, mainline and service pipe fittings in the pressure requirement calculations, Figures 12-8 and 12-9. As previously discussed, many designers use a percentage of pipe loss to cover losses that will occur in fittings. A table of example percentages for PVC zone piping is shown in Figure 12-5. Fitting losses included in the zone loss calculations, as a percentage of pipe length, are listed below:

Zone	Pipe: Total Length, ft	Fittings: Total Eqiv. Length, ft	Percent of Pipe Length
56.0 gpm	151	32	21%
42.0 gpm	114	26	23%

For additional reference, the total equivalent length included for fittings and plumbing valves in the copper tube and PVC mainline are listed below, as a percentage of the pipe length:

Type:	Pipe: Total Length, ft	Fittings/Valves: Total Equiv. Length, ft	Percent of Pipe Length
Service - Copper K	25	17.9	72%
P.V.B. - Copper M	12	13.9	116
56.0 gpm - PVC Main	394	78.0	20
42.0 gpm - PVC Main	410	107.0	26

The above percentages of pipe length illustrate the importance of including an allowance for the losses that will occur in "miscellaneous items." The higher percentages shown for copper K and M are due to the quantity of fittings and plumbing valves required in relatively short pipe lengths. These percentages can be compared to the fitting requirements of the spray system design in Chapter 11. Allowances for fitting losses are discussed in Chapter 11, Pipe Fitting Losses.

The number of individual zone calculations required for an irrigation design will depend on the number that is necessary to prove that all zones will have adequate operating pressure. The amount of "proof" that is necessary will depend on the experience of the designer.

The two calculations provided in Figures 12-8 and 12-9 are based on a selection of the "worst-case" zone in two different areas. The 56 gpm zone (Figure 12-8) was selected to determine the maximum pressure (and flow) requirement of the 4 zones in the South Area between Driveways. The 42 gpm zone (north-end of strip) was selected to determine the maximum requirement of the other 3 rotary zones.

Spray Zones. No pressure requirement calculations are necessary for the 4 spray zones in the exemplary system. These zones will have an additional 20 lb/in^2 available for pressure losses. This is due to the difference in head pressure requirement (rotary heads at 45 lb/in^2 and spray heads at 25 lb/in^2). Although a considerable amount of extra pressure is available for the spray zones, pipe sizes selected should include consideration for the maximum flow velocity recommended. Each spray zone electric valve will require adjustment to control the discharge performance into the zone piping.

The finalized exemplary system is shown in Figure 12-10. Rotary zones are numbered R-1 through R-7 and spray zones are numbered S-1 through S-4. The electric valve size is also included for each zone. Zone design flow is listed in the table provided on the plan. All flows shown are based on zone catalog flow x 1.06.

SUMMARY

Rotary system variations are primarily due to the size and type of property and the related requirements of pressure and flow. Although this chapter is limited to the design of one rotary system, the design considerations included for head layout, zoning and pipe sizing are typical for any type of rotary system.

Many design considerations that are often necessary for rotary systems, such as pumps, looped mains, drains, "dry-line" shock, valve wire sizing, etc. are discussed in other chapters.

CHAPTER 13

Micro Irrigation

Micro-irrigation is a term used in this text to cover a wide range of different methods for the application of moisture at very low flow rates. "Low Volume" and "Low Flow" are also descriptive terms used in the trade to cover this category of irrigation. Micro water application products are normally rated in gallons per hour (gph) or liters per hour (l/h) (lph).

This chapter is limited to basic design considerations relating to the use of micro-irrigation products as compared to broad coverage methods of landscape irrigation. It is not intended as a complete text that will provide all of the knowledge necessary for the design of micro-irrigation systems. There is a wide variety of literature available on the application of low volume products in agricultural and landscape irrigation. This includes several design manuals that are devoted exclusively to the design of micro-irrigation systems.

Many suggest that micro-irrigation products were first developed in the Middle East in the 1930's. In any event, agricultural irrigation in arid lands is the primary reason for the development of products that deliver minute quantities of water. Today, micro-irrigation is an accepted method for many types of agricultural crops. In landscape applications, the use of micro-irrigation has been somewhat limited to shrubs, trees, hedges and foundation plantings.

A variety of low-flow spray nozzles and porous piping materials were available for landscape irrigation in the U.S.A. before 1960. Several new types of agricultural irrigation products have been developed in recent years to provide flow rates less than 10 gph. Although most of these products have been used to some extent in landscape applications, agricultural irrigation methods are not always suitable or successful in landscape irrigation systems.

There are advantages and disadvantages to micro-irrigation zones or complete systems.

Advantages:

1. Water conservation due to reduced area of coverage and a reduction in loss due to evaporation, wind and run-off. In some climate regions, water conservation in landscaping may be regulated by local ordinances or state laws. Laws may include a variety of different limitations on landscape development and methods approved for irrigation.
2. Control of soil moisture within a desirable range to reduce stress and disease potential in plants.
3. Low Pressure/Low Flow products allow the use of small, low pressure water supplies. System pipe size requirements are reduced to a minimum.
4. Reduced weed growth in bed areas between plants.
5. System operation is normally not in conflict with the required use of land.
6. Reduced liability - no water on walks and driveways.
7. Improved performance for plants on steep slopes.
8. No spray on buildings when used for foundation planting.

Disadvantages:

1. High maintenance requirement. Regardless of product design and the use of filtration, there are inherent problems with water flowing through a very small passageway. Chemicals in the water

Micro Irrigation

Figure 13-1 Typical Controller(s) for Micro-irrigation systems.

can build up and clog the very small orifices. The requirement for periodic inspection of any water outlet will tend to increase as the flow rate decreases.

Scheduled maintenance as recommended can be time-consuming to check all water outlets, flush lines (unless automated) and clean filters.

2. Limited applications. Although some will recommend the use of micro-irrigation for all sizes and types of planting areas, many years of experience suggest that low volume products are limited to providing water to individual plants or small areas of coverage. This is due to the coverage limitations (water movement in soil or diameter of spray) of low pressure, low flow, water outlets. There is also a practical limitation on the quantity of outlets due to maintenance requirements.

3. Limited supply of moisture is available in the root zone. Frequent visual inspection of planting material condition is necessary with very low flow products which provide a small wetted area of coverage.

4. Filtration and Pressure Control. Almost all products will require the use of filters, even on domestic water supplies and pressure reduction of normal water pressures.

5. Pipe, tubing and other equipment exposed on the surface of the planting bed can be unsightly on a landscape project and subject to vandalism, unintentional damage and insect and rodent damage. In freezing climates, the frost may push the tubing up during winter.

6. Non-visible watering may result in a lack of customer confidence that plant material is being properly watered.

Note: Chapters 1 through 11 cover a variety of important subjects and design considerations that also relate to the design of a micro-irrigation system. Explanation provided in this chapter is based on the assumption that the reader is familiar with standard piping materials, hydraulics, cross-connection control, clean water, considerations for system performance, site data and pipe sizing methods.

SPECIAL EQUIPMENT

In addition to the water outlet products discussed later, there are a variety of different product requirements for micro-irrigation systems. This includes components that may be designed and manufactured specifically for use in micro-irrigation systems and standard types of products which are normally required in the piping system.

Controllers. Selection of an automatic controller for a micro-irrigation system is similar to the selection process used for any other type of system (See Controllers, Chapter 1). This includes the number of stations required for zone valves, basic features required or desired, and the type of housing (indoor/outdoor).

However, in most cases, the controller must also include features which are considered special for micro-irrigation systems. Some of the special requirements

Figure 13-2 Typical Electric Valve with Low Flow Characteristics

and necessary "standard" controller features are listed below:

1. *Long-Timing.* Due to the very low application rates of most micro-irrigation equipment, variable station timing of 0 - 9.9 hours in .1 hour increments is required for micro-irrigation stations.

   Controller must also provide variable station timing of 1 to 99 minutes in one minute increments if the system also includes standard spray and/or rotary sprinkler zones. On some controller models, as shown in Figure 13-1, "long-timing" is assignable on one or more of the available controller stations. Other models offer 0 to 99 minute

timing on one, or more, operating programs and 0 to 9.9 hours timing on a separate program.

2. *Watering Programs.* Two separate watering programs are often necessary for programming requirements.

3. *Stack Timing.* This feature assures that all starts will occur. This is very important as a particular operating cycle may extend beyond the next scheduled start time due to the long timing requirements of some stations.

4. *Calendar Options.* Standard water conservation ordinances in some regions, or short-term water rationing requirements may limit irrigation to specific days of the week, or for even-day, odd-day or some specific interval of days. Controller programming calendar must be as flexible as necessary for a particular requirement.

5. *Remote Sensor Circuit.* Although this is a standard feature with most controllers, it is considered a necessary requirement for a variety of different sensors that may be used with a system that is designed with special emphasis on water conservation. See Remote Sensors, Chapter 1.

Courtesy of Hendrickson

Figure 13-4 Pressure Regulator - Fixed Discharge Pressure

Electric Zone Valves. Electric control valves must be designed to open and close at very low flow rates. Solenoids should be of the best quality available due to the extended operating time requirements of micro-irrigation zones. Figure 13-2 illustrates an electric valve with flow characteristics as required for normal applications.

Courtesy of Agricultural Products, Inc.

Figure 13-3 Typical Wye Filter

Filters. All micro-irrigation systems need a filter to remove small particles from the water supply. Several types and models are available from many different

Micro Irrigation

**Figure 13-5 Pressure Regulator - Adjustable
Discharge Pressure**

manufacturers. A wye-type filter, as shown in Figure 13-3, is the most common type of filter used for normal flow and filtration requirements. Filter size depends on the total flow rate of the water outlets. Check product catalogs for recommendations.

Filter screens are rated by mesh number (openings per linear inch). See Chapter 7, Clean Water and Appendix, Table 29. Typical mesh sizes available for use with micro-irrigation systems are 100, 120, 140, 150 and 200.

Note: Standard screen filters are not adequate for biologically active water. Filters with stacked, serrated disks are commonly recommended. In general, filtration requirements should be considered carefully when non-potable water supplies are used for micro-irrigation systems.

Maintenance requirements should be considered when selecting a location for the filter. Maintenance schedule for cleaning of the filter will depend on the quality of the water supply. The property owner must be advised of

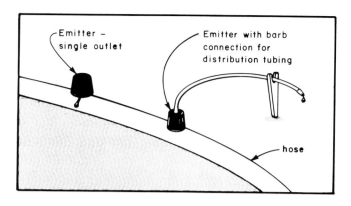

Figure 13-7 Drip Emitter

the filter location and procedures required to clean the filter.

Pressure Regulator. In most cases, a pressure regulator is required to reduce existing pressure for the low pressure requirements of micro-irrigation equipment. Since filter loss is variable, the regulator should be installed on the discharge side of the filter to maintain a constant system pressure. Regulators are selected for the discharge pressure requirement. The allowable range of flow will vary with different sizes and models.

The size of the regulator is very important and must not be undersized or oversized for the flow requirement. Many regulators will not regulate the discharge pressure if oversized.

Small, single zone regulators are available in either a fixed or adjustable type. Fixed outlet pressure regulators, as shown in Figure 13-4, are commonly available in 10, 15, 20, 25 and 30 lb/in^2 models. A schrader test valve is provided on the adjustable discharge pressure models, as shown in Figure 13-5.

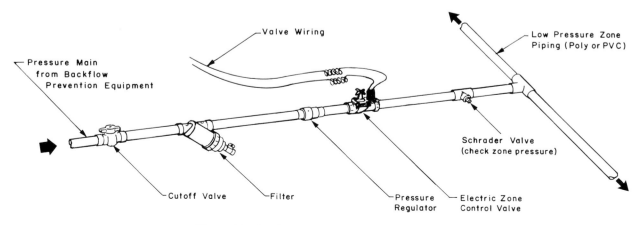

Figure 13-6 Typical Components For Zone Control

Installation should be in accordance with the manufacturer's recommendation including the possible requirement of an above-ground installation. Some design manuals include installation details that show the pressure regulator on the inlet side of the electric zone control valve. There are also manuals that show the pressure regulator installed on the discharge side of the electric zone control valve. Systems designers and installers should check with the electric valve manufacturer for the recommended location of the regulator. In some cases, valve performance may be affected by the location of the pressure regulator due to a very low flow rate.

Tubing/Hose/Pipe. Many different types and sizes of piping materials are used in micro-irrigation systems. This is primarily due to the fact that there are so many different variations of low volume systems. These include the "do-it-yourself" kits for homeowners; contractor installed residential and commercial; temporary systems and a wide range of different systems for agricultural crops.

In many cases, all of the low pressure piping materials are installed on the surface of the planting beds. Piping may be described as tubing or drip tubing or hose. A common material for this hose is LLDPE (Linear Low Density Polyethylene). The advantages of this material as compared to HDPE (High Density PE) are improved resistance to solar/environmental degradation, less expansion/contraction due to temperature changes and improvements in the long-term dependability of barb connections through the wall. Flexible PVC pipe is available from some manufacturers. Color coded (purple) pipe is also available for non-potable alert applications.

Nominal sizes available are ⅜ inch, ½ inch, ¾ inch and 1 inch. Actual inside and outside diameters will vary with different manufacturers. The absence of industry standards on pipe sizing can be confusing for the inexperienced systems designer. For example, several different inside diameters are available for ½ inch nominal tube size.

Compression and insert (barb) fittings are the most common types of fittings used with low volume, low pressure tubing. Solvent weld fittings are normally used with buried PVC pipe systems. Threaded connections on various components may have pipe-threads or hose-threads, or a combination of both. Many different types and brands of fittings, and special connectors are available for many different applications.

Small distribution tubing (sometimes referred to as spaghetti or micro-tubing) is used with some types of micro-irrigation outlets. Tubing is connected to the zone piping or riser, and routed to the water outlet device. It is also used to distribute water from drip emitters to the individual plants.

Drip Emitters and Micro Spray Emitters (heads) are the most common types of water outlets used in micro-irrigation systems.

Drip Emitters. Drip emitters are used primarily to water the root zone of individual plants as shown in Figure 13-7. Emitters are especially suitable for planting areas with widely-spaced shrubs and/or trees. The use of drip systems in large mass planting areas, such as flower beds and ground-cover, tends to vary by the climate region and individual designers.

City	ETo	City	ETo
Atlanta, GA	.24	Jacksonville, FL	.21
Bakersfield, CA	.26	Kansas City, MO	.20
Baltimore, MD	.19	Las Vegas, NV	.33
Billings, MT	.21	Lincoln, NE	.24
Biloxi, MS	.24	Little Rock, AR	.24
Birmingham, AL	.24	Los Angeles, CA	.23
Bismark, ND	.18	Memphis, TN	.24
Boston, MA	.20	Miami, FL	.24
Burlington, IA	.24	Minneapolis, MN	.21
Charleston, WV	.20	Newark, NJ	.20
Charlotte, NC	.21	New Orleans, LA	.24
Chicago, IL	.20	Norfork, VA	.20
Cincinnati, OH	.20	Oklahoma City, OK.	.24
Columbia, SC	.24	Philadelphia, PA	.20
Dallas, TX	.26	Portland, OR	.18
Denver, CO	.21	San Francisco, CA	.18
Detroit, MI	.21	Sioux Falls, SD	.24
Hartford, CT	.20	Spokane, WA	.18
Houston, TX	.26	Wichita, KS	.24
Indianapolis, IN	.20		

Note: Per day averages are based on average ETo/month. Obtain rates from a local source whenever possible.

Figure 13-8 Examples of ETo/Day - U.S.A. Cities Daily Average for Maximum ETo Month

Micro Irrigation

There are many different emitter devices available for use in landscape irrigation. Product features of primary importance relate to emission uniformity and resistance to plugging (number one problem for drip systems).

Emitter discharge rates listed in product catalogs are nominal flow rates. Actual flow rates will vary (plus or minus) depending on pressure, brand/model and variations in manufacture of individual products. Pressure compensating emitters are commonly used to reduce flow variations. However, the flow rate is not exactly the same at different pressures, and variations that will occur above and below the average rate will depend on the brand/model.

The greatest flow variation of all will occur when an emitter is plugged. Resistance to plugging will depend on the combination of features included in product design from inlet to discharge. Features that can improve plugging resistance include:

1. Barb design that locates the inlet off the inside wall surface of the hose. This will locate the inlet away from debris that tends to collect along the bottom edge and into an area of greater flow velocity.
2. Built-in inlet screen with large surface area.
3. Wide flow path in emitter, relative to flow.
4. Short flow path length, turbulent flow path, etc.

Drip irrigation design requires an estimate of the water required per plant, per day. Unlike agriculture, where an area of required coverage is normally limited to one type of crop, landscaped areas may include many different varieties of planting material. Although there are many variable factors relating to the actual water needs of an individual plant, estimates of irrigation requirement are determined by formula and/or tables. Due to the limitations of available data, variables are often limited to:

1. ETo (Reference Evapotranspiration) per day
2. Plant size
3. Plant type
4. Irrigation Efficiency

ETo inches/day. Reference Evapotranspiration (See Related Conditions, Chapter 8). The system design should be based on realistic ETo rates for the region in which the project is located. Standard rates for design purposes are normally based on average ETo values for the maximum temperature month.

Examples of ETo per day for a selected number of cities (U.S.A.) are shown in Figure 13-8. These values do not represent the absolute maximum ETo rate that may occur on any given day. Listed rates are the "average" per day for the maximum temperature month (July, in most cases). Calculated rates are based on historical weather data. The actual rate for any day or month may be more or less, depending on actual weather conditions.

In most cases, an extra allowance (safety factor) should be added to the average ETo rate per day for design purposes. The ETo rate should be obtained from a local agriculture extension service whenever possible. In addition to the maximum ETo rate for design, the average monthly rate for the normal irrigation season will be useful for irrigation scheduling. The best information for actual schedules (to cover normal variation) is ETo data based on current weather conditions.

Plant Size. Root zone area is estimated by using the canopy diameter of the plant, as illustrated in Figure 13-9. Square footage of the coverage area is also used when plantings are grouped together at close spacings.

In most cases, designs should be based on water use estimates of mature plants. When small plant sizes are used for a new landscape project, this method will minimize the need for future revisions and establish the maximum flow requirements of the piping system. Controller station timing can be adjusted as water requirements change with plant development.

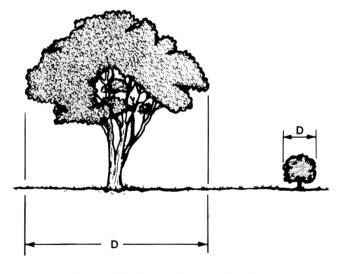

Figure 13-9 Canopy Diameter (Feet)

There are obvious limitations in using this method if new small plantings are mixed together with existing mature plants. Use of separate zones may be the only practical solution in some cases, to avoid periodic changes in quantity and/or size of emitters.

Plant Type. Unlike agricultural crops, the water requirements of ornamental plants are not well known. Consumptive water use of different varieties varies from very low to very high. In recent years, the need for water conservation in semi-arid and arid regions of the U.S.A., has created the need for more accurate information on water requirements of commonly used varieties.

Xeriscape is a landscape design concept to save water by selecting low water use plants (See Conservation by Landscape Design, Chapter 8). Although Xeriscape designs are based on several different principals to conserve water, the basic requirement is to use native or climate adaptable plants. Xeriscape design also considers plants with similar water use requirements when grouping plants together in the design.

In some climate regions of the U.S.A., the water requirement is known for many of the commonly used plant varieties. This information may also include seasonal variations in water requirement for improved irrigation scheduling throughout the year. However, in many regional areas, plant varieties are grouped together in a limited number of water use categories.

Plant Factors (PF) are used to determine the water requirement of different varieties by adjusting the base ETo rate. "Rule of Thumb" tables (example: Figure 13-10) should be used with caution since plant factors do not necessarily relate to individual varieties.

Plant factors can be calculated if plant water requirement (inches/day) is known.

Example: ETo = .30 inches/day.
　　　　　Requirement for a particular type
　　　　　= .22 inches/day

$$PlantFactor(PF) = \frac{Requirement\,(inches/day)}{ETo\,(inches/day)}$$

PF = .73 (.22/.30)

Landscape planting may also be located in a wide range of different environments. Some may be exposed to full sun, some in partial shade and others may be in complete shade. In many cases, zone separation of plant varieties or different areas is a practical way of eliminating too many known (or unknown) variables on a single operating valve.

Special attention is recommended for any large trees that have existed for many years without an irrigation system. In such cases, the systems designer should obtain professional advice on watering (or not watering) the trees. Unfortunately, there have been many cases where existing trees could not survive the new irrigation system.

Irrigation Efficiency. Efficiency is defined as the percentage of total irrigation water supplied to a given area which is made available within the root zone for beneficial use by plants.

Loss of moisture in drip irrigation is primarily due to evaporation. Temperature, wind, humidity and surface area are basic factors that will influence evaporation (see Water Evaporation, Chapter 6). Drip irrigation is considered to be very efficient due to the small area of coverage. Some designers use a standard percentage as a goal for all designs and others will vary the percentage depending on climatic conditions. Percentages of 80 to 95 percent are commonly used for drip irrigation system efficiency.

Gallons Required Per Day, Per Plant. The following examples are provided to illustrate a common method used to estimate gallons required per day, per plant:

　　ETo = .28 inches/day
　　Plants:　A. Small Shrub -- 1.5 ft. diameter
　　　　　　B. Large Shrub -- 5.0 ft. diameter
　　　　　　C. Shade Tree --15.0 ft. diameter

Gallonage Factor Table, Figure 13-11, is used to determine "GF" requirement. Maximum ETo of .30 inches per day is used in the table for average ETo of .28. Irrigation efficiency of 85 percent is used as a goal considering a warm, dry climate.

　　A. Small Shrub: GF　= .39 gallons
　　　　　　　　　　GPD (gallons required per plant)
　　　　　　　　　　= GF x PF
　　　　　　　　　　PF table, Figure 13-10, is used for
　　　　　　　　　　illustration - - PF = 1.0
　　　　　　　　　　GPD = .39 (.39 x 1)

Micro Irrigation

Plant Factor (PF)	Plant Types
1.00	Small shrubs (under 4 ft. dia.), Groundcover, Evergreens and Vines.
.80	Mature Shade Trees
.70	Shrubs (over 4 ft. dia.), Native plants (newly planted), and Shrubs (native to humid areas).
.40	Established Plants (native to region).

Figure 13-10 Example: "Rule of Thumb" Plant Factor Table

B. Large Shrub: GF = 4.3 gallons
GPD = GF x PF
PF table, Figure 13-10, PF = .70
GPD = 3.0 (4.3 x .70)

C. Shade Tree: Determine square footage of canopy area (Note: 15 ft. diameter canopy is not listed in table, Figure 13-11):

Diameter squared x .7854 (constant) = Area of circle
15^2 x .7854 = 176.72 sq. ft.
GF per sq. ft. = .22 (Figure 13-11)
GF = 176.72 x .22 = 38.9 gallons (PF = 1.0)
PF Table, Figure 13-10, PF = .80
GPD = GF x PF
GPD = 31 (38.9 x .80)

While there are many variables that can influence the actual water requirement of an individual plant, each must be considered as it relates to the particular type of plant. Accuracy of GPD values determined in the examples above are primarily limited by the accuracy of the PF multipliers. As previously mentioned, the systems designer should obtain the best information available on water requirements of the different plant species used in the landscape design.

Wetted Pattern (drip emitters). The wetted area on the surface and the shape of the wetted pattern below the surface are influenced by the type of soil. Figure 13-12 illustrates typical patterns of clay, loam and sand. The actual shape and size of the wetted area will depend on the soil conditions (including soil amendments commonly used in landscape beds), the application rate and the operating time of the zone. On site tests are recommended to determine the actual wetted profile.

Note: Typical wetted pattern shapes, as shown in different design manuals, are somewhat similar, except for the horizontal range of coverage. It is difficult to estimate the size of the wetted pattern without information from an actual test at the site. Emitters on slopes must be installed uphill from the plant to allow for the downhill shifting of the wetted pattern.

Root Zone Coverage. Fifty percent of the soil in the root zone is considered to be minimum coverage for landscape systems. Many recommend that 60% of the root zone should be within the wetted area for improved performance. In any case, 100% of the plant water requirement must be provided, regardless of the percentage of root zone coverage. Water requirement of plants is not changed by method of applying moisture. Salt build-up is a problem in some regions when a low percentage of the root zone is covered. It may be necessary to overlap the coverage (similar to sprinkler heads) and completely cover the root zone to move the salt to the outer perimeter of the wetted area.

Number of Emitters. Different methods are used to determine the number of emitters required for each individual plant or planting area. Regardless of the method used, the number and flow rate of the emitters must provide the water requirement per day (per week, if not operated daily) and provide the necessary coverage (percent of root zone).

Individual Plants. Number of emitters, flow rate and spacing requirements may be based on experience or "common practice guidelines", or calculated to determine the requirement in gallons or root zone coverage.

Example (based on gallons per day or per week):

Shrub A -- 1.5 ft. canopy | | |
| ETo = .25 | Efficiency
Shrub B -- 3.0 ft. canopy | | Estimate = 85%

Shrub "A": GF factor from Figure 13-11 is .32 and plant factor from Figure 13-10 is 1.0. Plant requirement is .32 gallons/day or 2.24 gallons/week (7 x .32).

Assuming three operations per week:
$\frac{2.24}{3}$ = .75 gallons required per operation.

Maximum ETo* in/day	Irrigation Efficiency %	GF - Gallonage Factors (PF = 1.0) Plant Canopy Diameter - Feet													Per Sq. Ft.
		1	1.5	2	2.5	3	3.5	4	5	6	7	8	10	12	
.10	80	.06	.14	.24	.38	.55	.75	.98	1.5	2.2	3.0	3.9	6.1	8.8	.08
	85	.06	.13	.23	.36	.52	.71	.92	1.5	2.1	2.8	3.7	5.8	8.3	.07
	90	.05	.12	.22	.34	.49	.67	.87	1.4	2.0	2.7	3.5	5.5	7.8	.07
.15	80	.09	.21	.37	.57	.83	1.1	1.5	2.3	3.3	4.5	5.9	9.2	13.2	.12
	85	.09	.19	.35	.54	.78	1.1	1.4	2.2	3.1	4.2	5.5	8.6	12.4	.11
	90	.08	.18	.33	.51	.73	1.0	1.3	2.0	2.9	4.0	5.2	8.2	11.7	.10
.20	80	.12	.28	.49	.76	1.1	1.5	2.0	3.1	4.4	6.0	7.8	12.2	17.6	.16
	85	.12	.26	.46	.72	1.0	1.4	1.8	2.9	4.1	5.6	7.4	11.5	16.6	.15
	90	.11	.24	.43	.68	1.0	1.3	1.7	2.7	3.9	5.3	7.0	10.9	15.7	.14
.25	80	.15	.34	.61	.96	1.4	1.9	2.5	3.8	5.5	7.5	9.8	15.3	22.0	.19
	85	.14	.32	.58	.90	1.3	1.8	2.3	3.6	5.2	7.1	9.2	14.4	20.7	.18
	90	.14	.31	.54	.85	1.2	1.7	2.2	3.4	4.9	6.7	8.7	13.6	19.6	.17
.30	80	.18	.41	.73	1.2	1.7	2.3	2.9	4.6	6.6	9.0	11.7	18.4	26.4	.23
	85	.17	.39	.69	1.1	1.6	2.1	2.8	4.3	6.2	8.5	11.1	17.3	24.9	.22
	90	.16	.37	.65	1.0	1.5	2.0	2.6	4.1	5.9	8.0	10.4	16.3	23.5	.21
.35	80	.21	.48	.86	1.3	1.9	2.6	3.4	5.4	7.7	10.5	13.7	21.4	30.8	.27
	85	.20	.45	.81	1.3	1.8	2.5	3.2	5.0	7.3	9.9	12.9	20.2	29.0	.26
	90	.19	.43	.76	1.2	1.7	2.3	3.0	4.8	6.9	9.3	12.2	19.0	27.4	.24
.40	80	.25	.55	.98	1.5	2.2	3.0	3.9	6.1	8.8	12.0	15.7	24.5	35.2	.31
	85	.23	.52	.92	1.4	2.1	2.8	3.7	5.8	8.3	11.3	14.7	23.0	33.2	.29
	90	.22	.49	.87	1.4	2.0	2.7	3.5	5.4	7.8	10.7	13.9	21.8	31.3	.28
.45	80	.28	.62	1.1	1.7	2.5	3.4	4.4	6.9	9.9	13.5	17.6	27.5	39.6	.35
	85	.26	.58	1.0	1.6	2.3	3.2	4.1	6.5	9.3	12.7	16.6	25.9	37.3	.33
	90	.24	.55	1.0	1.5	2.2	3.0	3.9	6.1	8.8	12.0	15.7	24.5	35.2	.31
.50	80	.31	.69	1.2	1.9	2.8	3.8	4.9	7.7	11.0	15.0	19.6	30.6	44.0	.39
	85	.29	.65	1.2	1.8	2.6	3.5	4.6	7.2	10.4	14.1	18.4	28.8	41.5	.37
	90	.27	.61	1.1	1.7	2.5	3.3	4.4	6.8	9.8	13.3	17.4	27.2	39.1	.35

* See Examples
Figure 13-8

GPD = GF x PF

Where: GPD = Gallons Required Per Day - Per Plant.
GF = Gallonage Factor - from above table
PF = Plant Factor - See Figure 13-10

Figure 13-11 GF Factors to Determine GPD Required Per Plant.

Duration time per operation using one 1 gph

$$emitter = \frac{.75\,gallons}{1\,gph} = .75 \text{ hours (45 minutes)}.$$

Shrub "B": GF factor from Figure 13-11 is 1.3 and plant factor from Figure 13-10 is 1.0. Plant requirement is 1.3 gallons/day or 9.1 gallons/week (7 x 1.3).
Assuming three operations per week:

$$\frac{9.1}{3} = 3.0 \text{ gallons required per operation}.$$

Duration time per operation using two 1 gph

$$emitter = \frac{3.0\,gallons}{2\,gph} = 1.5 \text{ hours (90 minutes)}$$

The number of emitters used in the above examples are typical of requirements for the size of the planting. Number can be changed as necessary for water requirements, root zone coverage or different watering frequency. Some designers use a minimum of 2 emitters per plant for safety (plugging protection).

The station duration times of the two examples are different and should not be on the same operating zone, unless flow rates and/or number of emitters are changed for compatible performance.

Unusual Soil Conditions. In landscape irrigation systems, root zone coverage below the surface is not the only problem of consideration for the systems designer. Building foundation damage is a problem in some regional areas due to unusual soil conditions. In some cases, systems should not be installed adjacent to the foundation. However, there are also areas that must maintain moisture in the soil to avoid sudden expansion of dry soil due to a short period of heavy rainfall.

Although systems designers cannot be responsible for existing problems with building foundations, it is important for the designer to obtain information on unknown soil conditions when designing a soil moisture supply system. Soils with poor drainage can also be a problem in some, or all planting bed locations at the site.

New Landscape Projects. In most cases, the number and flow rates of all emitters should be based on mature plant requirements. Future additions and alteration requirements for future plant development should be minimized when designing the system.

Operation/Programming. Scheduling irrigation is a process that requires careful attention. Operation may be based on estimated requirement, soil moisture measurement or visual appearance of plant material.

Systems with fertilizer injection equipment will require adequate station timing to move the fertilizer away from the emitter and into the root zone. A scheduled flush period will be necessary to remove the fertilizer from the system. Periodic injection of chemicals may also be necessary to control the growth of bacteria or slime.

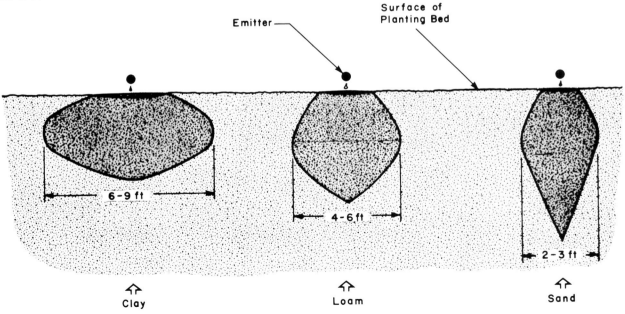

Figure 13-12 Examples of Wetted Pattern Shapes

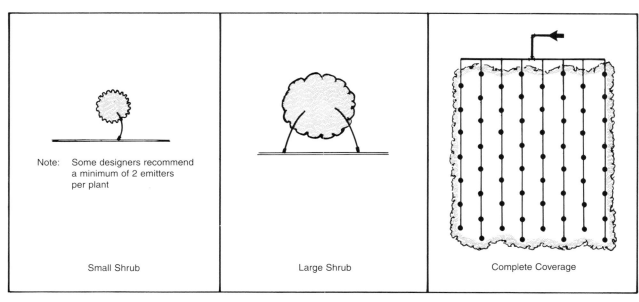

Figure 13-13 Typical Emitter Layouts

Frequency of irrigation will depend on the water requirement, type of plant and root depth, and the type of soil. Clay soils will hold moisture for a longer period of time. Sandy soils, with large pore spaces, will permit a higher rate of application, but will also allow the moisture to move through the soil and dry out quickly.

Complete Coverage. Emitter layout for ground cover or low shrub applications may be similar to a sprinkler layout, with complete coverage of the planting bed (See Figure 13-13). This is accomplished by using emitters at spacings of 12 to 30 inches on a square or triangular pattern. Drip tubing with pre-installed, in-line emitters is often used for this type of application. However, punch-in emitters can also be used at spacings as required. Water application can be measured in inches per hour for the area of coverage (assuming equal distribution).

Formulas : Application Rate

$$Application\ Rate\ (inches/hour) = \frac{GPH\ (one\ emitter)\ x\ 231}{Spacing\ on\ Row\ (inches)\ x\ Row\ Spacing\ (inches)}$$

$$Duration/hours = \frac{Inches\ Required}{Application\ Rate\ (inches/hour)}$$

Example: 1 gph emitters / 12 inch spacing on row / 18 inch row spacing.

$$Application\ Rate = \frac{1.0\ x\ 231}{12\ x\ 18} = \frac{231}{216} = 1.0\ {}^{in}/_{hr}$$

$$Duration\ Time = \frac{.3\ inches*}{1.0} = .3\ hours\ (18\ minutes)$$

*for example only

Zone Separation. Each emitter circuit should have a separate controller station to allow for duration time and irrigation frequency changes that may be necessary. In almost all cases, different plant groups and/or water use categories should not be mixed together on the same zone. Separate control circuits may also be necessary for plants in full sun, plants in complete shade or variations due to completely different soil conditions.

Caution: Although controller station and valve requirements are important for cost and programming, the systems designer should consider that "matched" frequency and duration time requirements, as determined

Courtesy of Antelco Corp.

Figure 13-14 Micro-Spray Sprinkler

Micro Irrigation

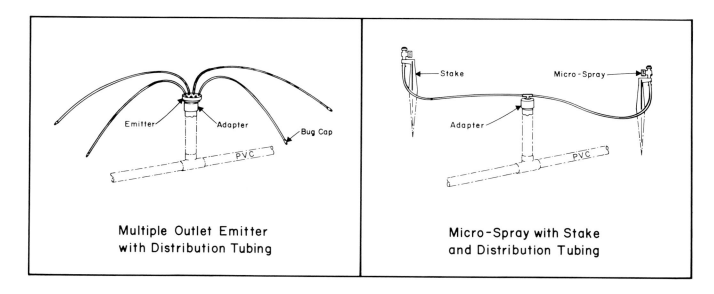

Multiple Outlet Emitter
with Distribution Tubing

Micro-Spray with Stake
and Distribution Tubing

Figure 13-15 Typical Risers - Buried PVC Pipe

during the design phase, may not be matched requirements at the site.

Micro-Spray Sprinklers

Micro-spray heads are a micro-flow alternative to drip emitters (See Figure 13-14). The spray sprinklers are useful for a variety of different requirements where increased surface coverage is desirable.

Spray (or stream spray) performance is available in full circle and a limited number of part circle or strip coverage patterns. Flow rates of nozzles range from 4 to 25 gph. Radius of the fine spray varies from 3 to 12 feet depending on the nozzle, operating pressure, arc of

coverage and brand and model. Operating pressure is in the 10 to 30 lb/in^2 range, although some flow control models are rated as high as 50 lb/in^2.

Some models can be adapted for use on pop-up heads. However, most of the nozzles are installed on fixed risers using a micro-irrigation stake and distribution tubing. Sprinkler layout is similar to the standard type of spray head layout (See Chapter 10). Spacing is equal to radius for head-to-head coverage of the very fine spray. Micro-spray heads should not be installed on the same circuit as drip emitters.

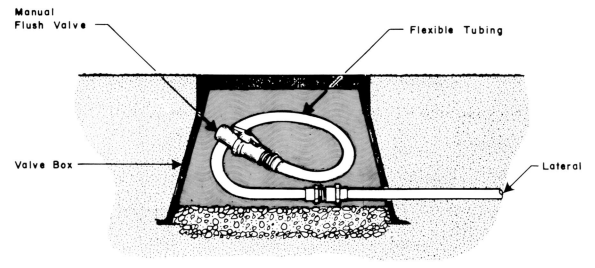

Figure 13-16 Flush Valve Required at End of Lateral

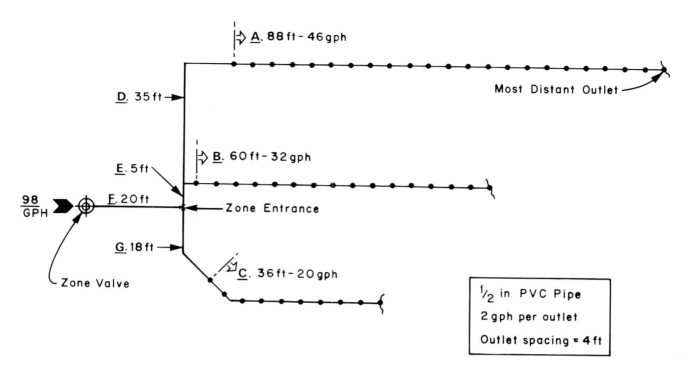

Figure 13-17 Drip Emitter Circuit - PVC Pipe

System Hydraulics. Pressure loss calculations for micro-irrigation systems are basically the same as for any other type of system (See Chapter 3). Pipe sizing and zone calculations are similar to requirements for spray systems, as discussed in Chapter 11. Although pressure requirement is somewhat less than that required for other types of irrigation equipment, the primary difference in sizing of pipe and components is due to the very low flow rates.

Mainline Piping. PVC - Poly (Vinyl Chloride) is the most common type of piping material used for mainline piping to the zone valves and/or pressure regulators. Pressure loss considerations in water meters, building supply lines, mainline pipe and fittings, backflow prevention equipment, filter and elevation differences (loss or gain) are the same as for any other type of irrigation system.

Zone Piping. PVC pipe and polyethylene tubing are the two most common types of piping materials used for zone piping. Some systems use only one type of pipe for all low pressure applications and others may be a combination of both types. Many landscape irrigation systems use buried PVC pipe for all zone piping lines, except for distribution tubing (PE) above grade (See Figure 13-15).

In most cases, pressure loss for zone piping can be estimated without the need for detailed calculations of each individual pipe section, as discussed for sprinkler heads in Chapter 11, Pipe Sizing and Zoning. Except for large systems, or complex piping arrangements, the systems designer can analyze the piping circuit and by applying logic, develop an estimate of the pressure loss within the zone. Many different types of tables, slide rules and design charts are available from different sources to assist the designer with lateral calculations.

Figure 13-17 illustrates a drip emitter circuit using ½ inch PVC pipe. Maximum pressure loss will normally occur in the piping between the "zone entrance" and the most distant outlet in the circuit. In this example, the most distant outlet (lateral length) is at the end of pipe lateral "A". Pressure loss to this outlet will be based on an estimate of losses in lateral A and pipe sections D, E, and F.

Lateral "A": Lateral length is 88 feet, flow is 46 gph and outlet spacing is 4 feet. Using Table "A", Figure 13-19, pressure loss per 100 feet for a multiple outlet lateral, pressure loss = .12 lb/in^2 (50 gph inlet flow at 4 ft outlet spacing). Table "A" includes an allowance for run-of-tee loss at each outlet (Note: Actual calculation of lateral pressure loss for 46 gph and 88 feet is .093 lb/in^2).

Micro Irrigation

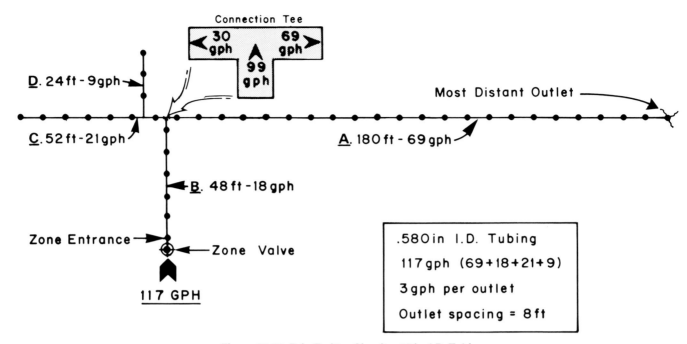

Connection Tee

30 gph   69 gph

99 gph

D. 24 ft - 9 gph

Most Distant Outlet

C. 52 ft - 21 gph

A. 180 ft - 69 gph

B. 48 ft - 18 gph

Zone Entrance   Zone Valve

117 GPH

.580 in I.D. Tubing

117 gph (69+18+21+9)

3 gph per outlet

Outlet spacing = 8 ft

Figure 13-18 Drip Emitter Circuit - .58 in. I.D. Tubing

Pipe Section "D": Pipe length allowance is 38 feet (35 ft plus 3 ft equivalent length for 90° elbow), flow is 46 gph. Using Table "C", Figure 13-22, pipe pressure loss per 100 feet, pressure loss for 50 gph = .07 lb/in^2 (.18 x .38).

Pipe Section "E": Pipe length allowance is 7 feet (5 ft plus 2 ft equivalent length for run-of-tee), flow is 78 gph (total of A and B laterals). Using Table "C", pressure loss at 80 gph = .03 lb/in^2 (.42 x .07).

Pipe Section "F": Pipe length allowance is 26 feet (20 ft. plus 6 ft equivalent length for branch-of-tee), flow is 98 gph (total of A, B, and C laterals). Using Table "C", pressure loss at 100 gph = .17 lb/in^2 (.64 x .26).

Total pressure loss in piping:

Lateral A	=	.12
Section D	=	.07
Section E	=	.03
Section F	=	.17
Total Pipe Loss	=	.39
Elevation (loss or gain)	=	-0-
Electric zone valve (if installed on the discharge side of the pressure regulator)	=	1.20 (example)
Emitter Operating Pressure	=	15.00 (example)
Minimum Pressure Required at Pressure Regulator Outlet	=	17 lb/in^2 (16.59)

Note: The filter is on the inlet side of the regulator and filter loss allowance is not included. Figure 13-18 illus-trates a drip emitter circuit using .58 inch I.D. drip tubing. The most distant outlet is at the end of lateral "A." Due to length, maximum pressure loss will occur in the 228 feet of lateral length (A at 180 + B at 48) from the zone entrance to the most distant outlet.

Lateral "A": Lateral length is 180 feet, flow is 69 gph and outlet spacing is 8 feet. Using Table "B", Figure 13-20, pressure loss per 100 feet for a multiple outlet lateral, loss is .51 lb/in^2 per 100 ft at 10 ft outlet spacing. (Note: 8 foot outlet spacing is not provided in Table "B." However, losses in the 5 and 10 foot columns are approximately the same at 70 gph lateral inlet flow). A loss allowance for emitter barbs is included in Table B.

Referring to the lateral length conversion table in Figure 13-21, the loss multiplier is 1.9 to convert the 100 foot loss listed in Table B to an approximate loss for 200 feet at 10 foot outlet spacing. Lateral "A" loss = .51 x 1.9 = .97 lb/in^2 (Note: Actual calculation of lateral loss for 69 gph, 8 ft outlet spacing and a lateral length of 180 ft is .9 lb/in^2).

Lateral "B": Lateral length is 48 feet, inlet flow is 117 gph (18 gph plus the flow requirements of the laterals A, C, and D). In this example, the loss can be estimated by assuming the 117 gph flows through the entire lateral length of 48 ft. (Note: If each segment of the lateral were calculated individually, the flow would be 99 gph in the first pipe section from the connecting tee and 117 gph in the last "zone entrance" section. Accumulation

Lateral Inlet Flow[1] GPH	Table A								
	Pressure Loss (lb/in^2) - 100 Ft. Lateral Length ½ in. PVC PIPE - SDR 13.5								
	Outlet Spacing - Feet								
	1	1.5	2	2.5	3	4	5	10	20
5	.01	.01	.01	.01	.01	.01	.01	.01	.01
10	.02	.02	.02	.01	.01	.01	.01	.01	.01
15	.03	.03	.02	.02	.02	.02	.02	.02	.02
20	.04	.04	.03	.03	.03	.03	.02	.02	.02
25	.05	.04	.04	.04	.03	.03	.03	.03	.03
30	.07	.06	.05	.05	.05	.05	.04	.04	.04
35	.10	.08	.07	.07	.06	.06	.06	.06	.06
40	.13	.11	.09	.09	.08	.08	.08	.07	.08
45	.16	.13	.12	.11	.10	.10	.09	.09	.10
50	.19	.16	.14	.13	.12	.12	.11	.11	.12
60	.26	.21	.19	.18	.17	.16	.15	.15	.16
70	.34	.28	.25	.23	.22	.21	.20	.19	.21
80	.42	.35	.31	.29	.27	.26	.25	.24	.26
90	.52	.43	.38	.36	.34	.32	.31	.30	.32
100	.62	.51	.46	.43	.40	.38	.37	.36	.38
120	.85	.70	.63	.58	.55	.52	.51	.49	.52
140	1.11	.92	.82	.76	.72	.68	.66	.64	.68
160	1.40	1.16	1.03	.96	.91	.86	.83	.80	.86
180	1.72	1.42	1.27	1.18	1.11	1.05	1.02	.98	1.05
200	2.06	1.71	1.52	1.41	1.33	1.27	1.22	1.18	1.26
220	2.43	2.01	1.79	1.67	1.58	1.50	1.44	1.39	1.49
240	2.83	2.34	2.09	1.94	1.83	1.74	1.68	1.62	1.73
260	3.25	2.69	2.40	2.24	2.11	2.00	1.94	1.87	2.00
280	3.70	3.07	2.73	2.54	2.40	2.28	2.20	2.12	2.27
300	4.18	3.46	3.08	2.87	2.71	2.57	2.48	2.39	2.56

(1) Listed flow is the total accumulated flow of all outlets (See Fig. 13-21)
(2) Loss includes an allowance for run-of-tee loss at each outlet.

Figure 13-19 Table A - Pressure Loss - Multiple Flow Outlets ½ in PVC Pipe - SDR 13.5

is in the opposite direction of flow. Calculated loss is 1.29).

Referring to Table "C", Figure 13-22, pressure loss per 100 feet is 3.19 lb/in^2 at a flow rate of 120 gph. Lateral "B" loss allowance = 1.53 lb/in^2 (3.19 x .48). Losses in six emitter barbs and the one tee are omitted as the estimated loss is on the entire length of the lateral. Minor loss will occur in the branch flow of the tee, assuming it is a compression-type of fitting (higher loss if an insert type).

Total loss in lateral piping:
Lateral A = .97
Lateral B = 1.53
Allowance for lateral losses = 2.50

The most distant outlet is 5 ft above the zone entrance (5 x .433 = 2.17)
Elevation Loss = 2.17
Electric zone valve (if installed on the discharge side of the pressure regulator) = 1.20 (example loss)
Emitter Operating Pressure = 20.00 (example)
Minimum Pressure Required at Pressure Regulator Outlet = 26 lb/in^2 (25.87)

Micro Irrigation

Lateral Inlet Flow[1] GPH	Table B Pressure Loss (lb/in²) - 100 Ft. Lateral Length .58 in. I.D. Tubing								
	Outlet Spacing - Feet								
	1	1.5	2	2.5	3	4	5	10	20
5	.02	.02	.02	.02	.02	.02	.02	.02	.02
10	.04	.03	.03	.03	.03	.03	.03	.03	.03
15	.05	.05	.05	.04	.04	.04	.04	.04	.04
20	.07	.07	.06	.06	.06	.06	.06	.06	.06
25	.10	.09	.09	.09	.08	.08	.08	.08	.09
30	.15	.13	.12	.12	.12	.11	.11	.12	.13
35	.19	.17	.17	.16	.16	.15	.15	.15	.16
40	.25	.22	.21	.20	.20	.19	.19	.19	.22
45	.30	.27	.26	.25	.24	.24	.24	.24	.26
50	.36	.33	.31	.30	.29	.29	.28	.29	.31
60	.50	.45	.42	.41	.40	.39	.39	.39	.44
70	.65	.58	.55	.53	.51	.51	.50	.51	.56
80	.82	.73	.69	.67	.65	.64	.63	.65	.71
90	1.00	.90	.85	.82	.80	.78	.78	.79	.87
100	1.20	1.08	1.02	.98	.95	.94	.93	.95	1.04
120	1.65	1.48	1.39	1.35	1.31	1.29	1.28	1.30	1.43
140	2.15	1.94	1.82	1.76	1.70	1.68	1.66	1.70	1.87
160	2.71	2.44	2.29	2.22	2.15	2.12	2.10	2.14	2.36
180	3.33	3.00	2.81	2.72	2.63	2.60	2.58	2.62	2.90
200	4.00	3.61	3.38	3.26	3.16	3.12	3.09	3.15	3.47
220	4.73	4.24	3.99	3.86	3.74	3.69	3.66	3.73	4.12
240	5.50	4.94	4.64	4.49	4.35	4.29	4.26	4.34	4.78

(1) Listed flow is the total accumulated flow of all outlets (See Fig. 13-21)
(2) Loss includes an allowance for emitter barbs. Fitting loss not included.

Figure 13-20 Table B - Pressure Loss - Multiple Flow Outlets .580 in I.D. Emitter Tubing

As previously discussed, each circuit will require careful analysis of the piping arrangement, location of flow outlets, etc., when estimating the pressure loss. To avoid detailed (and normally unnecessary) calculations of each lateral segment, logic used for estimating the loss must be realistic and with consideration for a degree of safety.

The following method of estimating the combined loss of laterals A and B is provided as an example of a different approach to estimating the lateral loss.

Referring to the connection tee detail in Figure 13-18, the combined flow of laterals A and B is the same as if it were a single outlet of 30 gph on the 228 foot lateral from the most distant outlet to the zone entrance (combined length of laterals A and B). A 228 foot single-line

Conversion Table: Use the following multipliers to convert losses listed in Tables A and B (loss/100 ft.) to pressure losses for 150, 200, 300 and 400 ft. lateral lengths.

Lateral Length Feet	Outlet Spacing - Feet								
	1	1.5	2	2.5	3	4	5	10	20
	Multipliers								
150	1.5	1.5	1.5	1.5	1.5	1.5	1.5	1.5	1.5
200	2.0	2.0	2.0	2.0	2.0	2.0	2.0	1.9	1.8
300	3.0	3.0	3.0	3.0	3.0	2.9	2.9	2.8	2.6
400	4.0	3.9	3.9	3.9	3.9	3.9	3.8	3.7	3.3

Example: 140 gph/10 ft. Spacing/ 200 ft. Lateral.

Psi Loss = ½ in. PVC Pipe (Table A): .64 (100 ft.) x 1.9 = 1.22

.58 I.D. Tubing (Table B): 1.70 (100 ft.) x 1.9 = 3.23

Lateral Inlet Flow, as listed in Tables A and B, indicates the total accumulated flow of all outlets in the lateral. Listed pressure loss is based on the same rate of flow at each outlet.

Example:

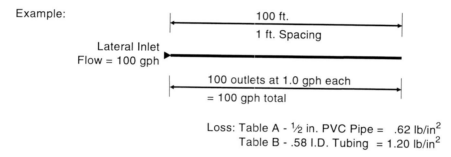

Loss: Table A - ½ in. PVC Pipe = .62 lb/in^2
Table B - .58 I.D. Tubing = 1.20 lb/in^2

Pressure loss per lateral length must be adjusted if rate of flow is not equal at each outlet. Actual loss will depend on the location and discharge rate of different outlets. Loss will be greater if higher rates of flow in the last half of the lateral length create an unequal distribution of flow.

Example:

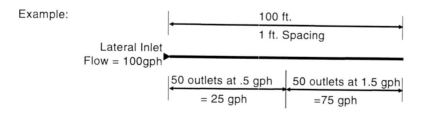

* 75% of inlet flow occurs in the last half of the lateral.

In this example, and for similar flow conditions, the following multipliers can be used to adjust the pressure loss. (Note: If two different spacings are required, use the listed loss for the lesser spacing).

Percentage of Total Flow in last half of the lateral length	Multiplier for 100, 150, 200, 300 and 400 ft. lateral loss
67%	1.25
75%	1.40
90%	1.65

Figure 13-21 - Notes and Multipliers for Pressure Loss Tables A and B

Micro Irrigation

Table C			
Pressure Loss (lb/in^2) Per 100 Feet*			
GPH	.58 in. I.D. Tubing	½ in. PVC SDR- 13.5	¾ in. PVC SDR - 21
5	.03		
10	.05		
15	.08		
20	.10	.03	
25	.22	.05	
30	.30	.07	
35	.39	.09	
40	.48	.12	.03
45	.59	.15	.04
50	.71	.18	.05
60	.97	.25	.07
70	1.26	.33	.09
80	1.59	.42	.11
90	1.94	.53	.14
100	2.35	.64	.17
120	3.19	.90	.24
140	4.20	1.19	.32
160	5.29	1.53	.41
180	6.54	1.90	.51
200	7.78	2.30	.63
220	9.29	2.75	.75
240	10.79	3.23	.88
260	12.34	3.74	1.02
280	14.14	4.29	1.17
300	16.02	4.88	1.32

* Barb and/or fitting losses not included.

Figure 13-22 Table C - Pressure Loss Per 100 Feet

lateral, with 117 gph inlet flow and 8 foot outlet spacing, will have a flow range of 100 to 117 gph in the first 40 feet. Therefore, a flow range of 99 to 117 gph in lateral B is similar, and the combined pressure loss of laterals A and B will be approximately equal to a 228 foot lateral with an inlet flow of 117 gph.

Estimate of lateral loss based on this method: Table B: Using 120 gph inlet flow and 10 foot outlet spacing, the pressure loss in a 100 foot lateral is 1.30 lb/in^2. A

multiplier for 228 feet can be estimated using factors provided in the length conversion table (Figure 13-21) or a direct ratio multiplier of 2.28 can be used: 1.30 x 2.28 = 2.96 lb/in^2 loss for laterals A and B.

Although Tables A and B are useful to estimate the loss of a multiple outlet lateral, the systems designer must understand the limitations of these tables. Listed pressure losses are not adequate for all of the possible flow variations that may occur at different locations within the lateral. Listed losses are based on an equal flow rate at each outlet and listed inlet flow is the total accumulated flow of all outlets at the listed spacing (See notes, Figure 13-21).

If, for example, a connection tee for a 30 gph requirement was located 60 feet from the most distant outlet (10 outlets in laterals C and D moved to a different location), pressure loss in the 228 foot (A and B combined) lateral would be greater, as some portion of lateral A would have a 30 gph increase in flow rate above the amount that would result from normal accumulation of flow from the most distant outlet.

In this revised example, the total of outlet flows in the last half (114) of the 228 foot lateral would be 75 gph. This flow is based on 15 outlets at 3 gph each, plus 30 gph requirement (10 at 3 gph each). The normal total flow of all outlets in the last half of the lateral would change from approximately 50% to 64% of the inlet flow.

Estimate of lateral loss based on a revised location of the 30 gph requirement:

First, the loss is estimated the same as in the previous example of a 228 foot lateral, loss = 2.96 lb/in^2. Second, the loss of 2.96 is adjusted for additional flow requirement in the last half of the lateral. Using the 67% adjustment multiplier from the table in Figure 13-21, 2.96 x 1.25 = 3.70 lb/in^2 loss for laterals A and B. (Note: Adjustment multipliers are also limited in application).

Other Types of Drip Products for Micro-Irrigation

As previously mentioned, there are other types of micro-irrigation products that can be used in landscape irrigation systems. These include "tape" or tubing with pre-drilled orifices at appropriate intervals, formed labyrinths and porous hose products.

Systems designers should always obtain design information from the suppliers or manufacturers of these products. This includes the suggested applications, lateral spacings, flow rates and filter and operating pressure requirements. In general, this type of equipment operates at lower pressure than other micro-irrigation products.

Low to Medium Flow Products

In some cases, designers will use other types of irrigation products to water individual plants and trees, small planting beds and special treatment areas. These products provide moisture at a higher rate of flow and are not classified as micro-irrigation products. In fact, the primary advantage of this equipment is to reduce the periodic monitoring and maintenance requirements of drip emitters and micro-spray heads in some, or all areas of a particular project.

The three most common types of heads used in this application are described in the Flood Head section, Chapter 1. Variations of these basic types are listed below for reference:

Adjustable Bubbler -- trickle flow
Adjustable Bubbler -- umbrella spray
Pressure-Compensating Bubbler -- trickle flow
Pressure-Compensating Bubbler -- umbrella spray
Jet Sprinklers -- stream outlets in full, half, quarter and strip patterns.
Spray Heads -- 5 to 8 ft. radius, low-angle trajectory in full and part-circle patterns.

Low flow, low-angle strip spray nozzles can also be used in some low planting bed applications (check product catalogs for overlap requirements).

In general, all of these products are unique and are not generally compatible. In most cases, different types should not be mixed together on the same zone control valve. Pressure requirement for most of these products is in the 10 to 20 lb/in^2 range. Flow will vary with type, application and brand/model. Part-circle spray nozzles are available with flow as low as 18 gph (.3 gpm).

BIBLIOGRAPHY

Many design manuals are available on the subject of micro-irrigation, including books and printed material developed by manufacturers of micro-irrigation products.

There are also several organizations directly involved in the design, operation and collection of research material relating to micro-irrigation systems. Three of the most notable trade associations are:

American Society of Agricultural Engineers
2950 Niles Road
St. Joseph, Michigan 49085-9659

The Irrigation Association
8260 Willow Oaks Corp. Drive, Ste. 120
Fairfax, VA 22031

Center for Irrigation Technology, CSUF
5370 North Chestnut
Fresno, CA 93740-0018

CHAPTER 14

Golf Course Systems

Terms used in this manual in reference to golf courses are listed below.

Tee: A maintained area of turfgrass from which golf ball is driven toward a green.

Green: Area of finely-tended, close-clipped grass containing a cup as target for golf ball, i.e., the putting surface.

Fairway: A strip of maintained turfgrass between *tee and green.*

Green approach: A part of the fairway extending from the green to a distance of about 100 feet. On many golf courses, the green approach is maintained in a condition superior to the rest of the fairway.

Fairway approach: A part of the fairway extending from the tee, narrower, and not as well maintained, as the rest of the fairway; not incorporated by all courses or all fairways on a given course. When used, length is slightly shorter than average distance ball is driven from tee.

Hole: Each combination of *tee, fairway and green.*

Rough: The area between holes which is generally only roughly maintained. Roughs are often not irrigated except in cases where normal rainfall is insufficient to establish or maintain hardy field grasses.

Figure 14-1 illustrates the areas described by the above terms.

Figure 14-1 Nomenclature of Golf Course Holes

HEAD LAYOUT

Pop-up rotary heads are used for automatically controlled irrigation of golf courses. The normal rules for rotary head layout apply. However, requirements of course irrigation cause some specialized deviations from normal. Due to the size and shape of irrigated areas, varied methods are almost always necessary to offset the effects of wind on sprinkler coverage.

The layout of sprinkler heads on each hole should be developed in segments; the segments corresponding to the five areas requiring different irrigation control (Figure 14-1). These areas, in order of importance, are:
Green
Green approach
Tee
Fairway
Fairway approach

Sprinkler coverage in each of the five segments of a hole must properly, and adequately, overlap with the sprinkler coverage of adjacent segments. Therefore, the proper sequence of layout is important. Because the location of heads around greens is highly restricted, the layout for green watering should be accomplished first.

The performance characteristics of heads used for irrigation of the golf course in this chapter are shown in the exemplary table of Figure 14-21.

Golf Course Systems

Putting area Apron Collar

Figure 14-2 Nomenclature of a GREEN

GREENS

Greens turf, although the finest of all turfs, is maintained under the most adverse conditions. It is mowed frequently and clipped extremely short. Greens turf must not retain too much moisture after watering, otherwise it would be too soft for ball play and could not withstand player foot traffic. To satisfy this requirement, porous soil is often used with a sub-soil drainage system. Watering is required frequently and consistently to compensate for the rapid drainage.

In addition to selecting the proper sprinkler for green watering, extra care is required in spacing and locating heads to provide reasonably equal water distribution over the entire area. This requires a plan which accurately portrays the size and shape of the putting area.

To more easily develop the relatively critical layouts for greens, many designers have "blow-ups" made of the green areas because of the necessarily small scale of over-all golf course plans commonly 1 in = 100 ft (metric equivalent, 1:1250). Most engineering supply stores provide enlargement services. The detailed layouts of greens are generally placed on a separate "detail sheet" with a scale of about 1 in = 30 ft.

In most cases, greens are watered with full-circle sprinklers located around the perimeter. This method is used as a practical compromise to provide coverage on the green and collar with the same sprinklers. In some cases, separate coverage and control with full-circle or part-circle heads is provided for the collar and area around the green.

Generally, part-circle sprinklers are used only for special requirements such as avoiding overthrow onto buildings, walks, streets, etc. If part-circles are required, they should be controlled separately from full-circles in order to provide equal precipitation.

GREEN LAYOUT RESTRICTIONS. Primary restrictions regarding layout for green watering can be summarized as follows:

Rule 1. Never locate heads in the putting area, or closer than one foot. Locating heads in the "apron" is usually permissible.

Rule 2. Heads on the approach side of the green should be located as far from center line of fairway as is consistent with good watering coverage.

Rule 3. Provide ample overlap of sprinkler coverage at center of green.

Rule 4. Extreme care must be exercised to provide coverage overlap with fairway sprinklers located in the green approach. Water from these sprinklers must not throw onto the green, otherwise distribution on the green will be upset. Therefore, a reference line intersecting heads at the front of the green should be in front of the green itself, or not over 5 ft behind (Figure 14-5).

GREEN LAYOUT GUIDELINES. The following general guidelines will be helpful for determining placement of heads.

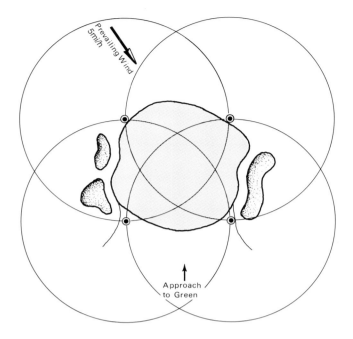

Figure 14-3 Exemplary Head Layout: Green Size - Approx. 5000 ft²

Guideline A. Except for very small greens, four or more sprinklers are usually required for good coverage.

Guideline B. Never exceed manufacturer spacing recommendations for the sprinklers that will be used, including spacing deration for prevailing winds.

Guideline C. Equal-space sprinklers around green as much as practical; over-all coverage is more important than equal spacing.

TYPICAL GREEN LAYOUT. Considering the restrictions and guidelines, head spacing and locations are controlled by the size and shape of the green, and the area around the green.

Figure 14-3 illustrates a green with 4 sprinklers on square spacing. Dimensions across the green, such as those shown in Figure 14-4, may be of limited use to determine the head spacing requirement, as heads are seldom located at the points of maximum width and length. For example, a 57 ft square spacing could be used on an 80 ft diameter green, or an 80 ft square green (heads located half-way along each side of the green).

A small spacing template can be very useful as a visual aid, since the best location of heads around the green is often not readily apparent. A simple, square spacing template is shown in Figure 14-4 (shaded area). The template was drawn to the proper scale on a small sheet of tracing paper.

Spacing requirements and head locations can be determined for each green, by using a selection of templates at different spacings and with different spacing patterns. In some cases, a single template may be adequate since the template is used only as a guide, and actual spacings required can be more or less than the spacing on the template.

Referring to Figure 14-21, exemplary rotary sprinkler performance tables, the 60 ft square spacing template shown in Figure 14-4 is based on the PK70AF (full circle) sprinkler with $7/32$ x $11/64$ nozzles at 60 lb/in². Spacing was determined using the wind deration table at 5 mi/h (120 ft diameter x .50 = 60 ft).

The template shown in Figure 14-4 was placed over the green and positioned with consideration of the fairway center line and approach to the green. Note that this places the row line of the two heads nearest the approach to a location that is approximately 8 ft behind the front edge of the green. Also, a slightly larger spacing is required to locate all heads approximately 1 ft from the edge of the putting area.

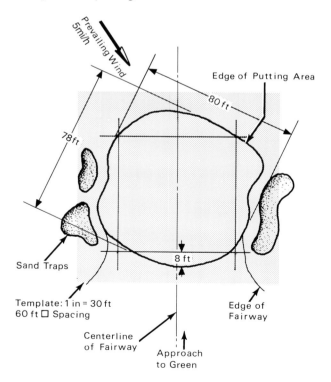

Figure 14-4 Using Template to Determine Head Locations at Green

Golf Course Systems

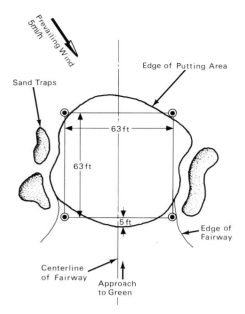

Figure 14-5 Adjusted Green Head Layout

An adjusted layout is shown in Figure 14-5 using a 63 ft (minimum) square spacing. The diameter of coverage required is 126 ft, using the wind deration method provided in Figure 14-21 for maximum spacing (63 ÷ .50 = 126 ft diameter). A PK70AF (full circle) sprinkler with $\frac{1}{4}$ x $\frac{11}{64}$ nozzles will provide a 126 ft diameter of coverage at 70 lb/in^2.

The precipitation rate is also very important and the nozzle flow rate is a factor of consideration when selecting the necessary sprinkler performance. The total operating time available per day is normally very limited, considering the amount of area that must be watered.

Sprinkler coverage on the collar and areas around the green can be checked by adding circles of coverage to the layout. In some cases, an additional head is required at the green to improve coverage in areas other than the putting surface. Coverage around greens is also improved with systems that include separate coverage along the golf cart path to the next tee.

USING GREEN CONTOURS FOR LAYOUT. The contours of odd shaped greens can often be used advantageously to minimize size of coverage diameters required when locating sprinklers around green. This reduces flow and pressure requirements which in turn reduces pipe and valve sizes.

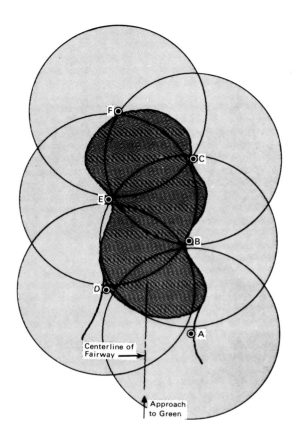

Figure 14-6 Using Green Contours for Head Layout

Figure 14-6 illustrates the use of contours for head layout. Heads (B), (C) and (E) were first located in contours providing least spacing. Spacings varied from 53 ft to 59 ft, triangularly. Other heads were then located to maintain triangular spacing of approximately the same maximum, 60 ft.

Head (F), located standard distance from putting area edge of 1.5 ft measured to center of head, fell 57 ft from heads (C) and (E).

Head (D) was located the maximum established for this layout of 60 ft from head (B); distance to head (E) is slightly less.

Head (A) was located 60 ft from heads (B) and (D) and approximately equi-distant from center line of fairway. While maintaining these maximum distances, head (A) was also moved into the fairway as far as possible to keep the row line between (A) and (D) close to the front edge of the putting area. Another reason for locating (A) in the fairway was to reduce overlap with heads (B) and (D).

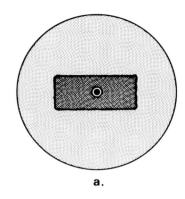

a.

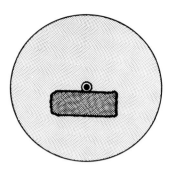

Figure 14-8 Watering with Single Sprinkler Off Narrow Tee

HEADS OFF TEES. If sprinkler heads in tees are not allowed, sprinklers are placed on the sides.

Narrow Tees. Full or part-circle coverage sprinklers can be used to water narrow tees from one side. Figure 14-8 illustrates this method with a single sprinkler.

Wider Tees. Multiple full or part-circle coverage sprinklers are used to water larger tees from the sides. Figure 14-9 shows a tee being watered by three full-circle sprinklers. If part-circles were preferred, the heads would be located in the same places using the same radius of coverage.

Wind effects, overthrow beyond boundaries, etc., must be considered when locating and spacing heads to water tees.

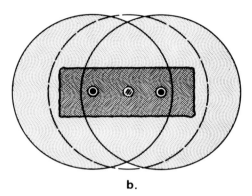

b.

Figure 14-7 Watering Small Tees

TEES

Tees are generally watered with full circle sprinklers; often the same sprinklers used around the greens. Although the coverage diameter may be larger than needed for small tees, it will provide extra watering around the tee. Also, this method reduces the variety of sprinkler models used in a system - an advantage in maintenance. However, the design should not be restricted by this advantage if a different sprinkler is more adaptable.

SMALL TEES. One Method is to locate a single sprinkler head in the center of the tee (Figure 14-7a). Adequate overthrow beyond borders of the tee is required to insure ample precipitation on the tee itself. This method is not recommended due to lack of uniform distribution, see Chapter 8.

In cases where overthrow is slight, as shown by sprinkler coverage indicated by dashed line circle in Figure 14-7b, two sprinklers provide ample coverage as shown by solid line circles in the illustration. This method, and other multiple head layouts for tees is used when overlap with fairway sprinklers must be provided.

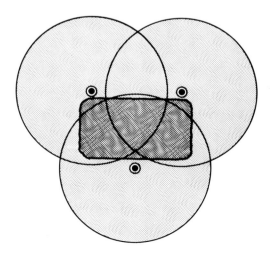

Figure 14-9 Watering with Multiple Sprinklers Off Wider Tee

Golf Course Systems

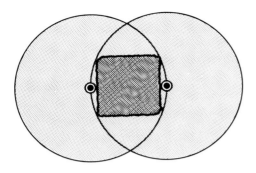

Figure 14-10 Small, Square Tee Watered from Front and Back

Square Tees. Square tees are usually watered from all sides. Small square tees can often be watered with two sprinklers located front and back. Figure 14-10 shows such a tee.

LARGE TEES. Some golf courses have large tees. Often these are actually two tees: Front Tee and Back Tee. Generally, the two tees form one large area of turfgrass.

Layout methods previously presented for watering tees and greens can be adapted for large tees. It is usually acceptable to locate heads in tees, at least when located on the line dividing the two tees.

APPROACHES AND FAIRWAYS

Watering requirements for the green approach generally differ from either the green or fairway. However, the treatment of the green approach is governed, to a large extent, by the type of system that will be used in the fairway. Therefore, discussion of these two areas must be handled simultaneously unless the approach is designed as an extension of the green layout.

Three commonly used methods of fairway watering may be described by the number of rows of heads used:

    Single row;
    Double row;
    Three row;
    etc.

Multiple-row systems provide important advantages over single-row systems.

1. Smaller diameters of coverage used are less affected by wind.
2. Smaller flows and pressures result in smaller pipe sizes.

3. Precipitation uniformity is improved.

Fairway sprinklers are equally spaced between the first fairway heads from the green and tee. First fairway head from the green may be located to merge coverage with the sprinklers watering the green or those watering the green approach. Methods are illustrated and discussed in the following text regarding approach and fairway watering.

The first fairway sprinkler from the tee may be located to merge coverage with the heads watering the tee or those watering the fairway approach. In instances where the fairway approach is not watered, the first head is located so its coverage overlaps well beyond the area that is to be maintained. Location of first sprinkler from tee is illustrated in the section of this chapter which discusses fairway approach watering.

FAIRWAY COVERAGE - GENERAL. The width of coverage provided for a fairway will depend on the head layout (spacing and number of rows), the sprinkler diameter of coverage, the effect of wind and the standard used to measure the area of coverage. Diameter of coverage, as listed in product catalogs, can be misleading since the radius may be based on the most distant point at which .01 in/hr precipitation will occur in a controlled sprinkler test. Sprinkler performance is discussed in Chapter 8.

The width of the wetted area (without wind effect) is normally obtained by using a scale to measure the distance on the plan or work sheet. If necessary, the width can be determined for different diameters of coverage and spacings, using the formulas listed below. In any case, the width is normally only useful as a very rough estimate or to compare one head layout to another. In addition to very low rates of application in some areas of the wetted pattern, the area will change in size and shape due to wind effect. See Figure 8-14.

Single-row: Width of wetted area (without wind effect) can be calculated using the following formula:

$$MW = \sqrt{D^2 - S^2}$$

Where:

    MW = maximum width, ft (wetted area without wind)

    D = diameter of coverage, ft
        (catalog diameter)

    S = head spacing, ft

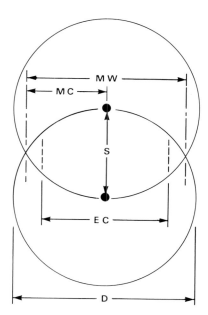

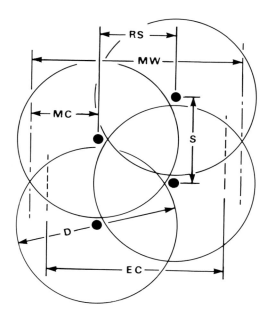

Example: 180 ft diameter of coverage sprinklers at 90 ft spacing.

$$MW = \sqrt{180^2 - 90^2}$$

$$MW = \sqrt{32400 - 8100}$$

$$MW = \sqrt{24300}$$

MW= 156 ft (155.88)

Multiple-row: Width of wetted area (without wind effect) can be calculated using the following formula:

$$MW = (\sqrt{D^2 - S^2}) + N\,(RS)$$

Where:
   MW = maximum width, ft
   (wetted area without wind)

   D = diameter of coverage, ft
       (catalog diameter)

   S = head spacing, ft

   N = number of spaces between rows

   RS = row spacing, ft

Example: 136 ft diameter of coverage sprinklers at 75 ft spacing. Two rows with 65 ft row spacing.

$$MW = (\sqrt{136^2 - S^2}) + 1\,(65)$$

$$MW = (\sqrt{18496 - 5625}) + 65$$

$$MW = (\sqrt{12871}) + 65$$

MW = 113.45 + 65

MW = 178 ft (178.45)

In a fairway head layout, some areas of coverage will have no overlap with adjacent sprinklers, or a limited amount of overlap as compared to other areas. The amount of moisture applied in the outer perimeter area of sprinkler coverage is not considered to be effective (without overlap) for the normal turfgrass requirement. Also, the total amount of application is not adequate in the area where the limits of two adjacent sprinklers overlap.

Effective Coverage. The term "effective coverage" is used to indicate the maximum radius (or diameter) of coverage for a specified minimum rate of application. The rate considered as minimum for effective coverage will depend on the average precipitation rate of the sprinkler or the maximum rate applied in any area. Although a compromise is necessary, the minimum rate selected for effective coverage must be realistic to maintain a degree of efficiency in system operation.

Consideration of effective coverage is necessary in system design to roughly estimate the width of fairway coverage that can be expected with a particular head layout, when operated for a reasonable period of time. The actual width and shape of the area that will receive the amount of moisture necessary for the turf quality desired will depend on the sprinkler distribution profile, wind conditions and the operating time per day (week, etc). Coverage may be approximately equal on each side of the fairway or different, depending on the prevailing wind direction as it relates to the individual fairway.

Since there are many variables that can affect the width of coverage, many designers use 50% to 70% of the listed radius to estimate the line of effective coverage from the outside row. This method is used to derate the MC distance for design. Percentage is selected based on the sprinkler performance (profile), wind conditions, irrigation requirement and experience.

Note: MC (mean coverage) is used for the maximum width of coverage on one side only. See explanation of (common) head layout factors in the Appendix (MC multipliers are listed in Tables 30 and 31).

For fairway coverage, a percentage of diameter is normally used to estimate the total width of coverage for the head layout. If EC in the single-row example was estimated at 70% of the diameter, the effective cover-age width would be 126 ft (180 x .70 = 126). At 70% of diameter for the two-row example, the total width would be 160 ft. This is based on 70% of diameter (same as 70% of radius on each side) plus row spacing (136 x .70 + 65 = 160.2).

Wind Compensation. As previously mentioned, the width of effective coverage may not be centered on the rows of heads. That is, the distance from the outer row of heads to the line of effective coverage may be less than calculated on the windward side because wind will blow the sprinkler streams back toward the heads. Conversely, the line of effective coverage will probably be greater on the leeward side where wind will extend the streams. Thus, further compensation may be necessary.

An old rule-of-thumb developed for single-row systems is still effective for wind compensation under certain conditions: *Install system 1 ft windward from center line of fairway for each 1 mi/h of average prevailing wind.* This rule is usable only in areas where wind direction is relatively constant during the watering season. It can also be applied to multi-row systems.

The above rule is somewhat arbitrary and is not suitable in areas where prevailing wind varies constantly or where wind direction varies considerably from season to season during period of watering. In these cases, systems are generally installed as designed. And, fairways are maintained only where grass is kept green.

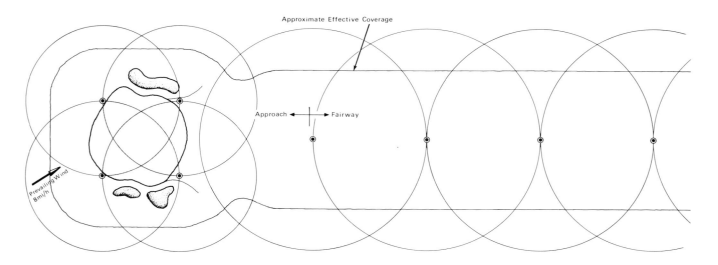

Figure 14-11 Single-Row Fairway Sprinkler Watering Green Approach

SINGLE-ROW SYSTEMS. Single-row fairway coverage is normally only considered for very narrow fairways, or in regions where a limited amount of irrigation is required (to improve turf quality in center of fairway), or when necessary due to a limited budget.

Large coverage pop-up sprinklers (160 to 200 ft diameter) are located down the center of the fairway. Selection of heads for a single-row system and coverage available are limited for practical reasons, including the pressure and flow requirement.

Spacing. Sprinklers in single-row systems are generally spaced at about 50% of the diameter of coverage of the sprinkler used. With more than moderate winds, spacing is often reduced to 45% or even 40% of the diameter of coverage.

Sprinklers are spaced closer than in multi-row systems to provide more overlap. This minimizes the amount of "scalloping" that occurs on borders where the large circumferences of coverage intersect, as shown in Figure 14-11.

Actual spacing may be slightly less than that selected when heads are equally spaced between the ends of the fairway.

The K90F, with $7/16$ x $11/64$ nozzles, Figure 14-21, was selected for the single-row system of Figures 14-11 and 14-12. The coverage diameter of 186 ft at 70 lb/in^2 was used with a spacing of 90 ft (48% of coverage diameter).

Sprinkler radius shown is equal to spacing. Diameters of coverage are normally not shown on final drawings except as desired in some locations for reference. Circles of coverage are included for illustration in this chapter.

Effective Coverage. Using the normal maximum percentage of diameter to estimate EC, the fairway width of coverage is 130 ft (186 x .70 = 130.2). Some designers use 60% as a compromise in estimating between the normal range of 50 to 70% of diameter. In this case, the width of coverage would be reduced to 112 ft (186 x .60 = 111.6), a reduction of 9 ft on each side. Regardless of the sprinkler performance (known or unknown) it would be reasonable to adjust the percentage somewhat in proportion to the wind deration factors used for head spacing.

The designer can consider the basic differences in system requirement (pipe, pumps, etc) with different diameters of coverage by comparing the flow and pressure requirements. An example comparison using 50% of diameter for head spacing is provided below:

K90F Nozzles	Coverage Diameter ft	Spacing (50% D) ft	EC Estimate (60% D) ft	Head Flow gpm	Head Pressure lb/in^2
$7/16$ x $11/64$	186	93	112	50.0	70
$1/2$ x $7/32$	200	100	120	74.5	90

Thus, to achieve approximately 7% more coverage (4 ft on each side of the fairway) the flow rate increases 49% and the pressure requirement 28%. The increase would require substantially larger pipe sizes and pumping capacity.

Green Approach. The first sprinkler of the fairway pattern must be properly blended with the coverage of the green sprinklers. Fairway sprinklers should not water onto the green. Locating fairway sprinklers so that the coverage circumference is at least 10 ft from the nearest edge of the putting area is desirable.

Note: In some cases, the layout for the approach is an extension of the green layout. In this case, the fairway layout is blended into the green approach layout.

Method 1. The first sprinkler of the single-row system has been located in Figure 14-11 so that its coverage blends with the coverage of the heads watering the square type green illustrated previously. Notice that because coverage of the fairway head was maintained 10 ft from the green, the effective coverage width has been reduced to less than the rest of the fairway; whereas, an approach wider than the fairway is generally desired. Coverage in the center of the approach is also less than desirable due to the spacing between the fairway head and the green heads.

Method 2. In Figure 14-12, the two sprinklers used in the approach were also located to maintain their circumference of coverage at 10 ft from the green. With the proper sprinkler coverage diameter, this method can provide an effective coverage width equal to, or greater than, that of the fairway. Coverage in the center of the approach is also improved as compared to the layout in Figure 14-11. Additional improvement would occur with reduced spacing between the fairway head and the approach heads.

Golf Course Systems

Precipitation. The formulas used for average precipitation within a square or triangularly spaced system (Chapter 8: System Distribution: Precipitation) are not suitable for single-row systems. It should be noted, too, that precipitation in single-row systems varies more than average throughout the system than multi-row systems do.

Several different formulas are available to calculate the average precipitation rate of a single-row layout. Variations are primarily due to the method used to determine the size of the area. Calculated rates will vary with different formulas, but most will provide rates which are similar to the precipitation rates calculated with the formula below:

$$\frac{gpm \times 96.25}{Spacing \times MC \times 2} = \,^{in}\!/_{h} \text{ precipitation}$$

Where:

gpm = flow, one sprinkler, gallons per minute
Spacing = S = distance between heads, ft
MC = mean coverage, ft, each side

Or:

$$\frac{m^{3}\!/_{h} \times 1000}{Spacing \times MC \times 2} = \,^{mm}\!/_{h} \text{ precipitation}$$

And:

$$\frac{^{l}\!/_{min} \times 60}{Spacing \times MC \times 2} = \,^{mm}\!/_{h} \text{ precipitation}$$

Where:

m3/h = flow, one sprinkler, cubic meters per hour
l/min = flow, one sprinkler, liters per minute
Spacing = S = distance between heads, meters
MC = mean coverage, meters, each side

Example: The sprinklers in Figures 14-11 and 14-12 have a coverage diameter of 186 ft with a flow of 50 gpm and are spaced at 48% of diameter. Precipitation in inches per hour is calculated using the above formula.

$$^{in}\!/_{h} = \frac{50 \times 96.25}{90 \times 81.58 \times 2}$$

$$^{in}\!/_{h} = \frac{4812.5}{14684.4}$$

$$^{in}\!/_{h} = .33 \quad (.3277)$$

Note: MC of 81.58 was determined using Table 30, Appendix. MC is approximate since spacing is actually 48.4% of diameter. MW from width calculation can be used in place of MC x 2.

Summary. In the final analysis, the exact width of effective coverage cannot be predetermined by formula, since sprinklers are installed in permanent locations and spacings, and operated in wind conditions that vary to some degree each time the system is operated.

TWO-ROW SYSTEMS. An exemplary two-row fairway system layout shown in Figure 14-13 uses PK70AF

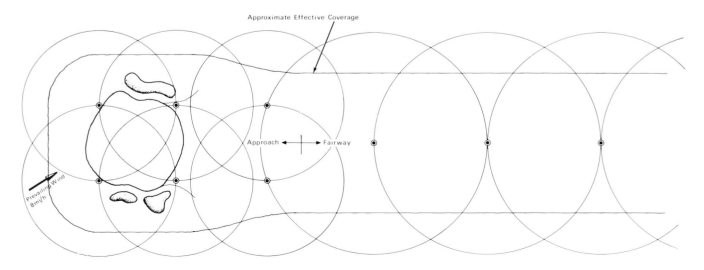

Figure 14-12 Approach Watered with Same Sprinklers Used for Greens

sprinklers with ¼ x ¹¹⁄₆₄ nozzles at 75 lb/in² (interpolated) with 127 ft diameter of coverage. Triangular spacing was used in the fairways.

Spacing. Head spacing in fairways is based on manufacturer's recommendation. See wind deration note, Figure 14-21. A spacing of 64 ft is used for winds up to 10 mi/h (127 x .50 = 63.5). Row spacing is 55.4 ft (64 x .866 = 55.4). Rows were located equi-distant from the center line of the fairway.

Note: Diameters of coverage (not to scale) are shown for illustration only.

The first head (A) from the green on one row was located so that its circumference of coverage is 10 ft from edge of putting surface. The first head from the tee on the same row (not shown) was located and heads on the row were equal spaced between the heads at each end of the fairway. Heads on the other row were located with consideration for triangular spacing and the row spacing requirement. A fill-in head (B) was added at reduced spacing between the green and the normal spacing layout in the fairway.

A fill-in head is normally required on one row when a square pattern is used for the green and approach, and a triangular pattern is used in the fairway. A smaller diameter of coverage may be required (or desired) for the fill-in head.

Effective Coverage. Using 60% of diameter to estimate the effective coverage, the total width of EC for the two-row system would be 132 ft (127 x .60 + 55.4 RS = 131.6).

Green Approach. Sprinklers in the approach to a green are often programmed separately from greens and fairways because irrigation and maintenance requirements vary for all three areas. In some cases, approach sprinklers will be programmed with green controllers.

Often the approach to a green is maintained wider than the fairway or green. Figure 14-14 shows one example. A row of three sprinklers, the same as those used at the green and in the fairway, were used in the approach. Row line is parallel to the row line of the two heads watering the green.

Head (D) was located first by triangulating from adjacent heads at the green, so that its circumference of coverage is 10 ft from the green's putting surface. Heads (C) and (E) provide the additional width of coverage.

Head (A) is on the standard spacing pattern for the fairway. Head (B) is a fill-in between the approach heads (D) and (E) and the fairway standard pattern.

Alternate Layouts. Square spacing is frequently used in fairways and approaches. If the greens also have square spacing, as in Figures 14-13 and 14-14, fill-in head (B) would be eliminated. Conversely, contiguous triangular spacing throughout all three areas does not require fill-in heads. As previously mentioned, fill-in heads are only required to join mis-matched square and triangular spacings.

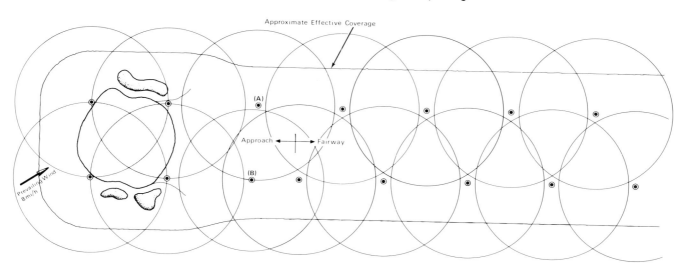

Figure 14-13 Exemplary 2-Row Head Layout for Fairway

Golf Course Systems

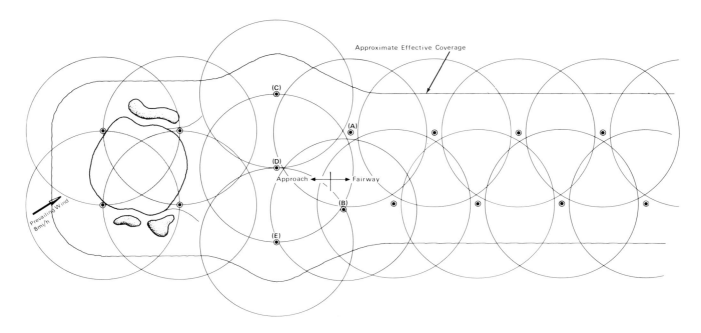

Figure 14-14 One Method to Increase Width of Approach Watering

Square spacing provides a slightly wider maintained fairway, but precipitation may not be as uniform within the system. And, more heads are required. For example, in Figures 14-13 and 14-14, spacing the length of the fairway would be reduced from 64 ft to 57 ft for square spacing.

In many two-row systems, larger diameter of coverage heads are used to obtain a greater width of coverage.

Precipitation. Average system precipitation within multiple-row systems is determined by formula pre-

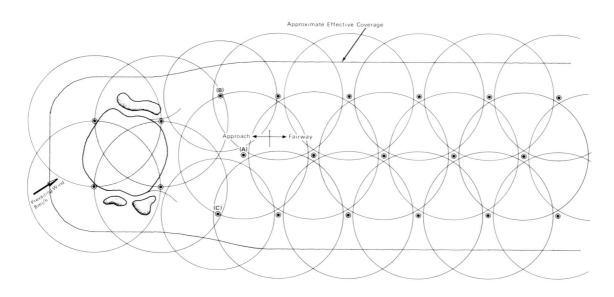

Figure 14-15 Exemplary 3-Row Head Layout for Fairway

sented in Chapter 8: System Distribution: Precipitation: Full-circle Sprinklers.

THREE-ROW SYSTEMS. With the exception of the complete coverage system, sometimes referred to as "wall-to-wall", the three-row system as shown in Figure 14-15 will provide the greatest width of fairway coverage. Many two-row systems will require a three-row layout on some of the extra-wide fairways.

In most cases, smaller coverage diameter sprinklers can be used with three-row systems. Better distribution

is provided, and with lower flow rates and pressure requirement, smaller pipe sizes are possible for much of the zone piping.

Effective Coverage. For comparison, a 55 ft increase in width of coverage would occur if the same sprinkler and spacing used for the two-row example layout were used for a three-row layout. Width of coverage would increase to 187 ft due to the addition of one row space (two-row EC of 131.6 + 55.4 = 187).

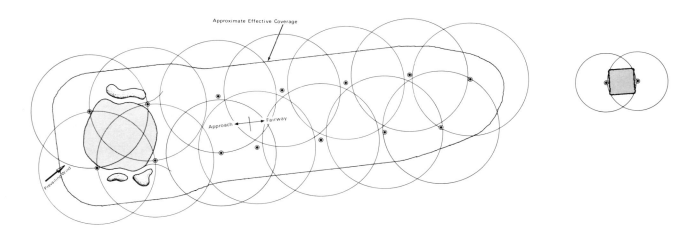

Figure 14-16 Fairway Approach Not Watered

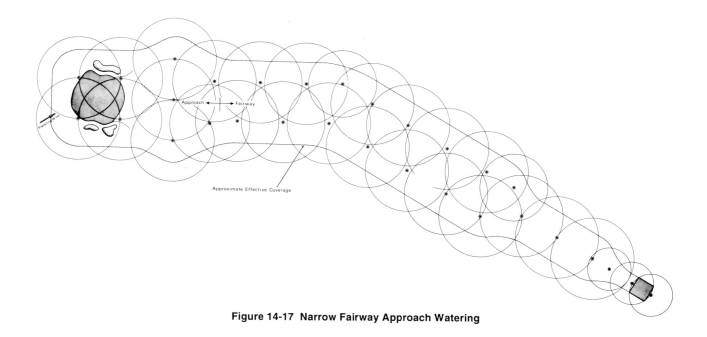

Figure 14-17 Narrow Fairway Approach Watering

Golf Course Systems

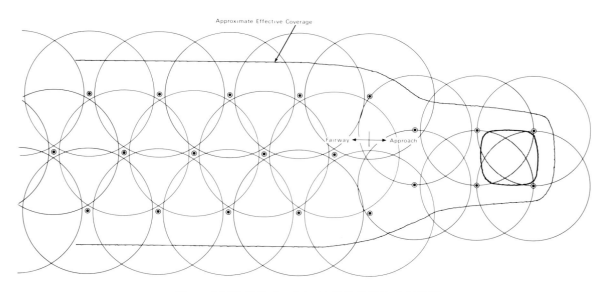

Figure 14-18 Watering Approach Full Fairway Width

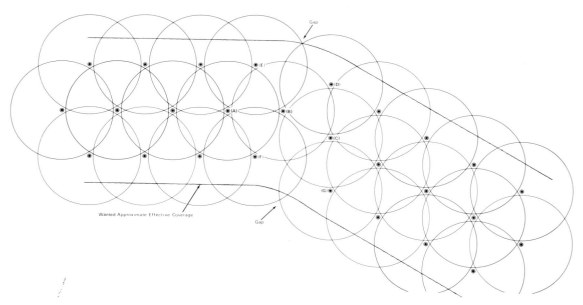

Figure 14-19 Development of Dog-Leg Layout

In Figure 14-15, the center row of heads was laid out first on center line of the fairway. (A) was located with its circumference of coverage 10 ft from putting surface of green. The rest of the heads in the row were equal spaced between head (A) and the first head from the tee. The two outside rows of heads were triangularly spaced with the center row.

Green Approach. Heads (A), (B), and (C) water the approach and, therefore, will be operated independently from heads watering the green and fairway.

Precipitation. For the example three-row fairway system, precipitation was calculated to be .61 in/h. Flow was interpolated at 22.4 gpm, Figure 14-21 at 75 lb/in^2.

$$Precipitation = \frac{gpm\,(one\ head)\ x\ 96.25}{spacing\ x\ row\ spacing} = {^{in}/_h}$$

Then:

$$Precipitation = \frac{22.4\ x\ 96.25}{64\ x\ 55.4} = {^{in}/_h}$$

$$Precipitation = .61\ {^{in}/_h}$$

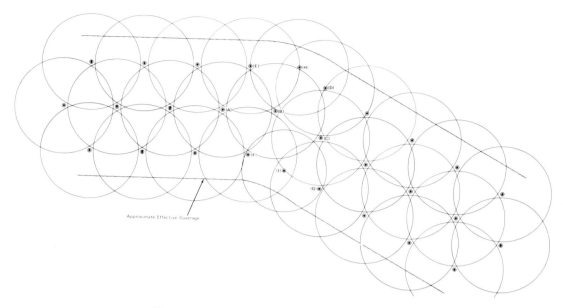

Figure 14-20 Completed Layout of Dog-Leg Fairway

FAIRWAY APPROACHES. When possible, fairway sprinklers are equally spaced between the green approach heads and the fairway approach heads. The following examples of fairway approach watering, and variations of same, are also applicable to other designs for fairway systems.

Fairway Approach Not Watered. Figure 14-16 illustrates a system for a hole where the fairway approach is not watered. On a golf course incorporating this feature, the fairway approach is maintained in a condition similar to the roughs. The last fairway head, or heads, are located so overthrow will provide sufficient watering on the maintained area.

Narrow Fairway Approach. The width of the fairway approach is often maintained much narrower than the rest of the fairway. In this case, a single row of sprinklers may be used in the approach to a fairway watered with a multi-row system. Figure 14-17 shows this method. In the example, the same sprinklers used in the fairway are also used in the approach.

Full-Width Fairway Approach. Fairways are also maintained at full width, almost to the tee. This method is often used with larger tees; the fairway narrows to the tee width as shown in Figure 14-18.

DOG-LEG FAIRWAYS. Systems should be laid out to emphasize dog-legs, as shown in Figure 14-20.

To develop the dog-leg layout, Figure 14-19, an equal spacing of the center row of heads was maintained

through the turn, heads (A), (B) and (C). The row of heads on the outside turn were then spaced properly with those on the center row. This left a sizeable gap in the layout pattern between heads (E) and (D). When the inside row of heads was properly spaced with the center row, insufficient coverage occurred between heads (F) and (G).

In Figure 14-20, fill-in head (H) was added to the outside row, and located to provide relatively equal overlap with heads (B), (E), and (D). Fill-in head (I) completed coverage inside the dog-leg. If normal spacing had been maintained on the outside row without a fill-in head, the turn on the dog-leg would have been straightened significantly.

Occasionaly, a "bulge" is required on the outside of the dog-leg turn for more emphasis. In this event, two or three sprinklers may be added.

For 2-row systems, dog-legs are handled similarly, Figure 14-17. The row of heads on the inside turn is laid out first. Equal spacing is maintained through the turn, same as with the center row of the 3-row system. The fill-in head is then located as needed in the outside row.

These procedures are the same for triangular or square spacing.

Golf Course Systems

PK60AF (FULL CIRCLE) Maximum Recommended Operating Pressure As Noted

Nozzle	Operating Pressure PSI	Flow GPM	Diameter Coverage (ft.)
B12 3/16	40	6.7	87
	50	7.5	89
	60	8.3	91
	70	9.1	93
	80	9.8	95
B13 13/64	40	7.2	88
	50	8.2	90
	60	9.1	92
	70	10.0	94
	80	10.8	96
B14 7/32	40	8.5	89
	50	9.6	91
	60	10.6	93
	70	11.6	95
	80	11.9	97
B15 15/64	40	9.6	90
	50	10.5	92
	60	11.6	94
	70	12.7	96
	80	13.3	98

PK60AP (PART CIRCLE) Maximum Recommended Operating Pressure As Noted

Nozzle	Operating Pressure PSI	Flow GPM	Radius Coverage (ft.)
B12 3/16	40	6.7	44
	50	7.5	45
	60	8.3	46
	70	9.1	47
	80	9.8	48
B13 13/64	40	7.1	45
	50	8.1	46
	60	9.1	47
	70	10.1	48
	80	11.1	49
B14 7/32	40	8.6	46
	50	9.6	47
	60	10.6	48
	70	11.6	49
	80	12.6	50
B15 15/64	40	9.8	47
	50	10.8	48
	60	11.8	49
	70	12.8	50
	80	13.8	51

PK70AF (FULL CIRCLE) Maximum Recommended Operating Pressure As Noted

Nozzle	Operating Pressure PSI	Flow GPM	Diameter Coverage (ft.)
E12 x A11 3/16 x 11/64	50	12.5	102
	60	13.8	105
	70	15.1	107
	80	16.4	110
	90	17.8	112
E13 x A11 13/64 x 11/64	50	15.0	110
	60	16.4	113
	70	17.8	117
	80	19.0	120
	90	20.2	122
E14 x A11 7/32 x 11/64	50	16.2	114
	60	17.5	120
	70	18.8	123
	80	20.1	126
	90	21.5	126
E16 x A11 1/4 x 11/64	50	19.0	116
	60	20.3	122
	70	21.7	126
	80	23.0	129
	90	24.3	129

PK70AP (PART CIRCLE) Maximum Recommended Operating Pressure As Noted

Nozzle	Operating Pressure PSI	Flow GPM	Radius Coverage (ft.)
B14X 7/32	50	10.5	53
	60	11.3	55
	70	12.0	56
	80	12.8	58
	90	13.5	59
B15X 15/64	55	12.5	55
	60	13.0	56
	70	14.0	57
	80	15.0	59
	90	16.0	60
B16X 1/4	60	14.0	57
	70	15.0	58
	80	16.0	60
	90	17.0	61
B17X 17/64	60	15.7	58
	70	16.8	59
	80	17.8	61
	90	19.0	62
B18X 9/32	65	18.1	59
	70	18.6	60
	80	19.7	62
	90	20.8	63

PK80AF (FULL CIRCLE) Maximum Recommended Operating Pressure As Noted

Nozzle	Operating Pressure PSI	Flow GPM	Diameter Coverage (ft.)
E18 xA12 9/32 x 3/16	60	22.0	114
	70	24.0	120
	80	26.0	126
	90	27.5	128
	100	29.0	130
E20 x A12 5/16 x 3/16	65	26.7	128
	70	27.7	133
	80	29.5	136
	90	31.4	141
	100	33.1	142
E22 xA13 11/32 x 13/64	70	31.5	138
	80	33.5	146
	90	35.7	147
	100	37.5	147
E24 x A13 3/8 x 13/64	75	35.5	146
	80	36.7	146
	90	38.7	147
	100	40.7	147

Wind Deration for Rotary Sprinklers

- Diameters of coverage shown in tables are for still air.

  Head Spacing = Diameter of coverage x Deration factor
  (selected from Perf. Table)   (listed below)

- Spacing with wind deration as follows:

Miles/Hour	Multiply Diameter in Table by:	
	Δ	⊐
5	.55	.50
10	.50	.45

K90F (FULL CIRCLE) Maximum Recommended Operating Pressure As Noted

Nozzle	Operating Pressure PSI	Flow GPM	Diameter Coverage (ft.)
F24 x A11 3/8 x 11/64	60	37.0	170
	70	39.0	180
	80	41.0	184
	90	42.0	187
	100	43.0	188
F28 x A11 7/16 x 11/64	65	48.0	184
	70	50.0	186
	80	52.0	190
	90	54.0	194
	100	56.0	194
F32 x A11 1/2 x 11/64	70	62.0	194
	80	67.0	198
	90	71.0	200
	100	76.0	202
F24 x A14 3/8 x 7/32	60	40.0	170
	70	42.8	180
	80	45.5	184
	90	48.1	187
	100	51.0	188
F28 x A14 7/16 x 7/32	65	51.5	184
	70	53.3	186
	80	57.0	190
	90	60.5	194
	100	64.1	194
F32 x A14 1/2 x 7/32	70	66.7	194
	80	70.5	198
	90	74.5	200
	100	78.3	202

K90P (PART CIRCLE) Maximum Recommended Operating Pressure As Noted

Nozzle	Operating Pressure PSI	Flow GPM	Radius Coverage (ft.)
F24 x A11 3/8 x 11/64	60	37.0	85
	70	39.0	90
	80	41.0	92
	90	42.0	93
	100	43.0	94
F28 x A11 7/16 x 11/64	65	48.0	92
	70	50.0	93
	80	52.0	95
	90	54.0	97
	100	56.0	97
F32 x A11 1/2 x 11/64	70	62.0	97
	80	67.0	99
	90	71.0	100
	100	76.0	101
F24 x A14 3/8 x 7/32	60	40.0	85
	70	42.8	90
	80	45.5	92
	90	48.1	93
	100	51.0	94
F28 x A14 7/16 x 7/32	65	51.5	92
	70	53.3	93
	80	57.0	95
	90	60.5	97
	100	64.1	97
F32 x A14 1/2 x 7/32	70	66.7	97
	80	70.5	99
	90	74.5	100
	100	78.3	101

Figure 14-21 Exemplary Rotary Sprinkler Performance Tables

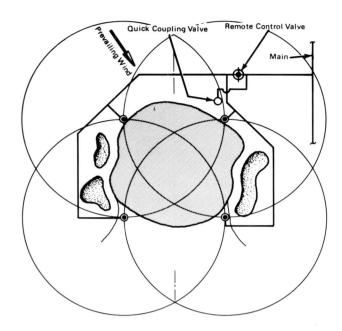

Figure 14-22 Block-Type Zone for Green

ZONING

Generally accepted practice today is to design golf course systems with small zones rather than block-type zones: (see Figure 14-32 for illustration of block-type zoning). Small zones provide many advantages:

1. Better control to offset effect of wind when watering critical areas such as greens.
2. Variable precipitation on small, adjoining areas with different uses.
3. Best control of precipitation for rolling terrain and soils with different absorption rates.
4. Use of smaller zone remote control valves (RCV) and piping.
5. Use of smaller mains by "scattering" zones that operate simultaneously.

GREENS--TEES
Several zoning methods are used.

BLOCK METHOD. Figure 14-22 shows a green watered by operation of a single control valve. This method doesn't allow control to offset effect of wind. Also, valve and pipe sizes are larger than those required when using multiple circuits as discussed in the following method.

MULTIPLE ZONES. Watering of the green in Figure 14-23 is controlled by two zones. Note that one zone

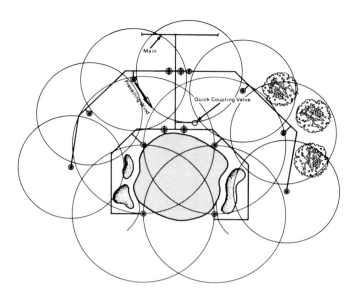

Figure 14-23 Multiple Zones for Green and Collar Watering

controls the sprinklers on the windward side of the green. And, the other zone controls watering on the leeward side. Sprinklers on the windward side are generally operated longest, providing the best total distribution on the green.

Figure 14-23 also shows sprinklers watering the collar area as often requested. Since this area normally requires a different amount of watering, sprinklers are operated separately from the green. The collar sprinklers in this example are also controlled in two zones to maintain the advantage of smaller pipe and valves inherent with small zones. The Quick Coupling Valve shown is used for supplemental hand watering when required.

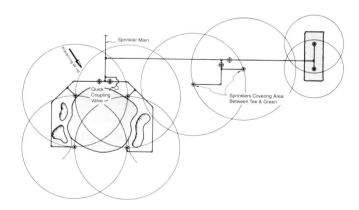

Figure 14-24 Zoning Green, Tee and Sprinklers Between

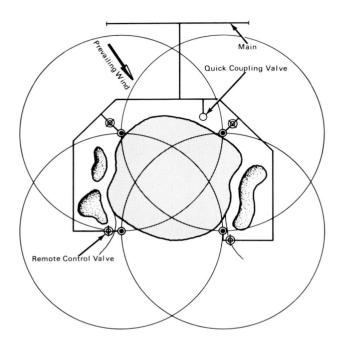

Figure 14-25 Separate Control Valve for Each Sprinkler Watering Green

The cart path area between each green and following tee is usually maintained like fairway turf. Number of heads and size of sprinkler coverage depends on distance between each green and the next tee. Width of area maintained usually requires only a single row of heads.

Figure 14-24 shows separate zoning of the sprinklers watering the area between the green and tee. Note that the head closest to the tee should be located so its circumference won't overlap onto the tee. Distance should be the same as recommended for greens: l0 ft. One additional head (connected to tee zone) between the tee and fairway head would improve coverage on the tee and fairway.

SEPARATE VALVES FOR HEADS. Figure 14-25 shows a separate control valve for each head, commonly referred to as valve-under-head or valve-in-head, which provides maximum flexibility for green watering. This level of control may or may not be effectively used, although it is often considered desirable. A schematic of valve-under-head is shown in Figure 14-27. With valve-in-head, the valve is an integral part of the head.

A system with a separate control valve for each head will require many additional controller stations (and controllers) since each valve must be on a separate station to provide maximum flexibility. However, the initial system cost is not the only factor of consideration, since system maintenance is also very important. Each extra valve represents some level of future maintenance and repair.

FAIRWAYS

In addition to the considerations previously listed, final sizing of fairway zones will vary depending on design of system, its operating characteristics and flow and pressure requirements of the sprinklers. Those sprinklers in the area known as the green approach are, however, usually operated as a separate zone.

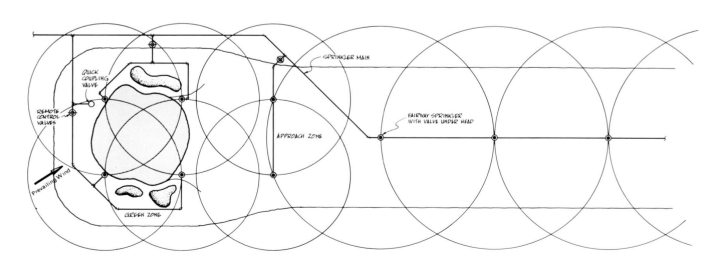

Figure 14-26 Single-Row Fairway System With Valve-Under-Head

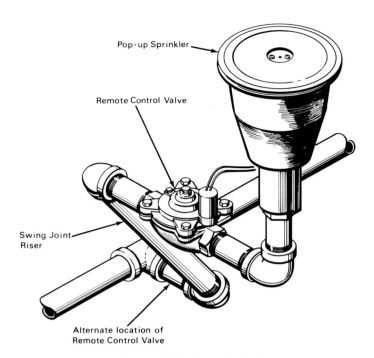

Figure 14-27 Valve-Under-Head

SINGLE ROW SYSTEMS. The supply main for single row systems is generally installed approximately under the row of fairway heads as shown in Figure 14-26.

A remote control valve is installed in a swing joint riser to each head as illustrated in Figure 14-27. The valve can also be installed in the leg of the swing joint connected to the main. However, this location is not desirable if the depth of the main would make maintenance of the valve difficult. *Note:* See Figure 14-53 for details of swing-joints.

MULTI-ROW SYSTEMS. There are several methods of zoning multi-row fairway systems depending on flow and pressure requirements, and grade of fairway. Some common zoning practices are reviewed for 2-row and 3-row systems along with some special considerations. With all methods, the green and fairway approach heads are zoned separately.

The sprinkler main is normally routed in the rough just outside the maintained fairway as shown in Figures 14-28 and 14-29. Although routing the main down the center of the fairway would reduce cost slightly, the advantages of the methods shown far outweigh the cost differential.

1. The mains and valves can be installed without interrupting play on the course.
2. Zone piping can be installed in substantially less time when mains have been installed previously. Also, trenches can be backfilled as piping installation of each zone is completed. Thus, interruption of play is further reduced.
3. If fairway sod is to be removed and replaced, it can be easily preserved for the short time it is out of place. Also, by placing the main in service first, each area can be tested and watered immediately after zone is completed.
4. Maintenance on the remote control valves, when required, does not disturb the fairway turfgrass.
5. Valve boxes should always be installed over remote control valves for ease of valve maintenance. Perhaps even more important, zones may be operated manually from the box to check and adjust sprinkler operation.

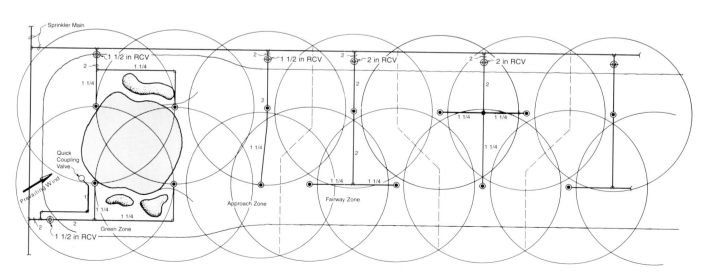

Figure 14-28 Two-Row System: 3 Heads Per Fairway Zone

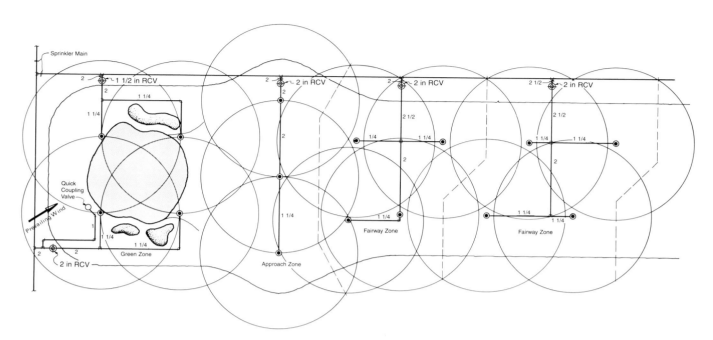

Figure 14-29 Two-Row Systems: 4 Heads Per Fairway Zone

6.With valves in the rough, there will be fewer complaints about balls bouncing off valve boxes.

Two-Row Systems. The 2-row sprinkler layout of Figure 14-13 has been zoned with three sprinklers per zone, a common method, (Figure 14-28). Note that varying precipitation can be programmed for relatively small areas throughout the length of the fairway. In this illustration, individual areas are approximately 14,000 ft^2; dashed lines indicate average coverage of zones.

Figure 14-29 illustrates 4-sprinkler fairway zones for the layout of Figure 14-14. Average of areas that can be watered separately (shown by dashed lines) is larger than 3-sprinkler zones; pipe and valve are also larger. Note that a wider approach is watered with three sprinklers.

Figure 14-30 illustrates some deviations in zoning methods discussed previously.
Zoning in this fairway is basically 3-head type. However, the lengthwise grade of the fairway, and the approach area, slope downward into zone F1 forming

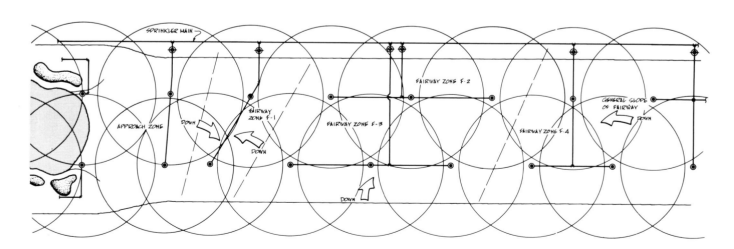

Figure 14-30 Alternate Zoning Methods

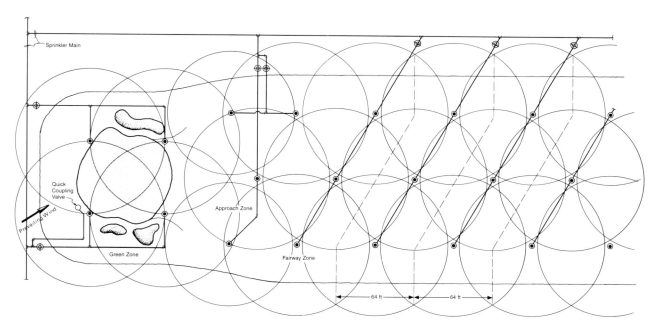

Figure 14-31 Zoning 3-Row Systems

a shallow gully. Because of the downward slopes there may be some runoff from the adjacent zones into Zone F-1. Therefore, the sprinklers in this area are zoned separately to reduce precipitation with a shorter watering period.

Figure 14-30 illustrates another method of altering zones to accommodate grade changes. The area of Zones F-2 and F-3 changes from a grade lengthwise of the fairway to crosswise. Compensation for run-off from one zone to another should be provided. Zoning lengthwise of the fairway for the distance of the cross grade permits separate watering times for two levels of the grade. Small zones permit change of zone shapes

even after design is completed and installation has started. Note that when grade returns to lengthwise, zoning reverts to normal.

Three-Row Systems. A common design practice of zoning 3-row systems is illustrated in Figure 14-31. This head layout was developed in Figure 14-15. The option of varying precipitation is provided in 64 ft wide strips for the length of the fairway. Although width of fairway coverage is greater than the 2-row system just discussed, sprinkler diameter of coverage and flow requirements for zones are less. Note, however, that one sprinkler which would normally be considered a fairway head is zoned with the approach. This was done to

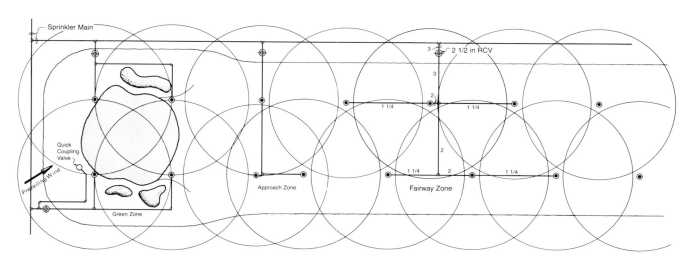

Figure 14-32 Block-Type Zoning

Golf Course Systems

	Heads Per Zone	Coverage Diameter ft	Spacing ft	Width Effective Coverage ft.	Flow, One head gpm	Flow, Average Zone gpm	Sprinkler Pressure required lb/in^2	Valve Size in	Average Precipitation in/h
Single-Row Figure 14-26:	1	186	90	112	50	50	70	2	.33
Two-Row: Figure 14-28:	3	127	64	132	22.4	67.2	75	2	.61
Figure 14-29:	4	127	64	132	22.4	89.6	75	2	.61
Figure 14-32:	6	127	64	132	22.4	134.4	75	2½	.61
Three-Row: * Figure 14-31:	3	127	64	187	22.4	67.2	75	2	.61

* Limited to EC comparison to two-row system.

Figure 14-33 Comparison of Different Type Fairway Systems and Zones

maintain symmetrical zones down the length of the fairway because of the change from square spacing at the green to triangular spacing. The approach could have been designed with four heads on one zone; however, using two zones provides more flexible control.

Methods of changing zone shapes illustrated for the 2-row system are readily adapted for 3-row systems.

BLOCK-TYPE FAIRWAY ZONES. Another method of zoning, Block-Type, is illustrated in Figure 14-32. As can be seen, larger valve and pipe sizes are required; mains are usually larger because of a greater concentration of flow; higher main pressures may be needed; and less control of varying precipitation results.

SUMMARY. The different zonings of fairway systems are compared in Figure 14-33.

ALLOWABLE OPERATING TIME

Golf courses must be irrigated at night when not in use. This is also true of other large turf areas like parks. The total time allowed for completion of an irrigation cycle can be quite restrictive.

Therefore, a program of operation must be established before designing the piping system. In addition, the water supply must be adequate for completion of the irrigation schedule within the time period allowed.

The number of hours of darkness, between sunset and sunrise, serves as a guideline for determining allowable operating time.

HOURS OF DARKNESS. The table in Figure 14-34 shows the minimum number of hours between sunset and sunrise for each month at various latitudes. For example, the shortest period of darkness for Seattle, Washington at an approximate latitude of 48N is 7 hours, 57 minutes in the month of June, in the midst of the irrigation season. Thus, operating time, normally, should not exceed 8 hours.

Since there may be other considerations and special circumstances affecting each golf course, project officials should be consulted for an acceptable "timetable" for starting and ending the period of watering.

EXEMPLARY GOLF COURSE DESIGN

The golf course sprinkler system illustrated in Figure 14-36 is reviewed in the following text. Although only the front nine holes (1-9) are shown because of space limitation, it is an eighteen hole course, and the piping and control system will be so designed. Assume therefore, for the sake of illustration, that the back nine holes (10 - 18) are exactly the same as the nine shown.

PRE-DESIGN CONFERENCE. It is important that a pre-design conference be held before beginning the design. Since there are almost as many ways to design a system as there are courses, the conference should be considered mandatory. Besides the designer, the conference should be attended by the superintendent and all other persons who will be involved in acceptance of the design.

Although many design decisions may be left to the discretion of the systems designer, the basic require-

NORTHERN HEMISPHERE: Read down and from left

Latitude	Jan		Feb		Mar		Apr		May		Jun		Jul		Aug		Sep		Oct		Nov		Dec		
°N	h	min	h	min	h	min	h	min	h	min	h	min	h	min	h	min	h	min	h	min	h	min	h	min	
0	11	53	11	53	11	53	11	53	11	53	11	52	11	52	11	53	11	54	11	53	11	53	11	53	0
5	12	05	11	58	11	51	11	42	11	37	11	35	11	35	11	42	11	47	11	55	12	03	12	08	5
10	12	19	12	04	11	47	11	32	11	21	11	18	11	18	11	27	11	42	11	58	12	13	12	25	10
15	12	31	12	09	11	45	11	20	11	03	10	59	10	59	11	13	11	36	12	00	12	25	12	42	15
20	12	47	12	16	11	40	11	08	10	45	10	40	10	40	11	00	11	29	12	03	12	35	12	59	20
25	12	59	12	21	11	37	10	55	10	25	10	17	10	20	10	42	11	23	12	05	12	48	13	18	25
30	13	15	12	29	11	32	10	41	10	04	9	56	9	57	10	26	11	15	12	07	13	01	13	38	30
32	13	23	12	32	11	31	10	35	9	54	9	43	9	46	10	18	11	11	12	10	13	07	13	48	32
34	13	30	12	35	11	29	10	27	9	44	9	33	9	36	10	08	11	07	12	10	13	13	13	58	34
36	13	37	12	38	11	27	10	21	9	32	9	21	9	24	10	04	11	03	12	12	13	19	14	08	36
38	13	45	12	39	11	25	10	13	9	20	9	11	9	14	9	51	11	00	12	12	13	25	14	18	38
40	13	53	12	44	11	22	10	08	9	12	9	00	9	03	9	44	10	56	12	14	13	21	14	27	40
42	14	03	12	48	11	20	9	59	9	01	8	45	8	48	9	34	10	53	12	15	13	39	14	40	42
44	14	13	12	52	11	18	9	51	8	44	8	31	8	35	9	24	10	47	12	17	13	46	14	52	44
46	14	23	12	56	11	14	9	41	8	30	8	14	8	18	9	14	10	43	12	18	13	54	15	06	46
48	14	33	13	00	11	12	9	31	8	14	7	57	8	00	9	06	10	37	12	20	14	04	15	20	48
50	14	46	13	05	11	08	9	21	7	57	*7	38	*7	43	8	47	10	31	12	22	14	13	15	36	50
52	15	00	13	10	11	06	9	08	*7	37	*7	16	*7	21	8	32	10	25	12	23	14	24	15	53	52
54	15	13	13	16	11	02	8	56	*7	16	*6	52	*6	57	8	15	10	17	12	26	14	35	16	12	54
56	15	29	13	22	10	58	8	42	*6	51	*6	22	*6	29	*7	55	10	10	12	28	14	47	16	36	56
58	15	49	13	29	10	53	*8	24	*6	22	*5	50	*5	57	*7	35	10	01	12	30	15	01	17	02	58
60	16	09	13	36	10	47	*8	05	*5	45	*5	08	*5	17	*7	11	9	51	12	32	15	18	17	32	60
	h	min	h	min	h	min	h	min	h	min	h	min	h	min	h	min	h	min	h	min	h	min	h	min	°S
	Jul		Aug		Sep		Oct		Nov		Dec		Jan		Feb		Mar		Apr		May		Jun		Latitude

*Twilight lasts all night during all or part of month

SOUTHERN HEMISPHERE: Read up and from right

Figure 14-34 Minimum Hours of Darkness: Sunset to Sunrise

ment for the fairways must be determined (or approved) by the golf course superintendent and/or other individuals responsible for the irrigation system.

In most cases, the number of sprinkler rows and related width of coverage provided, will be based on some level of compromise considering the average width of the fairways, width of irrigation desired, system cost, water consumption (volume available and cost) and system maintenance requirements.

The system shown in Figure 14-36 provides a "basic" two-row system as requested. The estimated width of coverage in the 125 to 130 ft range includes a degree of compromise (original request for expanded coverage in two fairways was not included).

Note: Depending on the width of fairways and the minimum width of coverage desired, a similar (or increased) level of compromise can occur with larger (or much larger) diameter of coverage sprinklers, or a three-row system.

GREENS. Two zones water the greens, one windward and one leeward, as requested by the course superin-

tendent. The practice green and greens 3, 7, and 9 which require more than four sprinklers each, are similar to the green head layout of Figure 14-6.

TEES. Tees are watered with two sprinklers each: one at the front and the other at the back like the example of Figure 14-10. There are a few exceptions.

FAIRWAYS. Because of grade changes, fairway 9 has several zones running lengthwise as illustrated in Figure 14-30. A portion of fairway 8 uses a single-row system because of special conditions. A widened dogleg and approach to green 7 required a 3-row system in this area.

PIPING SYSTEM. A simple looped supply main was best suited for the system. Two legs were routed to bisect the fairways as much as possible. Branch mains were located just outside the fairways in the rough. In two cases, fairways were close enough together that a single branch main serves both.

Note that two legs of the loop run parallel and adjacent to fairways, substituting for branch mains. Also note that one leg is part of the loop for the back nine.

Golf Course Systems

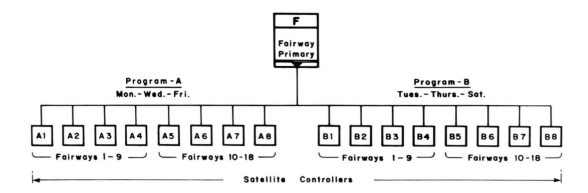

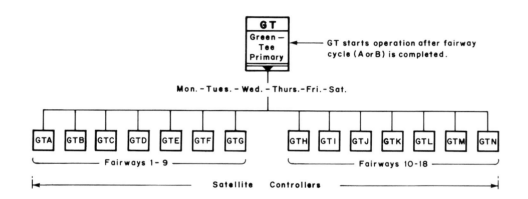

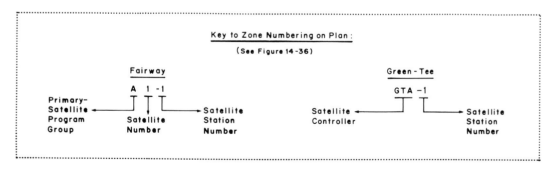

Figure 14-35 Schedule of Operation

It should be understood that Figure 14-36 is not necessarily designed as it would be in actual practice. Rather, the example is designed to present in the simplest form as many of the basics as possible. A "SUMMARY" at the end of this section reviews some alternates.

Before sizing mains a *Program of Operation* must be developed which entails several preliminary stages.

AUTOMATIC CONTROL SYSTEM

The basic method of control that will be used must be selected before development of the operating program. Golf course systems watering greens, tees and fairways commonly use a satellite system.

Primary/satellite systems are made by several manufacturers, each employing distinctive features of their own. There are so many variables in each product line that it is not feasible to discuss all functions, operating characteristics or terminology. These control systems also vary to the point that it is not realistic to establish categories, except by similar levels of water management available with different models.

Standard irrigation controllers and computer operated controllers are alternate methods of control for golf course systems. See "Summary" later in this section of the chapter.

Conventional satellite systems, as used in the example design, are similar to standard controllers but with improved programming and operating features. Controllers are linked together to form a system of control. The primary unit operates a number of satellite controllers. The satellites, in turn, operate a number of zone valves.

Programming features for the example design are limited to basic requirements of a primary/satellite system. Automatic operation occurs when the primary unit starts a number of satellite controllers simultaneously at a preset time. Each satellite then cycles by progressing from station to station. Assignment of primary and satellite controllers and schedule of operation are provided as examples only. Design decisions discussed are typical for a golf course watering program.

Each satellite unit is normally located so that operation of all zones can be seen from its location. This also tends to reduce the size and amount of wire needed from controller to valves.

When the design is finalized, a note should be included on the plan and in the operating instructions to advise the user as to the limits of the system hydraulics and electrical power supply. Manual or automatic operation of the system should never exceed the limits established in the design.

DEVELOPMENT OF OPERATION PROGRAM

Before sizing the sprinkler system mains, a program of operation must be developed so that watering can be accomplished within the allowable operating time; in the example, 9 hours as specified by the project officials. Theoretical precipitation rates of the various zones are calculated first; this determines how long each type zone must operate.

Note: The same sprinkler and nozzle sizes are used for the fairways, greens and tees to simplify the explanation of the exemplary design. An actual design may require several different sprinklers or nozzle combinations. Head spacings used for the example system are: Greens - 57 ft square (45% of D); Fairways - 64 ft triangular (50% of D); Tees - 60 ft single-row (47% of D).

PRECIPITATION RATES. The formula for determining average precipitation rate within a system, presented in Chapter 8: Precipitation, is used except for single-row systems. The formula is restated here for convenience.

$$\frac{gpm\ (one\ head)\ x\ 96.25}{head\ spacing,\ ft\ x\ row\ spacing,\ ft} = {}^{in}\!/_h\ precipitation$$

With most systems, it is necessary to determine precipitation rate only for the average of each type zone. Slight variations in other zones can be adjusted by operation time, since all of the allowable operating time is not normally utilized in the overall program.

Greens: (square spacing)

$$Precipitation = \frac{22.4\ x\ 96.25}{57\ x\ 57} = \frac{2156}{3249} = .66\ {}^{in}\!/_h$$

Fairways: (triangular spacing)

$$Precipitation = \frac{22.4\ x\ 96.25}{64\ x\ 55.4} = \frac{2156}{3545.6} = .61\ {}^{in}\!/_h$$

Tees: (single-row)

A special formula is required to determine approximate precipitation rate for single-row systems (previously explained in the detailed discussion of this type system).

$$Precipitation = \frac{gpm\ (one\ head)\ x\ 96.25}{spacing\ x\ MC\ x\ 2}$$

$$Precipitation = \frac{22.4\ x\ 96.25}{60\ x\ 56.0\ x\ 2}$$

$$Precipitation = \frac{2156}{6720}$$

$$Precipitation = .32\ {}^{in}\!/_h$$

Golf Course Systems

REQUIRED ZONE OPERATING TIME. With the precipitation rate of the various type zones known, the next step is to determine the zone duration time for each operation. This calculation is based on the precipitation rate, precipitation required per week and the frequency of operation wanted.

During the pre-design conference, the course superintendent specified how watering will be accomplished.

A six day irrigation week was requested to provide one day for some types of grounds maintenance, and to allow for additional irrigation if necessary.

Greens: 1½ inches precipitation per week, pro-rated daily, six days per week.

Fairways: 1 inch per week, pro-rated three days per week; i.e., every other day of a six day week.

Tees: About 1¼ inch per week, pro-rated daily, six days per week.

Note: The irrigation requirement (in/wk) provided by the superintendent (or others) may, or may not, include consideration for average rainfall and irrigation efficiency. In any case, the designer should understand how the irrigation requirements were determined. It may be necessary for the designer to check the requirements as specified, or to provide assistance in developing the normal maximum requirement for design purposes. This will include consideration for the maximum ETo rate, plant factors for turfgrass species, effective rainfall (if included) and a practical goal for irrigation efficiency; see Chapter 8: Related Considerations.

The irrigation requirement, the hours available for operation per day and days available per week, will directly affect the required flow rate, the water supply system (mains and pumps) and the controller system requirements.

Zone duration time required for each operation was determined as follows:

Greens:

$$\frac{1.5 \ ^{in}/_{wk}}{.66 \ ^{in}/_h \ rate} = 2.27h \ watering \ required \ per \ wk$$

Then:

$$\frac{2.27h}{6 \ ^{cycles}/_{wk}} = .378h \ x \ 60 = 22.7 \ min \ required \ per \ cycle$$

Or:

23 min each operation (rounded off) 6 times per wk

Fairways:

$$\frac{1.0 \ ^{in}/_{wk}}{.61 \ ^{in}/_h \ rate} = 1.64h \ watering \ required \ per \ wk$$

Then:

$$\frac{1.64h}{3 \ ^{cycles}/_{wk}} = .547h \ x \ 60 = 32.8 \ min \ per \ cycle$$

Or:

33 min/each operation (rounded off) 3 times per wk

Tees:

$$\frac{1.25 \ ^{in}/_{wk}}{.32 \ ^{in}/_h \ rate} = 3.91h \ watering \ required \ per \ wk$$

Then:

$$\frac{3.91h}{6 \ ^{cycles}/_{wk}} = .65h \ x \ 60 = 39.0 \ min \ per \ cycle$$

Or:

39 min/each operation 6 times per wk.

Note: The actual programming of the controllers for system operation will depend on the irrigation requirements at the time of installation. The possible use of multiple cycles to reduce run-off will also need to be considered for the final watering schedule.

CONTROLLERS REQUIRED. Many factors must be considered when deciding on the number of controllers to use. Considerations will vary with controller system selected.

1. *Valves per Station.* More valves operated by a single station reduces the number of satellites required. However, operating more than one valve per station reduces the flexibility of control. The example system was designed with each satellite station operating only one valve to provide the maximum flexibility specified by the superintendent. NOTE: Before designing a system using multiple valves per station, determine the limitations of the equipment that will be used.

2. Satellites. Using too few satellites can reduce the disadvantages of this type control system. Added length of wire runs to valves increases wire cost. Conversely, more satellites than necessary increase wire cost since powering the extra satellites usually entails more wire and larger size.

3. *Primary Controllers.* The number of primary controllers required depends on the type of controller system (brand and model) and the flexibility required in programming the system operation. The primary controller is only one unit of a minimum, two-component system, the second required unit is the satellite controller.

The total number of satellites that can be connected or operated at the same time from a single primary controller depends on the primary-satellite system. Communication wiring between the primary and satellite controllers (number of conductors and size) will also vary, depending on the control system.

4. *Example System.* A basic primary-satellite system is used in the example design. One primary controller will be provided to control the fairway satellite units and a separate primary controller will be used for all green-tee satellites. Each satellite controller station will be connected to only one electric valve. See "SUMMARY" later in this chapter for alternate equipment to the conventional satellite system.

Satellites Required. Approximately one-half of the fairways will be watered each night, except Sunday, to provide every other day watering. Greens and tees will be watered every night, except Sunday. Thus, one-half of satellites for fairways and all satellites for greens and tees must operate each night. Greens and tees are commonly watered after fairways.

Note: In some cases, it may be necessary for green and tee zones to operate at the same time as fairway zones due to limitations in the total cycle time available.

The total cycle time per night for fairway and green/tee zones cannot exceed 9 hours. The total of 85 fairway zones will be divided into two alternate night watering groups of 43 and 42 zones. There are 31 green and tee zones that must be operated each night. For this example system, it is assumed that fairways 10 - 18 will have the same zone requirement as fairways 1 - 9, as shown in Figure 14-36. Therefore, the combined totals

for the system will be 170 fairway zones and 62 green/tee zones.

Although there are limitations in operating a required number of zones for a required length of time each, and within a limited span of time, there are some variations available for automatic system operation.

Dividing the total time available for operation between the fairway zones and green/tee zones requires consideration of several factors, such as:

1. The total number of zones in each watering group.
2. The required operating time per night for each group.
3. The total system flow requirements of the operating program.
4. The total flow requirements in each fairway or group of fairways in one area of the golf course.
5. The number of satellite controllers required.
6. The location of controllers as related to zone locations (important for manual operation and wire length, and wire size).

Regardless of any other considerations that may be required for a particular golf course design, the flow requirement of the automatic system operation is very important since it will establish the basic requirement of the water supply system (pump station, mains, etc.). The maximum flow rate and variations in requirement during operation will depend on the operating program selected by the designer.

One method of developing a program of operation is to compare the water requirements of the fairway zones to the green/tee zones, and pro-rate the operating time available based on the difference in requirement.

For example, volume required (per night) is estimated using average zone flow (catalog) and zone duration time. An "average" duration time is used for greens/tees assuming half of the stations will be assigned to green zones (23 mins) and half will be tee zones (39 mins):

Fairways:
43 zones x 67.2 gpm x 33 min = 95356.8 gallons

Greens/Tees:
31 zones x 44.8 gpm x 31 min (avg) = 43052.8 gallons

Golf Course Systems

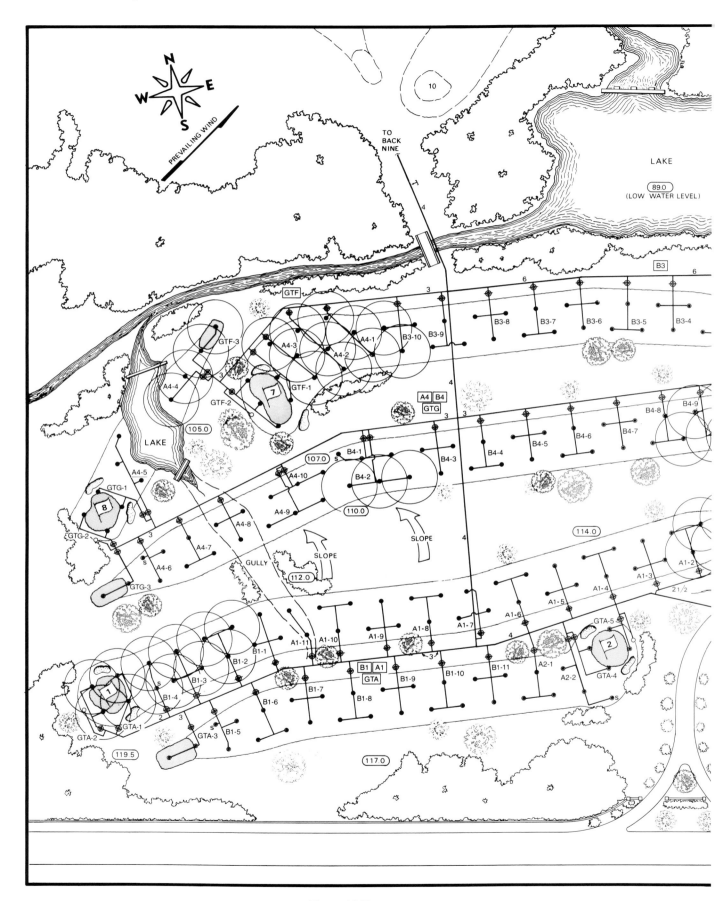

Figure 14-36

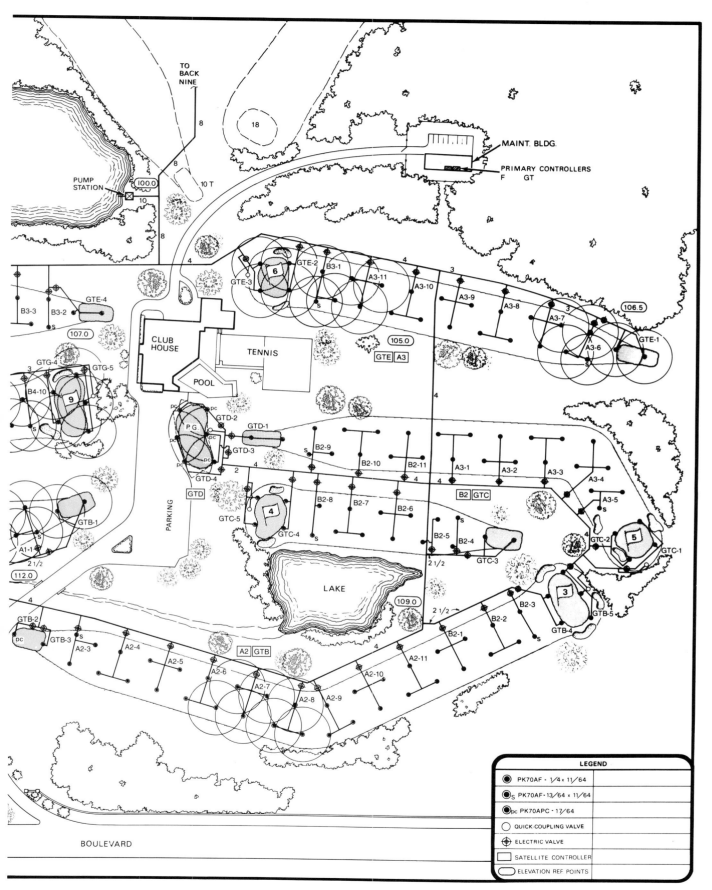

Exemplary Golf Course Sprinkler System

Golf Course Systems

The gallonage required for the greens and tees is 31.1% of the total gallons (138,409.6).

The initial cycle time allotment is based on maintaining a similar flow rate for the two watering groups. If the flow rate from the pump station to the green/tee zones was exactly equal to the flow rate of the fairway zones, the green/tee operation would require 31% of the total time available per night.

Therefore, the allotted cycle time for the green/tee operation is 2.8 h (9 h available x .31). The allotted time for the fairway irrigation cycle is 6.2 h (9 h – 2.8 h).

The maximum number of controller stations allowed for the cycle time can be determined by dividing the allotted time for each group, by the required (or average) station duration time.

$$Fairways: \frac{6.2h}{.55h} = 11 \ (11.27) \ stations$$

$$Greens/Tees: \frac{2.8h}{.51h \ (avg.)} \ 5 \ (5.49) \ stations$$

The actual time required for the maximum number of stations allowed is 6.05 h (11 x .55 h) for the fairway cycle and 2.55 h (5 x .51 h avg.) for the green/tee cycle. Total time required per night is 8.6 hours (6.05 + 2.55).

If the 43 fairway zones (one night/fairways 1 - 9) were assigned to controllers using up to 11 stations on each unit, 4 satellite controllers would be required. Total (catalog) flow required for the 4 zones (1 per satellite) operating at the same time is 268.8 gpm (4 x 67.2).

With 5 stations maximum used on the green/tee controllers, 7 satellite units would be required for the 31 green and tee zones (fairways 1 - 9). Total (catalog) flow required for the 7 zones (1 per satellite) operating at the same time is 313.6 gpm (7 x 44.8). Flow can be as high as 380.8 gpm since 3 greens have zones with 3 heads per zone.

The time allotment method described above is an example only and may not be suitable for use in some cases. Regardless of the method used to develop a program of operation, it may be desirable to analyze and compare possible variations in controlling the combined operation of the different watering groups.

In the exemplary system, the fairway controllers and zones are coded as "A" or "B" for the two alternate night watering groups. Fairway zones were assigned to an "A" group controller (up to a maximum of 11 stations), then to a "B" group controller, and so on, through the fairways to distribute the fairway flow requirement throughout the course. For example, only one "A" zone, or one "B" zone, on fairway 3 will operate automatically at the same time.

PRIMARY - SATELLITE ASSIGNMENT. The assignment of satellite controllers to primary controllers and schedule of operation for the exemplary system are shown in Figure 14-35.

Fairways. One primary controller (F) is connected to all fairway satellite controllers (A and B). Program "A" on the primary controller will be set for operation on Monday, Wednesday and Friday nights. All "A" satellites will start at the same time and operate the related zones as programmed on the individual "A" satellite controller.

Program "B" on the primary controller (F) will be set for operation on Tuesday, Thursday and Saturday nights. All "B" satellites will start at the same time and operate the related zones as programmed on the individual "B" satellite controller.

Greens and Tees. One primary controller (GT) is connected to all green/tee satellite controllers. Program "A" on the primary controller will be set for operation every day, Monday through Saturday. All "GT" satellites will start at the same time and operate the related zones as programmed on the individual "GT" satellite controller.

Start time on the primary controller for program "A" will be set for operation of the "GT" satellites after the fairway cycle is completed. Program "B" on the (GT) primary controller can be used for a syringe watering cycle if desired.

Note: The operation of the primary - satellite controller system described above is limited to the basic requirements for automatic operation of the system. The number of primary controllers required, the programming features available and the communication wiring requirements will vary with different brands and models of primary - satellite controller systems. See "SUMMARY" later in this chapter.

ITEM: (SCHEDULE 80 PVC pipe; see Appendix, Table 17)		Flow GPM	Length ft	Loss lb/in^2
1$\frac{1}{4}$ in pipe, nipples	2.0 ft (allowance)			
1$\frac{1}{4}$ in x 1 reducing bushing	1.8 (equiv. ft)			
3 ells @ 2.52 --	7.6 (equiv. ft)			
Total	(11.4) 12 ft	22.4	12	.53
1 in pipe, .5 ft (nipple)		22.4	1	.18
Total Loss Allowance for Swing-Joint				.71

Figure 14-37 Pressure Loss in Swing-Joint

ITEM: (200 psi, SDR-21 PVC pipe)	Flow GPM	Length ft	Loss lb/in^2 (a)	
1$\frac{1}{4}$ in swing - joint loss allowance [b]:	22.4		.71	
1$\frac{1}{4}$ pipe, 32 ft plus ell. 6 ft [c]:	22.4	38	.75	
2 in pipe, 56 ft plus tee branch-red. 16 ft [c]:	44.8	72	.88	
Zone Loss at Catalog Flow			2.34	
Zone Elevation Difference (+/-lb/in^2)				00
Adjusted Zone Loss (x 1.05)				2.46
Adjusted Zone Flow (67.2 x 1.05=70.6)				
2 in pipe, 70 ft plus run of tee, 5 ft [c]	70.6	75	2.13	
2 in Electric Valve:	70.6		3.30	
2 in pipe, 4 ft, valve to main plus ell, 7 ft[c]	70.6	11	.31	
Loss from Main to Zone Entrance				5.74
Sprinkler Operating Pressure				75.00
Operating Pressure Required in Main (at zone)				83.20

(a) Pipe loss calculated using Table 3, Appendix
(b) Swing-joint loss; see Figure 14-37.

Figure 14-38 Pressure Losses: Fairway Zone B1-2

SYSTEM PIPING

Pump discharge pressure must be sufficient to offset all pressure losses in the piping system and provide operating pressure required by the sprinklers. There are many methods and variations used by designers to determine the pressure requirements of a golf course or similar complex system. Some use a simple form of calculations which may or may not be close to actual requirements; others use computers. The majority, however, use methods with results somewhere between the two. In any case, sufficient pressure must be assured.

Pressure loss calculations should be close to actual, with a safety factor. If losses are greatly exaggerated

due to inaccurate calculations, costs may be increased significantly due to oversizing of pipe, fittings, pumps and related equipment. Conversely, such equipment could be under-sized resulting in an inadequate system.

The method of sizing pipe for the example is considered accurate within reason, realistic, and relatively simple in form. Flow and pressure requirement considerations are similar to those necessary for any type of sprinkler system.

PVC, SDR21, 200 Psi pipe is used exclusively in the example. Velocities should be maintained at 5 ft/s or less, if possible; (see Chapter 4: Water Hammer: Valve Closure: Pipe System Protection).

Golf Course Systems

ZONE PIPE SIZING

Sizes of zone piping are not shown on the example plan, Figure 14-36, because of its extreme reduced scale. For details of zone piping, see the zone detail plans previously reviewed in the "Zoning" section of this chapter.

There are only a few types of zones in systems such as the example. Therefore, zone piping pressure losses need to be calculated only for each type.

All full-circle sprinklers used in the exemplary plan, except fill-in heads, are PK70AF with $\frac{1}{4}$ x $\frac{11}{64}$ nozzles. Performance characteristics are 127 ft diameter and flow of 22.4 gpm at design head pressure of 75 lb/in^2. Although fill-in heads require less flow, all zone pressure loss calculations are based on this one sprinkler. This is considered good practice because unforeseen conditions may necessitate the use of the larger coverage sprinkler. Part-circle sprinklers at the practice green are PK70AP with $\frac{17}{64}$ nozzles.

Fairway head layouts and piping are as illustrated in detail, Figures 14-28 and 14-30. Four-head green layouts and piping are as illustrated in the same details.

Pressure loss calculations for zones are based on actual catalog listed (interpolated) flow. Flow and pressure loss will be adjusted, including a safety factor, after each zone calculation is completed. This is the same method of adjustment used in chapters 11 and 12 for spray and rotary systems. See Chapter 11, ZONE FLOW AND PRESSURE LOSS, for explanation of the method and example adjustment factors in Figure 12-6.

Note: Some designers increase the catalog flow by a standard (or variable) percentage before calculating zone pressure losses. Another method is based on estimating the flow rate of individual heads using actual head pressure. Pressure will be progressively higher at each successive head closer to the source by the amount of pressure lost in the piping between each two heads.

SWING JOINTS. A variety of different type swing-joint risers is used on golf course systems. These include variations of assembled units using PVC (schedule 80) threaded nipples and elbows (sch. 40 or 80), see Figure 14-52. Manufactured products with gaskets (O-rings) at swivel connections are also very common for large rotary heads and may offer advantages, especially for valve-in-head sprinklers.

Although the sprinklers (model used in the exemplary system) are threaded for one-inch pipe, a $1\frac{1}{4}$ in swing-joint will be specified to reduce the pressure loss in the riser assembly. The riser nipple (or threaded connection) into the sprinkler will be one-inch.

The pressure loss included in zone calculations is based on a "full" swing-joint (4 nipples and 3 elbows) and is used for an allowance only; see Figure 14-37.

FAIRWAY ZONES. The three basic type fairway 3-head zones for the 2-row system, such as B1-2, B1-3, and A4-9 all have about the same pressure losses. Pressure loss difference will be minor with the different piping arrangements. Zone B1-2, Fairway one, was selected for an example calculation; see Figure 14-38.

Minimum pressure required in the main for zone B1-2 is 83.2 lb/in^2 and is based on a calculation from the most distant head (choice of two at same distance) to the zone entrance (at location of head number 3). The pressure loss of 2.34 lb/in^2 and catalog flow of 67.2 gpm (3 heads at 22.4 each) are adjusted using a multiplier of 1.05. This adjustment is based on a minimum multiplier of 1.02 from the factors listed in Figure 12-6, plus a 3% safety factor for the zone loss and flow. Elevation difference within the zone (converted to lb/in^2) is listed for reference only, since there is no elevation difference in the example zone.

Pressure loss calculations shown in Figure 14-38 from the zone entrance to the mainline are based on a flow requirement of 70.6 gpm. The pressure loss in the 2 in electric valve was obtained from a manufacturer's pressure loss table (table is not provided).

The zone flow rate should be within the flow range recommended for the valve size by the manufacturer.

Note: The velocity in the 2 in pipe to the zone is 6 ft/s at the catalog flow rate of 67.2 gpm or 6.4 ft/s at the design flow rate of 70.6 gpm. This is above the general piping recommendation of 5 ft/s maximum. However, with the exception of the connection pipe at the valve, the pipe is not pressure-piping. Since this condition will exist in lateral piping to all fairway zones with 3 heads, the designer must also consider the cost difference if $2\frac{1}{2}$ in pipe is used for each zone. This is not intended as a recommendation to exceed normal piping design standards. However, it is an example of design decisions that may be necessary in some cases. A flow

ITEM: (200 psi, SDR-21 PVC pipe)	Flow gpm	Length ft	Loss lb/in^2 (a)	
1¼ in swing - joint loss allowance [b]:	22.4		.71	
1¼ pipe, 64 ft plus ell. 6 ft [c]:	22.4	70	1.38	
2 in pipe, 64 ft plus run of tee branch-red. 7 ft [c]:	44.8	71	.87	
Zone Loss at Catalog Flow			2.96	
Zone Elevation Difference (+/-lb/in^2)				00
Adjusted Zone Loss (x 1.05)				3.11
Adjusted Zone Flow (67.2 x 1.05=70.6)				
2 in pipe, 55 ft plus run of tee, 5 ft [c]:	70.6	60	1.70	
2 in Electric Valve:	70.6		3.30	
2 in pipe, 4 ft, valve to main plus ell, 7 ft [c]:	70.6	11	.31	
Loss from Main to Zone Entrance				5.31
Sprinkler Operating Pressure				75.00
Operating Pressure Required in Main (at zone)				83.42

(a) Pipe loss calculated using Table 3, Appendix
(b) Swing-joint loss; see Figure 14-37.
(c) Equivalent footage; see Figure 11-7

Figure 14-39 Pressure Losses: Fairway Zone A4-2

velocity of 6 ft/s (+/-) in "lateral" piping (or short runs of connection piping) is not uncommon.

The 3% safety factor in the flow and pressure adjustment was included only as an estimate of the basic requirement for an individual zone. Most designers will increase the zone flow rate a minimum of 10% for mainline sizing (branch and loop mains) and pump-station requirements. During automatic operation, zones nearer the source of supply will have greater pressure available and higher flow rates are common, even with pressure adjustment at the zone valves.

Additional Calculations. In many cases, additional pressure requirement calculations will be necessary due to variations in the piping arrangement, elevation differences within the zone, or some other reason. In the exemplary system, some zones are piped in a single-row style. Calculations for zone A4-2 are shown in Figure 14-39.

GREEN ZONES. Pressure requirement was calculated for a 2-head green zone. Calculations for GTA-1 are shown in Figure 11-40.

Many different fairway, green and tee zones can be related to a limited number of individual zone calculations. For example, the 3-head green zone GTG-5, number 9 green, will have a similar pressure requirement to the fairway zone A4-2, Figure 14-39. Most tee zones can be related to the 2-head green zone, Figure 14-40.

MAIN PIPE SIZING

Proper zoning and careful operational programming of golf course systems permit minimum sizing of main piping. General practice is to design for flow velocities not exceeding 5 ft/s. In the example, SDR2l, 200 psi PVC pipe is used (see Chapter 4: Water Hammer: Plastic Pipe Systems).

Fairway programming was scheduled so that only one fairway zone will operate at a time on any branch main. The same is true for green and tee zones, except for the branch main between fairways 4 and 5. Zones GTC-4 (or -5) and GTD-4 (or some other zone) will operate at the same time. In any case, only the "worst condition" for each branch main needs to be analyzed to determine the pipe size requirement.

Branch and loop mains will be sized with consideration for the 3 separate flow requirements of the automatic operation. This is very important since only one of the three (Fairway program "A" or "B" or the "GT" program) will operate at any one time; see Figure 14-35. A minimum of 85 lb/in^2 will be considered necessary for zone outlets on any branch mainline.

As previously discussed, zone flow rates are normally increased for sizing of the mainline piping. In this example system, the catalog flow rate of zones will be increased by 10% and rounded-off to the nearest gallon. Therefore, design flow for mains with 2-head zones will be 49 gpm (22.4 x 2 + 10% = 49.28). And for 3-head

Golf Course Systems

ITEM: (200 psi, SDR-21 PVC pipe)	Flow GPM	Length ft	Loss lb/in^2 (a)	
1¼ in swing - joint loss allowance [b]:	22.4		.71	
1¼ in pipe, 68 ft plus 2 ells and 45° ell, 15 ft [c]:	22.4	83	1.64	
Zone Loss at Catalog Flow			2.35	
Zone Elevation Difference (+/-lb/in^2)				00
Adjusted Zone Loss (x 1.05)				2.47
Adjusted Zone Flow (44.8 x 1.05=47.0)				
2 in pipe, 60 ft plus run of tee-red, 7 ft [c]:	47.0	67	.90	
1½ in Electric Valve:	47.0		4.10	
2 in pipe, 4 ft, valve to main plus ell, 7 ft[c]:	47.0	11	.15	
Loss from Main to Zone Entrance				5.15
Sprinkler Operating Pressure				75.00
Operating Pressure Required in Main (at zone)				82.62

(a) Pipe loss calculated using Table 3, Appendix
(b) Swing-joint loss; see Figure 14-37.
(c) Equivalent footage; see Figure 11-7.

Figure 14-40 Pressure Losses: Green Zone GTA-1

zones, the flow rate will be 74 gpm (22.4 x 3 + 10% = 73.92).

BRANCH MAINS. The branch main located between holes 1 and 2 is the longest, so it is sized first. "Worst condition" is the 3-head fairway zone B1-3 with a design flow of 74.0 gpm and 644 ft from the looped main to entrance of zone. Pipe size should not be less than 2½ in to limit flow velocity to not more than 5 ft/s. Pressure loss calculations for this zone are shown in Figure 14-41.

The zones for the green have only two heads, therefore the loss in the branch main to fairway zone B1-3 will be considerably less when only a green zone is being supplied. The portion of the branch main to zone GTA-1 is sized 2 in to balance the losses as nearly as possible. Calculations are shown in Figure 14-42.

The pressure loss calculation for the branch main to zone GTD-1, tee 5, is shown in Figure 14-43. Some combination of 2 zones can operate at the same time from the looped main to zone GTC-5, green 4. Zone GTD-1 was selected for the maximum GTD flow requirement.

All satellite controllers in an operating group will not be on the same station number during automatic operation. Although all units will start at the same time, each satellite will operate independently. Variation in station duration time, that may be necessary for some zones, will change the combination of zones operating at the same time. Many zone combinations are possible

with manual operation, even though manual operation of satellites will be limited to the same operating groups. This is an important consideration for the designer when sizing the branch mains. For example, the calculation shown in Figure 14-43, is based on the maximum flow condition for the branch main to GTC and GTD zones.

LOOPED MAIN. Determining pressure loss, and sizing of the looped main system, depends on the maximum flow it must supply at any one time. Normally this is accomplished by carefully considering the "worst-case" combination of zones operating at the same time in each operating group. Therefore, the combination selected for possible operation in each group may include one satellite controller operating on station 2, one unit operating on station 5, one unit on station 7, etc.

Some zones selected to analyze requirement will be supplied directly by the looped mains, and others will be located on branch mains. In most cases, it is not important where the zone is located on the branch, since looped mains are sized based on the flow requirement at the branch connection.

Although the combination of zones selected for possible operation at the same time in each group may not seem realistic, the objective is to determine the "worst-case" flow condition, and attempts to refine the possible flow combinations can be a time consuming task.

ITEM: (200 psi, SDR-21 PVC pipe)		Flow gpm	Pipe-Length ft	Branch Loss lb/in²
3 in pipe:	644 ft			
13 tees at 7 ft:	91			
	735 ft	74	735	3.39
Velocity: 3.1 ft/s				

Figure 14-41 Pressure Loss: Branch Main to Zone B1-3, Fairway 1

Maximum system flow for each operating group, using zone design flow established for mainline pipe sizing, will be as follows:

Fairway: Group "A" - Operates on Monday, Wednesday and Friday:

Holes   1- 9: 4 zones
Holes 10-18: 4 zones
8 zones will operate simultaneously.
8 zones at 74 gpm each = 592 gpm maximum.

Fairway: Group "B" - Operates on Tuesday, Thursday and Saturday:

Holes 1-9: 4 zones
Holes 10-18: 4 zones
8 zones will operate simultaneously.
8 at 74 gpm each = 592 gpm maximum
                     (same as "A")

Greens/Tees: Operates six nights per week, after "A" or "B":

Holes   1- 9: 7 zones
Holes 10-18: 7 zones
14 zones will operate simultaneously.

Typical flow:
14 at 49 gpm (2 head zones) = 686 gpm

Maximum flow if all 3 head zones operate at same time:
    8 at 49 gpm = 392 gpm
    6 at 74 gpm = <u>444</u> gpm
                836 gpm

The operation of the green-tee zones requires the greatest flow due to the number of zones (heads) that will be operating at the same time. A flow of 836 gpm would be required from the pump station if all 3-head

green zones operated at the same time. However, the looped main system must be designed with consideration for pressure loss, and the location of a 2-head zone may create more loss than a 3-head zone in a more suitable location.

The looped piping system will be sized with consideration for the flow requirements in each pipe section of the loop, as zones operating at the same time will be "scattered" throughout the system. Pressure loss and flow velocity are the two important items of consideration in sizing the pipe in each section. Mainline pipe sections will change at any point where the pipe size and/or flow rate changes.

Loop Loss Calculations. Pressure loss calculations for looped mains can be relatively simple or complex, depending on the number of loops, the number and location of zones operating at the same time, and the knowledge and experience of the designer. The accuracy of the calculated loss can range from a rough "guesstimate" to a fairly close estimate, depending on the amount of design time devoted to analyzing the possible flow and loss conditions, and refinement of the pressure loss calculations.

Calculations required for simple loop systems (one loop and one zone operating at a time) are discussed in Chapter 11, "LOOPED MAINS".

As previously discussed, the example golf course design shown in Figure 14-36 was developed to simplify the explanation of basic design requirements. This includes the simple loop layout shown for the front nine holes. One leg of the loop (along fairway 7) is also part of an adjacent loop that is used to supply the back nine loop. A total of 3 loops are required for the 18-hole golf course system. Flow requirements for the back nine are assumed to be exactly equal to the front nine requirement; see Figure 14-44.

The green-tee operation should be considered first for pipe sizing and pressure loss, since the total flow requirement is greater than the fairway operation (A or B). Pipe sizing for the loop main pipe sections may be based on flow velocity or pressure loss (estimate considering flow and length), or both. Initial pipe sizes selected are preliminary only, since sizes are based on a rough estimate of the flow rate in each portion of the loop system. The actual flow rate in each leg (or pipe section) of the loop will not be known until a flow ratio is established (by "trial and error" method) that will

ITEM: (200 psi, SDR-21 PVC pipe)		Flow gpm	Velocity ft/s	PipeLength ft	Loss lb/in^2
3 in pipe:	644 ft				
13 tees at 7 ft:	91				
	735 ft	49	2.0	735	1.58
2 in pipe:	137 ft				
2 tees at 5 ft:	10				
1 tee-branch:	13				
	160 ft	49	4.4	160	2.31
				Loss, Branch Main	3.89

Figure 14-42 Pressure Loss: Branch Main to Zone GTA-1, Green 1

ITEM: (200 psi, SDR-21 PVC pipe)		Flow gpm	Velocity ft/s	PipeLength ft	Loss lb/in^2
4 in pipe:	470 ft				
8 tees at 7.8 ft:	62 (table 17, Appendix)	98	2.5	532	1.22
	532 ft (2 zones)				
2 in pipe:	150 ft				
2 tees-branch at 13	26				
1 tee	5				
	181 ft (1 zone)	49	4.4	181	2.62
				Loss, Branch Main	3.84

Figure 14-43 Pressure Loss: Branch Main to Zone GTD-1, Tee 5

provide the same total pressure loss in each leg of the loop.

Calculations, flow rate changes and recalculations as necessary to establish approximately the same loss in each leg, is not difficult for a system with a single loop. However, with multiple loops, calculations can be a time-consuming task, since flow (or change in flow) in one loop will affect the flow in an adjacent loop. Some pipe sections, such as 8 and 18, and 9 and 21 in Figure 14-44, are common to two loops (same pipe with different numbers).

The flow rate in pipe sections to point "C" (1,2,3 and 4; and 5,6,7 and 8), as shown in Figure 14-45, can only be roughly estimated unless the actual flow rate in pipe section 19 (loop 3) is known. Therefore, the flow rate (or approximate rate) in all pipe sections for loops 2 and 3 must be known before the actual flow rate in pipe section 8 (or 18 on loop 3) is known for loop 1. However, the flow in pipe sections 1 and 7 (loop 1) will affect the

flow in pipe section 8 (or 18), which will affect the flow in section 19, and therefore, the distribution of flow in loops 2 and 3.

Calculations for multiple loops can be difficult, as the flow in all pipe sections and loops are interrelated, and as previously discussed, the accuracy of pressure loss calculation depends on the level of refinement.

The pressure loss calculations, shown in Figures 14-47 and 14-48, are limited to loop 1 (front nine) and are provided as an example to illustrate a typical loop calculation, flow adjustment and re-calculation. The flow rate in section 19 (loop 3) is based on an estimate only. Although calculations are not included for loops 2 and 3, similar calculations would be necessary for all loops. Example loop calculations (using a computer) are provided for all 3 loops later in this chapter.

The maximum flow rate normally used for mainline (pressure) piping is shown in Figure 14-46 for nominal pipe sizes, 3 in through 10 in. The average flow velocity of pipe sections in each leg of a loop will normally be considerably less than the maximum of 5 ft/s.

Flow velocity is a very important consideration for the systems designer; see Chapter 4, "Pipe System Protection."

The calculation shown in Figure 14-47 is based on four assumptions to establish a realistic set of flow conditions for the first pressure loss comparison of the left and right legs of loop 1, as shown in Figure 14-45. The four assumptions are as follows:

1. 100 gpm (rough estimate) will be required in pipe section 19 (loop 3), with the remaining 293 gpm requirement for the back nine being supplied through pipe section 22. Loops 2 and 3 will need to be checked to determine if this assumption is approximately correct. If the required flow in section 19 is greater than 100 gpm, the loss in loop 1 will increase, and if the flow is less than 100 gpm, the loss in loop 1 will be less than that indicated by the initial calculation.

2. The green-tee operation was analyzed to determine the possible flow requirements (not necessarily with all zones on the same controller station) around the loop that will result in the maximum pressure loss for the loop.

   Note: two of the 3-head green zones were included (GTF-2 and GTF-5). Zone GTB-5 was not included, although it may result in a slightly higher loop loss.

3. Point "C" was selected as the location on the loop where some portion of the flow requirement at that location (branch main connection) will be supplied by each leg of the loop. If point "C" is the wrong location for the flow distribution in the loop, it will become apparent as a balance in pressure loss will not be obtained in the two legs.

4. The flow requirement of 49 gpm at point "C" will be divided equally with 24.5 gpm in pipe section 5 and 24.5 gpm in section 4.

Footage equivalents for mainline fittings were not used in the loop calculation, shown in Figure 14-47. An allowance for fitting losses was included by adding an additional 10% to the actual length of each pipe section. The percentage used for fitting losses can be a standard

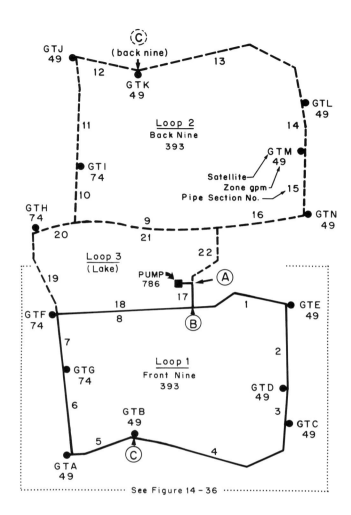

Figure 14-44 Green-Tee (Holes 1-18). Selected Flow Requirement Locations for Pressure Loss Calculations

(based on experience) or a percentage based on a simple check of the requirement in one area of the individual system.

The total loss of 5.8 lb/in^2 in the left leg is close to the 7.26 lb/in^2 total loss in the right leg. The actual loss in the loop will be somewhere between the two values.

The calculation shown in Figure 14-48 is included to illustrate a revised calculation. The flow in pipe section 5 has been increased by 10 gpm (approximately) and the flow in section 4 has been reduced by 10 gpm.

This minor refinement of the pressure loss for loop 1 includes the same estimate of flow (100 gpm) for pipe section 19. The calculated loss for the left leg is 6.47 lb/in^2 and 6.29 lb/in^2 for the right leg, or a loop loss of approximately 6.5 lb/in^2.

Golf Course Systems

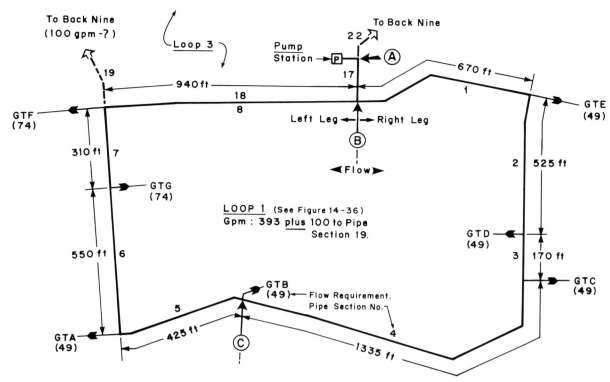

Figure 14-45 Green-Tee (Holes 1-9) Flow Requirements on Looped Main Indicated by Satellite. Pipe Sections 1 through 8.

Since loop 2 (not shown in Figure 14-36) for the back nine holes is considered to be similar for the exemplary system, the loop loss will also be similar (6.5 lb/in^2, plus or minus). However, the loss in loop 3 (around the lake) would also be a factor of consideration, and the total loss to the back nine would be greater than the loss to the front nine.

In many cases, the fairway automatic operation will have the greatest flow requirement and pressure loss. However, in the exemplary system, only 8 fairway zones operate at the same time, for a maximum flow

requirement of 592 gpm (8 at 74 each). The flow requirement locations for program "A" are shown in Figure 14-49 for all loops. The total loop pressure loss for fairway operations is as follows (calculations not provided):

Loss, lb/in^2 from Point "A":

| Program A | to satellite zones A1 - A2 --- 6.1 |
| (see Fig.14.49) | to satellite zone A7 --- 6.0 |

| Program B | to satellite zone B1 --- 3.4 (fairway 1) |
| | to satellite zone B7 --- 5.7 (fairway 15) |

Calculations by Computer. As previously discussed, complete calculations of all loops in a typical multiple loop system can be difficult for an inexperienced designer and time-consuming, regardless of experience.

Although some procedures are available to assist the designer with flow adjustments, and reduce the number of iterations required, all standard methods are based on some variation of trial and error. Complicated and repetitive calculations of this type are an excellent application for the use of a computer to provide the

SDR21. 200 psi PVC Pipe Size	gpm*
3 in	121
4 in	200
6 in	434
8 in	736
10 in	1144
	* See Table 5a, Appendix

Figure 14-46 Flow at Maximum Velocity of 5 ft/s

Pipe Section	Pipe Size	Flow Re: - gpm	Velocity ft/s[1]	Length ft [2]	Loss lb/in² [3]
Left Leg of Loop 1:					
5	4 in	½ GTB - 24.5	.6	468	.08
6	4 in	+ GTA - 73.5	1.8	605	.81
7	4 in	+ GTG -147.5	3.7	341	1.66
8	6 in	+ GTF & Sect 19 - 321.5	3.7	1034	3.25
				Total Loss, Left Leg:	5.80
Right Leg of Loop 1					
4	4 in	½ GTB - 24.5	.6	1469	.26
3	4 in	+ GTC - 73.5	1.8	187	.25
2	4 in	+ GTD - 122.5	3.1	578	2.00
1	4 in	+ GTE - 171.5	4.3	737	4.75
				Total Loss, Right Leg:	7.26

(1) Table 16, Appendix
(2) Plus 10% for fittings
(3) Table 3, Appendix

Figure 14-47 Pressure Loss Calculation for Loop 1 Based on Preliminary Estimate of Flow

designer with assistance in hydraulic design. As discussed in Chapter 11, "Computer-Aided Design", the use of computers in irrigation design is not limited to the use of CAD software to develop a design drawing.

Figure 14-50 illustrates a pressure loss calculation produced by a loop main program (software) and an inexpensive personal computer, as described in Chapter 11. The green/tee flow requirement of the exemplary design was used for comparison of the Loop 1 calculation in Figure 14-48, and to obtain the loss in all pipe sections, and loops.

Pipe sections 1 through 22 and points "A" and "C" relate to the loop main layout shown in Figure 14-44. Flow in each section is listed as a plus or minus value. This method is used to indicate the direction of flow in each section. A plus flow indicates the flow is in a clockwise direction around the loop. A minus flow indicates a counter-clockwise flow direction. Examination of notes and output data is, in most cases, self-explanatory.

The necessary data was obtained from the design plan. After input, the computer calculated, made adjustments and re-calculated all pipe sections and loops. Eight flow adjustments were required by the program to obtain the level of accuracy desired (+/- .1 lb/in²). The computer calculated 176 pipe sections for pressure loss and velocity (22 x 8 corrections) and checked 24 loops (3 x 8 cycles) in a total time span of a few minutes, including a printout.

The pressure loss of 7.8 lb/in² from point "A" to point "C" (back nine), as shown in Figure 14-50, will be the typical loop loss for the G-T operation. This loss is based on 4 of the 3-head G-T zones operating with 10 of the 2-head G-T zones, and a total flow of 786 gpm (see Figure 14-44).

A similar calculation (not provided) was produced to determine the maximum loss in the loop system if all 6 of the 3-head G-T zones were in operation at the same time with 8 of the 2-head G-T zones, and a total flow (maximum) of 836 gpm. This calculation indicates a "worst-case" loss of 9.3 lb/in² from point "A" to point "C" (back nine).

In most cases, the designer is limited to the worst-case flow condition, if multiple loop calculations are required without the use of a computer. In such cases, the designer should carefully examine the plan for all combinations of zones that may operate at the same time. Although many combinations are possible, the designer must select the combination that will require the greatest flow and/or pressure for operation.

DESIGN PRESSURE

Design pressure of the example system provides the information required for sizing the pumping station. Design pressure, in this case, will be the sum of the maximum sprinkler head pressure required and pressure losses in the zone piping, branch mains,

Golf Course Systems

looped main, supply piping from pumps to loop, any appurtenances in the supply piping, and difference in elevation between the pumps and other areas of the course. All pressure requirements have already been calculated, so these are added to the pressure required to offset losses in the supply piping and its appurtenances. This is determined in Figure 14-51 as 105 lb/in^2.

Data listed for losses and requirements in Figure 14-51 was determined as follows:

Item a. The above-ground piping from the pump station should be metal pipe (see Figure 6-28). Maximum design flow for the system (836 gpm) was used for sizing. Schedule 40 steel pipe was used for pressure loss; velocity at 3.4 ft/s.

Item b. Supply piping from the steel pipe to point "A" (loop 3) will be PVC, SDR-21.

Note: Any equipment in the supply piping (check valves, pressure control valves, etc) that will be used in the discharge piping should be included.

The following 4 items do not relate to the actual pressure requirement of an individual zone. Losses listed are maximum or typical for many different zones.

Item c. The loop loss of 9.3 lb/in^2 is the total loss from point "A" to point "C" on the back nine. This is the maximum loss in the area of pipe sections 12 and 13 on loop 2. Minor variations will occur in this area with different combinations of G-T zones in operation. The pressure loss to the same general area in loop 2 will be less (approximately 6 lb/in^2) for fairway operation.

Note: The 9.3 lb/in^2 loss is from the "worst-case" loop calculation at maximum flow, as previously discussed (calculation not provided).

Item d. The loss in the branch main of 3.39 lb/in^2 (see Figure 14-41) was used as an allowance for the pressure loss in any branch main with a 3-head zone in operation. Loss will be less for 2-head zones or mains with less total length.

Item e. The zone pressure requirement of 83.42 lb/in^2 is the maximum requirement for 2-head and 3-head zones (see Figures 14-38, 14-39 and 14-40).

Item f. The maximum elevation difference above the pump discharge is 19.5 ft, near the number 1 green (see Figure 14-36). For the example golf course, the same elevation difference is assumed in the area of pipe sections 11 and 12 (back nine).

Pressure will vary in different areas of the golf course system due to variations in pipe (friction) loss, and

Pipe Section	Pipe Size	Flow Re: - gpm	Velocity ft/s[1]	Length ft [2]	Loss lb/in^2 [3]
Left Leg of Loop 1:					
5	4 in	GTB - 34	.9	468	.15
6	4 in	+ GTA - 83	2.1	605	1.02
7	4 in	+ GTG -157	3.9	341	1.87
8	6 in	+ GTF & Sect 19 - 331	3.8	1034	3.43
				Total Loss, Left Leg:	6.47
Right Leg of Loop 1					
4	4 in	GTB - 15	.4	1469	.10
3	4 in	+ GTC - 64	1.6	187	.19
2	4 in	+ GTD - 113	2.8	578	1.72
1	4 in	+ GTE - 162	4.1	737	4.28
				Total Loss, Right Leg:	6.29

(1) Table 16, Appendix.
(2) Plus 10% for fittings
(3) Table 3, Appendix

Figure 14-48 Pressure Loss Calculation for Loop 1 with Flow Adjustment

variations in elevation (pressure loss or gain). Extreme elevation differences in one, or more, areas may require a separate mainline with special equipment to increase or decrease the pressure as necessary.

PUMPING SYSTEM

The maximum flow requirement of 836 gpm for the G-T operation will be used as the basic flow specification for the pump station. This flow rate was established using the design flow (catalog, plus 10%) for each zone and the satellite schedule of operation (automatic or manual), as shown in Figure 14-35.

In most golf course systems, a pre-engineered and pre-assembled pump station is used for the wide range of flow requirements that are necessary for the irrigation system. These automatic (supply on demand) pump stations include the necessary pumps, pump controllers, pressure and surge control equipment, and a variety of standard and optional safety features. These pumping systems are also engineered with consideration for the efficient use of energy.

The systems designer should consult with a pump engineer (with knowledge and experience in this type of pumping station) if a custom-designed pump system is desired, or required, for the sprinkler system. Pump stations and operation are discussed in Chapter 6.

In most cases, a safety factor should be included in the specification of pressure requirement at the pump station discharge. Many designers add 10% to the calculated design pressure requirement. Basic performances for selection (or design) of a pump system for the exemplary golf course system would be:

840 gpm at 115.0 lb/in^2 (105 + 10%)

Minimum flow from the pump station could be the manual operation of a single zone, or the use of a single quick-coupling valve.

WATER SUPPLY

The water supply (storage and refill) must be capable of supplying the amount of water required for each irrigation cycle. The design flows established for mainline pipe sizing (or catalog flow and some other allowance) can be used to determine the approximate total water requirement per cycle, per week, etc.

The amount required per cycle (6 nights per week for the example) can be based on a detailed list of sprinklers

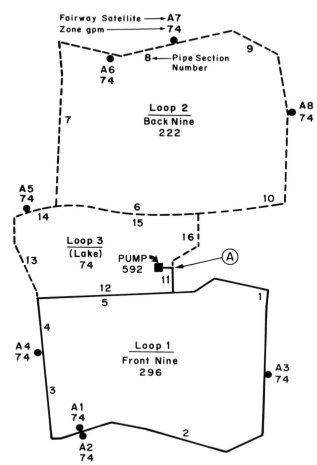

Figure 14-49 Fairway - Program "A". Selected Flow Requirement Locations for Pressure Loss Calculations (calculations not provided)

that will operate each night, including flow variations for full-circle, part-circle and different nozzle sizes. Since there are a limited number of part-circle sprinklers and nozzle sizes used in the exemplary system, an estimate based on the standard full-circle flow and the total number of heads, will provide the approximate total water requirement per cycle, example as follows:

	Heads Per Zone	Zone gpm		Duration Min.	Number Zones		Gallons
Greens:	2	49.0	x	23	x 36	=	40,572
	3	74.0	x	23	x 6	=	10,212
Tees:	1	24.0	x	39	x 4	=	3,822
	2	49.0	x	39	x 16	=	30,576
Fairways:	2	49.0	x	33	x 4	=	6,468
"A" Program	3	74.0	x	33	x 82	=	200,244

Approximate Gallons Required Per Night =   291,894

Golf Course Systems

```
****************************************************************
                   ** LOOP NUMBER  1 **

        SECT.   SIZE       FLOW      LGTH.    VEL.   LOSS   CODE
        NO.     IN.        GPM       FT.      FT/S   PSI
        ----    ----       ----      ----     ----   ----   ----
         1      4.00       161.0     670.0    4.0     4.2   20/ 15
         2      4.00       112.0     525.0    2.8     1.7   20/ 15
         3      4.00        63.0     170.0    1.6      .2   20/ 15
         4      4.00        14.0    1335.0     .3      .1   20/ 15
         5      4.00       -35.0     425.0     .9     -.2   20/ 15
         6      4.00       -84.0     550.0    2.1    -1.0   20/ 15
         7      4.00      -158.0     310.0    3.9    -1.9   20/ 15
         8      6.00      -313.8     940.0    3.6    -3.1   20/ 15<  3

     #=VELOCITY OVER 5 FPS      PIPE CODE=TYPE/'C'  <COMMON LOOP
                   REF.LOOP LOSS NO. 1 = 6.2

****************************************************************
                   ** LOOP NUMBER  2 **

        SECT.   SIZE       FLOW      LGTH.    VEL.   LOSS   CODE
        NO.     IN.        GPM       FT.      FT/S   PSI
        ----    ----       ----      ----     ----   ----   ----
         9      4.00       155.2     700.0    3.9     4.1   20/ 15<  3
        10      4.00       163.0     310.0    4.1     2.0   20/ 15
        11      4.00        89.0     550.0    2.2     1.2   20/ 15
        12      4.00        40.0     425.0    1.0      .2   20/ 15
        13      4.00        -9.0    1335.0     .2     0.0   20/ 15
        14      4.00       -58.0     170.0    1.4     -.2   20/ 15
        15      4.00      -107.0     250.0    2.7     -.7   20/ 15
        16      4.00      -156.0    1100.0    3.9    -6.5   20/ 15

     #=VELOCITY OVER 5 FPS      PIPE CODE=TYPE/'C'  <COMMON LOOP
                   REF.LOOP LOSS NO. 2 = 7.5

****************************************************************
                   ** LOOP NUMBER  3 **

        SECT.   SIZE       FLOW      LGTH.    VEL.   LOSS   CODE
        NO.     IN.        GPM       FT.      FT/S   PSI
        ----    ----       ----      ----     ----   ----   ----
        17      8.00       474.8     170.0    3.2      .3   20/ 15
        18      6.00       313.8     940.0    3.6     3.1   20/ 15<  1
        19      4.00        81.8     540.0    2.0     1.0   20/ 15
        20      4.00         7.8     370.0     .2     0.0   20/ 15
        21      4.00      -155.2     700.0    3.9    -4.1   20/ 15<  2
        22      8.00      -311.2     330.0    2.1     -.3   20/ 15

     #=VELOCITY OVER 5 FPS      PIPE CODE=TYPE/'C'  <COMMON LOOP
                   REF.LOOP LOSS NO. 3 = 4.4

****************************************************************
                   ** LOOP SYSTEM DATA **

PIPE SECTION NUMBERS:          (POINT A TO C)
  1 2 3 4 17=
                    ----> A TOTAL PRESSURE LOSS OF 6.5 PSI ┐
                                                           │
PIPE SECTION NUMBERS:          (POINT A TO C)              │
  5 6 7 8 17=                                              │
                    ----> A TOTAL PRESSURE LOSS OF 6.5 PSI ┘

PIPE SECTION NUMBERS:          (POINT A TO C -BACK 9)
  17 18 19 20 10 11 12=
                    ----> A TOTAL PRESSURE LOSS OF 7.8 PSI ┐
                                                           │
PIPE SECTION NUMBERS:          (POINT A TO C -BACK 9)      │
  13 14 15 16 22=                                          │
                    ----> A TOTAL PRESSURE LOSS OF 7.7 PSI ┘

-----------------------------------------------------------------

RE: +TO- DIFF.= .1  ( 8 )        TOTAL FLOW OF SYSTEM = 786 GPM

        PROJECT:EXEMPLARY GOLF COURSE          DATE:1-1-94
          RE : G/T FLOW -ALL LOOPS
           UNITS:USA        NOTE:LOSS INCLUDES FITTING ALLOW.OF 10%

+FLOW=CLOCKWISE      * RCII-885 *      -FLOW=COUNTER-CLOCKWISE
****************************************************************
```

Figure 14-50 Example of Pressure Loss Calculation by Computer. G-T Flow of Exemplary System

Item:	Re:	Flow gpm	Length ft	Loss lb/in²	
10 in [a]Supply pipe. Sch. 40 steel					
Pump discharge pipe:	20 ft				
2-45° ells at 13.4:	27 ft				
Total length =	47 ft	836	47	.15	
10 in [b]Supply pipe, SDR21, PVC					
Pump discharge pipe:	50 ft				
Branch of tee:	50 ft				
Total length =	100 ft	836	100	.17	
Loss, Pump Station to Point A:					.32
(c) Loop Main Loss, A to C (back nine)					9.30
(d) Loss in Branch Main:					3.39
(e) Pressure Required at zone:					83.42
(f) Elevation Loss (19.5 ft x .433)					8.44
Design Pressure:					(104.87) 105.00

Figure 14-51 Design Pressure of Exemplary System

The actual water supply available per night should be substantially more than the estimated requirement for several reasons.

1. Duration time may be increased on some zones (or all zones).

2. All water cannot be used from the reservoir. Inlets to pumps must be installed to avoid mud, silt, etc. from the bottom of the reservoir.

3. Loss of water due to seepage from the reservoir and evaporation from the surface can be substantial.

ADDITIONAL CONSIDERATIONS

Design considerations discussed for the exemplary system are typical, but limited to the basics of sprinkler layout, piping design, and control of the system operation. There are many additional design considerations that may be necessary for the average golf course system, and many alternates and additions that are possible for a particular system.

CONTROLLING ZONE PRESSURES. Zones closer to the source of the water supply will normally have more pressure than necessary for proper operation. An excessive amount of pressure will affect the distribution, flow and precipitation rate of the sprinkler. It will also affect the rotation, life-expectancy of the sprinkler and, in some cases, the product warranty. Manufacturers normally indicate the maximum operating pressure for each sprinkler model in the product catalog. Pressure to individual zones can be controlled by using electric control valves with pressure regulating devices, which are used to increase the pressure loss through the valves.

OPERATION TIME. Due to unforeseen circumstances, some means should be incorporated to provide for additional watering beyond the estimated time of system operation. Whenever possible, the daily operating program should require less time than the maximum allowed per day, or a six day program should be used to provide one additional irrigation cycle per week.

OPERATION. Many golf courses prefer to divide each day's watering application by using a repeat cycle. With this method, two or more cycles of operation are scheduled each night; the combined cycles are equal to the total time required. For the example system, assume that the absorption rate of the greens was low and 23 min of continuous watering would result in runoff. To eliminate run-off, the watering could be accomplished with two 12-min cycles. Water from the first cycle has time to "soak-in" before the second cycle commences. Depending on make of controllers, a short time delay

Golf Course Systems

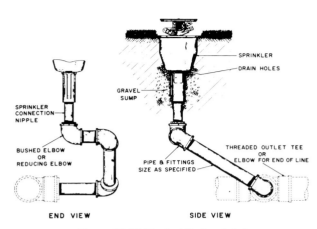

Figure 14-52 Typical Swing-Joint

may be required between cycles. Program of operation should provide for this delay, if required.

SYRINGE WATERING. Dew can damage greens. When known to be detrimental, the dew is removed near sunrise. Most automatic sprinkler controllers are available with a short *syringe cycle* which effectively washes dew off the grass. Length of cycle is variable; usually, about one to five minutes in one minute increments. When greens are watered with full-circle sprinklers, five minutes is usually allowed for syringing, because water is applied to the putting surface during only half of the full rotation. With part-circle sprinklers, the same amount of syringe is accomplished in about one-half the time. Syringe time is readily adjustable to suit most requirements. Syringe watering is also used to "cool" greens during the day.

SHUT-OFF VALVES. Valves to shut off segments of the system should be installed so that in case of break down of one portion, the balance of the system can be operated. Each branch main should be valved; the looped main should also be valved, at least in quarters. Some designs include a shut-off valve at the inlet to each electric zone control valve.

SUPPLEMENTAL WATERING. At least one quick-coupling valve is installed at each green for connection of a hose for maintenance, supplemental watering of newly-planted trees, shrubs, etc. Many designs will also include at least one quick-coupling valve at each tee. In addition, many golf course systems are installed with quick-coupling valves on pressure mains every few hundred feet along each fairway. Quick-couplers are recommended for hose connection which requires a special key (coupler) to obtain water. Standard hose

hydrants are not recommended because unknowing persons could drink non-potable water from the system.

SWING-JOINTS. Rotary heads are usually installed on swing-joints on large projects for two reasons.

1. Protection of lateral piping against damage from heavy maintenance equipment running over heads.
2. Facilitates setting heads to proper grade.

As previously discussed, a variety of different type swing-joint risers are used on golf course systems. These include variations of assembled units as shown in Figure 14-52. Threads at each joint provide the swivel action needed to counteract either top loading or side impact.

Manufactured swing-joint units are also commonly used for large rotary heads. These products have gaskets (o-rings) at swivel connections and can provide advantages as compared to pipe thread connection. A gravel sump is required under the head (and around the swing-joint) with some types of sprinklers.

CONTROLLER SYSTEM. In addition to the conventional satellite controller system, many different methods and levels of control are available.

Levels of control include controller systems that can be used with a variety of different remote sensors, such as: rain, wind, soil moisture, flow and pressure. Some central controllers provide additional irrigation management with PC software, which can process input data (telephone modem, on-site weather-station, etc.), calculate ET rates, and alter the schedule of operation if necessary. These systems offer the ability to review system performance from a video display and/or a computer printout.

The systems designer, golf course superintendent, and any other individuals who may be involved in the selection of the controller system, should understand the basic levels of irrigation management available, and the related cost and sophistication of different systems. The following five items are important considerations in selecting a control system for a particular golf course:

1. *Control Desired/Required* - Programming features, methods of communication, climatic sensors and calculated data provided with some systems, may or may not, be required or practical for some irriga-

tion systems. Equipment, regardless of type, must be dependable with a minimum amount of "downtime" to be practical and cost-effective. Assistance and maintenance support is an important consideration for some locations.

2. *Budget* - The installed cost, maintenance cost and possible replacement cost of different control systems will vary over a wide range. For example, the installed cost of some water management systems can be 2 or 3 times more than a conventional primary/satellite system.

3. Grounds Maintenance Personnel - training is required for the user, and the amount of training necessary will depend on the personnel who will use the equipment and the type of controller system. Some level of training may also be necessary in the future, with normal changes that occur in maintenance personnel.

4. *Location* - The location of the primary controller at the site is important for normal use. A clean and air-conditioned office environment is necessary for some types of controllers and related hardware. Sophisticated equipment of this type should not be located in work areas of the maintenance shop or similar buildings.

5. *Electrical* - The designer should obtain detailed information on all wiring requirements of the equip-

ment being considered. In many cases, the designer will require assistance in electrical requirement, including wire sizes, for the final design drawings or specifications.

SPRINKLERS WITH CHECK VALVES. Sprinklers with a standard, or optional, check valve feature, as discussed in Chapter 4, are normally recommended in golf course systems. Low-head drainage is a common problem due to elevation variations within the area of zone control. In some cases, sprinklers without check valves will allow the zone piping to drain after each operation and damage may occur due to the high velocity of uncontrolled flow from the valve into the empty lines.

COMPLETE COVERAGE SYSTEMS

Occasionally, golf course systems are designed to water all turf areas, including the roughs. These are commonly called "wall-to-wall" systems. Courses designed for complete coverage are usually in areas where rainfall is so deficient that turf will not grow without artificial watering.

Note: Complete coverage systems are very expensive and require a very large supply of water. Local or regional restrictions on the use of water may not allow this level of consumption.

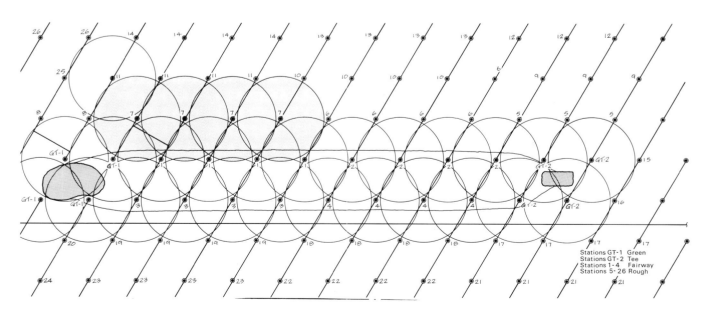

Figure 14-53 Valve-Under-Head, "Wall-to-Wall" Golf Course Sprinkler System

Golf Course Systems

The head layout is generally patterned without regard for fairways, tees or greens in the first stage. Adjustments are made in the second stage to coincide with guidelines previously outlined for proper coverage of the components of each hole.

1. Heads might be moved and added around Greens and Tees.

2. Pattern might be compressed in the fairway area, even to the extent of adding a row.

Zoning is similar to that already reviewed, except, because of pattern, fairway heads often water more of the rough. An alternate method of zoning and piping is illustrated in Figure 14-53.

Valve-under-head (or, in-head) operates sprinklers individually. Each lateral intersecting the main supplies a relatively large number of sprinklers. In many cases, only one head on each lateral will operate at a time. Therefore, lateral pipes can be only one size.

Pressure loss to the end head on each lateral, and flow velocity, determines size. Laterals usually operate one-half the sprinklers between each sprinkler main.

Zoning is accomplished by operating a pre-determined number of heads from each controller station. Figure 14-53 shows some typical zoning. Sprinklers bearing the same number operate simultaneously, and are connected to a corresponding station on one of many satellite controllers.

SYSTEM CONVERSION

Before considering conversion of older quick-coupling type golf course systems to modern, automatic systems, condition of the existing system should be investigated. Conversion is an unsound investment if the existing system is in a deteriorated condition.

PIPING. Condition of pipe can be judged from project records showing frequency of failures and amount of maintenance required.

Systems with old cast iron or steel pipe may have only a few additional years of life expectancy. In this case, a complete new system would be indicated.

Additionally, many existing systems are not adequately sized for flows and pressures required for an automatic system of acceptable design. In some cases, adding new supply lines and changing dead-end mains to loops may be sufficient. Or, new piping required may represent a very large percent of the total system and would result in an undesirable mixed network of old and new piping.

PUMPING SYSTEM. The existing pumping system may be below the performance required for an automatic system. The existing pump system may be revised,

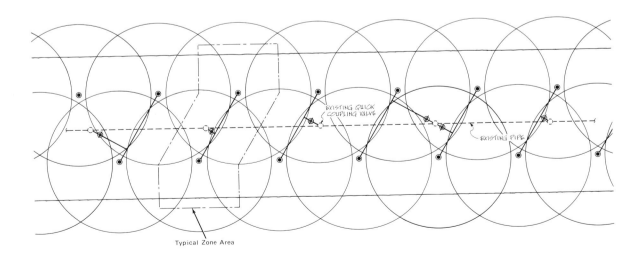

Figure 14-54 Existing System Converted to Automatic 2-Sprinkler Zone System

but more often than not, replacement is the best solution.

TESTING. Flow capacity, related to frictional resistance (condition) of old pipe in-place, is determined by comparing flow and pressures which provides approximate pressure losses. A flow test is made with different quantities of above-ground sprinklers connected to the quick-coupling valves in various locations. See Chapter 3: Hydraulics: Testing Pipe Lines.

SINGLE ROW SYSTEMS. Usually, the existing swing-joints and quick-coupling valves (Q.C.V.) can be removed, and replaced with new swing-joints, valve-under-head (or, valve-in-head) pop-up rotary sprinklers. The new head performance must be suitable for the existing spacing.

Additional piping is usually required, too, much the same as illustrated for multi-row systems reviewed below.

TWO ROW SYSTEMS. When possible, the tapped openings in sprinkler mains are used as connections for the conversion.
Figure 14-54 illustrates a two-row system using existing pipe as the supply. The same sprinkler with the same spacing as the exemplary plan reviewed previously is used. However, the openings for the original quick-coupling valves (Q.C.V.) are too small to supply more than two sprinklers. So, 2-sprinkler zones were utilized.

PROGRAMMING. Programming and operation of converted systems will be basically the same as described previously for a new system.

CHAPTER 15

Electrical

Controllers and electric remote control valves (RCV) must be properly wired together, otherwise operation of systems will be affected and become unreliable. Operation and function of controllers and valves were reviewed in Chapter 1, Equipment: System Operation: Automatic.

Satellite Systems, as discussed in Chapter 14, are made by several manufacturers, each employing distinctive features. Quantity of conductors required, voltage, methods of connection and terminology vary to the point that is not practical to provide an example requirement that could be considered typical. Detailed information on all wiring requirements should be obtained from the manufacturer of the equipment being used.

Controllers are furnished standard with a nominal voltage rating of 115V a.c., 60 Hz (Hertz for cycles) on the primary input side and an output of 24V a.c. on the secondary side for powering electric valve solenoids. There are many makes and models available. A large number of these can be ordered for other primary input voltages in both 50 and 60 Hz. 50 Hz is used in many countries, but has no application in the United States.

The current draw will vary with make and model, depending on the amount of current required to operate the controller itself and the number of valves that the controller is designed to operate per station.

A licensed electrician should be employed to install and connect the power supply to a controller with an internal-mounted transformer or, if required, the installation of a power supply outlet for a controller with an external, "plug-in" type transformer. In all cases, the installation must be in compliance with local codes. To avoid accidental power interruption, a separate, unswitched circuit with its own fuse or circuit breaker is recommended.

For the average system, wire size for the power supply is governed by local codes. The proper wire size(s) must be calculated on large projects using single or multiple controllers at remote distances from the power source. This will be discussed later.

VALVE WIRING

Most brands and models of electric control valves have an inrush rating in the 6 to 10VA range at 24V a.c., 60 Hz. Two wires are required to provide the secondary low voltage power supply for valve solenoids. The "common" serves all solenoids. A "station" or "hot" wire from the controller to each solenoid completes the circuit. A typical wiring schematic is shown in Figure 15-1.

If more than one controller is used on a system, a separate common wire (N) shown in Figure 15-1 is generally required for each controller and the group of valves it operates. In some cases, two or more controllers may be connected to the same common, but care must be taken to choose controllers suitable for this method of wiring. In all instances, you must comply with the manufacturer's instructions.

Note: The common wire and related points of connection are noted as "N" in some controller models and "C" in others.

TYPE OF WIRE
Type UF is the most common type of wire recommended for valve circuit (direct-burial) wiring in the U.S.A. Other types, including multi-conductor cables, are used in some applications and types of irrigation systems. In all cases, the type of wire and method of installation should be in accordance with local codes for Class 2 circuits of 30 volts or less.

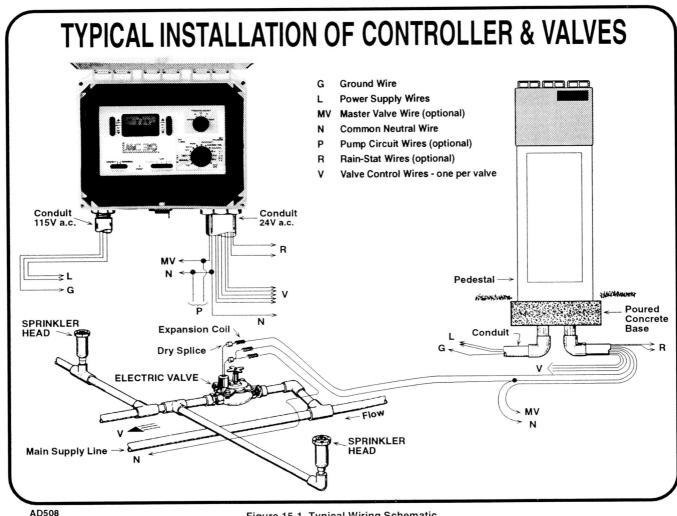

TYPICAL INSTALLATION OF CONTROLLER & VALVES

G   Ground Wire
L   Power Supply Wires
MV Master Valve Wire (optional)
N   Common Neutral Wire
P   Pump Circuit Wires (optional)
R   Rain-Stat Wires (optional)
V   Valve Control Wires - one per valve

AD508

Figure 15-1 Typical Wiring Schematic

Type UF has vinyl insulation and is considered moisture proof and resistant to practically all chemicals normally found in earth. Type UF also offers the advantage of greater protection as compared to other types, due to the extra thickness of the insulation.

Wires are generally color coded to distinguish between the station wires and the common. Red is commonly used for valve control (station) wire and white for the common wire to all valves. Color coding avoids the possibility of accidentally mixing the two sides of valve circuit wiring which would obviously cause problems.

WIRE SIZING WITH TABLES

Manufacturers of remote control valves furnish tables for sizing valve circuit wiring for average systems. Figure 15-2 is an example of such a table. *Caution: Use wire size recommendations provided by the manufacturer (or larger).*

Lengths shown are the maximum distance of the wire path or run from controller to valve. Sizing is based on the total length of wire from controller to valve, and return, with both wires being the same size. Therefore, wire size corresponding to distance may be selected direct from the table.

Note that the exemplary table is based on a controller (brand and model not provided) with an input voltage of 115V a.c. Some tables provided by manufacturers include information to cover additional variables, such as, the controller model, input voltage and different sizes for station and common wires.

In most cases, tables provided by manufacturers are limited to specific combinations of controller and valve models. Tables are not for use with other brands or different brands of controllers and valves in combination.

**WIRE SIZE - 1 VALVE PER STATION
CONTROLLER INPUT 115 V a.c.**

*Maximum length of wire run (feet) from controller to valve					
AWG SIZE	Static pressure not exceeding:				
Diameter, No. In	75 lb/in^2	85 lb/in^2	100 lb/in2	125 lb/in^2	150 lb/in^2
18 0.040	2,200	2,000	1,600	1,100	700
16 0.051	3,600	3,200	2,500	1,800	1,100
14 0.064	5,700	5,000	4,000	3,000	1,700
12 0.081	9,000	8,000	6,400	4,700	2,800
10 0.102	14,000	12,700	10,200	7,400	4,400
8 0.129	22,700	20,200	16,200	11,800	7,000
MULTIPLYING FACTOR: 2 Valves/Station	0.43	0.40	0.41	0.38	0.31

* Length of run (distance) includes station wire to valve and common return to controller. Both wires same size. American wire gauge solid copper.

Table shows wire size for 1 valve per station. For 2 valves per station, multiply length by factor given. Example: for 75 lb/in^2 pressure and No. 18 wire, length is 2200 x 0.43 = 946 feet.

Figure 15-2 Exemplary Table of Valve Circuit Wire Sizes

EFFECT OF WATER PRESSURE. Water pressure is a critical factor in determining wire size. Values shown in Figure 15-2 are the maximum static pressure under which the solenoid is required to operate. To avoid any misunderstanding in terminology, static pressure is meant to be the pressure gauged with no water flowing. This should be the highest seasonal pressure that will be encountered.

Higher water pressure requires a greater inrush of current to actuate the solenoid. Inrush current affects wire size for any given distance. If pressure is under estimated and the wire size used is too small, an excessive voltage drop may occur. In this event, voltage at the solenoid may be insufficient to operate the valve.

When the wire run distances exceed those given in Figure 15-2, or with more complex systems, wire size must be calculated by formula. This subject will be treated later.

ELECTRICAL FACTORS

Before proceeding with a discussion of wiring for the more complex systems involving greater distances, multiple controllers and multiple valves, a simple explanation of electricity will be made. The following definitions and terminology may appear over-simplified to experts in the field of electricity. However, they are stated in the simplest terms possible for the benefit of readers having little or no knowledge of the basics involved.

CURRENT. Current is the flow of electricity. It can be equated with the consumption of water. Examples:

A solenoid draws 0.25 amperes of current.
A sprinkler head flows 5 gallons/minute.

Current is designated by (I) and is measured in Amperes or Amps designated by (A).

The load of all electrical devices is rated in amps. An increased load (amperage) will cause a greater voltage loss and vice versa.

VOLTAGE. Voltage is the force applied to the flow of current. It can be equated to the pressure of water. Voltage is measured in Volts (E).

The use of current affects voltage. A small amount of current flowing through a large diameter wire of short length has an insignificant effect. A heavy load carried by a small wire of great length causes a substantial drop in voltage.

Wire sizes that are too small can cause voltage to drop below the minimum required to operate controllers and valves.

RESISTANCE. Resistance to the flow of current can be likened to friction caused by the flow of water in pipe. In electricity, resistance causes a drop in voltage. With water, friction causes a drop in pressure.

Resistance is measured in ohms designated as (R).

Resistance varies with wire diameter and length. The loss of voltage and consequential drop in voltage increases with the amount of resistance.

RELATION OF ELECTRIC FACTORS. These factors may be reduced to the following simple relationships:

1. $Current = \dfrac{voltage}{resistance}$

$$I \ (Amps) = \frac{E}{R}$$

2. Voltage $= current \times resistance$
   E (volts) $= IR$

3. $Resistance = \dfrac{voltage}{current}$

   $R \text{ (ohms)} = \dfrac{E}{I}$

4. $Power = voltage \times current$
   $Volt\ amperes\ (VA) = EI$

SIZING WIRE USING ELECTRIC FACTORS

Examples and solutions to the specific problems that follow are based on typical values which may or may not correspond to electrical ratings and other characteristics of all makes of controllers and electric valves. To be on the safe side, always calculate wire size based on data provided by the manufacturer of products that will be used. This is especially important if different brands are used for the controller and the valves.

Example 1.
Controller operates one electric valve per station. The same wire size will be used for each valve control wire and a single common wire to all valves. Determine wire size required from controller to the furthermost valve - i.e. - the worst condition on all stations. Wire size is determined by calculating allowable resistance in the wire.

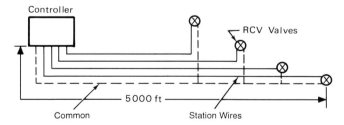

Conditions that must be considered in this example are:

1. Length of wire from controller to the furthermost valve (worst condition) is 5,000 feet.
2. The maximum static water pressure on-site will not exceed 75/in^2.
3. The primary input voltage to controller on-site will not be less than 115V a.c., as confirmed by the local electric company.
4. Only one electric valve will be operated at a time.

Resistance is determined by formula:

$$R_W = \frac{AVL \times 1000}{L \times 2 \times I_{vs}}$$

In which:

R_w=Resistance of wire (ohms)
AVL=Allowable voltage loss
L=Wire length, controller to valve
I_{vs}=Inrush current (for number of valves)

"L" is stated as wire length, controller to valve. Multiplier "2" in the equation is used to double the actual length to include the common return of same length.

Procedures:
a. Determine the maximum allowable voltage loss (AVL). This factor will be obtained by subtracting the valve operating voltage from the controller output voltage.

Controller output voltage from Figure 15-3 for 75 lb/in^2, 115V and 1 valve is 27.5 volts. Valve solenoid operating voltage from Figure 15-4 is 19.9 volts. Therefore, allowable voltage loss = 27.5 − 19.9 = 7.6 (AVL).

b. Determine the inrush current from Figure 15-4. For 1 valve @ 75 lb/in^2, inrush current = .265 (I_{vs}).

Then:

$$R_W = \frac{AVL \times 1000}{L \times 2 \times I_{vs}}$$

$$or,\ R_W = \frac{7.6 \times 1000}{5000 \times 2 \times .265}$$

$$and,\ R_W = \frac{7600}{2650} = 2.86\ ^{ohms}/_{1000}\ ft$$

Therefore, wire resistance must not exceed 2.86 ohms per 1000 feet, maximum. Select the proper wire size from the table in Figure 15-5. Since 16 AWG has a resistance of 4.02 and this exceeds the 2.86 allowable, 14 AWG must be used although the resistance for this wire size is only 2.52 ohms/1000 ft.

Caution: If a smaller wire with a higher resistance is used, the valve may not operate at maximum water pressure. In the example, No. 16 wire would cause a

STATIC WATER PRESSURE lb/in	CONTROLLER INPUT VOLTAGE a.c. 60 Hz.	CONTROLLER OUTPUT VOLTAGE		
		1 VALVE	2 VALVES	3 VALVES
50	110	26.3	25.4	24.6
	115	27.6	26.7	25.9
	120	28.8	27.9	27.1
60	110	26.3	25.3	24.5
	115	27.6	26.6	25.8
	120	28.8	27.8	27.0
75	110	26.2	25.2	24.3
	115	27.5	26.5	25.6
	120	28.7	27.7	26.8
85	110	26.2	25.2	24.2
	115	27.5	26.5	25.5
	120	28.7	27.7	26.7
100	110	26.1	25.1	24.0
	115	27.4	26.4	25.3
	120	28.6	27.6	26.5
125	110	26.0	24.9	23.8
	115	27.3	26.2	25.1
	120	28.5	27.4	26.3
150	110	25.9	24.8	23.7
	115	27.2	26.1	25.0
	120	28.4	27.3	26.2

Figure 15-3 Controller Output Voltage
(Example only)

voltage loss, between controller and valve, great enough to reduce the voltage below the minimum of 19.9 volts required to operate the valve at 75 lb/in^2.

Wire size may be calculated for each valve circuit on the assumption that smaller wire sizes may be suitable for the shorter runs. However, on small to average installations, mixed wire sizes have little to offer economically. And, there is always a danger that the installer may inadvertently use a small wire on a long run and a large wire on a short run. Based on this rationale, it is customary to use only one wire size being dictated by the "worst condition."

Example 2.
Controller operates 2 electric valves per station. The same wire size will be used for the control wires and common to all valves. Determine wire size required from controller to the furthermost valve - i.e. - the worst condition on all stations. In this example, Length (L) is 2000 feet.

All other conditions will be the same as in Example 1 - i.e. - water pressure 75 lb/in^2 and a primary input of 115 volts to controller.

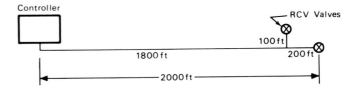

Allowable voltage loss is:

Controller output voltage for 2 valves (Figure 15-3)	26.5
Less valve operating voltage (Figure 15-4)	19.9
Allowable voltage loss	6.6 (AVL)
Inrush current for 2 valves (Figure 15-4)	.530 (Ivs)

Then:

$$R_w = \frac{AVL \times 1000}{L \times 2 \times I_{vs}}$$

$$or, R_w = \frac{6.6 \times 1000}{2000 \times 2 \times .530}$$

$$and, R_w = \frac{6600}{2120} = 3.11 \; ohms/1000 \; ft$$

Referring to Figure 15-5, it will be noted that the proper wire size is No. 14 with a resistance of 2.52 ohms/1000 ft. This is slightly less than the maximum allowable resistance calculated as 3.11 ohms. Wire size for the 100 foot branch will also be No. 14.

Example 3.
Determine the maximum length of a given wire size from controller to one valve per station. Wire size is No. 12. Controller input is 110 volts and water pressure is 100 lb/in^2.

Electrical

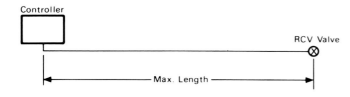

Allowable voltage loss is:

110V controller output voltage
for 1 valve @ 100 lb/in^2 = 26.1
    (Figure 15-3)

Less valve operating voltage   = <u>21.5</u>
    (Figure 15-4)

Allowable voltage loss   = 4.6 (AVL)

Inrush current for 1 valve @ 100 lb/in^2 = .289 (I_{vs})
    (Figure 15-4)
Resistance of No. 12 wire (Figure 15-5) = 1.59 (R_w)

$$Length = \frac{AVL \times 1000}{I_{vs} \times R_w \times 2}$$

In which:

AVL = Allowable voltage loss
Ivs = Inrush current (for number of valves)
Rw = Resistance of wire

WATER PRESSURE lb/in²	MINIMUM SOLENOID OPERATING VOLTAGE	INRUSH CURRENT (I_{vs})		
		1 VALVE	2 VALVES	3 VALVES
50	17.9	.240	.480	.720
75	19.9	.265	.530	.795
100	21.5	.289	.578	.867
125	22.7	.310	.620	.930
150	24.3	.328	.656	.984

Figure 15-4 Solenoid Operating Voltage and Inrush Current (Example only)

Then:

$$Length = \frac{4.6 \times 1000}{.289 \times 1.59 \times 2}$$

$$and, \; Length = \frac{4600}{.919} = 5000 \; ft \; (5005), \; maximum$$

Note: The maximum length of 5000 ft (controller to valve) actually includes the station wire and common wire, making the total footage 10,000 ft. Both wires will be the same size.

For the sake of simplicity, the formula used provides for a voltage loss in a double length of wire (controller to valve and return) in all cases. This also applies to several valves operating simultaneously from one station of the controller.

Example 4.
Determine the maximum length of a given wire size from controller to several valves operating simultaneously on one station. In this example, find maximum wire length for 3 valves supplied by No. 12 wire. Other

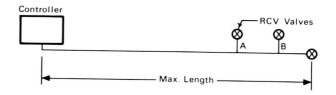

Wire Size AWG No.	Ohms/1000 ft*
18	6.39
16	4.02
14	2.52
12	1.59
10	1.00
8	0.63

*Data extracted from complete Table 33

Figure 15-5 Resistance of Copper Wire

conditions are same as Example 3 - i.e. - controller input, 110 volts and water pressure, 100 lb/in^2.

Allowable voltage loss is:

    110V controller output voltage
      for 3 valves @ 100 lb/in^2 = 24.0
      (Figure 15-3)

    Less valve operating voltage   = <u>21.5</u>
      (Figure 15-4)

    Allowable voltage loss   = 2.5 (AVL)
    Inrush current for 3 valves @ 100 lb/in^2 =   .867 (I_{vs})
      (Figure 15-4)

    Resistance of No. 12 wire (Figure 15-5) = 1.59 (R_w)

Thus:

$$Length = \frac{AVL \times 1000}{I_{vs} \times R_w \times 2}$$

$$or,\ Length = \frac{2.5 \times 1000}{0.867 \times 1.59 \times 2}$$

$$and,\ Length = \frac{2500}{2.757} = 900\ ft\ (906),\ maximum$$

Branches A and B, supplying intermediate valves, will also be No. 12 wire.

Note: Occasionally, the valve control wire and the common wire follow different routes to the valve. In these cases, actual combined total lengths of the two wires are substituted for L x 2 in the formulas.

INSTALLATION

There are certain procedures that should be followed in the installation of valve circuit wiring if long term failures and other more immediate problems are to be avoided:

1. Wiring may be laid in the same trench with pipe and should be laid at the same depth. When pipe is plastic or other non-metallic material, placing wire under pipe offers additional protection against damage from cultivation or other causes. Wiring should be separated from metal pipe to avoid the possibility of current leakage and short circuits.
2. Avoid placing rocks or other abrasive materials in direct contact with wire. Movement of either the wire

Courtesy of Global Span Products

Figure 15-6 Connector Failed the Water-Proof Test

or back-fill from expansion and contraction could easily damage the insulation.

3. Use expansion curls at the connections to all valves, at abrupt turns in the wire run, and at about 100 foot intervals in straight runs. Expansion curls are easily formed by wrapping approximately 5 turns around a pipe about 1 in diameter, then withdrawing pipe. Curls eliminate wire stressing or breakage when the earth expands or contracts due to vari-

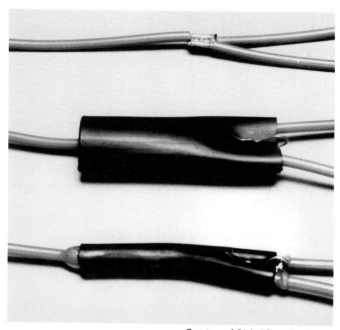

Courtesy of Global Span Products

Figure 15-7 Splice-Kote (heat shrink) Connector

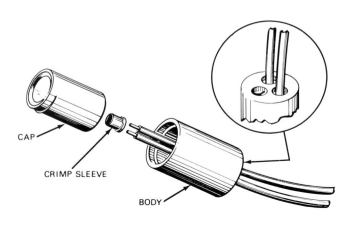

Figure 15-8 Dri-splice Wire Connector

ation in moisture content or extreme seasonal temperature fluctuations. Snaking wire in trenches, instead of laying it straight, will also relieve stressing to some extent.

4. Use only time-tested and approved connectors or splicing material on all underground connections to electric RCV valves and wire splices. It is essential that wire joints be carefully insulated against the admission of moisture and remain water-tight over the expected life of the system. Joints must also be made mechanically secure for the best electrical conductance. Faulty connections and imperfect insulation are the primary causes of electrical failure. Figure 15-6 illustrates a wire connector with insulating material removed for inspection. The connector failed to provide a water-tight connection for the underground wire splice.

There are several brands of waterproof connectors available for connection of the control wires to the electric valves, and any other splices that may be required between the controller and the zone control (RCV) valves. Various methods are used with these products to insulate the mechanical device used for the wire connection. These include heat-shrink materials and plastic sleeves (tubes, packs, etc.) which are pre-filled with a sealant to encapsulate the connection.

Figure 15-7 illlustrates the wire connection, the insulation sleeve in position and the final assembly of a heat-shrink product. Adhesive coating is provided inside the insulation sleeve.

An example of a pre-filled dri-splice connector is shown in Figure 15-8. This product is provided with a crimp sleeve for 10, 12 or 14 gauge wire sizes.

The importance of mechanically sound, well insulated and water-tight connections cannot be overemphasized. The most common problems caused by faulty connections are:

a. Exposed joints will eventually corrode and separate, causing an open circuit. If this happens on a valve control wire from controller, the affected valve will fail to open or cease to operate. If the common return wire separates, valves beyond the break become inoperative.

b. A severe short circuit between the common and valve station wiring through earth causes the secondary circuit breaker on controller to trip. Breaker will not hold-in until the short is located and repaired. Note: Some controller models use a fuse on the valve circuit.

c. Current leakage to earth can cause one or more valves to remain open, and continue operating, even when de-energized by controller. This can only happen while another valve is being energized and operating. This is due to the fact that once activated, only a small amount of current is required to hold a solenoid open. Thus, any current leakage from the valve being energized may be sufficient to cause the preceding valve to continue operating. This problem will be discussed later in more detail.

CONTROLLER WIRING

Controllers are often located some distance from the electrical power source. Procedures for sizing wire from power source to controller are similar to those for sizing valve circuit wiring. However, higher voltages are involved (U.S.A. - 115V nominal).

SINGLE CONTROLLERS
The following examples illustrate procedures used in determining the electric supply to single controllers.

Example 1.
The controller will be located some distance from its power source as shown in the following schematic. Determine wire size required to operate controller at its rated input voltage of 115V a.c. Three RCV valves will be operated simultaneously on one or more stations. Length of wire from power source to controller is 2500 ft.

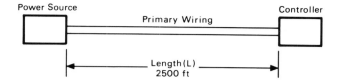

Power Source — Primary Wiring — Controller

Length (L)
2500 ft

Conditions that must be considered in this example are:

1. The voltage at power source is recorded as 118V with a voltmeter. This voltage will always be available under actual operating conditions as confirmed by the electric company.

    Note: If the voltage is unusually low or high, the electric company may be able to adjust the distribution transformer to provide a more suitable voltage.

2. Current required by controller for the greatest number of valves to be operated simultaneously on one or more stations. Obtain from manufacturer's data sheet. Assume 0.325 amps for 3 valves in this case.

The allowable voltage loss (AVL) is the maximum voltage that can be lost in the primary wiring between the controller and its power source. As previously stated, the source voltage is 118V and controller input is rated at 115V. Therefore, the allowable voltage loss is 118 − 115 = 3 (AVL).

Begin with the equation:

$$R_w = \frac{AVL \times 1000}{L \times 2 \times I_c}$$

In which:

- R_w = Resistance of wire (ohms)
- AVL = Allowable voltage loss
- L = Wire length, source voltage to controller
- I_c = Current required by controller for 3 valves

Then:

$$R_w = \frac{3 \times 1000}{2500 \times 2 \times .325}$$

and, $R_w = \frac{3000}{1625} = 1.84 \ ^{ohms}/1000 \ ft$

The proper wire size then, selected from Figure 15-5, is No. 12 with a resistance of 1.59 ohms/1000 ft which is somewhat less than the calculated allowable of 1.84.

Electrical

Example 2.
Voltage loss (VL) is the voltage actually lost in the wiring in a given situation. Determine voltage loss in the preceding example.

For two No. 12 wires 2500 ft long, and using the same electrical values, voltage loss (VL) will be:

$$VL = \frac{L \times 2 \times I_c \times R_w}{1000}$$

$$or, \ VL = \frac{2500 \times 2 \times .325 \times 1.59}{1000}$$

$$and, \ VL = \frac{2584}{1000} = 2.6 \ volts$$

MULTIPLE CONTROLLERS

Sizing wire for a single supply to more than one controller uses the same procedures already presented, although somewhat more complex.

Example:
The following schematic shows two groups of controllers operating from a single power source. Controllers 1, 3, and 5 operate simultaneously. Controllers 2 and 4 also operate simultaneously, but on alternate days. Therefore, each controller group will operate separately.

Determine wire size from power source to the group of controllers with the most critical conditions. Consider wire length and current load.

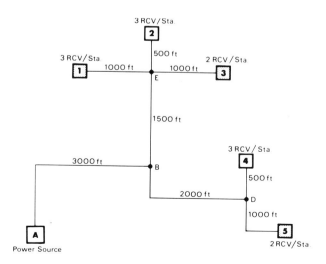

Electrical

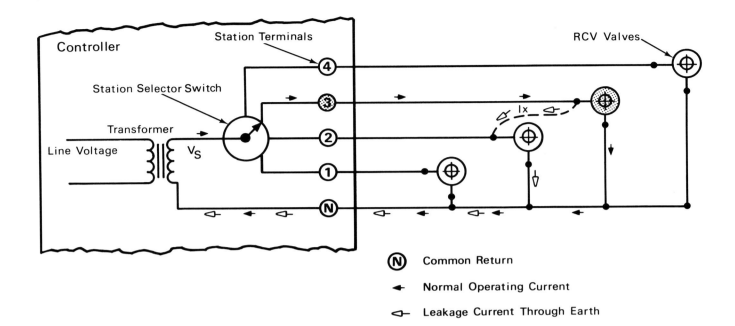

Figure 15-9 Current Leakage

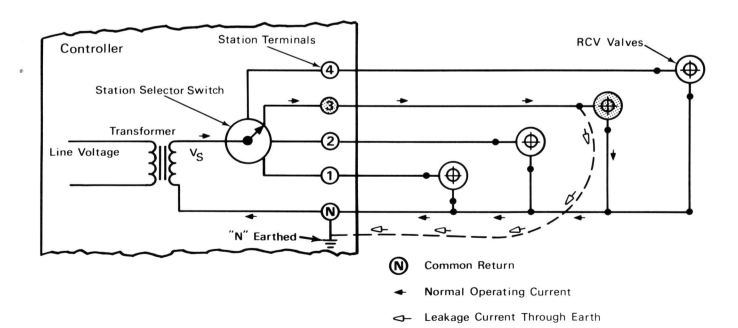

Figure 15-10 Grounding Common to Earth

First, determine the greatest wire length in both controller groups. This will be the distance from power source to the most remote controller in each group following the wire path. The most distant are controllers 4 and 5:

	Controller 4	Controller 5
Wire A-B	3000 ft	3000 ft
Wire B-D	2000	2000
Wire D-4	500	--
Wire D-5	--	1000
	5500 ft	6000 ft

Next, determine the current load from the manufacturer's data. In this example, current required by controllers and valves (I_c) is assumed to be:

Controller plus 2 valves = .260 amps (I_c)
Controller plus 3 valves = .325 amps (I_c)

Controllers 1, 3 and 5 will operate 7 valves at a time: (3 + 2 + 2 = 7). Current load is .845 amp: (.325 + .260 + .260 = .845).

Controllers 2 and 4 will operate 6 valves at a time: (3 + 3 = 6). Current load is .650 amp: (.325 + .325 = .650).

Since controllers 1, 3, and 5 have the greatest current load and require the most wire, wire size will be determined for this group.

The 3000 ft wire run A-B will carry the combined current load of controllers 1, 3, and 5 totaling .845 amp (Ic): (.325 + .260 + .260 = .845).

The 3000 ft wire run B-D-5 will carry the current load of controller No. 5 only = .260 amp (Ic).

Allowable voltage loss (AVL) is:

Power source voltage	120
Less voltage desired at controller	115
Allowable voltage loss	5 (AVL)

Now, determine resistance (R_w) and select a wire size accordingly from table, Figure 15-5. The formula is:

$$R_w = \frac{AVL \times 1000}{L \times 2 \times I_c}$$

Then:

$$R_w = \frac{5 \times 1000}{(3000 \times 2 \times .845) + (3000 \times 2 \times .260)}$$

$$\text{or, } R_w = \frac{5000}{5070 + 1560}$$

$$\text{and, } R_w = \frac{5000}{6630} = 0.75 \; ^{ohms}\!/_{1000} \; ft$$

The proper wire size for controller 5 selected from table Figure 15-5 is No. 8 with a resistance of 0.63 ohms/1000 ft. This is somewhat less than the calculated allowable of 0.75, as it should be.

Although controller No. 1 is closer to the power source (5500 ft instead of 6000 ft), it will operate one more valve (3 instead of 2), consequently its current load will be greater than controller No. 5.

Therefore, it will be necessary to determine wire size for this branch of the circuit, too.

The 3000 ft wire run A-B will carry the combined current load of controllers 1, 3, and 5, totaling .845 amp (I_c): (.325 + .260 + .260 = .845).

The 1500 ft wire run B-E will carry the combined current load of controllers 1 and 3, totaling .585 amp (I_c): (.325 + .260 = .585).

The 1000 ft wire run E-1 will carry the current load of controller No. 1 only of .325 amp (I_c).

Allowable voltage loss (AVL) will be 5 volts, same as in the preceding calculation.

Then:

$$R_w = \frac{5 \times 1000}{(3000 \times 2 \times .845) + (1500 \times 2 \times .585) + (1000 \times 2 \times .325)}$$

$$\text{or, } R_w = \frac{5000}{5070 + 1755 + 650}$$

$$\text{and, } R_w = \frac{5000}{7475} = 0.67 \; ^{ohms}\!/_{1000} \; ft$$

It is evident that No. 8 wire is also adequate for the A-B-E-1 branch of the circuit. The calculated allowable resistance of 0.67 ohms/1000 ft is very close to the actual resistance of 0.63 ohms that will occur in No. 8 wire. But, in both branches, not less than the desired voltage of 115V will be maintained at the most distant controllers 1, 3, and 5, with the greatest current loads.

Electrical

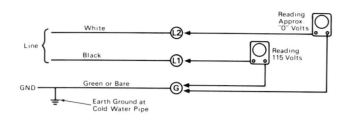

Figure 15-11 Earth Ground

Since wire length and current required by the remaining controllers are comparable, No. 8 wire will be used throughout for both lines of the power supply.

In actual practice, when there is an appreciable difference in wire length and current load between several branch circuits, it may be necessary to use more than one wire size for the power supply.

On larger projects of this kind, where a line feeds multiple controllers and the controllers operate a large number of valves, it may be more economical to increase the power supply lines one or more sizes. This would have the effect of delivering higher voltages to the controllers, thus making it possible to reduce the size (and cost) on a much greater quantity of valve circuit wiring.

There are no set rules in situations of this kind, so this option is left to the discretion of the designer.

GROUNDING CONTROLLER SYSTEMS

In an earlier discussion, it was pointed out that improperly insulated connections and splices and mechanically insecure joints in underground valve circuit wiring, can be a constant source of trouble.

This can be avoided if field wiring is done in a workman-like manner, and certain precautions are taken.

a. First, all underground (and above ground) connections must be mechanically secure to provide maximum electrical conductance. This is best accomplished by joining the wires with a standard crimp sleeve and crimping tool.

b. Second, insulate all wire joints carefully. For underground connections, insulate with one of the suitable materials discussed earlier (or comparable materials). The underground joints must be com-

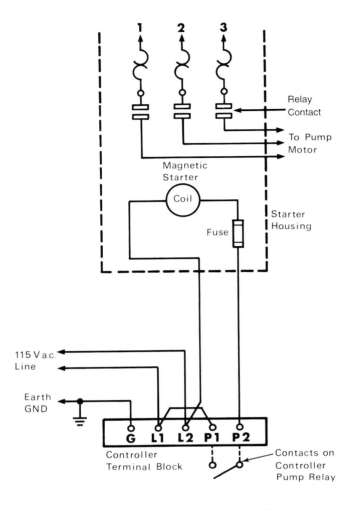

Figure 15-12 Controller Pump Circuit and Magnetic Starter

pletely waterproof and water-tight to prevent moisture in the soil environment from entering joints.

ELECTRICAL LEAKS

The problem caused by wire connections leaking electricity is illustrated in Figure 15-9, showing typical valve circuit wiring and power source from controller. Valve source voltage is designated by "V_s" originating from a transformer in the controller connected to line voltage. In the diagram, voltage is switched to valves 1 through 4 in sequence.

Note: A station selector switch for an electro-mechanical controller is shown in Figures 15-9 and 15-10 for illustration purposes. However, the problem discussed will occur with any type of controller.

When an electric RCV valve is first energized to open, it requires a momentary surge of power to activate its solenoid against an opposing force of water pressure.

The amount of voltage required for the inrush of current will vary from about 18 to 24 volts, depending on the amount of pressure. The required voltage will also vary with different brands and models. Once open, a small current will hold the solenoid actuator, consequently the valve can be held open and operating on as little as 7 to 8 volts.

In Figure 15-9, the solenoids on valves 2 and 3 have exposed wire connections. Valve 2 is operating and power is switched to valve 3. Valve 3 is energized and opened while valve 2 is de-energized. However, sufficient current can leak from valve 3 through earth between the faulty connections (dashed line) to hold valve 2 open. In this case, both valves will continue operating together until power is switched to circuit 4.

If the wire connections on all four circuits are exposed, one or more valves can be held open and continue operating with other valves. This depends on "I_x", which represents the leakage, which varies with:

a. proximity of valves
b. condition of wire splices and connections
c. conductivity of soil, which varies with its moisture content.

Ground current (I_x), in the example, can be equal to, or any part of, the current and voltage applied to an energized valve.

If the common wire "N" to all valves is properly grounded as shown in Figure 15-10, the problem of hanging valves due to ground currents can usually be eliminated. This method, of course, is not recommended as a substitute for good workmanship. Nevertheless, it will prevent problems from current leakage caused accidentally, such as punctures and abrasions to wiring, etc.

Common "N" may be grounded to earth separately as illustrated. Or, it may be more convenient to connect controller terminals "N" and "G" with a jumper wire; some controller models are supplied with this connection. For this last method, terminal "G" must be grounded to earth as outlined below. Note: Verify with controller manufacturer.

CONTROLLER EARTH GROUND

An earth ground shown in Figure 15-11, is required by the National Electrical Code. This should be provided even though not always required by local codes. Its

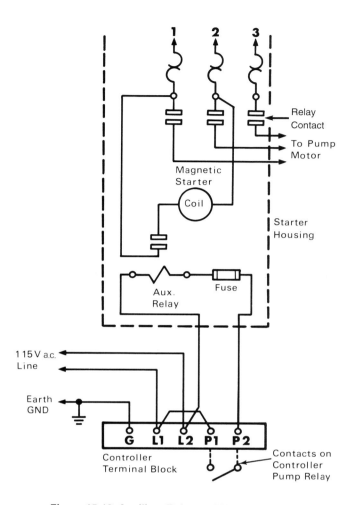

Figure 15-13 Auxiliary Relay and Magnetic Starter

purpose is to ground the controller housing to earth and thereby eliminate the possibility of any hazard of an electrical shock to the user. Always follow manufacturer's recommendations for controller earth grounding, especially with complex controller systems.

The earth ground connected from terminal "G" in the controller can be accomplished several ways. Most modern construction, both residential and commercial, includes a grounded electrical system which entails a third wire. A ground wire from terminal "G" can usually be connected to the third wire (ground wire) where power for the controller is obtained.

Alternate Method 1: an earth ground can be effected by connecting terminal "G" to a metallic cold water pipe using an approved electrical clamp.

Alternate Method 2: an earth ground can be made by use of an approved ground rod in the earth. Ground rod,

Electrical

clamp and method of installation should be in accordance with local codes.

Under no-load conditions, reading at a voltmeter connected to line "L2" and earth ground "G" will normally be about zero volts. Under load, depending on the amount of current and line voltage loss, this reading could show slight voltage without having any negative effect.

When power is connected to the controller, it is essential that the correct polarity be used. Line voltage, properly color coded for this purpose, is shown connected to terminals L1 and L2 in Figure 15-11 in the right relationship.

If there is any question about which line is "hot" or neutral, the polarity can be easily verified with a voltmeter as shown in the example.

PUMP CIRCUITS

When pumps are used as the source of water supply, controllers can be furnished with a pump control circuit. The control circuit closes at the beginning of an irrigation cycle, then opens when the last valve has finished operating, thus keeping a pump in operation throughout the entire watering cycle.

Pump circuits are furnished standard on some controller models and as an optional feature on others. The circuit may consist of a built-in relay or a completely separate relay controlled by the master valve circuit.

Note: Relays that are controlled by the master valve circuit must conform to the recommendations of the controller manufacturer.

Pumps are never powered direct from the pump circuit of an irrigation controller because contacts on the relays provided have a low current carrying capacity. Data relating to capacity should be obtained from the manufacturer since the contact rating will vary.

It is always necessary to supply power to pump motors independent of the controllers. The external power source is usually a Magnetic Motor Starter. Figure 15-12 illustrates a built-in pump relay, with the relay contact switching one side of the power supply to the coil of the magnetic starter.

MAGNETIC MOTOR STARTERS

Figure 15-12 illustrates a typical wiring schematic for a magnetic starter. The 115 volt coil and fuse are standard components. Purpose of the fuse is to protect the controller against an overload in case the 115V coil should ever develop a short circuit. Inrush power for the coil must not exceed the VA rating of the pump circuit. Coil voltage and frequency must be the same as controller line voltage L1 and L2.

The fuse illustrated must be rated with consideration for the inrush current requirements of the coil when energized. Voltage rating of the fuse must be equal to or greater than the controller line voltage L1 and L2.

AUXILIARY RELAY AND MAGNETIC STARTER

Figure 15-13 shows a wiring schematic for connecting a controller pump circuit to a magnetic starter with an auxiliary relay added. When the activating coil of a starter requires current in excess of the pump circuit VA rating, an auxiliary relay must be added to the circuit as illustrated. This must be a low current control relay, having contacts with a capacity sufficient for the current required by the activating coil of the starter.

Power required by the coil of the auxiliary relay must not exceed the pump circuit VA rating. Coil voltage and frequency rating must be the same as controller line voltage L1 and L2.

LIGHTNING SUPPRESSION

Occasionally lightning causes damage to controllers, electric RCV valves and other parts of the electrical control system. Such damage is not prevalent but does happen quite often in geographical areas that are lightning prone. Large irrigation systems connected to extensive power transmission lines, and having a great amount of valve circuit wiring spread out over large areas, are more exposed and more susceptible to lightning damage than the smaller and more compact systems.

Lightning seldom strikes a system directly. Damage, if any, is usually caused by strikes in the proximity of power transmission lines or valve circuit wiring. A strike in the vicinity of a system momentarily induces a surge of extremely high voltage that the equipment cannot withstand.

Damage is often caused by high voltage surges at the power input side to the controller. The surge of voltage, depending on its magnitude, can quite often be controlled and reduced to an acceptable level by installing a suppressor across the line. In more extreme cases, a suppressor with a third wire grounded to earth will offer still more protection to the controller.

Most of the damage to controllers is due to induced voltage in the valve wiring, and protection of the output side of the controller should be given careful consideration.

If necessary, suppressors may be used across each valve circuit provided that earth grounding in the controller is available. One suppressor is required for each station of the controller. This will give some protection to the secondary side of the controller against high voltage entering on one or more of the valve circuit stations.

The use of suppressors on valves to protect solenoids is generally impractical. Suppressors are difficult to waterproof and their replacement cost is comparable to the cost for replacing a damaged solenoid.

Note: Some controller models include input protection, and some include input and output protection as a standard feature.

Suppression devices will generally handle the normal surges incurred by induced voltage but offer no protection against direct lightning strikes on the wiring or other equipment. There are a number of suppressors available with different electrical characteristics and ratings. Most of these devices will take repeated surges within their rated capacity, but will eventually deteriorate and need to be replaced. In any event, suppressors must be considered expendable.

The controller manufacturer should be consulted for information on suitable lightning suppression devices, protection offered, and installation recommendations.

APPENDIX

APPENDIX

Appendix Contents

	TABLE	PAGE
Introduction		339
Technical Symbols and Abbreviations		
Explanation		339
Letter Symbols and Abbreviations	1	340
Graphic Symbols for Piping	2	341
Piping Pressure Losses and Velocities		342
Pressure Loss F- Factors ("RC" Method)	3	346
SDR 13.5 (315 psi PR) PVC Pipe	4	347
SDR 21(200 psi PR) PVC Pipe	5	349
SDR 26 (160 psi PR) PVC Pipe and Tubing	6	351
SDR 32.5 (125 psi PR) PVC Pipe	7	353
Schedule 40, 80, 120 PVC Pipe	8	355
Polyethylene Pipe and Tubing	9	357
Type K Copper Tube	10	359
Type M and L Copper Tube	11	361
Schedule 40, 80 Steel Pipe	12	363
Asbestos-Cement Pipe	13	365
Cast Iron Pipe	14	367
Water Hose	15	369
Flow Velocities		
Explanation		371
Multiplying Factors	16	372
Pressure Losses in Piping Appurtenances		
Explanation		373
Standard Plumbing Valves and Fittings	17	376
Standard Plumbing Valves and Copper Tube Fittings	18	377
Disc-Type Water Meters	19	378

	TABLE	PAGE
Equivalents		
Pressure (lb/in^2 to ft H$_2$O)	20	379
Pressure (ft H$_2$O to lb/in^2)	21	379
Pressure (lb/in^2 to kg/cm^2)	22	380
Precipitation (in/h to mm/h)	23	380
Wind Velocity (mi/h to km/h)	24	381
Flow (gpm to m^3/hr, l/s, l/min)	25	381
Length (ft to m)	26	382
Pumps		
Volume of Vertical Round Tanks	27	383
Volume of Horizontal Round	28	384
Water Supply		
Size Designations for Strainers	29	385
Head Layout		
Explanation		386
Head Layout Constants- Universal	30	387
Head Layout Constants (Feet to Meters)	31	387
Pipe Data		
Weight of Water in Pipes and Tubes	32	388
Electrical		
Wire Data-Standard Annealed Copper	33	389
Wire Resistance-Metric	34	389
Conversion Factors		
Length	35	390
Area	36	390
Volume	37	391
Flow	38	392
Velocity	39	393
Weight (Mass)	40	393
Density	41	393
Water Pressure	42	393

APPENDIX

ENGINEERING AND DESIGN DATA

Reference material provided in this section was compiled for the special requirements of landscape irrigation design. Many standard formulas have been reduced to tables of multiplying factors for quick reference and easy use. Any arithmetical requirements have been purposely arranged so they can be easily accomplished with an electronic calculator.

Although extreme care was exercised during preparation of all data in this Manual, neither the publisher nor the author shall be held responsible for any inaccuracy except to the extent that known errors will be corrected in future editions.

EXPLANATION OF TECHNICAL SYMBOLS AND ABBREVIATIONS

LETTER SYMBOLS

"Letter symbol" as a technical term does not have the same meaning as either "name" or "abbreviation". An abbreviation is a letter or a combination of letters (sometimes with an apostrophe or a period), which by convention represents a word or a name in a particular language, hence an abbreviation may be different in different languages. A symbol represents a quantity or a unit and is therefore independent of language**.

Example: For magnetomotive force, the symbol is F, whereas the abbreviation is mmf in English, fmm in French, MMK in German. The word "ampere" is sometimes abbreviated amp in some languages; the symbol for this unit is A.

    **Since letter symbols for units are internationally accepted, they should always be used in preference to abbreviations.[a]
Symbols are identical for both singular and plural.

TABLE 1

STANDARD SYMBOLS. Symbols listed are for United States Customary System of Weights and Measures which Irrigation System Designers may be expected to encounter. They have been developed by standards organizations such as American Society of Mechanical Engineers (ASME) and the U.S. National Bureau of Standards (NBS); nearly all have been approved as American National Standards.

[a] Extracted from American National Standard Glossary of Terms Concerning Letter Symbols (ANSI Y10.1-1972) with the permission of the publisher, The American Society of Mechanical Engineers, United Engineering Center, 345 East 47th Street, New York, New York 10017. by the International Organization for Standardization (ISO) for international use.

The standard symbols were developed in accordance with the principles for international symbols. Most of the standard symbols listed in Table 1 have been approved by the International Organization for Standardization (ISO) for international use.

Some SI (metric) symbols are used in conjunction with U.S. Customary Units; these are noted in the table. Also, a few symbols indicated with the comment "not universal" have not as yet been accepted as standard.

ABBREVIATIONS. In the United States, many abbreviations for quantities and units are referred to, and used, as symbols. Although such use is not correct, it will no doubt continue until such time as the U.S. converts entirely to the metric system. Table 1 also lists this type of abbreviation.

There are two primary reasons for continuation of some abbreviations of U.S. Customary quantities and units: (1) Habit, and (2) in some cases their greater brevity makes them useful for table headings.

Two of these abbreviations are used consistently in this Manual: "gpm" for "gallons per minute", and "psi" for "pounds per square inch." These are used for the reasons above and, in particular, to be in accordance with many standards and most U.S. equipment specifications.

AMERICAN NATIONAL STANDARD SYMBOLS FOR HYDRAULICS. These symbols, generally used in presenting formulas, are listed in Table 1 as reference for the reader.

TABLE 2

Graphic symbols for piping are shown in Table 2. Examples are included to illustrate the wide range of symbols that are commonly used in piping systems. This includes many custom symbols which are developed and used by individual designers.

A limited number of ASPE (American Society of Plumbing Engineers) symbols are included in Table 2. These are typical of the engineering symbols used on building and site plumbing plans.

Examples of ASAE (American Society of Agricultural Engineers) graphic symbols are also included for reference. Many designers use these (or similar) symbols for landscape irrigation designs. Additional symbols and variations for added detail are included in the complete set of ASAE standard symbols.

APPENDIX

TABLE 1

TECHNICAL SYMBOLS and ABBREVIATIONS

STANDARD SYMBOLS

Unit or Quantity	Symbol	Comments	Unit or Quantity	Symbol	Comments
acre	acre		mercury	Hg	
acre foot	acre-ft		mil	Mil	equals 0.001 in
acre inch	acre-in		mile (U.S. statute)	Mi	
ampere	A	SI symbol	mile per hour	mi/h	
area	A		million	M	mega
avoirdupois	avdp		minute (time)	min	SI symbol
			minute (plane angle)	$\ldots$ '	
breadth (width)	b		minus	$-$	
			month	mo	not universal
cubic foot	ft^3		multiplied by	$\cdot$, x	
cubic foot per minute	ft^3/min		ounce (avoirdupois)	oz	
cubic foot per second	ft^3/s		ounce (fluid)	fl oz	
cubic inch	in^3		per	/	function of division
cubic yard	yd^3		plus	+	
cycle per second (frequency)	Hz	SI symbol for hertz	pound	lb	
			pound per cubic foot	lb/ft^3	
day	d	SI symbol	pound per cubic inch	lb/in^3	not approved
degree Celsius (formerly Centigrade)	°C	SI symbol	pound—force	lb$f$	
degree Fahrenheit	°F		pound—force per square inch	lb$f$/in^2	(2)
degree (plane angle)	$\ldots$ °		radius	r	
diameter	d		revolution	r	
a divided by b	$\frac{a}{b}$, a/b	a/b preferred when in line of a text	revolution per minute	r/min	
			revolution per second	r/s	
foot	ft		second (time)	s	SI symbol
foot per minute	ft/min		second (plane angle)	$\ldots$ ''	
foot per second	ft/s		square foot	ft^2	
foot of water (head)	ftH$_2$O		square inch	in^2	
frequency	Hz	SI symbol for hertz	square yard	yd^2	
			temperature	T	
gallon	gal		ton (U.S. short)	ton	
gallons per minute	gal/min	not approved	velocity	v	
			volume	V	
height	h		volt	V	SI symbol
hertz	Hz	SI symbol	voltampere	VA	SI symbol
horsepower	hp	(1)	water	H$_2$O	
hour	h	SI symbol	watt	W	SI symbol
inch	in		week	wk	not universal
inch of mercury	inHg		(width) breadth	b	
kilowatt	kW	SI symbol	yard	yd	
length	l		year	yr	not universal

(1) Use of SI unit of power,
the watt (w), is preferred.

(2) When there is no chance of confusion,
the symbol for force, f, may be omitted.

ABBREVIATIONS SOMETIMES SUBSTITUTED FOR SYMBOLS

Item	Abbreviation	Comments	Item	Abbreviation	Comments
absolute	abs.		parts per million	ppm	
average	avg.		pounds per square inch	psi	not approved
gallons per minute	gpm	not approved	standard	std.	

AMERICAN NATIONAL STANDARD SYMBOLS for HYDRAULICS

Item	Symbol	Comments	Item	Symbol	Comments
atmosphere; standard	atm				
atmosphere, technical	at	at = kg$f$/cm^2	lift	L	
discharge (volume rate of flow)	Q		pressure	P	
"friction" factor	f		pressure, absolute	P_a	
head	h		pressure, gauge	P_g	
head-friction	h_f		pressure, vapor	P_v	
head-pressure rise for instantaneous closure	h_{max}		pressure increment	ΔP	
head-surge	h_s		radius (conduit)	R	
head = total	H		thickness	t	
			velocity, mean (Q/A)	V	

APPENDIX

TABLE 2

GRAPHIC SYMBOLS FOR PIPING

EXAMPLES OF CUSTOM SYMBOLS BY DESIGNERS

SYMBOL	DESCRIPTION	ABBREV.	SYMBOL	DESCRIPTION	ABBREV.
	GATE VALVE	GV		FLUSH LAWN HYDRANT	FLH
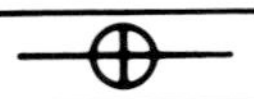	GLOBE VALVE	GLV		AUTOMATIC DRAIN VALVE	ADV
	ANGLE VALVE	ANV		BACKFLOW PREVENTER (INDICATE TYPE)	BFP
	CONTROL VALVE (ELECTRIC)	ECV		SPRINKLER HEADS (SEVERAL DIFFERENT SYMBOLS ARE USED FOR THE VARIOUS TYPES OF SPRINKLERS REQUIRED)	
	HOSE BIBB	HB			

EXAMPLES OF ASPE STANDARD PLUMBING SYMBOLS

SYMBOL	DESCRIPTION	ABBREV.	SYMBOL	DESCRIPTION	ABBREV.
	GATE VALVE	GV	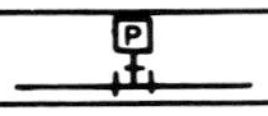	PRESSURE SWITCH	PS
	GLOBE VALVE	GLV		STRAINER–WYE TYPE	STR
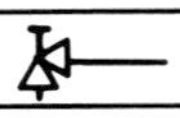	ANGLE VALVE	ANV		STRAINER-VERTICAL BASKET TYPE	STR
	SWING CHECK VALVE	CV	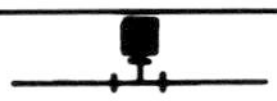	WATER HAMMER ARRESTOR	WHA
	NON-SLAM CHECK VALVE	NCV		AUTOMATIC AIR VENT	AAV
	BACKFLOW PREVENTER (INDICATE TYPE)	BFP		HOSE BIBB	HB
	SOLENOID OPERATED VALVE (ELECTRIC)	SVA		VALVE IN RISER (TYPE AS SPECIFIED OR NOTED)	
	PRESSURE REDUCING VALVE	PRV		VALVE IN YARD BOX (VALVE SYMBOL AS REQUIRED)	VIYB
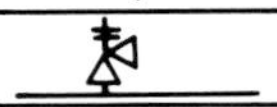	PRESSURE RELIEF VALVE	RV		EXPANSION JOINT	EJ
	FLOW SWITCH	FS		FLEXIBLE CONNECTOR	FC

EXAMPLES OF ASAE STANDARD SYMBOLS

SYMBOL	DESCRIPTION	SYMBOL	DESCRIPTION
	ROTARY SPRINKLER FULL-HALF-SPECIAL	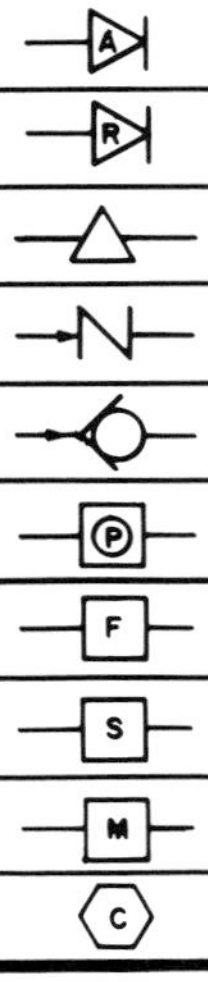	AUTOMATIC AIR VENT
	SPRAY SPRINKLER FULL-HALF-QUARTER		PRESSURE RELIEF VALVE
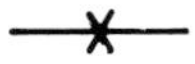	BUBBLER		QUICK COUPLER
	EMITTER		CHECK VALVE
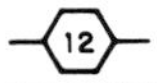	AUTOMATIC CONTROL VALVE NUMBER INDICATES ZONE		BACK FLOW PREVENTER
	MANUAL CONTROL VALVE		PUMP
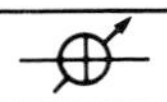	AUTOMATIC PRESSURE REGULATING VALVE		FILTER
	MANUAL PRESSURE REGULATING VALVE		STRAINER
	AUTOMATIC DRAIN VALVE		WATER METER
	ATMOSPHERIC VACUUM BREAKER		CONTROLLER

APPENDIX

EXPLANATION OF PRESSURE LOSSES IN PIPING

FORMULA
The tables of pressure losses due to friction of water flows were calculated using the Williams and Hazen formula in the form:

$$f = 0.2083 \left(\frac{100}{C} \right)^{1.85} \times \frac{Q^{1.85}}{d^{4.8655}}$$

Where:
- f = pressure loss in feet of head per 100 ft. of piping.
- C = coefficient accounting for inside pipe roughness.
- Q = flow in gpm.
- d = inside pipe diameter in inches.
- 2.309 ft head = 1 lb/in^2.

For use with SI (metric) system, the formula is:

$$f = .02081 \left(\frac{100}{C} \right)^{1.85} \times \frac{(4.403Q)^{1.85}}{(.039\,37\,d)^{4.8655}}$$

Where:
- f = pressure loss in kg/cm^2 per 100 meters of piping.
- C = coefficient accounting for inside pipe roughness.
- Q = flow in m^3/h.
- d = inside pipe diameter in millimeters.
- 1 kg/cm^2 = 1 at.
- 1 m^3/h = 16.67 l/min.

Analysis of the formula clearly shows that the loss of pressure that occurs when water is flowing through pipe is due to four causes:
1. LENGTH of piping
2. ROUGHNESS of the piping interior wall
3. RATE OF FLOW (and, consequently VELOCITY)
4. DIAMETER of piping

Pressure loss tables for water flowing through piping are constructed by formula. Any significant difference between tables for a given pipe occurs only when different roughness factors or diameters are used. And, of course, due to any varying degrees of accuracy in computations.

ROUGHNESS. The interior roughness of pipe varies, sometimes considerably, depending on kind of piping and age. Roughness of different kinds of new piping is the result of the method of manufacture and the kind of material from which the pipe is made. Deterioration is the major factor of roughness. Deterioration depends upon the material of the piping and the effect chemicals in the water have on the material.

The effects of deterioration are not consistent. Therefore, it is not possible to prepare tables which exactly reflect this factor, even though it is a prime cause of pressure loss. Each table of pressure losses (in this publication) is based on average deterioration of the kind of piping for which the table was prepared. It is recommended that prior experience be considered and local hydraulic engineers be consulted to determine if allowance for deterioration in the tables is sufficient for local conditions.

Roughness is accounted for in the Williams and Hazen formula by the coefficient "C". Average "C" values for new pipe and values commonly used for design of piping systems are shown below.

VALUES OF "C"

Type of Pipe	Average value for New, Straight Pipe	Commonly used Value for Design Purposes
Asbestos-Cement	150	140
Cast Iron, plain	130	100
Cast Iron, cement-mortar lined	140	130
Concrete	120	100
Copper; Brass; Lead	140	130
Steel, galvanized	140	100
Thermoplastic, PVC	160-150	150
Thermoplastic, PE	160-150	140

DIAMETER. The inside diameter of pipe affects pressure loss most drastically. Manufacturing tolerances, although limited to only thousandths of an inch in some kinds of pipe, must be considered when determining pressure losses in piping. For example: Due to tolerances, the maximum ID of $\frac{1}{2}$ in SDR 13.5 PVC pipe can be 0.720 in and the minimum 0.672 in or over 7% greater. With 4 gpm flowing through this pipe with the maximum ID, the pressure loss would be 2.74 lb/in^2; with the minimum ID, the loss for the same flow would be 3.83 lb/in^2, or an increase of almost 40%.

APPENDIX

Of course, the effect of diameter variations decreases as pipes become larger. However, it is still a factor that must be considered.

Varying diameters of pipe were considered in the preparation of pipe pressure loss tables of this publication. Since economics dictate that manufacturers of piping conserve material, it can be assumed that they will maintain wall thicknesses as near minimum as the manufacturing process reasonably allows. Thus, an average ID can be determined for each kind of pipe and tube. Use of average ID for calculating pressure losses by formula provides reasonable assurance that the calculated losses will be safe for designing piping systems but not overly conservative.

The method of determining average ID for different pipes is reviewed later in the explanation of pressure losses for each kind of pipe.

"RC" METHOD - PRESSURE LOSS (Table 3)
This method eliminates the need for standard pressure loss tables and interpolation of limited data when improved accuracy is desired or required. Pressure loss in pipe can be calculated for any flow rate using the multiplying factors provided in Table 3. Inside diameters, manufacturing tolerances and "C" values are the same as those described in this section for various types of pipe.

FORMAT OF TABLES (loss per 100 ft)
Pressure loss tables are included for pipe and tube types likely to be encountered. Multiplying factors, also provided, enable pressure losses to be determined for many other kinds of piping.

The last listed loss for each size thermoplastic and asbestos-cement pipe is for approximately 10 ft/s velocity flow. For other kinds of pipe (and hose) the last listed loss is for a velocity of approximately 15 ft/s; the only exception being for copper tube.

Pipe pressure loss tables do not provide allowances for turns, fittings, etc. and other appurtenances. See Tables 17, 18 and 19.

Included with each pressure loss table for a particular pipe or tube is a second page of tables providing additional data:

1. A table of flows occurring with velocities from 1 ft/s to 15 ft/s for the particular pipe for which losses are listed. Maximum flow velocities are critical with pipe to avoid damage.
Note: Table 16 provides multiplying factors to determine velocity with any flow and flow with any velocity. Multiplying factors are also provided for many pipes.
2. A table of multiplying factors to convert listed pressure losses for other values of "C."
3. A table of multiplying factors to determine pressure losses in odd sizes of pipe which are not listed in the loss table.
4. A table of multiplying factors to determine pressure losses for infrequently used types of the same kind of pipe.

POLY VINYL CHLORIDE (PVC) PLASTIC PIPE (Tables 4-8)
Pressure loss tables are provided for both SDR-PR and Schedule Wall PVC pipe.

Unlike many pipes, the standard wall thickness of PVC pipe has a plus tolerance only, ranging from 0.020 in to 0.090 in. Many pressure loss tables use the standard minimum wall (without tolerances) for computation purposes. Since manufacturing processes preclude achievement of this thickness, most all PVC pipe will have a thicker wall and consequently a smaller ID. Accordingly, use of the standard wall to prepare loss tables is not realistic. The loss tables in this manual use a wall thickness which includes one-half of the tolerances. This results in a more realistic average ID. This method of determining ID for calculation of pressure losses is recommended by the Plastic Pipe Institute (PPI).

Caution should be exercised to control velocities in PVC pipe to avoid damage from pressure surging (water hammer).

Note: PVC pressure loss tables can be used for any controlled OD thermoplastic pipe of the same SDR or Schedule number.

POLYETHYLENE (PE) PLASTIC PIPE (Table 9)
The pressure loss table for PE pipe is used for all controlled (IPS) ID PE pipe (both SDR and Schedule wall) since the ID for each nominal size is the same for all types. In accordance with general practice, the Standard ID dimensions (without tolerances) were used

as the average ID for computing pressure losses because tolerances are both plus and minus.

There is some disagreement as to the "C" factor that should be used when computing pressure losses in PE pipe and tube. The claim that PE is as smooth internally as PVC is disputed by some technicians. Also, many feel that because of its flexibility, when the pipe is bowed during installation and due to the weight of backfill, the circumferential orientation is forced out-of-round sufficiently to affect carrying capacity. Therefore, only "140" was used as the "C" factor in preparing the pressure loss table for PE pipe.

A multiplying factor is listed in one of the companion tables to determine loss in controlled (IPS) OD, SDR 11 PE pipe. For all other controlled (IPS) OD, SDR and Schedule Wall PE pipe, use the PVC pipe pressure loss table for the same SDR or Schedule wall (ID's are same). Before using a pressure loss in a PVC loss table, convert the listed loss to the equivalent of C = 140.

Caution should be exercised to control velocities in PE pipe to avoid damage from pressure surging (water hammer).

Note: The PE pressure loss table can be used for any controlled ID thermoplastic pipe.

COPPER WATER TUBE (Tables 10 and 11)
Standard OD and wall thickness dimensions were used to determine average ID, since both dimensions have plus and minus tolerances.

The value of "C" used to calculate pressure losses was "140." Five percent was added to the calculated losses as a safety factor for aging in service. The resultant calculated losses have proven safe over the years except for isolated areas with high concentration of chemicals in the water.

GALVANIZED STEEL PIPE (Table 12)
To construct the pressure loss table for galvanized steel pipe, the standard dimensions of steel pipe were used to determine average ID since both OD and wall thickness dimensions also have plus and minus tolerances. Losses are based on a "C" factor of "100" which is considered to represent the average roughness of fifteen-year-old galvanized steel pipe. An additional allowance should be made for older pipe or pipe

suspected of accumulating heavy deposits from extremely corrosive water.

ASBESTOS-CEMENT (A-C) PIPE (Table 13)
Only one pressure loss table is ordinarily provided for all classes of A-C pipe although, theoretically, some different classes have different inside diameters. However, because of the wide latitude for dimensions allowed by current standards, diameters of different classes overlap to a considerable extent. Therefore, a single safe average diameter for each size pipe is used in construction of pressure loss tables. This diameter is consistent with asbestos-cement pipe industry usage. The value of "C" recommended by manufacturers of A-C pipe is "140." And, this value was used in construction of the pressure loss table for A-C pipe.

CAST IRON PIPE - PLAIN (Table 14)
Standards of cast iron pipe allow the widest dimensional latitude of any pipe included in this Manual. Standard practice is to use the nominal size for the ID in computing pressure losses. This provides a safe average diameter.

The "C" factor normally used is "100." This value is considered to approximate the average roughness of 18-year-old pipe.

CAST IRON PIPE - CEMENT-MORTAR LINED
Cement-mortar lining of cast iron pipe reduces the inside diameter. However, the lining provides a long-lasting smooth interior surface which more than offsets the reduction of diameter in relation to carrying capacity. Therefore, general practice is to base pressure losses in this pipe on "C" = 130.

HOSE (Table 15)
Pressure loss in straight, smooth-bore hose was calculated in accordance with recommendations of the RMA[a]. The nominal size is used for the average ID. Note that the table was constructed with C = 140 and is suitable for smooth-bore hose only.

ACCURACY
It is strongly recommended that the user maintain the accuracy provided in the tables. Of necessity, two factors used in calculating pressure losses can vary from one length of pipe to another of the same kind:

---

a) Reference: RMA Handbook, published by Rubber Manufacturers
  Association 444 Madison Avenue, New York 10022

roughness and diameter. The factors used in calculation are average, although considered reliable. Thus if actual pipe used should deviate from average one way, and "loose" use of the listed losses deviate the same way, considerable inaccuracy can develop with possible disappointing results. On the other hand, accurate use of table losses should assure a reliable system design.

Normally, computations of pressure losses in a piping system are extended to only 0.1 lb/in^2. However, to simplify the designer's calculations, table losses are extended further:

1. To provide more accurate losses for long runs of pipe.
2. To allow accurate interpolation for unlisted flows visually where loss increments are small.

Nom. Size, in	PVC Pipe - C = 150[1]					PB Tube [4] SDR 13.5 C = 140[1]	PE-PB Pipe Controlled I.D.[5] C = 140
	315 psi SDR 13.5	200 psi SDR 21	160 psi SDR 26	Schedule 40	Schedule 80		
½	.4711	.4711[2]	.4711[2]	.6900	.9839	1.2634	.6784
¾	.2588	.2327	.2327[3]	.3224	.4277	.4373	.3238
1	.1410	.1204	.1188	.1685	.2161	.2233	.1716
1¼	.0758	.0645	.0612	.0809	.0999	.1314	.0834
1½	.0529	.0450	.0427	.0536	.0652	.0845	.0556
2	.0293	.0249	.0236	.0276	.0330	.0417	.0288
2½	.0177	.0150	.0142	.0173	.0205		.0181
3	.0105	.0089	.0085	.0097	.0114		.0102
4	.00545	.00460	.00435	.00475	.00548		.00499
6	.001971	.001664	.001573	.001610	.001859		
8		.000831	.000786	.000781	.000887		
10		.000466	.000440	.000428	.000488		
12		.000297	.000281	.000270	.000309		

Nom. Size, in	Copper Tube - C = 140 (+5%)			Galvanized Steel Sch. 40 C = 100	Asbestos-Cement Pipe C = 140	Cast Iron Pipe C = 100
	Type K	Type L	Type M			
½	1.0770	.9859	.8804	.9497		
¾	.4334	.3776	.3467	.4533		
1	.2024	.1872	.1736	.2402		
1¼	.1123	.1077	.1021	.1168		
1½	.0711	.0682	.0656	.0779		
2	.0341	.0329	.0319	.0404		.0440
2½	.0192	.0186	.0180	.0253		2¼=.0323
3	.0121	.0117	.0113	.0143	.0108	.0152
4	.00574	.00555	.00544	.00699	.00508	.00711
6	.002016	.001923	.001892	.002378	.001869	.002447
8	.000970	.000923	.000905	.001156	.000862	.001149
10	.000544	.000518	.000507	.000635	.000475	.000639
12	.000338	.000320	.000316	.000401	.000302	.000395

[1] Inside diameter reduced to include one-half of plus tolerance allowed for wall thickness.
[2] 315 psi, SDR 13.5
[3] 200 psi, SDR 21
[4] PB-ASTM D2666 (Cop. Tube O.D.)
[5] PE-ASTM D2239 / PB-ASTM D2662

PVC - Polyvinyl Chloride
PB - Polybutylene
PE - Polyethylene

MULTIPLYING FACTORS
FOR PIPE PRESSURE LOSSES

Irrigation designers can accurately compute the pressure loss in pipe using the following formula and 'F' factors provided for size and type of pipe variations. This method eliminates the need for standard pressure loss tables and interpolation of data when accuracy is required.

An inexpensive calculator with the key y^x (Function: y to the x power) is the only requirement for the chain calculation necessary with this method. Some models of calculators will allow commonly used data to be stored in memory. An entire program can be used in 'programmable' calculators or small computers.

"RC" Formula:
$(Q \times F)^{1.85} = PL_1$
$PL_1 \times L = PL_2$
therefore: $(Q \times F)^{1.85} \times L = PL_2$
where:
Q = flow, gpm.
F = factor from table.
PL_1 = pressure loss per 100 ft. of pipe length, psi.
L = pipe length in hundreds of feet $\frac{actual\ length}{100} = L$
PL_2 = pressure loss for pipe length, psi.
Example: Determine loss in 1¼ inch PVC pipe, 200 psi with a flow of 35.3 gpm through 67 ft of the pipe:
$(35.3 \times .0645)^{1.85} = 4.582 \times .67 = 3.07$ unit loss

Following is a typical calculator program for the example problem:
Enter: 35.3
Press Key: ×
Enter: .0645
Press Key: = (2.27685)
Press Key: y^x
Enter: 1.85
Press Key: = (4.5821434) = PL_1
Press Key: ×
Enter: .67
Press Key: = (3.0700361) = 3.07 = PL_2

Caution: The "RC" Formula and "F" multiplying factors listed are different than those provided in some previous editions.

APPENDIX

Table Losses Same for all Controlled OD SDR 13.5 thermoplastic pipe. For PE pipe, convert losses to equivalent of C = 140

TABLE 4
PRESSURE LOSS
315 psi PR SDR 13.5 PVC PIPE

C = 150

Pipe Sizes: Nominal — Losses per 100 ft: lb/in^2

gpm	1/2 in	3/4 in	1 in	1-1/4 in	1-1/2 in	2 in	gpm	2-1/2 in	3 in	4 in	6 in
1	0.248	0.082	0.027	0.008	0.004	0.001	105	3.15	1.21	0.356	0.054
2	0.896	.296	.096	.031	.016	.005	110	3.44	1.32	.388	.059
3	1.90	0.626	.204	.065	.033	.011	115	3.73	1.43	.421	.064
4	3.23	1.07	.347	.110	.057	.019	120	4.04	1.55	.455	.069
5	4.88	1.61	.524	.116	.086	.029	125	4.35	1.67	.491	.075
6	6.84	2.26	.734	.233	.120	.040	130	4.68	1.79	.528	.081
7	9.09	3.00	0.976	.310	.159	.053	135	5.02	1.92	.566	.086
8	11.64	3.84	1.25	.397	.204	.068	140	5.37	2.06	.606	.092
9	14.48	4.78	1.55	.493	.254	.085	145	5.73	2.19	.646	.099
10	17.59	5.81	1.89	0.599	0.308	0.103	150	6.10	2.34	0.688	0.105
11	20.98	6.93	2.25	.715	.368	.123	160		2.63	.775	.118
12	24.65	8.14	2.65	.840	.432	.144	170		2.95	.867	.132
13		9.44	3.07	0.974	.501	.167	180		3.27	0.964	.147
14		10.82	3.52	1.12	.575	.192	190		3.62	1.07	.163
15		12.30	4.00	1.27	.653	.218	200		3.98	1.17	.179
16		13.86	4.51	1.43	.736	.246	210		4.35	1.28	.196
17		15.50	5.04	1.60	.823	.275	220		4.75	1.40	.213
18		17.23	5.60	1.78	0.915	.305	230			1.52	.231
19		19.04	6.19	1.96	1.01	.338	240			1.64	.250
20		20.94	6.81	2.16	1.11	0.371	250			1.77	0.270
22			8.12	2.58	1.33	.443	260			1.90	.290
24			9.54	3.03	1.56	.520	270			2.04	.311
26	2-1/2 in		11.06	3.51	1.81	.603	280			2.18	.333
28			12.69	4.03	2.07	.692	290			2.33	.355
30	0.311		14.42	4.57	2.35	.786	300			2.48	.378
32	.350			5.15	2.65	.886	325			2.88	.439
34	.391			5.77	2.97	0.991	350			3.30	.503
36	.435	3 in		6.41	3.30	1.10	375			3.75	.572
38	.481			7.08	3.64	1.22	400				.644
40	.529	0.203		7.79	4.01	1.34	425				.721
42	.579	.222		8.52	4.39	1.46	450				.801
44	.631	.242		9.29	4.78	1.60	475				.885
46	.685	.262	4 in	10.09	5.19	1.73	500				0.973
48	.741	.284		10.91	5.61	1.88	550				1.16
50	0.799	0.306	0.090		6.05	2.02	600				1.36
52	.859	.329	.097		6.51	2.17	650				1.58
54	.921	.353	.104		6.98	2.33	700				1.81
56	0.985	.378	.111		7.47	2.49	800				2.32
58	1.05	.403	.119		7.97	2.66	900				
60	1.12	.429	.126		8.48	2.83	1000				
62	1.19	.456	.134		9.01	3.01	1100				
64	1.26	.483	.142			3.19	1200				
66	1.34	.512	.151			3.38	1300				
68	1.41	.541	.159			3.57	1400				
70	1.49	0.571	0.168			3.77	1500				
75	1.69	.648	.191			4.28	2000				
80	1.91	.730	.215			4.82	2500				
85	2.13	.817	.241			5.40	3000				
90	2.37	0.908	.267			6.00	3500				
95	2.62	1.00	.296			6.63	4000				
100	2.88	1.10	0.325			7.29	5000				

APPENDIX

Table VELOCITY FLOWS same for all
Controlled OD SDR 13.5 thermoplastic pipe.

TABLE 4a
VELOCITY FLOWS
SDR13.5 PVC PIPE

Velocity ft/s	Nominal Pipe Size: inches										Velocity ft/s
	1/2	3/4	1	1-1/4	1-1/2	2	2-1/2	3	4	6	
	Flow: gpm*										
1	1.2	1.9	3.0	4.8	6.3	9.8	14.4	21.3	35.2	76.3	1
2	2.4	3.7	5.9	9.5	12.5	19.6	28.7	42.6	70.5	152.7	2
3	3.6	5.6	8.9	14.3	18.8	25.4	43.1	64.0	105.7	229.0	3
4	4.7	7.5	11.9	19.0	25.0	39.2	57.5	85.3	140.9	305.3	4
5	5.9	9.3	14.8	23.8	31.3	49.1	71.9	106.6	176.2	381.7	5
6	7.1	11.2	17.8	28.5	37.5	58.9	86.2	127.9	211.4	458.0	6
7	8.3	13.1	20.8	33.3	43.8	68.7	100.6	149.2	246.7	534.3	7
8	9.5	15.0	23.7	38.1	50.0	78.5	115.0	170.5	281.9	610.6	8
9	10.7	16.8	26.7	42.8	56.3	88.3	129.3	191.9	317.1	687.0	9
10	11.9	18.7	29.7	47.6	62.5	98.1	143.7	213.2	352.4	763.3	10
11	13.0	20.6	32.6	52.3	68.8	107.9	158.1	234.5	387.6	839.6	11
12	14.2	22.4	35.6	57.1	75.0	117.7	172.5	255.8	422.8	916.0	12
13	15.4	24.3	38.6	61.8	81.3	127.5	186.8	277.1	458.1	992.3	13
14	16.6	26.2	41.5	66.6	87.5	137.4	201.2	298.5	493.3	1068.6	14
15	17.8	28.0	44.5	71.4	93.8	147.2	215.6	319.8	528.6	1145.0	15

*Flows calculated with factors in Table 16 may vary slightly due to rounding off of factors.

TABLE 4b
MULTIPLYING FACTORS TO CHANGE VALUE OF "C"
C = 150 TO OTHER VALUES

Value of "C"	To determine PRESSURE LOSSES with other values of "C", multiply Losses computed with C = 150 by following factors:											Value of "C"
	160	150	140	130	120	110	100	90	80	70	60	50	
Multiplier	0.887	1.0	1.14	1.30	1.51	1.77	2.12	2.57	3.20	4.10	5.45	7.63	Multiplier

TABLE 4c
PRESSURE LOSS
SDR 13.5 PVC PIPE
SIZES NOT LISTED OPPOSITE PAGE

To determine PRESSURE LOSSES of 1/8, 1/4 and 3/8 in SDR 13.5 PVC pipe, multiply Losses of 1/2 in SDR 13.5 by following factors:			
Nominal Size, in	1/8	1/4	3/8
	Multipliers		
SDR 13.5	109.8	14.80	3.60

To determine PRESSURE LOSSES of 3-1/2 and 5 in SDR 13.5 PVC pipe, multiply Losses of 4 in SDR 13.5 by following factors:		
Nominal Size, in	3-1/2(a)	5(a)
	Multipliers	
SDR 13.5	1.78	0.357

(a) Determine availability before designing systems with these sizes.

APPENDIX

Table Losses same for all
Controlled OD SDR 21 thermoplastic pipe.

C = 150

TABLE 5

PRESSURE LOSS
200 psi PR SDR 21 PVC PIPE

Pipe Sizes: Nominal   Losses per 100 ft: lb/in^2

gpm	1/2 in[1]	3/4 in	1 in	1-1/4 in	1-1/2 in	2 in	gpm	2 in	2-1/2 in	3 in	4 in	6 in	8 in
1	0.248	0.067	0.020	0.006	0.003	0.001	105	5.92	2.32	0.885	0.260	0.040	0.011
2	0.896	.243	.072	.023	.012	.004	110	6.45	2.53	0.964	.284	.043	.012
3	1.90	.515	.152	.048	.025	.008	115		2.74	1.05	.308	.047	.013
4	3.23	0.876	.259	.082	.042	.014	120		2.97	1.13	.333	.051	.014
5	4.88	1.32	.391	.123	.063	.021	125		3.20	1.22	.359	.055	.015
6	6.84	1.86	.548	.173	.089	.030	130		3.44	1.31	.386	.059	.016
7	9.09	2.47	.729	.230	.118	.039	135		3.69	1.41	.414	.063	.017
8	11.64	3.16	0.934	.294	.151	.051	140		3.95	1.51	.443	.068	.019
9	14.48	3.93	1.16	.366	.188	.063	145		4.21	1.61	.473	.072	.020
10	17.59	4.77	1.41	0.445	0.228	0.076	150		4.48	1.71	0.503	0.077	0.021
11	20.98	5.69	1.68	.531	.272	.091	160		5.05	1.93	.567	.086	.024
12	24.65	6.69	1.98	.623	.320	.107	170			2.16	.634	.097	.027
13		7.75	2.29	.723	.371	.124	180	10 in		2.40	.705	.108	.030
14		8.89	2.63	.829	.425	.142	190			2.65	.779	.119	.033
15		10.11	2.99	0.942	.483	.162	200	0.012		2.91	.857	.131	.036
16		11.39	3.37	1.06	.544	.182	210	.014		3.19	0.938	.143	.040
17		12.74	3.77	1.19	.609	.204	220	.015		3.48	1.02	.156	.043
18	2-1/2 in	14.16	4.19	1.32	.677	.226	230	.016		3.77	1.11	.169	.047
19		15.65	4.63	1.46	.748	.250	240	.017		4.08	1.20	.183	.051
20	0.108	17.21	5.09	1.60	0.823	0.275	250	.019			1.29	0.197	0.055
22	.129		6.07	1.91	0.981	.328	260	.020			1.39	.212	.059
24	.151		7.13	2.25	1.15	.386	270	.022			1.49	.228	.063
26	.175		8.27	2.61	1.34	.447	280	.023	12 in		1.60	.244	.067
28	.201		9.48	2.99	1.53	.513	290	.025			1.70	.260	.072
30	.228		10.77	3.40	1.74	.583	300	.026	0.011		1.81	.277	.076
32	.257		12.14	3.83	1.96	.657	325	.030	.013		2.10	.321	.089
34	.288		13.58	4.28	2.20	.735	350	.035	.015		2.41	.368	.102
36	.320	3 in		4.76	2.44	.816	375	.040	.017		2.74	.418	.116
38	.354			5.26	2.70	.902	400	.045	.019		3.09	.471	.130
40	0.389	0.148		5.78	2.97	0.992	425	.050	.022			.527	.146
42	.426	.162		6.33	3.25	1.09	450	.055	.024			0.586	0.162
44	.464	.177		6.90	3.54	1.18	475	.061	.027			.647	.179
46	.504	.192		7.49	3.84	1.28	500	.067	.029			.712	.197
48	.545	.208		8.10	4.15	1.39	550	.080	.035			.849	.235
50	.588	.224		8.74	4.48	1.50	600	.094	.041			0.997	.276
52	.632	.241		9.39	4.82	1.61	650	.110	.048			1.16	.320
54	.677	.259		10.07	5.17	1.73	700	.126	.055			1.33	.367
56	.725	.277	4 in		5.53	1.85	800	.161	.070			1.70	.470
58	.773	.295			5.90	1.97	900	.200	.087				.584
60	0.823	0.314	0.092		6.28	2.10	1000	0.243	0.106				.710
62	.875	.334	.098		6.67	2.23	1100	.290	.126				.846
64	.928	.354	.104		7.07	2.37	1200	.340	.148				0.994
66	0.982	.375	.110		7.49	2.51	1300	.395	.172				1.15
68	1.04	.396	.116		7.91	2.65	1400	.453	.197				1.32
70	1.09	.418	.123		8.35	2.79	1500	.514	.224				1.50
75	1.24	.475	.140			3.17	2000	0.876	.382				
80	1.40	.535	.157			3.58	2500	1.32	.577				
85	1.57	.599	.176			4.00	3000		0.809				
90	1.74	.665	.196			4.45	3500		1.08				
95	1.93	.735	.216			4.92	4000						
100	2.12	0.808	0.238			5.40	5000						

[1] 1/2 in SDR 21 not standard. For convenience, losses for SDR 13.5 listed.

APPENDIX

TABLE 5a
VELOCITY FLOWS
SDR 21 PVC PIPE

Velocity ft/s	1/2[1]	3/4	1	1-1/4	1-1/2	2	2-1/2	3	4	6	8	10	12	Velocity ft/s
							Flow: gpm*							
1	1.2	2.0	3.3	5.4	7.1	11.1	16.3	24.2	40.1	86.8	147.3	228.8	321.8	1
2	2.4	4.1	6.7	10.8	14.1	22.2	32.6	48.5	80.1	173.6	294.5	457.5	643.6	2
3	3.6	6.1	10.0	16.1	21.2	33.3	48.9	72.7	120.2	260.4	441.8	686.3	965.3	3
4	4.7	8.1	13.4	21.5	28.3	44.4	65.2	96.9	160.3	347.2	589.0	915.1	1287.1	4
5	5.9	10.1	16.7	26.9	35.4	55.5	81.5	121.1	200.4	434.1	736.3	1143.8	1608.9	5
6	7.1	12.2	20.1	32.3	42.4	66.6	97.8	145.4	240.4	520.9	883.6	1372.6	1930.7	6
7	8.3	14.2	23.4	37.6	49.5	77.7	114.2	169.6	280.5	607.7	1030.8	1601.4	2252.4	7
8	9.5	16.2	26.8	56.6	88.8	88.8	130.5	193.8	320.6	694.5	1178.1	1830.1	2574.2	8
9	10.7	18.2	30.1	48.4	63.7	99.9	146.8	218.1	360.7	781.3	1325.3	2058.9	2896.0	9
10	11.9	20.3	33.5	53.8	70.7	111.0	163.1	242.3	400.7	868.1	1472.6	2287.7	3217.8	10
11	13.0	22.3	36.8	59.1	77.8	122.1	179.4	266.5	440.8	954.9	1619.9	2516.4	3539.6	11
12	14.2	24.3	40.1	64.5	84.9	133.1	195.7	290.7	480.9	1041.7	1767.1	2745.2	3861.3	12
13	15.4	26.4	43.5	69.9	92.0	144.2	212.0	315.0	521.0	1128.5	1914.4	2974.0	4183.1	13
14	16.6	28.4	46.8	75.3	99.0	155.3	228.3	339.2	561.0	1215.4	2061.6	3202.7	4504.9	14
15	17.8	30.4	50.2	80.6	106.1	166.4	244.6	363.4	601.1	1302.2	2208.9	3431.5	4826.7	15

*Flows calculated with factors in Table 16 may vary slightly due to rounding off of factors.
[1]Flows for velocities in SDR 13.5 pipe.

TABLE 5b
MULTIPLYING FACTORS TO CHANGE VALUE OF "C"
C = 150 TO OTHER VALUES

Value of "C"	160	150	140	130	120	110	100	90	80	70	60	50	Value of "C"
	To determine PRESSURE LOSSES with other values of "C", multiply Losses computed with C = 150 by following factors:												
Multiplier	0.887	1.0	1.14	1.30	1.51	1.77	2.12	2.57	3.20	4.10	5.45	7.63	Multiplier

TABLE 5c
PRESSURE LOSS
SDR 21 PVC PIPE
SIZES NOT LISTED OPPOSITE PAGE

Nominal Size, in	3-1/2[a]	5[a]
To determine PRESSURE LOSSES of 3-1/2 and 5 in SDR 21 PVC pipe, multiply LOSSES of 4 in SDR 21 by following factors:		
	Multiplier	
SDR 21	1.78	0.357
SDR 17	2.02	0.406

[a] Determine availability before designing systems with these sizes.

TABLE 5d
PRESSURE LOSS
SDR 17 PVC PIPE

Size, in	3/4	1	1-1/4	1-1/2	2	2-1/2	3	4	6	8	10	12	Size, in
To determine PRESSURE LOSSES of SDR 17 PVC pipe, multiply losses of same size SDR 21 by following factors:													
	Multipliers												
SDR17	1.02	1.13	1.13	1.14	1.13	1.13	1.14	1.14	1.14	1.14	1.14	1.14	SDR17

APPENDIX

TABLE 6

Table losses same for all controlled OD SDR 26 thermoplastic pipe.

PRESSURE LOSS

160 psi PR SDR 26 PVC PIPE

C = 150

Pipe Sizes: Nominal • Losses per 100 ft: lb/in²

gpm	1/2 in [1]	3/4 in [1]	1 in	1-1/4 in	1-1/2 in	2 in
1	0.248	0.067	0.019	0.005	0.003	0.001
2	0.896	.243	.070	.021	.011	.004
3	1.90	.515	.148	.044	.022	.007
4	3.23	0.876	.253	.074	.038	.013
5	4.88	1.32	.382	.112	.057	.019
6	6.84	1.86	.535	.157	.081	.027
7	9.09	2.47	.711	.209	.107	.036
8	11.64	3.16	0.911	.267	.137	.046
9	14.48	3.93	1.13	.332	.171	.057
10	17.59	4.77	1.38	0.404	0.207	0.069
11	20.98	5.69	1.64	.481	.247	.082
12	24.65	6.69	1.93	.565	.290	.097
13		7.75	2.24	.656	.337	.112
14		8.89	2.56	.752	.386	.129
15		10.11	2.91	.854	.439	.146
16		11.39	3.28	0.963	.494	.165
17		12.74	3.67	1.08	.553	.184
18		14.16	4.08	1.20	.615	.205
19		15.65	4.51	1.32	.679	.227
20		17.21	4.96	1.45	.747	.249
22			5.92	1.74	0.891	0.297
24			6.95	2.04	1.05	.349
26	**2-1/2 in**		8.06	2.36	1.21	.405
28			9.25	2.71	1.39	.464
30	0.206		10.51	3.08	1.58	.527
32	.233		11.84	3.47	1.78	.594
34	.260		13.24	3.88	1.99	.665
36	.289	**3 in**		4.32	2.22	.739
38	.320			4.77	2.45	.817
40	.352	0.135		5.24	2.69	.898
42	.385	.147		5.74	2.95	0.983
44	.419	.161		6.26	3.21	1.07
46	.455	.174	**4 in**	6.79	3.49	1.16
48	.493	.189		7.35	3.77	1.26
50	0.531	0.203	0.059	7.92	4.07	1.36
52	.571	.219	.064	8.52	4.38	1.46
54	.613	.234	.069	9.14	4.69	1.56
56	.655	.251	.073	9.77	5.02	1.67
58	.699	.268	.078		5.35	1.79
60	.744	.285	.083		5.70	1.90
62	.791	.303	.089		6.06	2.02
64	.839	.321	.094		6.42	2.14
66	.888	.340	.099		6.80	2.27
68	.938	.359	.105		7.19	2.40
70	0.990	0.379	0.111		7.58	2.53
75	1.12	.430	.126		8.62	2.87
80	1.27	.485	..142			3.24
85	1.42	.543	.159			3.62
90	1.58	.603	.176			4.03
95	1.74	.667	.195			4.45
100	1.92	0.733	0.214			4.89

gpm	2 in	2-1/2 in	3 in	4 in	6 in	8 in
105	5.35	2.10	0.802	0.235	0.036	0.010
110	5.84	2.28	0.874	.256	.039	.011
115	6.34	2.48	0.949	.278	.042	.012
120	6.86	2.68	1.03	.300	.046	.013
125		2.89	1.11	.324	.049	.014
130		3.11	1.19	.348	.053	.015
135		3.34	1.28	.373	.057	.016
140		3.57	1.37	.399	.061	.017
145		3.81	1.46	.426	.065	.018
150		4.05	1.55	0.454	0.069	0.019
160		4.57	1.75	.511	.078	.022
170		5.11	1.96	.572	.087	.024
180	**10 in**		2.17	.636	.097	.027
190			2.40	.703	.107	.030
200	0.011		2.64	.773	.118	.033
210	.012		2.89	.846	.129	.036
220	.013		3.15	0.922	.140	.039
230	.014		3.42	1.00	.152	.042
240	.016		3.70	1.08	.165	.046
250	.017		3.99	1.17	0.178	0.049
260	.018			1.26	.191	.053
270	.019			1.35	.205	.057
280	.021	**12 in**		1.44	.219	.061
290	.022			1.54	.234	.065
300	.024	0.010		1.64	.249	.069
325	.027	.012		1.90	.289	.080
350	.031	.014		2.18	.332	.092
375	.036	.016		2.47	.377	.104
400	.040	.018		2.79	.424	.118
425	.045	.020		3.12	.475	.132
450	.050	.022			0.528	0.146
475	.055	.024			.583	.162
500	.061	.027			.641	.178
550	.073	.032			.765	.212
600	0.085	0.037			0.899	.249
650	.099	.043			1.04	.289
700	.113	.049			1.20	.331
800	.145	.063			1.53	.424
900	.180	.079			1.90	.527
1000	.219	.096				.640
1100	.261	.114				.764
1200	.307	.134				0.897
1300	.356	.155				1.04
1400	.408	.178				1.19
1500	.464	.202				1.36
2000	0.790	0.344				
2500	1.19	.521				
3000		.729				
3500		0.970				
4000						
5000						

(1)1/2 and 3/4 in SDR 26 not standard. For convenience, losses for 1/2 in SDR 13.5 and 3/4 in SDR 21 listed.

APPENDIX

Table Velocity Flows same for all controlled OD SDR 26 thermoplastic pipe.

TABLE 6a
VELOCITY FLOWS
SDR 26 PVC PIPE

Velocity ft/s	Nominal Pipe Size: inches — Flow: gpm*													Velocity ft/s
	1/2(1)	3/4(2)	1	1-1/4	1-1/2	2	2-1/2	3	4	6	8	10	12	
1	1.2	2.0	3.4	5.6	7.4	11.6	17.0	25.2	41.8	90.6	153.6	238.7	335.7	1
2	2.4	4.1	6.8	11.2	14.7	23.1	34.0	50.4	83.6	181.2	307.2	477.3	671.5	2
3	3.6	6.1	10.1	16.8	22.1	34.7	51.0	75.7	125.5	271.8	460.8	716.0	1007.2	3
4	4.7	8.1	13.5	22.4	29.4	46.2	68.0	100.9	167.3	362.4	614.4	954.7	1342.9	4
5	5.9	10.1	16.9	28.0	36.8	57.8	85.0	126.1	209.1	453.1	768.0	1193.3	1678.7	5
6	7.1	12.2	20.3	33.6	44.2	69.4	102.0	151.3	250.9	543.7	921.6	1432.0	2014.4	6
7	8.3	14.2	23.7	39.2	51.5	80.9	119.0	176.6	292.7	634.3	1075.1	1670.7	2350.2	7
8	9.5	16.2	27.0	44.8	58.9	92.5	136.0	201.8	334.5	724.9	1228.7	1909.3	2685.9	8
9	10.7	18.2	30.4	50.4	66.2	104.0	153.0	227.0	376.3	815.5	1382.3	2148.0	3021.6	9
10	11.9	20.3	33.8	56.0	73.6	115.6	170.0	252.2	418.2	906.1	1535.9	2386.7	3357.3	10
11	13.0	22.3	37.2	61.6	81.0	127.2	187.0	277.5	460.0	996.7	1689.5	2625.3	3693.1	11
12	14.2	24.3	40.6	67.2	88.3	138.7	204.0	302.7	501.8	1087.3	1843.1	2864.0	4028.8	12
13	15.4	26.4	43.9	72.8	95.7	150.3	221.0	327.9	543.6	1178.0	1996.7	3102.7	4364.5	13
14	16.6	28.4	47.3	78.4	103.0	161.8	238.0	353.1	585.4	1268.6	2150.3	3341.4	4700.3	14
15	17.8	30.4	50.7	83.9	110.4	173.4	255.0	378.4	627.2	1359.2	2303.9	3580.0	5036.0	15

*Flows calculated with factors in Table 16 may vary slightly due to rounding-off of factors.
(1) Flows are for velocities in SDR 13.5 pipe.
(2) Flows are for velocities in SDR 21 pipe.

TABLE 6b
MULTIPLYING FACTORS TO CHANGE VALUE OF "C"
C = 150 TO OTHER VALUES

To determine PRESSURE LOSSES with other values of "C", multiply losses computed with C = 150 by following factors:												
Value of "C"	160	150	140	130	120	110	100	90	80	70	60	50	Value of "C"
Multiplier	0.887	1.0	1.14	1.30	1.51	1.77	2.12	2.57	3.20	4.10	5.45	7.63	Multiplier

TABLE 6c
PRESSURE LOSS
SDR 26 PVC PIPE
SIZES NOT LISTED OPPOSITE PAGE

To determine PRESSURE LOSSES of 3-1/2 and 5 in SDR 26 PVC pipe, multiply Losses of 4 in SDR 26 PVC pipe by following factors:		
Nominal Size, in	3-1/2(a)	5(a)
	Multiplier	
SDR 26	1.78	0.357

(a) Determine availability before designing systems with these sizes.

TABLE 6d
PRESSURE LOSS
SDR 26 PVC TUBING

To determine PRESSURES of SDR 26 PVC TUBING, multiply Losses of 1 in SDR 26 PIPE by following factors:				
Size, in	1/2	3/4	1	1-1/4	Size, in
SDR 26 PVC Tubing	73.36	9.74	2.35	0.782	SDR 26 PVC Tubing

Table losses same for all Controlled OD
SDR 32.5 thermoplastic pipe.

C = 150

TABLE 7

PRESSURE LOSS

125 psi PR SDR 32.5 PVC PIPE

Pipe Sizes: Nominal — Losses per 100 ft: lb/in²

gpm	2 in[1]	2-1/2[1]	3 in	4 in	6 in
5	0.018	0.007	0.003	0.001	
10	.064	.025	.010	.003	
15	.135	.053	.020	.006	.001
20	.230	.090	.034	.010	.002
25	.348	.136	.052	.015	.002
30	.487	.190	.073	.021	.003
35	.648	.253	.097	.028	.004
40	.829	.324	.124	.036	.005
42	.907	.355	.136	.040	.006
44	0.989	.387	.148	.043	.007
46	1.07	.420	.161	.047	.007
48	1.16	.454	.174	.051	.008
50	1.25	0.490	0.187	0.055	0.008
52	1.35	.527	.202	.059	.009
54	1.44	.565	.216	.063	.010
56	1.55	.604	.231	.067	.010
58	1.65	.645	.247	.072	.011
60	1.76	.687	.263	.077	.012
62	1.87	.730	.279	.081	.012
64	1.98	.774	.296	.086	.013
66	2.09	.819	.313	.091	.014
68	2.21	.866	.331	.097	.015
70	2.33	.913	0.349	0.102	0.015
72	2.46	0.962	.368	.107	.016
74	2.59	1.01	.387	.113	.017
76	2.72	1.06	.407	.119	.018
78	2.85	1.12	.427	.125	.019
80	2.99	1.17	.447	.131	.020
85	3.34	1.31	.500	.146	.022
90	3.72	1.45	.556	.162	.025
95	4.11	1.61	.615	.179	.027
100	4.52	1.77	0.676	0.197	0.030
105	4.94	1.93	.740	.216	.033
110	5.39	2.11	.806	.235	.036
115	5.85	2.29	.875	.255	.039
120	6.33	2.48	0.947	.276	.042
125		2.67	1.02	.298	.045
130		2.87	1.10	.321	.049
135		3.08	1.18	.344	.052
140		3.29	1.26	.368	.056
145		3.51	1.34	.392	.060
150		3.74	1.43	0.418	0.063

gpm	2-1/2 in	3 in	4 in	6 in	8 in	10 in	12 in
160	4.22	1.61	0.471	0.071	0.020	0.007	0.003
170	4.72	1.80	.526	.080	.022	.008	.003
180	5.24	2.00	.585	.089	.025	.008	.004
190		2.22	.647	.098	.027	.009	.004
200		2.44	.711	.108	.030	.010	.004
210		2.67	.778	.118	.033	.011	.005
220		2.91	.848	.129	.036	.012	.005
230		3.16	.921	.140	.039	.013	.006
240		3.41	0.996	.151	.042	.014	.006
250		3.68	1.07	0.163	0.045	0.015	0.007
260		3.96	1.16	.175	.049	.017	.007
270			1.24	.188	.052	.018	.008
280			1.33	.201	.056	.019	.008
290			1.41	.215	.059	.020	.009
300			1.51	.229	.063	.022	.009
325			1.75	.265	.073	.025	.011
350			2.00	.304	.084	.029	.013
375			2.28	.346	.096	.033	.014
400			2.56	0.389	0.108	0.037	0.016
425			2.87	.436	.121	.041	.018
450			3.19	.484	.134	.046	.020
475				.535	.148	.051	.022
500				.588	.163	.056	.024
550				.702	.194	.067	.029
600				.824	.228	.078	.034
650				0.956	.265	.091	.040
700				1.10	.304	.104	.045
800				1.40	.389	.133	.058
900				1.75	.483	.166	.072
1000				2.12	0.587	0.201	0.088
1100					.701	.240	.105
1200					.823	.282	.123
1300					0.954	.327	.143
1400					1.09	.375	.163
1500					1.24	.426	.186
2000						0.726	.316
2500						1.10	.478
3000							0.669
3500							0.890
4000							
4500							
5000							

[1] Not ASTM Standard pipe.

APPENDIX

Table Velocity Flows same for all Controlled OD SDR 32.5 thermoplastic pipe.

TABLE 7a
VELOCITY FLOWS
SDR 32.5 PVC PIPE

Velocity ft/s	Nominal Pipe Sizes: inches								Velocity ft/s
	2[1]	2-1/2[1]	3	4	6	8	10	12	
	Flow: gpm*								
1	11.9	17.6	26.1	43.3	93.9	159.1	247.2	347.8	1
2	23.9	35.1	52.2	86.5	187.8	318.3	494.3	695.5	2
3	35.8	52.7	78.2	129.8	281.7	477.4	741.5	1043.3	3
4	47.8	70.3	104.3	173.1	375.6	636.6	988.6	1391.1	4
5	59.7	87.8	130.4	216.3	469.4	795.7	1235.8	1738.8	5
6	71.7	105.4	156.5	259.6	563.3	954.9	1482.9	2086.6	6
7	83.6	123.0	182.6	302.9	657.2	1114.0	1730.1	2434.4	7
8	95.6	140.6	208.6	346.1	751.1	1273.2	1977.2	2782.1	8
9	107.5	158.1	234.7	389.4	845.0	1432.3	2224.4	3129.9	9
10	119.5	175.7	260.8	432.6	938.9	1591.5	2471.5	3477.7	10
11	131.4	193.3	286.9	475.9	1032.8	1750.6	2781.7	3825.4	11
12	143.3	210.8	313.0	519.2	1126.7	1909.8	2965.8	4173.2	12
13	155.3	228.4	339.0	562.4	1220.5	2068.9	3213.0	4521.0	13
14	167.2	246.0	365.1	605.7	1314.4	2228.1	3460.2	4868.7	14
15	179.2	263.5	391.2	649.0	1408.3	2387.2	3707.3	5216.5	15

*Flows calculated with factors in Table 16 may vary slightly due to rounding-off of factors.
[1] Not ASTM standard pipe.

TABLE 7b
MULTIPLYING FACTORS TO CHANGE VALUE OF "C"
C = 150 TO OTHER VALUES

To determine PRESSURE LOSSES with other values of "C", multiply losses computed with "C" = 150 by following factors:												
Value of "C"	160	150	140	130	120	110	100	90	80	70	60	50	Value of "C"
Multiplier	0.887	1.0	1.14	1.30	1.51	1.77	2.12	2.57	3.20	4.10	5.45	7.63	Multiplier

TABLE 7c
PRESSURE LOSS
SDR 32.5 PVC PIPE
SIZES NOT LISTED OPPOSITE PAGE

To determine PRESSURE LOSSES in 3-1/2 and 5 in SDR 32.5 PVC pipe, multiply losses of 4 in SDR 32.5 by following factors:		
Nominal Size, in	3-1/2[a]	5[a]
	Multipliers	
SDR 32.5	1.78	0.355

[a] Determine availability before designing systems with these sizes.

APPENDIX

TABLE 8

PRESSURE LOSS

SCHEDULE 40 PVC PIPE

Table Losses same for all Controlled OD Schedule 40 thermoplastic pipe. For PE pipe, convert losses to equivalent of C=140.

C = 150

Pipe Sizes: Nominal — Loss per 100 ft: lb/in²

gpm	1/2 in	3/4 in	1 in	1-1/4 in	1-1/2 in	2 in
1	0.503	0.123	0.037	0.010	0.004	0.001
2	1.81	.444	.134	.034	.016	.005
3	3.84	0.940	.283	.073	.034	.010
4	6.54	1.60	.482	.124	.058	.017
5	9.88	2.42	0.728	.187	.088	.026
6	13.85	3.39	1.02	.263	.123	.036
7	18.42	4.51	1.36	.349	.163	.048
8	23.58	5.77	1.74	.447	.209	.061
9	29.32	7.17	2.16	.556	.260	.076
10		8.72	2.62	0.676	0.316	0.092
11		10.40	3.13	.806	.377	.110
12		12.22	3.68	0.947	.443	.129
13		14.17	4.26	1.10	.513	.150
14		16.25	4.89	1.26	.589	.172
15		18.46	5.56	1.43	.669	.196
16		20.80	6.26	1.61	.754	.220
17			7.01	1.80	.843	.247
18			7.79	2.00	0.937	0.274
19			8.61	2.22	1.04	.303
20			9.46	2.44	1.14	.333
22			11.29	2.91	1.36	.397
24			13.26	3.41	1.60	.467
26	*2-1/2 in*		15.37	3.96	1.85	.541
28				4.54	2.12	.621
30	0.297			5.16	2.41	.705
32	.335			5.81	2.72	.795
34	.375			6.50	3.04	.889
36	.416	*3 in*		7.23	3.38	0.988
38	.460			7.99	3.73	1.09
40	.506	0.175		8.78	4.11	1.20
42	.554	.191		9.61	4.49	1.31
44	.604	.208		10.47	4.90	1.43
46	.655	.226	*4 in*	11.37	5.32	1.56
48	.709	.245			5.75	1.68
50	0.765	0.264	0.070		6.20	1.81
52	.822	.284	.075		6.67	1.95
54	.882	.305	.081		7.15	2.09
56	0.943	.326	.086		7.65	2.24
58	1.01	.348	.092		8.16	2.39
60	1.07	.370	.098		8.69	2.54
62	1.14	.393	.104		9.24	2.70
64	1.21	.417	.110			2.87
66	1.28	.441	.117			3.03
68	1.35	.466	.123			3.21
70	1.42	0.492	0.130			3.38
75	1.62	.559	.148			3.84
80	1.82	.630	.167			4.33
85	2.04	.705	.186			4.84
90	2.27	.783	.207			5.38
95	2.51	.866	.229			5.98
100	2.76	0.952	0.252			6.54

gpm	2 in	2-1/2 in	3 in	4 in	6 in	8 in
105	7.16	3.02	1.04	0.276	0.037	0.010
110		3.29	1.14	.300	.041	.011
115		3.57	1.23	.326	.044	.012
120		3.86	1.33	.353	.048	.013
125		4.16	1.44	.381	.051	.013
130		4.48	1.55	.409	.055	.015
135		4.80	1.66	.439	.059	.016
140		5.14	1.77	.469	.064	.017
145		5.48	1.89	.501	.068	.018
150			2.02	0.533	0.072	0.019
160			2.27	.601	.081	.021
170			2.54	.672	.091	.024
180	*10 in*		2.82	.747	.101	.026
190			3.12	.826	.112	.029
200	0.011		3.43	.908	.123	.032
210	.012		3.76	0.994	.134	.035
220	.013		4.09	1.08	.147	.038
230	.014		4.45	1.18	.159	.042
240	.015			1.27	.172	.045
250	.016			1.37	0.186	0.049
260	.017			1.48	.200	.052
270	.018			1.58	.214	.056
280	.020	*12 in*		1.69	.229	.060
290	.021			1.81	.244	.064
300	0.022	0.010		1.92	.260	.068
325	.026	.011		2.23	.302	.079
350	.030	.013		2.56	.346	.091
375	.034	.014		2.91	.393	.103
400	.038	.016		3.27	.443	.116
425	.043	.018			.495	.130
450	.048	.020			0.551	0.144
475	.053	.022			.609	.160
500	.058	.025			.669	.175
550	.069	.029			.798	.209
600	0.081	0.035			0.938	.246
650	.094	.040			1.09	.285
700	.108	.046			1.25	.327
800	.138	.059			1.60	.418
900	.172	.073			1.99	.520
1000	.208	.089				.632
1100	.249	.106				.754
1200	.292	.124				0.886
1300	.339	.144				1.03
1400	.389	.165				1.18
1500	.441	.188				1.34
2000	0.752	0.320				
2500	1.14	.484				
3000		.678				
3500		0.901				
4000						
5000						

APPENDIX

TABLE 8a
VELOCITY FLOWS
SCHEDULE 40 PVC PIPE

Velocity ft/s	Nominal Pipe Size: inches													Velocity ft/s
	1/2	3/4	1	1-1/4	1-1/2	2	2-1/2	3	4	6	8	10	12	
	Flow: gpm*													
1	0.9	1.6	2.6	4.5	6.2	10.3	14.6	22.7	39.1	89.0	154.4	243.6	346.0	1
2	1.8	3.2	5.2	9.1	12.4	20.5	29.3	45.3	78.3	178.1	308.8	487.2	692.0	2
3	2.7	4.7	7.8	13.6	18.6	30.8	43.9	68.0	117.4	267.1	463.2	730.9	1038.1	3
4	3.5	6.3	10.4	18.1	24.8	41.0	58.5	90.6	156.5	356.2	617.6	974.5	1384.1	4
5	4.4	7.9	13.0	22.6	30.9	51.3	73.2	113.3	195.6	445.2	772.0	1218.1	1730.1	5
6	5.3	9.5	15.6	27.2	37.1	61.5	87.8	135.9	234.8	534.2	926.4	1461.7	2076.1	6
7	6.2	11.1	18.1	31.7	43.3	71.8	102.4	158.6	273.9	623.3	1080.9	1705.4	2422.1	7
8	7.1	12.7	20.7	36.2	49.5	82.1	117.1	181.2	313.0	712.3	1235.3	1949.0	2768.1	8
9	8.0	14.2	23.3	40.8	55.7	92.3	131.7	203.9	352.2	801.4	1389.7	2192.6	3114.2	9
10	8.9	15.8	25.9	45.3	61.9	102.6	146.3	226.5	391.3	890.4	1544.1	2436.2	3460.2	10
11	9.8	17.4	28.5	49.8	68.1	112.8	161.0	249.2	430.4	979.4	1698.5	2679.9	3806.2	11
12	10.6	19.0	31.1	54.3	74.3	123.1	175.6	271.8	469.5	1068.5	1852.9	2923.5	4152.2	12
13	11.5	20.6	33.7	58.9	80.5	133.3	190.2	294.5	508.7	1157.5	2007.3	3167.1	4498.2	13
14	12.4	22.2	36.3	63.4	86.6	143.6	204.9	317.1	547.8	1246.6	2161.7	3410.7	4844.3	14
15	13.3	23.7	38.9	67.9	92.8	153.9	219.5	339.8	586.9	1335.6	2316.1	3654.4	5190.3	15

*Flows calculated with factors in Table 16 may vary slightly due to rounding-off of factors.

TABLE 8b
MULTIPLYING FACTORS TO CHANGE VALUE OF "C"
C = 150 TO OTHER VALUES

To determine PRESSURE LOSSES with other values of "C", multiply losses computed with C = 150 by following factors:													
Value of "C"	160	150	140	130	120	110	100	90	80	70	60	50	Value of "C"
Multiplier	0.887	1.0	1.14	1.30	1.51	1.77	2.12	2.57	3.20	4.10	5.45	7.63	Multiplier

TABLE 8c
PRESSURE LOSS
SCHEDULE PVC PIPE
SIZES NOT LISTED OPPOSITE PAGE

To determine PRESSURE LOSSES of 1/8, 1/4 and 3/8 in schedule wall PVC pipe, multiply Losses of 1/2 in Schedule 40 by following factors:			
Nominal Size, in	1/8	1/4	3/8
	Multipliers		
Schedule 40	73.35	15.22	3.32
Schedule 80	241.0	40.03	7.05
Schedule 120	—	—	—

To determine PRESSURE LOSSES of 3-1/2 and 5 in schedule wall PVC pipe, multiply Losses of 4 in Schedule 40 by following factors:		
Nominal Size, in	3-1/2(a)	5(a)
	Multipliers	
Schedule 40	1.86	0.332
Schedule 80	2.45	0.424
Schedule 120	2.71	0.562

(a) Determine availability before designing systems with these sizes.

TABLE 8d
PRESSURE LOSS
SCHEDULE 80 and 120 PVC PIPE

To determine PRESSURE LOSSES of Schedule 80 and 120 PVC pipe, multiply Losses of same size Schedule 40 PVC by following factors:													
Size, in	1/2	3/4	1	1-1/4	1-1/2	2	2-1/2	3	4	6	8	10	12	Size, in
	Multipliers													
Schedule 80	1.93	1.69	1.59	1.48	1.44	1.39	1.38	1.34	1.30	1.31	1.27	1.27	1.28	Schedule 80
Schedule 120	3.01	2.10	2.02	1.81	1.72	1.66	1.54	1.61	1.73	1.66	1.72	1.68	1.72	Schedule 120

APPENDIX

TABLE 9

PRESSURE LOSS

ALL CONTROLLED ID PE PIPE

Table Losses same for all
Controlled ID Thermoplastic Pipe

C = 140

Pipe Sizes: Nominal — Losses per 100 ft: lb/in²

gpm	1/2 in	3/4 in	1 in	1-1/4 in	1-1/2 in	2 in
1	0.448	0.124	0.038	0.010	0.005	0.001
2	1.76	.448	.138	.036	.017	.005
3	3.72	0.948	.293	.077	.036	.011
4	6.34	1.61	.498	.131	.062	.018
5	9.58	2.44	0.753	.198	.094	.028
6	13.42	3.42	1.06	.278	.131	.039
7	17.85	4.54	1.40	.370	.175	.052
8	22.85	5.82	1.80	.473	.224	.066
9	28.42	7.23	2.23	.588	.278	.082
10	34.53	8.79	2.72	.715	.338	.100
11		10.48	3.24	0.853	0.403	0.119
12		12.32	3.80	1.00	.473	.140
13		14.28	4.41	1.16	.549	.163
14		16.38	5.06	1.33	.629	.187
15		18.61	5.75	1.51	.715	.212
16		20.97	6.48	1.71	.806	.239
17		23.46	7.25	1.91	0.901	.267
18	*2-1/2 in*		8.06	2.12	1.00	.297
19			8.90	2.34	1.11	.328
20	0.152		9.79	2.58	1.22	0.361
22	.181		11.68	3.07	1.45	.431
24	.213		13.72	3.61	1.71	.506
26	.247		15.91	4.19	1.98	.587
28	.283		18.24	4.80	2.27	.673
30	.322			5.46	2.58	.764
32	.363			6.15	2.90	.861
34	.406			6.88	3.25	0.964
36	.451	*3 in*		7.65	3.61	1.07
38	.499			8.45	3.99	1.18
40	0.548	0.191		9.29	4.39	1.30
42	.600	.209		10.17	4.80	1.42
44	.654	.227		11.08	5.24	1.55
46	.710	.247		12.04	5.68	1.69
48	.768	.267			6.15	1.82
50	.828	.288			6.63	1.97
52	.891	.310			7.13	2.11
54	0.955	.322			7.65	2.27
56	1.02	.355	*4 in*		8.18	2.43
58	1.09	.379			8.73	2.59
60	1.16	0.403	0.108		9.29	2.76
62	1.23	.429	.114		9.88	2.93
64	1.31	.455	.121		10.47	3.11
66	1.38	.481	.128			3.29
68	1.46	.508	.136			3.47
70	1.54	.536	.143			3.66
75	1.75	.610	.162			4.16
80	1.98	.687	.183			4.69
85	2.21	.768	.205			5.25
90	2.46	.854	.228			5.83
95	2.72	0.944	.252			6.45
100	2.99	1.04	0.277			7.09

gpm	2 in	2-1/2 in	3 in	4 in	6 in
105	7.76	3.27	1.14	0.303	0.041
110		3.56	1.24	.330	.045
115		3.87	1.34	.358	.049
120		4.18	1.45	.388	.053
125		4.51	1.57	.418	.057
130		4.85	1.69	.449	.061
135		5.20	1.81	.482	.066
140		5.56	1.93	.516	.070
145		5.94	2.06	.550	.075
150		6.32	2.20	0.586	0.080
160			2.48	.660	.090
170			2.77	.738	.101
180			3.08	.821	.112
190			3.40	.907	.124
200			3.74	0.997	.136
210			4.09	1.09	.149
220			4.46	1.19	.162
230			4.85	1.29	.176
240				1.40	.190
250				1.51	0.205
260				1.62	.221
270				1.74	.237
280				1.86	.253
290				1.98	.270
300				2.11	.288
325				2.45	.333
350				2.81	.382
375				3.19	.435
400				3.60	0.490
425					.548
450					.609
475					.673
500					.740
550					0.883
600					1.04
650					1.20
700					1.38
800					1.77
900					2.19
1000					
1100					
1200					
1300					
1400					
1500					
2000					
2500					
3000					
3500					
4000					
5000					

APPENDIX

Table velocity flows same for all controlled ID thermoplastic pipe

TABLE 9a
VELOCITY FLOWS
ALL CONTROLLED ID PE PIPE

Velocity ft/s	Nominal Pipe Sizes: inches										Velocity ft/s
	1/2	3/4	1	1-1/4	1-1/2	2	2-1/2	3	4	6	
	Flow: gpm*										
1	0.9	1.7	2.7	4.7	6.3	10.5	14.9	23.0	39.7	90.0	1
2	1.9	3.3	5.4	9.3	12.7	20.9	29.8	46.1	79.4	180.1	2
3	2.8	5.0	8.1	14.0	19.0	31.4	44.8	69.1	119.0	270.1	3
4	3.8	6.6	10.8	18.6	25.4	41.8	59.7	92.2	158.7	360.2	4
5	4.7	8.3	13.5	23.3	31.7	52.3	74.6	115.2	198.4	450.2	5
6	5.7	10.0	16.2	28.0	38.1	62.8	89.5	138.3	238.1	540.3	6
7	6.6	11.6	18.9	32.6	44.4	73.2	104.5	161.3	277.7	630.3	7
8	7.6	13.3	21.6	37.3	50.8	83.7	119.4	184.3	317.4	720.4	8
9	8.5	15.0	24.2	42.0	57.1	94.1	134.3	207.4	357.1	810.4	9
10	9.5	16.6	26.9	46.6	63.5	104.6	149.2	230.4	396.8	900.5	10
11	10.4	18.3	29.6	51.3	69.8	115.0	164.2	253.5	436.5	990.5	11
12	11.4	19.9	32.3	55.9	76.1	125.5	179.1	276.5	476.1	1080.6	12
13	12.3	21.6	35.0	60.6	82.5	136.0	194.0	299.5	515.8	1170.6	13
14	13.3	23.3	37.7	65.3	88.8	146.4	208.9	322.6	555.5	1260.7	14
15	14.2	24.9	40.4	69.9	95.2	156.9	223.8	345.6	595.2	1360.7	15

*Flows calculated with factors in Table 16 may vary slightly due to rounding-off of factors.

TABLE 9b
MULTIPLYING FACTORS TO CHANGE VALUE OF "C"
C = 140 TO OTHER VALUES

To determine PRESSURE LOSSES with other values of "C", multiply losses computed with C = 140 by following factors:													
Value of "C"	160	150	140	130	120	110	100	90	80	70	60	50	Value of "C"
Multiplier	0.781	0.880	1.0	1.15	1.33	1.56	1.86	2.26	2.82	3.61	4.79	6.72	Multiplier

TABLE 9c
PRESSURE LOSS
PE TUBING
SIZES NOT LISTED OPPOSITE PAGE

To determine PRESSURE LOSSES of 5/8 in PE tubing, multiply losses of 1/2 in PE Controlled ID pipe by following factors:	
Nominal Size, in	5/8
	Multipliers
SDR 9 Tubing (Controlled OD)	1.48
SDR 7.3 Tubing (Controlled OD)	2.10

TABLE 9d
PRESSURE LOSS
OTHER TYPES PE PIPING

To determine PRESSURE LOSSES of Controlled OD SDR 11 PE pipe and SDR 9 and SDR 7 PE tube, multiply losses of same size Controlled ID PE pipe by following factors:										
Nominal Size, in	1/2	3/4	1	1-1/4	1-1/2	2	3	4	6	Nominal Size, in
	Multipliers									
SDR 11 Pipe (Controlled OD)	0.707	0.916	0.991	1.19	1.29	1.44	1.49	1.69	1.84	SDR 11 Pipe (Controlled OD)
SDR 9 Tube (Controlled OD)	3.64	2.72	2.59	3.71	3.49	3.19	——	——	——	SDR 9 Tube (Controlled OD)
SDR 7.3 Tube (Controlled OD)	5.21	3.90	3.69	5.29	5.43	4.55	——	——	——	SDR 7.3 Tube (Controlled OD)

NOTE: For other Controlled OD SDR and Schedule Wall PE pipe, use pressure loss table for same SDR or schedule PVC pipe. Caution: Convert losses to equivalent for C = 140.

APPENDIX

TABLE 10

PRESSURE LOSS

TYPE "K" COPPER TUBE

C = 140*

Pipe Sizes: Nominal											Losses per 100 ft: lb/in^2	
gpm	1/2 in	3/4 in	1 in	1-1/4 in	1-1/2 in	2 in	gpm	2 in	2-1/2 in	3 in	4 in	6 in	8 in
1	1.15	0.213	0.052	0.018	0.008	0.002	105	10.58	3.67	1.55	0.392	0.057	0.015
2	4.14	0.767	.188	.063	.027	.007	110	11.53	4.00	1.69	.427	.062	.016
3	8.76	1.62	.398	.134	.057	.015	115	12.52	4.34	1.83	.463	.067	.017
4	14.91	2.77	0.677	.227	.098	.025	120	13.54	4.70	1.98	.501	.072	.019
5	22.53	4.18	1.02	.344	.148	.038	125	14.61	5.07	2.14	.541	.078	.020
6	31.57	5.86	1.43	.482	.207	.053	130	15.70	5.45	2.30	.581	.084	.022
7	41.98	7.79	1.91	.640	.275	.071	135	16.84	5.84	2.47	.624	.090	.023
8	53.75	9.97	2.44	0.820	.352	.090	140	18.01	6.25	2.64	.667	.096	.025
9	66.83	12.40	3.03	1.02	.438	.112	145	19.22	6.67	2.82	.712	.103	.027
10	81.22	15.07	3.69	1.24	0.532	0.137	150	20.46	7.10	3.00	0.758	0.109	0.028
11		17.98	4.40	1.48	.635	.163	160	23.06	8.00	3.38	.854	.123	.032
12		21.12	5.17	1.74	.746	.191	170		8.95	3.78	0.955	.138	.036
13		24.49	5.99	2.01	.865	.222	180	10 in	9.95	4.20	1.06	.153	.040
14		28.09	6.87	2.31	0.992	.254	190		11.00	4.64	1.17	.169	.044
15		31.91	7.81	2.62	1.13	.289	200	0.016	12.09	5.11	1.29	.186	.048
16		35.96	8.80	2.96	1.27	.326	210	.018	13.23	5.59	1.41	.204	.053
17		40.22	9.84	3.31	1.42	.364	220	.020	14.42	6.09	1.54	.222	.057
18	2-1/2 in	44.71	10.94	3.68	1.58	.405	230	.021		6.61	1.67	.241	.062
19		49.41	12.09	4.06	1.75	.448	240	.023		7.16	1.81	.261	.067
20	0.171	54.33	13.29	4.47	1.92	0.492	250	.025		7.72	1.95	0.281	0.073
22	.204	64.81	15.86	5.33	2.29	.587	260	.027		8.30	2.10	.303	.078
24	.239	76.13	18.63	6.26	2.69	.690	270	.029		8.90	2.25	.325	.084
26	.278	88.28	21.60	7.26	3.12	.800	280	.031	12 in	9.52	2.40	.347	.090
28	.318	101.25	24.77	8.32	3.58	0.917	290	.033		10.15	2.57	.370	.096
30	.362	115.03	28.14	9.46	4.06	1.04	300	0.035	0.015	10.81	2.73	.394	.102
32	.408		31.71	10.66	4.58	1.17	325	.040	.017		3.17	.457	.118
34	.456		35.48	11.92	5.12	1.31	350	.046	.019		3.63	.525	.135
36	.507	3 in	39.43	13.25	5.69	1.46	375	.053	.022		4.13	.596	.154
38	.560		43.58	14.64	6.29	1.61	400	.059	.025		4.65	.672	.173
40	0.616	0.260	47.92	16.10	6.92	1.77	425	.067	.028		5.20	.751	.194
42	.674	.285	52.45	17.62	7.57	1.94	450	.074	.031		5.78	.835	.216
44	.735	.310	57.16	19.21	8.25	2.12	475	.082	.034		6.39	0.923	0.238
46	.797	.337	62.06	20.85	8.96	2.30	500	.090	.037		7.03	1.01	.262
48	.863	.364	67.14	22.56	9.70	2.49	550	.107	.045		8.38	1.21	.313
50	0.930	.393	72.41	24.33	10.46	2.68	600	0.126	0.052			1.42	.367
52	1.00	.423		26.16	11.24	2.88	650	.146	.061			1.65	.426
54	1.07	.453		28.05	12.06	3.09	700	.167	.070			1.89	.488
56	1.15	.485	4 in	30.01	12.90	3.31	800	.214	.089			2.42	.625
58	1.22	.517		32.02	13.76	3.53	900	.267	.111			3.01	.777
60	1.30	0.551	0.139	34.09	14.65	3.76	1000	.324	.135			3.66	0.945
62	1.39	.585	.148	36.22	15.57	3.99	1100	.386	.161			4.36	1.13
64	1.47	.620	.157	38.42	16.51	4.23	1200	.454	.189			5.13	1.32
66	1.56	.657	.166	40.67	17.48	4.48	1300	.526	.219				1.53
68	1.64	.694	.175	42.97	18.47	4.74	1400	.604	.251				1.76
70	1.73	.732	.185	45.34	19.49	5.00	1500	0.686	0.285				2.00
75	1.97	.832	.210	51.52	22.14	5.68	2000	1.17	.486				3.41
80	2.22	0.937	.237	58.05	24.95	6.40	2500	1.76	0.734				
85	2.48	1.05	.265		27.91	7.16	3000	2.47	1.03				
90	2.76	1.17	.294		31.02	7.95	3500		1.37				
95	3.05	1.29	.325		34.28	8.79	4000		1.75				
100	3.35	1.42	0.358		37.69	9.67	5000						

*Note: 5% has been added to losses determined with a "C" factor of 140 as an allowance for aging.

APPENDIX

VELOCITY FLOWS
TYPE "K" COPPER TUBE

Velocity ft/s	Nominal Pipe Size: inches													Velocity ft/s
	1/2	3/4	1	1-1/4	1-1/2	2	2-1/2	3	4	6	8	10	12	
	Flow: gpm*													
1	0.7	1.4	2.4	3.8	5.4	9.4	14.5	20.7	36.4	80.7	140.8	218.6	313.4	1
2	1.4	2.7	4.8	7.6	10.7	18.8	29.0	41.4	72.8	161.4	281.5	437.1	626.8	2
3	2.0	4.1	7.3	11.4	16.1	28.2	43.5	62.1	109.3	242.0	422.3	655.7	940.2	3
4	2.7	5.4	9.7	15.2	21.5	37.6	58.1	82.7	145.7	322.7	563.1	874.3	1253.7	4
5	3.4	6.8	12.1	19.0	26.8	47.0	72.6	103.4	182.1	403.4	703.8	1092.8	1567.1	5
6	4.1	8.2	14.5	22.8	32.2	56.4	87.1	124.1	218.5	484.1	844.6	1311.4	1880.5	6
7	4.8	9.5	17.0	26.6	37.6	65.8	101.6	144.8	254.9	564.8	985.3	1530.0	2193.9	7
8	5.4	10.9	19.4	30.4	43.0	75.2	116.1	165.5	291.3	645.5	1126.1	1748.5	2507.3	8
9	6.1	12.2	21.8	34.1	48.3	84.6	130.6	186.2	327.8	726.1	1266.9	1967.1	2820.7	9
10	6.8	13.6	24.2	37.9	53.7	93.9	145.1	206.9	364.2	806.8	1407.6	2185.6	3134.1	10
11	7.5	14.9	26.7	41.7	59.1	103.3	159.7	227.6	400.6	887.5	1548.4	2404.2	3447.5	11
12	8.2	16.3	29.1	45.5	64.4	112.7	174.2	248.2	437.0	968.2	1689.2	2622.8	3761.0	12
13	8.8	17.7	31.5	49.3	69.8	122.1	188.7	268.9	473.4	1048.9	1829.9	2841.3	4074.4	13
14	9.5	19.0	33.9	53.1	75.2	131.5	203.2	289.6	509.8	1129.6	1970.7	3059.9	4387.8	14
15	10.2	20.4	36.4	56.9	80.5	140.9	217.7	310.3	546.3	1210.2	2111.5	3278.5	4701.2	15

*Flows calculated with factors in Table 16 may vary slightly due to rounding-off of factors.

MULTIPLYING FACTORS TO CHANGE VALUE OF "C"
C = 140 TO OTHER VALUES

To determine PRESSURE LOSSES with values of "C", multiply Losses computed with "C" = 140 by following factors*													
Value of "C"	160	150	140*	130	120	110	100	90	80	70	60	50	Value of "C"
Multiplier	0.781	0.880	1.0	1.15	1.33	1.56	1.86	2.26	2.82	3.61	4.79	6.72	Multiplier

*CAUTION: Table 10 was constructed with "C" = 140 and 5% added to calculated losses to allow for aging; before using above multiplying factors, losses in Table must be reduced to correct value of "C" = 140 by dividing by 1.05.

PRESSURE LOSS
TYPE "K" COPPER TUBE
SIZES NOT LISTED OPPOSITE PAGE

To determine PRESSURE LOSSES of 1/4, 3/8, and 5/8 in tube, multiply losses of 1/2 in Type "K" by following factors:			
Nominal Size, in	1/4	3/8	5/8
	Multipliers		
Type "K"	14.31	3.73	0.355

To determine PRESSURE LOSSES of 3-1/2 and 5 in tube, multiply losses of 4 in Type "K" by following factors:		
Nominal Size, in	3-1/2	5
	Multipliers	
Type "K"	1.89	0.343

TABLE 11
PRESSURE LOSS
TYPE "M" COPPER TUBE

C = 140*

Pipe Sizes: Nominal											Losses per 100 ft: lb/in²	
gpm	1/2 in	3/4 in	1 in	1-1/4 in	1-1/2 in	2 in	gpm	2 in	2-1/2 in	3 in	4 in	6 in	8 in
1	0.790	0.141	0.039	0.015	0.006	0.002	105	9.36	3.26	1.37	0.355	0.050	0.013
2	2.85	0.508	.141	.053	.023	.006	110	10.20	3.55	1.50	.387	.055	.014
3	6.03	1.08	.299	.112	.049	.013	115	11.07	3.86	1.62	.420	.060	.015
4	10.27	1.83	.509	.191	.084	.022	120	11.98	4.17	1.76	.455	.064	.016
5	15.51	2.77	0.769	.288	.127	.034	125	12.92	4.50	1.89	.491	.069	.018
6	21.74	3.88	1.08	.404	.178	.047	130	13.89	4.84	2.04	.527	.075	.019
7	28.91	5.15	1.43	.537	.237	.062	135	14.90	5.19	2.18	.566	.080	.020
8	37.01	6.60	1.84	.687	.304	.080	140	15.93	5.55	2.34	.605	.086	.022
9	46.02	8.21	2.28	0.855	.378	.099	145	17.00	5.93	2.49	.646	.091	.023
10	55.93	9.97	2.77	1.04	0.459	0.121	150	18.10	6.31	2.65	0.687	0.097	0.025
11	66.71	11.89	3.31	1.24	.547	.144	160	20.40	7.11	2.99	.775	.110	.028
12	78.36	13.97	3.89	1.46	.643	.169	170		7.95	3.35	.866	.123	.031
13		16.20	4.51	1.69	.745	.196	180	10 in	8.84	3.72	0.963	.136	.035
14		18.58	5.17	1.94	.855	.225	190		9.77	4.11	1.06	.151	.038
15		21.11	5.87	2.20	0.971	.256	200	0.015	10.74	4.52	1.17	.166	.042
16		23.79	6.62	2.48	1.09	.288	210	.016	11.76	4.95	1.28	.181	.046
17		26.61	7.40	2.77	1.22	.322	220	.017	12.81	5.39	1.40	.198	.050
18	2-1/2 in	29.58	8.23	3.08	1.36	.358	230	.019	13.91	5.85	1.52	.215	.055
19		32.69	9.09	3.40	1.50	.396	240	.020		6.33	1.64	.232	.059
20	0.152	35.95	10.00	3.74	1.65	0.435	250	.022		6.83	1.77	0.250	0.064
22	.181	42.88	11.93	4.47	1.97	.519	260	.024		7.34	1.90	.269	.069
24	.213	50.37	14.01	5.25	2.32	.610	270	.025		7.87	2.04	.289	.074
26	.247	58.41	16.24	6.08	2.69	.707	280	.027	12 in	8.42	2.18	.309	.079
28	.283	66.99	18.63	6.98	3.08	.811	290	.029		8.99	2.33	.329	.084
30	.321	76.11	21.17	7.93	3.50	0.922	300	0.031	0.013	9.57	2.48	.351	.090
32	.362		23.85	8.93	3.95	1.04	325	.036	.015	11.09	2.87	.407	.104
34	.405		26.68	9.99	4.41	1.16	350	.041	.017		3.30	.467	.119
36	.450	3 in	29.66	11.11	4.91	1.29	375	.046	.019		3.74	.530	.135
38	.497		32.78	12.27	5.42	1.43	400	.052	.022		4.22	0.597	0.153
40	0.547	0.230	36.04	13.50	5.96	1.57	425	.059	.024		4.72	.668	.171
42	.599	.252	39.45	14.77	6.53	1.72	450	.065	.027		5.25	.743	.190
44	.652	.274	42.99	16.10	7.11	1.87	475	.072	.030		5.80	.821	.210
46	.708	.298	46.68	17.48	7.72	2.03	500	.079	.033		6.38	0.903	.231
48	.766	.322	50.50	18.91	8.35	2.20	550	.094	.039		7.60	1.08	.275
50	.827	.348	54.46	20.39	9.01	2.37	600	0.111	0.046			1.26	.323
52	.889	.374		21.93	9.69	2.55	650	.128	.053			1.47	.375
54	0.953	.401		23.51	10.39	2.73	700	.147	.061			1.68	.430
56	1.02	.429	4 in	25.15	11.11	2.92	800	.189	.078			2.15	.550
58	1.09	.458		26.84	11.86	3.12	900	.234	.098			2.68	.684
60	1.16	0.487	0.126	28.57	12.62	3.32	1000	0.285	.119			3.25	0.831
62	1.23	.518	.134	30.36	13.41	3.53	1100	.340	.141			3.88	0.991
64	1.30	.549	.142	32.20	14.23	3.74	1200	.399	.166			4.56	1.16
66	1.38	.581	.151	34.08	15.06	3.96	1300	.463	.193			5.29	1.35
68	1.46	.614	.159	36.02	15.91	4.19	1400	.531	.221				1.55
70	1.54	.648	.168	38.00	16.79	4.42	1500	0.603	.251				1.76
75	1.75	.736	.191	43.18	19.08	5.02	2000	1.03	.427				3.00
80	1.97	.830	.215	48.65	21.50	5.66	2500	1.55	.646				4.53
85	2.21	0.928	.240		24.05	6.33	3000	2.17	0.905				
90	2.45	1.03	.267		26.73	7.04	3500		1.20				
95	2.71	1.14	.295		29.54	7.78	4000		1.54				
100	2.98	1.25	0.325		32.48	8.55	5000		2.33				

*NOTE: 5% has been added to losses determined with a "C" factor of 140 as an allowance for aging.

APPENDIX

| Velocity ft/s | \multicolumn{13}{c}{Nominal Tube Size: inches} | Velocity ft/s |
| | 1/2 | 3/4 | 1 | 1-1/4 | 1-1/2 | 2 | 2-1/2 | 3 | 4 | 6 | 8 | 10 | 12 | |
	\multicolumn{13}{c}{Flow: gpm*}	
1	0.8	1.6	2.7	4.1	5.7	9.9	15.2	21.8	37.9	84.7	148.4	230.4	330.4	1
2	1.6	3.2	5.4	8.2	11.4	19.8	·30.5	43.5	75.8	169.3	296.7	460.8	660.7	2
3	2.4	4.8	8.2	12.2	17.1	29.6	45.7	65.3	113.7	254.0	445.1	691.1	991.1	3
4	3.2	6.4	10.9	16.3	22.8	39.5	61.0	87.0	151.6	338.7	593.5	921.5	1321.5	4
5	4.0	8.1	13.6	20.4	28.5	49.4	76.2	108.8	189.5	423.3	741.8	1151.9	1651.8	5
6	4.8	9.7	16.3	24.5	34.2	59.3	91.4	130.5	227.4	508.0	890.2	1382.3	1982.2	6
7	5.5	11.3	19.1	28.6	40.0	69.2	106.7	152.3	265.3	592.7	1038.5	1612.6	2312.6	7
8	6.3	12.9	21.8	32.6	45.7	79.0	121.9	174.0	303.2	677.3	1186.9	1843.0	2642.9	8
9	7.1	14.5	24.5	36.7	51.4	88.9	137.1	195.8	341.1	762.0	1335.3	2073.4	2973.3	9
10	7.9	16.1	27.2	40.8	57.1	98.8	152.4	217.5	379.1	846.7	1483.6	2303.8	3303.7	10
11	8.7	17.7	30.0	44.9	62.8	108.7	167.6	239.3	417.0	931.3	1632.0	2534.2	3634.0	11
12	9.5	19.3	32.7	49.0	68.5	118.6	182.9	261.0	454.9	1016.0	1780.4	2764.5	3964.4	12
13	10.3	20.9	35.4	53.0	74.2	128.4	198.1	282.8	492.8	1100.7	1928.7	2994.9	4294.8	13
14	11.1	22.5	38.1	57.1	79.9	138.3	213.3	304.6	530.7	1185.3	2077.1	3225.3	4625.1	14
15	11.9	24.2	40.9	61.2	85.6	148.2	228.6	326.3	568.6	1270.0	2225.4	3455.7	4955.5	15

*Flows calculated with factors in Table 16 may vary slightly due to rounding-off of factors.

\multicolumn{13}{l}{To determine PRESSURE LOSSES with other values of "C", multiply losses computed with "C" = 140 by following factors:*}
Value of "C"	160	150	140	130	120	110	100	90	80	70	60	50	Value of "C"
Multiplier	0.781	0.880	1.0	1.15	1.33	1.56	1.86	2.26	2.82	3.61	4.79	6.72	Multiplier

*CAUTION: Table 11 was constructed with "C" = 140 and 5% added to calculated losses to allow for aging; before using above multiplying factors, losses in table must be reduced to correct value of "C" = 140 by dividing by 1.05.

To determine PRESSURE LOSSES of 1/4, 3/8, and 5/8 in tube, multiply losses of 1/2 in Type "M" by following factors:			
Nominal Size, in	1/4	3/8	5/8
	\multicolumn{3}{c}{Multipliers}
Type "M"	—	3.13	—
Type "L"	17.76	3.91	0.465

To determine PRESSURE LOSSES of 3-1/2 and 5 in tube, multiply losses of 4 in Type "M" by following factors:		
Nominal Size, in	3-1/2	5
	\multicolumn{2}{c}{Multipliers}
Type "M"	1.87	0.342
Type "L"	1.97	0.353

\multicolumn{15}{l}{To determine PRESSURE LOSSES of Type "L" copper tube, multiply losses of same size Type "M" by following factors:}
Size, in	1/2	3/4	1	1-1/4	1-1/2	2	2-1/2	3	4	6	8	10	12	Size, in
	\multicolumn{13}{c}{Multipliers}	
Type "L"	1.23	1.17	1.15	1.10	1.07	1.06	1.06	1.06	1.04	1.03	1.04	1.04	1.02	Type "L"

APPENDIX

TABLE 12

PRESSURE LOSS

C = 100

SCHEDULE 40 GALVANIZED STEEL PIPE

Pipe Sizes: Nominal											Losses per 100 ft: lb/in^2	
gpm	1/2 in	3/4 in	1 in	1-1/4 in	1-1/2 in	2 in	gpm	2 in	2-1/2 in	3 in	4 in	6 in	8 in
1	0.909	0.231	0.071	0.019	0.009	0.003	105	14.46	6.09	2.12	0.564	0.077	0.020
2	3.28	0.834	.258	.068	.032	.010	110	15.76	6.64	2.31	.615	.084	.022
3	6.94	1.77	.546	.144	.068	.020	115	17.11	7.21	2.50	.668	.091	.024
4	11.81	3.01	0.929	.245	.116	.034	120	18.51	7.80	2.71	.722	.098	.026
5	17.85	4.54	1.40	.370	.175	.052	125	19.96	8.41	2.92	.779	.106	.028
6	25.01	6.37	1.97	.518	.245	.073	130	21.47	9.04	3.14	.838	.114	.030
7	33.27	8.47	2.62	.689	.325	.096	135	23.02	9.70	3.37	.898	.122	.032
8	42.59	10.84	3.35	0.882	.417	.124	140	24.62	10.37	3.60	0.961	.131	.034
9	52.96	13.48	4.16	1.10	.518	.154	145	26.27	11.07	3.85	1.03	.140	.037
10	64.35	16.38	5.06	1.33	.629	.187	150	27.97	11.78	4.09	1.09	0.149	0.039
11	76.76	19.54	6.04	1.59	.751	.223	160	31.52	13.28	4.61	1.23	.168	.044
12	90.17	22.95	7.09	1.87	0.882	0.261	170		14.85	5.16	1.38	.187	.049
13	104.56	26.61	8.22	2.17	1.02	.303	180	10 in	16.51	5.74	1.53	.208	.055
14	119.93	30.53	9.43	2.48	1.17	.348	190		18.25	6.34	1.69	.230	.061
15		34.68	10.71	2.82	1.33	.395	200	0.022	20.06	6.97	1.86	.253	.067
16		39.08	12.07	3.18	1.50	.445	210	.024	21.96	7.63	2.03	.277	.073
17		43.72	13.51	3.56	1.68	.498	220	.026	23.93	8.32	2.22	.302	.079
18	2-1/2 in	48.59	15.01	3.95	1.87	.554	230	.028	25.98	9.03	2.41	.328	.086
19		53.71	16.59	4.37	2.06	.612	240	.031		9.77	2.60	.355	.093
20	0.283	59.05	18.24	4.80	2.27	.673	250	.033		10.54	2.81	0.382	0.101
22	.338	70.44	21.76	5.73	2.71	0.803	260	.036		11.33	3.02	.411	.108
24	.397	82.74	25.56	6.73	3.18	0.943	270	.038		12.15	3.24	.441	.116
26	.460	95.94	29.64	7.81	3.69	1.09	280	.041	12 in	12.99	3.46	.472	.124
28	.528		34.00	8.95	4.23	1.25	290	.044		13.86	3.70	.503	.132
30	.600		38.62	10.17	4.80	1.42	300	0.047	0.020	14.76	3.93	.536	.141
32	.676		43.52	11.46	5.41	1.61	325	.054	.023	17.12	4.56	.621	.163
34	.756		48.69	12.82	6.06	1.80	350	.062	.026	19.63	5.23	.713	.187
36	.841	3 in	54.12	14.25	6.73	2.00	375	.070	.030		5.95	.810	.213
38	0.929		59.81	15.75	7.44	2.21	400	.079	.034		6.70	0.912	0.240
40	1.02	0.355	65.76	17.32	8.18	2.43	425	.089	.038		7.49	1.02	.268
42	1.12	.389		18.95	8.95	2.65	450	.099	.042		8.33	1.13	.298
44	1.22	.424		20.66	9.76	2.89	475	.109	.046		9.21	1.25	.330
46	1.32	.460		22.43	10.59	3.14	500	.120	.051		10.12	1.38	.363
48	1.43	.497		24.26	11.46	3.40	550	.143	.061		12.08	1.64	.432
50	1.54	.536		26.17	12.36	3.66	600	0.168	0.072			1.93	.508
52	1.66	.577		28.14	13.29	3.94	650	.195	.083			2.24	.589
54	1.78	.619		30.17	14.25	4.23	700	.223	.095			2.57	.676
56	1.90	.662	4 in	32.27	15.24	4.52	800	.286	.122			3.29	0.865
58	2.03	.706		34.44	16.27	4.82	900	.356	.152			4.09	1.08
60	2.16	0.752	0.200	36.67	17.32	5.14	1000	.432	.184			4.97	1.31
62	2.30	.799	.213	38.96	18.40	5.46	1100	.515	.220			5.93	1.56
64	2.44	.847	.226	41.32	19.52	5.79	1200	.605	.258			6.96	1.83
66	2.58	.897	.239	43.74	20.66	6.13	1300	.702	.299			8.08	2.12
68	2.73	0.948	.253	46.22	21.83	6.47	1400	.805	.343				2.44
70	2.88	1.00	.266	48.77	23.03	6.83	1500	0.915	.390				2.77
75	3.27	1.14	.303		26.17	7.76	2000	1.56	0.664				4.71
80	3.68	1.28	.341		29.49	8.74	2500	2.35	1.00				7.12
85	4.12	1.43	.382		32.99	9.78	3000	3.30	1.41				
90	4.58	1.59	.424		36.67	10.87	3500	4.39	1.87				
95	5.06	1.76	.469		40.53	12.02	4000		2.39				
100	5.56	1.93	0.516			13.21	5000		3.62				

APPENDIX

TABLE 12a
VELOCITY FLOWS
SCHEDULE 40 GALVANIZED STEEL PIPE

Velocity ft/s	|	| 1/2	3/4	1	1-1/4	1-1/2	2	2-1/2	3	4	6	8	10	12	|	Velocity ft/s
							Flow: gpm*									
1		0.9	1.7	2.7	4.7	6.3	10.5	14.9	23.0	39.7	90.0	155.9	245.8	348.9		1
2		1.9	3.3	5.4	9.3	12.7	20.9	29.8	46.1	79.4	180.1	311.9	491.6	697.8		2
3		2.8	5.0	8.1	14.0	19.0	31.4	44.8	69.1	119.0	270.1	467.8	737.3	1046.6		3
4		3.8	6.6	10.8	18.6	25.4	41.8	59.7	92.2	158.7	360.2	623.7	983.1	1395.5		4
5		4.7	8.3	13.5	23.3	31.7	52.3	74.6	115.2	198.4	450.2	779.6	1228.9	1744.4		5
6		5.7	10.0	16.2	28.0	38.1	62.8	89.5	138.3	238.1	540.3	935.6	1474.7	2093.3		6
7		6.6	11.6	18.9	32.6	44.4	73.2	104.5	161.3	277.7	630.3	1091.5	1720.4	2442.1		7
8		7.6	13.3	21.6	37.3	50.8	83.7	119.4	184.3	317.4	720.4	1247.4	1966.2	2791.0		8
9		8.5	15.0	24.2	42.0	57.1	94.1	134.3	207.4	357.1	810.4	1403.3	2212.0	3139.9		9
10		9.5	16.6	26.9	46.6	63.5	104.6	149.2	230.4	396.8	900.5	1559.3	2457.8	3488.8		10
11		10.4	18.3	29.6	51.3	69.8	115.0	164.2	253.5	436.5	990.5	1715.2	2703.6	3837.6		11
12		11.4	19.9	32.3	55.9	76.1	125.5	179.1	276.5	476.1	1080.6	1871.1	2949.3	4186.5		12
13		12.3	21.6	35.0	60.6	82.5	136.0	194.0	299.5	515.8	1170.6	2027.1	3195.1	4535.4		13
14		13.3	23.3	37.7	65.3	88.8	146.4	208.9	322.6	555.5	1260.7	2183.0	3440.9	4884.3		14
15		14.2	24.9	40.4	69.9	95.2	156.9	223.8	345.6	595.2	1350.7	2338.9	3686.7	5233.1		15

*Flows calculated with factors in Table 16 may vary slightly due to rounding-off of factors.

TABLE 12b
MULTIPLYING FACTORS TO CHANGE VALUE OF "C"
C = 100 TO OTHER VALUES

	To determine PRESSURE LOSSES with other values of "C", multiply losses computed with "C" = 100 by following factors:												
Value of "C"	160	150	140	130	120	110	100	90	80	70	60	50	Value of "C"
Multiplier	0.419	0.472	0.537	0.615	0.714	0.838	1.0	1.22	1.51	1.93	2.57	3.61	Multiplier

TABLE 12c
PRESSURE LOSS
STEEL PIPE
SIZES NOT LISTED OPPOSITE PAGE

To determine PRESSURE LOSSES of 1/8, 1/4 and 3/8 in Schedule Wall Steel pipe, multiply losses of 1/2 in Schedule 40 by following factors:			
Nominal Size, in	1/8	1/4	3/8
	Multipliers		
Schedule 40	59.05	13.56	3.10
Schedule 80	175.7	33.63	6.53

To determine PRESSURE LOSSES of 3-1/2 and 5 in Schedule Wall Steel pipe, multiply losses of 4 in Schedule 40 by following factors:		
Nominal Size, in	3-1/2	5
	Multipliers	
Schedule 40	1.85	0.333
Schedule 80	2.40	0.420

TABLE 12d
PRESSURE LOSS
SCHEDULE 80 STEEL PIPE

	To determine PRESSURE LOSSES of Schedule 80 Steel pipe, multiply Losses of same size Schedule 40 steel by following factors:													
Size, in	1/2	3/4	1	1-1/4	1-1/2	2	2-1/2	3	4	6	8	10	12	Size, in
	Multipliers													
Schedule 80	1.89	1.67	1.56	1.45	1.41	1.37	1.35	1.32	1.28	1.28	1.25	1.26	1.27	Schedule 80

APPENDIX

TABLE 13

PRESSURE LOSS
ASBESTOS-CEMENT PIPE

C = 140

Pipe Sizes: Nominal								Loss per 100 ft: lb/in^2		
gpm	3 in	4 in	6 in	gpm	3 in	4 in	6 in	8 in	10 in	12 in
5	0.005	0.001		160	2.76	0.681	0.107	0.026	0.008	0.004
10	.016	.004	0.001	170	3.09	.762	.120	.029	.009	.004
15	.035	.009	.001	180	3.43	.847	.133	.032	.011	.005
20	.059	.015	.002	190	3.79	0.936	.147	.035	.012	.005
25	.089	.022	.003	200	4.17	1.03	.162	.039	.013	.006
30	.125	.031	.005	210	4.57	1.13	.177	.042	.014	.006
35	.166	.041	.006	220	4.98	1.23	.193	.046	.015	.007
40	.212	.052	.008	230		1.33	.210	.050	.017	.007
42	.233	.057	.009	240		1.44	.227	.054	.018	.008
44	.253	.063	.010	250		1.56	0.245	0.058	0.019	0.008
46	.275	.068	.011	260		1.67	.263	.063	.021	.009
48	.298	.073	.012	270		1.79	.282	.067	.022	.010
50	0.321	0.079	0.012	280		1.92	.302	.072	.024	.010
52	.345	.085	.013	290		2.05	.322	.077	.026	.011
54	.370	.091	.014	300		2.18	.343	.082	.027	.012
56	.396	.098	.015	325		2.53	.397	.095	.032	.014
58	.423	.104	.016	350		2.90	.456	.109	.036	.016
60	.450	.111	.017	375		3.29	.518	.124	.041	.018
62	.478	.118	.019	400			0.584	0.140	0.046	0.020
64	.507	.125	.020	425			.653	.156	.052	.022
66	.537	.132	.021	450			.726	.174	.058	.025
68	.567	.140	.022	475			.802	.192	.064	.028
70	0.598	0.148	0.023	500			0.882	.211	.070	.030
72	.630	.155	.024	550			1.05	.252	.083	.036
74	.663	.164	.026	600			1.24	.295	.098	.042
76	.697	.172	.027	650			1.43	.343	.114	.049
78	.731	.180	.028	700			1.64	.393	.130	.056
80	.766	.189	.030	800			2.10	.503	.167	.072
85	.857	.211	.033	900				.626	.207	.090
90	0.952	0.235	.037	1000				0.760	0.252	0.109
95	1.05	.260	.041	1100				0.907	.301	.130
100	1.16	0.285	0.045	1200				1.07	.353	.153
105	1.27	.312	.049	1300				1.24	.409	.177
110	1.38	.341	.054	1400				1.42	.470	.203
115	1.50	.370	.058	1500				1.61	.533	.231
120	1.62	.400	.063	2000					0.908	.393
125	1.75	.431	.068	2500					1.37	.594
130	1.88	.464	.073	3000						0.832
135	2.02	.497	.078	3500						
140	2.16	.532	.084	4000						
145	2.30	.568	.089	4500						
150	2.45	0.604	0.095	5000						

APPENDIX

TABLE 13a

VELOCITY FLOWS

ASBESTOS-CEMENT PIPE

Velocity ft/s	Nominal Pipe Sizes: inches						Velocity ft/s
	3	4	6	8	10	12	
	Flow: gpm*						
1	22.0	39.2	83.8	150.9	237.5	335.1	1
2	44.1	78.3	167.6	301.7	475.0	670.2	2
3	66.1	117.5	251.3	452.6	712.5	1005.3	3
4	88.1	156.7	335.1	603.4	950.0	1340.4	4
5	110.2	195.8	418.9	754.3	1187.5	1675.5	5
6	132.2	235.0	502.7	905.1	1425.1	2010.6	6
7	154.2	274.2	586.4	1056.0	1662.6	2345.7	7
8	176.3	313.3	670.2	1206.8	1900.1	2680.8	8
9	198.3	352.5	754.0	1357.7	2137.6	3015.9	9
10	220.3	391.7	837.8	1508.5	2375.1	3351.0	10
11	242.4	430.8	921.5	1659.4	2612.6	3686.1	11
12	264.4	470.0	1005.3	1810.2	2850.1	4021.2	12
13	286.4	509.2	1089.1	1961.1	3087.6	4356.4	13
14	308.4	548.3	1172.9	2111.9	3325.1	4691.5	14
15	330.5	587.5	1256.6	2262.8	3562.6	5026.6	15

*Flows calculated with factors in Table 16 may vary slightly due to rounding-off of factors.

TABLE 13b

MULTIPLYING FACTORS TO CHANGE VALUE OF "C"

C = 140 TO OTHER VALUES

	To determine PRESSURE LOSSES with other values of "C", multiply losses computed with "C" = 140 by following factors:												
Value of "C"	160	150	140	130	120	110	100	90	80	70	60	50	Value of "C"
Multiplier	0.781	0.880	1.0	1.15	1.33	1.56	1.86	2.26	2.82	3.61	4.79	6.72	Multiplier

APPENDIX

TABLE 14

PRESSURE LOSS

CAST IRON PIPE

C = 100

Pipe Sizes: Nominal											Losses per 100 ft: lb/in²	
gpm	2 in	2-1/4 in	3 in	4 in	6 in	gpm	2-1/4 in	3 in	4 in	6 in	8 in	10 in	12 in
5	0.061	0.034	0.008	0.002		160	20.86	5.15	1.27	0.177	0.044	0.015	0.006
10	.219	.124	.030	.008	0.001	170	23.34	5.76	1.42	.197	.049	.016	.007
15	.464	.262	.065	.016	.002	180	25.94	6.40	1.58	.219	.054	.018	.008
20	0.790	.445	.110	.027	.004	190	28.67	7.07	1.74	.243	.060	.020	.008
25	1.19	.673	.166	.041	.006	200		7.78	1.92	.267	.066	.022	.009
30	1.67	0.943	.233	.057	.008	210		8.51	2.10	.292	.072	.024	.010
35	2.22	1.25	.309	.076	.011	220		9.27	2.29	.318	.078	.027	.011
40	2.85	1.61	.396	.098	.014	230		10.07	2.48	.345	.085	.029	.012
42	3.12	1.76	.433	.107	.015	240		10.89	2.69	.374	.092	.031	.013
44	3.40	1.91	.472	.117	.016	250		11.75	2.90	0.403	0.099	0.034	0.014
46	3.69	2.08	.513	.126	.018	260		12.63	3.12	.433	.107	.036	.015
48	3.99	2.25	.555	.137	.019	270		13.55	3.34	.465	.115	.039	.016
50	4.30	2.43	0.598	0.148	0.021	280		14.49	3.57	.497	.123	.041	.017
52	4.63	2.61	.643	.159	.022	290		15.46	3.81	.530	.131	.044	.018
54	4.96	2.80	.690	.170	.024	300		16.46	4.06	.565	.139	.047	.019
56	5.31	2.99	.738	.182	.025	325		19.09	4.71	.655	.162	.055	.022
58	5.66	3.19	.787	.194	.027	350			5.40	.751	.185	.063	.026
60	6.03	3.40	.838	.207	.029	375			6.14	.853	.210	.071	.029
62	6.41	3.61	.891	.220	.031	400			6.91	0.962	0.237	0.080	0.033
64	6.79	3.83	0.945	.233	.032	425			7.74	1.08	.265	.090	.037
66	7.19	4.05	1.00	.247	.034	450			8.60	1.20	.295	.100	.041
68	7.60	4.28	1.06	.261	.036	475			9.50	1.32	.326	.110	.045
70	8.02	4.52	1.11	0.275	0.038	500			10.45	1.45	.358	.121	.050
72	8.45	4.76	1.17	.290	.040	550			12.46	1.73	.428	.144	.059
74	8.89	5.01	1.24	.305	.042	600			14.64	2.04	.502	.170	.070
76	9.33	5.26	1.30	.320	.045	650				2.36	.582	.197	.081
78	9.79	5.52	1.36	.336	.047	700				2.71	.668	.226	.093
80	10.26	5.79	1.43	.352	.049	800				3.47	0.855	.289	.119
85	11.48	6.47	1.60	.394	.055	900				4.31	1.06	.359	.148
90	12.76	7.20	1.77	.438	.061	1000				5.24	1.29	0.436	0.180
95	14.11	7.95	1.96	.484	.067	1100				6.25	1.54	.520	.214
100	15.51	8.74	2.16	0.532	0.074	1200				7.34	1.81	.611	.252
105	16.97	9.57	2.36	.582	.081	1300				8.51	2.10	.709	.292
110	18.50	10.43	2.57	.635	.088	1400					2.41	.813	.335
115	20.09	11.32	2.79	.689	.096	1500					2.74	0.924	.380
120	21.73	12.25	3.02	.745	.104	2000					4.66	1.57	.648
125	23.44	13.21	3.26	.804	.112	2500					7.04	2.38	0.979
130	25.20	14.21	3.50	.864	.120	3000						3.33	1.37
135	27.02	15.23	3.76	.927	.129	3500						4.43	1.82
140	28.90	16.30	4.02	0.991	.138	4000							2.34
145	30.84	17.39	4.29	1.06	.147	4500							2.90
150	32.84	18.51	4.57	1.13	0.157	5000							3.53

APPENDIX

VELOCITY FLOWS
CAST IRON PIPE

| Velocity ft/s | Nominal Pipe Size: inches | | | | | | | | Velocity ft/s |
| | 2 | 2-1/4 | 3 | 4 | 6 | 8 | 10 | 12 | |
	Flow: gpm*								
1	9.8	12.4	22.0	39.2	88.1	156.7	244.8	352.5	1
2	19.6	24.8	44.1	78.3	176.3	313.3	489.6	705.0	2
3	29.4	37.2	66.1	117.5	264.4	470.0	734.4	1057.5	3
4	39.2	49.6	88.1	156.7	352.5	626.7	979.2	1410.0	4
5	49.0	62.0	110.2	195.8	440.6	783.4	1224.0	1762.5	5
6	58.8	74.4	132.2	235.0	528.8	940.0	1468.8	2115.1	6
7	68.5	86.8	154.2	274.2	616.9	1096.7	1713.6	2467.6	7
8	78.3	99.1	176.3	313.3	705.0	1253.4	1958.4	2820.1	8
9	88.1	111.5	198.3	352.5	793.1	1410.0	2203.2	3172.6	9
10	97.9	123.9	220.3	391.7	881.3	1566.7	2448.0	3525.1	10
11	107.7	136.3	242.4	430.8	969.4	1723.4	2692.8	3877.6	11
12	117.5	148.7	264.4	470.0	1057.5	1880.0	2937.6	4230.1	12
13	127.3	161.1	286.4	509.2	1145.7	2036.7	3182.4	4582.6	13
14	137.1	173.5	308.4	548.3	1233.8	2193.4	3427.2	4935.1	14
15	146.9	185.9	330.5	587.5	1321.9	2350.1	3672.0	5287.6	15

*Flows calculated with factors in Table 16 may vary slightly due to rounding-off of factors.

MULTIPLYING FACTORS TO CHANGE VALUE OF "C"
C = 100 TO OTHER VALUES

| Value of "C" | To determine PRESSURE LOSSES with other values of "C", multiply Losses computed with C = 100 by following factors: | | | | | | | | | | | Value of "C" |
	160	150	140	130	120	110	100	90	80	70	60	50	
Multiplier	0.419	0.472	0.537	0.615	0.714	0.838	1.0	1.22	1.51	1.93	2.57	3.61	Multiplier

APPENDIX

TABLE 15

PRESSURE LOSS

C = 140 — STRAIGHT — SMOOTH BORE WATER HOSE

Hose Sizes: Nominal — Losses per 100 ft: lb/in^2

gpm	1/2 in	5/8 in	3/4 in	1 in	1-1/4 in	1-1/2 in	2 in	gpm	2 in	2-1/2 in	3 in	4 in	6 in
1	1.41	0.477	0.196	0.048	0.016	0.007	0.002	105	9.11	3.08	1.27	0.312	0.043
2	5.09	1.72	0.707	.175	.059	.024	.006	110	9.93	3.35	1.38	.341	.047
3	10.77	3.64	1.50	.369	.125	.051	.013	115	10.78	3.64	1.50	.370	.051
4	18.34	6.19	2.55	.629	.212	.087	.022	120	11.66	3.94	1.62	.400	.056
5	27.71	9.36	3.85	0.951	.321	.132	.033	125	12.58	4.25	1.75	.431	.060
6	38.83	13.11	5.40	1.33	.450	.185	.046	130	13.52	4.57	1.88	.464	.065
7	51.64	17.44	7.18	1.77	.598	.246	.061	135	14.50	4.90	2.02	.497	.069
8	66.12	22.32	9.19	2.27	.766	.315	.078	140	15.51	5.24	2.16	.532	.074
9	82.21	27.76	11.43	2.82	0.952	.392	.097	145	16.55	5.59	2.30	.568	.079
10	99.91	33.73	13.89	3.43	1.16	0.477	0.118	150		5.95	2.45	0.604	0.084
11		40.24	16.57	4.09	1.38	.569	.140	160		6.70	2.76	.681	.095
12		47.27	19.47	4.80	1.62	.668	.165	170		7.50	3.09	.762	.106
13		54.81	22.57	5.57	1.88	.774	.191	180	8 in	8.34	3.43	.847	.118
14		62.87	25.89	6.39	2.16	0.888	.219	190		9.21	3.79	0.936	.130
15		71.42	29.42	7.26	2.45	1.01	.249	200	0.035	10.13	4.17	1.03	.143
16			33.15	8.18	2.76	1.14	.280	210	.039	11.09	4.57	1.13	.157
17			37.08	9.15	3.09	1.27	.314	220	.042	12.08	4.98	1.23	.171
18	2-1/2 in		41.22	10.17	3.43	1.41	.349	230	.046	13.12	5.40	1.33	.185
19			45.55	11.24	3.79	1.56	.385	240	.049		5.85	1.44	.201
20	0.143		50.09	12.35	4.17	1.72	0.424	250	.053		6.30	1.56	0.216
22	.171			14.74	4.98	2.05	.506	260	.057		6.78	1.67	.233
24	.201			17.31	5.85	2.41	.594	270	.062		7.27	1.79	.249
26	.233			20.07	6.78	2.79	.689	280	.066		7.78	1.92	.267
28	.267			23.02	7.77	3.20	.790	290	.070		8.30	2.05	.285
30	.303			26.16	8.83	3.64	0.897	300	0.075		8.83	2.18	.303
32	.341			29.48	9.95	4.10	1.01	325	.087		10.24	2.53	.351
34	.382			32.97	11.13	4.59	1.13	350	.099			2.90	.403
36	.425	3 in		36.65	12.38	5.10	1.26	375	.113			3.29	.458
38	.469				13.68	5.63	1.39	400	.127			3.71	.516
40	0.516	0.212			15.04	6.19	1.53	425	.142			4.15	.577
42	.565	.233			16.46	6.78	1.67	450	.158			4.61	0.642
44	.615	.253			17.94	7.39	1.82	475	.175			5.10	.709
46	.668	.275			19.48	8.02	1.98	500	.192			5.61	.780
48	.723	.298			21.07	8.68	2.14	550	0.229			6.69	0.930
50	.780	.321			22.73	9.36	2.31	600	.269				1.09
52	.838	.345			24.44	10.06	2.48	650	.312				1.27
54	.899	.370			26.20	10.79	2.66	700	.358				1.45
56	0.961	.396	4 in		28.03	11.54	2.85	800	.459				1.86
58	1.03	.423			29.91	12.32	3.04	900	.571				2.31
60	1.09	0.450	0.111			13.11	3.23	1000	.693				2.81
62	1.16	.478	.118			13.93	3.44	1100	.827				3.35
64	1.23	.507	.125			14.78	3.65	1200	0.971				3.94
66	1.30	.537	.132			15.64	3.86	1300	1.13				4.57
68	1.38	.567	.140			16.53	4.08	1400	1.29				
70	1.45	.598	.148			17.44	4.30	1500	1.47				
75	1.65	.680	.168			19.82	4.89	2000	2.50				
80	1.86	.766	.189			22.33	5.51	2500	3.78				
85	2.08	.857	.211				6.16	3000					
90	2.31	0.952	.235				6.85	3500					
95	2.56	1.05	.260				7.57	4000					
100	2.81	1.16	0.285				8.32	5000					

APPENDIX

VELOCITY FLOWS

STRAIGHT-SMOOTH BORE WATER HOSE

Velocity	Nominal Hose Size: inches												Velocity
ft/s	1/2	5/8	3/4	1	1-1/4	1-1/2	2	2-1/2	3	4	6	8	ft/s
	Flow: gpm(1)												
1	0.6	1.0	1.4	2.4	3.8	5.5	9.8	15.3	22.0	39.2	88.1	156.7	1
2	1.2	1.9	2.8	4.9	7.6	11.0	19.6	30.6	44.1	78.3	176.3	313.3	2
3	1.8	2.9	4.1	7.3	11.5	16.5	29.4	45.9	66.1	117.5	264.4	470.0	3
4	2.4	3.8	5.5	9.8	15.3	22.0	39.2	61.2	88.1	156.7	352.5	626.7	4
5	3.1	4.8	6.9	12.2	19.1	27.5	49.0	76.5	110.2	195.8	440.6	783.4	5
6	3.7	5.7	8.3	14.7	22.9	33.0	58.8	91.8	132.2	235.0	528.8	940.0	6
7	4.3	6.7	9.6	17.1	26.8	38.6	68.5	107.1	154.2	274.2	616.9	1096.7	7
8	4.9	7.6	11.0	19.6	30.6	44.1	78.3	122.4	176.3	313.3	705.0	1253.4	8
9	5.5	8.6	12.4	22.0	34.4	49.6	88.1	137.7	198.3	352.5	793.1	1410.0	9
10	6.1	9.6	13.8	24.5	38.2	55.1	97.9	153.0	220.3	391.7	881.3	1566.7	10
11	6.7	10.5	15.1	26.9	42.1	60.6	107.7	168.3	242.4	430.8	969.4	1723.4	11
12	7.3	11.5	16.5	29.4	45.9	66.1	117.5	183.6	264.4	470.0	1057.5	1880.0	12
13	8.0	12.4	17.9	31.8	49.7	71.6	127.3	198.9	286.4	509.2	1145.7	2036.7	13
14	8.6	13.4	19.3	34.3	53.5	77.1	137.1	214.2	308.4	548.3	1233.8	2193.4	14
15	9.2	14.3	20.7	36.7	57.4	82.6	146.9	229.5	330.5	587.5	1321.9	2350.1	15

(1) Flows calculated with factors in Table 16 may vary slightly due to rounding-off of factors.

MULTIPLYING FACTORS TO CHANGE VALUE OF "C"

C = 140 TO OTHER VALUES

To determine PRESSURE LOSSES with other values of "C", Multiply losses computed with C = 140 by following factors:													
Value of "C"	160	150	140	130	120	110	100	90	80	70	60	50	Value of "C"
Multiplier	0.781	0.880	1.0	1.15	1.33	1.56	1.86	2.26	2.82	3.61	4.79	6.72	Multiplier

PRESSURE LOSS

STRAIGHT-SMOOTH BORE WATER HOSE

SIZES NOT LISTED OPPOSITE PAGE

To determine PRESSURE LOSSES of 5 in hose, multiply losses of 4 in hose by following factors:	
Nominal Size, in	5
	Multiplier
Hose	0.338

APPENDIX

EXPLANATION OF MULTIPLYING FACTORS FOR FLOW VELOCITIES

Mean velocity of water flow in piping, when flowing full, can be determined by the followings simplied formulas:

$$V = \frac{0.4085 \text{ gpm}}{d^2}$$

Where:

V = velocity in feet/second (ft/s)
gpm = flowing gallons per minute
d = pipe average interior diameter in inches

or,

$$V = \frac{353.68 \text{ m}^3/\text{h}}{d^2}$$

Where:

V= velocity in meters per second (m/s)
m^3/h = flow in cubic meters per hour
d = pipe average interior diameter in millimeters

The multiplying factors in Table 16 were derived from the formula above for determining velocity in U.S. Customary Units. Factors are listed for 19 different kinds of pipe and tubing and for water hose. The factors enable velocities to be determined easily with a degree of accuracy suitable for all practical purposes.

Example: Determine velocity when 15.5 gpm is flowing through 1 in, SDR 21 PVC (controlled OD) pipe:

        15.5   (gpm)
    x 0.299   (multiplying factor from table)
    = 4.6   ft/s velocity

The factors can also be used to determine flow for a given velocity.

Example: Determine flow through 1in, SDR 21 PVC (controlled OD) pipe for a velocity of 5.5 ft/s.

    (Velocity, ft/s) $\frac{5.5}{0.299}$ =18.4 gpm
    (multiplying factor)

Note: The interior pipe diameters (d) used to calculate the velocity multiplying factors were those determined for pressure loss tables.

Attention is called to the fact that flow velocities are always for new, straight pipe. True velocities in old, deteriorated pipe cannot be determined by formula. Therefore, when using such pipe, the designer should assume that the velocity is greater than calculated.

APPENDIX

TABLE 16
MULTIPLYING FACTORS
FLOW VELOCITIES

Nominal Size in	Controlled (IPS) OD Thermoplastic Pipe									Nominal Size in
	SDR 32.5	SDR 26	SDR 21	SDR 17	SDR 13.5	SDR 11	Schd. 40	Schd. 80	Schd. 120	
	To determine ft/s Velocity, multiply gpm Flow by following factors:									
1/8					5.82		6.59	10.7		1/8
1/4					2.55		3.45	5.14		1/4
3/8					1.43		1.83	2.52		3/8
1/2				0.843	0.843	0.915	1.13	1.48	1.77	1/2
3/4			0.493	.498	.535	.580	.632	.784	.858	3/4
1		0.296	.299	.314	.337	.370	.386	.466	.515	1
1-1/4		.179	.186	.196	.210	.230	.221	.259	.282	1-1/4
1-1/2		.136	.141	.149	.160	.175	.162	.188	.202	1-1/2
2	0.0837[1]	.0865	.0901	.0949	.102	.111	.0975	.112	.120	2
2-1/2	.0569[1]	.0588	.0613	.0645	.0696		.0683	.0779	.0815	2-1/2
3	0.0383	0.0396	0.0413	0.0435	0.0469	0.0512	0.0441	0.0498	0.0537	3
3-1/2	.0293	.0303	.0316	.0333	.0359		.0330	.0369	.0385	3-1/2
4	.0231	.0239	.0250	.0263	.0284	.0310	.0256	.0285	.0320	4
5	.0151	.0157	.0163	.0172	.0186		.0162	.0180	.0201	5
6	.0107	.0110	.0115	.0122	0.0131	0.0143	.0112	.0125	.0138	6
8	.006 28	.006 51	.006 79	.007 17			.006 48	.007 14	.008 10	8
10	.004 05	.004 19	.004 37	.004 61			.004 10	.004 53	.005 08	10
12	0.002 88	0.002 98	0.003 11	0.003 28			0.002 89	0.003 20	0.003 62	12

[1] Not ASTM Standard pipe.

Nominal Size in	Controlled OD (Copper Tube Size OD) Thermoplastic Tubing		PE Controlled (IPS) ID Thermoplastic Pipe	Copper Water Tube			Galv. Steel Pipe		Water Hose (Smooth-Bore)	Nominal Size in
	PVC SDR 26[2]	PE SDR 9[2]		Type M	Type L	Type K	Schd. 40	Schd. 80		
	To determine ft/s Velocity, multiply gpm Flow by following factors:									
1/8							5.65	8.84		1/8
1/4					4.12	4.39	3.08	4.48		1/4
3/8				2.02	2.21	2.53	1.68	2.28		3/8
1/2	1.73	1.80	1.06	1.26	1.38	1.47	1.06	1.37	1.63	1/2
5/8		1.24			0.921	0.961			1.05	5/8
3/4	0.754	0.906	0.602	0.621	.663	.736	0.602	0.742	0.726	3/4
1	.420	.548	.371	.367	.389	.413	.371	.446	.409	1
1-1/4	0.267	.368	.215	.245	.255	.264	.215	.250	.261	1-1/4
1-1/2		.264	.158	.175	.180	.186	.158	.182	.182	1-1/2
2		0.154	.956	.101	.104	.106	.0956	.109	.102	2
2-1/2			.670	.0656	.0672	.0689	.0670	.0757	.0654	2-1/2
3			0.434	0.0460	0.0471	0.0483	0.0434	0.0486	0.0454	3
3-1/2				.0341	.0348	.0357	.0325	.0361		3-1/2
4			.0252	.0264	.0268	.0275	.0252	.0279	.0255	4
5				.0170	.0172	.0177	.0160	.0176	.0163	5
6			0.0111	.0118	.0120	.0124	.0111	.0123	.0113	6
8				.006 74	.006 85	.007 10	.006 41	.007 03	0.006 38	8
10				.004 34	.004 11	.004 58	.004 07	.004 41		10
12				0.003 03	0.003 05	0.003 19	0.002 87	0.003 16		12

[2] CAUTION: Not same as Thermoplastic *pipe* of same SDR.

CAST IRON PIPE[3]	
Nominal Size, in	To determine ft/s Velocity, multiply gpm Flow by following factors:
2	0.102
2-1/4	0.0807
3	0.0454
4	0.0255
6	0.0114
8	0.006 38
10	0.004 09
12	0.002 84

ASBESTOS-CEMENT PIPE[3]	
Nominal Size, in	To determine ft/s Velocity, multiply gpm Flow by following factors:
3	0.0454
4	0.0255
6	0.0119
8	0.006 63
10	0.004 21
12	0.002 98

[3] Factors are same for all classes of pipe of the same nominal size.

See explanation of pressure loss in pipe for detailed information.

APPENDIX

EXPLANATION OF PRESSURE LOSS IN PIPING APPURTENANCES

Piping appurtenances maybe classed as two types:
1. Standard Plumbing Valves and Fittings
2. Specialty-Type Appurtenances

STANDARD PLUMBING VALVES AND FITTINGS

The pressure loss caused by a standard plumbing valve or fitting in a pipeline is usually determined by calculating the loss through an equivalent length of pipes supplying the appurtenance. Thus, pressure loss caused by a given standard plumbing valve or fitting is constant for a given flow regardless of the kind of pipe which supplies the item.

For determining the loss in the appurtenance, a pipe with a larger ID (and, consequently, less pressure loss per foot) requires a longer equivalent length than a smaller ID pipe. The end result will be the same loss for the two pipes). However, the loss through a given size and type appurtenance changes when its configuration changes. The following tables of "Equivalent Feet of Piping" were compiled using the most current information. However, available data is often conflicting and quite limited. In questionable areas, some compromise, extrapolation and assumption was required.

Tables 17 and 18 provide equivalent lengths of piping which cause approximately the same pressure loss as the listed valves and fittings (pipe is same nominal size as the item). The upper section of the tables lists base footage equivalents for each size valve or fitting. The next section lists multiplying factors to convert the base footage equivalents to footage equivalents for specific pipes. Never use the base footage equivalents without converting.

Examples: Determine pressure loss through a 1½ in straight globe valve with a flow of 60 gpm when supplied by:
a 1½ in SDR 13.5, 315 psi PVC pipe (Table 4)
a 1½ in SDR 26,160 psi PVC pipe (Table 6)

SDR 13.5 pipe		SDR 26 pipe
45.60	(Base Footage Equivalent)	45.60
x 1.10	(Conversion Multiplying Factor)	x 1.63
50.16 ft	(Equivalent Length)	74.33 ft

(Because the equivalents are approximate, it is recommended they be rounded off, upwards, before using.) Pressure loss will be as follows:

8.48 lb/in^2	(Loss per 100 ft)	5.70 lb/in^2
x .51 (50.16)		x.75 (74.33)
4.32 lb/in^2	(Loss in Valve)	4.28 lb/in^2

(Generally, calculations are rounded to one decimal place when designing a piping system; therefore, in the above examples, 4.3 lb/in^2 would be used as the pressure loss.)

Use of equivalent lengths simplifies calculations of pressure loss in piping systems since several calculations can be combined.

Example: Determine pressure loss through 42 ft of 1½ in SDR 21, 200 psi PVC pipe, a 1½ in angle globe valve which the pipe supplies, and a 1½ in by 1¼ in reducing bushing in the discharge side of the valve; flow is 52 gpm.

(a) Valve:
Base Footage	19.50
Multiplying Factor	x 1.48
Equivalent Feet	28.86

(b) Bushing:
Base Footage	1.70
Multiplying Factor	x 1.48
Equivalent Feet	2.52

(c) 1½ in SDR 21 PVC
	pipe	42 ft
	Valve	29
	Bushing	3
	Total	74 ft

(d)
Loss per 100 ft	4.82 lb/in^2	(From
Total equivalent ft	x .74	Table 5)
Loss all 3 items	3.57 lb/in^2	

The following explanations should make the tables easier to understand. Special conditions to enable determination of losses in fittings not directly listed are explained later.

VALVES

GATE and GLOBE VALVES. Pressure losses in valves determined by the table are based on good quality valves with ample passageways and full ports.

APPENDIX

Valves with undersized passageways and ports will have greater losses.

CHECK VALVES. The pressure losses through "conventional swing check valves" (no springs) determined with the tables are valid only if the disc is fully lifted. The disc of good quality check valves is fully-lifted at flow rates causing a loss of at least $\frac{1}{2}$ lb/in^2. Therefore, always use check valves of a size that will cause at least that loss, even if it the result is a check valve smaller than line size. The actual pressure drop will be little, if any, higher than that of a full (line) size valve which is used in other than a wide open position. Losses for reducing and increasing bushings (or couplings) must be added to loss of smaller (or larger) than line size valves.

SPECIAL NOTE. Some manufacturers of valves can furnish loss data for their valves based on actual tests. When available, this data should be used instead of the tables in this manual.

MATERIAL

All reference data for pressure loss in standard plumbing valves and fittings is based on new pipe and appurtenances; no recommendations are given for aging and deterioration. The following guidelines are based on reasonable assumption.

POLYETHYLENE

No authenticated data is available for pressure loss caused by" insert fittings" used in PE plastic pipe. Since they are installed inside the pipe, there is no doubt they cause a substantially greater loss than fittings used on the outside of pipe. Most designers offset this loss by using larger pipe than determined with the pressure loss table for PE pipe. One source recommends using pressure losses based on a "C" factor of 120 to provide a loss allowance for these fittings.

COPPER TUBE

The "equivalent lengths" of copper tube for valves provided in the table are for IPS (configuration) valves. The configuration of "copper-sweat" valves usually causes a greater loss.

STEEL AND CAST IRON

Fittings for galvanized steel and cast iron pipe, when made of the same material, no doubt deteriorate at a rate consistent with the pipe. Thus, the equivalent lengths, which are for new pipe, when used with the tables of pipe pressure losses for old pipe, provide an equal allowance for aging. Valves generally do not cause more pressure loss as they age. Therefore, the multiplying factors for valves used with steel and cast iron pipes have been adjusted to reflect non-deterioration with age when used with the tables for aged pipe.

ASBESTOS-CEMENT PIPE

When fittings made of cast iron or other ferrous-metal that can rust or corrode are used with A-C pipe, an allowance for such deterioration is required.

SPECIAL CONDITIONS

FITTINGS, GENERAL. Equivalent lengths for fittings listed in the table are for standard fittings for the pipe, i.e., deterioration, if any, of the fittings is the same as for the pipe. If the fitting is of another material, a suitable equivalent length must be substituted.

Example: A galvanized steel ell is used with PE pipe. Therefore, the equivalent length of that ell is used and the loss determined from the table of pipe pressure losses for galvanized steel pipe. Note: In this case, two plastic insert adapters would also be required. The losses of the adapters must then be added to the loss of the ell.

REDUCING TEES. Use the equivalent length for standard tees, run or branch, which ever is under consideration.

1. If the flow through the reduced portion is maintained at approximately the same, or less, than the flow velocity entering the tee, no adjustment of the equivalent length is required.
2. If the flow velocity through the reduced portion exceeds the velocity entering the tee, add the equivalent length of a reducing bushing or coupling to the equivalent length for the tee.

SPECIALTY-TYPE APPURTENANCES

Appurtenances classed as specialty type are those through which pressure losses do not relate to losses in piping. The cause of this non-relationship is, in general, due to the interior mechanisms of these appurtenances.

Except for water meters, pressure loss data for any specialty-type appurtenance must be obtained from the manufacturer. Because losses vary from manufacturer to manufacturer for the same type item, never use one manufacturer's loss data for another manufacturer's product. Also, pressure losses may vary by model of a particular item made by the same manufacturer.

WATER METERS
The tables of pressure losses caused by water meters are based on AWWA standards. The last listed loss for each meter is for the maximum flow that should occur through that meter. Never exceed that flow.

INTERPOLATION. Pressure Losses caused by a water meter for flows not listed in the tables can be interpolated with sufficient accuracy by use of the following procedure.

Example: Determine pressure loss caused by a 2 in water meter with a flow of 93.3 gpm.

Step 1.

$$\begin{array}{ll} 95 & \text{(nearest listed greater flow)} \\ \underline{-90} & \text{(nearest listed lesser flow)} \\ = 5.0 & \text{(gpm difference)} \end{array}$$

Step 2.

$$\begin{array}{ll} 7.0 & \text{(loss, lb/in}^2\text{, for nearest greater flow)} \\ \underline{-6.2} & \text{(loss, lb/in}^2\text{, for nearest lesser flow)} \\ = .8 & \text{(lb/in}^2 \text{ difference)} \end{array}$$

Step 3

$$\frac{.8}{5} = 0.16 \text{ lb/in}^2$$
(loss for each 1 gpm between *lesser* and *greater* flow)

Step 4.

$$\begin{array}{ll} 93.3 & \text{(gpm, \textit{required} flow)} \\ \underline{-90.0} & \text{(gpm, nearest listed \textit{lesser} flow)} \\ = 3.3 & \text{(gpm, difference)} \end{array}$$

Step 5.

$$\begin{array}{ll} & 0.16 & \text{(from Step 3)} \\ \times & \underline{3.3} & \text{(from Step 4)} \\ = & .53 & \\ + & \underline{6.2^*} & \text{(loss for lesser flow)} \\ = & 6.7 & \text{lb/in}^2 \text{ loss for 93.3 gpm} \end{array}$$

*Note: Always calculate from nearest lesser flow!

APPENDIX

TABLE 17
PRESSURE LOSS
STANDARD PLUMBING VALVES and FITTINGS
APPROXIMATE EQUIVALENT FEET OF PIPING

TYPE APPURTENANCE	Nominal Pipe Size: inches												
	1/2	3/4	1	1-1/4	1-1/2	2	2-1/2	3	4	6	8	10	12
	Base Footage Equivalents: CAUTION: Use only with conversion multiplying factors for correct kind of pipe												
Gate Valve	0.7	0.9	1.1	1.5	1.7	2.2	2.7	3.3	4.4	6.6	8.6	10.9	12.9
Straight Globe Valve	17.6	23.3	29.7	39.1	45.6	58.6	70.0	86.9	114.1	171.8	226.1	283.9	338.2
Angle Globe Valve	7.5	10.0	12.7	16.7	19.5	25.0	29.8	37.1	48.7	73.3	96.4	121.1	144.3
Conventional Check Valve[1]	7.0	9.3	11.8	15.5	18.1	23.3	27.8	34.5	45.3	68.2	89.8	112.7	134.3
Corporation Cock	14.2	10.1	9.0	12.9	12.2	11.3	—	—	—	—	—	—	—
Curb Stop	7.3	7.0	5.2	6.2	7.1	6.5	—	—	—	—	—	—	—
Straight Meter Cock	7.0	6.9	5.4	—	—	—	—	—	—	—	—	—	—
Angle Meter Cock	14.0	13.8	10.8	—	—	—	—	—	—	—	—	—	—
Stop and Waste Cock	14.0	10.3	—	—	—	—	—	—	—	—	—	—	—
90° Ell	1.6	2.1	2.6	3.5	4.0	5.2	6.2	7.7	10.1	15.2	20.0	25.1	29.9
45° Ell	0.8	1.1	1.4	1.8	2.2	2.8	3.3	4.1	5.4	8.1	10.6	13.4	15.9
90° Street Ell	2.6	3.4	4.4	5.8	6.7	8.6	10.3	12.8	16.8	25.3	33.3	41.8	49.7
Run of Straight Tee	1.0	1.4	1.8	2.3	2.7	3.5	4.1	5.1	6.7	10.1	13.3	16.7	19.9
Branch of Straight Tee	3.1	4.1	5.3	6.9	8.1	10.3	12.4	15.3	20.1	30.3	39.9	50.1	59.7
Reducing Bushing or Coupling[3]													
Reduced 1 Standard[2] Size	—	1.6	1.5	2.5	1.7	3.5	1.7	4.0	8.1	32.1	19.8	15.2	10.4
Reduced 2 Standard[2] Size	—	—	7.7	10.5	7.8	8.9	12.4	13.6	32.5	123.2	175.2	102.1	68.3
Increasing Bushing or Coupling[4]													
Increased 1 Standard[2] Size	0.4	0.5	0.7	0.3	1.0	0.7	1.4	2.2	5.5	5.2	5.0	4.4	—
Increased 2 Standard[2] Sizes	0.7	1.2	1.3	1.6	2.1	2.6	4.2	7.5	10.5	12.2	12.1	—	—
Ordinary Entrance	1.1	1.5	1.9	2.7	3.2	4.3	5.4	6.8	9.5	15.3	20.9	27.6	33.7

[1] Check valve with less than 0.5 psi loss should not be used.
   See explanation text.
[2] Standard sizes are those used in this table.
[3] Calculate loss with larger pipe.
[4] Calculate loss with smaller pipe.

KIND OF PIPING	Multiplying Factors To Convert Base Footage Equivalents To Footage Equivalents for Specific Pipes — Nominal Pipe Size: inches												
	1/2	3/4	1	1-1/4	1-1/2	2	2-1/2	3	4	6	8	10	12
Controlled OD Thermoplastic													
SDR 11 Pipe	1.42	1.09	1.01	0.84	0.78	0.69	—	0.67	0.61	0.54	—	—	—
SDR 13.5 Pipe	1.96	1.51	1.44	1.19	1.10	0.97	1.04	0.94	0.85	0.76	—	—	—
SDR 17 Pipe	—	1.80	1.71	1.42	1.30	1.16	1.25	1.13	1.02	0.91	0.87	0.84	0.82
SDR 21 Pipe	—	1.84	1.92	1.61	1.48	1.31	1.41	1.28	1.16	1.04	0.99	0.95	0.93
SDR 26 Pipe	—	—	1.97	1.77	1.63	1.45	1.56	1.42	1.29	1.15	1.10	1.06	1.04
SDR 32.5 Pipe	—	—	—	—	—	1.57	1.69	1.54	1.40	1.26	1.19	1.15	1.13
Schedule 40 Pipe	0.97	1.01	1.03	1.06	1.07	1.08	1.08	1.09	1.10	1.11	1.11	1.11	1.11
Schedule 80 Pipe	0.50	0.60	0.65	0.72	0.74	0.78	0.79	0.81	0.84	0.85	0.88	0.87	0.87
SDR 26 PVC Tubing	0.29	0.55	0.70	0.56	—	—	—	—	—	—	—	—	—
PE SDR 7.3 Tubing	0.19	0.26	0.27	0.19	0.18	0.22	—	—	—	—	—	—	—
PE SDR 9 Tubing	0.28	0.37	0.39	0.27	0.29	0.31	—	—	—	—	—	—	—
Controlled ID PE Pipe	1.00	1.00	1.00	1.00	1.00	1.00	1.00	1.00	1.00	1.00	—	—	—
Schedule 40 Galvanized Steel Pipe													
Valves	0.54	0.54	0.54	0.54	0.54	0.54	0.54	0.54	0.54	0.54	0.54	0.54	0.54
Galvanized Fitting	1.00	1.00	1.00	1.00	1.00	1.00	1.00	1.00	1.00	1.00	1.00	1.00	1.00
Asbestos-Cement Pipe													
Valves								0.90	0.97	0.84	0.92	0.92	0.91
Non-rusting or non-deteriorating Fittings								0.70	0.67	0.56	0.54	0.54	0.50
Rusting or deteriorating Fittings								1.30	1.25	1.04	1.00	1.00	0.93
Cast Iron Pipe							(2-1/4)[5]						
Valves						0.46	0.35	0.49	0.52	0.51	0.55	0.53	0.56
Fittings						0.65	0.64	0.62	0.65	0.61	0.60	0.58	0.57

[5] 2-1/4 in cast iron pipe; Equivalent of 2-1/4 in pipe represents pressure loss in 2-1/2 in valve.

APPENDIX

NOTE: This table is for use with pipe pressure loss tables in this manual.

TABLE 18

PRESSURE LOSS
STANDARD PLUMBING VALVES and TUBE FITTINGS
APPROXIMATE EQUIVALENT FEET COPPER WATER TUBING

TYPE APPURTENANCE	Nominal Tube Size: Inches												
	1/2	3/4	1	1-1/4	1-1/2	2	2-1/2	3	4	6	8	10	12
	Base Footage Equivalents: Caution: Use only with conversion multiplying factors for correct types of Tubing												
IPS Gate Valve, Full Open	0.3	0.5	0.9	0.9	1.1	1.7	2.4	2.5	3.4	4.8	6.4	7.8	9.6
IPS Straight Globe Valve, Full Open	7.8	13.5	22.0	22.8	28.7	43.3	62.3	64.3	87.8	125.4	167.3	204.4	250.3
IPS Angle Globe Valve, Full Open	3.2	5.8	9.4	9.7	12.3	18.5	26.6	27.4	37.5	53.5	71.4	87.2	106.8
IPS Conventional Check Valve, Full Open[1]	3.0	5.4	8.7	9.0	11.4	17.2	24.7	25.6	34.9	49.8	66.4	81.2	99.4
Corporation Cock, Full Open	6.7	6.4	7.3	8.2	8.4	9.2	—	—	—	—	—	—	—
Curb Stop, Full Open	3.4	4.4	4.2	3.9	4.8	5.2	—	—	—	—	—	—	—
Straight Meter Cock, Full Open	3.3	4.4	4.4	—	—	—	—	—	—	—	—	—	—
Angle Meter Cock, Full Open	6.6	8.7	8.7	—	—	—	—	—	—	—	—	—	—
Stop and Waste Cocks, Full Open	6.6	6.6	—	—	—	—	—	—	—	—	—	—	—
Wrought Tube Fittings:													
90° Ell	1.0	1.3	1.5	2.0	2.5	3.5	4.0	5.0	7.0	10.0	15.1	—	—
45° Ell	0.6	0.8	1.0	1.2	1.5	2.0	2.5	3.0	4.0	6.0	7.9	—	—
90° Street Ell													
Run of Straight Tee	0.3	0.4	0.5	0.6	0.8	1.0	1.3	1.5	2.0	3.0	4.0	—	—
Branch of Straight Tee	1.5	2.0	2.5	3.0	3.5	5.0	6.0	7.5	10.5	15.0	19.8	—	—
Cast Fittings:													
90° Ell	1.0	2.0	4.0	5.0	8.0	11.0	14.0	18.0	28.0	52.0	68.4	85.9	102.3
45° Ell	0.6	1.0	2.0	2.0	3.0	5.0	8.0	11.0	17.0	28.0	36.6	46.3	55.0
90° Street Ell													
Run of Straight Tee	0.5	0.5	0.5	1.0	1.0	2.0	2.0	2.0	2.0	3.0	4.0	5.0	5.9
Branch of Straight Tee	2.0	3.0	5.0	7.0	9.0	12.0	16.0	20.0	37.0	61.0	80.3	100.9	120.2
Straight Coupling	0.3	0.4	0.5	0.6	0.8	1.0	1.3	1.5	2.0	3.0	4.0	5.0	5.9
Reducing Bushing or Coupling:[3]													
Reduced 1 Standard[2] Size	—	1.9	2.0	1.3	0.9	3.9	2.8	2.0	8.5	27.8	18.5	13.2	10.4
Reduced 2 Standard[2] Sizes	—	—	12.0	8.7	5.9	10.9	17.5	12.5	25.0	111.6	152.0	88.1	62.3
Increasing Bushing or Coupling:[4]													
Increased 1 Standard[2] Size	0.4	0.5	0.4	0.4	1.0	1.0	0.9	2.3	5.1	5.1	4.5	4.3	—
Increased 2 Standard[2] Sizes	0.9	1.0	1.1	1.6	2.2	2.3	3.6	6.8	9.4	7.8	11.4	—	—
Ordinary Entrance	0.9	1.3	1.8	2.3	2.8	3.9	5.0	6.2	8.6	13.7	18.9	24.1	29.9

[1] Check valve with less than 0.5 psi loss should not be used. See explanation text.
[2] Standard sizes are those used in this table.
[3] Calculate loss with larger pipe.
[4] Calculate loss with smaller pipe.

TYPE COPPER TUBE	Multiplying Factors to Convert Base Footage Equivalents to Footage Equivalents for Specific Tubes												
	Nominal Pipe Size: inches												
	1/2	3/4	1	1-1/4	1-1/2	2	2-1/2	3	4	6	8	10	12
Type K	1.00	1.00	1.00	1.00	1.00	1.00	1.00	1.00	1.00	1.00	1.00	1.00	1.00
Type L	1.18	1.29	1.16	1.08	1.08	1.07	1.06	1.07	1.06	1.09	1.09	1.09	1.11
Type M	1.45	1.51	1.33	1.19	1.16	1.13	1.13	1.13	1.10	1.12	1.14	1.14	1.14

APPENDIX

TABLE 19
PRESSURE LOSS
DISC-TYPE WATER METERS

Meter Size: inches — Losses: lb/in²

gpm	5/8	3/4	1	1-1/4[1]	1-1/2	2
5	0.88	0.41	0.23	0.25	0.15	0.10
6	1.3	.56	.28	.29	.21	.13
7	1.8	0.75	.33	.33	.25	.15
8	2.3	1.0	.39	.38	.29	.17
9	2.9	1.3	.47	.43	.33	.19
10	3.7	1.6	.55	.49	.37	.22
11	4.4	1.9	.67	.55	.41	.25
12	5.2	2.2	.79	.62	.46	.27
13	6.3	2.7	0.95	.69	.51	.29
14	7.3	3.1	1.1	.75	.55	.32
15	8.4	3.6	1.3	.80	.60	.34
16	9.5	4.1	1.4	.88	.66	.37
17	10.8	4.7	1.6	0.95	.70	.40
18	12.1	5.2	1.8	1.0	.76	.42
19	13.5	5.9	2.0	1.2	.83	.45
20	15.0	6.5	2.2	1.3	.89	.49
21		7.2	2.5	1.4	0.95	.51
22		7.9	2.7	1.6	1.0	.55
23		8.7	3.0	1.7	1.1	.58
24		9.4	3.3	1.9	1.2	.60
25		10.3	3.6	2.0	1.3	.63
26		11.2	3.9	2.1	1.4	.67
27		12.1	4.2	2.2	1.5	.69
28		13.2	4.6	2.4	1.6	.72
29		14.1	4.9	2.6	1.7	.76
30		15.0	5.3	2.8	1.8	.79
31			5.7	3.0	1.9	.83
32			6.1	3.1	2.0	.87
33			6.5	3.3	2.1	.90
34			6.9	3.5	2.2	.94
35			7.3	3.7	2.4	.97
36			7.7	4.0	2.5	0.99
37			8.2	4.2	2.7	1.0
38			8.7	4.4	2.8	1.1
39			9.1	4.6	2.9	1.2
40			9.6	4.9	3.1	1.2
41			10.1	5.1	3.3	1.3
42			10.6	5.4	3.5	1.3
43			11.1	5.7	3.7	1.4
44			11.6	6.0	3.8	1.5
45			12.1	6.2	4.0	1.6
46			12.8	6.5	4.2	1.6
47			13.3	6.8	4.3	1.7
48			13.9	7.1	4.5	1.8
49			14.4	7.4	4.7	1.8
50			15.0	7.8	4.9	1.9

gpm	1-1/4[1]	1-1/2	2	3	4	6
50	7.8	4.9	1.9	0.80	0.42	0.19
55	9.3	5.9	2.2	.88	.45	.20
60	11.1	7.1	2.7	0.98	.52	.23
65	12.9	8.3	3.1	1.1	.55	.24
70	15.1	9.7	3.7	1.2	.60	.26
75	17.3	11.1	4.2	1.4	.64	.27
80	20.0	12.7	4.8	1.6	.69	.29
85		14.5	5.5	1.8	.75	.31
90		16.1	6.2	2.0	.81	.34
95		18.0	7.0	2.2	.86	.36
100		20.0	7.8	2.4	0.92	0.38
110			9.4	2.9	1.0	.42
120			11.3	3.3	1.2	.46
130			13.3	3.9	1.4	.51
140			15.4	4.5	1.6	.55
150			17.7	5.0	1.9	.60
160			20.0	5.8	2.1	.65
170				6.5	2.3	.70
180				7.4	2.6	.75
190				8.1	2.9	.81
200				8.9	3.2	.86
220				10.9	3.9	0.96
240				12.8	4.6	1.1
260				15.2	5.4	1.3
280				17.4	6.3	1.5
300				20.0	7.3	1.8
320					8.3	2.0
340					9.4	2.3
360					10.4	2.5
380					11.7	2.8
400					12.9	3.1
420					14.2	3.4
440					15.5	3.8
460					17.1	4.1
480					18.5	4.5
500					20.0	4.9
550						6.1
600						7.1
650						8.5
700						9.8
750						11.3
800						12.9
850						14.7
900						16.4
950						18.0
1000						20.0

[1] Not AWWA STANDARD. Losses are for Hershey Model HD.

NOTE: The greatest flows listed above are the maximum safe capacities for meters.

APPENDIX

Conversion factor
1 lb/in² = 2.3089 ft H₂O
(Water at 60° F)

TABLE 20
PRESSURE EQUIVALENTS

POUNDS PER SQUARE INCH (lb/in²) TO (HEAD) FEET of WATER (ft H²0)

Base Table

lb/in²	0	1	2	3	4	5	6	7	8	9
					Head: ft H₂O					
0	0.0	2.3	4.6	6.9	9.2	11.5	13.9	16.2	18.5	20.8
10	23.1	25.4	27.7	30.0	32.3	34.6	36.9	39.3	41.6	43.9
20	46.2	48.5	50.8	53.1	55.4	57.7	60.0	62.3	64.6	67.0
30	69.3	71.6	73.9	76.2	78.5	80.8	83.1	85.4	87.7	90.0
40	92.4	94.7	97.0	99.3	101.6	103.9	106.2	108.5	110.8	113.1
50	115.4	117.8	120.1	122.4	124.7	127.0	129.3	131.6	133.9	136.2
60	138.5	140.8	143.2	145.5	147.8	150.1	152.4	154.7	157.0	159.3
70	161.6	163.9	166.2	168.5	170.9	173.2	175.5	177.8	180.1	182.4
80	184.7	187.0	189.3	191.6	193.9	196.3	198.6	200.9	203.2	205.5
90	207.8	210.1	212.4	214.7	217.0	219.3	221.7	224.0	226.3	228.6
100	230.9	233.2	235.5	237.8	240.1	242.4	244.7	247.1	249.4	251.7
110	254.0	256.3	258.6	260.9	263.2	265.5	267.8	270.1	272.5	274.8
120	277.1	279.4	281.7	284.0	286.3	288.6	290.9	293.2	295.5	297.8
130	300.2	302.5	304.8	307.1	309.4	311.7	314.0	316.3	318.6	320.9
140	323.3	325.6	327.9	330.2	332.5	334.8	337.1	339.4	341.7	344.0
150	346.3	348.6	351.0	353.3	355.6	357.9	360.2	362.5	364.8	367.1

Supplemental Table

lb/in²	0.1	0.2	0.3	0.4	0.5	0.6	0.7	0.8	0.9
Head: ft H₂O	0.2	0.5	0.7	0.9	1.2	1.4	1.6	1.8	2.1

Conversion Factor:
1 ft H₂O = 0.4331 lb/in²
(Water at 60⁰ F)

TABLE 21
PRESSURE EQUIVALENTS
(HEAD) FEET of WATER (ft H²O) to POUNDS PER SQUARE INCH (lb/in²)

Base Table

ft H₂O	0	1	2	3	4	5	6	7	8	9
					lb/in²					
0	0.00	0.43	0.87	1.30	1.73	2.17	2.60	3.03	3.46	3.90
10	4.33	4.76	5.20	5.63	6.06	6.50	6.93	7.36	7.80	8.23
20	8.66	9.10	9.53	9.96	10.39	10.83	11.26	11.69	12.13	12.56
30	12.99	13.43	13.86	14.29	14.73	15.16	15.59	16.02	16.46	16.89
40	17.32	17.76	18.19	18.62	19.06	19.49	19.92	20.36	20.79	21.22
50	21.66	22.09	22.52	22.95	23.39	23.82	24.25	24.69	25.12	25.55
60	25.99	26.42	26.85	27.29	27.72	28.15	28.58	29.02	29.45	29.88
70	30.32	30.75	31.18	31.62	32.05	32.48	32.92	33.35	33.78	34.21
80	34.65	35.08	35.51	35.95	36.38	36.81	37.25	37.68	38.11	38.55
90	38.98	39.41	39.85	40.28	40.71	41.14	41.58	42.01	42.44	42.88
100	43.31	43.74	44.18	44.61	45.04	45.48	45.91	46.34	46.77	47.21
110	47.64	48.07	48.51	48.94	49.37	49.81	50.24	50.67	51.11	51.54
120	51.97	52.41	52.84	53.27	53.70	54.14	54.57	55.00	55.44	55.87
130	56.30	56.74	57.17	57.60	58.04	58.47	58.90	59.33	59.77	60.20
140	60.63	61.07	61.50	61.93	62.37	62.80	63.23	63.67	64.10	64.53
150	64.97	65.40	65.83	66.26	66.70	67.13	67.56	68.00	68.43	68.86
160	69.30	69.73	70.16	70.60	71.03	71.46	71.89	72.33	72.76	73.19
170	73.63	74.06	74.49	74.93	75.36	75.79	76.23	76.66	77.09	77.52
180	77.96	78.39	78.82	79.26	79.69	80.12	80.56	80.99	81.42	81.86
190	82.29	82.72	83.16	83.59	84.02	84.45	84.89	85.32	85.75	86.19
200	86.62	87.05	87.49	87.92	88.35	88.79	89.22	89.65	90.08	90.52
210	90.95	91.38	91.82	92.25	92.68	93.12	93.55	93.98	94.42	94.85
220	95.28	95.72	96.15	96.58	97.01	97.45	97.88	98.31	98.75	99.18
230	99.61	100.05	100.48	100.91	101.35	101.78	102.21	102.64	103.08	103.51
240	103.94	104.38	104.81	105.24	105.68	106.11	106.54	106.98	107.41	107.84
250	108.28	108.71	109.14	109.57	110.01	110.44	110.87	111.31	111.74	112.17
260	112.61	113.04	113.47	113.91	114.34	114.77	115.20	115.64	116.07	116.50
270	116.94	117.37	117.80	118.24	118.67	119.10	119.54	119.97	120.40	120.83
280	121.27	121.70	122.13	122.57	123.00	123.43	123.87	124.30	124.73	125.17
290	125.60	126.03	126.47	126.90	127.33	127.76	128.20	128.63	129.06	129.50
300	129.93	130.36	130.80	131.23	131.66	132.10	132.53	132.96	133.39	133.83
310	134.26	134.69	135.13	135.56	135.99	136.43	136.86	137.29	137.73	138.16
320	138.59	139.03	139.46	139.89	140.32	140.76	141.19	141.62	142.06	142.49
330	142.92	143.36	143.79	144.22	144.66	145.09	145.52	145.95	146.39	146.82
340	147.25	147.69	148.12	148.55	148.99	149.42	149.85	150.29	150.72	151.15
350	151.59	152.02	152.45	152.88	153.32	153.75	154.18	154.62	155.05	155.48

Supplemental Table

Head: ft H₂O	0.1	0.2	0.3	0.4	0.5	0.6	0.7	0.8	0.9
lb/in²	0.04	0.09	0.13	0.17	0.22	0.26	0.30	.35	0.39

Use of Tables

Read down left column and across row of base table; equivalent is for combined headings of column and row.
Adding extends equivalents beyond limits of base tables.

Example: Determine ft H₂O for 172.7 lb/in²:

    150.0 lb/in = 346.3 ft H₂O (base table)
    +22.0 lb/in² = +50.8 ft H₂O (base table)
    + 0.7 lb/in² = + 1.6 ft H₂O (supplemental table)
    172.7 lb/in² = 398.7 ft H₂O

Example: Determine lb/in² for 53.7 ft H₂O

    53.0 ft H₂O = 22.95 lb/in² (base table)
    +0.7 ft H₂O = +0.30 lb/in² (supplemental table)
    53.7 ft H₂O = 23.25 lb/in²

379

APPENDIX

TABLE 22

PRESSURE EQUIVALENTS

POUNDS PER SQUARE INCH (lb/in²) to KILOGRAMS PER SQUARE CENTIMETRE (kg/cm²)

Base Table

lb/in²	0.0	1.0	2.0	3.0	4.0	5.0	6.0	7.0	8.0	9.0
					kg/cm²					
0.	0.00	0.07	0.14	0.21	0.28	0.35	0.42	0.49	0.56	0.63
10.	0.70	0.77	0.84	0.91	0.98	1.05	1.12	1.20	1.27	1.34
20.	1.41	1.48	1.55	1.62	1.69	1.76	1.83	1.90	1.97	2.04
30.	2.11	2.18	2.25	2.32	2.39	2.46	2.53	2.60	2.67	2.74
40.	2.81	2.88	2.95	3.02	3.09	3.16	3.23	3.30	3.37	3.45
50.	3.52	3.59	3.66	3.73	3.80	3.87	3.94	4.01	4.08	4.15
60.	4.22	4.29	4.36	4.43	4.50	4.57	4.64	4.71	4.78	4.85
70.	4.92	4.99	5.06	5.13	5.20	5.27	5.34	5.41	5.48	5.55
80.	5.62	5.69	5.77	5.84	5.91	5.98	6.05	6.12	6.19	6.26
90.	6.33	6.40	6.47	6.54	6.61	6.68	6.75	6.82	6.89	6.96
100.	7.03	7.10	7.17	7.24	7.31	7.38	7.45	7.52	7.59	7.66
110.	7.73	7.80	7.87	7.95	8.01	8.09	8.16	8.23	8.30	8.37
120.	8.44	8.51	8.58	8.65	8.72	8.79	8.86	8.93	9.00	9.07
130.	9.14	9.21	9.28	9.35	9.42	9.49	9.56	9.63	9.70	9.77
140.	9.84	9.91	9.98	10.05	10.12	10.19	10.26	10.34	10.41	10.48
150.	10.55	10.62	10.69	10.76	10.83	10.90	10.97	11.04	11.11	11.18

Supplemental Table

lb/in²	0.1	0.2	0.3	0.4	0.5	0.6	0.7	0.8	0.9
kg/cm²	0.007	0.014	0.021	0.028	0.035	0.042	0.049	0.056	0.063

Note: 1 kg/cm² = 1 at (technical atmosphere).

1 kg/cm² = 10.009 mH₂0 at 15°C (59.6 °F); (in common practice, mH₂0 is rounded to 10.0).

TABLE 23

PRECIPITATION EQUIVALENTS
INCHES PER HOUR (in/h) to MILLIMETRES PER HOUR (mm/h)

Base Table

in	0.0	0.1	0.2	0.3	0.4	0.5	0.6	0.7	0.8	0.9
					mm					
0.0		2.5	5.1	7.6	10.2	12.7	15.2	17.8	20.3	22.9
1.0	25.4	27.9	30.5	33.0	35.6	38.1	40.6	43.2	45.7	48.3
2.0	50.8	53.3	55.9	58.4	61.0	63.5	66.0	68.6	71.1	73.7
3.0	76.2	78.7	81.3	83.8	86.4	88.9	91.4	94.0	96.5	99.1
4.0	101.6	104.1	106.7	109.2	111.8	114.3	116.8	119.4	121.9	124.5
5.0	127.0	129.5	132.1	134.6	137.2	139.7	142.2	144.8	147.3	149.9
6.0	152.4	154.9	157.5	160.0	162.6	165.1	167.6	170.2	172.7	175.3
7.0	177.8	180.3	182.9	185.4	188.0	190.5	193.0	195.6	198.1	200.7
8.0	203.2₄	205.7	208.3	210.8	213.4	215.9	218.4	221.0	223.5	226.1
9.0	228.6	231.1	233.7	236.2	238.8	241.3	243.8	246.4	248.9	251.5
10.0	254.0	256.5	259.1	261.6	264.2	266.7	269.2	271.8	274.3	276.9

Supplemental Table

in	0.00	0.01	0.02	0.03	0.04	0.05	0.06	0.07	0.08	0.09
					mm					
0.00		0.3	0.5	0.8	1.0	1.3	1.5	1.8	2.0	2.3
0.10	2.5	2.8	3.0	3.3	3.6	3.8	4.1	4.3	4.6	4.8
0.20	5.1	5.3	5.6	5.8	6.1	6.4	6.6	6.9	7.1	7.4
0.30	7.6	7.9	8.1	8.4	8.6	8.9	9.1	9.4	9.7	9.9
0.40	10.2	10.4	10.7	10.9	11.2	11.4	11.7	11.9	12.2	12.4
0.50	12.7	13.0	13.2	13.5	13.7	14.0	14.2	14.5	14.7	15.0
0.60	15.2	15.5	15.7	16.0	16.3	16.5	16.8	17.0	17.3	17.5
0.70	17.8	18.0	18.3	18.5	18.8	19.1	19.3	19.6	19.8	20.1
0.80	20.3	20.6	20.8	21.1	21.3	21.6	21.8	22.1	22.4	22.6
0.90	22.9	23.1	23.4	23.6	23.9	24.1	24.4	24.6	24.9	25.1

Use of Tables

Read down left column and across row of base table; equivalent is for combined headings of column and row. Adding extends equivalents beyond limits of base table.

Example: Determine pressure in kg/cm² for 162.7 lb/in²

    150   lb/in² = 10.55 kg/cm² (base table)
    +12   lb/in² = +0.84 kg/cm² (base table)
    + 0.7 lb/in² = +0.05 kg/cm² (supplemental table)
    162.7 lb/in² = 11.44 kg/cm²

Example: Precipitation equivalents:
    (Note: Supplemental table read same as base Table.)
A sprinkler system has an average precipitation of 1.15 in/h; determine rate in mm/h:

    1.0   in/h = 25.4 mm/h (base table)
    +0.15 in/h = +3.8 mm/h (supplemental Table)
    1.15 in/h = 29.2 mm/h

APPENDIX

TABLE 24

WIND VELOCITY EQUIVALENTS

MILES PER HOUR (mi/h) (mph*) to KILOMETRES PER HOUR (km/h)

mi/h	0.0	1.0	2.0	3.0	4.0	5.0	6.0	7.0	8.0	9.0
	km/h									
0.	0.0	1.6	3.2	4.8	6.4	8.0	9.7	11.3	12.9	14.5
10.	16.1	17.7	19.3	20.9	22.5	24.1	25.7	27.4	29.0	30.6
20.	32.2	33.8	35.4	37.0	38.6	40.2	41.8	43.5	45.1	46.7

*Commonly used U. S. abbreviation for miles per hour.

Use of Table

Read down left column and across row of table; equivalent is for combined headings of column and row.
Example: 11 mi/h = 17.7 km/h

Conversion factors:

1 gpm = 0.227 124 707 m³/h (cubic metres per hour).
= 0.063 090 196 l/s (litres per second).
= 3.785 411 784 l/min (litres per minute) exactly.

TABLE 25

FLOW EQUIVALENTS

to GALLONS PER MINUTE (gpm)

Base Table

gpm	m³/h	l/s	l/min	gpm	m³/h	l/s	l/min	gpm	m³/h	l/s	l/min	gpm	m³/h	l/s	l/min
1.0	0.23	0.063	3.8	26.0	5.91	1.640	98.4	51.0	11.58	3.218	193.1	76.0	17.26	4.795	287.7
2.	0.45	0.126	7.6	27.	6.13	1.703	102.2	52.	11.81	3.281	196.8	77.	17.49	4.858	291.5
3.	0.68	0.189	11.4	28.	6.36	1.767	106.0	53.	12.04	3.344	200.6	78.	17.72	4.921	295.3
4.	0.91	0.252	15.1	29.	6.59	1.830	109.8	54.	12.26	3.407	204.4	79.	17.94	4.984	299.1
5.	1.14	0.315	18.9	30.	6.81	1.893	113.6	55.	12.49	3.470	208.2	80.	18.17	5.047	302.8
6.	1.36	0.379	22.7	31.	7.04	1.956	117.3	56.	12.72	3.533	212.0	81.	18.40	5.110	306.6
7.	1.59	0.442	26.5	32.	7.27	2.019	121.1	57.	12.95	3.596	215.8	82.	18.62	5.173	310.4
8.	1.82	0.505	30.3	33.	7.50	2.082	124.9	58.	13.17	3.659	219.6	83.	18.85	5.236	314.2
9.	2.04	0.568	34.1	34.	7.72	2.145	128.7	59.	13.40	3.722	223.3	84.	19.08	5.300	318.0
10.	2.27	0.631	37.9	35.	7.95	2.208	132.5	60.	13.63	3.785	227.1	85.	19.31	5.363	321.8
11.	2.50	0.694	41.6	36.	8.18	2.271	136.3	61.	13.85	3.849	230.9	86.	19.53	5.426	325.5
12.	2.73	0.757	45.4	37.	8.40	2.334	140.1	62.	14.08	3.912	234.7	87.	19.76	5.489	329.3
13.	2.95	0.820	49.2	38.	8.63	2.397	143.8	63.	14.31	3.975	238.5	88.	19.99	5.552	333.1
14.	3.18	0.883	53.0	39.	8.86	2.461	147.6	64.	14.54	4.038	242.3	89.	20.21	5.615	336.9
15.	3.41	0.946	56.8	40.	9.08	2.524	151.4	65.	14.76	4.101	246.1	90.	20.44	5.678	340.7
16.	3.63	1.009	60.6	41.	9.31	2.587	155.2	66.	14.99	4.164	249.8	91.	20.67	5.741	344.5
17.	3.86	1.073	64.4	42.	9.54	2.650	159.0	67.	15.22	4.227	253.6	92.	20.90	5.804	348.3
18.	4.09	1.136	68.1	43.	9.77	2.713	162.8	68.	15.44	4.290	257.4	93.	21.12	5.867	352.0
19.	4.32	1.199	71.9	44.	9.99	2.776	166.6	69.	15.67	4.353	261.2	94.	21.35	5.930	355.8
20.	4.54	1.262	75.7	45.	10.22	2.839	170.3	70.	15.90	4.416	265.0	95.	21.58	5.994	359.6
21.	4.77	1.325	79.5	46.	10.45	2.902	174.1	71.	16.13	4.479	268.8	96.	21.80	6.057	363.4
22.	5.00	1.388	83.3	47.	10.67	2.965	177.9	72.	16.35	4.452	272.5	97.	22.03	6.120	367.2
23.	5.22	1.451	87.1	48.	10.90	3.028	181.7	73.	16.58	4.606	276.3	98.	22.26	6.183	371.0
24.	5.45	1.514	90.8	49.	11.13	3.091	185.5	74.	16.81	4.669	280.1	99.	22.49	6.246	374.8
25.0	5.68	1.577	94.6	50.0	11.36	3.155	189.3	75.0	17.03	4.732	283.9	100.0	22.71	6.309	378.5

Supplemental Table A

gpm	0.1	0.2	0.3	0.4	0.5	0.6	0.7	0.8	0.9	1.0
m³/hr	0.02	0.05	0.07	0.09	0.11	0.14	0.16	0.18	0.20	0.23
l/s	0.006	0.013	0.019	0.025	0.032	0.038	0.044	0.050	0.057	0.063
l / min	0.4	0.8	1.1	1.5	1.9	2.3	2.6	3.0	3.4	3.8

Supplemental Table B

gpm	100.0	200.0	300.0	400.0	500.0	600.0	700.0	800.0	900.0	1000.0
m³/h	22.71	45.42	68.14	90.85	113.56	136.27	158.99	181.70	204.41	227.12
l/s	6.309	12.618	18.927	25.236	31.545	37.854	44.163	50.472	56.781	63.090
l/min	378.5	757.1	1135.6	1514.2	1892.7	2271.3	2649.8	3028.3	3406.9	3785.4

1 l (litre) = 1 dm³ (cubic decimetre) exactly.

Use of Tables

Adding extends equivalents beyond limits of base tables.

Example: Determine l/min for 267.79 gpm
200.0 gpm = 757.1 l/min (Supplemental Table B)
+ 67.0 gpm = +253.6 l/min (Base table)
0.7 gpm = + 2.6 l/min (Supplemental Table A)
267.7 gpm = 1013.3 l/min

APPENDIX

TABLE 26

LENGTH EQUIVALENTS

FEET (ft) to METERS (m)

Base Table

feet	0.0	1.0	2.0	3.0	4.0	5.0	6.0	7.0	8.0	9.0
					metres					
0.0	0.0	0.30	0.61	0.91	1.22	1.52	1.83	2.13	2.44	2.74
10.	3.05	3.35	3.66	3.96	4.27	4.57	4.88	5.18	5.49	5.79
20.	6.10	6.40	6.71	7.01	7.32	7.62	7.92	8.23	8.53	8.84
30.	9.14	9.45	9.75	10.06	10.36	10.67	10.97	11.28	11.58	11.89
40.	12.19	12.50	12.80	13.11	13.41	13.72	14.02	14.33	14.63	14.94
50.	15.24	15.54	15.85	16.15	16.46	16.76	17.07	17.37	17.68	17.98
60.	18.29	18.59	18.90	19.20	19.51	19.81	20.12	20.42	20.73	21.03
70.	21.34	21.64	21.95	22.25	22.56	22.86	23.16	23.47	23.77	24.08
80	24.38	24.69	24.99	25.30	25.60	25.91	26.21	26.52	26.82	27.13
90.	27.43	27.74	28.04	28.35	28.65	28.96	29.26	29.57	29.87	30.18
100.	30.48	30.78	31.09	31.39	31.70	32.00	32.31	32.61	32.92	33.22
110.	33.53	33.83	34.14	34.44	34.75	35.05	35.36	35.66	35.97	36.27
120.	36.58	36.88	37.19	37.49	37.80	38.10	38.40	38.71	39.01	39.32
130.	39.62	39.93	40.23	40.54	40.84	41.15	41.45	41.76	42.06	42.37
140.	42.67	42.98	43.28	43.59	43.89	44.20	44.50	44.81	45.11	45.42
150.	45.72	46.02	46.33	46.63	46.94	47.24	47.55	47.85	48.16	48.46
160.	48.77	49.07	49.38	49.68	49.99	50.29	50.60	50.90	51.21	51.51
170.	51.82	52.12	52.43	52.73	53.04	53.34	53.64	53.95	54.25	54.56
180.	54.86	55.17	55.47	55.78	56.08	56.39	56.69	57.00	57.30	57.61
190.	57.91	58.22	58.52	58.83	59.13	59.44	59.74	60.05	60.35	60.66
200.	60.96	61.26	61.57	61.87	62.18	62.48	62.79	63.09	63.40	63.70
210.	64.01	64.31	64.62	64.92	65.23	65.53	65.84	66.14	66.45	66.75
220.	67.06	67.36	67.67	67.97	68.28	68.58	68.88	69.19	69.49	69.80
230.	70.10	70.41	70.71	71.02	71.32	71.63	71.93	72.24	72.54	72.85
240.	73.15	73.46	73.76	74.07	74.37	74.68	74.98	75.29	75.59	75.90
250.	76.20	76.50	76.81	77.11	77.42	77.72	78.03	78.33	78.64	78.94
260.	79.25	79.55	79.86	80.16	80.47	80.77	81.08	81.38	81.69	81.99
270.	82.30	82.60	82.91	83.21	83.52	83.82	84.12	84.43	84.73	85.04
280.	85.34	85.65	85.95	86.26	86.56	86.87	87.17	87.48	87.78	88.09
290.	88.39	88.70	89.00	89.31	89.61	89.92	90.22	90.53	90.83	91.14
300.	91.44	91.74	92.05	92.35	92.66	92.96	93.27	93.57	93.88	94.18
310.	94.49	94.79	95.10	95.40	95.71	96.01	96.32	96.62	96.93	97.23
320.	97.54	97.84	98.15	98.45	98.76	99.06	99.36	99.67	99.97	100.28
330.	100.58	100.89	101.19	101.50	101.80	102.11	102.41	102.72	103.02	103.33
340.	103.63	103.94	104.24	104.55	104.85	105.16	105.46	105.77	106.07	106.38
350.	106.68	106.98	107.29	107.59	107.90	108.20	108.51	108.81	109.12	109.42
360.	109.73	110.03	110.34	110.64	110.95	111.25	111.56	111.86	112.17	112.47
370.	112.78	113.08	113.39	113.69	114.00	114.30	114.60	114.91	115.21	115.52
380.	115.82	116.13	116.43	116.74	117.04	117.35	117.65	117.96	118.26	118.57
390.	118.87	119.18	119.48	119.79	120.09	120.40	120.70	121.01	121.31	121.62
400.	121.92	122.22	122.53	122.83	123.14	123.44	123.75	124.05	124.36	124.66
410.	124.97	125.27	125.58	125.88	126.19	126.49	126.80	127.10	127.41	127.71
420.	128.02	128.32	128.63	128.93	129.24	129.54	129.84	130.15	130.45	130.76
430.	131.06	131.37	131.67	131.98	132.28	132.59	132.89	133.20	133.50	133.81
440.	134.11	134.42	134.72	135.03	135.33	135.64	135.94	136.25	136.55	136.86
450.	137.16	137.46	137.77	138.07	138.38	138.68	138.99	139.29	139.60	139.90
460.	140.21	140.51	140.82	141.12	141.43	141.73	142.04	142.34	142.65	142.95
470.	143.26	143.56	143.87	144.17	144.48	144.78	145.08	145.39	145.69	146.00
480.	146.30	146.61	146.91	147.22	147.52	147.83	148.13	148.44	148.74	149.05
490.	149.35	149.66	149.96	150.27	150.57	150.88	151.18	151.49	151.79	152.10
500.0	152.40	152.70	153.01	153.31	153.62	153.92	154.23	154.53	154.84	155.15

Supplemental Table A

feet	0.1	0.2	0.3	0.4	0.5	0.6	0.7	0.8	0.9	1.0
meters	0.03	0.06	0.09	0.12	0.15	0.18	0.21	0.24	0.27	0.30

Supplemental Table B

feet	1000.0	2000.0	3000.0	4000.0	5000.0	6000.0	7000.0	8000.0	9000.0	10 000.0
meters	304.8	609.6	914.4	1219.2	1524.0	1828.8	2133.6	2438.4	2743.2	3048.0

Use of Table

Read down left column and across row of base table; equivalent is for combined headings of column and row.
Adding extends equivalents beyond limits of base table.

Example: Determine equivalent length in meters for 112.8 feet:

1000.0 ft = 304.80 m (Supplemental table B)
+112.0 ft = +34.14 m (base table)
0.8 ft = + 0.24 m (Supplemental Table A)
1112.8 ft = 339.2 m

APPENDIX

TABLE 27
VOLUME (gallons)
IN ROUND TANKS SET VERTICALLY

\multicolumn{12}{c}{Per Foot of Depth}											
Diameter		Diameter		Diameter		Diameter		Diameter		Diameter	
ft	Gallons	ft	Gallons	ft	Gallons	ft	Gallons	ft	Gallons	ft	Gallons
0.5	1.5	5.5	177.7	10.5	647.7	15.5	1411.5	20.5	2469.0	25.5	3820.3
1.0	5.9	6.0	211.5	11.0	710.9	16.0	1504.0	21.0	2591.0	26.0	3971.6
1.5	13.2	6.5	248.2	11.5	777.0	16.5	1599.5	21.5	2715.8	26.5	4125.8
2.0	23.5	7.0	287.9	12.0	846.0	17.0	1697.9	22.0	2843.6	27.0	4283.0
2.5	36.7	7.5	330.5	12.5	918.0	17.5	1799.3	22.5	2974.3	27.5	4443.1
3.0	52.9	8.0	376.0	13.0	992.9	18.0	1903.6	23.0	3108.0	28.0	4606.1
3.5	72.0	8.5	424.5	13.5	1070.8	18.5	2010.8	23.5	3244.6	28.5	4772.1
4.0	94.0	9.0	475.9	14.0	1151.5	19.0	2120.9	24.0	3384.1	29.0	4941.0
4.5	119.0	9.5	530.2	14.5	1235.3	19.5	2234.0	24.5	3526.6	29.5	5112.9
5.0	146.9	10.0	587.5	15.0	1321.9	20.0	2350.1	25.0	3672.0	30.0	5287.7

1 gallon = 0.133 68 cubic feet

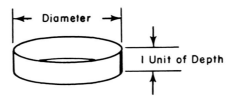

HOW TO USE TABLES 27 AND 27A

Example 1: Determine volume in a round tank set vertically with a diameter of 15.5 ft and 5.0 ft deep:

a. Read from Table 27 opposite 15.5 ft diameter, 1411.5 gallons per foot of depth.

b. Volume for 5 ft depth equals: volume per foot depth x total depth or,
1411.5 x 5 = 7057.5 gallons for 5.0 ft depth.

Example 2: Determine volume in a round tank set vertically with a diameter of 4.75 m and 1.5 m deep:

a. Read from Table 27A opposite 4.75 m diameter, 17.72 m³ per metre of depth.

b. Volume for 1.5 m depth equals: volume per metre depth x total depth or,
17.72 x 1.5 = 26.50 m³ for 1.5 m depth.

TABLE 27A
VOLUME (M³)
IN ROUND TANKS SET VERTICALLY

\multicolumn{8}{c}{Per Metre of Depth}							
Diameter		Diameter		Diameter		Diameter	
m	m³	m	m³	m	m³	m	m³
0.25	0.049	2.75	5.94	5.25	21.65	7.75	47.17
0.50	0.20	3.00	7.07	5.50	23.76	8.00	50.27
0.75	0.44	3.25	8.30	5.75	25.97	8.25	53.46
1.00	0.79	3.50	9.62	6.00	28.27	8.50	56.75
1.25	1.23	3.75	11.04	6.25	30.68	8.75	60.13
1.50	1.77	4.00	12.57	6.50	33.18	9.00	63.62
1.75	2.41	4.25	14.19	6.75	35.78	9.25	67.20
2.00	3.14	4.50	15.90	7.00	38.48	9.50	70.88
2.25	3.98	4.75	17.72	7.25	41.28	9.75	74.66
2.50	4.91	5.00	19.63	7.50	44.18	10.00	78.54

1 cubic metre = 1000 litres

APPENDIX

TABLE 28

APPROXIMATE VOLUME
IN ROUND TANKS SET HORIZONTALLY

$\frac{h}{D}$	K	$\frac{h}{D}$	K	$\frac{h}{D}$	K	$\frac{h}{D}$	K	$\frac{h}{D}$	K	$\frac{h}{D}$	K	$\frac{h}{D}$	K
0.0050	0.0006	0.1550	0.0986	0.3050	0.2582	0.4550	0.4428	0.6050	0.6327	0.7550	0.8100	0.9050	0.9517
.0100	.0017	.1600	.1033	.3100	.2640	.4600	.4491	.6100	.6389	.7600	.8155	.9100	.9554
.0150	.0031	.1650	.1080	.3150	.2699	.4650	.4555	.6150	.6451	.7650	.8209	.9150	.9590
.0200	.0048	.1700	.1127	.3200	.2759	.4700	.4618	.6200	.6513	.7700	.8262	.9200	.9625
.0250	.0067	.1750	.1175	.3250	.2818	.4750	.4682	.6250	.6575	.7750	.8316	.9250	.9659
.0300	.0087	.1800	.1224	.3300	.2878	.4800	.4745	.6300	.6636	.7800	.8369	.9300	.9692
.0350	.0110	.1850	.1273	.3350	.2938	.4850	.4809	.6350	.6698	.7850	.8421	.9350	.9724
.0400	.0134	.1900	.1323	.3400	.2998	.4900	.4873	.6400	.6759	.7900	.8473	.9400	.9755
.0450	.0160	.1950	.1373	.3450	.3059	.4950	.4936	.6450	.6820	.7950	.8525	.9450	.9785
0.0500	0.0187	0.2000	0.1424	0.3500	0.3119	0.5000	0.5000	0.6500	0.6881	0.8000	0.8576	0.9500	0.9813
.0550	.0215	.2050	.1475	.3550	.3180	.5050	.5064	.6550	.6941	.8050	.8627	.9550	.9840
.0600	.0245	.2100	.1527	.3600	.3241	.5100	.5127	.6600	.7002	.8100	.8677	.9600	.9866
.0650	.0276	.2150	.1579	.3650	.3302	.5150	.5191	.6650	.7062	.8150	.8727	.9650	.9890
.0700	.0308	.2200	.1631	.3700	.3364	.5200	.5255	.6700	.7122	.8200	.8776	.9700	.9913
.0750	.0341	.2250	.1684	.3750	.3425	.5250	.5318	.6750	.7182	.8250	.8825	.9750	.9933
.0800	.0375	.2300	.1738	.3800	.3487	.5300	.5382	.6800	.7241	.8300	.8873	.9800	.9952
.0850	.0410	.2350	.1791	.3850	.3549	.5350	.5445	.6850	.7301	.8350	.8920	.9850	.9969
.0900	.0446	.2400	.1845	.3900	.3611	.5400	.5509	.6900	.7360	.8400	.8967	.9900	.9983
.0950	.0483	.2450	.1900	.3950	.3673	.5450	.5572	.6950	.7418	.8450	.9014	.9950	.9994
0.1000	0.0520	0.2500	0.1955	0.4000	0.3735	0.5500	0.5636	0.7000	0.7477	0.8500	0.9059	1.0000	1.0000
.1050	.0559	.2550	.2010	.4050	.3798	.5550	.5699	.7050	.7535	.8550	.9105		
.1100	.0598	.2600	.2066	.4100	.3860	.5600	.5762	.7100	.7593	.8600	.9149		
.1150	.0639	.2650	.2122	.4150	.3923	.5650	.5825	.7150	.7651	.8650	.9193		
.1200	.0680	.2700	.2178	.4200	.3986	.5700	.5888	.7200	.7708	.8700	.9236		
.1250	.0721	.2750	.2235	.4250	.4049	.5750	.5951	.7250	.7765	.8750	.9279		
.1300	.0764	.2800	.2292	.4300	.4112	.5800	.6014	.7300	.7822	.8800	.9320		
.1350	.0807	.2850	.2349	.4350	.4175	.5850	.6077	.7350	.7878	.8850	.9361		
.1400	.0851	.2900	.2407	.4400	.4238	.5900	.6140	.7400	.7934	.8900	.9402		
.1450	.0895	.2950	.2465	.4450	.4301	.5950	.6202	.7450	.7990	.8950	.9441		
0.1500	0.0941	0.3000	0.2523	0.4500	0.4364	0.6000	0.6265	0.7500	0.8045	0.9000	0.9480		

HOW TO USE TABLE 28

For round tanks set horizontally, table is used to determine:
1. Height of water level, h, for a known volume.
2. Volume with a known water level.

Table can be used with any system of measurement. Dimensions D, h, and L in feet:

Volume is in gallons when full tank capacity is gallons;

Volume is in cubic feet when full tank capacity is cubic feet.

Dimensions D, h, and L in metres:

Volume is in cubic metres when full tank capacity is cubic metres;

Volume is in litres when full tank capacity is litres.

Example 1: Determine h when a tank 6.0 ft diameter (D) and 12.0 ft long (L) is required to be 66% full by volume.

a. Referring to Table 27, each foot of a 6.0 ft diameter tank contains 211.5 gal; therefore, when full, the example tank contains 2538.0 gal: 211.5 x 12 = 2538.0 gal. When 66% full by volume, tank contains 1675 gal: 2538.0 × 0.66 = 1675 gal.

b. K is used as percent of full tank in solution for h.
Read opposite K = 0.6600 $\frac{h}{D}$ = 0.6275.*

(*Approximate interpolation between K = 0.6575 and 0.6636.)

Thus, $\frac{h}{6}$ = 0.6275

c. Then: h = 6 × 0.6275 = 3.8 ft

Example 2: Determine volume of water in a tank 5.0 ft in diameter and 16.0 ft long when height of water level, h, is 3.0 ft.

a. Each foot of a full 5.0 diameter tank contains 146.9 gal, Table 27. Therefore, when full, the example tank contains 2350.4 gal: 146.9 × 16 = 2350.4 gal.

b. $\frac{h}{D} = \frac{3}{5}$ = 0.6000

c. Then: read opposite $\frac{h}{D}$ = 0.6000 K = 0.6265

d. Thus: volume of water to height 3.0 ft: K × volume of full tank = volume of segment = 0.6265 × 2350.4 = 1472 gal.

e. And: with water level at 3.0 ft in example tank, it is approximately 63% full by volume.

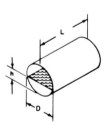

Note: Table 28 is for tanks with flat ends. Semiellipsoidal ends will make no practical difference for irrigation.

APPENDIX

TABLE 29
STRAINERS
SIZE DESIGNATIONS

Most strainer manufacturers use the ASTM Standard Test Sieve nominal dimensions for designation of strainer sizes; that portion of ASTM standard dimensions for sieves less than 1/4 inch in size is listed below. Also listed is a compilation of sub-sieve sizes used by many manufacturers. Tolerances of manufacture result in some aperture openings larger than nominal as indicated in table; this permissible deviation should be considered when selecting strainer sizes. Comparable information is not available for sub-sieve sizes.

Strainers may be specified by RETENTION SIZE; i.e., the size of the largest spherical solid particle that will normally pass through the straining element.

ASTM Standard Specification E11
(U.S.A. Standard Series)

Sieve Designation		Nominal Opening	Permissible Variation of Average Opening from the Standard Sieve Designation	Maximum Opening Size for Not More than 5 percent of Openings	Maximum Individual Opening
Standard	Alternative (a)	(b)			
mm	No.	in	± mm	mm	mm
* 5.60	3-1/2	0.223	0.18	5.90	6.04
4.75	4	0.187	0.15	5.02	5.14
* 4.00	5	0.157	0.13	4.23	4.35
3.35	6	0.132	0.11	3.55	3.66
* 2.80	7	0.111	0.095	2.975	3.070
2.36	8	0.0937	0.080	2.515	2.600
* 2.00	10	0.0787	0.070	2.135	2.215
1.70	12	0.0661	0.060	1.820	1.890
* 1.40	14	0.0555	0.050	1.505	1.565
1.18	16	0.0469	0.045	1.270	1.330
* 1.00	18	0.0394	0.040	1.080	1.135
μm	NO.	in	±μm	μm	μm
850	20	0.0331	35	925	970
* 710	25	0.0278	30	775	815
600	30	0.0234	25	660	695
* 500	35	0.0197	20	550	585
425	40	0.0165	19	471	502
* 355	45	0.0139	16	396	425
300	50	0.0117	14	337	363
* 250	60	0.0098	12	283	306
212	70	0.0083	10	242	263
* 180	80	0.0070	9	207	227
150	100	0.0059	8	174	192
* 125	120	0.0049	7	147	163
106	140	0.0041	6	126	141
* 90	170	0.0035	5	108	122
75	200	0.0029	5	91	103
* 63	230	0.0025	4	77	89
53	270	0.0021	4	66	76
* 45	325	0.0017	3	57	66
38	400	0.0015	3	48	57

(1)Sub-Sieve Sizes Commonly-Used by Strainer Manufacturers	
μm	in
30	0.001 18
25	0.000 98
20	0.000 79
15	0.000 59
10	0.000 394
8	0.000 315
5	0.000 197
2.5	0.000 098
1	0.000 0394

(1)Not a part of ASTM Standards

ASTM Standard E11 reprinted by special permission of American Society Testing and Materials.

* These standard designations correspond to the values for test sieve apertures recommended by the International Standards Organization (ISO).

(a) These numbers, 3-1/2 to 400, are the approximate number of openings per linear inch but it is preferred that the sieve be identified by the standard designation in millimetres or μm.

(b) Only approximately equivalent to the metric values.

Note: 1000 μm = 1 mm; 1 μm (*micrometre) = 0.000 001 m
*The special name, micron, and symbol, μ, was abolished in 1968 by The General (International) Conference on Weights and Measures.

μm Comparisons
Talcum powder equivalent to 8-10 μm
Table Salt equivalent to 100 μm
Average diameter human hair is 50-70 μm

EXPLANATION OF HEAD LAYOUT MULTIPLYING FACTORS

Tables 30 and 31 provide an easy means for determining layout dimensions for sprinkler heads when spacing is a percentage of rated coverage diameter. The tables provide multiplying factors for spacings of 45% to 75% of diameter. The factors apply to equilateral triangular and square spacing.

Equilateral Triangular Spacing ($\triangle$)
Layout Dimensions

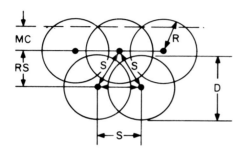

Square Spacing ($\square$)
Layout Dimensions

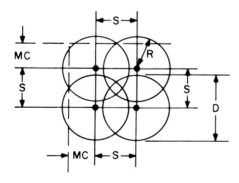

S = Head Spacing
RS = Row Spacing
MC = Mean coverage of streams from row

Table 30 lists *universal* multiplying factors. These factors can be used with any unit of measurement. *Do not mix units.* Dimensions determined will be in unit used for diameter. That is, diameter in feet provides dimensions in feet; diameter in meters provides dimensions in meters.

Example A: Determine layout dimensions for sprinkler with rated coverage diameter of 100 ft. and recommended $\triangle$ spacing 60% of diameter:

$$S = 100 \times 0.60 \quad = 60.0 \text{ ft}$$
$$RS = 100 \times 0.5196 = 52.0 \text{ ft}$$
$$MC = 100 \times 0.4000 = 40.0 \text{ ft}$$

Example B: Same sprinkler as used in Example A, except rated diameter is given in meters:
100 ft.= 30.48 m
$$S = 30.48 \times 0.60 = 18.3 \text{ m}$$
$$RS = 30.48 \times 0.5196 = 15.8 \text{ m}$$
$$MC = 30.48 \times 0.4000 = 12.2 \text{ m}$$

Table 31 provides layout dimensions in meters only for rated coverage diameters listed in feet.

Example C: Same sprinkler as used in Example A:
$$S = 100 \text{ ft.} \times 0.1829 = 18.3 \text{ m}$$
$$RS = 100 \text{ ft.} \times 0.1584 = 15.8 \text{ m}$$
$$MC = 100 \text{ ft.} \times 0.1219 = 12.2 \text{ m}$$

MEAN COVERAGE (MC)

All head layout dimensions are based on the manufacturer's listed diameter of coverage (maximum distance). The precipitation rate of the sprinkler stream reduces rapidly at the extreme distance of coverage; often to .01 in/hr. Specified spacings compensate for this phenomenon for the area between sprinklers. However, spacing does not compensate for mean coverage deficiency in areas not overlapped by more than two sprinklers; for example: the outer rows of sprinklers on a golf course fairway. The designer must allow for this deficiency.

APPENDIX

TABLE 30

HEAD LAYOUT (multipliers) CONSTANTS
UNIVERSAL*

For Equilateral Triangular (△) and Square (□) Spacing.

Spacing of % Diameter (D)	To determine Layout Dimensions			Spacing of % Diameter (D)	To determine Layout Dimensions		
	S	RS	MC		S	RS	MC
	Multiply Diameter (D) by:				Multiply Diameter (D) by:		
75	0.75	0.6495	0.3307	60	0.60	0.5196	0.4000
74	0.74	0.6408	0.3363	59	0.59	0.5109	0.4037
73	0.73	0.6322	0.3417	58	0.58	0.5023	0.4073
72	0.72	0.6235	0.3470	57	0.57	0.4936	0.4108
71	0.71	0.6149	0.3521	56	0.56	0.4850	0.4143
70	0.70	0.6062	0.3571	55	0.55	0.4763	0.4176
69	0.69	0.5975	0.3619	54	0.54	0.4676	0.4208
68	0.68	0.5889	0.3666	53	0.53	0.4590	0.4240
67	0.67	0.5802	0.3712	52	0.52	0.4503	0.4271
66	0.66	0.5716	0.3756	51	0.51	0.4417	0.4301
65	0.65	0.5629	0.3800	50	0.50	0.4330	0.4330
64	0.64	0.5542	0.3842	49	0.49	0.4243	0.4359
63	0.63	0.5456	0.3883	48	0.48	0.4157	0.4386
62	0.62	0.5369	0.3923	47	0.47	0.4070	0.4413
61	0.61	0.5283	0.3962	46	0.46	0.3984	0.4440
				45	0.45	0.3897	0.4465

*Multiplying factors listed above can be used with any units of measurements.
Do not mix units. For example: 57.25 ft; not 57 ft - 3 in.
Factors provide head layout dimensions in same units as diameter.

TABLE 31

HEAD LAYOUT (multipliers) CONSTANTS
FEET COVERAGE DIAMETER TO DIMENSIONS IN METERS *

For Equilateral Triangular (△) and Square (□) Spacing

Spacing of % Diameter (D)	To Determine Layout Dimensions In Meters			Spacing of % Diameter (D)	To Determine Layout Dimensions In Meters		
	S	RS	MC		S	RS	MC
	Multiply Feet of Diameter (D) by:				Multiply Feet of Diameter (D) by:		
75	0.2286	0.1980	0.1008	60	0.1829	0.1584	0.1219
74	0.2256	0.1953	0.1025	59	0.1798	0.1557	0.1230
73	0.2225	0.1927	0.1042	58	0.1768	0.1531	0.1241
72	0.2195	0.1900	0.1058	57	0.1737	0.1505	0.1252
71	0.2164	0.1874	0.1073	56	0.1707	0.1478	0.1263
70	0.2134	0.1848	0.1088	55	0.1676	0.1452	0.1273
69	0.2103	0.1821	0.1103	54	0.1646	0.1425	0.1283
68	0.2073	0.1795	0.1117	53	0.1615	0.1399	0.1292
67	0.2042	0.1769	0.1131	52	0.1585	0.1373	0.1302
66	0.2012	0.1742	0.1145	51	0.1554	0.1346	0.1311
65	0.1981	0.1716	0.1158	50	0.1524	0.1320	0.1320
64	0.1951	0.1689	0.1171	49	0.1494	0.1293	0.1329
63	0.1920	0.1663	0.1184	48	0.1463	0.1267	0.1337
62	0.1890	0.1637	0.1196	47	0.1433	0.1241	0.1345
61	0.1859	0.1610	0.1208	46	0.1402	0.1214	0.1353
				45	0.1372	0.1188	0.1361

*Multiplying factors suitable only to determine head layout dimensions in meters when diameter of sprinkler coverage is in feet.

APPENDIX

TABLE 32

WEIGHT (MASS) of WATER*
IN PIPES and TUBES

Nominal Size in	Controlled OD Thermoplastic Pipe								Nominal Size in
	SDR 32.5 lb/ft	SDR 26 lb/ft	SDR 21 lb/ft	SDR 17 lb/ft	SDR 13.5 lb/ft	SDR 11 lb/ft	Schd. 40 lb/ft	Schd. 80 lb/ft	
1/8					0.0276		0.0246	0.0157	1/8
1/4					.0600		.0451	.0310	1/4
3/8					.105		.0827	.0609	3/8
1/2					.174	0.161	.132	.101	1/2
3/4			0.294	0.292	.272	.252	.231	.187	3/4
1		0.486	.481	.459	.427	.395	.374	.312	1
1-1/4		0.798	0.767	.729	.680	.627	.648	.556	1-1/4
1-1/2		1.05	1.01	0.955	0.891	0.821	0.882	0.765	1-1/2
2	1.69(1)	1.64	1.57	1.49	1.39	1.28	1.45	1.28	2
2-1/2	2.48(1)	2.40	2.30	2.19	2.04		2.07	1.84	2-1/2
3	3.67	3.55	3.41	3.24	3.02	2.79	3.20	2.86	3
3-1/2	4.79	4.64	4.46	4.24	3.95		4.28	3.85	3-1/2
4	6.07	5.87	5.64	5.36	5.00	4.61	5.51	4.98	4
5	9.27	8.97	8.62	8.20	7.64		8.66	7.88	5
6	13.15	12.72	12.22	11.62	10.83	10.00	12.51	11.29	6
8	22.29	21.56	20.72	19.69			21.67	19.78	8
10	34.62	33.50	32.19	30.61			34.15	31.11	10
12	48.71	47.12	45.28	43.05			48.48	44.02	12

(1)Not ASTM standard pipe

Nominal Size in	Controlled ID PE Pipe lb/ft	Controlled OD PE Tube SDR 9 lb/ft	Controlled OD PE Tube SDR 7.3 lb/ft	Controlled OD PVC Tube SDR 26 lb/ft
1/2	0.132	0.0807	0.0698	0.0854
5/8		.116	.101	
3/4	.231	.158	.137	.192
1	.374	.260	.227	.341
1-1/4	.648	.389	.339	0.532
1-1/2	0.882	.543	.457	
2	1.45	0.929	0.810	
2-1/2	2.07			
3	3.20			
4	5.51			
6	12.51			

Nominal Size in	Copper Water Tube		
	M lb/ft	L lb/ft	K lb/ft
1/4		0.0338	0.0316
3/8	0.0689	.0629	.0550
1/2	.110	.101	.0945
5/8		.151	.145
3/4	.224	.210	.189
1	.379	.357	.337
1-1/4	.567	.544	.527
1-1/2	0.793	0.770	0.746
2	1.37	1.34	1.31
2-1/2	2.12	2.07	2.02
3	3.02	2.95	2.87
3-1/2	4.07	3.99	3.90
4	5.27	5.19	5.06
5	8.19	8.08	7.85
6	11.76	11.62	11.21
8	20.62	20.30	19.56
10	32.01	31.51	30.37
12	45.91	45.50	43.55

Schedule 40 Steel Pipe	
Nominal Size, in	lb/ft
1/8	0.0246
1/4	.0451
3/8	.0827
1/2	.132
3/4	.231
1	.374
1-1/4	.648
1-1/2	0.882
2	1.45
2-1/2	2.07
3	3.20
3-1/2	4.28
4	5.51
5	8.66
6	12.51
8	21.67
10	34.15
12	48.48

Asbestos-Cement Pipe	
Nominal Size, in	lb/ft
3	3.06
4	5.44
6	12.25
8	21.27
10	34.02
12	48.98

Cast-Iron Pipe	
Nominal Size, in	lb/ft
2	1.36
2-1/4	1.72
3	3.75
4	5.72
6	12.82
8	23.04
10	35.53
12	50.96

*Data based on standard dimensions without tolerances.

APPENDIX

TABLE 33

WIRE DATA (1)

STANDARD ANNEALED COPPER AT 20°C (68°F)

American Wire Gage	Millimetre Wire Gage	Diameter, Mils	Diameter, mm	Resistance[2]	
				per 1000 ft., ohms[3]	per kilometre, ohms[3]
1		289.3	7.348	0.1239	0.4065
	7.0		7.000		.4480
2		257.6	6.543	.1563	.5128
	6.0		6.000		.6098
3		229.4	5.827	.1971	.6466
4		204.3	5.189	.2485	.8152
	5.0		5.000		0.8781
5		181.9	4.620	.3134	1.028
	4.5		4.500		1.084
6		162.0	4.115	.3952	1.297
	4.0		4.000		1.372
7		144.3	3.665	.4981	1.634
	3.5		3.500		1.792
8		128.5	3.264	.6281	2.061
	3.0		3.000		2.439
9		114.4	2.906	.7925	2.600
10		101.9	2.588	0.9988	3.277
	2.5		2.500		3.512
11		90.7	2.30	1.26	4.14
12		80.8	2.05	1.59	5.21
	2.0		2.00		5.49
13		72.0	1.83	2.00	6.56
	1.8		1.80		6.78
14		64.1	1.63	2.52	8.28
	1.6		1.60		8.58
15		57.1	1.45	3.18	10.4
	1.4		1.40		11.2
16		50.8	1.29	4.02	13.2
	1.2		1.20		15.2
17		45.3	1.15	5.05	16.6
18		40.3	1.02	6.39	21.0
	1.0		1.000		22.0
19		35.9	0.912	8.05	26.4
	0.90		.900		27.1
20		32.0	0.813	10.1	33.2

[1] Extracted from National Bureau of Standards Handbook 100
[2] The fundamental resistivity used in calculating the tables is the International Annealed Copper Standard
[3] The values given in the table are for annealed copper of the standard resistivity. The user of the table must apply the proper correction for copper of any other resistivity. Hard-drawn copper may be taken as about 2.5 percent higher resistivity than annealed copper.

TABLE 34

RESISTANCE-METRIC WIRE SIZES

COPPER CONDUCTORS AT 20°C (68°F)

Conductor Size[1] mm^2	Resistance[2]	
	per 1000 ft., ohms	per kilometer, ohms
.5	11.03	36.20
.75	7.35	24.13
1.0	5.52	18.10
1.5	3.69	12.10
2.5	2.26	7.41
4.0	1.41	4.61
6.0	.939	3.08
10.0	.558	1.83
16.0	.351	1.15
25.0	.222	.727
35.0	.160	.524
50.0	.118	.387

(1) Nominal cross-sectional area/mm^2.
(2) Maximum resistance allowed may vary with different copper wire standards.

APPENDIX

TABLE 35

CONVERSION FACTORS

LENGTH

To convert from		in	ft	yd	mi
		Multiply by			
Inches	(in)	1	0.083 333	0.027 777	
Feet	(ft)	*12.	1	0.333 33	0.000 189 39
Yards	(yd)	*36.	*3.	1	0.000 568 18
Miles	(mi)		*5 280.	*1 760.	1
Millimetres		0.039 370	0.003 280 84	0.001 093 6	
Centimetres		0.393 70	0.032 808 4	0.010 936	
Metres		39.370	3.280 84	1.093 6	0.000 621 37
Kilometres			3 280.84	1 093.6	0.621 37

To convert from		mm	cm	dm	m	km
		Multiply by				
Inches		*25.4	*2.54	*0.254	*0.025 4	
Feet		*304.8	*30.48	*3.048	*0.304 8	*0.000 304 8
Yards		*914.4	*91.44	*9.144	*0.914 4	*0.000 914 4
Miles					*1 609.344	*1.609 344
Millimetres	(mm)	1	*0.1	*0.01	*0.001	
Centimetres	(cm)	*10.	1	*0.1	*0.01	
Decimetres	(dm)	*100.	*10.	1	*0.1	
Metres	(m)	*1 000.	*100.	*10.	1	*0.001
Kilometres	(km)				*1 000.	1

*Exact values

Note: obsolete length of measurement still in common usage:

1 micron = *0.001 mm   1 micron = 0.000 039 370 in
1 mm = *1 000. microns   1 inch = *25 400. microns
                                0.001 = *25.4 microns
The correct unit, of the same value, is: micrometre (μm)

TABLE 36

CONVERSION FACTORS

AREA

To convert from		in²	ft²	yd²	acre
		Multiply by			
Square inches	(in²)	1	0.006 944	0.000 771	
Square feet	(ft²)	*144.	1	0.111 11	0.000 022 957
Square yards	(yd²)	*1 296.	*9.	1	0.000 206 61
Acres	(acre)		*43 560.	*4 840.	1
Square centimetres		0.1550	0.001 076 4	0.000 119 60	
Square metres		1 550.0	10.764	1.195 60	0.000 247 11
Ares		155 000.3	1 076.4	119.60	0.024 711
Hectares		15 500 031.	107 639.	11 959.9	2.471 1

To Convert from		cm²	m²	a	ha
		Multiply by			
Square inches		*6.451 6	*0.000 645 16		
Square feet		929.030	0.092 903 0	0.000 929 030	0.000 009 290 30
Square yards		8 361.3	0.836 13	0.008 361 3	0.000 083 613
Acres			4 046.9	40.469	0.404 69
Square centimetres	(cm²)	1	*0.000 1		
Square metres	(m²)	*10 000.	1	*0.01	*0.000 1
Ares	(a)		*100.	1	*0.01
Hectares	(ha)		*10 000.	*100.	1

*Exact values

APPENDIX

TABLE 37
CONVERSION FACTORS
VOLUME

To convert from		in³	ft³	yd³
		Multiply by		
Cubic inches	(in³)	1	0.000 578 70	
Cubic feet	(ft³)	*1 728.	1	0.037 037
Cubic yards	(yd³)		*27.	1
Gallons		*231.	0.133 68	
Million gallons			133 680.5	
Acre — inches			*3 630.	
Acre — feet			*43 560.	
Cubic centimetres		0.061 024	0.000 035 315	
Litres**		61.024	0.035 315	
Cubic metres		61 024.	35.315	1.308 0
Hectare — millimetres			353.15	

To convert from		gal	M gal	acre — in	acre — ft
		Multiply by			
Cubic inches		0.004 329 0			
Cubic feet		7.480 5	0.000 007 480 5	0.000 275 48	0.000 022 957
Gallons	(gal)	1	*0.000 001	0.000 036 827	0.000 003 068 9
Million gallons	(M gal)	*1 000 000.	1	36.827	3.068 9
Acre — inches	(acre—in)	27 154.	0.027 154	1	0.083 333
Acre — feet	(acre—ft)	325 851.	0.325 85	*12.	1
Litres**		0.264 17			
Cubic metres		264.17	0.000 264 17	0.009 728 6	0.000 810 71
Hectare — millimetres		2 641.7	0.002 641 7	0.097 286	0.008 107 1

To convert from		cm³	l	m³	ha — mm
		Multiply by			
Cubic inches		16.387	0.016 387	0.000 016 387	
Cubic feet			28.317	0.028 317	0.002 831 7
Gallons			3.785 4	0.003 785 4	0.000 378 54
Million gallons			3 785 412.	3 785.4	378.54
Acre — inches			102 790.	102.790	10.279 0
Acre — feet			1 233 482.	1 233.5	123.35
Cubic centimetres	cm³	1	*0.001		
Litres**	(l)		1	*0.001	*0.000 1
Cubic metres	(m³)		*1 000.	1	*0.1
Hectare — millimetres	(ha·mm)		*10 000.	*10.	1

*Exact value   **1 litre = 1 dm³ exactly

Note: 1 liquid ounce (liq oz) = *0.007 8125 gallons
                             = 1.8047   cubic inches
                             = 29.574   millilitres
                             = 0.029 574 litres

APPENDIX

TABLE 38

CONVERSION FACTORS

FLOW

To convert from	ft³/S	gal / min (gpm)[1]	gal/d (gpd)[1]	Mgal/d (mgd)[1]
		multiply by		
Cubic feet per second (ft³/s)	1	448.83	646 317.	0.646 32
Gallons per minute (gal/min)	0.002 228 0	1	*1 440.	0.001 44
Gallons per day (gal/d)	0.000 001 547 2	0.000 694 44	1	*0.000 001
Million gallons per day (M gal/d)	1.547 2	694.44	*1 000 000.	1
Acre – inches per hour	1.008 3	452.57	651 703.	0.651 70
Acre – inches per day	0.042 013 8	18.857	27 154.	0.027 154
Acre – feet per hour	*12.1	5 430.9	7 820 434.	7.820 4
Acre – feet per day	0.504 16	226.29	325 851.	0.325 85
Litres per second	0.035 315	15.850	22 824.	0.022 824
Litres per minute	0.000 588 58	0.264 17	380.41	0.000 380 41
Cubic metres per hour	0.009 809 6	4.402 9	6 340.1	0.006 340 1
Hectare – millimetres per hour	0.098 096	44.029	63 401.	0.063 401
Hectare – millimetres per day	0.004 087 3	1.834 5	2 641.7	0.002 641 7

To convert from	acre – in/h	acre – in/d	acre – ft/h	acre – ft/d
		multiply by		
Cubic feet per second	0.991 735 5	23.802	0.082 645	1.983 5
Gallons per minute	0.002 209 59	0.053 03	0.000 184 133	0.004 419
Gallons per day	0.000 001 534 44	0.000 036 826 6	0.000 000 127 870	0.000 003 068 9
Million gallons per day	1.534 44	36.826 6	0.127 870	3.068 9
Acre – inches per hour (acre-in/h)	1	*24.	0.083 333	*2.
Acre – inches per day (acre-in/d)	0.041 666	1	0.003 472 2	0.083 333
Acre – feet per hour (acre-in/h)	*12.	*288.	1	*24.
Acre – feet per day (acre-ft/d)	*0.5	*12.	0.041 666	1
Litres per second**	0.035 023	0.840 55	0.002 918 6	0.070 045 6
Litres per minute**	0.000 583 71	0.014 009	0.000 048 643	0.001 167 43
Cubic metres per hour	0.009 728 6	0.233 49	0.000 810 713	0.019 457
Hectare – millimetres per hour	0.097 286	2.334 9	0.008 107 13	0.194 57
Hectare – millimetres per day	0.004 053 57	0.097 286	0.000 337 80	0.008 107 13

**1 litre = 1 dm³ exactly

To convert from	1/S	1/min	m³/h	ha–mm/h	ha–mm/d
		multiply by			
Cubic feet per second	28.317	1 699.0	101.94	10.194	244.66
Gallons per minute	0.063 090	3.785 4	0.227 13	0.022 712 5	0.545 1
Gallons per day	0.000 043 813	0.002 628 76	0.000 157 73	0.000 015 773	0.000 378 54
Million gallons per day	43.813	2 628.76	157.73	15.773	378.54
Acre – inches per hour	28.553	1 713.2	102.790	10.279 0	246.7
Acre – inches per day	1.189 70	71.382	4.2829	0.428 29	10.279 0
Acre – feet per hour	342.634	20 558.0	1233.5	123.35	2 960.4
Acre – feet per day	14.276 4	856.585	51.395	5.139 5	123.35
Litres per second** (1/S)	1	*60.	*3.6	*0.36	*8.64
Litres per minute** (1/min)	0.016 666	1	*0.06	*0.006	*0.144
Cubic metres per hour (m³/h)	0.277 77	16.666	1	*0.1	*2.4
Hectare – millimetres per hour (ha–mm/h)	2.777 7	166.66	*10.0	1	*24.
Hectare – millimetres per day (ha/mm/d)	0.115 74	6.944 4	0.416 66	0.041 666	1

*Exact value   [1]Commonly used U. S. abbreviations   ** 1 litre = 1 dm³ exactly

APPENDIX

TABLE 39

CONVERSION FACTORS

VELOCITY

To convert from	To	ft/s (fps)[1]	mi /h (mph)[1]	m/s	km / h
Feet per second	(ft/s)	1	0.681 818	*0.304 8	*1.097 28
Miles per hour	(mi/h)	1.466 6	1	*0.447 04	*1.609 344
Metres per second		3.280 84	2.236 9	1	*3.6
Kilometres per hour		0.911 34	0.621 37	0.277 77	1

*Exact value   [1]Commonly used U. S. abbreviations

TABLE 40

CONVERSION FACTORS

(weight) MASS

To convert from	To	oz avdp	lb	g	kg
			multiply by		
Ounce[1], avoirdupois	(oz avdp)	1	*0.062 5	28.350	0.028 350
Pound[1], avoirdupois	(lb avdp)	*16.0	1	*453.592 37	*0.453 592 37
Gram	(g)	0.035 274	0.002 204 6	1	*0.001
Kilogram	(kg)	35.274	2.204 6	* 1 000.	1

*Exact Value

TABLE 41

CONVERSION FACTORS

DENSITY

To convert from	To	lb/in^3	lb / gal	kg / cm^3	kg / l
			multiply by		
Pounds per cubic inch	(lb/in^3)	1	*231.	0.027 680	27.680
Pounds per gallon	(lb/gal)	0.004 329 00	1	0.000 119 83	0.119 83
Kilograms per cubic centimetre	(kg/cm^3)	36.127	8 345.4	1	* 1 000.
Kilograms per litre**	(kg/l)	0.036 127	8.345 4	*0.000 1	1

*Exact value   **1 litre = 1 dm^3 exactly

TABLE 42

CONVERSION FACTORS

WATER PRESSURE

To convert from	To	atm	lbf/in^2 (psi)[1]	kgf/cm^2	mH$_2$O @ 15° C	ftH$_2$O @ 60° F	bar
				multiply by			
Standard atmospheres	(atm)	1	14.696	*1.0332775 [a]	10.342	33.932	1.0133
Pounds per square inch [b]	(lbf/in^2)	0.068046	1	0.070307	0.70370	2.3089	0.068947
Kilograms per square centimeter[b]	(kgf/cm^2)	0.96784	14.223	1	10.009	32.841	0.98067
Feet water @ 60° F	(ft H$_2$O @ 60° F F)	0.029471	0.433100	0.030450	0.30477	1	0.029890
Meters water @ 15° C	(m H$_2$O @ 15° C)	0.096697	1.4211	0.099910	1	3.2811	0.098064
Bar		0.98692	14.504	1.0197	10.197	33.456	1

* Exact value   (a) ICAO standard   [1]Commonly used U.S. abbreviation

Index

A

Air
  control 115
  gap 94
  relief 82,111
Algae 133, 137
Appurtenances, pressure loss 59
Arrester, water hammer 76
Atmospheric, vacuum breaker 88
Automatic
  air relief 82, 111
  controllers 22, 253, 297, 315
  drain valves 33
  priming 110
  pump stations 112, 121
  strainers 130
  system operation 21

B

Backflow
  prevention 87
  types of 85
Backwashing (see Strainers)
Ball drive heads 14
Bedspray heads 10
Blow-down (see Strainers)
Booster pumps 125
Borders, layout 153, 186, 187
Box, planter 195
Bubbler 10, 18, 270

C

Catch-can test 167
Cavitation 103
Check valve 80, 82, 92, 316
Climatic sensors 32, 315
Clock (see Controller)
Computer
  aided design (CAD) 227
  calculations, pressure 228, 309
  controllers 22, 315
Contaminants
  algae/peat moss 133,137
  general 128
  strainers/filters 130, 254
Control
  cross-connection 84, 95
  flow 27, 72, 80, 213, 302
  pump 111, 112, 121, 312
Controller
  electric 28
  features 24, 253, 295, 315
  grounding 331
  hydraulic 30
  primary (command) 298
  satellite (field) 298
  wiring 327
Copper water tube 38, 211, 243

Creep, plastic pipe 41
Cross-connection 86

D

Desanders (separators) 138
Distribution, sprinkler (coverage)
  adjustment, effects of 6, 146
  diameter, catalog listed 146
  droplet size 147
  patterns (profiles) 145
  pressure, effect of 148
  rotation, effect of 148
  uniformity 144, 148, 150
  wind, effect of 147
Dog-leg (fairways) 286
Double check assembly 92
Drip (see Micro)

E

Effective
  coverage 278, 280, 282, 284
  radius 190, 207
Efficiency, irrigation 15, 18, 161, 258
Electrical
  factors 322
  leaks 331
  wiring 320
Electrolysis 38
Elevation, effect of 55
Emitter 18, 256
Evaporation 124, 159
Evapotranspiration 159, 257, 297
ETo inches/day 257

F

Fairways, layout of 277
Fatigue, plastic pipe 41
Filters 130, 254
Fittings
  compression 39, 256
  flared 39
  gasket (O-ring) 40, 46
  insert 45, 256
  mechanical joint 40
  pressure loss 59, 208, 241, 251, 308
  solder 39
  solvent-weld 46
  theaded 48
Flow
  control 27, 80
  design adjustment 105, 204 213, 241, 249, 304, 312
  sensor (switch) 32, 126
  variation 204
  velocity 59, 72, 74, 213, 217, 232, 243, 303, 304, 308
  zone 206, 241, 243

G

Gauge, pressure/vacuum 69, 102
Gear drive
  heads 14
  selection of 233
Golf course systems
  automatic control of 295, 315
  conversion of 317
  layout, sprinkler
    fairways 277
    greens 273
    tees 276
  operation program 296
  piping 302
  syringe 315
  water supply 312
Grid patterns, development of 181
Grounding, controller systems 331

H

Head (also see Sprinkler)
  feet of 54
  flood 10
  layout 178, 233, 262, 272
  rotary 12
  micro 18
  spray 4
High shrubs 193
Holding tank 94, 137
Hours of darkness 293
Hydraulics 54
Hydro-pneumatic pressure
  systems 112, 121

I

I.D. (inside diameter) 37
Impact drive heads 13, 19, 287
Installation
  controllers 26, 28, 320
  cross-connection devices 84, 85, 87, 88, 89, 90, 92, 93, 95
  piping 39, 40, 47
  pumps 98, 104, 108, 112, 113, 117, 120, 125
  spray heads
    lawn 8
    shrub 9, 201
  strainers/filters 131, 132, 133
  swing-joints 8, 303, 315
  valves 24, 26, 28, 34
  wire 324, 326
Irrigation
  audits 166
  method of 4, 163

394

Index

J

Jockey pumps 120

K

Kinetic energy 77

L

Landscape design,
  conservation by 164
Lawn heads (pop up) 5, 12
Layout (also see Spacing)
  borders 153, 186
  corners 186
  curves 187
  emitters 259, 262
  fairways 277
  flood watering 194, 262
  greens 273
  high shrubs 193
  individual shrubs 196, 259
  lawn and shrubs 192
  parkways 189, 199
  patterns 149, 180, 183, 233, 272
  planter boxes 195
  rotary heads 179, 233, 272
  special methods 185
  spray heads 180, 196, 238, 263
  strips 189
  tees 276
Leakage, electrical 331
Lightning suppression 333
Looped Mains 221, 305
Low flow/volume irrigation 252, 270

M

Mains
  branch 305
  city supply 55, 64, 75, 211, 213, 232
  looped 221, 305
  pressure 72, 217, 241, 246, 264, 304
Manual control 21
Mean coverage (or effective) 153, 190, 278, 280, 282, 284
Micro
  products 18, 252, 256, 263, 269
  spray 18, 263
  systems 252

N

Net positive suction head
  (NPSH) 103
Non-potable
  sprinkler alert 16, 20
  piping alert 47, 256, 315
  water 86, 94, 128
Nozzle
  adjustable 6
  fixed 6

flow, variance of 204
inner 13
low angle 8
pop-up spray 5
pressure compensating 8
range 13
special 8
stream spray 9
strip 8

O

OD (outside diameter) 37
Operation
  controllers 22, 295
  pumps 111, 112, 333
  system 21, 243, 295
  valves 29, 30

P

Parkway (see Layout)
Patterns (see Layout)
Pipe
  A-C 40
  cast iron 40
  copper tube 38
  creep (plastic pipe) 41
  electrolysis 40
  fatigue (plastic pipe) 41
  galvanized steel 37
  I.D. 37
  I.P.S. 37
  micro 256, 264
  nominal size 37
  non-potable 47, 256
  O.D. 37
  P.B. 47
  P.E. 44
  porous 252, 269
  PVC 46
  schedule 37, 38, 42, 46
  SDR 43, 45, 46
  wall 37
  working pressure 37, 38, 40
Planting
  beds 192
  boxes 195
  gallons per day 258
  special 195
  variations 161, 258
Plot plans 168
Potable water 86
Precipitation
  calculation of 154, 243, 262, 281, 296
  variations 212
Pressure
  absolute 101
  atmospheric 101
  design 61, 246, 310
  effects on distribution 148
  equivalents 55
  gauge 54, 69, 102
  loss tables for micro 266, 267, 268, 269

operating 57, 204
regulator 27, 28, 255, 314
static 57, 64
surge (see Water hammer)
vapor 103
Programming 24, 243, 261, 296
Pump
  booster 125
  cavitation 103
  centrifugal 98
  circuits 111, 333
  hydro-pneumatic systems 112
  jockey 120
  NPSH 103
  priming 110
  selection 105, 107
  static suction head 102
  static suction lift 102
  station, manufactured 121
  suction 108
  terms and definitions 100
  VFD 122

Q

Quick-coupler equipment 19, 315

R

Rain sensors 31
Reduced pressure assembly 94
Relay, auxiliary pump 333
Remote control valves 24, 25, 27
Remote valve operator 30
Reservoirs 124
Resistance, electrical 322
Riser
  micro systems 263
  pop-up 8
  shrub, fixed 9
  swing-joint 8, 303, 315
Root zone 259
Rotary (also see Sprinkler)
  check valve equipped 17, 316
  head patterns 233
  layout 233
  rubber covers 16
  systems 230
Row spacing, calculation of 155, 182
Rule of proportion (spacing) 184

S

Sand, removal of 138
Satellite controllers 295, 297
Scheduling (see system operation)
Sensors, remote
  climatic 32
  flow/pressure 32
  rain 31
  soil moisture 31
  temperature, low 32
Separators 138

Index

Shrub
  heads (also see Sprinkler)   9
  watering of   192, 240, 256, 262
Soil absorption   160, 261
Soil-water-plant   160
Solvent, pipe   48
Solenoid, valve   29
Spacing
  design   151
  emitter   259, 262
  equal   181
  half   183
  rotary   17, 233, 272
  row   179
  spray   6, 179, 197
  square   149, 179, 238,
            274, 282
  templates   197
  triangular   149, 179, 197, 233,
               238, 274, 282
  wind effects   147
Spray (also see Sprinkler)
  head patterns   6, 179
  layout   180, 196
  spacing   6, 179
  systems   4, 196
Sprinkler
  ball drive   14
  distribution   144
  flood type   10, 194
  gear drive   14
  impact   13
  jet   10
  micro   18, 263
  performance   144
  pop-up   5
  pressure compensating   8
  pressure, differential of   204, 212
  rotary   12, 230, 272
  shrub   9, 201, 240
  spray   4, 180, 196, 238
  test, catch-can   167
Strainers/Filters
  algae/peat moss   133, 137
  automatic   134
  backwashing   134
  blow-down   132
  cleaning   132, 254
  dump valve   132
  installation   131
  mesh size   131, 133, 255
  pressure loss   131
  pressure switch alarms   135
  selection   131, 254
Strip nozzle   8
Suction friction head   103
Suction lift   102, 103
Surge protection
  electrical   333
  hydraulic   72
Swing-joint   8, 303, 315
Syringe watering   315
System, operation program   296

T

Tank, holding   94, 137
Tees, head layout of   276
Temperature sensor   32
Template, spacing   197
Test
  catch-can   167
  pipe flow   65, 318
Thrust blocks   75
Transpiration   160
Trees, watering of   256
Trickle (see Micro)
Tubing
  copper   38
  hydraulic   30
  micro   256

V

Vacuum breaker
  atmospheric   88
  pressure-type   89
Valve
  automatic drain   33
  check   17, 80, 83, 92, 316
  contamination resistant   27
  electric diaphragm   27, 29
  flow adjustment   27
  foot   106
  gate (shut-off)   21, 315
  globe   21
  hydraulic diaphragm   27, 28, 30
  in-head   289, 317
  installation   24, 326
  operator, remote   30
  pressure
    control   112, 122
    reducing   27, 28, 255
    relief   116
  quick coupler   20
  solenoid   29, 320
  tubing, control   30
  wiring   28, 320
  zone   27, 254
Vapor pressure   103
Variable frequency drive   122
Velocity, flow   59, 72, 74, 213,
               217, 232, 243, 303, 304, 308
Vents, automatic air   82
Voltage   322

W

Water
  audit irrigation   166
  conservation   163, 252
  gray   129
  loss
    evapotranpiration   159, 257
    supply   124
  non-potable   128
  quality   128, 195, 252
  recycled   128
  requirement   124, 158
  source   128

strainers/filters   130, 254
supply
  city   55, 211, 243
  private   128, 137, 312
  treated waste   129
Water hammer
  air entrapment   81
  arrester   76
  causes   72
  pipe protection   73
  uncontrolled flow   79
Wells   137
Wetted pattern   259
Wind
  data sources   156
  effect of   147, 279
Wire
  connectors   326
  installation   320, 326
  resistance   322
  sizing   321, 323, 327
  type   320

Z

Zone entrance (ZE)   206, 246
Zoning
  golf courses   288
  micro systems   262
  rotary systems   241, 288
  spray systems   211